VITAL RECORDS

OF

CHELMSFORD

MASSACHUSETTS

TO THE END OF THE YEAR 1849

PUBLISHED BY
THE ESSEX INSTITUTE
SALEM, MASS.
1914

Notice

In many older books, foxing (or discoloration) occurs and, in some instances, print lightens with wear and age. Reprinted books, such as this, often duplicate these flaws, notwithstanding efforts to reduce or eliminate them. The pages of this reprint have been digitally enhanced and, where possible, the flaws eliminated in order to provide clarity of content and a pleasant reading experience.

Originally published
Salem, Massachusetts
1914

Reprinted by:

Janaway Publishing
2412 Nicklaus Dr.
Santa Maria, California 93455
(805) 925-1038
www.JanawayGenealogy.com

2002, 2007

ISBN 10: 1-59641-104-X
ISBN 13: 978-1-59641-104-3

Made in the United States of America

EXPLANATIONS

The following records of births, marriages and deaths include all entries to be found in the books of record kept by the town clerks; in the church records; in the returns made to the Middlesex Co. Quarterly Court; in the cemetery inscriptions; and in private records found in family Bibles, etc. These records are printed in a condensed form in which every essential particular has been preserved. All duplication of the town clerk's record has been eliminated, but differences in entry and other explanatory matter appear in brackets. Parentheses are used when they occur in the original record; also to indicate the maiden name of a married woman.

When places other than Chelmsford and Massachusetts are named in the original records, they are given in the printed copy. Marriages and intentions of marriage are printed under the names of both parties. Double-dating is used in the months of January, February and March, prior to 1752, whenever it appears in the original, and also, whenever from the sequence of entry in the original, the date may be easily determined. In all records the original spelling of names is followed, and in the alphabetical arrangement the various forms should be examined, as items about the same family may be found under different spellings.

CHELMSFORD

On May 18, 1653, the General Court granted the petition of several of the inhabitants of "Concord & Woobourne for the erecting of a new plantacon on Merremacke River, neere to Pawtuckett," and May 29, 1655, the Court granted the name thereof to be called Chelmsford.

May 14, 1656, land granted to Chelmsford.

May 31, 1660, bounds between Chelmsford and the Indian plantation at Patucket established.

June 27, 1701, bounds between Chelmsford and Billerica established.

Nov. 23, 1725, part of Chelmsford annexed to Littleton.

June 13, 1726, "Wameset" annexed.

Sept. 23, 1729, part of Chelmsford established as Westford.

Apr. 24, 1755, part of Chelmsford annexed to Dunstable.

Apr. 28, 1780, part of Chelmsford included in the second district of Carlisle.

Mar. 1, 1783, part of the second district of Carlisle annexed.

Mar. 1, 1826, part of Chelmsford established as Lowell.

The population of Chelmsford at different periods was as follows:

1765,	1,012.	1810,	1,396.	1850,	2,097.
1776,	1,341.	1820,	1,535.	1900,	3,984.
1790,	1,144.	1830,	1,387.	1910,	5,010.
1800,	1,290.	1840,	1,697.		

ABBREVIATIONS

a.—age.
abt.—about.
b.—born.
bef.—before.
bet.—between.
bp.—baptized.
bur.—buried.
c. r. 1.—church record, First Congregational Church (now Unitarian), Chelmsford Centre.
c. r. 2.—church record, First Baptist Church, South Chelmsford.
c. r. 3.—church record, Second Congregational Church, North Chelmsford.
c. r. 4.—church record, Second Church (now First Unitarian), of Westford.
c. r. 5.—church record, St. Anne's Church (Episcopal), of Lowell.
ch.—child.
chn.—children.
Co.—county.
ct. r.—court record, Middlesex Co. Quarterly Court.
d.—daughter; day; died.
Dea.—deacon.
dup.—duplicate entry.
g. r. 1.—gravestone record, Forefather's Cemetery, Chelmsford Centre.
g. r. 2.—gravestone record, Hart Pond Cemetery, South Chelmsford.
g. r. 3.—gravestone record, Riverview Cemetery, North Chelmsford.
g. r. 4.—gravestone record, Fairview Cemetery, West Chelmsford.

ABBREVIATIONS

G. R. 5.—gravestone record, Fairview Cemetery, Westford.
G. R. 6.—gravestone record, Cemetery No. One, Lowell.
G. R. 7.—gravestone record, Cemetery No. Two (English), Lowell.
h.—husband; hour.
inf.—infant.
int.—intention of marriage.
jr.—junior.
m.—male; married; month.
P. R. 1.—Extracts from Rev. John Fiske's note-book, now in possession of the Massachusetts Historical Society.
P. R. 2.—Copy of inscriptions in Forefather's Cemetery made by Roland Parkhurst.
P. R. 3.—Cemetery commissioners' records now in possession of William Hall.
P. R. 4.—Copy of diary of Rev. Ebenezer Bridge, now in possession of Rev. Wilson Waters.
P. R. 5.—Bible record now in possession of Mrs. Amos B. Adams.
P. R. 6.—Framed record now in possession of Miss Cecilia Richardson.
P. R. 7.—Bible record now in possession of Mrs. Julia E. Warren.
P. R. 8.—Sampler record now in possession of Mrs. Julia E. Warren.
P. R. 9.—Bible record now in possession of Judge Samuel P. Hadley of Lowell.
P. R. 10.—Bible record now in possession of Wallace A. Josselyn of North Chelmsford.
P. R. 11.—Sampler record now in possession of Joseph Bowers of Lowell.
P. R. 12.—Bible record now in possession of Mrs. Mary A. Tyler of Lowell.
P. R. 13.—Bible record now in possession of Daniel Byam.
P. R. 14.—Bible record now in possession of Mrs. Almon Holt.
P. R. 15.—Framed record now in possession of Mrs. Henry Perham.
P. R. 16.—Bible record now in possession of Miss Abigail Smith of Lowell.

P. R. 17.—Bible record now in possession of Mrs. George A. Parkhurst.

P. R. 18.—Family record now in possession of Miss L. Rosamond Spaulding.

P. R. 19.—Scrap-book record now in possession of Mrs. M. E. Bean of Lowell.

P. R. 20.—Family Register now in possession of George Mansfield.

P. R. 21.—Bible record now in possession of George Mansfield.

P. R. 22.—Bible record now in possession of Mrs. Octavia Parkhurst.

P. R. 23.—Bible record now in possession of Mrs. Octavia Parkhurst.

P. R. 24.—Copy of Bible record now in possession of Mrs. M. E. Perham.

P. R. 25.—Copy of Bible record now in possession of Mrs. M. E. Perham.

P. R. 26.—Copy of Bible record now in possession of Mrs. M. E. Perham.

P. R. 27.—Bible record now in possession of Frank Byam.

P. R. 28.—Bible record now in possession of Mrs. Otis Adams.

P. R. 29.—Bible record now in possession of Miss Emma E. Proctor.

P. R. 30.—Copy of Bible record now in possession of Mrs. A. M. Batchelder.

P. R. 31.—Copy of Middlesex Co. Court Records now in possession of William H. Manning of West Somerville.

rec.—recorded.

s.—son.

sr.—senior.

T. C.—town copy.

unm.—unmarried.

w.—wife ; week.

wid.—widow.

widr.—widower.

y.—year.

CHELMSFORD BIRTHS

TO THE END OF THE YEAR 1849

ABBOT (see also Abbott), Caleb Fletcher, s. [Capt. C. R. 1.] Caleb and Marcy, Sept. 8, 1812.
Evelina [Maria. C. R. 1.] Antoinett, d. Capt. Caleb and Mercy, Sept. 14, 1817.
Joshua, s. William and Bridget, bp. Apr. 9, 1780. C. R. 1.
Josiah Gardner, s. Capt. Caleb and Mercy, Nov. 1, 1814.
Lucy Ann Lovejoy, d. [Capt. C. R. 1.] Caleb and Marcy, Sept. 16, 1809.
Marcy Maria Richardson [Mary Maria. C. R. 1.], d. Caleb and Marcy, Jan. 24, 1808.
Sally [Susanna. P. R. 4.], d. Jeremiah and Susanna, bp. Apr. 1, 1792. C. R. 1.
Sally, bp. Apr. 19, 1801, a. 17 y. C. R. 1.
William, s. William and Bridget, bp. Apr. 12, 1778. C. R. 1.

ABBOTT (see also Abbot, Abott), Bridget, d. William and Bridget, Dec. 13, 1770.
Hannah, d. Jeremiah and Susannah, Jan. 30, 1774.
Jedathan, s. William and Bridget, Feb. 9, 1773.
Jeremiah, s. Jeremiah and Susanna, Feb. 26, 1772.
Jessa, s. Jeremiah and Susannah, Sept. 22, 1776.
Jonas, s. Jeremiah and Susannah, Apr. 29, 1781.
Rebeckah, d. Jeremiah and Susannah, Aug. 26, 1778.
Sarah, d. William and Briggit, Oct. 1, 1775.
Susanna, d. Jeremiah and Susannah, June 12, 1769.
William, s. Jeremiah and Susanna, Nov. 3, 1787.

ABOTT (see also Abbott), Silas, s. Jeremiah and Susanna, bp. July 25, 1784. C. R. 1.

ADAMES (see also Adams), Elisabeth, d. Pelatiah, Apr. 26, 1680.
Ester [Hester. CT. R.], d. Samuell and Ester [Hester. CT. R.], 9 : 2 m : 1669.

CHELMSFORD BIRTHS

ADAMES, Jane, d. Thomas and Judah, Dec. 2, 1704.
Ruth, d. Pelitiah and Ruth, Mar. 8, 1673.
Salathiel, s. Jonas and Rebecca, Dec. 13, 1753.
Samuell, s. Samuell and Ester, Mar. 7, 1671.
Sarah, d. Pelitiah and Ruth, July 12, 16[91. T. C.].
Sarah, d. Samuel and Esther, June 2, 1754.

ADAMS (see also Adames, Addams), Abel, s. Jonas and Rebecca, May 26, 1746.
Abel, s. Abel and Olive, Aug. 17, 1776.
Abel, s. Salathiel and Sarah, Jan. 14, 1809.
Abi, w. Solomon Byam, July 17, 1773. P. R. 13.
Abigail, d. Cornet Otis and Abigail O., Mar. 25, 1823.
Abigal, d. Palitiah and Ruth, June 7, 1697.
[Ab]igall, d. Jonathan and Leah, Nov. 9, 1693.
Anna, d. Timothy and Joanna, Sept. 12, 1787.
Benjamen, s. Joseph and Mary, Dec. 1, 1701.
Benjamin, s. Capt. Samuell and Ester, May 29, 1679.
Benjamin, s. Benjamin and Olive, Feb. 25, 1727-8.
Benjamin, s. John and Esther, Nov. 5, 1744.
Benjamin, s. William and Elizebeth, Dec. 5, 1760.
Benjamin, s. Oliver and Rachil, Apr. 28, 1771.
Benja[min], s. William and Polly, May 10, 1801.
Benjamin Franklin, s. Richard and Sally, Aug. 5, 1815.
Benjamin Franklin, s. Benja[min] and Adeline, Dec. 25, 1838.
Bettey, d. Samuel and Esther, Dec. 29, 1768.
Bridget, d. Samuel and Esther, Feb. 10, 1739.
Calvin Waldo, s. Capt. Otis and Abigail O. [(Reed). P. R. 5.], Apr. 12, 1828.
Caroline Melvina, d. Benj[ami]n F. and Frances C., July 24, 1841.
Charles, s. Isaac and Hannah, Apr. 11, 1800.
Charles Edwin, s. Joel and Catharine Mary, Dec. 31, 1811.
Easter, d. Samuel and Easter, Nov. 3, 1737.
Easter, d. Samuel and Easter, Jan. 22, 1762.
Edath, d. Timothy and Dorithy, Dec. 31, 1716.
Edeth, d. Tho[mas] and Mare ———. [Feb. 21, 1655. CT. R.]
Edeth, d. Jonathan and Leaeh, Dec. 1, 1683.
Edith, d. Pelatiah and Ruth, June 25, 1688. CT. R.
Elisabeth, d. William and Polly, Dec. 8, 1794.
Eliza Ann Jane Bush, d. Capt. Benja[min] and Eliza Ann, Apr. 6, 1833.
Eliza Jane B., d. Benjamin and Eliza, Feb. 10, 1835.
Elizabeth, d. Timothy and Dorithy, Oct. 26, 1705.
Elizabeth, d. Benjamin and Abigail, Sept. 18, 1726.

CHELMSFORD BIRTHS 11

ADAMS, Ella Elizabeth, d. Gen. Benj[ami]n, farmer, and Adeline, at North Chelmsford, July 31, 1847.
Ephraim, s. John and Esther, Jan. 13, 1750-51.
Ephraim, s. Ephraim and Betty, of Limerick, bp. Nov. 1, 1778. C. R. 1.
Ephraim, s. Joseph and Lucey [(Blodget). P. R. 24.], Sept. 10, 1789.
Ephriam, s. Thomas and Judah, Nov. 14, 1712.
Ester, d. Thomas and Judah, Aug. 18, 1706.
Esther, d. Benjamin and Abigail, Mar. 24, 1721-2.
Esther, d. Jonas and Rebecca, bp. May 29, 1743. C. R. 1.
Esther, d. John and Esther, Sept. 25, 1748.
Fitz Edward, s. W[illia]m, jr. and Sarah S., June 12, 1835.
Francis Perkins, s. Gen. Benjamin and Adeline, Mar. 5, 1843.
George Abijah, s. William, jr. and Sarah S., Feb. 23, 1828.
Hanah, d. Capt. Joseph and Mary, Sept. 17, 1717.
Hanah, d. twin, Thomas and Jude, May 7, 1724.
Hanah, d. John, 3d and Mary, Mar. 8, 1778.
Hannah, d. Oliver and Rachel, Apr. 12, 1764.
Hannah, d. [Capt. C. R. 1.] William and Polly, July 14, 1803.
Hannah Mariah, d. Isaac and Hannah, June 26, 1813.
Henery, s. Thomas and Judah, May 20, 1708.
Henery, s. Lt. Abel and Olive, Mar. 34 [sic], 1784. [bp. Mar. 28. C. R. 1.]
Henry Kirkland, s. Joel and Catharine Mary, Feb. 1, 1819.
Hester, d. Joseph and Mary, Mar. 10, 1704-5.
Isaac, s. Isaac and Hannah, Apr. 22, 1808.
Isabel J., d. Gen. Benj[ami]n, trader, and Adeline, at North Chelmsford, Mar. 3, 1845.
Jesse, s. Jonas and Rebecca, Jan. 11, 1743-4.
Joanah, d. Samuel and Easter, Jan. 23, 1756.
Joel, s. Timothy and Joanna, Nov. 4, 1783.
John, s. Benjamin and Mary, Apr. 16, 1711.
John, s. Timothy and Dorothy, Aug. 13, 1719.
John, s. John and Esther, June 28, 1746.
John, s. John and Sarah, May 20, 1747.
John, s. Timothy and Joanna, Dec. 12, 1785.
John, s. Samuel and Sarah, May 3, 1787.
John, s. Isaac and Hannah, June 27, 1805.
John Henry, s. Joel and Catharine Mary, Feb. 8, 1822.
John Joseph, s. Joseph, 2d and Dolly, July 5, 1840.
John Richardson, s. W[illia]m and Polly, Dec. 7, 1798.
John Thornton Kirkland, s. Joel and Catharine Mary, Sept. 2, 1827.
Jonas, s. Joseph and Mary, Dec. 16, 1712.
Jonas, s. Jonas and Rebecka, Jan. 24, 1741-2.

ADAMS, Jonas, s. Abel and Olive, Aug. 30, 1772.
Jonas, s. Capt. Abel and Olive, June 5, 1789.
Jonathan, s. Th[omas], bp. 1: 12 m: 1656. P. R. 1.
Jonathan, s. Timothy and Mary, Aug. 3, 1688. CT. R.
Jonathan, s. Jonathan and Leah [torn]2 [torn. Mar. 28, 1695-6. T. C.].
Jonathan, s. Timothy and Dorithy, Aug. 7, 1714.
Jonathan, s. William and Elizabeth, Aug. 24, 1766.
Joseph, s. Capt. Samuell and Easter, 27: 11 m: 1672.
Joseph, s. Joseph and Marey, July 8, 1698.
Joseph, s. Joseph and Mary, July 8, 1726.
Joseph, s. Joseph and Lidya, Nov. 5, 1758.
Joseph, s. Joseph and Lucy [(Blodget). P. R. 24.], May 16, 1786.
Joseph, s. Ephraim and Tabitha, Oct. 27, 1814.
Josiah Francis, s. W[illia]m, jr. and Sarah S., Oct. 27, 1832.
Julia Maria, d. Joseph Miller and Dorothy, at Mill Row, July 27, 1843. [July 28. dup.]
Kathrin, d. Benjamin and Mary, Apr. 20, 1710.
Lemuel, s. Jonas and Rebecca, bp. Nov. 6, 1748. C. R. 1.
Levi, s. Joseph and Lydia, June 30, 1751.
Levi, s. Joseph and Lydia, June 14, 1764.
Lideah, d. Peletiah and Lidea, Mar. 26, 1716.
Lidiah, d. Jonathan and Leah, Apr. 2, 1691.
Lucina M., w. Solomon Parkhurst, Jan. 26, 1811. P. R. 17.
Lucy, d. Benjamin and Abigail, June 8, 1724.
Lucy, d. Joseph, jr. and Lucy [(Blodget). P. R. 24.], Sept. 26, 1784.
Lucy, d. Lt. Samuel and Sarah, Feb. 26, 1793.
Lucy Ann, d. Ephraim and Tabitha, Sept. 30, 1817.
Lydia, d. Joseph and Lydia, Dec. 12, 1748.
Lydia, d. Samuel and Easter, May 3, 1749.
Marah, d. Benjamin and Mary, Dec. 27, 1715.
Margaret, d. Jonathan and Leah, June 24, 1688. CT. R.
Maria Juliet, d. Joel and Catharine Mary, Mar. 15, 1810.
Mary, d. Th[omas], bp. 1: 12 m: 1656. P. R. 1.
Mary, d. Temothy and Mary, Sept. 25, 1684.
Mary, d. Joseph and Mary, July 1, 1707.
Mary, d. Timothy and Dorithy, Apr. 14, 1710.
Mary, d. Joseph and Mary, July 24, 1721.
Mary, d. Lucy, July 2, 1747.
Mary, d. John, 3d and Molley, Sept. 18, 1770.
Mary, d. John and Mary, July 17, 1773.
Mary, d. Samuel and Sarah, Mar. 10, 1785.
Mary, d. Ephraim and Tabitha, Apr. 20, 1824.
Mary Adeline, d. Benj[ami]n and Adeline, Dec. 27, 1840.

ADAMS, Nabby, d. Oliver and Rachil, July 4, 1769.
Nathaniell, s. Samuell and Rebekah, Feb. 28, 1662.
Noris, s. Capt. Salathiel and Sarah, Dec. 18, 1817.
Olive, d. Benjamin and Olive, Dec. 14, 1724.
Olive, d. Oliver and Rachil, Sept. 27, 1759.
Olive, d. Abel and Olive, Jan. 26, 1780.
Oliver, s. Benjamin and Olive, Oct. 27, 1729.
Oliver, s. Oliver and Rachil, Jan. 7, 1767.
Otis, s. Joseph and Lucy [(Blodget). P. R. 24.], June 5, 1798.
Otis, s. Lt. Otis and Abigail O. [(Reed). P. R. 5.], Jan. 6, 1826.
Patte, d. Samuel and Thankfull, Apr. 23, 1771.
Pelatiah, s. Th[omas], bp. 1: 12 m: 1656. P. R. 1.
Pelatiah, s. Pelatiah and Ruth, Nov. 17, 1682.
Pelatiah, s. Samuel and Esther, June 1, 1751.
Phebe, d. Thomas and Jude, Dec. 3, 1716.
Pheneas, s. twin, Thomas and Jude, May 7, 1724.
Polly, d. William and Polly, Jan. 4, 1788.
Procter, s. Salathial and Susanna, Dec. 15, 1806.
Rebecca, d. Jonas and Rebecca, Apr. 6, 1751.
Rebecca, d. Samuel and Esther, May 17, 1764.
Rebecca, d. Williams and Polly, July 29, 1792.
Rebeckah, d. Joseph and Lydia, June 20, 1767.
Rebekah, d. Joseph and Mary, Nov. 28, 1709.
Reuben, s. Robert and Rachel, Mar. 12, 1783.
Reufas, s. Robert and Rachel, June 10, 1791.
Richard, s. Robert and Rachel, Sept. 6, 1785.
Robert, s. John and Sarah, Feb. 21, 1751-2.
Robert, s. Robert and Rachel, May 3, 1780.
Rufus, s. Capt. Salathiel and Sarah, Mar. 27, 1814.
Rufus, s. Isaac and Hannah, Jan. 28, 1817.
Salathial, jr., s. Salathial and Susanna, Dec. 3, 1804.
Salethial, s. Abel and Olive, May 28, 1782.
Salla, d. Samuel and Sarah, Apr. 29, 1783.
Sally, d. Capt. Timothy and Joanna, Nov. 30, 1791.
Samuel, s. Th[omas], bp. 1: 12 m: 1656. P. R. 1.
Samuel, s. Pelitiah and Liddiah, Feb. 29, 1712.
Samuel, s. Joseph and Mary, Sept. 5, 1734.
Samuel, s. Samuel and Easter, Sept. 5, 1735.
Samuel, s. Samuel and Esther, Sept. 7, 1747.
Samuel, s. Samuel and Lucy, bp. Mar. 28, 1773. C. R. 1.
Samuel, s. Samuel and Sarah, Sept. 17, 1781.
Samuel Webber, s. Samuel, jr. and Betsy, Apr. 2, 1807.
Samuell, s. Pelatiah [and Ruth. CT. R.], Mar. 28, 1685.
Samuell, s. Josaph and Mercy, July 30, 1696.
Sam[ue]ll, s. Timothy and Dorithy, Nov. 15, 1700.
Sam[ue]ll, s. Peletiah and Lediah, July 21, 1714.

ADAMS, Sarah, d. John and Sarah, Aug. 26, 1744.
Sarah, d. John and Esther, Dec. 29, 1752.
Sarah, d. John and Sarah, Sept. 18, 1760.
Sarah, d. William and Polly, Mar. 9, 1808.
Sarah Elizabeth, d. William, jr. and Sarah S., Apr. 16, 1838.
Sary, d. Joseph and Mary, Oct. 5, 1723.
Sibel, d. Oliver and Rachel, Sept. 12, 1761.
Simeon, s. Joseph and Lucy [(Blodget). P. R. 24.], May 22, 1796.
Solomon, s. William and Elizebeth, Dec. 7, 1758.
Solomon, s. [Capt. C. R. 1.] William and Polly, Sept. 19, 1796.
Stephen, s. Thomas and Judah, Feb. 4, 1715.
Stephen, s. Timothy and Joanna, Feb. 22, 1782.
Sumner, s. Isaac and Hannah, Apr. 3, 1803.
Susan Elizabeth, d. Abiel C., carpenter, b. Boxborough, and Elizabeth H., b. Dracut, at Andover, Sept. 13, 1848.
Susanah, d. Pellatiah and Liddia, July 22, 1723.
Susanna, d. Robert and Rachel, Oct. 16, 1789.
Sybbill, d. Josep and Mary, Aug. 14, 1714.
Tabitha Maria, d. Ephraim and Tabitha, Sept. 7, 1819.
Thankfull, d. Joseph and Mary, Nov. 13, 1729.
Thankfull, d. Joseph and Lydia, May 3, 1755.
Thomas, s. Timothy and Dorithy, June 3, 1707.
Thomas, s. John and Sarah, Jan. 23, 1749-50.
Thomas Jefferson, s. William and Polly, May 4, 1805.
Thomas Minott, s. Isaac and Hannah, Sept. 12, 1810.
Timothy, s. Th[omas], bp. 1: 12 m: 1656. P. R. 1.
Timothy, s. Timothy and Dorethy, Aug. 13, 1703.
Timothy, s. John and Sary, Sept. 7, 1754.
Timothy, s. John and Sarah, Aug. 14, 1757.
Timothy, jr., s. Timothy and Joanna, June 6, 1789.
William, s. Benjamin and Olive, June 8, 1732.
William, s. William and Elizebeth, Apr. 13, 1762.
William, s. Joseph, jr. and Lydia, May 30, 1770.
William, s. William and Polly, Oct. 11, 1790.
Zacceos, s. Pellitiah and Lidia, Mar. 20, 1719.
Zacceus, s. Pellitiah and Liddiah, July 1, 1714.
Zachariah, s. Thomas and Judah, Nov. 5, 1718.
——, ch. Jo[seph], jr., Apr. 9, 1754. C. R. 1. [Apr. 8. P. R. 4.]
——, ch. Jonas, Apr. 3, 1758. P. R. 4.

ADDAMS (see also Adams), David, s. Jonathan and Leah, Mar. 29, 1699.
Marah, d. Samuell and Rebeckah [Deborah. CT. R.], Sept. 8, 1664.
Rachil, d. Oliver and Rachil, Aug. 19, 1757.

ADDAMS, Thomas, s. Tho[mas] and Mare, July 22, 1660.

ALEN (see also Allen), Israel, s. W. and M., bp. Jan. 15, 1815, a. 7 w. c. r. 1.

ALEXANDER (see also Elexander, Ellexander), Lucinda, d. Hannah, bp. Oct. 12, 1794. c. r. 1.

ALLEN (see also Alen), Charles Hastings, s. Rev. Wilks and Mary, Mar. 11, 1809.
James Morrell, s. Rev. Wilkes and Mary, Oct. 5, 1806.
John Clark, s. Rev. Wilkes and Mary, Nov. 15, 1812.
Mary, d. Rev. Wilkes and Mary, bp. May 24, 1818. c. r. 1.
Nathaniel Glover, s. Rev. Wilkes and Mary, Jan. 22, 1816.
Sarah, d. Wilkes and Mary, bp. June 11, 1820. c. r. 1.
Wilkes, s. Rev. Wilkes and Mary, Dec. 30, 1810.

AMES, Eliza, d. Nathan and Pheby, Feb. 21, 1799.
Francis Gorham, s. Nathan and Pheby, Jan. 30, 1798.
Jeremiah Tylor, s. Nathan and Pheby, Sept. 16, 1801.

ANDERSON, Charles H., s. Evans and Mary Ann, Feb. 3, 1837.

ANDREWS, Abel, s. Ammi and Mary, bp. July 8, 1770. c. r. 1.
Amaziah, s. Ammi and Mary, bp. July 8, 1770. c. r. 1.
Charles Haskell, s. Benj[ami]n C., painter, and Abigail A., at North Chelmsford, Nov. 23, 1847.
Elizabeth, d. Ammi and Mary, bp. July 8, 1770. c. r. 1.
Issachar, s. Ammi and Mary, bp. July 8, 1770. c. r. 1.
Mary, d. Ammi and Mary, bp. July 8, 1770. c. r. 1.
Samuel Ingalls, s. Ammi and Mary, bp. July 8, 1770. c. r. 1.
Sarah, d. Ammi and Mary, bp. Dec. 23, 1770. c. r. 1.
Stephen, s. Ammi and Mary, bp. July 8, 1770. c. r. 1.

ANTHONY, ——, d. Joseph, watchman, b. Island of Field, Western Isles, and Mary Ann, b. Yorkshire, Eng., May 1, 1849.

ATWOOD, Easter, d. Joshua and Easter, May 27, 1759.
Lydia, d. Joshua and Esther, bp. Apr. 21, 1765. c. r. 1.
Sarah, d. Joshua and Easter, Aug. 9, 1762.
Thomas, s. Joshua and Easter, Jan. 22, 1760.

AUSTIN, Daniel H., s. Daniel F., laborer, and Martha, at North Chelmsford, Jan. 31, 1844.

AYER (see also Ayers), Jane, d. Phineas and Betsy, Aug. 16, 1813.

AYERS (see also Ayer), Lucia, d. Joseph, at Dunstable, N. H., bp. Oct. 4, 1767. P. R. 4.

BAILEY, Esther, d. Joseph and Martha, Jan. 19, 1814.
Grenville, s. Joseph and Martha, Jan. 6, 1810.
Joseph Augustus, s. Joseph and Martha, Mar. 24, 1808.
Louisa, d. Joseph and Martha, Nov. 8, 1819.
Martha Emerson, d. Joseph and Martha, Nov. 7, 1805.
Mary Ann, d. Geo[rge] Azro, stone-cutter, b. Compton, Canada, and Mary Ann, b. Nashua, N. H., July 26, 1849.
Mary Smith, d. Joseph and Martha, Sept. 29, 1804.
Sarah, d. Joseph and Martha, Dec. 27, 1816.

BAKER, Josiph [Bowker. CT. R.], s. Josiph and Hanah, Dec. 5, 1690. [Dec. 1. CT. R.]

BALDWIN, Charles Richardson, s. Lt. Cyrus and Elizbeth, Oct. 16, 1808.
Elizabeth, d. Cyrus and Elizabeth, May 14, 1813.
Mary [Fowle. C. R. 1.], d. Cyres and Elizabeth, Nov. 25, 1802.

BALKE, see Bauke.

BALLARD, Mary Ann, d. Sam[ue]l F. and Sarah A., Oct. 16, 1842.

BANCROFT, Hannah Elizabeth, d. Isaac and Hannah, July 1, 1814.

BANKE (see also Bauke), [Hannah Ban. CT. R.]ke, d. John and H[torn. Hannah, May 7, 1666. CT. R.].

BARBER, Simon Frederick, s. ——, bp. Nov. —, 1810. C. R. 1.

BARETT (see also Barrett), Meriam, d. Joseph and Marth[a], Apr. 29, 1686.

BARIT (see also Barrett), Abigal, d. Josaph and Abigal, Oct. 11, 1697.
Benjamin, s. Jonathan and Abagill, Feb. 14, 1705.
Benjamin, s. Benjamin and Anne, Jan. 5, 1709.
Benjamin, s. Joseph and Abagill, Sept. 30, 1711.
Benjamin, s. Benjamin and Elizabeth, Nov. 27, 1733.

CHELMSFORD BIRTHS 17

BARIT, David, s. Moses and Sary, Feb. 18, 1709-10.
Dorcass, d. Joseph and Abagill, Feb. 4, 1713-14.
Ebenezar, s. Joseph and Abagell, July 28, 1706.
Eleizar, s. Joseph, Aug. 1, 1708.
Elenar, d. John and Margret, May 26, 1706.
Elizibeth, d. Benjamin and Elizabeth, Nov. 6, 1732.
Ezekiell, s. John and Margret, Sept. 18, 1709.
Hanah, d. Benjamin and Anna, June 23, 1706.
Hanah, d. Moses and Sary, Nov. 2, 1711.
Hanah, d. John and Margret, Oct. 10, 1714.
John, s. Jonathan and Abagill, Dec. 13, 1709.
Josiah, s. Josiah and Mary, Dec. 14, 1711.
Josiah, s. Josiah and Mary, Jan. 19, 1718-19.
Lideah, d. John and Sarah, Sept. 22, 1659.
Lideah, d. Joseph and Mary, Sept. 22, 1717.
Lidia, d. Benjamin and Elizabeth, Mar. 26, 1738.
Mahitabell, d. Thomas and Francis, Apr. 12, 1665.
Mare, d. John and Sarah, Mar 13, 1662-3.
Margret, d. John and Sarah, Nov. 10, 1667.
[M]argrit, d. Thomas and Franscis, Mar. 31, 1660.
Mary, d. Josiah and Mary, Feb. 28, 1712-13.
Moses, s. Thomas and Francis [torn] 25, 1662.
Moses, s. Thomas and Rachell, Feb. 1, 1718-19.
Oliver, s. Moses and Sary, Nov. 2, 1713.
[Samuel. CT. R.], s. John and Sarah [torn. June 16, 1660. CT. R. 1661?].
Samuell, s. Samuell and Sarah, Apr. 24, 1697.
Sary, d. John and Margret, Jan. 14, 1712.
Sary, d. Jonathan and Sary, May 4, 1714.
Sary, d. Thomas and Rachil, May 6, 1734.

BARITE (see also Barrett), Bengamin, s. twin, John and Dorathy, Oct. 20, 1690.
Deli[ve]ranc, d. Jonathan and Sarah, Feb. 24, 1689-90. [Jan. 24. CT. R.]
Experi[e]n[ce], d. Jonathan and Sara, Jan. 3, 1694-5.
Josiph, s. twin, John and Dorathy, Oct. 20, 1690.
Marah, d. John and Dorathy, Jan. 9, 1694-5.
Wilyam, s. Sameuell and Sarah, Nov. 21, 1689.

BARITT (see also Barrett), Abigill, d. Jonathan and Lidia, Mar. 4, 1730-31.
Ebenezer, s. Jonathan and Lidia, Feb. 14, 1735-6.
Joel, s. Thomas and Rachel, Nov. 30, 1737.
Mary, d. Benjamin and Elizabeth, July 25, 1736.
Rebeckah, d. Jonathan and Lidy, Aug. 5, 1733.

BARITT, Ruth, d. Benjam[in] and Elizibeth, Jan. 5, 1734-5.
Zacheus, s. Thomas and Rachil, Mar. 31, 1728.

BARKE (see also Bauke), Sarah [Bucke. CT. R.; Balke. P. R. 1.], d. John and Hanna, Mar. 30, 1668.

BARKER, Asa, s. Asa and Sally, May 16, 1795.
Ebenezer, s. Asa and Sally, Jan. 10, 1797.
Henry, s. Asa and Nancy, Sept. 16, 1811.
Mary, d. Asa and Nancy, July 8, 1810.
Mehetebell, d. Stephen and Mary, Jan. 16, 1716-17.
Nancy, d. Asa and Nancy, Jan. 2, 1809.
Sally, d. Asa and Sally, Nov. 11, 1805.
Samuel Healy, s. Asa and Sally, Dec. 3, 1807.
Stephen, s. Stephen and Mary, Apr. 19, 1719.
William Foster, s. Asa and Sally, Nov. 6, 1799.

BARNES, Samuel, s. Oliver, bp. at Concord, Aug. 11, 1765. P. R. 4.

BARON (see also Barron), Hanah, d. Moses and Lucy, May 15, 1736.
Jonathan, s. Moses and Mary, June 28, 1698.
Lucy, d. Jonathan and Rebeckeh, Sept. 29, 1728.
Lucy, d. Moses and Lucy, Mar. 12, 1733-4.
Martha, d. Samuel and Sary, Feb. 24, 1730-31.
Mary, d. Isack and Sarah, Sept. 11, 1698.
Sarah, d. Isack and Sarah, Sept. 29, 1695.
Sarah, d. Samuel and Sarah, Oct. 9, 1734.

BARRAT (see also Barrett), Billy, s. Benjamin and Olive, bp. May 2, 1779. C. R. 1.
Jonathan, s. Jonathan and Abigail, bp. Jan. 26, 1772. C. R. 1.
Joseph, s. Nathaniel and Martha, bp. Dec. 31, 1749. C. R. 1.
Oliver, s. Oliver and Anna, bp. Mar. 16, 1760. C. R. 1.
Patty, d. Nath[anie]ll and Martha, bp. May 19, 1751. C. R. 1.
Stephen, s. John and Martha, bp. July 1, 1759. C. R. 1.
Sybil, d. Christopher and Mary, bp. Apr. 28, 1771. C. R. 1.
Sybil, d. Benjamin and Olive, bp. Mar. 9, 1777. C. R. 1.

BARRATT (see also Barrett), Sarah, d. Joseph and Mary, Feb. 8, 1731-2.

BARRET (see also Barrett), Abigail, d. John and Martha, Dec. 29, 1748.
Betty, d. Benjamin and Elizabeth, Jan. 26, 1742-3.

BARRET, Briget, d. Jonathan and Abbigal, Apr. 11 [faded]7 [170-. T. C. 1702?].
Christepher, s. Benjamin and Elizebath, Feb. 6, 1739.
Ephraim, s. Joseph and Abigal, Sept. 15, 1700.
Hester, d. Joseph and Abigall, Apr. 17, 1699.
Jam[e]s, s. Thomas and Rachel, Sept. 4, 1716.
John, s. John and Martha, Feb. 12, 1738-9.
John, s. Joseph and Sarah, Jan. 16, 1747-8.
Jonas, s. Thomas and Rachel, Jan. 4, 1721-2.
Jonathan, s. Jonathan and Sarah, Oct. 28, 1687. CT. R.
Jonathan, s. John and Martha, Oct. 27, 1746.
Joseph, s. Joseph and Sarah, June 30, 1744.
Josiah, s. Joseph and Martha, July 2, 1688. CT. R.
Lemuel, s. Benjamin and Olive, Oct. 12, 1763.
Liddia, d. Jonathan and Liddia, June 3, 1719.
Lucy, d. Jonathan and Lydia, Aug. 14, 1738.
Martha, d. Joseph and Mary, May 27, 1720.
Mary, d. Jonathan and Lidia, Nov. 10, 1721.
Mary, d. Benjamin and Olive, Mar. 8, 1766.
Oliver, s. Oliver and Anna, Oct. 13, 1764.
Pattee, d. John and Martha, Jan. 20, 1740-41.
Rachel, d. Jonathan and Abigal, Aug. 9, 1699.
Rachel, d. Thomas and Rachel, Feb. 17, 1723-4.
Rebeca, d. John and Martha, Sept. 26, 1744.
Sarah, d. Josiah and Mary, Aug. 14, 1720.
Simeon, s. John and Martha, Nov. 2, 1750.
Tabitha, d. Jonathan and Lydia, Mar. 3, 1728-9.
William, s. Joseph and Sarah, May 17, 1746.
Zebulon, s. Christopher and Mary, Feb. 9, 1766.
——, s. Patric, forger, and Jane, both b. "Latham Co.," Ireland, Dec. 15, 1849.

BARRETT (see also Barett, Barit, Barite, Baritt, Barrat, Barratt, Barret, Barrit, Barrite, Barritt), Amos, s. Thomas and Rachell, Mar. 23, 1725-6.
Anna, d. Thomas and Francis, Dec. 7, 1668.
Elizabeth, d. Jonathan and Lidia, Feb. 14, 1726-7.
Hannah, d. Jonathan and Lidya, Jan. 8, 1724-5.
Hannah, d. Thomas and Rachel, Apr. 10, 1730.
Henry Oliver, s. Oliver S. and Lucy S., Jan. 27, 1843.
John, s. John and Dorothy, Apr. 22, 1686.
Joseph, s. Joseph and Martha, Feb. 24, 1690. CT. R.
Joseph, s. Joseph and Mary, Jan. 31, 1722-3.
Lucy, d. Thomas and Rachell, Apr. 17, 1732.
Margreat, d. Joseph and Martha, Apr. 28, 1683.
Mary, d. Jonathan, Jan. 14 [torn. 1679-80?].

BARRETT, Mary, d. Jonathan and Sarah, 20: 9 m: 1684.
Moses, s. Moses and Hannah, Oct. 27, 1685.
Nathaniel, s. Joseph and Mary, Dec. 1, 1724.
Oliver, s. Joseph and Mary, Jan. 9, 1726-7.
Rebeckah, d. Joseph and Martha, July 4, 1673.
Samuell, s. Samuell and Sarah, Nov. 23, 1686.
Sarah, d. Samuell and Sarah, Mar. 20, 1685.
Sarah, d. John and Martha, Sept. 11, 1741.
[torn], d. Joseph and Martha, July 8, 1678.

BARRIT (see also Barrett), Benjamin, s. Christopher and Mary, May 27, 1767.
Benjamin, s. Benjamin and Olive, Apr. 30, 17[torn. bp. 1771. C. R. 1.].
Ebenezer, s. Oliver and Anna, Mar. 10, 1762.
John, s. Nathaniel and Martha, Dec. 29, 1756.
Jonathan, s. Jonathan and Sarrah, May 16, 1716.
Joseph, s. Oliver and Anna, Sept. 2, 1767.
Lucy, d. Joseph and Marcy, Dec. 28, 1761.
Luke, s. Benjamin and Olive, Feb. 15, 1761.
Martha, d. Nathaniel and Martha, Feb. 17, 1759.
Mary, d. Joseph and Mary, Aug. 12, 1715.
Molle, d. Oliver and Anne, Oct. 10, 1757.
Molle, d. Joseph and Marcy, July 23, 1758.
Olive, d. Benjamin and Olive, Feb. 7, 17[torn. bp. 1774. C. R. 1.].
Rebeca, d. Josiah and Mary, Feb. 26, 1715-16.
Ruth, d. Nathaniel and Martha, May 5, 1761.
Sarah, d. Joseph and Abigal, Sept. 25, 170[2. T. C.].
Smith, s. Moses and Sary, Jan. 2, 1716-17.
Steven, s. John and Martha, Oct. 1, 1756.
Thaddeas, s. Benjamin and Olive, Aug. 11, 176[faded. 1769?].

BARRITE (see also Barrett), Elisabeth, d. Sameuell and Sarah, Dec. 10, 1692.

BARRITT (see also Barrett), Anna, d. Oliver and Anna, June 12, 1755.
John, s. Christopher and Mary, Mar. 4, 1769.

BARRON (see also Baron), Abigail, d. Elliz., Jan. 10, 1670. CT. R.
Abigail, d. Oliver and Abigail, bp. Jan. 14, 1759. C. R. 1.
Benjamin, s. Jonathan [deceased. C. R. 1.] and Rachel, Nov. 17, 1755.
Charls, s. Jonathan and Rebeckeh, June 4, 1731.

BARRON, Eliseus, s. Samuel [jr. P. R. 4.] and Sarah, Aug. 24, 1749.
Elisseus, s. Moses and Mary, Mar. 16, 1682.
Elizabeth, d. Isaac and Sarah, Dec. 9, 1700.
Elizabeth, d. Samuel and Mary, July 14, 1722.
Elizabeth, d. twin, Samuel and Sarah, May 2, 1742.
Elizeus, s. Sam[ue]ll and Mary, July 23, 1727.
Georg [Bancroft. C. R. 1.], s. Jonathan and Mary Dandrig, Mar 22, 1803.
Hanah, d. Isaac and Sarah, Oct. 14, 1703.
Harriet, d. Jonathan and Mary D., May 29, 1800.
Isaac, s. Moses and Mary, Dec. 1, 1671.
Isaac, s. Sam[ue]ll and Mary, Jan. 15, 1713-14.
Isaac, s. Samuel and Sarah, Sept. 13, 1747.
Joanna, d. Samuel and Sarah, Nov. 24, 1750.
Jonathan, s. Jonathan and Rebecka, Nov. 12, 1726.
Jonathan, s. Jonathan and Rachel, Nov. 3, 1750.
Jonathan, s. Jonathan and Rachel, Nov. 28, 1751.
Jonathan, s. Capt. Oliver and Abigail, Aug. 22, 1769.
Joseph, s. Moses and Mary, Sept. —, 1688. [Aug. 27. CT. R.]
Joshua, s. Elizabeth, bp. July 21, 1771. C. R. 1.
Lucia, d. Jonathan and Rachil, Dec. 19, 1753.
Lucy, d. Capt. Oliver and Abigal, Mar. 9, 1764.
Lydia, d. Ens. Samuel and Sarah, Oct. 16, 1753.
Mary, d. Moses and Mary, Mar. 1, 1673.
Mary, d. Samuel and Mary, Sept. 14, 1719.
Mary, d. Samuel and Sarah, Sept. 24, 1732.
Mary, d. Jonathan and Mary D., Sept. 15, 1796.
Moses, s. Moses [Elyas. CT. R.] and Mary, Oct. 28, 1669.
Moses, s. Samuell and Mary, July 3, 1709.
Moses, s. Moses and Lucy, June 1, 1738.
Olive, d. twin, Samuel and Sarah, May 2, 1742.
Oliver, s. Jonathan and Rebeceh, Jan. 7, 1733.
Oliver, s. Capt. Oliver and Abigal, Oct. 28, 1766.
Oliver, s. Jonathan and Mary D., July 11, 1798.
Rebecca, d. Oliver and Abigail, bp. Dec. 12, 1756. C. R. 1.
Rebecca D[andredge. C. R. 1.], d. Jonathan and Mary D[andrig. dup.], Aug. 26, 1805. [Aug. 27. dup.]
Rhoda, d. Samuel and Sarah, Oct. 14, 1744.
Samuell, s. Moses and Mary, May 3, 1679.
Samuell, s. Samuell and Mary, June 4, 1706.
Wiliam, s. Moses and Mary, Nov. 19, 1685.
William, s. Jonathan and Rebeckeh, Oct. 17, 1737.
William, s. Jonathan and Mary D., Sept. 24, 1810.

BARRUS, Joshaua, s. Joshaue and Mary, Oct. 24, 1696.

BARRY, Honora, d. Daniel, laborer, and Catharine, both b. Ireland, at Middlesex Village, Nov. —, 1849.
Julia, d. Daniel, laborer, and Catharine, both b. Ireland, at Middlesex Village, Mar. —, 1848.

BARTLETT, Charles Edwin Adams, s. Dr. John C. and Maria Juliett, Sept. 5, 1836.
George Henry, 2d, s. Dr. J. C. and Maria J., bp. June 30, 1839. C. R. 1.
Joel Adams, s. Dr. J. C. and Maria Juliett, Aug. 22, 1842.

BATCHELDER, John Montgomery, s. Samuel and Mary M., bp. Oct. 2, 1825. C. R. 5.

BATEMAN (see also Batman), Charles, s. Jonas and Lydia, Dec. 9, 1793.
Charlotte, d. Lt. John, bp. June 30, 1799. C. R. 1.
Ephraim, s. Lt. John and Hannah, Dec. 15, 1803.
Nabby, d. Lt. John and Hannah, Dec. 1, 1790.
Sally, d. Lt. John and Hannah, Feb. 17, 1793.

BATES (see also Batties), Betty, d. John and Deborah, May 5, 1713.
Betty, d. Edward, bp. Dec. 3, 1727. C. R. 4.
Betty, d. Robert and Lydia, Aug. 12, 1755.
Hannah, d. John and Deborah, Nov. 24, 17[torn. 1701?].
John, s. John and Mary, Dec. 22, 1668.
John, s. John and Deborah, Nov. 29, 1706.
John, s. Jonathan and Abigail, Apr. 23, 1748.
Jonathan, s. John and Deborah, Mar. 31, 1709.
Jonathan, s. Jonathan and Abigail, Feb. 13, 1749-50.
Joseph, s. Edward and Mary, Nov. 3, 1725.
Lydia, d. Robert and Lydia, May 2, 1750.
Lydia, d. Samuel and Sybil, bp. Sept. 21, 1783. P. R. 4.
Olive, d. Robert and Lydia, Jan. 16, 1752.
Oliver, s. Edward and Mary, Jan. 13, 1720-21.
Robert, s. John and Deborah, Jan. 16, 1711.
Sibell, d. Robert and Lydia, Feb. 27, 1759.

BATMAN (see also Bateman), Anna, d. Lt. John and Hannah, Nov. 9, 1795.
John, s. Lt. John and Hannah, Mar. 18, 1801.
Lucy, d. Lt. John and Hannah, Aug. 11, 1797.
Lydia, d. John and Hannah, Apr. 15, 1788.

BATS (see also Batties), Debarah, d. John and Deborah, Oct. 21, 1694.
Edward, s. John and Daborah, Apr. 14, 1696.
Mary, d. John and Mary, May 8, 1667.
Mary, d. John and Debora, Feb. 1, 1705.

BATTES (see also Batties), Elisabeth, d. John and Mary, Dec. 22, 1671.
Lidiah, d. John and Mary, Feb. 25, 1673.

BATTIES (see also Bates, Bats, Battes, Batty, Betties, Betty), Andrew, s. Andrew and Mary, Dec. 22, 1740.
Benjamin [Betty. C. R. 1.], s. Andrew and Mary, June 2, 1745.
Robert [Betty. C. R. 1.], s. Andrew and Mary, Nov. 2, 1746.
William [Betty. C. R. 1.], s. Andrew and Mary, June 13, 1749.

BATTY (see also Batties), James [Betty. C. R. 1.], s. Andrew and Mary, Oct. 4, 1752.

BAUKE (see also Banke, Barke), Mary, d. John and Hanna, Jan. 7, 1670.

BEAN, Mary Charlotte, d. Eldad P. and Mary, Nov. 26, 1840.

BEARSE, Clara Arvilla, d. Elijah D., moulder, and Sarah, both b. Hanson, July 24, 1849.

BELL, John Franklin, s. W[illia]m, manufacturer, b. Hillsborough, N. H., and Polly, b. Stonington, Nov. 11, 1849.

BETTIES (see also Batties), Andrew, s. Robert and Hannah, Jan. 16, 1767.
John, s. Andrew and Mary, July 7, 1757.

BETTY (see also Batties), John, s. Andrew and Mary, bp. June 3, 1744. C. R. 1.
Joseph, s. Andrew and Mary, Nov. 13, 1751. [bp. Nov. 18, 1750. C. R. 1.]

BIAM (see also Byam), Abraham, s. Abraham and Exspariens, Sept. 29, 1680. [Oct. 1. dup.]
Anna, d. Abraham and Exsperience, Oct. 14, 1673.
George, s. Abraham and Mary, May 16, 1710.
Isacke, s. Abraham and Sarah, Jan. 4, 1691.
Jacob, s. Abraham and Sari, July 18, 1692.
Jona, d. Abraham and Hanah, June 4, 1718.

BIAM, Susanah, d. Abraham and Experience, Oct. 2, 1682.
Tabatha, d. Abraham and Mary, Jan. 4, 1712.
[torn], d. Abraham and Exsperienc, May 4, 1678.

BICKFORD, Mary Isadore, d. Geo[rge] W., carpenter, b. Tyngsborough, and Lydia, b. Dracut, at Lowell, June 10, 1848.

BIGSBY (see also Bixby), Jacob, s. David, bp. Aug. 18, 1728. c. r. 4.

BINGHAM, George H., s. George, milkman, and Caroline, at Baptist Village, Dec. 13, 1846.

BIRCH (see also Burch), Caroline Isidore, d. Benjamin, boatman, and Carolin, at Middlesex Village, Sept. 17, 1843.

BIRD, Charles Henry, s. Charles T. and Sarah H., July 15, 1841.
Charles Shelden, s. Charles T., founder, and Sarah H., at North Chelmsford, Sept. 18, 1847.
Ella Louisa, d. Ch[arles] T., iron-founder, b. Mansfield, and Sarah H., b. Easton, Sept. 1, 1849.
Hellen Eluthera, d. Charles T. and Sarah H., Jan. 28, 1843.
Mary Frances, d. Henry M., moulder, and Olive C., at North Chelmsford, Jan. 5, 1848.
Sarah Sheldon, d. Charles T. and Sarah H., Oct. 9, 1839.

BIXBY (see also Bigsby), Abigall, d. David, Apr. 13, 1717.
Daniel, s. Thomas and Phebe, Aug. 31, 1746.
Edward, s. Thomas and Phebe, Sept. 8, 1744.
Jonathan, s. David and Abagall, Nov. 17, 1714.
Thomas, s. Thomas and Deborah, May 17, 1722.

BLAISDEL (see also Blasdell), William, s. William and Sarah, bp. Sept. 16, 1759. p. r. 4.

BLAKE, Frank L. L., s. Lyman, milk merchant, and Zeruah, Dec. 29, 1848.
Jeraldine Florella, d. Isaac W., tailor, and Cynthia, at North Chelmsford, Nov. 3, 1845.

BLANCHARD, Benjamin, s. twin, John and Hanah, Mar. 15, 1664-5.
Benjamin, s. Thomas and Ruth, Dec. 28, 1706.
Elizabath, d. Thomas and Ruth, Jan. 19, 1705.

BLANCHARD, Esther, d. Thomas and Dorcas, of Dunstable [N. H. P. R. 4.], bp. Nov. 11, 1753. C. R. 1.
Esther, d. Joshua and Sarah, of Hollis, Nov. 9, 1763.
Gosiah, s. twin, John and Hanah, Mar. 15, 1664-5.
James, s. John and Hanah, Mar. 10, 1666-7.
James, s. Thomas and Ruth, Dec. 29, 1711.
Joseph, s. John and Hannah, 1 : 9 m : 1672.
Nathanell, s. John and Hannah, Sept. 23, 1674.
Nathaniell, s. Thomas and Ruth, Sept. 30, 1709.
Rebecca, d. Eleazer and Lucy Butterfield, Oct. 11, 1752.
[torn], d. Hannah, Nov. 30, 1678.

BLASDEL (see also Blasdell), Mary, d. He[n]ry and Liddia, Aug. 27, 1720.

BLASDELL (see also Blaisdel, Blasdel, Blazdel, Blazedell, Blazedil, Blazedill, Blazedle), John, s. Henry and Lydia, Nov. 23, 1732.
Sarrah, d. Henry and Lydia, Mar. 23, 1729-30.

BLAZDEL (see also Blasdell), Henry, s. William and Sary, Nov. 23, 1760.
William, s. William and Sary, Nov. 30, 1756.

BLAZEDELL (see also Blasdell), Aron, s. William and Sarah, Nov. 2, 1762.
Isaac, s. William and Sarah, May 17, 1770.
Lydia, d. William and Sarah, May 13, 1768. [bp. Sept. 27, 1767. C. R. 1.]

BLAZEDIL (see also Blasdell), Sarah, d. Henery and Sarah, Feb. 10, 1735-6.
William, s. Henery and Lidya, June 6, 1735.

BLAZEDILL (see also Blasdell), Ann, d. Henery and Lidia, Mar. 3, 1727.
Anna, d. Henery and Lydia, Apr. 7, 1725.
Lidia, d. Henery and Lidya, May 7, 1723.

BLAZEDLE (see also Blasdell), John Sawyer, s. John and Mary, Nov. 3, 1757.

BLODGET (see also Blodgett, Blodgit, Bloged, Bloget, Blogett, Blogged, Blogget, Bloggett, Blogit, Blotchid), Abagell, d. Willam and Mary, Apr. 4, 1707.
Anna, d. Benjamin and Mary, Jan. 19, 1686-7.

BLODGET, Anne, d. Thomas and Mary, May 9, 1714.
Bettey, d. Simeon and Lydia, June 5, 1767.
Daniel, s. Benjamin and Mary, Feb. 1, 1689-90.
Elizabath, d. Willam and Mary, Mar. 10, 1705.
Ephraim, s. Simeon and Lydia, Nov. 5, 1769.
Esther, d. William and Eleziabeth, Nov. 6, 1739.
Hanah, d. Willam and Mary, Dec. 6, 1715.
Hannah, d. Simeon and Lidya, Dec. 10, 1757.
John, s. Thomis and Mary, Nov. 26, 1698.
John Warren, s. Frederick W. and Betsey, Apr. 13, 1839.
Josiah, s. Willam and Mary, July 27, 1709.
Mary, d. Thomas and Mary, Jan. 4, 1706.
Persis, d. Willam and Mary, Mar. 7, 1712.
Rebecka, d. Oliver and Rebecka, July 31, 1758.
Sam[ue]ll, s. Thomas and Mary, Sept. 27, 1702.
Sibill, d. Simeon and Lidya, Mar. 17, 1759.
Simeon, s. Simeon and Lydia, May 5, 1764.
Thankful, d. Esther, bp. May 13, 1759. C. R. 1.
Thankfull, d. Willam and Mary, Apr. 28, 1719.
Thankfull, d. Esther, Dec. 29, 1769.

BLODGETT (see also Blodget), Lydia, d. Simeon and Lydia, June 7, 1754.
Sarah Francelia, d. Fred[eri]c W., stable-keeper, and Betsey B., at North Chelmsford, July 10, 1846.

BLODGIT (see also Blodget), Frederic Floyer, s. Fred[eri]c W., stable-keeper, and Betsey B., at Furnace Village, Aug. 30, 1843.
Lucy, d. Simeon and Lydia, July 27, 1761.
Ruben, s. William and Elizibeth, May 25, 1737.

BLOGED (see also Blodget), Anna, d. Daniell and [Mary. T. C.], Nov. 9, 1655. [Nov. 2, 1654. CT. R.; 2: 9 m: 1655. P. R. 1.]
Daniell [torn. s. Daniel. CT. R.], Jan. [torn. Jan. 6, 1656. CT. R.; 7: 11 m: P. R. 1.]
Jonathan, s. Daniell and Mare, Sept. 18, 1660.
Sarah, d. Wilyam and Mary, Jan. 6, 1698-9.
Thomas, s. Daniell and Mare, June 25, 1654. [24: 11 m: P. R. 1.]
William, s. William and Mary, Mar. 13, 1697.

BLOGET (see also Blodget), Elisabeth, d. Benjamin and Mary, Dec. 15, 1699.
Jacob, s. William and Mary, Mar. 23, 17[02]-3.

BLOGET, Josiph, s. Thomas and Mary, Oct. 10, 1689-90.
Mary, d. William and Mary, Jan. 22, 1701.
Samuel, s. John and Abigail, Aug. 28, 1724.
Tabatha, d. Thomas and Tabatha, Jan. 2, 1719-20.
[torn], d. Bengamin and Marai, Oct. 31, 1694.

BLOGETT (see also Blodget), Ebenezer, s. William and Elizabeth, July 18, 1729.
Olliver, s. Jacob and Mary, Mar. 24, 1727-8.
Zacheus, s. Jacob and Mary, Mar. 17, 1726-7.

BLOGGED (see also Blodget), Nathaniell, s. Daniell and Mary, Oct. 22, 1664.
Samuell, s. Daniell and Mare, Oct. 12, 1662.

BLOGGET (see also Blodget), [Benoni. T. C.], s. Thomas and Marie, Oct. 22, 1694.
Olive, d. William and Elisabeth, June 27, 1742.
Thomas, s. Thomas, jr., bp. Aug. 10, 1729. C. R. 4.

BLOGGETT (see also Blodget), Nathaniell, s. Daniell and Sarah, Mar. 16, 1670.
Rebeckah, d. Thomas and Mary, Apr. 12, 1684.

BLOGIT (see also Blodget), Benjamin, s. Banjamin and Mery, Mar. 6, 1697.

BLOOD, Abigail, d. Josiah and Tabathy, June 6, 1787.
Ada Frances, d. Charles Augustus, miller, and Sarah M., b. Stockbridge, Vt., at North Chelmsford, Jan. 8, 1849.
Ambrose L., s. Samuel, farmer, b. Concord, and Sarah, b. Washington, Me., at Manchester, N. H., Feb. 21, 1848.
Augustus Wayland, s. Benj[ami]n, laborer, and Betsey Ann, at Furnace Village, Oct. 7, 1843.
Betty, d. Ephraim and Elizabeth, Mar. 7, 1746-7.
Darcos, d. Josiah and Tabatha, Jan. 16, 1768.
Easter, d. Jonathan and Lydia, Feb. 16, 1761.
Elener, d. James and Kathrin, Sept. 12, 1712.
Elizebeth, d. Josiah and Tabatha, June 24, 1770.
Harriett Elizabeth, d. Benja[min], laborer, and Betsey, at North Chelmsford, Nov. 18, 1845.
Josiah, s. Josiah and Tabathy, Feb. 1, 1773.
Lucy, d. Ephraim and Betty, bp. Dec. 19, 1756. C. R. 1.
Mary Persons, d. Nathaniel, farmer, and Sarah, at North Chelmsford, Oct. 21, 1846.
Molly, d. Josiah and Tabathy, Aug. 1, 1775.

BLOOD, Nathaniel Leavitt, s. Nathaniel, farmer, b. Tyngsborough, and Sarah, b. Meredith, N. H., at North Chelmsford, Nov. 6, 1848.
Oliver, s. Josiah and Tabathy, Jan. 31, 1778.
Sally Mery, d. Oliver and Sally, Feb. 16, 1809.
Samuel L., s. Samuel, farmer, b. Concord, and Sarah, b. Washington, Me., at Dracut, Feb. 20, 1846.
Sarah Catharine, d. Nathaniel, farmer, and Sarah, at North Chelmsford, Sept. 3, 1845.
Tabathy, d. Josiah and Tabathy, Nov. 15, 1781.
Willard, s. Ephraim and Betty, June 10, 1743.

BLOTCHID (see also Blodget), Elizabeth, d. William and Elizabeth, Oct. 4, 1722.
Hanah, d. William and Elizibeth, Jan. 7, 1731-2.
Nehemiah, s. Jacob, ———. [1732 or 1733?]
Ruth, d. William and Elizibeth, Mar. 5, 1734-5.
Simion, s. William and Elizabeth, Feb. 6, 1727.
William, s. William and Elizabeth, Dec. 1, 1724.

BOINTON (see also Boynton), Hannah, d. Nathaniell and Hannah, Jan. 14, 1725-6.
Nathaniel, s. Nathaniel and Hannah, June 8, 1724.

BOOMER, John Luce, s. James C., Baptist clergyman, and Eliza, Oct. 25, 1848.

BOOTMAN (see also Butman), Edson, s. Jonathan and Amy W., Nov. 27, 1826.
Henry Burton, s. Jonathan and Amy W., Feb. 1, 1829.

BOOTT, John Wright, s. Kirk and Anne, bp. Mar. 20, 1825. c. r. 5.

BORN (see also Borne), James, s. James and Mary, June 18, 1690.

BORNE (see also Born), Mary, d. James and Mary, May 14, 1685.
———, d. James and Mary, Nov. 6, 1686.

BOSWORTH, Harriett Newell, d. Henry E. and Lucy, Dec. 12, 1841.
Hellen Arabella, d. Henry E., machinist, and Lucy, at North Chelmsford, Nov. 18, 1844.
Joanna Harlow, d. Henry E. and Lucy, May 31, 1840.

CHELMSFORD BIRTHS 29

BOSWORTH, Tryphena Adgate, d. [Dea. c. R. 3.] Henry E., machinist, and Lucy, at North Chelmsford, Sept. 26, 1846.

BOWARS (see also Bowers), Benjamin, s. Jonathan and Hanah, Mar. 7, 1713-14.
John, s. Jonathan and Hanah, Sept. 20, 1707.
Luce, d. Jerathmell and Sary, July 21, 1715.
Sary, d. Jonathan and Hanah, Feb. 25, 1712.
Sary, d. Jeramuell and Sary, Nov. 12, 1713.
Willam, s. Jonathan and Hanah, Jan. 8, 1709.

BOWERS (see also Bowars), Alpheus, s. Capt. Joseph and Rhoda [(Butterfield). P. R. 11.], May 17, 1807.
Alpheus, s. Alpheus, farmer, and Julia A., at Middlesex Village, July 20, 1849.
Benjamin, s. Jonathan and Mary, bp. July 19, 1741. C. R. 1.
Benja[min], s. Francis and Elizibeth, Mar. 6, 1782.
Betty, d. Jerahmeel and Sarah, June 15, 1725.
Betty, d. Oliver and Esther, bp. Jan. 30, 1757. C. R. 1.
Betty, d. Oliver and Ester, Feb. 22, 1757.
Charles, s. Jerahmael and Sarah, Feb. 27, 1716-17.
Charles Henry, s. M. and M., bp. Oct. 5, 1828. C. R. 3.
David, s. Francis and Elizabeth, bp. Apr. 13, 1777. C. R. 1.
Ebenezer, s. Jerahmeel and Elizabeth, bp. Mar. 17, 1751. C. R. 1.
Esther, d. Oliver and Esther, bp. Mar. 13, 1763. C. R. 1.
Frances, s. Frances and Elisabeth, May 20, 1775.
Francis, s. Jonathan and Mary, bp. July 22, 1744. C. R. 1.
George, s. Sewall, farmer, and Philinda, b. Whitefield, N. H., at Middlesex Village, Oct. 30, 1848.
Hannah, d. Jonathan and Hannah, Nov. 11, 1703.
Hannah, d. William and Hannah, May 14, 1765.
Harbart, s. Frances and Elizabath, Feb. 25, 1793.
Henry, s. Oliver and Esther, July 23, 1759.
Irene, d. Capt. Joseph and Rhoda [(Butterfield). P. R. 11.], May 27, 1804.
Isaac, s. Jonathan and Mary, Jan. 1, 1732-3.
Jerahmeel, s. Jerahmeel and Sarah, Oct. 31, 1719.
Jerahmeel, s. Jerahmeel [jr. C. R. 1.] and Elizabeth, July 7, 1749.
Jerahmeel, s. Oliver and Esther, Mar. 11, 1765.
Jerahmell, s. Jonathan and Hannah, Jan. 5, 1700.
Jerathmell, s. Jerathmell and Elisabeth, Dec. 17, 1685.
Jesse, s. William and Hannah, Nov. 13, 1785. [bp. Nov. 28, 1784. C. R. 1.]

BOWERS, John, s. Oliver and Elisabeth, Oct. 17, 1769.
John Frie, s. Philip and Chole, July 13, 1799.
John Fry, s. Philip and Chloe, bp. Oct. 1, 1797. C. R. 1.
Jonathan, s. Jerathmell and Elisabeth, Apr. 13, 1674.
Jonathan, s. Jonathan and Hannah, July 5, 1701.
Jonathan, s. Jonathan and Mary, Nov. 18, 1726.
Jonathan, s. William and Hannah, Feb. 18, 1761.
Joseph, s. William and Hannah, Dec. 31, 1780.
Joseph Alpheus, s. Alpheus, farmer, and Julia, at Middlesex Village, Sept. 8, 1845.
Josiah, s. Capt. Jonathan and Hanah, Jan. 10, 1719-20.
Lewis, s. Philip and Chloe, bp. May 6, 1804. C. R. 1.
Lucy, d. Oliver and Esther, Apr. 27, 1767.
Luke, s. Jonathan and Mary, bp. Sept. 28, 1746. C. R. 1.
Luke, s. William and Hannah, Feb. 25, 1763.
Mary, d. Jonathan and Mary, Dec. 29, 1729.
Mary, d. William and Elizabeth, bp. Nov. 15, 1761. P. R. 4.
Mary, d. M. and M., bp. Oct. 5, 1828. C. R. 3.
Mary Ann, d. M., bp. July 21, 1829. C. R. 3.
Mary S., d. Joseph and Rhoda (Butterfield), Feb. 14, 1818. P. R. 11.
Matthias, s. Hannah, bp. June 25, 1786. C. R. 1.
Micagah, s. M. and M., bp. Oct. 5, 1828. C. R. 3.
Nathaniel, s. Jerahmeel and Sarai, Mar. 27, 1722.
Olive, d. William and Hannah, Mar. 24, 1772.
Oliver, s. Jerahmeel and Sarah, Apr. 14, 1728.
Oliver, s. Oliver and Easter, Nov. 25, 1754.
Philip, s. William and Hannah, Jan. 15, 1774.
Samuel, s. Jerathmeel, jr. and Elizabeth, Mar. 11, 1750-51.
Sarah, d. Olever and Esther, May 7, 1753.
Sarah, d. William and Hannah, Aug. 17, 1767.
Sewell, s. Philip, bp. Apr. 18, 1802. C. R. 1.
Sewell, s. Capt. Joseph and Rhoda [(Butterfield). P. R. 11.], July 27, 1810.
Susan Butterfield, d. Capt. Joseph and Rhoda [(Butterfield). P. R. 11.], Aug. 19, 1813.
Tabitha, d. Francis and Elizabeth, bp. Dec. 24, 1780. C. R. 1.
Timothy, s. William and Hannah, Nov. 12, 1777.
William, s. William and Hannah, Nov. 21, 1769. [bp. Nov. 19. C. R. 1.]
William Francis, s. M. and M., bp. Oct. 5, 1828. C. R. 3.
——, ch. Jonathan, Dec. —, 1716.

BOYAM (see also Byam), James, s. Henry and Lucia, Apr. 5, 1752.

BOYNTON (see also Bointon), Bridget, d. Nath[aniel], bp. Dec. 31, 1727. c. R. 4.
Sarah, d. Natha[n]iel and Hannah, Mar. 12, 1721.

BRABROOK, Anna, d. Joseph and Hannah, Aug. 6, 1781.
William, s. Joseph and Hannah, Jan. 6, 1783.

BRACKLEY, Julietta, d. John, boatman, and Lois, at Middlesex Village, Oct. 5, 1847.

BRADFORD, Clara Edna, d. Henry, painter, and Augusta, May 6, 1847.

BRADT, Garrat James, s. ——, bp. Nov. —, 1810. c. R. 1.

BRANNON, Ellen Elizabeth, d. George, moulder, and Joanna, at Furnace Village, Apr. 5, 1844.
George, s. George, moulder, b. Ireland, and Joanna, b. "Barton Ms.", at North Chelmsford, Oct. 7, 1848.
Margarett Maria, d. George, moulder, and Joanna, at North Chelmsford, Aug. 11, 1846.

BRIDGE, Ebenezer, s. Rev. Ebenezer and Sarah, Apr. 23, 1744.
Elizabath, d. William and Rachel, Dec. 17, 1776.
Elizabeth, d. Rev. Ebenezer and Sarah, July 1, 1748.
John, s. Rev. Ebenezer and Sarah, Jan. 31, 1745-6.
Katherine, d. Ebenezer and Sarah [Feb. 16, 1755. p. r. 4.]. c. r. 1.
Lucretia, d. Rev. Ebenezer and Sarah, Mar. 6, 1757.
Mary, d. Rev. Ebenezer and Sarah, Nov. 14, 1750.
Sarah, d. Rev. Ebenezer and Sarah, July 23, 1742.
William, s. Rev. Ebenezer and Sarah, Jan. 11, 1753.
William Stoddard, s. William and Rachel, Aug. 23, 1779.
——, d. Rev. Ebenezer, Apr. 2, 1760. p. r. 4.

BROOKS, Ruth, d. Noah, bp. at Concord, Aug. 23, 1767. p. r. 4.

BROWN (see also Browne), Betsey B., d. Samuel and Lucy, Oct. 28, 1798.
Eliazer, s. Eliazer and Abbigall, Mar. 20, 1702-3.
Ellen Louisa, d. Gardner H., farmer, and Betsey T., Dec. 2, 1846.
Erastus, s. Samuel and Lucy, Oct. 21, 1803.
Hannah Frances, d. John, machinist, and Hannah N., at North Chelmsford, Sept. 30, 1844.

BROWN, Jacob Prescott, s. Samuel and Lucy, Aug. 17, 1814.
Joel, s. Samuel and Lucy, Dec. 22, 1800.
Lucy, d. Samuel and Lucy, Sept. 26, 1802.
Lucy, d. Samuel and Lucy, Feb. 15, 1806.
Mary, d. Samuel and Lucy, Dec. 12, 1812.
Sam[ue]ll, s. Elliazer and Abigal, Dec. 8, 1700.

BROWNE (see also Brown), Benjamin, s. Eliazar and Dinah, Feb. 27, 1682.
Briggett, d. Eliazer and Dinah, July 7, 1685.
Deliveranc, s. Eliazar and Dinah, Dec. 4, 1689.
Dinah, d. Eliazar and Dinah, Feb. 4, 1677.
Eliazar, s. Eliazar and Dinah, Apr. 2, 1676.
Thomas, s. Eliazar and Dinah, May 9, 1680.

BRYANT, Hervy, jr., s. Hervy and Lydia B., Oct. 2, 1827.
Lydia Amelia, d. Hervy and Lydia B., July 19, 1834.

BUELL, Abba Louisa, d. John H., carpenter, b. Newport, N. H., and Abba P., b. Williamstown, Vt., at Nashua, N. H., July 11, 1848.

BURCH (see also Birch), Charles Edward, s. Benj[amin], boatman, and Caroline, at Middlesex Village, Nov. 18, 1847.

BURDG (see also Burge), John, s. David and Rebecca, Sept. 28, 1765.

BURDGE (see also Burge), David, s. John and Sarah, Apr. 17, 1727.
Elezabeth, d. John and Sarai, May 14, 1739.
Joseph, s. John and Sarah, July 28, 1722.
Josiah, s. John and Sarah, Dec. 12, 1723.
Samuel, s. Josiah and Susana, Oct. 16, 1726.

BURG (see also Burge), Josiah, s. John and Triall, Mar. 12, 1696.

BURGE (see also Burdg, Burdge, Burg), David, s. David and Rebeckah, July 16, 1761.
Deborah, d. John and Triall, May 26, 1685.
Easter, d. John and Sary, Mar. 3, 1733-4.
Elisabath, d. John and Tryall, July 12, 1698.
Elisebeth, d. David and Rebecka, Aug. 7, 1770.
Hana, d. John and Triall, Jan. 12, 1689.

BURGE, Hanah, d. John and Tryall, June 12, 1690.
John, s. John and Tryall, Oct. 20, 1688. [Oct. 21, 1687. CT. R.]
John, s. John and Sary, July 21, 1719.
Lidiah, d. John and Sarah, Feb. 16, 1730-31.
Lucy, d. John and Sarah, May 28, 1737.
Lydia, d. David and Rebecca, May 26, 1774.
Mary, d. John and Tryall, Oct. 25, 1678.
Moses, s. Josiah and Susanah, Oct. 19, 1728.
Ratchel, d. John and Tryall, Dec. 21, 1692.
Rebecka, d. David and Rebecka, Dec. 29, 1757.
Rebeckah, d. John and Triall, Nov. 5, 1683.
Sarah, d. John and Triall, May 21, 1691.
Sarah, d. John and Sarah, May 30, 1728.
Susannah, d. John and Tryal, June 27, 1694.

BURGESS, Charles Gilmore, s. James and Susan, at Lowell, Feb. 25, 1844.
George Clarke, s. James C. and Susan A., at Boston, Apr. 13, 1834.
Harriott Maria, d. James C. and Susan A., at Boston, Oct. 11, 1838.
Susan Jane, d. James C. and Susan A., at Boston, July 11, 1836.

BURNETT, James Hervey, s. Hervey, bp. Oct. 12, 1823. C. R. 1.

BURROWS, Charles F., s. W[illia]m F., farmer, and Louisa, at Baptist Village, Jan. 18, 1845.
James, s. James and Catharine, May 14, 1842.
Nancy Mary Eloisa, d. W[illia]m F. and Louisa E., May 11, 1842.

BUTERFEELD (see also Butterfield), David, s. Jonathan and Jane, Dec. 16, 1700. [1702?]

BUTERFEILD (see also Butterfield), Febee, d. Samuell and Mary, 5: 9 m: 1684.
Mary, d. Samuel and Mary, Feb. 4, 1673.

BUTERFELD (see also Butterfield), Abigal, d. twin, Josiph and Lidiah, June 4, 1693.
Abraham, s. twin, Josiph and Lidiah, June 4, 1693.
Benjamin, s. Benjamin and Elizebeth, May 25, 1702.
Isack, s. twin, Josiph and Lidiah, Oct. 14, 1689-90. [Oct. 1. CT. R.]
Jacobe, s. twin, Josiph and Lidiah, Oct. 14, 1689-90. [Oct. 1. CT. R.]

BUTERFELD, Lideah, d. Nathanell and Sarah, Sept. 19, 1698.
Sarah, d. Nathanill and Debrah, Mar. 6, 1689.
Sarah, d. Josepeh and Eunies, Apr. 12, 1698.

BUTERFIELD (see also Butterfield), Abiel, d. Benjamin, deceased, and Sarrah, Apr. 2, 1716.
Benjamin, s. Joseph, Feb. 24, 1679.
Deborah, d. Nathanell and Deborah, June 1, 1660. [1670?]
Deborah, d. Lt. Joseph and Sarah, Jan. 11, 1711.
Deborah, d. Benjamin and Elizabeth, Aug. 18, 1714.
Dinah, d. Jacob and Pheabe, Jan. 21, 1713-14.
Ebenezar, s. Sam[ue]ll and Rachell, July 13, 1707.
Ester, d. Benjamin and Elizebeth, Mar. 19, 1709.
Hanah, d. Samuell and Rachell, Aug. 20, 1714.
Johana, d. Samuell and Rachell, Apr. 30, 1718.
Jonas, s. Jacob and Febe, Sept. 5, 1717.
Jonathan, s. Jonathan and Elizabeth, July 11, 1713-14.
Mary, d. Benjamin and Sary, Aug. 25, 1706.
Rachell, d. Sam[ue]ll and Rachell, July 3, 1709.
Willam, s. Benjamin and Elisibeth, Nov. 28, 1706.
Willam, s. Sam[ue]ll and Rachell, Mar. 16, 1712.
Zachariah, s. Jacob and Febe, May 13, 1716.

BUTERFILD (see also Butterfield), John, s. Benjamin and Sarah, Jan. 12, 1697-8.
Nathaniell, s. Nathaniell and Deborah, 28: 1 m: 1673.
[torn], d. Josiph and Lidiah, July 8, 1678.

BUTLER, Hannah, d. Hezekiah and Pricilla, July 9, 1721.

BUTMAN (see also Bootman), Evander Melburn, s. Willard and Mary, Aug. 27, 1834.
Jonathan Warren, s. Jonathan and Amey, Jan. 31, 1823.
Joseph Edward, s. Jonathan and Amey, Jan. 15, 1825.
Loiza Willard, d. Jona[than] and Amey, bp. Apr. 27, 1823.
c. r. 1.

BUTTERFEILD (see also Butterfield), Abial, d. John and Anna, June 16, 1738.
Bathsheba, d. William and Bathshaeba, Sept. 17, 1727.
Benjamin, s. Benjamin, bp. 1: 12 m: 1656, a. abt. 20 y. p. r. 1.
Benjamin, s. David and Keziah, Oct. 17, 1732.
Benjamin, s. John and Anna, Aug. 10, 1735.
Bridgit, d. John and Anna, Nov. 20, 1727.
Elijah, s. Nathaniel and Abigail, Oct. 31, 1736.

CHELMSFORD BIRTHS

BUTTERFEILD, John, s. John and Anna, Feb. 20, 1730-31.
Jonathan, s. Benjamin, bp. 1: 12 m: 1656, a. abt. 15 y. P. R. 1.
Joseph, s. Benjamin, bp. 1: 12 m: 1656, a. abt. 6 y. P. R. 1.
Keziah, d. David and Keziah, Feb. 25, 1733-4.
Lucy, d. John and Anna, June 15, 1733.
Mary, d. Mary, bp. 8: 3 m: 1670. P. R. 1.
Nathaniel, s. Benjamin, bp. 1: 12 m: 1656, a. abt. 11 1-2 y. P. R. 1.
Nathaniel, s. Nathaniel and Abigail, Jan. 28, 1733-4.
Rebecka, d. Samuel and Rachil, May 19, 1728.
Samuel, s. Benjamin, bp. 1: 12 m: 1656, a. abt. 8 y. P. R. 1.
Sarah, d. Nathaniel and Abigail, Dec. 31, 1738.
William, s. William and Rebeckeh, Nov. 4, 1737.

BUTTERFIELD (see also Buterfeeld, Buterfeild, Buterfeld, Buterfield, Buterfild, Butterfeild, Butterfild), Abigail, d. Nathaniel [jr. C. R. 1.] and Abigail, Dec. 29, 1742. [bp. Nov. 21. C. R. 1.]
Abigail, d. Sam[ue]l and Hannah, Sept. 13, 1812.
Anna, d. John and Anna, Aug. 29, 1723.
Anna, d. Benjamin and Olive, Feb. 5, 1771.
Anna, d. Benjamin and Olive, bp. Jan. 19, 1777. C. R. 1.
Annah, d. Samuell and Mary, Sept. 2, 168[0. T. C.].
Augustus, s. Reuben and Jamima, June 19, 1815.
Benjamin, s. Benjamin and Kezia, May 15, 1726.
Benjamin, s. Benjamin and Olive, May 25, 1759.
Caroline, d. Sam[ue]l and Hannah, July 6, 1814.
Clarissa Maria, d. Ralph and Jemima, Mar. 31, 1816.
Daniel, s. Jonathan and Lydia, Dec. 18, 1759.
Deborah, d. Samuel and Mary, Aug. 20, 1687. CT. R.
Deborah, d. Samuel and Rachel, Dec. 6, 1720.
Elesibeth, d. Benjamin and Elesibeth, Sept. 15, 1704.
Elijah, s. Nathaniel and Elizabeth, Aug. 14, 1763.
Elizabeth, d. Jonathan and Susanna, bp. Apr. 1, 1744. C. R. 1.
Elizabeth, d. Nathaniel and Elizabeth, Aug. 13, 1765.
Emeline, d. Sam[ue]l and Hannah, June 21, 1820.
Emeline, d. Stephen and Mary Ann, Aug. 25, 1835.
Ephraim, s. Capt. John and Anna, July 28, 1741.
Ester, d. Nathan[ie]ll and Sarah, Nov. 14, 1703.
Esther, d. David and Keziah, Nov. 13, 1738.
Esther, d. Nathaniel and Abigal, Jan. 4, 1744-5.
Hannah, d. Samuel and Hannah, at Billerica, Oct. 9, 1801.
Hannah, d. Stephen and Mary Ann, Mar. 12, 1840.
Huldah, d. Nathaniel and Elizabeth, Apr. 27, 1773.
Jacob, s. Jacob and Phebe, Apr. 2, 1724.
Jane, d. David and Keziah, Jan. 9, 1736-7.

BUTTERFIELD, Jeramiah, s. Nathaniel and Abigail, June 1, 1740.
Joanna, d. Jacob and Phebe, Sept. 7, 1721.
Joanna, d. David and Keziah, Oct. 6, 1741.
John, s. Ben[jamin] bp. June 30, 1728. C. R. 4.
John, s. Jonathan and Lydia, Jan. 18, 1762.
John, s. Benjamin and Olive, May 31, 1766.
Jonathan, s. Samuel and Rachel, Jan. 3, 1721-2.
Jonathan, s. Jonathan and Lidia, Nov. 23, 1753.
Joseph, s. Joseph and Eunic, July 19, 1703.
Joseph, s. Samuel and Hannah, May 19, 1805.
Julia Ann, d. Sam[ue]l and Hannah, June 15, 1803.
Julia Ann, d. Ralph and Jemima, Mar. 16, 1813.
Lidiah, d. Benjamin and Sary, Nov. 11, 1711.
Lowal, s. Lt. Benja[min] and Sarah, Feb. 5, 1797.
Lucius, s. Stephen and Mary Ann, Apr. 18, 1842.
Lucy, d. John and Rebecca, bp. Sept. 23, 1798. C. R. 1.
Lura, d. Lt. Benja[min] and Sarah, Dec. 1, 1800.
Lydia, d. Nathaniel and Abigail, Nov. 5, 1747.
Lydia, d. Jonathan and Lydia, Feb. 27, 1752.
Marcy, d. Jonathan and Lydia, Aug. 23, 1755.
Martha, d. Sam[ue]l and Hannah, Mar. 20, 1818.
Mary, d. Sam[ue]ll and Rachell, Nov. 8, 1723.
Mary, d. Jonathan and Elizabeth, Jan. 19, 1726-7.
Mary, d. Capt. John and Anna, Nov. 1, 1746.
Mary, d. Nathaniel and Abigail, July 29, 1754.
Mary, d. Nathaniel and Elizebeth, May 30, 1759.
Mary, d. Sam[ue]l and Hannah, Dec. 26, 1808.
Mary Ann, d. Stephen and Mary Ann, July 29, 1837.
Mary Jane, d. Ralph and Jemima, Jan. 13, 1811.
Meriam, d. Jonathan and Lidya, Feb. 11, 1758.
Molley, d. Jeremiah and Mary, Jan. 29, 1767.
Nathaniel, s. Nathaniel and Sarah, Dec. 25, 1711.
Nathaniel, s. Nathaniel and Elizebeth, Apr. 14, 1761.
Olive, d. Benjamin and Olive, Oct. 11, 1761.
Oliver, s. Jeremiah and Mary, Feb. 19, 1769.
Patty, d. Ens. Benjamin and Sarah, Mar. 21, 1784.
Ralph, s. Ens. Benjamin and Sarah, Feb. 25, 1788.
Ralph, s. Ralph and Jemima, Mar. 27, 1818.
Rebecca, d. W[illia]m, bp. Aug. 31, 1729. C. R. 4.
Rebecca, d. Lucy, bp. Apr. 15, 1753. C. R. 1.
Rebecka, d. Benjamin and Olive, Jan. 19, 1769.
Reuben, s. Benjamin and Olive, Feb. 26, 1764.
Rhoda, d. Benjamin and Olive, bp. Apr. 18, 1779. C. R. 1.
Rhoda, w. Joseph Bowers, Apr. 10, 1780. P. R. 11.
Rhoda, d. Sam[ue]l and Hannah, Apr. 6, 1816.

BUTTERFIELD, Robbert, s. Jonathan and Elizabeth, Sept. 16, 1716.
Ruben, s. Benja[min], jr. and Sarah, July 3, 1782.
Ruth, d. Benjamin and Kezia, Apr. 13, 1724.
Salley, d. Benja[min], jr. and Sarah, Aug. 1, 1779.
Samuel, s. David and Keziah, Dec. 9, 1748.
Samuel, s. Samuel and Hannah, at Billerica, Nov. 8, 1799.
Samuel, s. Sam[ue]l and Hannah, Dec. 3, 1810.
Samuell, s. Samuell and Rachell, Oct. 24, 1704.
Sarah, d. Benjamin and Sarah, Sept. 23, 1701.
Sarah, d. Jonathan and Elizabeth, July 14, 1719.
Sarah, d. John and Anna, Sept. 3, 1725.
Sarah, d. Capt. John and Anna, May 4, 1744.
Sarah, d. David and Keziah, May 20, 1744.
Sarah, d. Jeremiah and Mary, Jan. 17, 1773.
Sevil, d. Ens. Benjamin and Sarah, Mar. 5, 1792.
Sharribeah, s. Nathaniel and Elizabeth, July 26, 1768.
Silas, s. Ens. Benjamin and Sarah, Mar. 7, 1786.
Silos, s. Benjamin and Olive, Apr. 24, 1773.
Solomon, s. Jeremiah and Mary, June 23, 1765.
Stephen, s. Sam[ue]l and Hannah, Jan. 23, 1807.
Stephen Spaulding, s. Stephen and Mary Ann, May 2, 1834.
Supply, s. Nathaniel and Elizabeth, Sept. 21, 1769.
Susan, d. John and Rebecca, bp. Oct. 23, 1796. C. R. 1.
Susanna, d. David and Keziah, bp. Nov. 8, 1741. C. R. 1.
Tabitha, d. Joseph and Lydia, May 29, 1687. CT. R.
Thomas, s. Jonathan and Susanna, bp. June 29, 1746. C. R. 1.
William, s. Nathaniel and Deborah, Jan. 5, 1686. CT. R.

BUTTERFILD (see also Butterfield), Joseph, s. Nathaniell and Deborah, June 6, 1680.

BUTTRICK, Charles, s. Charles and Betcy, Mar. 15, 1801.
Henry Oscar, s. Nathan, jr., turner and cabinet-maker, and Martha B., Apr. 10, 1844.
James G., s. Nathan, turner, and Martha, at Baptist Village, Jan. 18, 1846.
Mehitabel, d. Ephraim and Mehitabel, Mar. 24, 1805.
Olvin, s. Charles and Betsy, bp. Mar. —, 1804. C. R. 1.

BYAM (see also Biam, Boyam, Byham), Abigail, d. Abraham and Hannah, Sept. 29, 1731.
Abraham, s. Abraham and Mary, Feb. 10, 1713.
Amos, s. Henry and Lucy, July 3, 1754.
Amos, s. Amos and Sarah [(Peirce). P. R. 25.], Apr. 24, 1784.
Amos Adams, s. Amos and Lucy, Sept. 9, 1808.

BYAM, Ann Relief, d. Henry and Relief, July 25, 1827.
Anna, d. John and Sarah, July 5, 1791.
Arabella Parker, d. Josiah and Sophronia, Mar. 13, 1830.
Aseph, s. Amos and Sarah [(Peirce). P. R. 25.], Jan. 29, 1791.
Augustus Bateman, s. W[illia]m A., farmer, and Mercy M., Oct. 4, 1849.
Austin Grosvener, s. Henry and Relief, Oct. 2, 1836.
Benjamin, s. Abraham and Hanah, Nov. 29, 1733.
Benja[min], s. Benja[min] and Mary, July 15, 1769.
Betsy Procter, d. Solomon and Abi, Dec. 20, 1803.
Betty, d. Benja[min] and Mary, Dec. 10, 1766.
Charles Wellington, s. Henry and Relief, June 19, 1832.
Chellis Carpenter, s. Stillman, wheelwright, and Mary A., at Baptist Village, Mar. 8, 1847.
Clarina A., d. Solomon and Abi (Adams), Apr. 18, 1808. P. R. 13.
Daniel Proctor, s. Marcus D. and Mary [(Proctor). P. R. 13.], Nov. 8, 1841.
Deliverance, d. John and Sarah, Dec. 4, 1789.
Diliverance, d. John and Sarah, Dec. 4, 1768.
Ephraim Albert, s. Stillman, wheelwright, and Mary Ann, at Baptist Village, Nov. 7, 1844.
Ephraim L., s. Solomon and Abi (Adams), Aug. 16, 1812. P. R. 13.
Ezekel, s. William and Rebeckah, Sept. 13, 1795.
Francis Charles, s. W[illia]m A., farmer, and Mercy, at Baptist Village, Aug. 18, 1847.
Frank Colby, s. Solomon E., farmer, and Hannah, at Baptist Village, Mar. 26, 1848.
George Henry, s. Henry and Relief, Sept. 7, 1829.
George Otis, s. Otis and Lavinia, at Boston, Apr. 2, 1829.
Hannah, d. John and Sarah, May 10, 1785.
Henry, s. Amos and Sarah [(Peirce). P. R. 25.], Oct. 23, 1788. [Oct. 2. P. R. 25.]
Henry Augustus, s. Henry and Relief, July 10, 1825.
Henry Stillman, s. Stillman and Mary Ann, Sept. 20, 1841.
James, s. John and Sary, Feb. 18, 1764.
Jemimah, d. Abraham and Hannah, Jan. 24, 1735-6.
Joanna, d. Jacob and Sary, June 24, 1734.
John, s. Isaac and Mary, Feb. 7, 1730-31.
John, s. John and Sary, June 28, 1761.
John, s. Josiah and Sophronia, Feb. 5, 1832.
John Bateman, s. Ezekiel and Charlotte, Mar. 21, 1823.
Jonathan, s. Jacob, jr. and Sarah [of No. 6. C. R. 1.], Dec. 9, 1753.
Josephine, d. Josiah and Sophronia, Nov. 15, 1840.

BYAM, Josiah, s. Solomon and Abi, May 8, 1795.
Laura, d. Solomon and Abi (Adams), Jan. 13, 1815. P. R. 13.
Laura Jane, d. Marcus D. and Rebecca [(Chamberlain). P. R. 13.], June 24, 1834.
Lucinda Catharine, d. Josiah and Sophronia, Sept. 10, 1825.
Lucy, d. Amos and Sarah [(Peirce). P. R. 25.], Sept. 17, 1780.
Lucy Marind[a], d. Amos and Lucy, Feb. 15, 1811.
Lysander Marcus, s. Marcus D. and Rebecca [(Chamberlain). P. R. 13.], Nov. 26, 1837.
Marcus D., s. Solomon and Abi (Adams), Apr. 15, 1805. P. R. 13.
Mary, d. Abraham and Mary, Nov. 8, 1708.
Mary, d. Henry and Lucy, Dec. 13, 1757.
Mary, d. John and Sarah, Jan. 25, 1776.
Mary, d. Solomon and Abi, Sept. 20, 1801.
Mary Savell, d. Henry, farmer, and Relief S., May 4, 1845.
Mercy Elzina, d. W[illia]m A., farmer, and Mercy M. [at Baptist Village. dup.], Sept. 11, 1844.
Molley, d. Amos and Sarah [(Peirce). P. R. 25.], July 8, 1782.
Olive, d. John and Sary, Oct. 29, 1762.
Oliver, s. Henry and Lucey, May 30, 1762.
Otis, s. Solomon and Abi, Feb. 27, 1799.
Patty, d. Solomon and Abi [(Adams). P. R. 13.], June 8, 1791.
Raymond Stratton, s. Otis and Lavina, Nov. 15, 1839.
Rebeckah, d. Henry and Lucey, Dec. 7, 1759.
Rebeckah, d. Amos and Sarah [(Peirce). P. R. 25.], July 23, 1787.
Roxanna, d. Josiah and Sophronia, Sept. 3, 1836.
Rufus, s. Amos and Lucy, Sept. 9, 1816.
Rufus G., s. Rufus, farmer, and Eunice G., May 15, 1845.
Salathial, s. Solomon and Abi, Feb. 5, 1797.
Sally, d. John and Sarah, Jan. 12, 1787.
Samuel, s. Isaac and Mary, Feb. 14, 1729-30.
Samuel, s. Jacob and Sarah, Aug. 13, 1736.
Samuel Leander, s. Otis and Lavina, May 10, 1837.
Sarah, d. Jacob and Sarah, June 26, 1729.
Sarah, d. John and Sarah, Dec. 15, 1758.
Sarah Lavinia, d. Otis and Lavina, at Boston, Feb. 27, 1835.
Sarah Parkhurst, d. Henry and Relief, Oct. 3, 1834.
Simeon, s. John and Sarah, Jan. 30, 1767.
Solomon, s. John and Sarah, May 17, 1770.
Solomon E., s. Solomon and Abi (Adams), July 13, 1810. P. R. 13.
Sophronia Ann, d. Josiah and Sophronia, Apr. 25, 1824.
Stillman, s. Solomon and Abi (Adams), Sept. 11, 1817. P. R. 13.
Susanna, d. John and Sary, Mar. 18, 1760.

BYAM, Susanna, d. Josiah and Sophronia, Sept. 12, 1838.
Thankfull, d. John and Sarah, Nov. 1, 1765.
Tryphena, d. Solomon and Abi, Feb. 20, 1793.
Willard, s. Henry and Lucy, Mar. 16, 1756.
Willard, s. John and Sarah, Jan. 23, 1778.
William, s. John and Sarah, Oct. 28, 1772.
William Augustus, s. Ezekiel and Charlotte, July 20, 1820.
Zebediah, s. Benjamin and Mary, Jan. 10, 1761.

BYHAM (see also Byam), Abel, s. Jacob, jr. and Sarah, Jan. 4, 1747-8.
Abel, s. Lt. Benjamin and Mary, Oct. 18, 1762.
Dorcas, d. Abraham and Hanah, Feb. 16, 1729-30.
Elizabeth, d. Jacob and Sarah, Mar. 11, 1731-2.
Experiance, d. Abraham and Mary, May 4, 1723.
Henry, s. Abraham and Mary, Sept. 27, 1720.
Henry, s. Henry and Lucy, May 15, 1750.
Jacob, s. Jacob and Sarah, July 3, 1724.
Jacob, s. Jacob, jr. and Sarah, Apr. 16, 1749.
Jessee, s. Jacob and Sarah, Oct. 22, 1750.
Joseph, s. Jacob and Sarah, Aug. 15, 1744.
Mary, d. Isaac and Mary, Feb. 12, 1725-6.
Patty, d. John and Sarah, bp. July 31, 1774. C. R. 1.
Pheneas, s. Jacob and Sarah, Feb. 25, 1725-6.
Rachal, d. Jacob and Sarah, May 20, 1739.
Sarah, d. Jacob and Sarah, Mar. 27, 1722.
Sarah, d. Lt. Benjamin and Mary, Oct. 25, 1764.
Thomus, s. Abraham and Mary, Feb. 24, 1715-16.

CAMPBELL, Hannah, d. William, bp. Sept. 30, 1770. C. R. 1.
John, s. William, bp. Sept. 29, 1771. C. R. 1.
John Warren, s. John, machinist, and Nancy, at North Chelmsford, May 5, 1844.
Martha Jane, d. John and Nancy, June 13, 1836.
Mary Elizabeth, d. John and Nancy, Sept. 22, 1839.

CARLTON, Amos, Mar. 4, 1766. P. R. 7.
Amos, s. Amos and Esther (Manning), Aug. 7, 1798. P. R. 7.
Daniel, s. Amos and Esther (Manning), Aug. 24, 1806. P. R. 7.
Esther, d. Amos and Esther (Manning), Oct. 18, 1796. P. R. 7.
George, s. Amos and Esther (Manning), Jan. 10, 1812. P. R. 7.
John, s. David, bp. July 15, 1823. C. R. 1.
Julia Ann, d. David and Sarah, Mar. 9, 1842.
Martha, d. Amos and Esther (Manning), Sept. 7, 1800. P. R. 7.
Mehitabel, d. Amos and Esther (Manning), Jan. 17, 1803. P. R. 7.

CARLTON, Sarah Chase, d. David, bp. July 15, 1823. C. R. 1.

CARROLL (see also Caryl), Catharine, d. Thomas and Anne, Nov. 8, 1838.
Charles David, s. Thomas and Anne, Apr. 15, 1840.
William, s. Thomas and Anne, Jan. 8, 1842.

CARRY (see also Cory), Jacob, s. Thomas and Abigail, June 23, 1688. CT. R.

CARYL (see also Carroll), Mary H., d. John C., trader, and Abby D., at Middlesex Village, July 6, 1846.

CHAIMBERLEN (see also Chamberlin), Bridget, d. Jacob and Lydia, Oct. 28, 1767.
Jacob, s. Jacob and Lydia, Feb. 17, 1769.
Nathaniel, s. Aron and Thankfull, Mar. 30, 1768.
Olive, d. Benjamin and Susanna, Aug. 10, 1768.
Samuel, s. Benjamin and Susanna, Dec. 15, 1758.
Sybel, d. Aron and Thankfull, July 17, 1757.

CHAIMBERLIN (see also Chamberlin), John, s. Jonathan and Elizebeth, both of Londonderry, Sept. 16, 1759.
Moly, d. Jonathan and Elizebeth, both of Londonderry, May 10, 1756.
Samuel, s. Aaron and Thankfull, Mar. 26, 1771.
Susanna, d. Benjamin and Susanna, Aug. 3, 1760.

CHAMBARLIN (see also Chamberlin), Rebecah, d. Joseph and Elizibeth, Aug. 31, 1735.

CHAMBELIN (see also Chamberlin), [torn], ch. Thomas and Sarah [torn. 1678?].

CHAMBERLAIN (see also Chamberlin), Aaron, s. Samuel and Abigail, Aug. 23, 1725.
Adams, s. Joseph and Martha, May 10, 1839.
Benjamin, s. Benjamin and Susanna, bp. Oct. 30, 1763. C. R. 1.
Elisabeth, d. Jonathan and Elisabeth, both of "Tyingstown so Cald," Apr. 30, 1742.
Eliza Jane, d. Isaac and Olive, Jan. 25, 1831.
Ephraim, s. Samuel and Rebecka, Sept. 28, 1725.
Harriet Mial, d. Isaac, jr. and Ollive, Apr. 29, 1817.
Isaac Albro, s. Isaac and Olive, Dec. 15, 1827.

CHAMBERLAIN, Jacob, s. Samuel and Abigail, Apr. 25, 1729.
John Franklin, s. Joseph and Martha, Mar. 4, 1832.
Jonathan, s. Samuel and Abigail, Feb. 11, 1711-12.
Joseph, s. Joseph and Elizabeth, Oct. 27, 1742.
Joseph, s. Benjamin, 3d and Susanna, bp. Dec. 10, 1769. C. R. 1.
Joseph, s. Phineas and Rebecca, bp. Dec. 5, 1773. C. R. 1.
Joseph Augustus, s. Joseph and Martha, Oct. 11, 1829.
Lydia, d. Benjamin and Easther, May 27, 1739.
Martha Ann, d. Joseph and Martha, Mar. 1, 1834.
Mary, d. Benjamin, jr. and Susanna, bp. Dec. 15, 1771. C. R. 1.
Olive, d. Abia, bp. July 30, 1758. C. R. 1.
Phineas, s. Phineas and Rebecca, bp. Apr. 19, 1772. C. R. 1.
Rebecca, d. Phineas and Rebecca, bp. Aug. 6, 1775. C. R. 1.
Robert Bates, s. Robert Bates and Lydia, Aug. 29, 1816.
Sarah, d. Benjamin, July 12, 1740.
Susanna, d. Benjamin and Susanna, bp. Nov. 27, 1763. C. R. 1.

CHAMBERLEN (see also Chamberlin), Sarah, d. Aron and Thankfull, June 1, 1759.

CHAMBERLIN (see also Chaimberlen, Chaimberlin, Chambarlin, Chambelin, Chamberlain, Chamberlen, Chamberline, Chamberlyn, Chamberlyne, Chambrlin, Chambrling, Chemberlin), Aaron, s. Aaron and Thankfull, Sept. 21, 1753.
Aaron, s. Aaron and Mary, May 26, 1791.
Abagill, d. Sam[ue]ll and Abigell, Dec. 28, 1707.
Abel, s. Jacob and Lydia, Sept. 23, 1763.
Abigail, d. Benjamin and Easter, Feb. 17, 1734-5.
Abigail, d. Aaron and Thankfull, June 18, 1761.
Abigal, d. Jonathan and Elizabeth, both of Londonderry, N. H., July 8, 1763.
Anna, d. Tho[mas], bp. 1: 12 m: 1656, a. abt. 20 y. P. R. 1.
Annah, d. Samuel and Annah, Dec. 26, 1715-16.
Anne, d. twin, Samuel and Anne, Apr. 15, 1720.
Benjamin, s. Joseph and Elizibeth, Oct. 23, 1733.
Benjamin, s. Benjamin and Easter, Feb. 18, 1736-7.
Benjamin, s. Benjamin, jr. and Susanna, July 27, 1766.
Benjamin, s. Ens. Isaac and Bettey, Aug. 17, 1786.
Benj[ami]n Franklin, s. Jacob, bp. Oct. 29, 1801. C. R. 1.
Calvin Thomas, s. Isaac, jr. and Olive, May 31, 1822.
Clarissa, d. Jacob, bp. Nov. 15, 1801. C. R. 1.
Easther, d. Benjamin and Easther, Sept. 8, 1732.
Elisabeth, d. Edmond, bp. 1: 12 m: 1656, a. abt. 5 y. P. R. 1.
Elisabeth, d. twin, Sam[ue]ll and Elisabeth, May 29, 1699.
Elisabeth, d. Ens. Isaac and Bettey, Mar. 29, 1793.
Elizabeth, d. twin, Joseph and Elizabeth, Aug. 17, 1720.

CHELMSFORD BIRTHS 43

CHAMBERLIN, Elizabeth, d. Joseph and Elizabeth, July 2, 1724.
Elizebeth, d. Benjamin and Susannah, July 17, 1762.
Ellis, s. Benjamin and Susanna, Apr. 21, 1774.
Ephraim, s. Phinehas and Sibbel, Mar. 20, 1778.
George Evans, s. Robert B. and Lydia, Sept. 30, 1826.
Girshum, s. Thomas and Elizabeth, Oct. 18, 1697.
Hanah, d. twin, Benjamin and Susanah, Jan. 3, 1779.
Harriot Moriah, d. Isaac, jr. and Olive, June 12, 1824.
Horatio, s. Jacob, bp. Nov. 15, 1801. C. R. 1.
Ichabod, s. Capt. Isaac and Sarah, Feb. 3, 1807.
Ira, s. Aaron, jr. and Sarah, July 22, 1782.
Isaac, s. Ens. Isaac and Bettey, Nov. 4, 1788.
Jacob, s. Edmon and Mare, Oct. 15, 1658.
Jane, d. Thomas and Sarah, 19: 11 m: 168[torn. 1682-3?].
Jane, d. Samuel and Abigail, Aug. 6, 1723.
Joanna, d. Aaron and Thankful, Aug. 22, 1764.
John, s. Edmond, bp. 1: 12 m: 1656, a. abt. 3 y. P. R. 1.
John, s. Thomas and Elisabeth, Mar. 29, 1692.
John, s. Dea. Aaron and Thankfull, Jan. 16, 1774.
John, s. Aaron, jr. and Sarah, Apr. 20, 1784.
Jonathan, s. Jonathan, and Elizabeth, Feb. 26, 1743-4.
Joseph, s. Samuel and Elizabeth, Nov. 5, 1687. CT. R.
Joseph, s. Samuel and Abagail, July 25, 1716.
Joseph, s. Benjamin and Easther, May 24, 1743.
Joseph, s. Jacob and Lydia, June 8, 1765.
Joseph, s. twin, Aaron and Mary, Mar. 5, 1797.
Joseph, s. Joseph and Mary, Feb. 27, 1798.
Josiph, s. Thomas and Elisabeth, Oct. 11, 1693.
Judith, d. Jacob, bp. Oct. 29, 1801. C. R. 1.
Lidia, d. twin, Benjamin and Susanah, Jan. 3, 1779.
Loammi, s. Ens. Isaac and Bettey, June 6, 1791.
Loammi. s. Robert B. and Lydia, Nov. 1, 1813.
Lucy, d. Benjamin and Susanna, Mar. 17, 1772.
Lydia, d. Jacob and Lydia, June 11, 1762.
Lydia Elizabeth, d. Robert B. and Lydia, July 24, 1820.
Marah, d. twin, Samuel and Anne, Apr. 15, 1720.
Martha, d. Benja[min], jr. [2d C. R. 1.] and Susanna, Feb. 20, 1770.
Martha Howard, d. Benj[amin], bp. Oct. 28, 1821. C. R. 1.
Mary, d. Edmond, bp. 1: 12 m: 1656, a. abt. 8 y. P. R. 1.
Mary, d. Tho[mas], bp. 1: 12 m: 1656, a. abt. 6 y. P. R. 1.
Mary, d. twin, Sam[ue]ll and Elisabeth, May 29, 1699.
Mary, d. Benjamin and Mary, Aug. 24, 1723.
Mary, d. Aaron and Thankfull, Aug. 27, 1755.
Mary, d. twin, Aaron and Mary, Mar. 5, 1797.

CHAMBERLIN, Olive, d. Jonathan and Elizabeth, Aug. 16, 1750.
Parker, s. Joseph and Mary, Feb. 7, 1803.
Patta, d. Aaron and Sarah, Jan. 13, 1789.
Patty, d. Jacob, bp. Nov. 15, 1801. c. r. 1.
Phinehas, s. Joseph and Sueshanah, Mar. 12, 1715-16.
Polle, d. Phinehas and Mary, June 30, 1788.
Rebecca, d. Joseph and Mary, Dec. 17, 1805.
Rebekah, d. Samuel and Rebekah, Feb. 26, 1727-8.
Robert Bates, s. Isaacc and Bettey, May 10, 1784.
Rhoda, d. Aaron and Mary, July 12, 1793.
Samuel, s. Tho[mas], bp. 1: 12 m: 1656, a. abt. 10 y. p. r. 1.
Samuel, s. Jonathan and Elizabeth, Apr. 4, 1748.
Samuell, s. Thomas and Sa[rah. t. c.], Jan. 11 [1679. t. c.].
Sam[ue]ll, s. Sam[ue]ll and Anne, Dec. 29, 1711.
Samuell, s. Samuell and Abagill, July 15, 1714.
Sam[ue]ll, s. Sam[ue]ll and Rebeckah, Oct. 26, 1723.
Sarah, d. Edmond, bp. 1: 12 m: 1656, a. abt. 7 y. p. r. 1.
Sarah, d. Joseph and Elizabeth, Dec. 5, 1722.
Sarah, d. Jonathan and Elezebeth, Apr. 6, 1753.
Sarah, d. Benjamin, jr. and Susanna, Aug. 19, 1764.
Sarah, d. Aaron and Sarah, Dec. 14, 1786.
Susanah, d. twin, Joseph and Elizabeth, Aug. 17, 1720.
Thankfull, d. Aaron and Thankfull, Nov. 12, 1751.
Thomas, s. Tho[mas], bp. 1: 12 m: 1656, a. abt. 17 y. p. r. 1.
Thomas, s. Thomas and Abagill, June 21, 1714.
Thomas, s. Samuel and Abigail, Mar. 28, 1718.
Thomas, s. Joseph and Elizibeth, Jan. 18, 1727-8.
Thomas, s. Benjamin and Esther, Sept. 24, 1750.
Willard, s. Benjamin and Susanna, Oct. 23, 1776.

CHAMBERLINE (see also Chamberlin), Benjamin, s. Sam[ue]ll and Abbigall, Aug. 11, 170[4. t. c.].
Edmund, s. Edm[und], May 30, 1656. ct. r.
Thomas, s. Thomas and Sarah, May 30, 1667.

CHAMBERLYN (see also Chamberlin), Aaron, s. twin, Tho[mas] and Elizebeth, July [3, 1695. t. c.].
Moses, s. twin, Tho[mas] and Elizebeth, July [3, 1695. t. c.].

CHAMBERLYNE (see also Chamberlin), Benjamin, s. twin, Samuel and Elezebeth, Nov. 4, 1694.
Elizebeth, d. twin, Samuel and Elezebeth, Nov. 4, 1694.

CHAMBRLIN (see also Chamberlin), Elisabeth, d. Thomas and Sarah, July 21, 1685.

CHAMBRLIN, Elizabeth, d. Samuell and Abigill, Jan. 8, 1709-10.
John, s. Thomas and Abagill, Feb. 1, 1717-18.
Joseph, s. Sam[ue]ll and Anna, Jan. 27, 1713-14.
Lidiah, d. Samuell and Elizabath, Aug. 8, 1706.
Samuell, s. Samuell and Elisabeth, Oct. 28, 1685.

CHAMBRLING (see also Chamberlin), Eleazer, s. Joseph and Susanah, Nov. 25, 1717.
Eleizer, s. Samuell and Anna, Dec. 27, 1717.

CHANDLER, Elizabeth, d. Rev. John and Elizabeth, of Billerica, bp. Aug. 17, 1760. C. R. 1.
George, s. John, dyer, and Ann, at Scythe Factory Village, Jan. 11, 1848.
Henry, s. William and Susanah, Mar. 29, 1727.
John, s. William and Susanah, Sept. 7, 1725.
Joseph, s. William, bp. Mar. 30, 1729. C. R. 4.
Nyrhe, w. Edwin Josselyn, Aug. 31, 1815. P. R. 10.
Sarai, d. Ephraim and Sarai, Oct. 20, 1724.

CHAPMAN, Ann Eliza, d. John, machinist, b. Peterborough, N. H., and Eliza R., b. Winchendon, Jan. 29, 1849.

CHARLES, Roland, s. Osgood, farmer, b. Fryeburg, Me., and Alice A., b. Lovell, Me., May 13, 1848.

CHASE, Celeste Uberte, d. John E., shoemaker, and Susan B., at Middlesex Village, July 9, 1847.
Susan Elizabeth, d. John E., shoemaker, b. Andover, and Susan E., b. Boston, at Middlesex Village, Sept. 9, 1849.

CHEMBERLIN (see also Chamberlin), John, s. Samuell and Abagill, Feb. 11, 1706.

CLARCK (see also Clark), Elizabeth, d. Lt. Jonas and Elizabeth, Feb. 25, 1719-20.

CLARK (see also Clarck, Clarke), Abba Jane Frances, d. David P., moulder, b. Stockbridge, Vt., and Eliza Jane, at North Chelmsford, Jan. 3, 1849.
Abigall, d. Thomas and Elizabethe, Jan. 28, 1705.
Benjamin, s. Maj. Jonas and Elizabeth, Jan. 25, 1730-31.
Emely Frances, d. Carlos C., machinist, and Emely, at North Chelmsford, Aug. 8, 1844.
Francelia O[riann. C. R. 3.], d. Benj[ami]n F., clergyman, and Mehitabel A., at North Chelmsford, Feb. 1, 1844.

CLARK, Isabella Louisa, d. David P., shoemaker, and Mary, deaf-mutes, at North Chelmsford, Sept. 9, 1846.
Jeremy, s. Lt. Isaac and Bridget, Jan. 16, 1789.
Jonas, s. Thomas and Mary, Dec. 2, 1684. [Dec. 22. CT. R.]
Jonathan, s. Lt. Isaac and Bridget, Apr. 12, 1786.
Lucy, d. Jonas and Elisabeth, Nov. 10, 1721.
Mary, d. Jonas and Elizabeth, June 25, 1711.
Mary Ella, d. Benj[ami]n F., clergyman, and Mahitabel A., at North Chelmsford, Nov. 1, 1847.
Rebecka, d. Capt. Jonas and Elizabeth, Aug. 22, 1724.
Thomas, s. Jonas and Elizabeth, Aug. 24, 1713.
Timothy, s. Thomas and Eliza, Apr. 29, 1702.
Timothy, s. Jonas and Elisabeth, Oct. 10, 1726.
William Henry, s. Peter, formerly a potter, now a boarding-house-keeper, and Lucy G., at North Chelmsford, Nov. 15, 1844.

CLARKE (see also Clark), Jonas, s. Jonas and Elizebath, Feb. 20, 1715-16.
Margaret, d. Thomas and Mary, Oct. 28, 1687. CT. R.
Thomas, s. Thomas, Sept. 28, ———. [1694?]

CLEAVELAND (see also Cleveland), John, s. Josiah and Mary, June 28, 1696.
Jonathan, s. Josiah and Mary, Mar. 2, 1698.
Josiph, s. Sameuell and Pearsis, July 18, 1689-90.
[M. T. C.]ari, d. Josiah and Mary, Mar. 17, 1693-4.

CLEAVELANDE (see also Cleveland), Heniry, s. Josiah and Mary, ——— 22, 1699.

CLEVELAND (see also Cleaveland, Cleavelande, Clevland), Ephraim, s. Samuel and Persis, Apr. 10, 1687. CT. R.
Josiah, s. Josiah and Marah, Oct. 7, 1690.
Josiph, s. Josiah and Marah, June 13, 1692.
Samuell, s. Samuell and Persis, Jan. 12, 1684.

CLEVLAND (see also Cleveland), Persis, d. Samuell and Persis, Apr. 21, 1683.

COBORN (see also Colburn), Daniell, s. Daniell and Sarah, July 25, 1686.
Edward, s. Danill and Sarah, Dec. 21, 1691.
Elisabeth, d. John and Elisabeth, Apr. 8, 1679.
Hanah, d. Ezerah and Hanah, Aug. 14 [1695. T. C.].

CHELMSFORD BIRTHS 47

COBORN, Hannah, d. Joseph and Hannah, Sept. 9, 1684.
John, s. Esdras and Hanah, Apr. 15, 1690.
Johnathán, s. Thomas and Mary, Dec. 22, 169[torn. 1694?].
Jonathan, s. Thomas and Mary, Mar. 15, 1684-5.
Josiph, s. John and Elisabeth, July 26, 1680.
Lidiah, d. Josiph and Hanah, Jan. 18, 169[2. T. C.].
Marie, d. Josiph and Hana, Oct. [22. T. C.], 1688.
Mary, d. John and Susanah, 23: 8 m: 167[torn. 1672?].
Mary, d. Robertt and Mary, Jan. 22, 1673.
Mary, d. Thomis and Mary, Mar. 1, 1699.
Samuell, s. Ezarah and Hannah, Sept. 18, 1684.
Sarah, d. Danill and Sarah, Jan. 14, 1688-90. [1689-90. CT. R.]
Sarah, d. Josiph and Hana, Oct. 18, 1690.
Sarie, d. John and Elisabeth, Dec. 8, 1685.
[Si. T. C.]mon, s. Danill and Sara, June 12, 1694.
Simon, s. Daniel and Sary, May 30, 1695.
[Thomas. T. C.], s. Thomas and Hannah, May [14. T. C.], 1675.

COBORNE (see also Colburn), Hanah, d. John and Elisabeth, June 10, 1689.
Jeams, s. Thomas and Marie, Jan. 31, 1689-90.
Lidiah, d. John and Elisabeth, Dec. 14, 168[7. T. C.].
Marah [Margarett. CT. R.], d. Thomas and Marie, Mar. 12, 1691-2.
Robarte, s. John and Elisabeth, Jan. 28, 1682.
Wilyam, s. John and Elisabeth, July 17, 1693.

COBOURN (see also Colburn), Joseph, s. Joseph and Hanah, Apr. 4, 1695.

COBURN (see also Colburn), Anna, d. W[illia]m, bp. at Dracut, Aug. 23, 1781. P. R. 4.
Anna, d. Henry and Sarah, Feb. 14, 1794.
Carolin, d. [Thomas. C. R. 1.], Oct. 16, 1813.
Catharine Leonora, d. James B., carpenter, and Betsey, at North Chelmsford, Mar. 3, 1848.
Ezekiel H[ildreth. C. R. 1.] T. [Fletcher. C. R. 1.], s. [Thomas. C. R. 1.], Nov. 20, 1817.
Hannah, d. Aaron and Marcy, Mar. 22, 1724.
Henry, s. Henry and Sarah, Dec. 16, 1780.
Lucy Robbins, d. [Thomas. C. R. 1.], May 30, 1815.
Sarah, d. Silas and Esther, Jan. 13, 1779.
Sarah, d. Henry and Sarah, Aug. 1, 1782.
Thomas, s. Henry and Sarah, Dec. 16, 1785.
Timothy Varnum, s. Timothy and Hannah, Apr. 12, 1810.

CHELMSFORD BIRTHS

COBURNE (see also Colburn), Abraham, s. Ezra and Hannah, Aug. 7, 1687. CT. R.
Edward, s. Thomas and Mary, Aug. 13, 1687. CT. R.

COCHRAN, Alphonso Dunning [Oscar Alphonzo Dunning. C. R. 1.], s. W[illia]m K. [H. C. R. 1.] and Lydia, Nov. 23, 1842.
Ellen Louisa, d. W. H., bp. Feb. 21, 1841. C. R. 3.
William Henry, s. W[illia]m K. and Lydia, Dec. 29, 1837.

COLBORN (see also Colburn), Ephariam, s. Thomas and Mary, Apr. 24, 1706.
Hanah, d. John and Joanah, Aug. 6, 1713.
Jacob, s. Daniell and Sarah, Sept. 6, 1696.
Jane, d. John and Johana, Nov. 26, 1706.
John, s. Susanah, Jan. 31, 1695-6.
Rachell, d. John and Johana, Sept. 2, 1704.
Timothy, s. John and Joanah, Oct. 20, 1716.
Zacariah, s. Thomas and Mary, Apr. 26, 1697.

COLBURN (see also Coborn, Coborne, Cobourn, Coburn, Coburne, Colborn, Coulborn), Aron, s. Joseph and Hannah, May 27, 1700.
Charles Butterfield, s. Henry, bp. Sept. 1, 1827. C. R. 1.
Edward, s. Joseph and Hannah, July 9, 1697.
Franklin, s. Henry, bp. Sept. 1, 1827. C. R. 1.
Henniry, s. Thomas and Mary, May 2, 1700.
Henry Albert, s. Henry, bp. Sept. 1, 1827. C. R. 1.
Jerahmeel, s. Oliver and Lucy, of Dunstable, bp. July 19, 1752. C. R. 1.
Joanah, d. John and Joanah, Nov. 18, 1702.
John, s. John and Joanna, Mar. 29, 1701.
Olive, d. Timothy and Olive, of Dracut, bp. May 10, 1752. C. R. 1.
Phineas, s. Silos and Esther, Apr. 23, 1776.
Sarah, d. Ezra and Hannah, Nov. 10, 16[torn. 169-. T. C. 1699?].
Sarah, d. Thomas and Mary, Oct. 7, 170[torn. 1703?].
Stephen Adams, s. Henry, bp. Sept. 1, 1827. C. R. 1.

COLE, John Richardson, s. John and Polly, June 5, 1795.
Mary Lauria, d. W[illia]m E., carpenter, and Susan H., at Sutton, Nov. 3, 1846.

COLLAR (see also Color), Jeams, s. Nathanell and Mary, Aug. 11, 1698.

CHELMSFORD BIRTHS 49

COLOR (see also Collar), John, s. Nathaniell and Mery, Oct. 16, 1696.

COMING (see also Cummings), Mary, d. John and Elizabeth, July 5, 1708.

COMINGS (see also Cummings), Bridget, d. John and Elizabeth, Nov. 15, 1722.
Ebenezer, s. John and Elizabeth, July 4, 1726.
John, s. John and Elizabeth, June 1, 1710.
Thomas, s. John and Elizabeth, Aug. 4, 1714.

COMINS (see also Cummings), Elizabeth, d. John and Elizabeth, Aug. 29, 1706.

COMMINGS (see also Cummings) Ephraim, s. John and Elizabeth, Nov. 13, 1720.

CONANT (see also Connant), Easther, d. Robert and Easther, Mar. 3, 1726.
Josiah, s. Robert and Esther, Nov. 4, 1723.
Peter, s. Robert and Easter, Oct. 29, 1727.

CONLEY (see also Connelly), Mary Elizabeth, d. James, moulder, and Mary, at North Chelmsford, June 27, 1845.

CONNANT (see also Conant), Samuel, s. Robbert and Esther, July 25, 1722.

CONNELLY (see also Conley), James Francis, s. James, moulder, and Mary, at North Chelmsford, Aug. 25, 1847.

COREY (see also Cory), Abial, d. Ephraim [deceased. c. r. 1.] and Hannah, Oct. 3, 1741.
Eunice, d. John and Ruth, Sept. 5, 1741.
John, s. Thomas and Abigall, Jan. 26, 1666.
Josyah, s. John and Elezebeath, Aug. 22, 1698.
Lois, d. John and Ruth, Feb. 1, 1742-3.
Nathanell, s. Thomas and Abigaill, Dec. 1, 1674.
Ruben, s. twin, Ephraim and Hannah, Apr. 29, 1730.
Simeon, s. twin, Ephraim and Hannah, Apr. 29, 1730.

CORIE (see also Cory), John, s. John and Elisabeth, Dec. 4, 1694-5.
Sameuell, s. John and Elisabeth, Sept. 20, 1691.

CHELMSFORD BIRTHS

CORRY (see also Cory), Amme, d. Thomas, Mar. 7, 1686.
Elisabeth, d. Thomas and Abagaill, Dec. 21, 1683.

CORY (see also Carry, Corey, Corie, Corry), Abigaill, d. Thomas and Abigaill, —— [torn. 1672?].
Anis, d. Ephraim and Hannah, Nov. 4, 1735.
Benoni, s. John and Ruth, May 11, 1752.
Ebenezer, s. Josiah and Easter, July 1, 1730.
Ebenezer, s. Ebenezer and Hannah, Nov. 15, 1753.
Eleazer, s. Oliver and Hannah, Aug. 23, 1753. [Aug. 28. dup.]
Eliazer, s. Josiah and Ester, Sept. 4, 1719.
Elisabeth, d. Oliver and Hannah, Mar. 3, 1761.
Elisebeth, d. Solomon and Elizabeth [Rebecca. c. r. 1.], Sept. 16, 1770.
Elizibeth, d. John and Ruth, Mar. 4, 1729.
Ephraim, s. John and Elesabeth, Sept. 1, 1700.
Ephraim, s. Oliver and Hannah, Oct. 29, 1750. [Oct 30. dup.]
Esther, d. Josiah and Esther, Nov. 17, 1722.
Ezra, s. John and Ruth, Apr. 15, 1744.
Hanah, d. John and Elizabeth [May 30, 1705. t. c.].
Hannah, d. Ephraim and Hannah, July 30, 1728.
Hannah, d. Oliver and Hannah, June 16, 1768.
Hezekiah, s. John and Elizabeth, Jan. 23, 1710.
Hezikiah, s. John and Ruth, June 22, 1736.
Jesse, s. Oliver and Hannah, Aug. 15, 1758.
Joanna, d. John and Ruth, Nov. 17, 1748.
John, s. John and Ruth, Nov. 8, 1726.
Joseph, s. Tho[mas] and Hanah, Sept 6, 1695.
Josiah, s. Josiah and Easther, Apr. 5, 1734.
Mary, d. John and Ruth, Aug. 24, 1724.
Mary, d. Ephraim and Hannah, Dec. 20, 1738.
Mary, d. Eleazer and Rachel, July 28, 1743.
Mehettabel, d. Eleazer and Rachel, Mar. 28, 1745.
Olive, d. Reuben and Olive, Oct. 29, 1758.
Olive, d. Reuben and Olive, bp. Nov. 9, 1760. c. r. 1.
Oliver, s. Josiah and Easther, Aug. 26, 1728.
Oliver, s. Oliver and Hannah, Jan. 21, 1756.
Phebe, d. Reuben and Olive, Oct. 15, 1764.
Phinias, s. Josiah and Easter, Mar. 5, 1735-6.
Priscilla, d. John and Ruth, Feb. 5, 1745-6.
Rebecah, d. Reuben and Olive, July 29, 1763.
Rebecca, d. Reuben and Olive, bp. Apr. 12, 1761. c. r. 1.
Ruth, d. John and Reuth, Jan. 3, 1730.
Ruth, d. John and Ruth, bp. June 5, 1743. c. r. 1.
Samuell, s. Thomas and Abigaill, Feb. 6, 167[0. t. c.].

CORY, Samuell, s. Sam[ue]ll and Mary, Feb. 25, 1714-15.
Sarah, d. Jona[t]han and Sarah, July 17, 1701.
Sarah, d. Ephraim and Hanah, June 2, 1733.
Sarah, d. Reuben and Olive, bp. Oct. 23, 1763. C. R. 1.
Simeon, s. Oliver and Hannah, June 10, 1763.
Solomon, s. John and Ruth, Nov. 20, 1737.
Solomon, s. Solomon and Rebeckah, Feb. 12, 1769.
Stephen, s. Oliver and Hannah, July 10, 1765.
Thankfull, d. Reuben and Olive, Mar. 8, 1767.
Thomas, s. Thomas and Abigaill, 28: 4 m: 1669.
Townsend, s. Annis, bp. Dec. 4, 1763. C. R. 1.
William, s. John and Ruth, July 15, 1734.
Zebediah, s. John and Ruth, Sept. 10, 1732.
[torn], s. [torn], Jan. 4, 1679.

COULBORN (see also Colburn), Moses, s. Joseph and Hanah, Jan. 1, 1702-3.

COWDRY, Charles Isaac, s. Isaac B., laborer, and Rhoda, July 7, 1844.
Samuel, s. Rebecca, bp. June 6, 1773. C. R. 1.

CROOKER, Paschal Young Wilkins, s. Isaac, housewright, and Mary Ann, Sept. 15, 1843.

CROSBY, Aaron, s. Nathan, jr. and Bettey, Dec. 11, 1771.
Hannah, d. Benjamin and Mary, May 18, 1773.
Jeremiah, s. Nathun and Bettey, Sept. 22, 1766.
Joanna, d. Joel and Hannah, lately of Ipswich, bp. July 14, 1771. C. R. 1.
John, s. Nathan and Anne [Anna. C. R. 1.], Mar. 26, 1760.
John, s. Simon and Dorothy, bp. May 9, 1773. C. R. 1.
Lydia, d. Nathan, jr. and Betty, Sept. 6, 1765.
Molley, d. Benjamin and Mary, Nov. 1, 1767.
Rhoda, d. Benjamin and Mary, Nov. 2, 1769.

CROSMAN, Betsy, d. Elder Abisha and Experience, May 9, 1783.
Silas Cutler, s. Elder Abisha and Experieance, Nov. 13, 1785.

CROSS, Sarah Elizabeth, d. Charles, machinist, and Elizabeth, at North Chelmsford, Nov. 6, 1845.

CUMINGS (see also Cummings), Abagill, d. John and Elizthbeth, Nov. —, 1716.

CUMINGS, Becca, d. Nathaniel and Rebecca, Aug. 19, 1776.
Samuell, s. John and Elizabeth, Nov. 16, 1718.
Willam, s. John and Elizabeth, July 27, 1712.
Willard, s. John and Sarah, of Dunstable, bp. Dec. 12, 1779.
C. R. 1.

CUMMINGS (see also Coming, Comings, Comins, Commings, Cumings, Cummins), John, s. John and Sarah, of Dunstable, bp. Oct. 26, 1777. C. R. 1.
Sarah Warren, d. Jepthah and Asenath, at Middlesex Village, Feb. 25, 1839.

CUMMINS (see also Cummings), Isaac, s. Isaac and Elizabeth, of Westford, bp. Feb. 25, 1781. C. R. 1.

CURTIS (see also Curtiss), Albert, s. James, shoemaker, and Jane, at Factory Village, Dec. 9, 1846.
Edward James, s. John, mechanic, and Fanny, at Worsted Mills, Jan. 25, 1846.

CURTISS (see also Curtis), Alfred, s. John, carder, and Fanny, at Scythe Factory Village, Jan. 9, 1848.

DADMUN, Arabella A., d. Nathan P., blacksmith, and Martha, Dec. 27, 1844.
Gerard Prescott, s. Nathan P., blacksmith, and Martha, Aug. 30, 1846.
Martha Ellen, d. Nathan P., blacksmith, b. Charlestown, and Martha, Oct. 27, 1848.
Nathan Prescutt, s. Nathan and Abigail P., at Charlestown, Apr. 1, 1818.

DAILEY, Mary, d. Patrick, laborer, b. Anascaul, Ireland, and Joanna, b. Bandon, Ireland, June 7, 1849.

DAKIN, Levy, s. Ebenezer and Abigail, July 20, 1743.
Sherebiah, s. Levi and Sarah, Nov. 26, 1789.

DALTON, Charles Henry, s. Dr. J. C. and Julia Ann, bp. Dec. 16, 1826. C. R. 1.
Edward, s. Dr. J. C., bp. Nov. 17, 1828. C. R. 1.
John Call, s. Dr. John C. and Julia Ann, bp. Nov. 16, 1823. C. R. 1.
John Call, s. Dr. John C., bp. May 8, 1825. C. R. 1.
Julia Anne, d. Dr. J. C. and Julia Anne, bp. Sept. 4, 1831. C. R. 1.

DANE, Allice [Dana. P. R. 4.], d. Joseph and Allice, Mar. 8, 1789.

DANFORTH, Benja[min] Pierce, s. David and Elizabeth, Feb. 22, 1780.
David, s. David and Elizabeth, May 11, 1784.
Eli, s. David and Hannah, of Camden, bp. Jan. 28, 1776. C. R. 1.
Elizebeth, d. David and Elizabeth, Feb. 21, 1782.
Hannah, d. David and Joanna, bp. Nov. 11, 1770. C. R. 1.
Israel, s. David and Hannah, of Camden, bp. Jan. 28, 1776. C. R. 1.
Jessa, s. David and Elizabeth, Aug. 27, 1776.
John, s. David and Joanna, Oct. 27, 1768.
Kimbell, s. Jacob and Mehetibel, Apr. 14, 1792.
Oliver, s. Jacob and Mehetibel, June 22, 1788.
Timothy, s. David and Elizabeth, Apr. 2, 1778.
William, s. Jacob and Mehetibel, Aug. 10, 1790.

DAVERSON (see also Davidson), Polly, d. William and Polly, Sept. 30, 1796.

DAVICE (see also Davis), Amos, s. Sam[ue]ll and Hanah, Oct. 15, 1705.
Anne, d. Sam[ue]ll and Hanah, May 24, 1697.
Barnabus, s. Sam[ue]ll and Hanah, Dec. 19, 1700.
Elizabeth, d. Sam[ue]ll and Hanah, Jan. 16, 1708.
Experienc, d. Sam[ue]ll and Hanah, Nov. 23, 1707.
Mary, d. Sam[ue]ll and Hanah, May 20, 1699.
Samuell, s. Sam[ue]ll and Hanah, Aug. 16, 1695.
Simon, s. Sam[ue]ll and Hanah, Nov. 15, 1702.
Stephen, s. Sam[ue]ll and Hanah, Jan. 31, 1711.

DAVIDSON (see also Daverson), James R. P., s. John, machinist, and Salome, at North Chelmsford, Dec. 18, 1844.
Rebecca Richardson, d. Francis and Rebeca, deceased, bp. Apr. 2, 1780. C. R. 1. [a. 2 m. P. R. 4.]

DAVIES (see also Davis), Susanna, d. Moses and Lydia, Mar. 20, 1767.

DAVIS (see also Davice, Davies, Davise), Augusta, d. Abijah and Sally, Feb. 12, 1798.
Betey, d. Abijah and Sally, at Tyngsborough, Aug. 10, 1794.
Betsey Ann, d. Lucy, Nov. 1, 1840.

CHELMSFORD BIRTHS

DAVIS, Caroline, d. James R. and Civonia, Dec. 7, 1842.
Charles, s. Ruben and Bettey, Apr. 30, 1786.
Charles, s. Abijah and Sally, Jan. 15, 1800.
Ebenezer, s. Samuel and Anna, Mar. 16, 1710. [1712. T. C.]
Eliza, d. Joshua and Betcey, Aug. 3, 1798.
Elizebeth, d. Thomas and Ruhamah, Dec. 27, 1775.
Elnathan, s. Reuben and Bettey, July 25, 1793.
Eunice, d. Thomas and Ruhamah, at Stow, June 8, 1772.
Faney, d. Joshua and Betcy, Apr. 15, 1801.
Harriett, d. Erasmus P., printer, and Harriett, at Lowell, July 7, 1847.
Isaac, s. Reuben and Bettey, July 26, 1795.
James E., s. James R., scythe maker, and Savonia, at Worsted Factory, Jan. 20, 1845.
John, s. Joshua and Elisabeth, Nov. 15, 1771.
Joshua Barron, s. Joshua and Eliz[abe]th, bp. May 20, 1804. C. R. 1.
Lucy, d. Sam[ue]l and Phebe, bp. May 26, 1805. C. R. 1.
Lydia, d. Abel, bp. at Harvard, Nov. 13, 1768. P. R. 4.
Martha Francis, d. James R. and Civonia, Sept. 6, 1839.
Mary, d. Thomas and Ruhamah, Mar. 12, 1778.
Mary, d. Abijah and Sally, Jan. 22, 1796.
Mary Jane, d. James R. and Civonia, Apr. 27, 1841.
Otis, s. Joshua and Eliza, bp. May 25, 1800. C. R. 1.
Polly, d. Benjamin and Mary, Aug. 8, 1778.
Polly, d. Reuben and Bettey, Dec. 7, 1791.
Rhoday, d. Joshua and Betcey, Sept. 21, 1802.
Ruhamah, d. Thomas and Ruhamah, at Stow, Dec. 13, 1773.
Sally, d. Abijah and Sally, at Tyngsborough, Apr. 14, 1793.
Susanna, d. Reuben and Bettey, Feb. 26, 1789.

DAVISE (see also Davis), Ann, d. John and Ann, Oct. 22, 1722.
Benjamin, s. Jabez and Ruth, Jan. 16, 1725-6.
John, s. John and Anna, Apr. 2, 1720.
Mary, d. John and Anna, Sept. 25, 1724.

DEUREN (see also Duren), Sally [Durrant. C. R. 1.], d. Jacob and Mercy, June 16, 1769.

DEXTER, Harriott, d. twin, Bartlett W. and Mercy F., July 6, 1840.
Maria, d. twin, Bartlett W. and Mercy F., July 6, 1840.

DICKINSON, Augustine Marcelline, s. E., bp. Sept. 28, 1829. C. R. 1.

DICKINSON, Barney Prescott, s. ——, bp. July 2, 1826. C. R. 1.
Ellen Josephine, d. E., bp. Sept. 15, 1827. C. R. 1.

DIMOND, Elizabeth, d. Francis and Elizabeth, bp. Aug. 30, 1747. C. R. 1.

DIX, Almira, d. Joel and Prissiller, Jan. 25, 1819.
Clarisea, d. Joel and Prissiller, Nov. 17, 1811.
Joel, s. Joel and Prissiller, Mar. 26, 1817.
Mary, d. Joel and Pressillia, June 11, 1815.
Sibbil, d. Joel and Prissillia, Nov. 3, 1813.

DOWNS, ——, s. Luther, machinist, and Mary A., at North Chelmsford, Feb. 10, 1848.

DRAKE, ——, d. Nathaniel, laborer, and Susanna, at North Chelmsford, June 6, 1844.

DUDLEY, Jesse, s. Daniel, bp. Apr. 26, 1761. C. R. 1.
Martha Ann, d. Otis B., blacksmith, and Martha A., at Baptist Village, Oct. 12, 1846.

DUNN, Abi, d. Benjamin and Phebe, Dec. 1, 1769.
Benjamin, s. James and Elizabeth, May 22, 1743.
Bettey, d. Joseph and Mary, Aug. 13, 1771.
Bettey, d. James and Rachel, Feb. 11, 1790.
Betty, d. James and Elizabeth, Aug. 28, 1745.
Betty, d. wid. Lefey, bp. Aug. 24, 1800. C. R. 1.
Center, s. James, bp. Oct. 18, 1801. C. R. 1.
Charity Lund, s. James and Rachel, Feb. 26, 1792.
Charlottey, d. James and Rachel, Mar. 21, 1794.
George N., s. Center, farmer, and Mary, Apr. 24, 1844.
Jam[e]s, s. Jam[e]s and Elizebeth, May 16, 1751.
James, s. James and Rachel, at Merrimack, Nov. 14, 1797.
James Dustin, s. Center and Mary, Jan. 23, 1838.
John, s. James and Elisabeth, Mar. 15, 1739-40.
John, s. John and Hannah, May 24, 1773.
Jonas, s. Benjamin and Phebe, at Dunstable, Dec. 12, 1767.
Joseph, s. James and Elisabeth, May 29, 1737.
Leafe, d. Joseph and Mary, Dec. 26, 1767.
Loammi, s. James [jr. C. R. 1.] and Rachel, Mar. 3, 1796.
Lucy, d. James and Rachel, June 4, 1788.
Mary Jane, d. Center and Mary, at Harvard, Nov. 9, 1836.
Molly, d. Joseph and Mary, Nov. 27, 1765.
Polly, d. James and Rachel [of Westford. C. R. 1.], May 4, 1781.

DUNN, Rachel, d. James and Rachel [of Westford. C. R. 1.], at Westford, July 23, 1779.
Rebecka, d. James and Elizabeth, June 29, 1748. [Jan. dup.]
Roxana, d. James, bp. Apr. 7, 1805. C. R. 1.
Roxana Rosamond, d. Center and Mary, May 16, 1839.
Sabra, d. James [jr. C. R. 1.] and Rachel, Nov. 9, 1798.
Salla, d. James and Rachel, Feb. 4, 1783.
Samuel, s. wid. Lefey, bp. Aug. 24, 1800. C. R. 1.
Sarah, d. James and Elizabeth, Oct. 6, 1759.
Senter, s. James and Rachel, Nov. 10, 1802.
William, s. James and Elezebeth, Sept. 21, 1754.
William, s. James and Rachel, Mar. 29, 1786.
William, s. Benjamin and Phebe, of Stoddard, N. H., bp. Nov. 16, 1788. C. R. 1.

DURANT (see also Durent), George E[dward. C. R. 3.], s. Thomas, blacksmith, and Elizabeth C., at North Chelmsford, Dec. 26, 1843.

DUREN (see also Deuren), John Adams, s. Silvester, bp. Apr. 25, 1813. C. R. 1.
Thomas, s. Silvester, bp. Apr. 25, 1813. C. R. 1.

DURENT (see also Durant), Abby Elizabeth, d. Thomas, bp. July 22, 1844. C. R. 3.
Nancy Jane, d. Thomas, bp. July 22, 1844. C. R. 3.

DUTTEN (see also Dutton), Abigail, d. James and Ruth, May 11, 1755.
Abner, s. Esther, deceased, bp. Mar. 3, 1751. C. R. 1.
John, s. Jonas [deceased. C. R. 1.] and Rebeckah, Dec. 28, 1760.
Jonas, s. Jonas and Rebecca, Aug. 17, 1754.
Rebeckah, d. Jonas and Rebeckah, Feb. 14, 1756.

DUTTON (see also Dutten), Amos Wright, s. David and Hannah, Dec. 14, 1805.
Benjamin, s. Mary, bp. June 24, 1744. C. R. 1.
Darcis, d. Jam[e]s and Pheebe, Aug. 21, 1732.
Darius, s. David and Hannah, Mar. 4, 1803.
Dorcas, d. David and Hannah, July 26, 1804.
Easter, d. James and Phebe, Oct. 13, 1734.
Edwin Elbridge, s. Elbridge and Laura M., Aug. 2, 1841.
Elbridge, s. David and Hannah, June 4, 1810.
James, s. James and Phebe, Sept. 1, 1729.
Jonas, s. James and Phebe, Oct. 27, 1727.

CHELMSFORD BIRTHS

DUTTON, Levi, s. David and Hannah, Mar. 4, 1808.
Lewis Maverick, s. Elbridge, farmer, and Laura M., b. Westford, Jan. 17, 1849.
Mary, d. James and Phebe, June 19, 1726.
Mary Elizabeth, d. Hildreth P., butcher, b. Greenfield, N. H., and Abigail A., Oct. 15, 1849.
Sarah, d. Jonas and Rebecka, May 28, 1758.
Stephen, s. James, jr. and Edith, Jan. 7, 1753.
Susanna, d. James and Ruth, Oct. 24, 1756.
———, s. Parker, stone-cutter, and Lucretia, at North Chelmsford, Apr. 27, 1844.

EDMANDS, Josephine E., d. Thomas S., bookbinder, and Harriet S., at "Concord River," Mar. 3, 1847.
Laroy Sunderland, s. Phillip D., bookbinder, and Susan H., at "Concord River," Jan. 26, 1847.

EDWARDS, Abby Howard, d. Isaiah, painter, and Harriett N., at Middlesex Village, Mar. 10, 1847.
Alice Amanda, d. Moses, wool sorter, b. Manchester, Eng., and Mary E., b. Loudon, N. H., Apr. 3, 1849.
George Henry, s. Nathan B., physician, and Maria H., at North Chelmsford, Jan. 14, 1848.

ELEXANDER (see also Alexander), James, s. James and Joanna, Aug. 20, 1776.

ELLEXANDER (see also Alexander), Hannah Gordon, d. wid. Joanna, Jan. 11, 1781.

ELLIOTT, Clarry J., d. Jotham P., teamster, and Clarinda P., at Lowell, Sept. 21, 1846.

EMERSON, Bryant, s. Owen and Mary, Jan. 29, 1801.
Charles Franklin, s. Owen, farmer, and Louisa, Sept. 28, 1843.
Edward, s. Edward and Rebecah, May 8, 1702.
Elesabeth, d. Edward and Rebecka, Apr. 19, 1701.
Elisabeth, d. Dea. Oen and Mary, July 23, 1808.
Elizebeth, d. Joseph and Ruth, Aug. 27, 1779.
Franklin, s. Dea. Oen and Mary, Sept. 4, 1806.
George Edgar, s. Franklin and Rebecca A., Dec. 2, 1837.
Hannah Eliza, d. Bryant and Hannah, June 9, 1836.
John, s. Joseph and Elizabeth, bp. Feb. 9, 1772. C. R. 1.
John Bryant, s. Bryant and Hannah, Feb. 8, 1831.
Joseph, s. Edward and Rebeka, Apr. 20, 17[00. T. C.].
Joseph, s. Joseph and Elizabeth, May 26, 1770.

CHELMSFORD BIRTHS

EMERSON, Joseph, s. Owen and Mary, May 31, 1799.
Joseph Bradford, s. Bryant and Hannah, Mar. 15, 1833.
Luther, s. Lt. Joseph and Ruth, Apr. 18, 1785.
Mary, d. Owen and Mary, Apr. 20, 1798.
Owen, s. Joseph and Elizabeth, bp. Oct. 3, 1773. C. R. 1.
Owen, s. Owen and Mary, Oct. 24, 1796.
Parker, s. Parker and Rebeckah, Apr. 5, 1775.
Patty, d. Parker and Rebeckah, Nov. 17, 1777.
Rufas, s. Dea. Oen and Mary, Mar. 3, 1810.
Rufus Francis, s. Franklin and Rebecca Adams, Sept. 19, 1835.
Rufus Webster, s. Bryant and Hannah, Aug. 26, 1834.
Samuel, s. Joseph and Ruth, Mar. 10, 1777.
Samuel, s. Samuel and Hanah, July 26, 1798.

EMERY (see also Emmery), Clement, s. Dr. Anthony and Abigail, Jan. 20, 1747-8.
Daniel, s. Zacheriah and Sarah, May 5, 1730.
Ebenezer, s. Ebenezer and Agness, Nov. 23, 1769.
John, s. Zachariah and Sarai, Jan. 2, 1724-5.
John, s. Anthoney and Abigal, Mar. 23, 1739.
Joseph, s. Dr. Anthoney and Abigal, May 12, 1744.
Mary, d. Samuel and Mary, Apr. 1, 1775.
Noah, s. Zachariah and Sary, Oct. 15, 1714.
Noah, s. Zachariah and Sarah, June 18, 1720.
Samuel, s. Zachariah and Thankfull, June 3, 1753.
Sarah, d. Zachary and Sarah, Aug. 17, 1727.
Sarah, d. Anthony and Abigail, Dec. 31, 1740.
Sary, d. Zachariah and Sary, Oct. 20, 1713.
Silos, s. Ebenezer and Agness, Mar. 14, 1773.
Thankful, d. Samuel and Mary, bp. Dec. 14, 1777. C. R. 1.
Thankfull, d. Zachariah and Thankfull, July 3, 1749.
Thomas, s. Dr. Anthony and Abigail, May 13, 1746.
William, s. Anthony and Abigail, Apr. 16, 1742.
Zachriah, s. Zachriah and Sarah, Aug. 26, 1716.

EMMERY (see also Emery), Ebenezer, s. Zachery, "and a former wife," bp. Mar. 24, 1745. C. R. 1.
Joseph, s. Zachery and Thankful, bp. Mar. 24, 1745. C. R. 1.
Samuel, s. Zachariah and Sarah, Aug. 2, 1722.

ESTABROOKS (see also Esterbrooks), Josiah, s. Moses and Esther, bp. Dec. 15, 1745. C. R. 1.
Moses, s. Moses [deceased. C. R. 1.] and Esther, Mar. 30, 1747.

ESTERBROOKS (see also Estabrooks, Estherbrooks), Hannah, d. Aron and Hannah, Oct. 3, 1757.

CHELMSFORD BIRTHS 59

ESTERBROOKS, John, s. Moses and Sarah, Mar. 11, 1773.
Sally, d. Moses and Sarah, Jan. 6, 1777.

ESTHERBROOKS (see also Esterbrooks), Betey, d. Moses and Sarah, July 28, 1785.
Walter, s. Moses and Sarah, Nov. 8, 1782.

FALKNER (see also Foulkner), Eleziabeth, d. Timothy and Deborah, Dec. 4, 1739.

FARLEY, William, s. Timothy and Mary, July 25, 1761.

FARMER, Charles Granville, s. Oliver, carpenter, and Adeline E., b. Ludlow, Nov. 2, 1848.
Charlotta, d. Dea. John and Lydia, July 19, 1792.
Eleazer, s. Simeon and Mary, bp. Feb. 1, 1767. C. R. 1.
Elijah, s. Simeon and Mary, bp. Mar. 23, 1777. C. R. 1.
Elizabeth, d. Jonas and Easther, Mar. 20, 1744-5.
Hiram, s. Abigail, Aug. 16, 1786.
Jedediah, s. Dea. John and Lydia, bp. June 27, 1802. C. R. 1.
Jesse, s. Simeon and Mary, bp. July 2, 1769. C. R. 1.
John, s. Dea. John and Lydia, June 12, 1789.
Jonas, s. Thomas and Elizebeth, at Billerica, May 10, 1719.
Jonas, s. Jonas and Esther, Aug. 26, 1741.
Joseph, s. Simeon and Mary, bp. Nov. 5, 1780. C. R. 1.
Jotham, s. Simeon and Mary, bp. Aug. 8, 1771. C. R. 1.
Lucy, d. Jonas and Esther, bp. Jan. 18, 1747. C. R. 1.
Mary, d. Dea. John and Lydia, Aug. 31, 1794.
Miles, s. Dea. John and Lydia, Jan. 18, 1791.
Oliver, s. Jonas and Easter, Oct. 2, 1754.
Simeon, s. Jonas and Esther, Jan. 26, 1739.
Simeon, s. Simeon and Mary, bp. July 24, 1774. C. R. 1.
Solomon, s. Jonas and Easther, Nov. 24, 1751.
William, s. Esther, bp. Nov. 25, 1781. C. R. 1.

FARR, Ellen Augusta, d. John Harvey, mason, b. Springfield, Vt., and Lucy A., b. Tyngsborough, at North Chelmsford, Oct. 18, 1848.

FARRAR (see also Farrer), Bridgett, d. Joseph and Deberar, Jan. 11, 1753.
Hannah, d. Joseph and Deborah, June 6, 1770.
John, s. Joseph and Deborah, Aug. 16, 1767.
Jonas, s. Joseph and Deborah, Sept. 5, 1762.
Nathaniel, s. Nathaniel and Rachel, bp. Oct. 25, 1778. C. R. 1.
Oliver, s. Nathaniel and Rachil, Aug. 23, 1774.

FARRAR, Rebecka, d. Joseph and Deborah, May 1, 1757.
Ruth, d. Joseph and Deborah, Feb. 4, 1755.
Sally, d. Nathanael and Rachel, bp. Apr. 14, 1776. C. R. 1.
Timothy, s. Joseph and Deborah, Mar. 8, 1759.

FARRER (see also Farrar), Debbe, d. Joseph and Deborah, Apr. 29, 1749.
Joseph, s. Joseph and Deborah, Feb. 10, 1744-5.
Mary, d. Joseph and Deborah, July 4, 1743.
Mercy, d. Joseph and Deborah, June 17, 1747.
Peter, s. Joseph and Deborah, Jan. 4, 1765.
Sarah, d. Joseph and Deborah, Feb. 20, 1750-51.

FARRINGTON, Thomas, s. Capt. (now in ye army), bp. at Groton, Oct. 12, 1760. P. R. 4.

FARRON, see Ferrin.

FARWALL (see also Farwell), Hanory, s. Hanory and Susanah, Oct. 14, 1696.

FARWELL (see also Farwall), Elisabeth, d. Joseph and Hanna, June 9, 1672.
Hannah, d. Joseph and Hannah, Jan. 20, 1667.
Hannah Thurston, d. Tho[ma]s T. and Sally, Feb. 21, 1838.
[Henry. T. C.], s. Joseph and Hannah, Dec. 18, 1674.
Isadora Fratonia, d. Asa T. and Mary Ann, Mar. 16, 1843.
John, s. Joseph and Hanna, June 15, 1686.
Josaph, s. Josaph and Hanah, Aug. 5, 1696.
Joseph, s. Joseph and Hannah, 24 : 5 m : 1670.
Josyah, s. Hennarry and Susanah, Aug. 27, 1698.
Kate Francelia, d. Asa T., scythe maker, b. Fitchburg, and Mary Ann, b. Westford, at Millbury, Dec. 13, 1848.
Maria Augusta, d. Tho[ma]s T. and Sally, July 10, 1842.
Maria Isadore, d. Asa T., scythe maker, and Mary Ann, at Worsted Factory, Sept. 14, 1844.
Oliver, s. Josiph and Hanah, Nov. 25, 1692.
Sarah, d. Joseph and Hannah, 2 : 7 m : 1683.
Stephen Thurston, s. Tho[ma]s T. and Sally, May 9, 1840.
Thomas Thurston, s. Thomas T. and Sally, Sept. 29, 1832.
Thomis, s. Josepeh and Hannah, Oct. 11, 1698.
Willam, s. Joseph and Hanah, Jan. 15, 1688. [Jan. 21. dup.]

FELLOWS, Unis, d. Samuel and Unis, May 23, 1736.

CHELMSFORD BIRTHS   61

FERRIN, Geo[rge] Washington, s. Aaron, milk pedler, and Elizabeth, at Middlesex Village, Sept. 14, 1845.

FISH, John Linzy, s. John B. and Mary H., Mar. 2, 1839.
Martha Ann, d. John B. and Mary H., Mar. 13, 1841.

FISHER, Charlott Ann, d. twin, John and Lucy, Jan. 23, 1818.
George Abbot, s. twin, John and Lucy, Apr. 17, 1814.
John Adams, s. twin, John and Lucy, Apr. 17, 1814.
Mary Jane, d. twin, John and Lucy, Jan. 23, 1818.

FISK (see also Fiske), Chloe, d. William and Rachel, Apr. 4, 1782.
Louisa, d. Benjamin and Betey, May 30, 1801.

FISKE (see also Fisk), Charles, s. Benjamin and Elizabeth, Nov. 17, 1807.

FLACHER (see also Fletcher), Daniall, s. William and Sareh, Mar. 3, 1697.

FLANDERS, Abby Anna Grace, d. W[illia]m S., machinist, and Mary L. L., at North Chelmsford, Jan. 1, 1847.
Lydia Elizabeth, d. Parker and Hannah, Apr. 13, 1841.

FLATCHER (see also Fletcher), Hannah, d. Samuell and Hannah, July 30, 1676.
Samuell, s. Samuell and Mary, Feb. 1, 1698.

FLECHER (see also Fletcher), Elisabath, d. Joshua and Sarah, June 10, 1698.
Elisabeth, d. Samuell, jr., Mar. 6, 1678-9.
Ezekill, s. Wilyam and Sarie, Nov. 24, 16[94. T. C.].
Jonah, s. Josaway and Sara, Dec. 25, 1[torn. 1694?].
Jonathan, s. Joshway and Sararah, Aug. 10, 1693.
Josiph, s. Josheuaye and Sarah, June 10, 1689.
Lydia, d. Sam[ue]ll and Hannah, May 29, 1689. CT. R.
Rachell, d. Joshuah and Sarah, June 27, 1683.
Robbarte, s. Willyam and Sarah, Jan. 9, 1690-91. [1689-90. CT. R.]
Samuell, s. Samuell and Hannah, Sept. 5, 1684.
[Sa. T. C.]rah, d. William and Sarah, May 26, 1679.
Sarah, d. Josheway and Sarah, Jan. 21, 1690-91. [Jan. 27. CT. R.]
Susana, d. Sameuell and Hanah, May 17, 1692.
Temothy, s. Joshuah and Sarah, Oct. 20, 1685.

FLECHER, Thomas, s. Sameuel and Mare, May 31, 1693.
William, s. Samuell [sr. P. R. 1.] and Margreatt, Jan. 1, 1673.
William, s. Samuell and Hannah, Oct. 23, 1673.
William, s. William and Sarah, Apr. 1, 1688. CT. R.
[torn], s. Joshuah and Grisill, Oct. 23, 1679.

FLETCHER (see also Flacher, Flatcher, Flecher), Aaron, s. Andrew and Mary, bp. Aug. 16, 1778. C. R. 1.
Adams, s. Adams and Betsy, Jan. 10, 1807.
Albart, s. Aaron and Sally, Nov. 21, 1808.
Alpheus, s. Maj. Joseph and Lucy, Feb. 6, 1805.
Alzina, d. Adams and Betsey, Apr. 17, 1810.
Amoss, s. Willam and Mary, July 11, 1717.
An, d. Simeon and Mary, Apr. 28, 1757.
Andrew, s. Josiah and Joana, Oct. 23, 1721.
Andrew, s. Andrew and Elizabeth, Feb. 2, 1748-9.
Andrew, s. Josiah and Mary, Apr. 23, 1762.
Ann Maria, d. Jonathan T., stone-cutter, and Joanna, at North Chelmsford, Nov. 4, 1846.
Anna, d. Capt. Benja[min] and Anna, July 20, 1780.
Asa, s. Robert and Remembrance, bp. Mar. 25, 1759. C. R. 1.
Benjamen, s. Joseph and Sary, Aug. 8, 1716.
Benjamin, s. Willam and Mary, Feb. 22, 1715-16.
Benjamin, s. Josiah and Mary, Sept. 18, 1746.
Benjamin, s. Andrew [deceased. C. R. 1.] and Elizebeth, Oct. 29, 1759.
Benjamin, s. Benjamin and Hannah, bp. June 28, 1772. C. R. 1.
Benjamin Chamberlin, s. Maj. Joseph and Lucy, Sept. 18, 1815.
Benjamin Franklin, s. Aaron and Sally, Sept. 22, 1807.
Benjamin Franklin, s. William B. and Sarry, Jan. 7, 1811.
Benjamin William, s. Benjamin and Rachil, Nov. 1, 1772.
Betsey, d. Henry [deceased in May 1781. C. R. 1.] and Remembrance, Apr. 19, 1777.
Betsy, d. Adams and Betsy, Sept. 12, 1808.
Betsy Woods, d. Solomon, bp. Oct. 4, 1812. C. R. 1.
Bridget, d. Paull and Deliverenc, Dec. 2, 1717.
Brigett, d. Robert and Remembrance, June 28, 1754.
Charles, s. Joseph and Lucy, Jan. 31, 1803.
Charles Ballard, s. William Benjamin and Marah, Mar. 5, 1813.
Charles Frederic, s. William, farmer, and Diantha, July 4, 1846.
Charles Washington, s. Josiah, jr., bp. Apr. 22, 1832. C. R. 1.
Charls, s. Robert and Remembrance, Jan. 2, 1748-9.
Daniel, s. Josiah and Zilpah, bp. Mar. 21, 1790. C. R. 1.
Daniel, s. Capt. Joseph and Lucy, Aug. 28, 1796.

CHELMSFORD BIRTHS

FLETCHER, David, s. Samuell and Hanah, Mar. 9, 1717.
Deborah, d. William and Sarah, Mar. 18, 1699.
Deborah, d. Paul and Diliverance, June 15, 1724.
Deborah, d. Samuel and Deborah, Feb. 14, 1770.
Dorithy, d. Joshua and Dorithy, Mar. 17, 1715-16.
Easter, d. William and Lideah, Apr. 12, 1664.
Ebinezer, s. Samuell and Mary, May 16, 1699.
Ede, d. Joseph and Sary, Apr. 8, 1725.
Edward, s. Robert and Remembrance, Apr. 3, 1746.
Elezebeth, d. Andrew and Elezebeth, Mar. 24, 1754.
Eliazer, s. Sam[ue]ll and Mary, Apr. 19, 1704.
Eliza Adeline, d. Benj[ami]n and Mary, Sept. 12, 1841.
Elizabath, d. Joshua and Dorithy, Feb. 9, 1705.
Elizabeth, d. Samuel and Hanna, Mar. 9, 1719-20.
Elizabeth, d. Jonas and Elizabeth, Oct. 21, 1723.
Elizabeth, d. Andrew and Elizabeth, bp. Mar. 25, 1753. C. R. 1.
Elizabeth Bulah, d. William B. and Marah, Aug. 9, 1814.
Ep[h]raim, s. Isaac and Percis, July 2, 1724.
Ephraim, s. Samuel and Deborah, Aug. 11, 1763.
Ephraim, s. Samuel and Bulah, Feb. 21, 1789. [bp. Feb. 28, 1790. C. R. 1.]
Ephrim, s. Joshua and Dorithy, Mar. 12, 1710.
Ester, d. Paull and Deliverance, Jan. 20, 1712-13.
Eunice, d. Joshua and Dorothy, Nov. 9, 1720.
Ezekiel Hildreth, s. Capt. William and Orpah, Dec. 10, 1821.
Ezekil Hildreth, s. William and Lucy, Feb. 23, 1786.
Francis Tyler, s. Jona[than] T., stone-cutter, b. Westford, and Joanna, b. Billerica, at North Chelmsford, Oct. 2, 1848.
Gardner, s. Capt. Josiah and Zilpah, July 9, 1792.
Georg Andrew, s. Jonathan and Polly, Jan. 22, 1812.
George Washington, s. twin, Maj. Joseph and Lucy, Sept. 12, 1806.
Gershom, s. Joshua and Dorithy, July 27, 1712.
Hanah, d. Samuell and Marg[ret], Sept. 14, 1666.
Hanah, d. Joshua and Dorithy, Sept. 21, 1706.
Hanah, d. Samuel and Hanah, Nov. 9, 1718.
Hanah, d. Isaac and Perses, Dec. 16, 1719.
Hannah, d. Benjamin and Hannah, Nov. 18, 1767.
Hannah, d. Joseph and Lucy, Sept. 17, 1794.
Hannah Rogers, d. Capt. Josiah, jr. and Hannah, Feb. 14, 1826.
Hariot, d. Nehemiah and Polly, Apr. 6, 1800.
Hariot Maria, d. William B. and Sarah, Nov. 30, 1816.
Henry, s. Josiah and Joana, May 4, 1729.
Henry, s. Henry and Sarah, Jan. 17, 1754.

FLETCHER, Henry, s. Henry [deceased in May, 1781. C. R. 1.] and Rememberanc, Nov. 12, 1778.
Isaac, s. Samuel and Hanah, Aug. 27, 1694.
J. Merrill, s. Josiah and Hannah, Oct. 1, 1828.
Jacob, s. Sam[ue]ll and Hanah, Mar. 17, 1714-15.
Jacob, s. Samuel and Hanah, Apr. 4, 1725.
James, s. Paull and Deliverence, Jan. 17, 1715.
Jemima, d. William and Lydia, Nov. 25, 1774.
Jeptha, s. Ens. Benjamin and Hannah, Sept. 20, 1775.
Joana, d. Josiah and Joana, Mar. 10, 1726.
Joanna, d. Sam[ue]l, bp. June 8, 1729. C. R. 4.
Joanna, d. Thomas and Mary, Nov. 4, 1756.
Joanna, d. Seth and Joanna, of Westford, bp. Sept. 10, 1780. C. R. 1.
Joanna Stevens, d. David and Joanna, deceased, of Westford, bp. Nov. 12, 1780. C. R. 1.
John, s. Joshua and Sarah, May 7, 1687. CT. R.
John, s. Paul and Deliverance, June 3, 1709.
John, s. Capt. Benja[min] and Anna, Aug. 3, 1782.
John Adams, s. twin, Maj. Joseph and Lucy, Sept. 12, 1806.
John Bateman, s. Ezra and Hannah, Nov. 9, 1803.
John Bates, s. W[illia]m, bp. 1 : 12 m : 1656, a. 15 y. P. R. 1.
Jonas, s. Jonas, bp. Aug. 10, 1729. C. R. 4.
Jonathan, s. Lt. William and Mary, July 20, 1721.
Jonathan, s. Jonas and Elizabeth, July 31, 1725.
Jonathan, s. Joseph, bp. Aug. 17, 1729. C. R. 4.
Jonathan, s. William and Mary, Dec. 18, 1748.
Jonathan, s. William and Mary, May 15, 1755.
Jonathan, s. Andrew and Elizebeth, Sept. 18, 1755.
Jonathan, s. Andrew and Mary, bp. Aug. 25, 1782. C. R. 1.
Joseph, s. Abigail Parker, Nov. 1, 1711.
Joseph, s. Joseph and Sary, July 6, 1713.
Joseph, s. Josiah and Mary, Mar. 22, 1765.
Joseph, s. Joseph and Lucy, May 9, 1793.
Joseph, s. Ens. Joseph and Frances Grant, Dec. 22, 1794.
Jos[h]ua, s. W[illia]m, bp. 1 : 12 m : 1656, a. abt. 12 y. P. R. 1.
Joshua, s. Joshua and Grisell, Jan. 4, 1677.
Joshua, s. Joshua and Dorithy, May 1, 1701.
Joshua, s. Joshua and Elizabeth, July 10, 1724.
Josiah, s. William and Sarah, Apr. 8, 1687. CT. R.
Josiah, s. Josiah and Joana, Oct. 30, 1719.
Josiah, s. Henry and Sarah, June 27, 1758.
Josiah, s. Josiah and Mary, Mar. 20, 1759.
Josiah, s. Josiah, jr. and Marcy, Mar. 2, 1785.
Josiah Richardson, s. Capt. Josiah, jr. and Hannah, Mar. 2, 1822.

FLETCHER, Leafy, d. William and Mary, bp. July 15, 1753.
  c. r. 1.
Leefe, d. William and Mary, May 14, 1762.
Lefee, d. Levi and Phebe, Mar. 28, 1802.
Levi, s. William and Mary, Mar. 3, 1757.
Lidia, d. W[illia]m, bp. 1 : 12 m : 1656, a. abt. 9 y. p. r. 1.
Lidiah, d. Samuell and Margreat, 26 : 7 m : 1669.
Lidya, d. William and Mary, June 1, 1724.
Lowel [Lovell. c. r. 1.], s. Capt. Josiah and Zilpha, Aug. 21, 1795. [bp. Aug. 24, 1794. c. r. 1.]
Lucy, d. Paul and Deliverance, Jan. 20, 1721-2.
Lucy, d. Jonas and Elizibeth, Apr. 22, 1727-8.
Lucy, d. Stephen and Susannah, Feb. 25, 1744-5.
Lucy, d. William and Lucy, Feb. 9, 1791.
Lucy, d. Maj. Josiph and Lucy, Aug. 17, 1808.
Luse, d. William and Tabitha, Feb. 21, 1710.
Lydia, d. Andrew and Lydia, Jan. 29, 1746-7.
Lydia, d. Thomas and Mary, July 15, 1755.
Marcellus H., s. John B. and Susannah, Nov. 10, 1828.
Marcy, d. Josiah, 3d and Marcey, Oct. 29, 1782.
Mare, d. William and Lidiah, Oct. 4, 1658.
Mariah Hartwell, d. Gardner and Francis Grant, Aug. 23, 1819.
Martha, d. Oliver and Grace, Oct. 29, 1767.
Mary, d. Samuel and Mary, Sept. 11, 169[5. t. c.].
Mary, d. Paull, Apr. 15, 1706.
Mary, d. Willam and Mary, Feb. 1, 1718-19.
Mary, d. Josiah and Mary, Dec. 10, 1748.
Mary, d. Simeon and Mary, July 13, 1755.
Mary, d. William and Mary, Oct. 15, 1760. [bp. Oct. 21, 1759. c. r. 1.]
Mary, d. Benjamin and Hannah, Dec. 25, 1769.
Mary, d. Ezra and Hannah, July 3, 1808.
Mary Chamberlain, d. Capt. Josiah and Zilpha, June 30, 1805.
Mary Jane, d. Capt. William and Orpah, Oct. 2, 1816.
Mary Kate, d. W[illia]m, farmer, and Diantha, b. Vermont, Sept. 2, 1849.
Mary Robbins, d. Maj. Joseph and Lucy, Aug. 3, 1810.
Mercy, d. Stephen and Susannah, Feb. 17, 1741-2.
Mercy Ann, d. Benjamin and Mary, Sept. 13, 1831.
Merril, s. Capt. Joseph and Lucy, Apr. 1, 1799.
Miah, s. Andrew and Mary, Nov. 30, 1776.
Moses, s. Andrew and Mary, bp. July 9, 1780. c. r. 1.
Nancy Jones, d. Benj[ami]n and Mary, Apr. 18, 1836.
Obadiah, s. Stephen and Susanna, bp. Jan. 21, 1750. c. r. 1. [1749-50. p. r. 4.]
Obadiah, s. Stephen and Susanna, Apr. 14, 1761.

FLETCHER, Oliver, s. Willam and Mary, Sept. 10, 1708.
Oliver, s. Steephen and Susanna, Sept. 6, 1743.
Oliver, s. Robert and Remembrance, Jan. 14, 1750-51.
Pattey, d. Nehemiah and Polly, Dec. 2, 1798.
Paule, s. W[illia]m, bp. 1: 12 m: 1656, a. abt. 2 y. P. R. 1.
Pelitiah, s. Joseph and Sary, May 3, 1727.
Persis, d. Simeon and Mary, Apr. 7, 1750.
Phebe, d. William and Sarah, Nov. 24, 1700.
Phebe, d. Levi and Phebe, Apr. 1, 1794.
Philip, s. Simeon and Mary, Mar. 20, 1752.
Polly, d. Andrew and Mary, bp. Nov. 25, 1787. C. R. 1.
Porter, s. Andrew and Mary, bp. Oct. 31, 1784. C. R. 1.
Prescott Varnum, s. Jonathan and Polly, Sept. 20, 1810.
Rachel, d. Josiah and Joanna, Jan. 14, 1723-4.
Rebecah, d. Will[ia]m and Sarah, Jan. 29, 17[02. T. C.].
Rebecca, d. Thomas and Mary, Dec. 6, 1753.
Rebecca, d. Benjamin and Hannah, bp. Apr. 20, 1777. C. R. 1.
Rebekah, d. Robert and Sarah, May 3, 1772.
Rebeckeh, d. Paul and Deliverance, Sept. 12, 1728.
Remembrance, d. Robert and Remembrance, Dec. 23, 1752.
Rhoda Butterfield, d. Benj[ami]n and Mary, June 14, 1833.
Robert, s. Willam and Mary, Apr. 20, 1713.
Robert, s. Robert and Remembrance, July 14, 1744.
Ruben, s. William and Mary, July 2, 1720.
Ruth, d. Jacob and Ruth, Sept. 24, 1747.
Salle, d. Capt. Benjamin and Anna, Sept. 26, 1785.
Samson, s. Willam and Mary, Feb. 13, 1719.
Samueil, s. Isaac and Pearcis, Feb. 15, 1728.
Samuel, s. W[illia]m, bp. 1: 12 m: 1656, a. abt. 4 y. P. R. 1.
Samuel, s. Samuel and Hanah, Apr. 10, 1722.
Samuel, s. Samuel and Deborah, Apr. 13, 1765.
Samuel, s. Samuel, jr. and Buler, Oct. 19, 1787.
Samuell, s. Samuell and Marget, July 23, 1664.
Sam[ue]ll, s. Sam[ue]ll and Hanah, Sept. 28, 1683.
Samuell, s. Willam and Mary, Aug. 26, 1706. [Sept. 26. dup.]
Samuell, s. Sam[ue]ll and Hanah, Mar. 7, 1713.
Sarah, d. Samuel and Hannah, Feb. 1, 1686. CT. R.
Sarah, d. Joshua and Doretha, Feb. 25, 1703-4.
Sarah, d. Stephen and Susanna, Aug. 16, 1752.
Sarah, d. Robert and Rememberance, Jan. 24, 1756.
Sarah, d. Thomas and Mary, June 26, 1758.
Sarah, d. Henry and Sarah, June 11, 1763.
Sarah, d. Benjamin and Hannah, June 25, 1773.
Sarah Ann, d. William B. and Sarah, Mar. 21, 1809.
Sary, d. Paul and Deliverance, Feb. 15, 1711.
Sary, d. Josiah and Johana, Oct. 7, 1717.

FLETCHER, Sary, d. Joshua and Dorithy, Mar. 29, 1719.
Sary, d. Joseph and Sary, May 16, 1723.
Sary, d. Josiah and Mary, June 2, 1750.
Sheribiah, s. Henry and Sarah, Nov. 4, 1760.
Shuar Holt, d. Levi and Phebe, Mar. 24, 1796.
Simeon, s. Isaac and Peirces, May 2, 1722.
Solomon, s. Samuel and Deborah, July 1, 1767.
Stephen, s. Willam and Tabith[a], Apr. 3, 1713.
Stephen, s. Stephen and Susanna, July 2, 1748.
Suel, s. Capt. Joseph and Lucy, Mar. 2, 1801.
Susan Pierce, d. Capt. William, jr. and Orpha, Oct. 10, 1828.
Susan [Susanna. C. R. 1.] Proctor, d. Maj. Joseph and Lucy, May 28, 1813.
Susana, d. William B. and Sarah, July 22, 1806.
Susanna, d. Samuel and Hannah, Dec. 29, 1723.
Susanna, d. Stephen and Susanna, bp. Sept. 7, 1755. C. R. 1.
Susun, d. William, jr. and Lucy, Aug. 20, 1779.
Sybil, d. William and Rebecca [(Adams). P. R. 4.], now of Temple, bp. Mar. 1, 1789. C. R. 1.
Tabitha, d. William and Tabitha, Dec. 26, 1721.
Tabitha, d. Stephen and Susanna, Sept. 30, 1751.
Thankful, d. Stephen and Susanna, bp. Oct. 2, 1757. C. R. 1.
Thankfull, d. Sam[ue]ll and Mary, July 19, 1701.
Thankfull, d. William and Tabitha, Sept. 25, 1731.
Thomas, s. Willam and Mary, Jan. 18, 1711.
Thomas, s. Joseph and Sary, Mar. 16, 1721.
Thomas, s. Thomas and Mary, Feb. 13, 1761.
Timothy, s. Paull and Deliverance, Sept. 30, 1707.
Timothy, s. Joseph and Sary, Apr. 12, 1719.
Uriah, s. Steaphen and Susanna, Sept. 15, 1746.
Willam, s. Willam and Mary, Sept. 22, 1702. [Sept. 23. dup.]
William, s. William and Lidiah, Feb. 22, 1656. [Feb. 21. CT. R.]
William, s. William and Tabitha, Oct. 16, 1716.
William, s. Robert and Remembrance, Aug. 23, 1747.
William, s. Josiah and Mary, Dec. 22, 1754.
William, s. William and Leucy, May 18, 1782.
William, s. Levi and Phebe, Sept. 2, 1791.
William, s. William B. and Sarah, Mar. 13, 1805.
William, s. Capt. William and Orpah, July 10, 1819.
William Benjamin, s. Benja[min], deceased, and Rachel, bp. May 2, 1773. C. R. 1.
Zaccheus, s. William and Mary, Dec. 27, 1751. [bp. Dec. 30, 1750. C. R. 1.]
Zachariah, s. Joshua and Dorithy, Oct. 28, 1714.
Zacheus, s. Levi and Phebe, Aug. 9, 1798.

FLINT, Alvan Sawyer, s. Warren and Lucinda, at Groton, Dec. 15, 1832.
Benj[ami]n Franklin, s. Warren and Lucinda, at Canton, July 1, 1838.
Curtis Washington, s. Warren and Lucenday, at Dracut, Feb. 22, 1840.
Ellen Viola, d. Warren, machinist, and Lucinda, Feb. 12, 1844.
Forest Newton, s. Warren and Lucinda, at Dracut, Jan. 13, 1842.
George Henry, s. Warren and Lucinda, at Lowell, Aug. 22, 1836.
Lucy Sawyer, d. Warren and Lucinda, at Dunstable, N. H., Sept. 9, 1834.
Warren Byron, s. Warren and Lucinda, at Boston, Mar. 25, 1831.

FORBUSH (see also Furbush), Benj[amin] Franklin, s. Silas, bp. Sept. 11, 1808. C. R. 1.
Clarissa, d. Silas and Anna, bp. July 10, 1803. C. R. 1.
Rufus, s. Silas, bp. June 7, 1807. C. R. 1.
Silas Butterfield, s. Silas and Anna, bp. Oct. 14, 1804. C. R. 1.

FORD, Iekeli, s. Elisha, bp. Feb. 27, 1812. C. R. 1.

FOSTER, Aaron, s. William and Hannah, Jan. 26, 1750-51.
Aaron, s. Obediah and Mary, Mar. 7, 1791.
Abigail, d. Joseph [deceased. C. R. 1.] and Thankful, July 6, 1741.
Abigail, d. James and Betsy, Sept. 28, 1808.
Abram, s. Samuell and Hester [Ester. CT. R.], Oct. 27, 1664.
Adams, s. Joseph and Mary, May 5, 1794.
[And. T. C.]rew, s. Eli and Judah, Mar. 28, 1694.
Andrew, s. Sameuell and Sara, Mar. 28, 1[694-5. T. C.].
Androoe, s. Samewell and Hester [torn] 30, 1662.
Anna, d. Samuell and Sarah, Dec. 3, 1684.
Anna, d. Isaiah and Anna, Apr. 4, 1744.
Asa, s. Asa, bp. at Pelham, July 24, 1765. P. R. 4.
Benjamin, s. Elias and Hanah, Feb. 18, 1712-13.
Benony, s. Joseph and Thankfull, Jan. 23, 1733-4.
Betty, d. Robert and Mary, bp. Sept. 30, 1770. C. R. 1.
Bridget, d. William and Hannah, Feb. 17, 1760.
Bridgitt, d. Edward and Remembrance, June 12, 1739.
Charles T., s. James and Betsy, Sept. 28, 1816.
Coburn, s. Obediah and Mary, Dec. 13, 1792.
Daniel, s. Elias and Hannah, Aug. 7, 1721.
Daniel, s. Andrew and Mary, Apr. 17, 1726.

CHELMSFORD BIRTHS 69

FOSTER, Darkes, d. Ely and Judah, Sept. 24, 1705.
[Easter. CT. R.], d. Samuell and Easter [torn. Nov. CT. R.] 1, 1659.
Ebenezer, s. Ebenezer and Liddia, Sept. 14, 1718.
Ebenezer, s. Ebenezer and Sarah, July 23, 1744.
Edwar[d], s. Samewell and Easter, Apr. 30, 1657. [Apr. 29. CT. R.]
Edward, s. Sameuell and Sarah, Jan. 29, 1689.
Edward, s. Edward and Remembrance, Jan. 28, 1714.
Edward, s. William and Hannah, Apr. 3, 1747.
Eli, ch. Br[other], bp. 1 : 12 m : 1656, a. abt. 3 y. P. R. 1.
Elias, s. Ely and Judith, Feb. 15, 1686. CT. R.
Elias, s. Elias and Hannah, Apr. 11, 1716.
Elizabeth, d. John and Elizabeth, Mar. 10, 1723-4.
Elizabeth, d. James and Betsy, Mar. 21, 1799.
Ester, d. Ely and Judah, Aug. 5 [torn. 170-. T. C. 1700?].
Franklin, s. Joseph and Mary, Nov. 6, 1798.
George W., s. James and Betsy, Mar. 24, 1814.
Hanah, d. Ely and Judah, May 11, 1698.
Hannah, d. Bro[ther], bp. 1 : 12 m : 1656, a. abt. 7 y. P. R. 1.
Hannah, d. William and Hannah, Feb. 7, 1748-9.
Hannah, d. Edward and Phebe, Nov. 4, 1772.
Hannah, d. Obediah and Mary, July 1, 1800.
Hannah, d. James and Betsy, Sept. 30, 1802.
Hapzibab, d. Eli and Judah, Mar. 12, 1696.
Henery, s. John and Elizabeth, Aug. 11, 1726.
Hezekiah, s. Obadiah, bp. Feb. 23, 1806. C. R. 1.
Isaac, s. Isaac and Lydia, Sept. 25, 1770.
Isaiah, s. Ebenezer and Liddia, Nov. 16, 1720.
Isaiah, s. Isaiah and Anna, Feb. 8, 1749-50.
Jacob, s. Robert and Mary, May 1, 1768.
James, s. James and Betsy, July 4, 1800.
Jane, d. Samuell and Sarah, Oct. 8, 1696.
Joana, d. Daniel and Sary, Oct. 12, 1755.
John, s. Samuell and Ester, 28 : 7 m : 16[71. T. C.].
[Jo. T. C.]hn, s. Edward and Rebeka, July 30, 1694.
Jonathan, s. Robert and Mary, bp. May 9, 1773. C. R. 1.
Joseph, s. Samuell and Sarah, Nov. 14, 1686.
Joseph, s. Sam[ue]ll and Sarah, Oct. 23, 1690. CT. R.
Joseph, s. Robert and Mary, Mar. 14, 1766.
Josiah, s. Edward and Rememberance, July 25, 1728.
Josiah, s. Isaac and Lydia, July 7, 1774.
Jude, d. Ely and Jude, Mar. 20, 1683.
Lenord, s. Lenord [deceased. C. R. 1.] and Abigail, Nov. 15, 1759.
Leonard, s. twin, Joseph and Thankfull, July 12, 1738.

FOSTER, Lidia, d. Ebenezer and Lidya, Nov. 16, 1722.
Lidyah, d. Nathaniel and Frances, Nov. 17 [torn. 170-. T. C. 1702?].
Lydia, d. Isaiah and Anna, Aug. 10, 1747.
Lydia, d. Isaac and Lydia, Apr. 9, 1772.
Mariah, d. James and Betsy, July 9, 1805.
Martha, d. Cler[k?] William and Hannah, Feb. 10, 1765.
Martha, d. James and Betsy, Dec. 28, 1806.
Mary, d. Edward and Remembrance, Apr. 25, 1725.
Mary, d. Andrew and Mary, Feb. 11, 1728-9.
Mary, d. Ebenezer and Mary, Feb. 7, 1742-3.
Mary, d. Joseph and Mary, May 7, 1792.
Moses, s. Joseph and Mary, Feb. 14, 1790.
Mosis, s. Sameuel and Sarah, Oct. 4, 1692.
Namoie, d. Nathaniel and Francies, July 15, 1718.
Nathaniel, s. Ebenezer and Lidia, Dec. 23, 1730.
Nathaniell, s. Samuel and Hester, Oct. 14, 1667.
Noah, s. William and Hannah, Aug. 28, 1757.
Noah, s. Robert and Mary, Nov. 3, 1778.
Noah, s. Obediah and Mary, Dec. 21, 1797.
Obadiah, s. William and Hannah, July 17, 1762.
Oliver, s. Ebenezer and Hannah, Nov. 28, 1773.
Phebe, d. Eli and Judah, June 20, 1691.
Rachel, d. Obediah and Mary, June 20, 1803.
Rebecah, d. Ebenezer and Lidiah, July 11, 1733.
Rebecca, d. Josiah and Sarah, Nov. 25, 1766.
Rebecka, d. Ebenezer and Sarah, Jan. 14, 1750-51.
Rebekah, d. Edward and Rebekah, Mar. 25, 1690.
Remembrance, d. William and Hannah, Feb. 23, 1753.
Remembrence, d. Edward and Remembrence, Mar. 2, 1718.
Reuben, s. Betsey, bp. May 4, 1800. C. R. 1.
Robert, s. Joseph and Thankfull, Jan. 4, 1735-6.
Robert, s. twin, Joseph and Thankfull, July 12, 1738.
Robert, s. Robert and Mary, bp. July 23, 1775. C. R. 1.
Ruben, s. Ebenezer and Lidya, Feb. 19, 1726-7.
Rubin, s. Isaiah and Hannah, Sept. 23, 1753.
Ruth, d. Eli and Judah, Apr. 9, 1689.
Ruth, d. Daniel and Sarah, Sept. 7, 1753.
Ruth, d. Ebenezer and Hannah, July 11, 1771.
Sampson, s. Joseph and Thankfull, Mar. 16, 1736-7.
Samuel, s. Bro[ther], bp. 1: 12 m: 1656, a. abt. 6 y. P. R. 1.
Samuel, s. Edward and Remembrance, Mar. 23, 1731-2.
Samuel Emery, s. Robert and Mary, Mar. 19, 1781.
Samuel Emery, s. Samuel Emery and Mary [wid. in May, 1805. C. R. 1.], May 10, 1804.
Samuell, s. Moses and Mary, Oct. 31, 1718.

FOSTER, [Sarah, d. Sa. T. C.]meuell and Sarie, Aug. 16, 1694.
Sarah, d. Ebenezer and Sarah, Jan. 1, 1746-7.
Sarah, d. Daniel and Sarah, Oct. 6, 1750.
Sarah, d. Josiah and Sarah, Oct. 24, 1764.
Sarah, d. Edward and Phebe, bp. Jan. 8, 1775. C. R. 1.
Sarah, d. Isaac and Lydia, July 29, 1776.
Sarah, d. Joseph and Mary, May 3, 1796.
Sarah A., d. James and Betsy, Aug. 25, 1818.
Solomon, s. Ely and Judetth, Feb. 14, 1684.
Stephen, s. Eli and Judah, Jan. 20, 1702[-3.].
Stephen, s. Andrew and Mary, Apr. 6, 1724.
Thankful, d. Robart and Mary, Mar. 9, 1764.
Walter C., s. James and Betsy, June 2, 1812.
William, s. William and Hannah, Sept. 12, 1745.
William, s. William and Hannah, Apr. 28, 1755.
William, s. Ebenezer and Hannah, Aug. 10, 1769.
William, s. Obediah and Mary, Feb. 7, 1796.
William Bacon, s. Isaac and Lydia, Nov. 15, 1778.
William P., s. James and Betsy, Dec. 28, 1810.
Willum, s. Edward and Rememberance, Nov. 11, 1716.

FOULKNER (see also Falkner), Sarah, d. Timothy and Deborah, Sept. 17, 1737.

FOX, Josiah, s. Eliphalet, bp. at Dracut, July 29, 1781. P. R. 4.

FRENCH, ——, ch. Samuell, 5 : 1 m : 1[torn. 1678-9?].

FROST, Abigail, d. Ebenezer and Hannah, Feb. 7, 1734-5.
Asa, s. Ebenezer and Hannah, Mar. 28, 1742.
Asa, s. Ebenezer and Esther, Mar. 13, 1767.
Asa, s. Asa and Rhode, May 29, 1790.
Betty, d. Ebenezer and Hannah, Jan. 16, 1743-4.
Charles Andrew, s. Levi, farmer, and Lucretia, July 29, 1847.
Ebenezer, s. Ebenezer and Hannah, Aug. 8, 1731.
Ebenezer, s. Ebenezer and Esther, Dec. 16, 1770.
Hannah, d. Ebenezer and Hannah, Feb. 2, 1732-3.
Hannah, d. Ebenezer, jr. and Esther, Jan. 9, 1769.
Hannah, d. Asa and Rhoda, bp. Aug. 1, 1802. C. R. 1.
Jesse, s. Jesse and Joanna, Sept. 6, 1762. [bp. Sept. 13, 1761. C. R. 1.]
Joanna, d. Jesse and Joanna, July 6, 1763.
Levy, s. Ebenezer and Esther, Sept. 25, 1772.
Olive, d. Eben[eze]r and Olive, bp. Apr. 8, 1798. C. R. 1.

FROST, Patty, d. Ebenezer [and Esther. C. R. 1.], Sept. 7, 177 [torn. bp. 1774. C. R. 1.].
Porter, s. Asa and Rhoda, bp. Aug. 1, 1802. C. R. 1.
Rhode, d. Asa and Rhode, Aug. 12, 1794.
Salathiel, s. Eben[eze]r and Olive, bp. Apr. 8, 1798. C. R. 1.
Salethial, s. Ebinezer and Esther, May 18, 1781.
Sarah, d. Ebenezer and Hannah, Jan. 29, 1737-8.
Sarah, d. Ebenezer and Esther, bp. Apr. 27, 1777. C. R. 1.

FURBER, John, s. Andrew S. and Ann, Jan. 28, 1843.
Mary Ann, d. Andrew S., machinist, and Ann, at North Chelmsford, Apr. 21, 1845.

FURBUSH (see also Forbush), Milo, s. Silas and Anna, June 23, 1798.
Suel, s. Silas and Anna, Apr. 17, 1800.

GALUSHA (see also Galusiah, Galutiah, Gelusha, Golushaw, Golushua), Nathanell, s. Danell and Hanah, Dec. 22, 1691. [Dec. 24. dup.]

GALUSIAH (see also Galusha), Daniel, s. Daniel and Hanah, Mar. 31, 1686-7.
Dinah, d. Daniel and Hanah, Jan. 14, 1695-6.
Hanah, d. Danil and Hanah, Sept. 12, 1677.
Jacob, s. Daniel and Hanah, June 24, 1680. [June 22. dup.]
Ratchel, d. Daniel and Hanah, Sept. 14, 1683. [18: 7 m: dup.]

GALUTIAH (see also Galusha), Daniel, s. Daniel and Hannah, Apr. 3, 1688. CT. R.

GEER, George F., s. Frederic S., trader, b. Shelburne, Vt., and Louisa, b. Tyngsborough, at Middlesex Village, Sept. 4, 1849.

GELUSHA (see also Galusha), Richard, s. Hannah, Dec. 4, 1696.

GIBSON, James Kimball, s. James, Oct. 31, 1836.

GILLSON (see also Gilson), Mare, d. Joseph and Mare, Nov. 17, 1662.

GILMORE, Emeline, d. W[illia]m S., hatter, and Emeline, at Middlesex Village, Sept. 3, 1847.

CHELMSFORD BIRTHS 73

GILMORE, William Parkenson, s. William P., hatter, and Emily, at Middlesex Village, Apr. 18, 1844.

GILSON (see also Gillson), Anna, d. Joseph, Feb. 22, 1670. CT. R.

GLEASON, Ella Florence, d. Alpheus, scythe maker, b. Orford, N. H., and Cornelia, b. Auburn, Jan. 10, 1849.

GLOAD (see also Glode, Glood), Dolly, d. Elnathan and Dolly, June 26, 1807.
Elizabeth, d. Elnathan and Dolly, Apr. 19, 1809.
Jannett, d. Elnathan and Dolly, Aug. 15, 1805.
John, s. Elnathan and Dolly, Apr. 3, 1803.

GLODE (see also Gload), Esther, d. John and Esther, bp. Jan. 5, 1772. C. R. 1.
William, s. John and Esther, July 10, 1770.

GLOOD (see also Gload), Nancy, d. William and Sally, Oct. 18, 1794.

GLOVER, Caroline Sophia, w. Otis Adams, jr., Jan. 12, 1829. P. R. 28.

GOLD (see also Gould), John, s. Samuell and Mehettebell, Jan. 24, 1693.

GOLDE (see also Gould), Anna, d. Sam[ue]ll and Mehettebel, Sept. 12, 1689.
Margret, d. Sam[ue]ll and Mehettabel, May 12, 168[torn. bef. 1689.].
Sam[ue]ll, s. Sam[ue]ll and Mehettebell, Nov. 10, 1691.

GOLE (see also Gould), Elisabeth, d. Francis and Rose, Jan. 15, 1664.
Marcy [Mary Goole. CT. R.], d. Francis and Roase, Feb. 23, 1666.

GOLUSHAW (see also Galusha), Nathaniel, s. Sam[ue]ll and Easter, Sept. —, 1741.

GOLUSHUA (see also Galusha), Elijah, s. Samuel and Esther, Dec. 23, 1743.

GOODHUE, Jemmy, s. Daniel and Sarah, of Westford, bp. Aug. 27, 1780. C. R. 1.

GOOLD (see also Gould), Abijah, s. Adam and Elizibeth, Dec. 12, 1735.
Alpheus, s. Benjamin and Sarah, bp. Aug. 21, 1791. C. R. 1.
Benjamin, s. Ebenezer and Olive, June 13, 1758.
Benjamin, s. Benjamin and Sarah, Mar. 19, 1788.
Deborah, d. Benjamin [jr. P. R. 4.] and Easter, Nov. 8, 1761.
Easter, d. Benjamin and Easter, Jan. 11, 1763.
Ebenezer, s. Benjamin and Sarrah, Feb. 21, 1725-6.
Ebenezer, s. Ebenezer and Olive, Feb. 27, 1755.
Elijah, s. Benjamin, jr. and Esther, July 20, 1764.
Jemima, d. Samuell and Mehitabell, June 30, 1696.
Lidia, d. Benjamin and Sarah, July 7, 1738.
Lucy, d. Adam and Elizebeth, Feb. 4, 1732-3.
Lucy, d. Ebenezer and Olive, Aug. 31, 1760.
Mary, d. Benjamin and Sarah, Jan. 12, 1730-31.
Mary, d. Cornet Benjamin and Sarah, Aug. 29, 1746.
Mary Phillips, d. wid. Martha, bp. Dec. 2, 1819. C. R. 1.
Nathaniel, s. Benjamin and Sarah, May 21, 1741.
Olive, d. Ebenezer and Olive, Nov. 2, 1751.
Phebe, d. Reuben and Deborah, Dec. 21, 1772.
Reuben, s. Reuben and Deborah, bp. June 23, 1765. P. R. 4.
Reuben Benjamin Hammatt, s. wid. Martha, bp. Dec. 2, 1819. C. R. 1.
Ruben, s. Benjamin and Sarah, Apr. 30, 1736.
Ruben, s. Ruben and Deborah, June 21, 1765.
Ruth, d. Ebenezer and Olive, Oct. 4, 1762.
Salla, d. Benjamin and Sarah, Dec. 16, 1785.
Sarah, d. Ruben and Deborah, May 21, 1768.
Sary, d. Benjamin and Sary, June 15, 1728.
Simeon, s. Simeon and Elizebeth, Apr. 17, 1761.
Simion, s. Benjamin and Sarah, Aug. 17, 1733.

GOOLDE (see also Gould), Isaac, s. twin, Sam[ue]ll and Mehettebel, Mar. 6, 1699.
Moses, s. twin, Sam[ue]ll and Mehettebel, Mar. 6, 1699.

GOOLE (see also Gould), Isack, s. Francis and Rose, Mar. 3, 1669.
Leah, d. twin, Francis and Roase, May 4, 1663.
Rachell, d. twin, Francis and Roase, May 4, 1663.
Thankefull, d. Francis and Rose, 31: 11 m: 1671.

GORMAN, Cyrus, s. Patric, laborer, and Ann, at Middlesex Village, May 16, 1843.
Thomas, s. Patric, laborer, and Ann, at North Chelmsford, Jan. 7, 1846.

GOSSLING, Samuel, s. Thomas and Mary, of Boston, bp. June 2, 1776. c. r. 1.

GOULD (see also Gold, Golde, Gole, Goold, Goolde, Goole, Guod), Benjamin, s. Benjamin and Sary, Aug. 7, 1723.
Benjamin, s. Adam and Elisabeth, Aug. 29, 1742.
Charles Edwin, s. Charles and Eliza Ann, Feb. 22, 1842.
Ebenezer, s. Benjamin and Sarah, Oct. 31, 1794.
Joanna, d. Reuben and Mathew, June 5, 1798.
Joseph, s. Reuben and Mathew, Feb. 22, 1805.
Mary, d. Benjamin and Sarah, Jan. 18, 1797.
Mary Phillips, d. Reuben and Mathew, May 26, 1790.
Nancy, d. Benj[ami]n and Sarah, May 12, 1798.
Pamely, d. Benjamin and Sarah, Aug. 5, 1789.
Rachel, d. Ebenezer and Olliv, Feb. 28, 1753.
Ruth, d. Benjamin and Sarah, —— 23, 1792. [bp. Dec. 9. c. r. 1.]

GRAVES, James, s. Sam[ue]ll and Sary, Apr. 22, 1714.
Sam[ue]ll, s. Sam[ue]ll and Sary, Apr. 16, 1711.
Sary, d. Sam[ue]ll, Dec. 19, 1709.

GREEN, Amos, s. Amos and Louisa, Mar. 14, 1832.
Charles, s. Amos and Louisa, Dec. 28, 1833.
George, s. Amos and Louisa, Jan. 29, 1830.
Perley, s. John, laborer, and Hannah, at Carlisle, July 6, 1844.
William, s. Amos, farmer, and Looisa, Dec. 13, 1845.

GUOD (see also Gould), [Jo. t. c.]hn [Goold. ct. r.], s. Francis and Ros [torn. —— 21, 16. t. c.] 61. [Aug. 21. ct. r.]

HADLEY, Belinda Page, d. Samuel P[age. p. r. 9.] and Belinda R. [Butler. p. r. 9.], Apr. 21, 1823.
Samuel Page, s. Samuel P[age. p. r. 9.] and Belinda B[utler. p. r. 9.], Oct. 22, 1831.

HALE, Edward Clarence, s. Calvin G., scythe maker, b. Norridgewock, Me., and Cordelia Ann, b. Winthrop, Me., Oct. 13, 1848.

HALE, Harriot, d. Moses and Sussanna, Aug. 21, 1794.
Lidia, d. Moses and Susanna, Apr. 29, 1791.
Sophronia, d. Moses and Susanna, Mar. 13, 1799.

HALL, Esther Antoinette, d. Darius, laborer, and Sarah A., Dec. 9, 1846.
Franklin, s. Joseph C. and Rhoda, Nov. 19, 1822.
Frederic William, s. Harrison, harness-maker, and Esther, at North Chelmsford, Mar. 17, 1845.
Harriot, d. Joseph C. and Rhoda, Aug. 4, 1813.
John Adams, s. Darius and Sarah Ann, Sept. 10, 1842.
Mary Moore, d. Harrisson, trunk and harness-maker, and Esther S., at North Chelmsford, July 13, 1847.
Sarah, d. Christopher, Dec. 4, 1670. CT. R.
Willard, s. Willis and Mehetable, of Westford, bp. Apr. 29, 1781. C. R. 1.
——, d. Darius, laborer, and Sarah Ann, Apr. 26, 1844.

HAMBLET, Deborah, d. Ruben and Deborah [bp. at Dracut. P. R. 4.], Dec. 4, 1764.
Ruben, s. Ruben and Deborah, Sept. 27, 1760.
William, s. Ruben and Deborah, Nov. 1, 1762.

HARDY, Sarah, d. Ezekiel and Sarah, June 24, 1764.

HARIS (see also Harriss), Hephsibeth, d. Ebenazer and Elizibeth, Oct. 19, 1734.

HARISS (see also Harriss), Ebenezer, s. Ebenez[er] and Elizabeth, June 12, 1731.
Hannah, d. Ebenezer and Elazeb[e]th, June 26, 1737.

HARRINGTON, Rufus, s. [Dr. C. R. 1.] Timothy and Sarah, Mar. 10, 1791.
Salley, d. Dr. Timothy and Sarah, July 5, 1786.

HARRISS (see also Haris, Hariss), Thomas, s. Ebenezer and Elizabeth, Aug. 2, 1742.
William, s. Ebenezer and Elizabeth, Oct. 7, 1744.

HARTWELL, Amy Frances, d. Geo[rge] H., scythe maker, b. Littleton, and Mary F., b. Smithfield, R. I., at Fitchburg, June 18, 1849.
Oliver, s. Jonathan and Sarah, Mar. 9, 1728-9.
Peter, s. Jonathan and Sarah, Mar. 5, 1724-5.
Sarah, d. Jonathan and Sarah, Sept. 22, 1723.
Thomas, s. Jonathan and Sarah, Mar. 6, 1726-7.

HARVIL, John, s. John and Easter, Apr. 24, 1736.

HARWOD (see also Harwood), Elesabeth, d. Nathan[ie]ll and Mary, Jan. 28, 1701.
Jonathan, s. Nathaniell and Mary, Apr. 21, 1710.
Mary, d. James —— [torn. 1680?].
Sary, d. Nath[anie]ll and Mary, Aug. 28, 1707.
Susanah, d. Nath[anie]ll and Mary, Apr. 14, 1713.

HARWOOD (see also Harwod, Herod), Abel, s. John and Sarah, Apr. 4, 1790.
Abigal, d. James and Lidya, May 18, 1699.
Anna, d. John, bp. Nov. —, 1817. c. r. 1.
Betcey, d. John and Sarah, Apr. 17, 1794.
Charles Albert, s. Rufus, laborer, and Sarah, Aug. 28, 1846.
Easter, d. Jonathan and Judith, Dec. 2, 1762.
Elizabeth, d. Jonathan and Mary, May 8, 1745.
Ephraim, s. John and Sarah, Nov. 19, 1787.
Hannah, d. Nathanell and Mary, July 28, 1698.
James, s. twin, James and Lidyah, Sept. 30, 169[5. t. c.].
Joana, d. Jonathan and Joana, Mar. 27, 1732.
Joana, d. Jonathan and Mary, Dec. 17, 1738.
Joanna, d. John and Sarah, Dec. 19, 1784.
John, s. twin, James and Lidyah, Sept. 30, 169[5. t. c.].
John, s. James and Lidya, May 27, 1703.
John, s. Jonathan and Mary, Dec. 2, 1752.
John, s. John and Sary, Dec. 26, 1776.
Jonas, s. Jonathan and Mary, Feb. 27, 1742-3.
Jonathan, s. Jonathan and Mary, Jan. 9, 1740-41.
Jonathan, s. Jonathan, jr. and Olive, Oct. 26, 1767.
Jonathan, s. John and Sarah, Oct. 4, 1782.
Martha Washington, d. Solomon, farmer, and Mardany D., Nov. 22, 1843.
Mary, d. Jonathan and Joanna, Jan. 16, 1732-3.
Molly, d. John and Sary, Oct. 9, 1774.
Nathaniel, s. Ens. Jonathan and Jude [Judith. c. r. 1.], July 2, 1760.
Olive, d. Jonathan and Joana, Feb. 8, 1734-5.
Rachell, d. Nathan[ie]ll and Mary, Dec. 2, 1703.
Sarah, d. John and Sarah, Oct. 3, 1779.
[torn], d. James and Lidiah, Dec. 25, 1678.

HASTINGS, Jonathan Cotton, s. Walter and Lucretia, bp. Feb. 10, 1782. c. r. 1.
Walter, s. [Dr. p. r. 4.] Walter and Lucretia [grands. Rev. Ebenezer Bridge. p. r. 4.], bp. Jan. 3, 1779. c. r. 1.

HATHAWAY, Solon Albertes, s. John, hatter, and Agnes, at Middlesex Village, Aug. 15, 1843.

HAWARD (see also Howard), Bengamin, s. Nathanill and Sarah, Apr. 9, 1691.
Marie, d. Nathanill and Sarah, Aug. 17, 1693.
Rebeca [Howard. CT. R.], d. Nathanill and Sarah, May 9, 1688. [June 24. CT. R.]

HAWOOD (see also Heywood), James [Haywood. C. R. 1.], s. James and Sarah, Oct. 13, 1758.

HAYDEN, Abigail, d. Daniel and Sarah, June 9, 1811.
Elizabeth Farwell, d. Daniel and Sarah, May 17, 1813.
Francis Augusta, d. Daniel and Sarah, Apr. 7, 1808.
Sarah Ann, d. Daniel and Sarah, June 14, 1806.

HAYNES, Amanda L., d. Charles B., painter, and Lucy, Oct. 25, 1844.

HAYWOOD (see also Heywood), Adelia Elizabeth, d. Benj[ami]n, farmer, and Esther, b. Townsend, Jan. 7, 1843.
Benjamin, s. Josiph and Susanna, Apr. 30, 1798.
Betey, d. Joseph and Susanna, Nov. 6, 1790.
Emeline Maria, d. Benj[ami]n, farmer, and Esther, b. Townsend, Jan. 27, 1848.
Hannah, d. Joseph and Susanna, Sept. 14, 1793.
Hermon Florion, s. Benjamin, farmer, and Esther, b. Townsend, Sept. 27, 1849.
Jesse, s. James and Sary, Aug. 30, 1755.
Joseph, s. James and Sary, Apr. 10, 1761.
Joseph, s. Joseph and Susanna, June 4, 1792.
Joseph Lyman, s. Joseph E., laborer, and Nancy, at Furnace Village, Dec. 3, 1843.
Julia Ella, d. Benj[ami]n, farmer, and Esther, b. Townsend, Dec. 7, 1834.
Polly, d. Joseph and Susanna, May 14, 1796.
Rufus Benjamin, s. Benj[ami]n, farmer, and Esther, b. Townsend, Oct. 1, 1839.
Sarah, d. Joseph and Susanna, Dec. 27, 1799.
Susanna, d. Joseph and Susanna, Sept. 20, 1789.
———, d. Benjamin, farmer, and Esther, at Baptist Corner, Jan. 7, 1844.

HEALD (see also Heild), Ephraim, s. Thomas, bp. Jan. 12, 1729. C. R. 4.
Lucy Ann, d. E. and H., bp. Dec. 2, 1832. C. R. 3.

CHELMSFORD BIRTHS 79

HEARRICK (see also Herrick), Pattey, d. Abnor and Elizebeth, Apr. 26, 1783.

HEILD (see also Heald), Gershom, s. Gershom and Sarah, Sept. 4, 1727.

HELDRETH (see also Hildreth), Ana, d. Ephram and Anne, Sept. 3, 1705.
Benjamin, s. Richard and Darkos, Feb. 18, 1706.
David, s. Ephraim and Anna, Aug. 16, 1711.
Epharim, s. Ephraim and Marsye, Jan. 18, 1708.
Isack, s. Isack and Elesabath, Aug. 1, 1698.
Jacob, s. Ephriam and Ana, July 18, 1709.
Jaems, s. Ephram and Ane, Dec. 23, 1698.
John, s. Josepeh and Abegale, June 9, 1698.
Jonas, s. Richard and Darkes, May 10, 1713. [May 7. dup.]
Jonas, s. Richard and Dorcas, Aug. 1, 1716.
Jonathan, s. Joseph and Deliveranc, Dec. 24, 1712.
Josiah, s. Ephrim and Marsy, Feb. 14, 1710.
Sam[ue]ll, s. Richard and Darkus, Oct. 10, 1709.
Thomas, s. Epharim and Anne, Sept. 25, 1707.
Thomas, s. Richard and Darkes, Sept. 26, 1708.

HELDRITH (see also Hildreth), Josiph, s. Ephrime and Anah, Feb. 22, 1688.

HERICK (see also Herrick), Jamima, d. Abner and Elizebeth, Oct. 29, 1778.

HEROD (see also Harwood), Abigall, d. twin, Jeams and Lidiah, Sept. 2, 1692.
Andrew, s. twin, Jeams and Lidiah, Sept. 2, 1692.

HERRICK (see also Hearrick, Herick), Bethiah, d. Joseph and Lois, bp. Dec. 2, 1750. C. R. 1.
Elizebeth, d. Abnor and Elizebeth, Jan. 29, 1781.
Jonathan, s. Joseph and Lois, bp. Dec. 2, 1750. C. R. 1.
Lois, d. Joseph and Lois, Aug. 17, 1749.
Molley, d. Joseph and Lois, bp. Dec. 2, 1750. C. R. 1.
Polly, d. Abner and Elizabath, Sept. 14, 1786.
Rebecca, d. Abner and Elisebeth, Nov. 21, 1776.
Sarah, d. Abner and Elizabeth, bp. May 28, 1785. C. R. 1.

HEYWARD (see also Heywood), ——, d. Benjamin, farmer, and Esther, —— 27, 1848.

HEYWOOD (see also Hawood, Haywood, Heyward), Benjamin, s. James and Sarah, Oct. 22, 1753.
Charles, s. Joseph and Fidelia, Jan. 20, 1832.
Elizabeth, d. Joseph and Fidelia, Mar. 10, 1824.
Isaac Bancroft, s. Joseph and Fidelia, Mar. 1, 1827.
James, s. James and Sarah, Jan. 7, 1770.
John Stratton, s. Joseph and Fidelia, Oct. 6, 1822.
Joseph, s. Joseph and Sarah, June 8, 1749.
Joseph E., s. Joseph and Fidella, Jan. 23, 1821.
Joseph Emery, s. Joseph and Fidelia, Jan. 23, 1820.
Lydia, d. Joseph and Sarah, July 4, 1746.
Lydia Ann, d. Joseph and Fidelia, June 14, 1837.
Mary Elizabeth, d. Joseph and Fidelia, July 29, 1835.
Sarah, d. Joseph and Sarah, July 16, 1747.
Sarah, d. James and Sarah, Sept. 22, 1764.
Susan Maria, d. Joseph and Fidelia, Jan. 14, 1829.
Thankful, d. James and Sarah, Jan. 25, 1752.

HIBBARD, Eli Henry, s. Eli B., machinist, and Laura P., at North Chelmsford, Jan. 23, 1845.

HILDERETH (see also Hildreth), Persis, d. Richard and Elisabeth, Feb. 8, 1659.

HILDREATH (see also Hildreth), Jeams, s. Ephrim and Anah, Apr. 19, 1692.

HILDRETH (see also Heldreth, Heldrith, Hildereth, Hildreath, Hildrith, Hilldereth, Hilldrith), Abigail, d. Joseph and Abigail, Mar. 8, 1687-8. CT. R.
Abigail, d. Ezekiel [deceased in Mar. 1776. c. R. 1.] and Lucy, Nov. 30, 1775.
Abigaill, d. James and Margreat, Oct. 3, 1672.
Abigall, d. Josiph and Abig[a]ll, Oct. 20, 1691.
Bridget, d. Joseph and Lydia, bp. June 19, 1763. C. R. 1.
Darcas, d. Richard and Darcas, Apr. 1, 1719.
Easter, d. Isaac and Easter, Mar. 3, 1755.
Ebenezer, s. Ebenezer and Sarai, Apr. 20, 1721.
Ebinezer, s. Ephrim and Anna, May 22, 1696.
Edward, s. Isaac and Rachell, Oct. 14, 1740.
Elesibeth, d. Joseph and Abbigall, July 29, 1703.
[El]isabeth, d. Joseph and Abigall, Oct. 14, 1693-4.
Ephraim, s. Ephräim and Anna, Oct. 28, 1687. CT. R.
Ephraim, s. Joseph and Abigal, Aug. 25, 1700.
Ephraim, s. Joseph and Deleveranc, Feb. 21, 1718-19.

CHELMSFORD BIRTHS

HILDRETH, Ephraim, s. Ephraim and Mary, May 31, 1725.
Ephraim, s. Lt. Jonathan and Hannah, June 26, 1743.
Esther, d. Isaac [jr. C. R. 1.] and Esther [of Nichewaug. C. R. 1.], Apr. 4, 1752.
Hanah, d. James and Margratt, Oct. 2, 167[0. T. C.].
Hanah, d. Jonathan and Hanah, Oct. 28, 1727.
Hannah, d. Joseph and Abigaill, Jan. 19, 1684.
Hannah, d. Eben[ezer], bp. Mar. 16, 1729. C. R. 4.
Isaac, s. Isaac and Rachel, Feb. 4, 1726-7.
James, s. Richard and Dorkis, May 18, 1701.
Jesse, s. Isaac and Easter, Sept. 30, 1756.
John, s. Richard and Dorcis, Aug. 18, 1703.
John, s. Ebenezer and Sarah, Sept. 3, 1725.
John, s. Isaac and Rachel, Mar. 21, 1745-6.
John Massillon, s. John C. and Harriott M., Nov. 29, 1838.
Jonathan, s. Jonathan and Hannah, Dec. 31, 1739.
Joseph, s. Richard and Elisabeth, Apr. 16, 1658.
Joseph, s. twin, Joseph and Abigaill, May 18, 1686.
Joseph, s. Joseph and Abigall, Nov. 30, 16[95. T. C.].
Joseph, s. Joseph and Phebe, Feb. 21, 1723-4.
Julia Ann, d. Moses, laborer, and Eliza A., Jan. 8, 1844.
Leonard, s. Lt. Jonath[an] and Hannah, Apr. 6, 1745.
Lucy, d. Joseph and Lydia, bp. July 28, 1765. C. R. 1.
Lydia, d. Sampson and Lydia, Dec. 3, 1752.
Mary, d. Ephraim and Mary, Feb. 24, 1723-4.
Oliver, s. James and Dorothy, July 11, 1723.
Phebe, d. Joseph and Phebe, Oct. 1, 1721.
Phineas, s. Joseph and Diliveranc, Aug. 6, 1725.
Rebecca, d. James and Dorothy, Mar. 31, 1726.
Richard, s. twin, Joseph and Abigaill, May 18, 1686.
Richard, s. Ephraim and Annah, Apr. 17, 1691. CT. R.
Sampson, s. Jona[than], bp. Apr. 27, 1729. C. R. 4.
Samson, s. Jonathan and Hanah, May 5, 1730.
Sarah, d. Isaac and Elesibeth, Nov. 21, 170[0. T. C.].
Sarah, d. Ebenezer and Sarah, Feb. 12, 1720-21.
Sarah, d. Ephraim and Mary, Oct. 3, 1726.
Sarah, d. Jonas and Sarah, Nov. 2, 1746.
Thomas, s. James and Margreatt, Aug. 12, 1668.
Thomas, s. Thomas and Mary, Apr. 30, 1686.
William, s. Isaac and Rachel, May 25, 1743.
Zachariah, s. James and Dorothy, Dec. 28, 1728.
——, d. Dorithy, Aug. 17, 1697.

HILDRITH (see also Hildreth), Anna, d. Ebenezer and Sary, Mar. 12, 1729.
Easter, d. Jacob and Abigill, Aug. 26, 1731.

HILDRITH, Elizibeth, d. Isaac and Rachil, May 12, 1738.
Ezekiel, s. twin, Timothy and Hannah, June 2, 1782.
Hanah, d. Joseph and Pheebe, Mar. 19, 1738.
Hosiah, s. twin, Timothy and Hannah, June 2, 1782.
Joseph, s. Timothy and Hannah, Apr. 27, 1780.
Leah, d. twin, Isaac and Rachel, Sept. 4, 1731.
Mary, d. Jonathan and Hannah, Aug. 14, 1737.
Rachel, d. twin, Isaac and Rachel, Sept. 4, 1731.
Samuel, s. Isaac and Rachel, July 25, 1735.
Timothy, s. Timothy and Hannah, Feb. 7, 1779.
William, s. Joseph and Phebee, June 15, 1728.

HILL (see also Hills), Joseph Henry, s. Joseph, laborer, and Susan M., at Dracut, Oct. 18, 1847.

HILLDERETH (see also Hildreth), Elisabeth, d. twin, James and Margret [Mary. CT. R.], Mar. 28, 1666.
Isake, s. Richard and Elisabeth, July [20, 1661. T. C.; 1663?].
James, s. James [and Margarett. CT. R.], Apr. 9, 1664.
Mare, d. twin, James and Margret [Mary. CT. R.], Mar. 28, 1666.
Margret, d. James and Margret, May 22, 1660.
Sarah, d. James and Margrit, Feb. 22, 1661.
Thomas, s. Richard and Elisabeth, Feb. 1, 1661.

HILLDRITH (see also Hildreth), Elizabeth, d. James [jr. C. R. 4.] and Lidia, June 25, 1728.
Simion, s. Ephraim and Mary, Mar. 27, 1728-9. [bp. Apr. 14, 1728. C. R. 4.]

HILLS (see also Hill), William, jr., s. William and Polly, Mar. 28, 1813.
Wingate, s. William and Polly, Aug. 11, 1815.

HODGES, Charles Henry, s. Benj[ami]n F., farmer, and Julia, at Mill Row, Oct. 1, 1844.
Hannah Augusta, d. Benja[min] F. and Julia A., Sept. 25, 1842.
Horace J., s. Jeremiah, blacksmith, and Julia A., at North Chelmsford, Oct. 31, 1846.
Mary Jane, d. Benja[min] F., farmer, b. Sharon, and Julia A., b. Foxborough, June 30, 1848.

HODGMAN, Abigail, d. Josiah and Dorothy, bp. Aug. 17, 1760. C. R. 1.
Alva, s. Asa and Sally (Spaulding), Nov. 23, 1824.

HODGMAN, Asa, s. Asa and Sibbel, Jan. 18, 1795.
Augustus, s. Asa and Sally, Oct. 7, 1834.
Betty, d. Asa and Sibble, June 28, 1783.
Clorinda, d. Asa and Sally, Feb. 24, 1833.
Hannah, d. Asa and Sibbel, Sept. 30, 1799.
Lucy, d. Josiah and Dorothy, bp. Aug. 28, 1763. C. R. 1.
Lucy, d. Asa and Sibble, Oct. 6, 1785.
Lydia, d. Asa and Sibbel, Mar. 23, 1792.
Malvina, d. Asa and Sally, Jan. 17, 1837.
Rebekah, d. Asa and Sibbel, Dec. 23, 1796.
Romanus, s. Asa and Sally, Apr. 3, 1827.
Sarah, d. Asa and Sally, Jan. 6, 1830.
Sibbel, d. Asa and Sibbel, May 4, 1788.

HOLDEN, Benjamin Franklin, s. Artemos and Jerusha, June 16, 1817.
Frederic Artemas, s. Artemas and Jerusha, Aug. 14, 1812.
Mary Ann, d. Artamas and Jerusha, Sept. 16, 1810.
Sarah Jane, d. Artemas and Ann, Dec. 18, 1824.

HOLDGATE, Mary Ann, d. Abraham, finisher of worsted goods, and Eliza, at Scythe Factory Village, Feb. 15, 1848.

HOLLAND, Henry, s. Michael, ware dresser, and Mary, both b. Ireland, at Lowell, Oct. 15, 1849.
Patric, s. Michael, laborer, and Mary, at North Chelmsford, Apr. 5, 1846.

HOLMES, Charles, s. John, laborer, b. Hull, Eng., and Ann, b. Leicester, Eng., Apr. 5, 1849.

HOLT, Abba Josephine, d. Dean and Sarah, Feb. 27, 1842.
Ballard, s. Dean and Sarah, Mar. 20, 1837.
Dean, s. Dean and Sarah, Oct. 1, 1835.
Ellen, d. Dean and Sarah, Apr. 14, 1834.
Hannah Abbott, d. Dean and Sarah, Nov. 4, 1838.
Mary H., d. Dean and Sarah, Oct. 3, 1840.
Sarah Elizabeth, d. Dean, butcher, and Sarah, at Middlesex Village, July 10, 1844.

HORSELEY, Bridget, d. Samuel, bp. Aug. 23, 1747. C. R. 1.

HOWARD (see also Haward, Howerd), Abigail, d. Jacob and Rachil, June 27, 1757.
Benjamin, s. Benjamin and Mary, Nov. 26, 1724.

HOWARD, Benjamin, s. Samuel and Mary, Aug. 15, 1759.
Caroline, d. Jacob and Rachel, Apr. 23, 1804.
Chearls, s. Jacob and Rachel, Sept. 16, 1796.
Clarissa, d. Jacob and Rachel, Nov. 23, 1800.
Cotten, s. Benjamin and Mary, Nov. 3, 1736.
Elizabeth, d. Benjamin and Mary, Apr. 21, 1717.
Hannah, d. Nathaniel and Hannah, Dec. 31, 1798.
Harriott, d. Jacob and Rachel, June 14, 1815.
Jacob, s. Jonathan and Sarai, Oct. 12, 1719.
Jacob, s. Jacob and Rachel, Aug. 30, 1765.
Joanna, d. Jacob and Rachel, Nov. 26, 1754.
Jonathan, s. Jonathan and Sary, Apr. 4, 1708.
Jonathan, s. Jonathan and Sary, June 19, 1714.
Jonathan, s. Samuel and Mary, Apr. 21, 1769.
Lidya, d. Benjamin and Mary, Feb. 5, 1722-3.
Lowel, s. Lt. Nathaniel and Hannah, July 19, 1802.
Lydia, d. Benjamin and Martha, Mar. 29, 1754.
Lydia, d. Samuel and Mary, May 24, 1775.
Martha, d. Benjamin and Martha, June 18, 1750.
Mary, d. Benjamin and Mary, Aug. 3, 1715.
Mary, d. Samuel and Mary, June 5, 1761.
Mary, d. Jacob and Rachel, Mar. 21, 1813.
Molley, d. Samuel and Mary, June 5, 1773.
Nathaniel, s. Benjamin and Mary, Sept. 6, 1719.
Nathaniel, s. Samuel and Mary, May 26, 1771.
Olive, d. Jonathan and Sary, Feb. 9, 1728-9.
Otis, s. Lt. Nathaniel and Hannah, Oct. 2, 1804.
Rachel, d. Benjamin and Mary, Mar. 2, 1729.
Rachel, d. Jacob and Rachel, Nov. 6, 1745.
Rebecah, d. Benjamin and Mary, Nov. 26, 1733.
Sameuell, s. Nathanell and Sarah, Mar. 27, 1684.
Samuel, s. Benjamin and Mary, Aug. 10, 1731.
Samuel, s. Samuel and Mary, Apr. 26, 1763.
Samuel, s. Samuel and Mary, Mar. 30, 1767.
Samuel, s. Maj. Nathanil and Hannah, Sept. 18, 1808.
Sarah, d. Jacob and Rachel, May 24, 1751.
Sary, d. Jonathan and Sary, Apr. 4, 1710.
Timothy, s. Samuel and Mary, Feb. 2, 1765.
Willam, s. Jonathand and Sary, Mar. 17, 1717-18.
Willard, s. Jacob and Rachel, Mar. 26, 1748.

HOWERD (see also Howard), Timothy, s. Benjamen and Mary, Aug. 3, 1727.

HUNT, Benjamin Peter, s. Joshua and Olive, May 18, 1808.
David Wilson, s. Eliphalet and Persis, Apr. 27, 1839.

CHELMSFORD BIRTHS 85

HUNT, Eliphalet, s. Joshua and Olive, Feb. 10, 1806.
Marian, d. Joshua and Olive, Aug. 30, 1803.
Martha, d. Joshua and Olive, Jan. 14, 1811.
Olivia, d. Jushua and Olive, Mar. 17, 1801.

HUNTER, Sarah Augusta, d. Gilman, milkman, b. Stow, and Sarah, b. Carlisle, Oct. 5, 1848.
——, s. Gilman, farmer, and Sarah, Apr. 18, 1846.

HUTCHENS (see also Hutchins), Anna, d. Thomas and Anna, Jan. 3, 1765.
David Williams, s. Samuel and Mercy, Mar. 25, 1746.
Dorothy, d. Samuel [deceased. C. R. 1.] and Marcy, June 16, 1755.
Ruth, d. Samuel and Mercy, June 16, 1744.
Samuel, s. Samuel and Mercy, Sept. 3, 1749.
Thomas, s. Thomas and Anna, July 21, 1763.

HUTCHINGS (see also Hutchins), Eliakim, s. Thomas and Anna, Mar. 29, 1769.
Moley, d. Thomas and Anna, Jan. 12, 1767.

HUTCHINS (see also Hutchens, Hutchings), Dolley, d. Samuel and Mercy, bp. Aug. 4, 1751. C. R. 1.
Elimah [Ellinah. C. R. 1.], d. Thomas and Anna, June 10, 1772.
Eliza Jane, d. David, blacksmith, and Melinda, at Lowell, Jan. 19, 1847.
Ruth, d. twin, Thomas and Anna, bp. Feb. 3, 1771. C. R. 1.
Stephen, s. twin, Thomas and Anna, bp. Feb. 3, 1771. C. R. 1.

HUTCHINSON, Mary, d. Nathanel and Rebecca, bp. Mar. 27, 1768. C. R. 1.
Sarah, d. Nathaniel and Rebecca, bp. Aug. 12, 1770. C. R. 1.

INGRAHAM, William, s. Joseph and Mary, of Boston, now resident in Chelmsford, July 19, 1777.

JEFFRAEY, Emeline Jane, d. John, farmer, b. Three Rivers, Canada, and Harriett, b. Gloucestershire, Eng., at F[actory] Village, Apr. 3, 1849.

JEWETT, Abner Augustus, s. Francis, butcher, b. Nelson, and Selina, b. Stoddard, N. H., at Middlesex Village, Aug. 4, 1848.

JEWETT, John, s. Edward and Sarah, Nov. 6, 1749.
Oliver, s. Edward and Sarah, Feb. 24, 1746-7.
Sarah, d. Edward and Sarah, May 29, 1744.

JOHNSON, Andrew W., s. Mark, farmer, and Charlotte, at Lowell, July 15, 1846.
Horace Erving, s. Horace, machinist, b. Vershire, Vt., and Mary Ann, b. Merrimack, N. H., June 30, 1849.

JONES, Francis Norman Pratt, s. Archible R. and Lucy A., Nov. 7, 1841.

JOSLIN (see also Josselyn), Richard James, s. ———, bp. Nov. —, 1810. C. R. 1.

JOSLYN (see also Josselyn), Edwin Forest, s. Edwin and Mira [Nyrhe (Chandler). P. R. 10.], Oct. 14, 1838. [1837. P. R. 10.]
Harriet Maria, d. Elbridge and Sally P., Feb. 3, 1828.

JOSSELYN (see also Joslin, Joslyn), Albert Warren, s. Edwin and Nyrhe (Chandler), Sept. 18, 1842. P. R. 10.
Edwin, June 23, 1810. P. R. 10.
Eliza Ann, d. Edwin and Nyrhe (Chandler), Sept. 9, 1840. P. R. 10.
Wallace Andrew, s. Edwin and Nyrhe (Chandler), June 2, 1839. P. R. 10.

KEEMP (see also Kemp), Amos, s. Jacob and Mathew, Sept. 29, 1759.
Joseph, s. Bethiah, Aug. 30, 1713.
Martha, d. Benjamin and Judith, Aug. 27, 1768.

KEIES (see also Keyes), John, s. Solomon and Francis, Aug. 14, 1674.
Moses, s. Solomon and Francis, Mar. 25 [torn. 1671.].
Ruth, d. Solmon and Francis, Apr. 4, 1669.

KELLEY, Eliza Ann, d. Andrew K., spinner, b. Sandwich, N. H., and Almira A., b. Granville, Vt., at North Chelmsford, Mar. 25, 1849.
Ella, d. Moses, butcher, and Harriete, July 27, 1846.

KEMP (see also Keemp, Keymp), Albert Hartwell, s. Abel H. and Susan, Apr. 28, 1841.
Anna, d. Mary, Jan. 3, 1722-3.

CHELMSFORD BIRTHS 87

KEMP, Annes, d. Josiah and Rachel, Sept. 7, 1753.
Benjamin, s. Jacob and Martha, Sept. 15, 1761.
Benjamin, s. Benjamin and Judith, Feb. 22, 1764.
John, s. Jonathan and Mary, Sept. 26, 1714.
Jonathan, s. Jonathan and Sarai, Apr. 6, 1723.
Josiah, s. Jonathan and Mary, Mar. 8, 1708.
Josiah, s. Josiah and Rachel, Jan. 26, 1732-3.
Judith, d. Benjamin and Judith, Feb. 10, 1762.
Lidiah, d. Josiah and Rachil, Nov. 29, 1734. [Oct. dup.]
Nathaniel, s. Josiah and Rachil, Feb. 6, 1736-7.
Phinehas, s. Josiah and Rachel, Feb. 18, 1730-31.
Prudence, d. Jacob and Martha, bp. Aug. 7, 1763. C. R. 1.
Simeon, s. Josiah and Rachel, Oct. 23, 1750.
Susanna, d. John and Susanna, bp. June 14, 1741. C. R. 1.

KENDAL (see also Kendall), Hannah, d. Nathan and Rachel, Mar. 7, 1731-2.

KENDALL (see also Kendal), Annette Varnum, d. Geo[rge] W., carpenter, b. Tyngsborough, and Mary Ann, b. Dracut, at North Chelmsford, June 28, 1849.
——, ch. Joel [on a journey, at John Butterfields. P. R. 4.], Jan. 3, 1792. C. R. 1.

KENNINGTON, Charles Edward, s. Edward, moulder, and Ann, both b. Kilkenny Co., Ireland, at "Barton, Ms.," Dec. 30, 1848.

KENT, Eliza[beth], d. Abner, bp. Aug. 31, 1729. C. R. 4.

KEY (see also Keyes), Ruth, d. Soloman and Mary, June 8, 1707.

KEYES (see also Keies, Key, Keys, Kyes), Aaron, s. Abel and Olive, bp. Feb. 28, 1773. C. R. 1.
Abel, s. Zachariah and Dinah, Apr. 29, 1743.
Abel, s. Abel and Olive, bp. Nov. 25, 1770. C. R. 1.
Abigail, d. Ezekiel and Abigail, June 8, 1731.
Abigail, d. Moses and Susannah, May 18, 1736.
Abner, s. Ezekiel and Abigail, Dec. 11, 1738.
Anna, d. Daniel and Byal, Nov. 7, 1766.
Annes [Agnis. C. R. 1.], d. Zachariah and Dinah, Dec. 26, 1757.
Betty, d. Abel and Olive, bp. Oct. 10, 1779. C. R. 1.
Daniel, s. Moses and Susannah, Nov. 30, 1731.
Daniel, s. Zebadiah and Mary, June 4, 1741.
David, s. Moses and Susan, June 2, 1724.

KEYES, Easther, d. Zebadiah and Mary, June 3, 1744.
Ebenezer, s. Ephraim and Rebeckah, Nov. 18, 1755.
Ebenezer Bradley, s. David and Sarah, June 17, 1797.
Elias, s. Solomon and Marah, Sept. 28, 1692. CT. R.
Elias, s. Soloman and Mary, Oct. 17, 1692.
Elisebath, d. Moses and Mehitable, Mar. 14, 1701-2.
Elizabeth, d. Joseph and Elizabeth, Apr. 3, 1720.
Elizabeth, d. Moses and Susan, Jan. 3, 1728.
Ella Maria, d. Marcus, butcher, and Maria, at North Chelmsford, Feb. —, 1844.
Ephraim, s. Ezekiel and Abigail, Aug. 14, 1727.
Ephraim, s. Ephraim and Rebeckah, Dec. 11, 1752.
Ephriam, s. Elias and Mary, July 5, 1715.
[Eunice. T. C.], d. Sollomon and Marry, Dec. [15. T. C.], 1704.
Ezekiel, s. Ephraim and Rebeccah, Aug. 24, 1752.
Hanah, d. Moses and Susan, Jan. 11, 1726.
Hannah, d. Soloman and Mary, Jan. 28, 1698.
Henarry, s. Solloman and Mary, Jan. 23, 1698-9.
Issacer, s. Zachariah and Dinah, July 30, 1747.
[Jan. T. C.]e, d. Mosis and Mahitabel, Sept. 24, 1694.
Joanna, d. Zacheriah and Dinah, May 20, 1755.
Johanah, d. Joseph and Johanah, Feb. 10, 16[95. T. C.].
John, s. Zebediah and Mary, June 7, 1749.
Jonas, s. Stephen and Anah, Aug. 3, 1709.
Jonathan, s. Joseph and Elizabeth, Jan. 21, 1721-2.
Josepeh, s. Josepeh and Johannah, May 1, 1698.
Joseph, s. Solloman and Francis, May 24, 1667.
Levi, s. Abel and Olive, bp. June 29, 1777. C. R. 1.
Lidiah, d. Joseph and Johanah, Aug. 10, 1693.
Lucy, d. Daniel and Abiel, of Limerick, bp. Feb. 24, 1782. C. R. 1.
Lydia, d. Zachariah and Dinah, May 31, 1741.
Mary, d. Moses and Susanah, Dec. 12, 1720.
Mary, d. Zebadiah and Mary, Mar. 9, 1738-9.
Mary Elizabeth, d. Marcus, butcher, b. Westford, and Maria W., b. Troy, N. Y., Feb. 16, 1849.
Mercy, d. Solomon and Mary, Mar. 30, 1688. CT. R.
Miriam, d. Joseph and Joannah, Mar. 29, 1691. CT. R.
Molly, d. Daniel and Abial, bp. July 29, 1770. C. R. 1.
Olliv, d. Zachariah and Dinah, May 9, 1739.
Pheabe, d. S[t]even and Anna, Dec. 10, 1706.
Phebe, d. Moses and Susanah, Apr. 23, 1734.
Rachell, d. Moses and Mehitabell, Feb. 8, 1709.
Rebeckah, d. Ephraim and Rebeckah, May 29, 1762.
Robert, s. Stephen and Anne, Sept. 21, 1711.
Ruth, d. Moses and Susanah, Dec. 9, 1729.

KEYES, Sally, d. Daniel and Abiel, of Limerick, bp. Sept. 19, 1779. C. R. 1.
Samuel, s. Moses and Susan, Feb. 17, 1723.
Sarah, d. Ezekiel and Abigail, Jan. 1, 1723-4.
Sarah, d. Daniel and Abiel, bp. Oct. 3, 1773. C. R. 1.
Sarah, d. David and Sarah, Oct. 22, 1795.
Saray, d. Moses, of Westford, and Susanna, Apr. 11, 1740.
Sibel, d. Zacheriah and Dinah, July 23, 1737.
Sollomon, s. Sollomon and Francis, June 24, 1665.
Sollomon, s. Sollomon and Mary, May 11, 1701.
Solomon, s. Zebediah and Mary, July 18, 1752.
Stephen, s. Elias and Mary, July 15, 1717.
Stephen, s. Ephraim and Rebeckah, Jan. 24, 1760.
Susana, d. Moses and Susana, May 28, 1719.
Susanna, d. David and Sarah, May 4, 1801.
Tabatha, d. Moses and Susanah, May 27, 1738.
Thankfull, d. Zachariah and Dinah, Sept. 23, 1752.
Uriah, s. Zachariah and Dinah, bp. Apr. 1, 1750. C. R. 1.
William, s. Uriah and Hannah, Oct. 21, 1775.
Zachria, s. Moses and Mehetable, Feb. 18, 1713-14.
Zebadiah, s. Zebadiah and Mary, May 17, 1746.
Zebediah, s. Solomon and Persila, Jan. 11, 1710.
Zebediah, s. Daniel and Abiel, bp. Jan. 19, 1777. C. R. 1.
Zebulon, s. Zachariah and Dinah, June 9, 1745.
Zebulon, s. Abel and Olive, bp. July 2, 1775. C. R. 1.

KEYMP (see also Kemp), John Read, s. Benjamin and Judith, May 19, 1766.
Jonas, s. Josiah and Rachel, July 5, 1745.
Martha, d. Josiah and Rachel, July 14, 1748.

KEYS (see also Keyes), Ezekell, s. Moses and Mehetable, Mar. 19, 1699.
Lidiah, d. Joseph and Elizabeth, Aug. 26, 1724.
Mosis, s. Mosis and Mehitiball, Nov. 24, 1696.
Pattey, d. David and Sarah, Feb. 16, 1793.

KIDDER (see also Kider), Aaron, s. Thomas and Joana, Dec. 22, 1719.
Amos, s. John and Mary, Feb. 4, 1729-30.
Anna, d. John and Lidiah, Sept. 12, 1685.
Ebenezer, s. David and Esther, bp. May 16, 1762. C. R. 1.
Elizabeth, d. James and Sarah, Dec. 26, 1738.
Elizabeth Daviss, d. Jacob and Hannah, bp. May 20, 1804. C. R. 1.
Esther, d. David and Esther, Jan. 6, 1751-2.

KIDDER, Hannah, d. Jacob and Hannah, bp. May 20, 1804.
C. R. 1.
Isaac, s. John and Mary, June 1, 1722.
Isaac, s. [twin. C. R. 1.] James and Sarah [deceased. C. R. 1.],
Apr. 14, 1749.
James, s. John and Lidya, Jan. 28, 170[0. T. C.].
James, s. James and Sarah, May 3. 1745.
Jamse, s. Jeams and Abigill, Jan. 4, 1730-1.
John, s. John and Lidiah, Dec. 23, 1687.
Jonas, s. John and Mary, Jan. 9, 1723-4.
[J]onathan, s. John and Lydia, Jan. 14, 1701-2.
Joseph, s. Thomas and Joana, Oct. 13, 1725.
Joseph, s. Jacob and Hannah, bp. May 20, 1804. C. R. 1.
Lydia, d. James and Sarah, Aug. 2, 1743.
Mary, d. John and Lidyah, Apr. 9, 1695.
Mary, d. John and Mary, May 11, 1719.
Mary, d. Amos and Mercy, of Carlisle, bp. May 4, 1783. C. R. 1.
Nathanill, s. John and Lidia, Dec. 13, 1692.
Phebe, d. David and Easther, May 20, 1759.
Phineas, s. David and Ester, July 17, 1756. [bp. June 20.
C. R. 1.]
Reuben, s. Thomas and Joana, June 1, 1723.
Samuel, s. James and Sarah, Oct. 2, 1740.
Sarah, d. James and Sarah, Mar. 15, 1741-2.
Stephen, s. David and Esther, Apr. 24, 1754.
Thomas, s. James and Sarah, Nov. 8, 1746.
Zimry, s. Jacob and Hannah, Apr. 23, 1801.

KIDER (see also Kidder), Benjamin, s. twin, John and Lidya,
Aug. 11, 1697.
David, s. John and Lidiah, Oct. 11, 1706.
Easther, d. Benjamin and Sairy, Dec. 27, 1732.
Elesibeth, d. John and Lydia, July 12, 170[4. T. C.].
Isaiah, s. Thomas and Joanna, Feb. 20, 1727-8.
Josaph, s. twin, John and Lidya, Aug. 11, 1697.
Lidya, d. John and Mary, Apr. 6, 1726.
Rachil, d. John and Mary, Oct. 23, 1728.
Sary, d. John and Lidiah, June 2, 1709.
Thomas, s. John and Lidah, Oct. 13, 1690.
Thomas, s. Thomas and Johanah, Feb. 2, 1717-18.

KIMBALL, Mary An, d. Sally Brooks, May 5, 1805.

KING, Bening, s. Richard and Lucy, July 11, 1767.
Betty, d. Richard and Lucy, June 26, 1764.
Daniel Edward, s. Samuel, boatman, b. Albany, Me., and
Sophia, b. Dracut, at Middlesex Village, Jan. 12, 1849.

KING, Hannah, d. Dr. Samuel and Hannah, Feb. 5, 1754.
Hannah, d. Samuel and Hannah, Dec. 12, 1755.
Lucy, d. Richard and Lucy, May 18, 1760.
Lydia, d. Samuel and Hannah, bp. Mar. 12, 1758. C. R. 1.
Mary, d. Richard and Lucy, May 24, 1762.
Samuel, s. Samuel and Hannah, Dec. 14, 1751.

KITTERAGE (see also Kittredge), Asa, s. Ebenezer and Abigail, Sept. 27, 1760.
Daniel, s. Ebenezer and Abigail, Jan. 26, 1757.

KITTERIDGE (see also Kittredge), Jacob, s. Jacob and Rebecca, bp. June 13, 1773. C. R. 1.

KITTREDGE (see also Kitterage, Kitteridge, Kittridge), Cullena Fordyce, d. Cullen F., machinist, and Amy H., Nov. 14, 1844.
Dorcas Melvina, d. Dr. Francis M. and Tirzah Almira, Oct. 31, 1837.
Estelle Sophia, d. Cullen F., machinist, and Amy H., Oct. 21, 1843.
Henry Mead, s. Francis M. and Tirza Almira, Feb. 6, 1843.
Reuel Williams, s. Francis M. and Tirza Almira, Sept. 12, 1839.

KITTRIDGE (see also Kittredge), Fastina Ann Dilutia, d. Paul C. and Susan, Jan. 23, 1835.
Nancy Martin, d. Paul and Rebecca, Apr. 21, 1834.

KNECTTLE, Emely, d. John R., glass-blower, and Harriett S., at Middlesex Village, July 12, 1844.

KNOWLES, Emeline, d. Rebecah, bp. Feb. 26, 1815. C. R. 1.
Lewis Lumber, s. Jona[than], bp. July 21, 1816. C. R. 1.
Moses Lewis, s. Jona[than], bp. May 18, 1821. C. R. 1.
Rebecca, d. Jona[than], bp. Oct. 28, 1819. C. R. 1.
Willard, s. ——, bp. Sept. 21, 1818. C. R. 1.

KYES (see also Keyes), Anna, d. Stephen and Anna, Dec. 29, 1707.

LANCEY, George, s. Samuel and Elisabeth, Aug. 1, 1796.
Polly, d. Samuel and Elizabath, Aug. 25, 1789.
Rebeckah, d. Samuel and Elisabeth, Nov. 16, 1793.
Samuel, s. Samuel and Elizabath, June 25, 1786.
Thomas, s. Samuel and Elizabath, Nov. 28, 1791.
William, s. Samuel and Elizabath, Dec. 25, 1784.

LANGLE (see also Longley), Mary, d. Willam and Debroah, Feb. 27, 1709.

LANGLEE (see also Langley), Mary, d. Nathaniel and Lidiah, Nov. 3, 1728.
William, s. Nathaniel and Lidia, Apr. 25, 1731.

LANGLEY (see also Langlee), Deborah, d. Nathaniel and Lidya, Dec. 25, 1723.
Lydia, d. Nathaniel and Lydia, May 12, 1726.
Mary, d. Nathaniel and Lidia, Dec. 22, 1733.
Naomi, d. Nathaniel and Lydia, May 18, 1741.
Nathaniel, s. Nathaniel and Lydea, May 22, 1739.

LAPHAM, Eldorada, s. W[illia]m, miller, b. Boston, and Elizabeth, b. Littleton, Aug. 30, 1849.

LARCOM, Franklin Hersey, s. Jonathan, carpenter, and Harriett, at Mill Row, Nov. 22, 1847.

LARNED (see also Lernet), Benoni, s. Izak and Mare, Nov. 29, 1657. [Dec. 4. CT. R.]
Izak, s. Izak and Mare, Sept. 16, 1655. [Oct. 5. CT. R.]
Sarah, d. Izake and Mare, Oct. 28, 1653. [a. 4 y. 15: 9 m: 1656. P. R. 1.]

LEACH, Jacob Haskell, s. Jacob and Clarissa Ann, Sept. 27, 1831.
Solomon, s. Jacob and Clarissa Ann, Nov. 28, 1833.
Susan Ann, d. Jacob and Clarissa Ann, May 31, 1830.

LEMON, Mary, d. Samuel, Jan. 11, 1670. CT. R.

LEONARD, see Larned.

LERNET (see also Larned), Anna, d. Isaac, bp. 1: 12 m: 1656, a. 8 y. 11: 6 m: 1656. P. R. 1.
Mary, d. Isaac, bp. 1: 12 m: 1656, a. abt. 10 y. 15: 5 m: 1656. P. R. 1.
William, s. Isaac, bp. 1: 12 m: 1656, a. 6 y. 1 day: 8 m: 1656. P. R. 1.

LEVINGSTON (see also Livingston), Charlotte, d. Seth and Abigail, Jan. 30, 1793.
Larken, s. Seth and Abigail, Mar. 2, 1796.
Seth, s. Seth and Abigail, Apr. 23, 1778.

CHELMSFORD BIRTHS 93

LEVINGSTON, Sprake, s. Seth and Abigail, May 28, 1787.
William, s. Seth and Abigail, Oct. 25, 1782.

LEVINGSTONE (see also Livingston), Benjamin, s. Seth and Abigail, Aug. 17, 1789.

LEWIS, Abi, d. Reuben and Abihail, July 9, 1771.
Joseph, s. Samuel and Betty, Sept. 2, 1775.
Reuben, s. Reuben and Abihail, Nov. 25, 1772.
Samuel, s. Samuel and Betty, Mar. 29, 1774.

LIBBEE, Betsey Amanda, d. James, blacksmith, and Betsey, at Furnace Village, June 17, 1843.
George Francis, s. James and Betsey, May 4, 1840.

LINCOLN, Albert H., s. Isaac L. and Mary, Mar. 10, 1840.
Francis Maltby, s. Otis and Hannah, Oct. 4, 1836.
Hannah Jane, d. Otis and Hannah W., Jan. 19, 1831.
Mary, d. w. of Peter Marshal, bp. Oct. 6, 1805. C. R. 1.
Otis Bradford, s. Otis and Hannah W., Mar. 28, 1834.
Varnum, s. Abel and Phebe, Sept. 25, 1819.

LINKFIELD, Edward, s. Benjamin and Martha, bp. Aug. 30, 1762. C. R. 1. [Aug. 29. P. R. 4.] [formerly of Derry and Bedford. P. R. 4.]
Martha, d. Benjamin and Martha, bp. Aug. 30, 1762. C. R. 1. [Aug. 29. P. R. 4.] [formerly of Derry and Bedford. P. R. 1.]

LITTLEHALE, Hannah Jaques, d. Richard and Susan, bp. Oct. 27, 1816. C. R. 1.
Susan Burt, d. Richard and Susan, bp. Oct. 27, 1816. C. R. 1.

Martha, d. Jonathan and Martha, Oct. 21, 1776.

LIVINGSTON (see also Leviagston, Levingstone, Livingstone), Benjamin Franklin, s. Benjamin and Clarissa, Mar. 16, 1827.
Clarissa Jane, d. Benjamin and Clarissa, June 5, 1824.
Laura Ann, d. Benjamin and Clarissa, June 23, 1832.

LIVINGSTONE (see also Livingston), Abigail Prudence Ford, d. Sprake and Betsey, Dec. 31, 1836.
William Damon, s. Benj[ami]n and Clarissa, Aug. 19, 1840.

LOCK (see also Loock), Abigail, d. Daniel and Abigail, Nov. 17, 1747.
Elezebeth, d. Daniel and Abigail, June 17, 1754.
Mary, d. Daniel and Abigail, Oct. 21, 1751.
Susannah, d. Daniel and Abigail, Apr. 30, 1749.

LONGLEY (see also Langle, Longly), Emma Adelaid, d. Jonas B., scythe maker, b. Millbury, and Eliza, b. "Scituate, R. I.," Oct. 20, 1848.
Herbert Eugene, s. James B., scythe maker, and Eliza, at Millbury, May. —, 1847.

LONGLY (see also Longley), Nathaniell, s. William and Daborah, Dec. 16, 1697.

LOOCK (see also Lock), Enos, s. Daniel and Abigail, Sept. 2, 1764.

LORD, Hallis, d. Robert, mechanic, and Anna, at Worsted Mills, Dec. 11, 1845.
Hannah, d. Robert, farmer, and Ann, both b. Rochdale, Eng., at Factory Village, Apr. 22, 1849.
Mary A., d. Robert, laborer, and Ann O., at Farwell Village, Apr. 4, 1844.

LORING, Mary Elizabeth, d. Jefferson, Feb. 18, 1839.

LYON, Albert E., s. Joseph E., farmer, and Sophia, Mar. 21, 1848.
Ella Leora, d. Joseph E., farmer, b. Plymouth, Vt., and Sophia, b. Chester, Vt., Nov. 9, 1849.

McCARTHY, John, s. John, farmer, and Joanna, both b. Ireland, Sept. 29, 1849.

McCLENCHE, John, s. John and Elizabeth, Apr. 13, 1744.

McCLUSKEY (see also McClusky), Dennis, s. Pattrick and Elizabeth, Nov. 1, 1839.

McCLUSKY (see also McCluskey), John Francis, s. Patrick, moulder, and Elizabeth, at North Chelmsford, Aug. 11, 1844.

McCOY, Mary Ann, d. John, iron cleaner, and Margaret, at North Chelmsford, May 12, 1846.
Michael Francis, s. John L., teamster, and Margaret, at North Chelmsford, Jan. 22, 1848.

McEMERY (see also McEneaney, McEneany), Mary Ann, d. Arthur, ware dresser, and Mary, both b. Monaghan Co., Ireland, at North Chelmsford, Sept. 23, 1849.

McENEANEY (see also McEmery), Lawrence, s. Owen, watchman, and Mary, at North Chelmsford, Aug. 15, 1847.

McENEANY (see also McEmery), Mary Jane, d. Owen, watchman, and Mary, at North Chelmsford, May 2, 1845.

McGLAUTHLIA (see also McGlauthlin), ———, d. Hiram L., moulder, b. Pembroke, N. H., and Hannah, b. Easton, at North Chelmsford, Sept. 13, 1849.

McGLAUTHLIN (see also McGlauthlia), Mary Elizabeth, d. Hiram, moulder, and Hannah, at Furnace Village, Oct. 11, 1843.

McGUINAS, Bridgett, d. Phillip, carpenter, and Rosanna, at Scythe Factory Village, Jan. 5, 1848.

McINTIRE, Josiphene, d. Warren, butcher, and Harriett, at Middlesex Village, Oct. 13, 1843.
———, s. Amos B., butcher, and Mary A., at Middlesex Village, Mar. 17, 1845.
———, s. Warren, butcher, and Harriett, at Middlesex Village, Dec. 13, 1845.
———, s. Warren, butcher, b. Stoddard, N. H., and Harriett, b. Nelson, N. H., at Middlesex Village, Aug. 4, 1849.

MACKASLIN, Solomon, s. Rose, Mar. 14, 1727.

McKEE, Elizabeth R., d. William and Rebecca, Sept. 10, 1841.
Rebecca Rosette, d. William and Rebecca, Sept. 10, 1841.
Warren Ellis, s. William, laborer, and Rebecca, at Mill Row, Dec. 15, 1843.

MACKENEY, William, s. John and Sarah, June 24, 1738.

MACLAIN (see also Maclaine, Maclane), Anna, d. Dennis and Joanna, Dec. 26, 1773. [bp. Feb. 7, 1773. c. r. 1.]

MACLAIN, Charls, s. Dennis and Cristian, Sept. 22, 1719.
Dennis, s. Charles and Susanna, June 21, 1742.
Lucy, d. Charles and Susannah, Jan. 22, 1753.
Obed, s. Charls and Susanna, Oct. 9, 1757.
Sarah, d. Charls and Susannah, Feb. 21, 1755.
Susanna, d. Charles and Susanna, Mar. 13, 1740-41.
Willard, s. Dennis and Joanna, bp. May 1, 1763. c. r. 1.

MACLAINE (see also Maclain), Charls, s. Charls and Susannah, Dec. 10, 1743.
Elizabeth, d. Charls and Susanna, Feb. 15, 1744-5.
Mary, d. Charls and Susanna, Aug. 23, 1746.

MACLANE (see also Maclain), Sibyll, d. Charls and Susanna, Mar. 22, 1748-9.
Uri, s. Charls and Susanna, Nov. 5, 1750.

MAHARS, James Thomas, s. James and Rosanna, June 19, 1840.

MANING (see also Manning), Jacob, s. Jacob and Lucy, Oct. 31, 1796.
Joseph, s. Jonathan and Martha, Apr. 21, 1795.

MANNING (see also Maning), Asa, s. Timothy and Mary, Aug. 31, 1780.
Asenath, d. Jonathan and Martha, June 29, 1791.
Benja[min], s. Jonathan and Marthea, Aug. 27, 1778.
Charlotte Ann, d. William, farmer, and Mary, at "Concord River," Feb. 19, 1847.
Elizebeth, d. Jonathan and Martha, June 8, 1786.
Esther, d. Timothy and Mary, Dec. 4, 1786.
George Joseph, s. Joseph and Julia Maria, Jan. 23, 1836.
Jane Howard, d. Joseph and Julia Maria, Oct. 11, 1831.
John Hawood [Heywood. c. r. 1.], s. Timothy and Mary, Jan. 25, 1779.
Jonathan, s. Jonathan and Martha, Dec. 31, 1774.
Julia Elizabeth, d. Joseph and Julia Maria, Mar. 28, 1830.
Lidia, d. Jonathan and Martha, May 30, 1782.
Martha, d. Jonathan and Martha, Oct. 21, 1776.
Mary, d. Timothy and Mary, July 27, 1782.
Mary, d. Timothy and Mary, Oct. 16, 1790.
Meheteble, d. Jonathan and Marthar, Nov. 13, 1788.
Nathaniel, s. Timothy and Mary, Oct. 9, 1784.
Salethial, s. Jonathan and Mathew [Martha. c. r. 1.], June 17, 1780.

MANNING, Solomon Andrews, s. Jacob and Lucy, May 16, 1799.
Timothy, s. Timothy and Mary, bp. May 11, 1777. C. R. 1.

MANSFIELD, Abiah, d. John and Lois, Sept. 5, 1762.
Asa, s. John and Loies, Feb. 19, 1778.
Asaph, Oct. 11, 1818. P. R. 21.
Aseph, s. John and Loies, Aug. 1, 1780.
Charles T., s. Asaph, farmer, and Sylvia, b. Westford, Feb. 15, 1849.
Elbridge B., grands. Joel, Nov. 16, 1847. P. R. 21.
Elizabeth Ann, d. Leonard J[arvis. dup.], farmer, and Mary E. [grandd. Joel. P. R. 21.], at Baptist Village, Apr. 30, 1845.
Ellen Maria Louisa [Ellen Mary. P. R. 20.], d. Jeremiah C., farmer, and Susan E[(Parkhurst). P. R. 20.], Jan. 27, 1848.
George Albert, s. Asaph and Sylvia E. [grands. Joel. P. R. 21.], Nov. 28, 1841.
Hellen Marion [Maria. dup.], d. Leonard J[arvis. dup.], farmer, and Mary E., b. Bedford [Westford. dup.], Feb. 5, 1849.
Jeremiah C., Jan. 6, 1817. P. R. 20.
John, s. John and Loies, Sept. 14, 1775.
John, grands. Joel, June 4, 1845. P. R. 21.
Jonathan, s. John and Loies, Sept. 1, 1770.
Leonard J., Oct. 29, 1820. P. R. 21.
Leonard Jarvis, s. Leonard J., farmer and Mary, at Baptist Village, Dec. 17, 1846.
Mary J., grandd. Joel, Mar. 31, 1843. P. R. 21.
Rachel, d. John and Loies, Mar. 7, 1773.
Rebeckah E., grandd. Joel, Sept. 8, 1843. P. R. 21.
Sarah, d. John and Loes, Aug. 28, 1768.
Susan Emma, d. Jeremiah C., farmer, and Susan [E. (Parkhurst). P. R. 20; grandd. Joel Mansfield. P. R. 21.], June 4, 1845.
Willard, s. John and Loes, June 24, 1764.
William, s. John and Loes, Apr. 17, 1766.
Zarah, s. John and Loies, Nov. 30, 1782.
Zela, s. John and Lois, bp. Jan. 11, 1761. C. R. 1.

MARCY, Sarah, d. Aaron, bp. at Dracut, Aug. 24, 1766. P. R. 4.

MARSHAL (see also Marshall), Abel, s. Samuel and Esther, Sept. 9, 1764.
Abel, s. Peter, bp. Oct. 6, 1805. C. R. 1.

MARSHAL, Ebenezer, s. Joseph and Sarah, Mar. 12, 1764.
Hannah, d. Abel and Polly, at Lyme, N. H., Dec. 7, 1794.
Phebe, d. Dr. Jonas and Abigail, Apr. 30, 1782.
Polly, d. Abel and Polly, at Lyme, N. H., Jan. 3, 1793.

MARSHALL (see also Marshal), Aaron, s. Samuel and Esther, Mar. 22, 1770.
Aaron, s. Joshua and Esther, of Halestown, bp. Sept. 30, 1781. c. r. 1.
Abel, s. Abel and Polley, Dec. 17, 1788.
Anna, d. Samuel and Sibbel, July 12, 1789.
Asa, s. Joseph and Sarah, Mar. 14, 1759.
Assenath, d. ———, bp. Mar. 24, 1799. c. r. 1.
Augustus, s. Willard and Olive, Feb. 25, 1796.
Avery, s. Samuel and Sibbel, Oct. 22, 1798.
Benjamin, s. twin, Joseph and Sarah, Nov. 8, 1760.
Benjamin, s. Jonas and Mary, Dec. 25, 1771.
Benjamin Parker, s. Peter and Mary, Nov. 18, 1810.
Bettey, d. Joseph and Susanna, Oct. 30, 1772.
Bradley, s. Peter and Mary, July 30, 1817.
Charlottee, d. Joshua and Esther, bp. Mar. 2, 1794. c. r. 1.
David, s. Thomas and Hannah, Mar. 19, 1762.
Dorcas, d. Samuel and Sybil, bp. Apr. 1, 1792. c. r. 1.
Eben Russell, s. Eben H., blacksmith, and Phebe, Dec. 5, 1846.
Eliza Adams, d. Peter and Mary, Sept. 15, 1812.
Elizabeth, d. Isaac and Elizabeth, bp. Nov. 13, 1785. c. r. 1.
Emma Jane, d. Eben[ezer. dup.] H., blacksmith, and Phebe R., Aug. 17, 1843.
Esther, d. Samuel and Esther, Aug. 27, 1758.
Fordyce, s. Samuel [jr. c. r. 1.] and Sibbel, June 22, 1796.
George, s. Abel and Polly, Oct. 1, 1808.
Hannah, d. Thomas and Hannah, Mar. 28, 1756.
Hannah, d. Joseph and Susanna [of N. H. p. r. 4.], bp. Oct. 4, 1778. c. r. 1.
Hannah, d. Isaac and Elizabeth, bp. July 15, 1787. c. r. 1.
Harr[i]ot, d. Abel and Polly, Apr. 28, 1807.
Hezekiah, s. Samuel and Sibbel, Jan. 22, 1794.
Isaac, s. Thomas and Hannah, Dec. 25, 1757.
Isaac, s. Isaac and Elizabeth, bp. June 26, 1785. c. r. 1.
Jacob, s. Thomas and Hannah, June 12, 1760.
James, s. Samuel and Easter, May 1, 1760.
James, s. James and Joanna, bp. July 12, 1789. c. r. 1.
Jemime, d. Samuel and Sibbel, Nov. 3, 1787.
Jesse, s. Thomas and Hannah, Aug. 21, 1754.
Jesse, s. Joshua, bp. Jan. 10, 1796. c. r. 1.
Joanna, d. James and Joanna, bp. Jan. 29, 1786. c. r. 1.

MARSHALL, Joel Moor, s. Elon and Lucy, May 22, 1818.
John, s. Thomas and Hannah, bp. Apr. 22, 1764. C. R. 1.
John, s. Joseph and Susanna, Oct. 23, 1770.
John, s. Dr. Jonas and Mary, Dec. 13, 1776.
John, s. Abel and Polly, Jan. 12, 1802.
Jonas, s. Jonas and Mary, Nov. 21, 1768.
Jonathan, s. Joseph and Susanna, Mar. 13, 1767.
Joseph, s. twin, Joseph and Sarah, Nov. 8, 1760.
Joseph, s. James, bp. Apr. 11, 1802. C. R. 1.
Joseph Adams, s. Dr. Jonas and Abigail, Jan. 29, 1781.
Joseph Adams, s. Peter and Mary, May 27, 1804.
Josh[u]a, s. Samuel and Easter, Oct. 6, 1756.
Levi, s. James and Joanna, bp. Apr. 27, 1794. C. R. 1.
Lidia Chandler, d. Peter and Mary, Dec. 3, 1805.
Loring, s. Peter and Mary, July 2, 1807.
Luther, s. Samuel and Sibbel, June 26, 1781.
Lydia, d. Thomas and Lydia, Dec. 19, 177 [faded. bp. 1774. C. R. 1.].
Lydia, d. Samuel and Sibbel, Sept. 25, 1783. [bp. Sept. 20. C. R. 1.]
Martha, d. Peter and Mary, Apr. 28, 1809.
Mary, d. Jonas and Mary, bp. May 30, 1773. C. R. 1.
Mary, d. Thomas and Lydia, bp. Aug. 25, 1775. C. R. 1.
Mary, d. Joseph and Susanna, May [faded. 1776?].
Mary, d. James and Joanna, bp. Jan. 1, 1792. C. R. 1.
Mary Ann, d. Thomas, farmer, and Ann F., at "Concord River", July 19, 1846.
Mary Ann Elizabeth, d. George, farmer, and Eliza Ann, at Concord River Neck, Aug. 31, 1844.
Mary Frances, d. Joseph and Lois, Nov. 29, 1837.
Micajah, s. Abel and Polley, Jan. 30, 1790.
Mira, d. Peter and Mary, July 7, 1814.
Otis, s. James, bp. Sept. 22, 1806. C. R. 1.
Peter, s. Thomas and Lydia, Apr. 17, 1773.
Rachel, d. James and Joanna, bp. Oct. 21, 1787. C. R. 1.
Rebeckah, d. Samuel and Easter, June 30, 1762.
Reuben, s. Isaac, of Nottingham, bp. Oct. 19, 1794. C. R. 1.
Rhoda, d. Isaac and Elizabeth, bp. Aug. 24, 1788. C. R. 1.
Rhoda, d. Abel and Polly, Dec. 19, 1803.
Rufus, s. Joseph and Susanna, Jan. [torn. bp. 1775. C. R. 1.].
Rufus Weeks, s. James, bp. May 20, 1810. C. R. 1.
Ruth, d. Dr. Jonas and Mary, Mar. 24, 1770.
Ruth, d. Thomas and Lydia, bp. Sept. 5, 1779. C. R. 1.
Ruth, d. Isaac, of Nottingham, bp. Oct. 19, 1794. C. R. 1.
Sally, d. Abel and Polly, Jan. 4, 1797.
Samuel, s. Samuel and Easter, Apr. 22, 1755.

MARSHALL, Samuel, s. Abel and Polly, Mar. 29, 1799.
Samuel Adams, s. Thomas and Mary, Mar. 14, 1836.
Sarah, d. Joseph and Susanna, Dec. 4, 1768.
Sibbel, d. Samuel and Sibbel, Oct. 16, 1785.
Sibyl, d. Dr. Jonas and Mary, Sept. 29, 1775.
Thomas, s. Thomas and Hannah, May 25, 1753.
Thomas, s. Peter and Mary, Aug. 18, 1802.
Willard, s. Samuel and Esther, July 30, 1766.

MARSTON, William Alvin, s. Jonathan Calvin, machinist, and Susan Elizabeth, at North Chelmsford, Sept. 19, 1847.

MARTEN (see also Martin), Sarah, d. Asa and Molly, Mar. 21, 1751.

MARTIN (see also Marten), Asa, s. William and Hannah, Oct. 19, 1727.
Asa, s. Asa and Molly, bp. Nov. 3, 1765. C. R. 1.
Elizabeth, d. Asa and Molley, bp. Jan. 20, 1754. C. R. 1.
Hannah, d. Asa and Molley, bp. Feb. 20, 1757. C. R. 1.
Molly, d. Asa and Mary, Nov. 4, 1749.
Olive, d. Asa and Molley, bp. Aug. 8, 1762. C. R. 1.
Sarah, d. William and Hannah, May 10, 1718.
William, s. William and Hannah, Aug. 7, 1721.
William, s. Asa and Molley, bp. July 5, 1752. C. R. 1.

MASON, Laura A., d. Jonathan, moulder, and Laura A., at North Chelmsford, Apr. 29, 1842.
Mary, d. William D. and Mary Ann, Nov. 30, 1824.

MEADS, Lydia, d. John and Lydia, deceased [late of Lyndeborough. P. R. 4.], bp. July 14, 1776. C. R. 1.

MEARS (see also Meers), Darkis, d. Robert and Darkis, Oct. 7, 1790.
Pattey, d. William and Esther, Jan. 31, 1785.
Rebeckah, d. Robert and Darkes, Aug. 29, 1793.

MEERS (see also Mears), Betsy, d. William and Esther, bp. Nov. 9, 1788. C. R. 1.

MELVIN, Abiah, d. Benjamin and Joanna, July 1, 1782.
Benjamin, jr., s. Benjamin and Joanna, June 22, 1786.
Charles, s. Benjamin and Joanna, Feb. 26, 1795.
Charles Butterfield, s. Charles and Susanna, May 5, 1824.
Dawes, s. Benjamin and Joanna, July 17, 1799.

MELVIN, James, s. Benjamin and Joanna, Aug. 29, 1777. [Mar. 19. dup.]
James Fletcher, s. Benjamin and Joanna, Mar. 14, 1779.
Joanna, d. Benjamin and Joanna, Mar. 6, 1793.
Lucretia, d. Benjamin and Joanna, Feb. 13, 1797.
Lydia, d. Benjamin and Joanna, Aug. 30, 1788.
Nathaniel Pettengell Hunt, s. Charles and Susanna, Nov. 27, 1825.
Rhoda, d. Benjamin and Joanna, bp. Feb. 18, 1781. C. R. 1.
Rhoda, d. Benjamin and Joanna, Mar. 30, 1791.
Rufus, s. Benjamin and Joanna, Aug. 30, 1801.
Thomas Fletcher, s. Benja[min] and Joanna, Mar. 14, 1779.

MERRIAM, Lydia Grace, d. Darius G., farmer, b. Concord, and Elizabeth E., b. Eaton, Canada, at Lowell, July 31, 1845.
Mary, d. John and Hannah, bp. at Littleton, Feb. 11, 1728. C. R. 4.
Nehemiah Flint, s. Darius G., farmer, b. Concord, and Elizabeth E., b. Eaton, Canada, June 28, 1849.

MERRICK, Stephen, s. Reuhamah Juel, Sept. 24, 1785.

MERRILL, Orlando, s. Enoch and Adeline Eliza, July 14, 1829.

MINOT (see also Minott), Elizabeth, d. Jonathan and Elizabeth, Jan. 30, 1717.
Elizebeth, d. Samuel and Elizebeth, June 27, 1737.
Elizebeth, d. Jonathan and Easter, June 13, 1755.
Esther, d. Jonathan and Esther, May 23, 1747.
Jonathan, s. Jonathan and Elizabeth, Jan. 19, 1722-3.
Jonathan, s. Jonathan and Esther, Aug. 23, 1749.
Rebeckca, d. Jonathan and Elizabeth, Apr. 2, 1719.
Samuell, s. Jonathan and Elizabeth, Sept. 10, 1714.

MINOTT (see also Minot), Anna, d. Jonathan and Elizabeth, Sept. 13, 1725.
Hannah, d. Samuel and Elizabeth, Dec. 20, 1739.
John, s. Jonathan and Elizabeth, Dec. 16, 1730.
Joseph, s. Jonathan, jr. and Esther, June 13, 1751.
Mary, d. Samuel and Elisabeth, Feb. 28, 1741-2.
Ollive, d. Jonathan and Esther, June 14, 1753.

MOARS (see also Moores), Charlotte, d. Simeon and Joanna, Nov. 21, 1770.

MOARS, Ester, d. Simeon and Joanna, Jan. 6, 1757.
Joseph, s. Simeon and Joanna, Oct. 17, 1759.
Larkin, s. Simeon and Joanna, Aug. 27, 1772.
Micajah, s. Simeon and Joanna, Oct. 17, 1768.

MOOERS (see also Moores), George, s. David and Tamer, Jan. 6, 1793.

MOORE (see also Moores), Frederic Lewis, s. Ephraim S., mason, b. Wayland, and Henrietta A., at Middlesex Village, May 20, 1849.
George Edward S., s. Ephraim S., mason, and Henrietta, at Middlesex Village, May 7, 1844.
William A., s. Ashleel, shoemaker, b. Acworth, N. H., and Martha H., b. St. Johnsbury, Vt., May 20, 1848.

MOORES (see also Moars, Mooers, Moore, Moors, Mores, Mors), Jesse, s. Miel and Sarah, Aug. 25, 1795.
Loammi, s. David and Tamer, Mar. 6, 1795.

MOORS (see also Moores), Augustus Parker, s. Simeon and Betsy, Feb. 11, 1822.
Charlotte, d. Miel and Sarah, Aug. 27, 1801.
Elizabeth, d. Capt. Simeon and Betsy, Nov. 21, 1825.
Hannah, d. Mial and Sarah, June 3, 1806.
Herbert, s. Simeon and Joanna, July 20, 1766.
John Appleton, s. Lt. Simeon and Betsy, Oct. 4, 1824.
Miel, s. Simeon and Joanna, Apr. 11, 1764.
Miranda, d. Miel and Sarah, Aug. 17, 1810.
Permela, d. Mial and Sarah, Nov. 16, 1803.
Sabra, d. Simeon and Joanna, bp. June 8, 1777. C. R. 1.
Sabra, d. Miel and Sarah, July 23, 1799.
Salathial, s. Mial, May 4, 1808.
Salla, d. Miel and Sarah, Sept. 3, 1797.
Simeon, s. Miel and Sarah, Aug. 28, 1793.

MORES (see also Moores), Daniel, s. David and Tamer, Nov. 1, 1786.
David, s. David and Tamar, Dec. 26, 1782.
Jonathan, s. David and Tamer, Aug. 31, 1788.
Leucrietia, d. Simeon and Joanna, Apr. 12, 1780.
Simeon, s. Joseph and Esther, Dec. 6, 1732.
Timothy, s. David and Tamer, Apr. 24, 1785.

MORS (see also Moores), Joanna, d. Simeon and Joannah, Nov. 17, 1761.

MORSE, George Warren, s. Seneca P., machinist, and Cordelia A., at North Chelmsford, Mar. 15, 1848.
——, s. Seneca P., machinist, and Cordelia, at North Chelmsford, Feb. 10, 1846.

MUNGER, Luthera, d. Harvey, machinist, and Nancy, at North Chelmsford, Dec. 27, 1844.

MYRICK, Horace Allen, s. Freeman H., clerk, and Eliza, at North Chelmsford, Nov. 7, 1847.

NICHOLS (see also Nickles), David, s. David and Rebecca, bp. Oct. 8, 1769. C. R. 1. [Oct. 7. P. R. 4.]
Kendal, s. David and Rebeca, July 5, 1768.
——, s. W[illia]m Edward, spinner, b. Hillsborough, N. H., and Elizabeth B., b. Tyngsborough, Dec. 30, 1849.

NICKLES (see also Nichols), Robert, s. Robert, bp. at Billerica, Nov. 28, 1760. P. R. 4.

NOLTE, George Justus, s. Justus, hatter, and Dorotha, at Middlesex Village, June 4, 1843.
Mary Louisa, d. Justus, hatter, and Dorothy, at Middlesex Village, Oct. 25, 1846.

NUTTING, James, s. John, bp. 3: 6 m: 1656, a. 3 y. 30: 4 m: 1656. P. R. 1.
John, s. John, bp. 3: 6 m: 1656, a. 5 y. 25: 6 m: 1656. P. R. 1.
Josiah, s. John and Sarah, June 10, 1658.
Mare, d. John and Sarah, Jan. 10, 1655. [Jan. 16. CT. R.]
Sarah, d. John and Sarah, Jan. 7, 1659.

OBEAR (see also Ober), Albert Warren, s. Benj[ami]n I., formerly carpenter, now farmer, and Rebecca, Aug. 28, 1847.
Benjamin, s. Tho[ma]s W. and Emily, Aug. 24, 1842.
Charles Thomas, s. Tho[ma]s W., carpenter, and Emily, Aug. 10, 1844.
Frances Elizabeth, d. Benja[min] I. and Rebecca, Oct. 10, 1838.
Harriett Augusta, d. Thomas W., carpenter, and Emily, Sept. 22, 1846.
Oliver, s. Benja[min] I. and Harriott, June 12, 1826.
Priscilla, d. Benjamin I. and Rebecca, July 20, 1842.
Samuel Ives, s. Benja[min] I. and Rebecca, June 21, 1832.
Sarah Jane, d. Benja[min] I. and Rebecca, Oct. 12, 1835.

OBER (see also Obear), Harriet, d. Benjamin I. and Harriet, Sept. 13, 1816.
Thomas Woodberry, s. Benjamin I. and Harriet, Jan. 25, 1821.

ONG, Jacob, s. Jacob, Feb. 9, 1671. CT. R.

OSBORN (see also Osburn), James Byam, s. James and Mary, Dec. 18, 1811.
John Freeland, s. James and Mary, bp. June 9, 1816. C. R. 1.

OSBURN (see also Osborn), Mary Maria, d. James and Mary, bp. Nov. 6, 1814. C. R. 1.
Sarah Abigail, d. James, bp. June 21, 1818. C. R. 1.

OSGOOD, Abigal, d. Ephraim and Abigal, Nov. 1, 1800.
Benjamin, s. Benjamin and Triphena, of Westford, bp. June 10, 1781. C. R. 1.
Charles, s. Ephraim and Abigal, Jan. 31, 1811.
Dorcas, d. Ephraim and Abigal, Feb. 8, 1804.
Jacob, s. Benjamin and Tryphena, of Westford, bp. May 6, 1787. C. R. 1.
Josiah, s. Benjamin and Triphena, of Westford, bp. Dec. 1, 1782. C. R. 1.
Laura Maria, d. Tho[ma]s T. and Laura, May 28, 1840.
Mary Elizabeth, d. Augustus, butcher, b. Nelson, N. H., and Mary, b. Franklin, N. H., at Middlesex Village, Aug. 3, 1849.
Phena, d. Benjamin and Triphena, of Westford, bp. July 2, 1780. C. R. 1.
Rebecca, d. Joseph and Sarah, Feb. 3, 1754.

PACKARD, Alpheus Spring, s. Rev. Hezekiah and Mary, Dec. 23, 1798.
Charles, s. Rev. Hezekiah and Mary, Apr. 12, 1801.

PAGE, Alma Malvina, d. Hector M., manufacturer, and Mary, at Worsted Factory, Sept. 25, 1844.

PALMER, Abby Joanna, d. Moses, blacksmith, and Abby L., at North Chelmsford, Sept. 24, 1847.

PARCHURST (see also Parkhurst), William, s. Jonathan and Brigett, May 16, 1754.

PARIS, Thomas, s. Roberd and Seaborne, July 23, 1663.

PARK, Harriett Elizabeth, d. John N., manufacturer, b. Windham, N. H., and Harriett M., b. Cabot, Vt., Apr. 8, 1849.

PARKER (see also Perker), Aaron, s. William and Abiel, bp. Apr. 16, 1775. C. R. 1.
Abel, s. twin, Capt. Moses and Sarah, Oct. 31, 1769.
Abel, s. Lt. Joseph and Tabothy [(Warren). P. R. 8.], Aug. 16, 1799.
Abiel, d. William and Abiel, bp. June 7, 1767. C. R. 1.
Abigail, d. Aaron and Abigail, Oct. 17, 1720.
Abigail, d. Lt. Isaacc and Elizebeth, Nov. 10, 1772.
Abigail, d. Daniel and Abigail, Nov. 10, 1816.
Abigaile, d. Moses and Abigaill, May 8, 1685.
Abraha[m], s. Abrah[am], bp. 1: 12 m: 1656, a. 4 y. in 6 m: 1656. P. R. 1.
Alice Caroline, d. Samuel G., butcher, b. Nelson, N. H., and Sarah, b. Stoddard, N. H., at Middlesex Village, Jan. 29, 1849.
Anah, d. Joseph and Marget, Nov. 16, 1663.
Anah [Hannah. CT. R.], d. John and Marie, Apr. 2, 1692. [Apr. 13. CT. R.]
Anna, d. Joseph and Marget, Feb. 2, 1655. [Feb. 7. CT. R.]
Anna, d. Abrah[am], bp. 1: 12 m: 1656, a. 11 y. in 8 m: 1656. P. R. 1.
Anna, d. James, bp. 1: 12 m: 1656, a. 10 y. 14 d. P. R. 1.
Anna, d. Thomas and Ester, June 11, 1715.
Anna, d. Willard and Anna, May 26, 1766.
Anna, d. Philip and Anna, Mar. 3, 1770.
Anna, d. Philip [and Anna. C. R. 1.], Oct. 1, 1777.
Anna Maria, d. Jona[than], bp. Sept. 1, 1827. C. R. 1.
Aron, s. Aron and Abigall, Aug. 19, 1713.
Aron, s. twin, Capt. Moses and Sarah, Oct. 31, 1769.
Arone, s. Mosis and Abigall, Apr. 9, 1689.
Artemos, s. Artemos and Sibbel, June 7, 1807.
Asa, s. Reuben and Sarah, Jan. 28, 1776.
Benjamin, s. Jacob and Sarah [Aug. 8, 1663. CT. R.].
Benjamin, s. Mosis and Abigell, Apr. 14, 1696.
Benjamin, s. Benjamin and Sarah, Sept. 12, 16[torn. 169-. T. C. 1699?].
Benjamin, s. Benjamin and Elizabeth, Mar. 26, 1723.
Benjamin, s. Benjamin, jr. and Elesebeth, Nov. 6, 1753.
Benjamin, s. David and Lucy, June 18, 1774.
Benjamin, s. Joseph, jr. and Tabetha [(Warren). P. R. 8.], Feb. 8, 1786.
Benjamin, s. Benjamin and Bettey, Jan. 13, 1789.
Benjamin, s. Jeduthan and Phebe, July 6, 1803.

PARKER, Benoni, s. Thomas and Marie, Feb. 2, 1690.
Betey, d. Simon and Susanna, Oct. 4, 1793.
Betty, d. David and Lucey, Nov. 18, 1765.
Betty, d. William and Abiel, bp. Mar. 21, 1779. C. R. 1.
Betty, d. Lt. Isaac and Elezebeth, May 1, 1779.
Bradley, s. Zebulon and Rachel, Dec. 22, 1799.
Bridgitt, d. Joseph and Rebecka, Apr. 11, 1734.
Charles, s. Isaiah and Debrah, bp. Apr. 20, 1806. C. R. 1.
Charles, s. Jona[than], bp. Sept. 1, 1827. C. R. 1.
Charlotte, d. Ebenezer and Rebekah, Feb. 19, 1806.
Charlottee, d. Ebenezer and Rebecca, Jan. 28, 1802.
Clarise, d. Ebenezer and Rebackah, Oct. 31, 1799.
Clarise, d. Ebenezer and Rebecca, Apr. 8, 1804.
Clifford, s. Jepthah, farmer, and M. Amanda, b. Carlisle, June 11, 1848.
Clifton, s. Jepthah, farmer, and Amanda, at Baptist Village, Oct. 26, 1846.
Daniel, s. Willard and Anne, Oct. 21, 1790.
Daniel A., s. Daniel and Abigail, Nov. 11, 1818.
Daniell, s. Abraham and Martha, July 15, 1683.
Darcos, d. Philip [and Anna. C. R. 1.], June 23, 1779.
Darcus, d. Philip, Sept. 2, 177[faded. bp. 1774. C. R. 1.].
David, s. Benjamin and Elizabeth, Mar. 19, 1731-2.
David, s. David and Lucy, Aug. 25, 1768.
David, s. David and Phebe, at Billerica, July 19, 1772.
Deborah, d. Isaiah and Debrah, bp. Apr. 20, 1806. C. R. 1.
Ebenezer, s. Ebenezer and Elizabeth, June 4, 1720.
Ebenezer, s. Jacob and Rachel, Dec. 6, 1748.
Ebenezer, s. William and Sarah, Apr. 26, 1754.
Ebenezer, s. David and Lucy, May 25, 1760.
Ebenezer, s. William and Hanah, June 17, 1778.
Ebinesar, s. Thomas and Marie, Dec. 17, 1690.
Edward Francis, s. Francis B. and Mary [(Richardson). P. R. 26.], Sept. 24, 1838.
Eleazar, s. James and Elisabeth, Nov. 9, 1661.
Elisabeth d., Abraham and Rose, Apr. 10, 1663.
Elisabeth, d. John and Mary, May 30, 1680.
Elisabeth, d. Joseph and Hannah, Dec. 4, 1684.
Elisabeth, d. Mosis and Abigall, Dec. 26, 1691.
Elisabeth, d. Reuben and Sarah, Sept. 11, 17[faded. bp. 1773. C. R. 1.].
Elizabeth, d. James, bp. 1: 12 m: 1656, a. 12 y. on 4: 1 m: 1657. P. R. 1.
Elizabeth, d. Ebenezer and Elizabeth, Apr. 3, 1713.
Elizabeth, d. Benjamin and Elizabeth, Aug. 18, 1726.

PARKER, Elizabeth, d. Aaron, bp. July 14, 1728. C. R. 4.
Elizabeth, d. Matthew, bp. May 14, 1769. P. R. 4.
Elizabeth, d. twin, Isaac and Elizabeth, bp. Dec. 30, 1770. C. R. 1. [b. Dec. 24. P. R. 4.]
Ester, d. Isack and Ester, Nov. 13, 1686.
Ester, d. Thomas and Ester, Oct. 26, 1711.
Ester, d. Thomas and Ester, Oct. 26, 1712.
Esther, d. Joseph and Rebeca, July 25, 1726.
Ephraim, s. John and Hannah, Oct. 20, 1738.
Ephraim, s. Ephraim and Sybel, Oct. 6, 1769. [bp. Oct. 9, 1768. C. R. 1.]
Fanny, d. Artemos and Sibbel, Dec. 18, 1815.
Francilla Elizabeth, d. Eli P., carpenter, and Nancy B., July 29, 1847.
Francis Bowers, s. Eli and Elizabeth, bp. July 9, 1809. C. R. 1.
George Alvah, s. Francis B., farmer, and Mary [(Richardson). P. R. 26.], Mar. 15, 1842.
Gillbert, s. Zebulon and Rachel, Mar. 27, 1797.
[Grace. T. C.], d. Abraham and Marth[a], May 27, 1693.
Granvil, s. Jonathan, 3d and Hannah, Dec. 31, 1808.
Hannah, d. Jonathan and Rachel, Jan. 28, 1744-5.
Hannah, d. Jonathan [deceased. C. R. 1.] and Joanna, Mar. 14, 1745-6.
Hannah, d. John and Hannah, June 9, 1749.
Hannah, d. Obadiah and Ruth, "belonging to a new Township above Townsend," bp. Oct. 6, 1754. P. R. 4.
Hannah, d. Josiah and Hannah, bp. Apr. 29, 1764. C. R. 1.
Hannah, d. David, bp. at Dracut, May 12, 1765. P. R. 4.
Hannah, d. David and Phebe, at Billerica, Sept. 13, 1767.
Hannah, d. William and Hannah, Apr. 27, 1774.
Hannah, d. Isaac and Elizabeth, bp. Aug. 21, 1774. C. R. 1.
Hannah, d. Jonathan and Sarah, bp. Jan. 26, 1777. C. R. 1.
Hannah, d. Lt. Isaac and Elezebeth, Aug. 12, 1781.
Hannah, d. Simon and Susannah, Feb. 15, 1796.
Hannah, d. Jonathan, 3d [jr. C. R. 1.] and Hannah, July 9, 1803.
Hannah Fletcher, d. Ebenezer and Rebeckah, May 29, 1797.
Harriott, d. Daniel and Abigail, Sept. 2, 1821.
Henery, s. Benjamin and Sary, Jan. 21, 1705.
Henry Spaulding, s. William and Abiel, bp. Oct. 25, 1772. C. R. 1.
Isaac, s. Isaac and Esther, Apr. 4, 1688. CT. R.
Isaac, s. John and Hannah, May 8, 1747.
Isaac, s. Lt. Isaac and Elezebeth, Dec. 27, 1776.
Isack, s. Isack and Ester, July 26, 1685.
Isaiah, s. Willard and Anna, Mar. 31, 1778.

PARKER, Isake, s. Abraham and Roas, Sept. 13, 1660.
Jacob, s. Jacob and Sarah, [torn] 30 [torn. bef. 1653; a. 4 y. in 3 m: 1656. P. R. 1.]
Jacob, s. Abraham and Rose, Mar. 24, 1669.
Jacob, s. John and Rebecka, Dec. 15, 1720-21.
James, s. James, bp. 1: 12 m: 1656, a. 5 y. on 15: 2 m: 1657. P. R. 1.
James, s. twin, William and Abiel, bp. May 19, 1776. C. R. 1.
Jeduthan, s. Jeduthun and Phebe, Jan. 7, 1794.
Jeduthun, s. Benja[min] and El[i]zebeth, Nov. 18, 1762.
Jepther, s. Ebenezer and Rebeckah, June 8, 1795.
Jesse, s. Natt[haniel], bp. at Groton, Oct. 12, 1760. P. R. 4.
Jesse, s. Jeduthan and Phebe, Aug. 28, 1797.
Joana, d. Joseph and Rebecka, May 8, 1724.
Joanna, d. Jonathan and Joanna, Oct. 29, 1743.
John, s. Abrah[am], bp. 1: 12 m: 1656, a. 9 y. in 8 m: 1656. P. R. 1.
John, s. James, bp. 1: 12 m: 1656, a. 8 y. 12 d. P. R. 1.
John, s. Joseph and Marget [Mary, July 31, 1659. CT. R.].
John, s. Joseph and Margret, Nov. 24, 1661.
John, s. John and Rebeckah, Jan. 13, 1711-12.
John, s. John and Hannah, Jan. 25, 1743-4.
John, s. Ephraim and Sybel, Oct. 20, 1763.
John, s. Ebenezer and Hannah, at Princeton, Aug. 25, 1788.
John, s. Ebenezer and Hannah, bp. Sept. 1, 1790. C. R. 1.
Jonas, s. Jonathan and Joanna, Nov. 8, 1739.
Jonathan, s. John and Mary, Jan. 2, 1683.
Jonathan, s. Benjamin and Sary, Aug. 1, 1709.
Jonathan, s. John and Rebecah, June 2, 1714.
Jonathan, s. Jonathan and Rachal, Sept. 18, 1748.
Jonathan, s. David and Lucy, Dec. 30, 1771. [bp. Dec. 30, 1770. C. R. 1.]
Jonathan, s. Willard and Anna, June 10, 17[faded. bp. 1774. C. R. 1.].
Jonathan, s. Jonathan and Sarah, bp. Mar. 18, 1781. C. R. 1.
Joseph, s. Joseph and Marget, Mar. 30, 1653.
Joseph, s. Joseph and Rebecka, Nov. 16, 1728.
Joseph, s. Benjamin and Elezebeth, Aug. 21, 1756.
Joseph, s. Capt. Moses and Sary, Feb. 18, 1763.
Joseph, s. Joseph and Tabathy [(Warren). P. R. 8.], Sept. 19, 1794.
Joshewaie, s. Jam[e]s and Elisabeth, Mar. 23, 1658.
Josiah, s. James, bp. 1: 12 m: 1656, a. 4 y. 4 m. P. R. 1.
Josiah, s. John and Mery, Jan. 10, 1696-7.
Josiah, s. Thomas and Esther, Dec. 19, 1721.
Josiah, s. Josiah and Hannah, May 12, 1760.

PARKER, [Jos. T. C.]ip [H. T. C.], s. Mosis and Ab[i]gall, Mar. 25, 1693-4.
Julia Maria, d. Lt. Joseph and Tabatha [(Warren). P. R. 8.], Apr. 9, 1807.
Leonard, s. William and Abiel, bp. Mar. 3, 1765. C. R. 1.
Levy, s. Levy and Sarah, May 4, 1768.
Lidiah, d. Abraham and Rose, Feb. 17, 1665.
Loiza, d. Thaddeus and Lydia, Mar. 24, 1819.
Louisa, d. Ebenezer and Rebekah, Feb. 4, 1809.
Lucretia, d. Lt. Isaac and Elizebeth, Mar. 29, 1787.
Lucy, d. Ebenezer and Elizabeth, Feb. 24, 1714-15.
Lucy, d. Aaron and Abigaill, Jan. 11, 1725-6.
[Lydia. T. C.], d. Abraham and Marth[a], July 11, 1691.
Lydia, d. Josiah and Hannah, Jan. 28, 1759.
Lydia, d. Willard and Hannah [Anna. C. R. 1.], Mar. 22, 1768.
Lydia, d. Thaddeus and Lydia, Mar. 14, 1824.
[Lydi. T. C.]ah, d. John and Marie, Apr. 13, 1694.
[M. T. C.]ara, d. Bengamin and Sara, May 3, 1694.
Marah, d. Joseph and Rebeckah, May 12, 1738.
Marcy, d. Artemos and Sibbel, June 30, 1818.
Mare, d. Abraham and Roas, Nov. 15, 1655. [Nov. 20. CT. R.]
Mare, d. Joseph and Marget, Oct. 28, 1657.
Maria, d. Artemas, stone-cutter, and Lucinda, at Middlesex Village, May 8, 1845.
Martha, d. Oliver and Sarah, July 25, 1782.
Mary, d. Jacob and Sarah, Sept. 8, 1667.
Mary, d. Thomas and Mary, Nov. 26, 1684.
Mary, d. John and Mare, Apr. 4, 1690.
Mary, d. Moses and Abegall, Sept. 6, 1698.
Mary, d. Ebenezer and Elizabeth, Jan. 14, 1716-17.
Mary, d. Aaron and Abigail, Oct. 20, 1723.
Mary, d. Benjamin, jr. and Elezebeth, Sept. 17, 1739.
Mary, d. William and Abiel, bp. Dec. 3, 1769. C. R. 1.
Mary, d. Willard and Anna, bp. May 26, 1776. C. R. 1.
Mary, d. Jeduthan and Phebe, July 2, 1799.
Mary, d. Artemos and Sibbel, Aug. 28, 1813.
Mary E., d. Artemas, stone-cutter, and Lorinda, at North Chelmsford, July 26, 1843.
Molley, d. Jacob, bp. at Groton, Oct. 12, 1760. P. R. 4.
Molly, d. David and Phebe, at Billerica, June 19, 1769.
Molly, d. Jonathan and Sarah, bp. Jan. 31, 1779. C. R. 1.
Moses, s. Abraham and Roas[torn. after 1655.].
Moses, s. Moses and Abigail, Nov. 24, 1686. CT. R.
Moses, s. Aaron and Abigill, May 16, 1718.
Moses, s. Joseph and Rebeckah, May 13, 1731.

PARKER, Moses, s. Capt. Moses and Sarah, Nov. 18, 1767.
Moses, s. Joseph and Tabethy [(Warren). P. R. 8.], Aug. 26, 1783. [1784. P. R. 8.]
Nehemiah Abbott, s. Capt. Moses and Sarah, Sept. 9, 1765.
Newell Edgar, s. Eli P. and Nancy, Dec. 11, 1841.
Obediah, s. Zebulon and Rachel, Nov. 25, 1802.
Olive, d. Ebenezer and Elizibeth, June 12, 1731.
Oliver, s. John and Hannah, Apr. 3, 1741.
Peter Clark, s. Jonathan, 3d [jr. C. R. 1.] and Hannah, June 7, 1805.
Phebe, d. David and Phebe, at Billerica, Oct. 16, 1770.
Phebe, d. Jeduthan and Phebe, Jan. 29, 1796.
Pheneus, s. Obadiah and Hannah, ——, 1725.
Philip, s. Zebulon and Rachel, Jan. 20, 1795.
Phillip, s. Benjamin and Elizibeth, July 19, 1734.
Rachel, d. Ebenezer and Elizabeth, July 21, 1725.
Rachel, d. Jonathan and Rachel, Sept. 3, 1737.
Rachel, d. Jacob and Rachel, Apr. 4, 1741. [bp. Sept. 12, 1742. C. R. 1.]
Rachel, d. Thaddeus and Lydia, Aug. 4, 1818.
Rachell, d. Jacob and Sarah, Mar. 9, 1664-5.
Rachell, d. Thom[as] and Mary, Nov. 6, 169[5. T. C.].
Rachil, d. Willard and Anna, Dec. 22, 1769.
Rebacah, d. Ebenezer and Rebacah, Apr. 29, 1793.
Rebecah, d. Joseph and Rebecah, Dec. 16, 1719.
Rebecca, d. Col. Moses and Sarah, May 7, 1775.
Rebecca, d. William and Hannah, Apr. 6, 1776.
Rebecca, d. twin, William and Abiel, bp. May 19, 1776. C. R. 1.
Rebecca, d. Phillip and Anna, bp. June 20, 1790. C. R. 1.
Rebecca, d. Eben[eze]r and Rebecca, bp. Sept. 14, 1794. C. R. 1.
Rebecca, d. Lt. Joseph and Tabatha [(Warren). P. R. 8], Sept. 9, 1804.
Rebecca, d. Jeduthan and Phebe, Jan. 18, 1806.
Rebecka, d. Oliver and Sarah, Mar. 18, 1771.
Rebeckah, d. Jacob and Sarah, 29: 3 m: 1661.
Rebeckah, d. John and Rebeckah, June 22, 1719.
Rebeckah, d. John and Hannah, Nov. 17, 1735.
Rebeckah, d. Johnathan and Joanna, Jan. 31, 1737.
Rebeckah, d. Jonas and Rebeckah, Jan. 26, 1762.
Rebeckah, d. Lt. Isaac and Elizabath, at Springfield, Vt., June 13, 1790.
Rebekah, d. Benjemin and Sarah, Feb. 28, 1697.
Reuben, s. Benjamin and Elizabeth, Nov. 26, 1750.
Reuben, s. Reuben and Sarah, Dec. 20, 1771.
Reuben, s. David and Phebe, June 4, 1775.
Reuben, s. Betcy Foster, May 27, 1799.

PARKER, Rhoda, d. Philip and Anna, bp. May 28, 1786. C. R. 1.
Rodolfo, s. Artemos and Sibbel, Mar. 19, 1809.
Ruben, s. Willard and Anna, May 21, 1780.
Rufus, s. Joseph and Tabathy [(Warren). P. R. 8.], May 9, 1797.
Ruth, d. Benjamin and Elizabeth, Oct. 2, 1729.
Samuel, s. James, bp. 1: 12 m: 1656, a. 6 m. P. R. 1.
Samuel, s. John and Mary, Mar. 10, 1687-8. CT. R.
Samuel, s. Abraham and Mathew, Apr. 13, 17[00. T. C.].
Samuel, s. John and Rebeckah, June 1, 1723.
Samuell, s. Aaron and Abigell, Jan. 1, 1716.
Sara, d. Joseph and Tabetha [(Warren). P. R. 8.], Mar. 13, 1789.
Sarah, d. Jacob and Sarah, Jan. 14, 1653.
Sarah, d. Jacob, bp. 1: 12 m: 1656, a. 2 y. in 2 m: 1656. P. R. 1.
Sarah, d. Thomas and Mary, Mar. 13, 1686. CT. R.
Sarah, d. Bengamin and Sara, Oct. 1, 1691.
Sarah, d. Joseph and Rebeckah, Apr. 6, 1722.
Sarah, d. Jonathan and Rachel, Nov. 15, 1735.
Sarah, d. Benjamin and Elizibeth, Sept. 21, 1736.
Sarah, d. William and Sarah, Dec. 21, 1755.
Sarah, d. Josiah and Hannah, bp. Apr. 25, 1762. C. R. 1.
Sarah, d. Oliver and Sarah, May 24, 1768.
Sarah, d. Levi and Sarah, Aug. 5, 1770.
Sarah, d. Capt. Moses and Sarah, Jan. 23, 1772.
Sarah, d. Philip and Anna, Feb. [faded. bp. Feb. 14, 1773. C. R. 1.].
Sarah, d. Jonathan and Sarah, bp. May 7, 1775. C. R. 1.
Sarah, d. David and Phebe, Aug. 19, 1776.
Sarah, d. Jeduthan and Phebe, July 20, 1801.
Sary, d. Ebenezer and Elizabeth, Nov. 14, 1722.
Sewel, s. Lt. Joseph and Talbatha [(Warren). P. R. 8.], Nov. 23, 1801.
Sibbel Spalding, d. Artemos and Sibbel, Feb. 1, 1811.
Silos, s. William and Sarah, Aug. 6, 1759.
Simon [Simeon. P. R. 4.], s. Benjamin and Elizebeth, Oct. 25, 1759.
Simon, s. Simon and Susanna, Jan. 25, 1798.
Solomon, s. Willard and Anna, June 11, 1784.
Stephen, s. Thaddeus and Lydia, Apr. 21, 1822.
Sybel, d. Ephraim and Sybel, Aug. 30, 1766.
Tabitha, d. Jacob and Sarah, Feb. 28, 1658.
Tabitha, d. Benjamin and Sary, Feb. [torn. 1701-2?].
Tabitha, d. Jonathan and Rachell, Nov. 4, 1739.

PARKER, Tabitha, d. Joseph and Tabitha [(Warren). P. R. 8.], July 17, 1791.
Thaddeus, s. Thaddeus and Lydia, May 20, 1828.
Thankfull, d. Lt. Isaac and Elezebeth, Apr. 10, 1784.
Thomas, s. Jacob and Sarah [Mar. T. C.] 28, 1656.
Thomas, s. John and Mary, Dec. 18, 1685.
Thomas, s. Thomas and Ester, Aug. 24, 1717.
Thomas, s. Ebenezer and Elizabeth, May 25, 1718.
Thomas, s. Josiah and Hannah, Aug. 25, 1757.
Thomas, s. Levy and Sarah, Nov. 16, 1767. [bp. Feb. 1, 1767. C. R. 1.]
Willard, s. Jonathan and Rachel, June 10, 1742-3.
Willard, s. Willard and Anna, June 22, 1772.
Willard, s. Jonathan and Remembrance, bp. Apr. 7, 1793. C. R. 1.
Willard, s. Jonathan, 3d [jr. C. R. 1.] and Hannah, —— 2, 1800.
Willard, s. Daniel and Abigail, Apr. 18, 1826.
William, s. John and Rebeca, Jan. 26, 1725-6.
William, s. Ebenezer and Elizabeth, Nov. 18, 1727.
William, s. Jonathan and Joanna, Sept. 8, 1741.
William, s. William and Sarah, Oct. 7, 1751.
William Foster, s. Silas and Matthew, Feb. 28, 1789.
Wilyam, s. Thomas and Marah, Dec. 21, 1692.
Zebulon, s. Benjamin, jr. and Elizabeth, July 24, 1764.
Zebulon, s. Zebulon and Rachel, Mar. 2, 1793.
Zechariah, s. James and Elisabeth, Jan. 14, 1659.
[torn], d. Abraham and Marth[a], July 3, 1687.
——, d. twin, Isaac and Elizabeth, Dec. 24, 1770. P. R. 4.
——, d. Jona[than], bp. Nov. 7, 1813. C. R. 1.

PARKHURST (see also Parchurst, Parkhust, Parkis, Perkhast, Perkhust), Abigail, d. Joel and Polly, Apr. 2, 1804.
Abraham, s. John and Surviah, bp. June 20, 1813. C. R. 1.
Adaline, d. John, bp. June 11, 1815. C. R. 1.
Andrew, s. Jonathan and Bridgget, Sept. 6, 1759.
Andrew, s. Philip and Mary, Mar. 16, 1773.
Benjamin, s. James and Abigail, Oct. 26, 1732.
Benjamin, s. James and Abigail, Jan. 25, 1740-41.
Benjamin, s. Benjamin and Elizebeth, May 30, 1773.
Benjamin, s. Benj[amin], deceased, and Elizabeth, bp. Dec. 31, 1820. C. R. 1.
Betty, d. Samuel and Bettey, July 15, 1796.
Caroline Augusta, d. Solomon and Lucina M. [(Adams). P. R. 17.], Sept. 9, 1842.
Celia Ellen, d. Rev. John and Celia, Jan. 7, 1829.
Charles, s. John, bp. Jan. 9, 1826. C. R. 1.

CHELMSFORD BIRTHS

PARKHURST, Charles Henry, s. Sewall and Sarah, Mar. 13, 1831.
Charles William, s. Rev. John and Celia, Dec. 3, 1838.
Ebinezer, s. Ebinezer and Mary, Dec. 25, 1699.
Edgar S., s. Sewall and Sarah, Apr. 1, 1834.
Edwin King, s. Josiah King and Ruth, Feb. 28, 1828.
Elisabeth Ann, d. John and Celia, June 11, 1823.
Elizabeth, d. Benjamin and Elizabeth, Jan. 11, 1812.
Elizebeth, d. Benjamin and Elizebeth, Mar. 3, 1769.
Ellen Lucina, d. Capt. Solomon and Lucina M. [(Adams). P. R. 17.], Mar. 9, 1839.
Eustace Micajah, s. Rev. John and Celia, Dec. 11, 1830.
George Adams, s. Capt. Solomon and Lucina M. [(Adams). P. R. 17.], Aug. 11, 1833.
George W. K., s. Edwin K., carpenter, and Charlotte M., at Wilmington, Oct. 28, 1847.
Hannah Stevens, d. Dea. Josiah and Rachel, Apr. 30, 1813.
Harriot Lucretia, d. John and Surviah, bp. Nov. 21, 1818. C. R. 1.
Henry, s. Philip and Mary, bp. Aug. 15, 1779. C. R. 1.
Hezekiah, s. Josiah and Rachel, Feb. 16, 1797.
Isaac, s. Jonathan and Bridget, Aug. 23, 1767.
James, s. [twin. P. R. 4.], James and Abigail, bp. July 7, 1754. C. R. 1.
Jepthah, s. John and Surviah, bp. June 25, 1809. C. R. 1.
Jerome B., s. John, stone-cutter, and Elizabeth R., Nov. —, 1847.
Jerusha Jaine, d. John, bp. Apr. 22, 1827. C. R. 1.
Jesse, s. Jonathan and Bridget, Oct. 19, 1756. [bp. Sept. 26. C. R. 1.]
Joel, s. Benjamin and Elisabeth, Nov. 5, 1776.
John, s. Philip and Mary, June 5, 1775.
John, s. Samuel and Bettey, Jan. 17, 1789.
John, s. John and Seviah, bp. Aug. 16, 1807. C. R. 1.
Jonathan, s. Ebenezer and Mary, Dec. 2, 170[1. T. C.].
Jonathan, s. Jonathan and Hanah, May 12, 1725.
Jonathan, s. Jonathan and Bridget, Apr. 15, 1752.
Joseph, s. Joseph and Eunis, Aug. [5, 1695. T. C.].
Joseph, s. Ebenezer and Sarah, Aug. 30, 1725.
Josiah King, s. Josiah and Rachel, Mar. 24, 1793.
Julia Augustia, d. Dea. Josiah and Rachel, Mar. 15, 1809.
Julia Louisa, d. Rev. John and Celia, June 17, 1840.
Lucinda, d. John, bp. Jan. 9, 1826. C. R. 1.
Martha, d. Dea. Josiah and Rachel, May 24, 1815.
Martha Lucinda, d. Rev. John and Celia, Nov. 1, 1832.
Martha Spalding, d. Josiah K. and Ruth, Nov. 16, 1822.
Matthias, s. Josiah and Rachel, June 10, 1795.
Mary, d. Ebenezar and Mary, Sept. 27, 1[695. T. C.].

PARKHURST, Micajah, s. Samuel and Bettey, Aug. 14, 1793.
Oliver, s. Josiah and Elizebeth, June 27, 1767.
Osgood, s. Joel and Polly, May 17, 1807. [bp. Oct., 1806. C. R. 1.]
Polley, d. Phillip and Mary, Dec. 5, 1788.
Polly, d. Joel and Polly, Oct. 15, 1802.
Rachel, d. Josarah and Rachil, Feb. 5, 1799.
Rufus, s. Joel and Polly, Nov. 6, 1809.
Ruth Pierce, d. John and Ruth, bp. May 19, 1805. C. R. 1.
Sally, d. Joel and Polly, Aug. 22, 1812.
Samuel, s. Josiah and Elizeb[e]th, Nov. 4, 1759.
Samuel, s. Samuel and Betcey, May 18, 1799.
Samuel Stevens, s. Dea. Josiah and Rachel, Nov. 13, 1806. [Nov. 18. P. R. 22.]
Sam[ue]ll, s. Joseph and Unec, Apr. 25, 1701.
Sarah, d. Ebenezer and Mary, Dec. 6, 1703.
Sarah, d. Ebenezer and Sarah, Aug. 6, 1722.
Sarah, d. Benja[min] and Elisabeth, Jan. 4, 1771.
Sarah, d. Rev. John and Celia, Feb. 13, 1825.
Sarah Jane, d. Amos, farmer, and Mary J. A., July 25, 1846.
Sarah Haywood, d. John, bp. Jan. 9, 1826. C. R. 1.
Sewel, s. Dea. Josiah and Rachel, Apr. 25, 1801.
Silas, s. Phillip and Mary, Nov. 7, 1785.
Solomon, s. Dea. Josiah and Rachel, July 12, 1804.
Solomon Waldo, s. Capt. Solomon and Lucina M. [(Adams). P. R. 17.], May 10, 1836.
Suel, s. John and Serviah, bp. Aug. 18, 1811. C. R. 1.
Surviah Manning, d. John and Surviah, bp. Dec. 8, 1805. C. R. 1.
Susan, d. Joel and Polly, Nov. 25, 1816.
Susan Emma, d. Rev. John and Celia, Nov. 23, 1836.
Susanna, d. Samuel and Bettey, Mar. 18, 1791.
Susanna Elizabeth, d. Samuel and Anna, Nov. 14, 1818.
Tabitha Elizabeth, d. Dea. Josiah and Rachel, Feb. 13, 1811.
William Manning, s. John, bp. Feb. 23, 1817. C. R. 1.
——, ch. Philip, Jan. 3, 1772. P. R. 4.

PARKHUST (see also Parkhurst), Abigail, d. James and Abigail, Dec. 5, 1734.
Abigal, d. Benjamin and Elizabeth, Nov. 26, 1764.
Andrew, s. James and Abigail, Apr. 10, 1743.
Betty, d. Josiah and Elizabeth, Sept. 10, 1764.
Ephraim, s. James and Abigail, Sept. 24, 1746.
Ephraim, s. Philip and Mary, Apr. 11, 1783.
Hanah, d. Josaph, July 24, 1697.
Hannah, d. Josepeh and Euines, Aug. 25, 1698.
Henery, s. Philip and Mary, Sept. 14, 1779.

PARKHURST, James, s. Benjamin and Elizabeth, Aug. 3, 1766.
John, s. Joseph and Eunice, Mar. 1, 1691. CT. R.
John, s. Jonathan and Hannah, Jan. 23, 1733-4.
John, s. Jonathan and Bridget, May 28, 1762.
Josiah, s. Jonathan and Hannah, Dec. 15, 1728.
Josiah, s. Josiah and Elizebeth, Jan. 20, 1763.
Lidia, d. Ebinezer and Mary, Feb. 11, 1697.
Mary, d. Jonathan and Hanah, Dec. 28, 1736.
Mary, d. Philip and Mary, June 1, 1777.
Philip, s. James and Abigail, Apr. 17, 1745.
Sarah, d. James and Abigail, Apr. 29, 1737.
Sarah, d. Jonathan and Bridget, Oct. 10, 1750.
Thaddeus, s. Jonathan and Bridget, July 8, 1765.

PARKIS (see also Parkhurst), Abigal, d. Joseph and Rebekah [Sarah. dup. CT. R.] Mar. 11, 1664-5.
Eunis, d. Josiph and Eunis, June 4, 1693.
Joseph, s. Joseph and Rebeckah, Jan. 12, 1661.
Mare, d. Joseph and Rebeckah, Aug. 10, 1657.
Rebeckah [Parks. CT. R.], d. Joseph and Rebeckah, Aug. 14, 1659.

PARRT, Mary, d. Rowel, Apr. 15, 1671. CT. R.

PARRY (see also Perry), James, s. John and Sarah, June 24, 1737.
Joseph, s. John and Sarah, Nov. 22, 1750.
Molly, d. John and Mary, Sept. 2, 1756.

PATTEN (see also Pattin), Isaac, s. Isaac and Lydia, Feb. 25, 1785.
James Pollard, s. Isaac and Lydia, Dec. 4, 1784.

PATTIN (see also Patten), Isaac, s. Isaac and Lydia, Mar. 6, 1761.
Oliver, s. twin, Isaac and Lydia, Jan. 24, 1763.
Thomas, s. twin, Isaac and Lydiah, Jan. 24, 1763.

PAYSON, Elizabeth French, d. A. M. and H. D., bp. Oct. 26, 1845. C. R. 3.

PEARCE (see also Pierce), Ann, d. Oliver and Ann, Sept. 13, 1736.
Ephraim, s. Robert and Mary, Jan. 1, 1733.
Joel, s. Stephen, jr., bp. Jan. 23, 1802. C. R. 1.
Rachel, d. Joseph and Barbary, Oct. 31, 1735.
William, s. Robert and Mary, Oct. 29, 1735.

PEARSON, Abel Goodridge, s. Amos and Rebecca, June 7, 1824.
George Warren, s. Amos and Rebecca, Sept. 22, 1825.
Jonathan, s. George and Elizabeth, bp. Aug. 18, 1765. C. R. 1.

PEIRCE (see also Pierce), Abigail, d. Oliver and Daborah, Feb. 7, 1792.
An, d. Steven and Betty, Oct. 19, 1756.
Anna, d. William and Elizebeth, Jan. 30, 1770.
Benjamin, s. Stephen and Esther, Nov. 25, 1726.
Benjamin, s. Stephen and Phebe, Dec. 7, 1790.
Bettey, d. Lt. Jonas and Bettey, May 7, 1782.
Betty, d. Stephen and Betty, Nov. 17, 1751.
Bradley, s. William and Elizebeth, May 4, 1772.
Dolle, d. William and Elizebeth, Oct. 31, 1763.
Easter, d. Benjamin and Elizebeth, June 12, 1761.
Eben, s. Stephen, jr., bp. May —, 1799. C. R. 1.
Elizabeth, d. Benja[min] and Elizabeth, bp. Oct. 22, 1752. C. R. 1.
Elizabeth, d. William and Elizabeth, Sept. 2, 1765.
Elizibeth, d. Oliver and Anna, Dec. 30, 1734.
Ephraim, s. Ephraim and Bridgit, Sept. 1, 1761.
Esther, d. Stephen and Ester, Apr. 24, 1711.
Esther, d. Oliver and Hannah, Aug. 23, 1748.
George, s. Stephen, jr. and Abigail, Jan. 28, 1815.
Hannah, d. Oliver and Hannah, Feb. 5, 1744-5.
Hannah, d. Oliver and Deborah, July 3, 1774. [bp. July 9, 1775. C. R. 1.]
Hannah, d. Stephen, jr. and Hannah, Dec. 7, 1778.
Jesse, s. twin, Benjamin and Elizabeth, Dec. 21, 1748.
Jesse, s. Stephen and Hannah, Feb. 2, 1790.
Joanna, d. Joseph, jr. and Mary, Mar. 24, 1764.
John, s. Stephen, jr. and Hannah, June 20, 1782.
Jonas, s. Oliver and Hannah, June 22, 1750.
Jonas, s. Jonas and Betey, Jan. 20, 1780.
Jonathan, s. Oliver and Hannah, Apr. 7, 1752.
Jonathan, s. Stephen and Hannah, Oct. 16, 1796.
Joseph, s. Silos and Elisabeth, Mar. 5, 1775.
Leafe, d. Benjamin and Elizebeth, May 1, 1759.
Levi, s. Levi and Remembrance, of Temple, bp. Feb. 15, 1779. C. R. 1.
Levy, s. Joseph [jr. C. R. 1.] and Mary, Feb. 20, 1747-8.
Lucy, d. Steaphen and Betty, Oct. 14, 1748.
Lydia, d. Benjamin and Elizabeth, Sept. 11, 1750.
Lydia, d. Stephen, bp. May 18, 1800. C. R. 1.
Marshall, s. Stephen, 3d and Hannah, Nov. 14, 1793.

PEIRCE, Mary, d. Stephen and Esther, Dec. 14, 1722.
Mary, d. Robart and Mary, Aug. 5, 1742.
Mary, d. Joseph and Mary, May 16, 1755.
Mary, d. William and Elizebeth, Nov. 10, 1761.
Mary, d. Silos and Lucy, July 24, 1772.
Merril, s. Benjamin and Elizabeth, Jan. 29, 1764.
Moses, s. Stephan and Hannah, Jan. 22, 1792.
Olive, d. Oliver and Hannah, July 13, 1759.
Olive, d. Silas and Elizabeth, bp. Oct. 27, 1776. C. R. 1.
Oliver, s. Stephen and Ester, May 15, 1709.
Oliver, s. Oliver and Hannah, May 30, 1742.
Oliver, s. Oliver, jr. and Deberah, July 2, 1783.
Oliver, s. Capt. Jonas and Bettey, Nov. 7, 1789.
Pamely, d. Stephen and Phebe, Aug. 9, 1792.
Parker, s. Ephraim and Bridgett, Aug. 19, 1770.
Pattee, d. Stephen and Hannah, Jan. 21, 1788.
Phebe, d. twin, Benjamin and Elizabeth, Dec. 21, 1748.
Polley, d. Capt. Jonas and Bettey, Feb. 17, 1787.
Ra[c]hel, d. Joseph and Mary, May 15, 1762.
Rebecca, d. Benjamin and Elizabeth, Feb. 24, 1746-7.
Rebecca, d. Ephraim and Bridget, Oct. 31, 1763.
Rebeckah, d. Oliver, jr. and Deborough, Jan. 1, 1780.
Remembrance, d. Stephen and Ester, Feb. 11, 1719.
Robert, s. Stephen and Ester, Jan. 19, 1708.
Robert, s. Steven and Betty, Apr. 13, 1754.
Robert, s. Ephraim and Bridget, Sept. 24, 1767.
Roda, d. Silas and Elizebe[t]h, Sept. 14, 1779.
Ruth, d. Oliver and Hannah, Sept. —, 1756. [bp. Sept. 26. C. R. 1.]
Ruth, d. Oliver, jr. and Deborah, Apr. 11, 1773.
Sarah, d. Steven and Tabitha, Mar. 25, 1685-6.
Sarah, d. Stephen and Betty, Dec. 20, 1745.
Sarah, d. Joseph and Mary, Dec. 30, 1759.
Sarah, d. Lt. Jonas and Bettey, Sept. 8, 1784.
Sarai, d. Stephen and Esther, Jan. 10, 1720-21.
Sibel, d. William and Elisabeth, Sept. 13, 1775.
Silas, s. Joseph and Mary, July 22, 1744.
Stephen, s. Stephen and Tabatha, Apr. 10, 1715.
Stephen, s. Olever and Hannah, Aug. 15, 1754.
Stephen, s. Stephen and Betty, Feb. 5, 1759.
Stephen, s. Stephen and Hannah, Apr. 5, 1786.
Susanna, d. Benjamin and Elizabeth, Nov. 11, 1754.
Sybill, d. Oliver and Hannah, Oct. 5, 1746.
Tabitha, d. Stephen and Ester, Feb. 28, 1716.
Than[k]full, d. Joseph, jr. and Mary, Jan. 9, 1751-2.
Thomas, s. Stephen, bp. Dec. 25, 1796. C. R. 1.

PEIRCE, Willard, s. Joseph and Mary, Dec. 1, 1746.
William, s. Steaphen and Esther, May 7, 1713.
William, s. William and Elizebeth, Oct. 7, 1767.
William Stearns, s. Jesse and Hannah, Sept. 14, 1815.

PEIRS (see also Pierce), Tabartha, d. Steven and Tabartha, Feb. 17, 1689-90. [Feb. 24. CT. R.]

PELSUE, Betey, d. Benjamin and Ruth, July 11, 1797.
William, s. Ens. William and Betsy, Apr. 27, 1805.

PERAM (see also Perham), [J. T. C.]am[e]s, s. Josiph and Dorathi, May 6, 1694.

PERCE (see also Pierce), Benjamin, s. Steven and Tabitha, June 4, 1682.

PEREM (see also Perham), Dorithy, d. Josaph and Dorithy, July 9, 1696.

PERHAM (see also Peram, Perem, Perrum), Albert Proctor, s. Samuel P., farmer, b. Wilton, N. H., and Assenath [(Lewis). P. R. 14.], b. Francestown, N. H., June 25, 1849. [June 23. P. R. 14.]
Anna, d. Lidia, bp. 13: 5 m: 1673. P. R. 1.
Benjamin, s. John and Lidiah, Feb. 23, 1709.
Benony, s. Samuel and Sarah, Feb. 22, 1749-50.
Benony, s. Samuel, jr. and Dolle, Dec. 14, 1777.
Caroline Rebecca, d. David [jr. P. R. 15.] and Elutheria W. [(Wait). P. R. 15.], Jan. 5, 1842.
David, s. Samuel, jr. and Dolle, Mar. 20, 1784.
David, s. David and Rebecah, Dec. 16, 1813.
Dolle, d. Samuel and Dolle, Aug. 1, 1786.
Edwin P., s. Samuel P. and Rebecca (Perham), Aug. 21, 1842. P. R. 14.
Elisabeth, d. John [torn. 1680?].
Eliza Butterfield, d. Samuel P., farmer, and Assenath [(Lewis). P. R. 14.], Jan. 17, 1847.
Elizabeth, d. Jonathan and Mary, Feb. 28, 1806.
Ester, d. Benony and Sary, Aug. 28, 1713.
George Washington, s. Jonathan and Mary, Sept. 23, 1808.
Hanah, d. Bennony and Sarah, Feb. 23, 1716-17.
Hannah, d. Josepeh and Doratey, Aug. 6, 1698.
Hannah, d. Samuel and Sarah, bp. July 12, 1752. C. R. 1.
Henry Spalding, s. David [jr. P. R. 15.], farmer, and Elutheria W. [(Wait). P. R. 15.], Nov. 16, 1843.

PERHAM, Joel, s. David and Rebecah, Apr. 17, 1821.
John, s. John and Lidiah, Jan. 12, 1695.
John, s. Samuel and Sarah, Mar. 6, 1811.
Jonathan, s. Joseph and Dorothy, Mar. 21, 1706-7.
Jonathan, s. Benony and Sary, July 25, 1711.
Jonathan, s. Samuel and Elizabath, Apr. 2, 1776.
Joseph, s. John and Lidiah, 22: 10 m: 1669. [Dec. 26. CT. R.]
Josiph, s. Josiph and Dorathie, Mar. 13, 1691-2.
Lidah, d. John and Lidia, Oct. 20, 1693.
Lidia, d. Benony and Sarah, Sept. 24, 1722.
Lidiah, d. John and Lidiah, Feb. 19, 1673.
Lidiah, d. Joseph and Dorithy, July 27, 1703.
Lidiah, d. Benony and Sary, Aug. 17, 1707.
Louisa E., d. Perley P., milkman, and Emeline A., Nov. —, 1847.
Maria Asenath, d. Samuel P., farmer, and Asenath [(Lewis). P. R. 14.], May 15, 1845.
Mary, d. John and Lidiah, Dec. 24, 1700.
Mary, d. Benony and Sary, Aug. 1, 1709.
Mary, d. Samuel and Sarah, July 14, 1745.
Mary Ann, d. Jonathan and Mary, Jan. 7, 1801.
Mary Elizabeth, d. David and Eluthena [Elutheria. dup.] W., at Boston, Mar. 16, 1840.
Oliver, s. Samuel and Sary, July 5, 1762.
Otis, s. Capt. Jonathan and Mary, Mar. 2, 1813.
Rebecah, d. David and Rebecah, Sept. 8, 1817.
Samuel, s. Benony and Sarrah, Mar. 4, 1715-16.
Samuel, s. Samuel and Mary Graves, May 14, 1736.
Samuel, s. Samuel and Sarah, bp. Oct. 9, 1746. C. R. 1.
Samuel, s. Samuel and Sary, May 27, 1754.
Samuel, s. Samuel, jr. and Dolle, Nov. 28, 1779.
Samuel, s. Samuel and Sarah, June 29, 1809.
Samuel, s. David and Rebecca, Oct. 25, 1829.
Samuel, s. Samuel and Eliza, Oct. 26, 1831.
Sam[ue]ll, s. John and Lidiah, May 6, 1698.
Sam[ue]ll, s. Samuel and Sary, July 25, 1756.
Sarah, d. Samuel and Sarah, May 26, 1742.
Sarah, d. Samuel and Sarah, bp. Mar. 13, 1748. C. R. 1.
Sarah, d. Samuel, jr. and Dolle, Jan. 20, 1782.
Sary, d. John and Lidiah, Oct. 16, 1703.
Sary, d. Benony, Nov. 1, 1705.
Willam, s. John and Lidiah, July 16, 1706.

PERIGO, Hellen Maria, d. James M., pattern-maker, b. Wrentham, and Sarah B., b. Easton, Sept. 7, 1849.

PERKER (see also Parker), Elizabeth, d. Aaron and Abigal, July 18, 1728.
Isaac, s. John and Rebeccah, Nov. 14, 1728.

PERKHAST (see also Parkhurst), James, s. James and Abigail, May 3, 1739.

PERKHUST (see also Parkhurst), Elizibeth, d. Jonathan and Hannah, Dec. 27, 1731.
Hannah, d. Jonathan and Hannah, Dec. 31, 1729.
James, s. Ebenezar and Mary, Nov. 18, 1707.
Philip, s. Ebenezer and Sary, Sept. 5, 1726.

PERRUM (see also Perham), John, s. John and Liddiah, Jan. 27, 1667.
Mare, d. John and Lidiah, Jan. 8, 1665.

PERRY (see also Parry), William Henry, s. W[illia]m H., farmer, and Charlotte, at Westford, Nov. 9, 1844.

PIERCE (see also Pearce, Peirce, Peirs, Perce), Ann Elizabeth, d. Stephen and Mary, Nov. 20, 1832.
Benjamin, s. Benjamin and Elizabeth, bp. Dec. 12, 1756. c. r. 1.
Charles H., s. Stephen and Mary, Apr. 13, 1840.
Charles Henry, s. Joseph B., machinist, and Mary B., at North Chelmsford, Jan. 5, 1845.
Cynthia Ellen, d. Ruel and Cynthia, at North Chelmsford, Nov. —, 1846.
Edwin, s. Capt. Jesse and Hannah, Jan. 18, 1818.
Eliza Jane, d. Ruel, farmer, and Cynthia, at North Chelmsford, July 16, 1844.
Frank Warren, s. Joseph Brooks, machinist, b. Merrimack, N. H., and Mary B., b. Hillsborough, N. H., at North Chelmsford, Dec. 17, 1848.
Frederic, s. Ruel, farmer, and Cynthia, b. Danvers, at North Chelmsford, Nov. 29, 1849.
Hermon, s. Jonathan and Hannah, Sept. 26, 1829.
Hezekiah Hildreth, s. Jonas, jr. and Suky, Jan. 3, 1810.
Ira, s. W[illia]m S. and Sarah, Apr. 30, 1842.
James, s. Joseph, bp. Mar. 12, 1826. c. r. 1.
Joel E., s. Stephen and Mary, Mar. 27, 1836.
John, s. Stephen, blacksmith, and Mary, July 18, 1845.
Joseph, s. Joseph, bp. Mar. 12, 1826. c. r. 1.
Julia M., d. Stephen and Mary, May 31, 1838.
Lucinda, d. Stephen, jr. and Abigail, Oct. 30, 1820.

PIERCE, Maria, d. Jonathan and Hannah, Jan. 21, 1828.
Milo, s. Stephen, jr. and Abigal, May 29, 1818.
Milo Spalding, s. Milo, trader, and Mary A., at Middlesex Village, Dec. 8, 1844.
Nancy B., d. Stephen, jr. and Abigal, Oct. 9, 1816.
Sanborn, s. Marshall and Mary, Dec. 6, 1818.
Sarah Jane, d. Capt. Jesse and Hannah, Aug. 19, 1820.
Susanna, d. Marshall and Mary, Aug. 22, 1822.
Walace Whitney, s. Joseph B., machinist, and Mary [B. dup.], at Furnace Village, Nov. 11, 1843.
Washington Brooks, s. Joseph B. and Mary, May 27, 1841.

PIKE, Harriett S., d. James, blacksmith, and Betsey B., at North Chelmsford, June 18, 1843.

PIPER, W[illia]m Henry, s. W[illia]m Henry and Elizabeth S., May 9, 1836.

PITTS, Samuel, s. Samuel and Joanna, bp. May 1, 1791. C. R. 1.
William Lendall, s. Samuel and Joanna, bp. Mar. 15, 1789. C. R. 1.

POLLARD, Charles Dawson, s. Dawson, carpenter, and Julia Ann, at Worsted Factory Village, May 13, 1847.
James, s. James and Molly, bp. Feb. 22, 1767. C. R. 1.

POOR, Charles Ira, s. twin, Daniel, innholder, and Elisabeth Ann, at Middlesex Village, Jan. 25, 1844.
Climena, d. Thomas, farmer, and Olive, at Middlesex Village, Sept. 22, 1847.
——, s. twin, Daniel, innholder, and Elisabeth Ann, at Middlesex Village, Jan. 25, 1844.

POWARS (see also Power), Hanah, d. Isaac and Mary, Mar. 21, 1709.
Tripheana, d. Isaac and Mary, May 22, 1711.

POWER (see also Powars, Powers), ——, d. John, shoemaker, b. Limerick, Ireland, and Bridgett, b. Monaghan Co., Ireland, at North Chelmsford, Dec. 29, 1849.

POWERS (see also Power), John, s. William and Remembrance, bp. Jan. 11, 1747. C. R. 1.
Lydia, d. William and Remembrance, Nov. 5, 1745.
Nahum, s. Peter and Hannah, of Nisscitisset, bp. Aug. 9, 1741. C. R. 1.

POWERS, Remembrance, d. wid. Rememb[ran]ce, now of Sutton, bp. July 15, 1753. C. R. 1.
Steaphen, s. William and Remembrance, May 16, 1742. [bp. 1741. C. R. 1.]
William, s. William and Rem[em]brance, Mar. 3, 1741-2.
William, s. William and Remembrance, Aug. 13, 1743.

PRATT, Abby Issabel, d. Joshua, moulder, and Cynthia, at North Chelmsford, Nov. 27, 1847.
Albert Gallatin, s. John R. and Lydia, Sept. 25, 1838.
Clara Isabel, d. W[illia]m A., miller, b. Woodstock, Vt., and Letitia, b. Plymouth, Vt., Feb. 14, 1849.
Elnora Malinda, d. Oliver R., moulder, and Mary Ann, at North Chelmsford, July 29, 1844.
Henry Francis, s. Oliver R. and Mary Ann, Dec. 2, 1837.
Lydia Ann, d. John R. and Lydia, May 29, 1836.
Mary Esterla, d. Oliver R. and Mary Ann, Mar. 5, 1839.
Susan P., d. Joshua, moulder, and Cynthia, at Furnace Village, Aug. 9, 1843.

PRAY, Hellen Elizabeth, d. Abraham F., soap maker, b. Portsmouth, N. H., and Diantha M., b. Fitchburg, at Middlesex Village, Aug. 27, 1849.

PRENTISS, ——, d. Amos E., drover, and Mary A., Apr. 18, 1844.

PRESCUTT, Jonas, s. Jonas and Ester, Apr. 7, 1727.
Timothy, s. Jonas [jr. C. R. 4.] and Easter, Nov. 21, 1728.

PRESTON, Joshua, s. Joshua and Anna, bp. Oct. 10, 1742. C. R. 1.
Sarah Jane, d. Erasmus D., shoemaker, and Sarah, at North Chelmsford, Mar. 17, 1848.

PROCKTER (see also Proctor), Abigail, d. Josiah, bp. at Harvard, Nov. 13, 1768. P. R. 4.
Benjamin, s. John and Miriam, Oct. 20, 1704.
Benjamin, s. Benjamin and Rachel, of New Ipswich, bp. July 13, 1760. C. R. 1.
Betty, d. Benjamin and Lidia, Mar. 7, 1730-31.
Charls, s. Sam[ue]ll and Sary, June 31, 1710.
Daniel, s. Daniel and Susanah, Nov. 3, 1728.
Daniell, s. Samuell and Sary, Nov. 1, 1706.
David, s. Sam[ue]ll and Hannah, Feb. 1, 1701.
Ebinezer, s. Gershom and Sarah, Jan. 16, 1703-4.

PROCKTER, Ester, d. Peter and Mary, July 9, 1700.
Ester, d. Gershom and Sarah, Oct. 25, 1710.
Hannah, d. John and Mirriam, May 9, 1701.
Hannah, d. Gershom and Sarah, Oct. 3 [torn. Oct. 31, 170-.
    T. C. 1701?].
Isaac, s. Josiah, bp. at Harvard, Nov. 13, 1768. P. R. 4.
Jane, d. Gershom and Sary, Mar. 10, 1706.
Jonas, s. Sam[ue]ll and Sary, Apr. 9, 1712.
Joseph, s. Peter and Rebecka, Nov. 8, 170[3. T. C.].
Josiah, s. Josiah, bp. at Harvard, Nov. 13, 1768. P. R. 4.
Luce, d. Sam[ue]ll and Sary, Aug. 19, 1708.
Lucy, d. Israel and Sarah, bp. July 21, 1754. C. R. 1.
Lydia, d. Nathan and Lydia, of Camden, bp. Jan. 28, 1776.
    C. R. 1.
Marah, d. Samuel and Lidia, July 27, 1731.
Mary, d. John and Mary, Mar. 27, 1719.
Molly, d. Elijah and Esther, bp. Sept. 22, 1776. C. R. 1.
Molly, d. Nathan and Lydia, of Camden, bp. Nov. 8, 1778.
    C. R. 1.
Moses, s. John and Meream, Nov. 19, 1706.
Rachil, d. Peter and Hannah, Sept. 12, 1731.
Robert, s. Robert and Mary, Apr. 8, 1719.
Ruhamah, d. Sybil, bp. July 3, 1768. C. R. 1.
Samuell, s. Samuell and Sarah, Jan. 16, 1696-7.
Sarah, d. Samuel and Sarah, Sept. 30, 1715.
Uriah, s. Dan[ie]ll and Susan[n]a, bp. Oct. 1, 1749. P. R. 4.
William, s. Sam[ue]ll and Sarah, Aug. 14, 1704.

PROCTER (see also Proctor), Aaron, s. Oliver and Mary,
    May 12, 1747.
Abel, s. Simeon and Rebeca, July 18, 1754.
Abel, s. Peter and Molly, Feb. 10, 1787.
Abigail, d. Israel and Sarah, Mar. 29, 1738-9.
Abigil, d. Peter and Hannah, Dec. 16, 1733.
Achsah, d. Azariah and Azubah, Nov. 15, 1778.
Anna Parker, d. Eldad and Rachel [(Parker). P. R. 13.], Nov.
    27, 1802.
Asa, s. Simeon and Rebecca, May 23, 1764.
Asa, s. Asa and Sarah, Aug. 8, 1784.
Azariah, s. Cornet Daniel and Susanna, Sept. 20, 1749.
Azeriah, s. Azeriah and Azubah, Aug. 13, 1782.
Benjamin, s. Benjamin and Lidiah, June 5, 1733.
Caroline, d. Azariah and Lucy (Hodgman), Sept. 13, 1824.
    P. R. 29.
Cotton, s. Samuel and Lydia, Apr. 18, 1725.
Daniel, s. Cornet Daniel and Susanna, Nov. 20, 1744.

PROCTER, Daniel, s. Azeriah and Azubah, Aug. 4, 1784.
Daniel, s. Elldad and Rachel [(Parker). P. R. 13.], Nov. 16, 1794. [1795. P. R. 13.]
Easter, d. Daniel and Susanah, Mar. 29, 1738.
Edward, s. John and Meream, Feb. 15, 1698-9.
Edwin, s. Azariah and Lucy (Hodgman), Sept. 13, 1830. P. R. 29.
Elezebeth, d. Garshom [deceased in Sept. 1751. C. R. 1.] and Elezebeth, Mar. 29, 1751.
Elijah, s. Benjamin and Lidya, July 6, 1736.
Elizabeth, d. Jonathan and Elizabeth, Mar. 17, 1721.
Elizabeth, d. John and Marai, Oct. 18, 1724.
Elizabeth, d. Daniel and Susanah, Sept. 21, 1733.
Ephraim, s. Jonathan and Elizabeth, Oct. 24, 1726.
Ephraim, s. Capt. Azariah and Azubah, May 26, 1790.
Esther, d. Joseph and Agness, Nov. 27, 1725.
Esther, d. Simeon and Rebecca, Mar. 18, 1766.
Esther, d. Elijah and Esther, Dec. 27, 1769.
George, s. Azariah and Lucy [(Hodgman). P. R. 29.], Sept. 5, 1814.
[Ge. T. C.]rshom, s. Gershom and Sara, Apr. 24, 1691. [Apr. 7. CT. R.]
Gershom, s. Gershom and Rebeckah, Mar. 29, 1722-3.
Gershom, s. Gershom and Elizabeth, May 30, 1748.
Hannah, d. Peter and Hannah, Jan. 10, 1722-3.
Hannah, d. Israel and Sarah, Feb. 2, 1743-4.
Hannah, d. Simeon and Rebeckah, Jan. 3, 1757.
Hannah, d. Peter and Moley, Feb. 7, 1777.
Harbad, s. Samuel and Sally, Oct. 5, 1797.
Henry, s. Gershom and Rebecka, Mar. 15, 1728-9.
Henry, s. Henry and Sarah, July 21, 1770.
Henry Byam, s. Azariah, jr. and Lucy [(Hodgman). P. R. 29.], Apr. 2, 1819.
Isaac, s. Peter and Hannah, Dec. 8, 1738.
Isaac, s. Simeon and Rebackah, Feb. 16, 1770.
Isaac, s. Peter and Molly, Oct. 29, 1783.
Israel, s. Gershom and Sarai, Oct. 4, 1708.
Israel, s. Israel and Sarah, Mar. 2, 1741-2.
Jacob, s. Jonathan and Elizabeth, Nov. 24, 1724.
James, s. John and Mary, Nov. 14, 1720.
Jane, d. Gershom and Rebecka, Aug. 1, 1730.
Jeptha, s. Asa and Sarah, Feb. 17, 1782.
Joanna, d. Daniel and Susanna, July 31, 1742.
[John. T. C.], s. John and Miriam, Oct. 6, 1694.
John, s. Benj[a]min and Lydia, Apr. 20, 1750.
John, s. Lt. Elijah and Esther, July 18, 1781.

PROCTER, Jonas Robins, s. Azariah and Azubah, June 11, 1786.
[torn]hom [Jonathan. T. C.], s. Gershom and Sara, July 8, 1693.
Jonathan, s. Jonathan and Elizabeth, Mar. 22, 1722-3.
Josiah, s. Isarell and Margret, Jan. 10, 1691-2.
Levy, s. William and Lucy, Aug. 31, 1740.
Lidia, d. Benjamin and Lidya, May 28, 1729.
Louise, d. Azariah and Lucy (Hodgman), Jan. 9, 1826. P. R. 29.
Lucia, d. William and Lucia [Lucy. C. R. 1.], Feb. 25, 1747-8.
Lucy, d. Gershom and Rebeckah, Dec. 15, 1738.
Lucy, d. Cornet Daniel and Susanna, Nov. 28, 1746.
Lucy, d. Gershom and Elizabeth, Feb. 6, 1746-7.
Lucy, d. Henry and Sary, Mar. 22, 1763.
Lucy, d. Peter and Molly, Aug. 29, 1780.
Lucy, d. Azariah and Lucy (Hodgman), Nov. 6, 1806. P. R. 29.
Lydia, d. Samuel and Lydia, May 1, 1729.
Lydia, d. Simeon and Rebeckah, Aug. 25, 1755.
Martha Ann, d. Azariah and Lucy (Hodgman), Jan. 28, 1829. P. R. 29.
Mary, d. Peeter and Mary, Mar. 10, 1697.
Mary, d. Benjamin and Lydia, Aug. 10, 1744.
Mary, d. Israel and Sarah, Apr. 20, 1746.
Mary, d. Israel and Sarah, Feb. 11, 1753.
Mary, d. Elldad and Rachel [(Parker). P. R. 13.] [May 30. P. R. 13.], May 31, 1799.
Maryim, d. John and Maryim, June 30, 1696.
Mercy, d. Peter and Hannah, Feb. 10, 1724-5.
Miriam, d. Benjamin and Lydia, July 22, 1741.
Moley, d. Peter and Moly, Oct. 7, 1778.
Molley, d. William and Mary, Apr. 16, 1770.
Nathan, s. Israel and Sarah, Apr. 20, 1751. [bp. Apr. 29, 1750. C. R. 1.]
Olive, d. John, bp. Mar. 2, 1729. C. R. 4.
Olive, d. Gershom and Rebeckah, Mar. 29, 1736.
Oliver, s. Peter and Hannah, Mar. 14, 1720-21.
Oliver, s. John, bp. Mar. 2, 1729. C. R. 4.
Oliver, s. Oliver and Mary, Apr. 14, 1745.
Peter, s. Peter and Hannah, Jan. 17, 1735-6.
Pheneas, s. John and Mary, Nov. 10, 1722.
Philip, s. Thomas and Hanah, Jan. 3, 1725-6.
Porter, s. Samuel and Sally, Mar. 4, 1794.
Ratchel, d. Sam[ue]ll and Hanah, Jan. 5, 1702[-3.].
Rebecah, d. Gershom and Rebecah, Oct. 11, 1733.
Rebeckah, d. Azariah and Lucy [(Hodgman). P. R. 29.], Oct. 27, 1812.

PROCTER, Rebekah, d. Peter and Marah, Apr. 29, 1692.
Robbart, s. Peter and Marie, Jan. 3, 1689-90.
Samuel, s. Samuel and Lydia, Feb. 28, 1726-7.
Samuel, s. Asa and Sarah, Jan. 28, 1789.
[Sarah. T. C.], d. Sameuel and Sarah, Apr. 15, 1694.
Sarah, d. Gershom and Rebecka, Dec. 26, 1725.
Sarah, d. Joseph, bp. Dec. 15, 1728. C. R. 4.
Sarah, d. Daniel and Susannah, Oct. 12, 1731.
Sarah, d. Israel and Sarah, Nov. 2, 1736.
Sarah, d. Henry and Sarah, Apr. 25, 1761.
Sarah, d. Lt. Elijah and Esther, Sept. 9, 1779.
Sarah, d. Azariah and Lucy (Hodgman), May 18, 1822. P. R. 29.
Sary, d. Gershom and Sary, Sept. [torn. 1673. T. C.].
Sibbill, d. Samuel and Lydia, May 15, 1740.
Simeon, s. Peter and Hanah, July 19, 1729.
Simeon, s. Azariah and Lucy (Hodgman), Dec. 2, 1816. P. R. 29.
Sukey Amanda [Susan. P. R. 29.], d. Azeriah and Lucy [(Hodgman). P. R. 29.], Oct. 10, 1808.
Susana, d. Daniel and Susana, Oct. 19, 1729.
Susanah, d. Joseph and Agness, Feb. 29, 1723-4.
Susanah, d. Daniel and Susanah, Jan. 7, 1735-6.
Susanna, d. Azeriah and Azubah, July 28, 1780.
Thankfull, d. Peter and Hanah, Feb. 8, 1726-7.
Thomis, s. Sameuell and Sarah, Dec. 12, 1698.
Timothy, s. Simeon and Rebeckah, July 29, 1762.
Ueriah, s. Daniel and Susanna, Mar. 17, 1739.
Willard, s. Elldad and Rachel [(Parker). P. R. 13.], Mar. 6, 1797.
William, s. William and Lucy, Oct. 30, 1734.
William, s. Israel and Sarah, Feb. 20, 1747-8.

PROCTOR (see also Prockter, Procter, Proctter, Prookter), Abigail Maria, d. George, clergyman, and Susan M., at Sterling, July 8, 1844.
Alfred, s. Jonas R. and Sybil, July 8, 1822.
Asubah, d. Peter and Molley, Sept. 6, 1770. [bp. July 8. C. R. 1.]
Azariah, s. Azariah and Lucy [(Hodgman). P. R. 29.], Oct. 8, 1810.
Azubah, d. Azariah and Azubah, Apr. 8, 1776.
Benjamin, s. Elijah and Esther, Jan. 14, 1768.
Betsey Carolina, d. Calvin, farmer, b. Dunstable, and Honora, b. Brookline, N. H., Nov. 19, 1849.
Charles, s. Jonas R. and Sybil, June 9, 1815.

CHELMSFORD BIRTHS 127

PROCTOR, Eldad, s. Daniel, jr. and Mary, Oct. 14, 1769. [1770. P. R. 13.]
Elizabeth, d. Roberd and Jane, Dec. 16, 1656. [Jan. 21. CT. R.]
Gaius, s. Peter and Molly, Sept. 9, 1771. [bp. July 14. C. R. 1.]
Gershom, s. Henry and Sarah, Sept. 22, 1767.
Hannah, w. Daniel Byam, jr., Feb. 28, 1745. P. R. 13.
Harriett Louisa, d. Daniel, farmer, and Betsey, at Baptist Village, Apr. 19, 1845.
Hiram, s. Azariah and Azubah, Mar. 30, 1772.
Israel, s. William and Mary, Dec. 30, 1773.
Israell, s. Robertt and Jane, Apr. 29, 1668.
James, s. Roberd and Jane, Jan. 8, 1658.
John, s. Roberd and Sarah, Aug. 17, 1663.
Jonas R., s. Jonas R. and Sybil, Sept. 15, 1810.
Josiah Kendall, s. Calvin, farmer, and Honora, Mar. 4, 1848.
Julia Ann, d. Jonas R. and Sybil, Dec. 18, 1825.
Lideah, d. Roberd and Jane [torn], 1660. [Feb. 19. CT. R.]
Lidiah, d. Isarell and Margrett, Apr. 20, 1690.
Lucy, d. Daniel and Mary, Feb. 22, 1773. [1772. P. R. 13.]
Lydia, d. Elijah and Esther, Sept. 10, 1771.
Mary, d. Simeon and Rebecka, Jan. 9, 1759.
Mary B., d. Alfred, wheelwright, and Harriett E., Feb. 28, 1848.
Milo Jefferson, s. Jonas R. and Sybil, Oct. 3, 1831.
Molley, d. Azariah and Azubah, Nov. 28, 1773.
Rebeca, d. Henry and Sarah, May 28, 1765.
Rebeckah, d. Simeon and Rebeckah, Feb. 22, 1768.
Rufus, s. Jonas R. and Sybil, Dec. 11, 1812.
Samuell, s. Roberd and Sarah, Sept. 15, 1665.
Sarah, d. William and Mary, Feb. 6, 1772.
Simeon, s. Simeon and Rebeca, Oct. 16, 1760.
Sybil Mariah, d. Jonas R. and Sybil, Aug. 9, 1817.
Sybil Mariah, d. Jonas R. and Sybil, Aug. 15, 1820.
Thomas, s. Robertt and Jane, Apr. 30, 1671.
Zilpah, d. Daniel, jr. and Mary, Dec. 4, 1767. [1768. P. R. 13.]

PROCTTER (see also Proctor), Nathan, s. Gershom and Sarah, Oct. 1, 1698.
[Peter. T. C.], s. Peter and Sarah, Aug. 14, 1694.

PROOKTER (see also Proctor), Ezekiell, s. Peter and Mary, Nov. 19, 1709.

PROVANCHA, Isadore Fratonia, d. George, laborer, and Olive G., at North Chelmsford, July 17, 1844.

CHELMSFORD BIRTHS

PRO[torn], Benoni, s. Elisabeth [torn. 1679-80?].

PUTMAN (see also Putnam), Israel, s. Jonathan and Hannah, June 19, 1773.
Joseph, s. Jonathan and Hannah, Mar. 6, 1771.
Stephen, s. Jonathan and Hannah, Mar. 20, 1776. [bp. Mar. 17. c. r. 1.]

PUTNAM (see also Putman), Ann, d. Joseph, bp. July 7, 1816. c. r. 1.
Daniel, s. Daniel and Hannah, bp. Feb. 10, 1799. c. r. 1.
Eliel, s. Joseph, bp. July 7, 1816. c. r. 1.
Franklin, s. Joseph, bp. July 7, 1816. c. r. 1.
Hannah, d. Daniel and Hannah, bp. May 11, 1800. c. r. 1.
Hannah W., d. twin, Israel, farmer, and Mary, at Mill Row, Sept. 2, 1845.
Israel, s. Joseph, bp. July 7, 1816. c. r. 1.
Julia Amanda, d. Joseph, bp. July 7, 1816. c. r. 1.
Martha Trask, d. Joseph, bp. July 7, 1816. c. r. 1.
Osgood, s. Joseph, bp. July 7, 1816. c. r. 1.
Pattey, d. Jonathan and Hannah [formerly of Townsend. p. r. 4.], May 28, 1769.
Sarah Lee, d. twin, Israel, farmer, and Mary, at Mill Row, Sept. 2, 1845.
Stephen, s. Joseph, bp. July 7, 1816. c. r. 1.

PUTNEY, Adelaide Augusta, d. Jonas K. [B. dup.], farmer, and superintendent of almshouse, and Phebe, at almshouse, May 30, 1843.

QUESEY, John Baptist Actor, s. Henry, laborer, and Sarah, at North Chelmsford, Mar. 3, 1843.

RAND, Mary, d. Robert and Mary, of Boston, bp. Jan. 19, 1777. c. r. 1.
Susanna, d. Bartholomew and Mary, of Boston, bp. Apr. 6, 1777. c. r. 1.

RAYMENT (see also Raymond), Elizabeth, d. Edward and Abigail, bp. July 20, 1760. c. r. 1.
Stephen, s. Edward and Abigail, bp. June 18, 1769. c. r. 1.

RAYMOND (see also Rayment), Abigail, d. Edward and Abigail, May 8, 1752.
Anna, d. Edward and Abigail, June 17, 1756.
Edward, s. Edward and Abigail, bp. June 5, 1763. c. r. 1.

RAYMOND, Ruth, d. Edward and Abigail, Apr. 12, 1754.
Sarah, d. Edward and Abigail, bp. Sept. 29, 1765. C. R. 1.
William, s. Edward and Abigail, Apr. 30, 1758.

REA, Pelatiah, s. Jeremiah and Bridget, July 31, 1771.

READ (see also Reed), Benjamin, s. Jacob and Lucy, Feb. 22, 1752. [bp. Feb. 2. P. R. 4.]
Benjeman, s. Thomis and Hannah, Oct. 23, 1698.
Betey, d. Jonathan and Margret, Jan. 15, 1716-17.
Bethiah, d. Esdras, bp. 1 : 12 m : 1656, a. abt. 19 y. P. R. 1.
Betty, d. John and Jane, May 27, 1721.
Deborah, d. W[illia]m, bp. July 13, 1729. C. R. 4.
Ephraim, s. James, bp. at Harvard, Nov. 13, 1768. P. R. 4.
Hanah, d. Jonathan and Margret, May 17, 1715.
Hanah, d. John and Jane, Jan. 15, 1722-3.
Hanah, d. Thomas and Sarah, Apr. 26, 1724.
Jane, d. John and Jane, Apr. 1, 1717.
John, s. John and Jane, Feb. 3, 1709.
John, s. Jacob and Lucy, May 22, 1758.
Joseph, s. Thomas and Sarrah, June 4, 1716.
Lucy, d. John and Jane, July 16, 1727.
Mary, d. John and Jane, July 3, 1707.
Mary Ann, d. Timothy and Sarah, Aug. 10, 1817.
Obadiah, s. Esdras, bp. 1 : 12 m : 1656, a. abt. 17 y. P. R. 1.
Priscilla, d. Jacob and Lucy, June 3, 1756.
Rebeckeh, d. Thomas and Sarah, May 26, 1727.
Robert, s. William and Hanah, Dec. 25, 1720.
Samuel, s. John and Jane, Aug. 7, 1711.
Sarah Elizabeth, d. Timothy and Sarah, Sept. 15, 1815.
Sarai, d. John and Jane, Feb. 22, 1718-19.
Sary, d. Thomas and Sary, Mar. 25, 1711.
Sary, d. Thomas and Sary, Aug. 17, 1712.
Thomas, s. John and Jane, Oct. 25, 1713.
Timothy, s. Thomas and Sary, Mar. 21, 1714.
William, s. John and Jane, Apr. 2, 1715.
William, s. William and Hannah, Feb. 25, 1724-5.

REDDING, Bridget, d. Robart and Hannah, June 11, 1745.
Sarah, d. Robert and Hannah, Mar. 9, 1743-4.

REED (see also Read), Abigail, d. Oliver and Abigail, of Westford, bp. Apr. 22, 1781. C. R. 1.
Abigail O., w. Otis Adams, May 26, 1801. P. R. 5.
Andrew Jackson, s. Joseph, innholder, and Maria E., Mar. 16, 1844.

REED, Caroline Augusta, d. Joseph and Maria, Nov. 1, 1839.
Catharine Augusta, d. Joseph, farmer, and Maria, Oct. 4, 1846.
Charles Spalding, s. Joseph and Leonora, Apr. 29, 1835.
Elizabeth, d. Jacob and Lucy, bp. Apr. 25, 1756. C. R. 1.
George Eaton, s. Joseph and Maria, Jan. 17, 1838.
Henry Ransford, s. Josiah Ransford and Lucinda Graves, Aug. 23, 1837.
Hulday, d. John and Sarah, at Hollis, N. H., July 14, 1781.
Jacob, s. Jacob and Lucy, bp. Sept. 22, 1754, a. abt. 6 or 7 y. C. R. 1.
Joseph Willard, s. Joseph and Leonora, Mar. 25, 1833.
Leonora Maria, d. Joseph and Maria, Nov. 21, 1836.
Lydia, d. John and Sarah, in the District of Carlisle, Jan. 25, 1784.
Martina, d. Joseph, innholder, and Maria, Aug. 10, 1845.
Oliver, s. Oliver and Abigail, of Westford, bp. Oct. 22, 1780. C. R. 1.
Priscilla, d. Jacob and Lucy, bp. Sept. 22, 1754, a. abt. 3 m. C. R. 1.
Robert Foster, s. John and Sarah, Apr. 28, 1786.
Sarah, d. John and Sarah, July 13, 1780.
Thankfull, d. John and Sarah, Mar. 11, 1783.
Zachery Taylor, s. Joseph, farmer, and Maria, Jan. 21, 1848.
Zadock, s. W[illia]m and Lucy, bp. at Litchfield, Oct. 1, 1752. P. R. 4.

RICHARDSON (see also Richardsun, Richarson, Richerdson, Richerson, Richeson, Ritchardson, Ritchardsun, Ritcherdson, Ritcheson), Abi, d. John and Esther, Sept. 23, 1751.
Alva [Alva Howard. C. R. 1.], d. Elijah and Polly [(Howard). P. R. 26.], Jan. 7, 1807.
Alvah Howard, s. Elijah, jr. and Elisabeth [(Emerson). P. R. 6.], Sept. 4, 1833.
Ann Prudence, d. Robert and Sybil, Mar. 13, 1831.
Asa Edwin, s. George and Assenath, May 31, 1836.
Asenath Louisa, d. George and Asenath, Dec. 21, 1823.
Benjamin, s. Benj[amin], bp. Apr. 20, 1729. C. R. 4.
Benjamin, s. Jonathan and Lydia, July 20, 1788.
Benoni, s. Josiah and Lydia, May 27, 1775.
Bridget, d. Zachary and Sarah, Apr. 23, 1726.
Brigett, d. James and Brigett, Mar. 17, 1674.
Cecelia Ann, d. Elijah, jr., farmer, and Elizabeth [(Emerson). P. R. 6.], Aug. 4, 1843. [Aug. 5. P. R. 6.]
Charles, s. Oliver and Chloa, July 18, 1793.
Cloe, d. Oliver and Cloe, Nov. 14, 1806.

CHELMSFORD BIRTHS 131

RICHARDSON, Deborah, d. Zachary and Sarah, June 1, 1727.
Dolly, d. Josiah, jr. and Sibyl, Dec. 15, 1795.
Easter, d. John and Ester, June 11, 1736.
Ebenezer, s. Oliver and Chloa, Mar. 1, 1799.
Elijah [s. Zachariah and Sarah. C. R. 1.], Oct. 19, 1767. P. R. 26.
Elijah, jr., s. Elijah and Mary [(Howard). P. R. 26.], Nov. 12, 1803.
Elisibath, d. Jonathan and Elisibath, Oct. 19, 1696.
Elizabath, d. Ezekiell and Mary, "Later End of" Nov., 1692.
Elizar, s. Sam[ue]ll and Rachell, Oct. 9, 1718.
Ellen Louisa, d. Elijah, jr., farmer, and Elizabeth [(Emerson). P. R. 6.], Nov. 17, 1846. [Nov. 16. P. R. 6.]
Ellen M., d. George and Assenath, Dec. 1, 1830.
Emmerson, s. Elijah, jr. and Elisabeth, Oct. 28, 1835.
Esther, d. Josiah and Lydia, Dec. 10, 1770.
Esther, d. Josiah, jr. and Sibyl, Dec. 27, 1797.
Febe, d. John and Elesibeth, Mar. [torn. Mar. 9. T. C. 1700?].
Frances Adelaid, d. Elijah, jr. and Elizabeth [(Emerson). P. R. 6.], Oct. 5, 1841. [Oct. 4. P. R. 6.]
Fran[c]is, s. Oliver and Chloa, Mar. 1, 1795.
Gedeon, s. Josiah and Experience, June 5, 1730.
George Robert, s. Robert and Sybil, May 18, 1834.
Hanah, d. Josyah and Mercy, Sept. 28, 1698.
Hannah, d. John and Elesibeth, Mar. 18, 1702-3.
Hannah, d. Eleazer and Lydia, Feb. 17, 1761.
Hannah, d. Zachariah, jr. and Sarah, Jan. 14, 1765.
Hannah, d. Jonathan and Lydia, bp. Mar. 3, 1782. C. R. 1.
Henery, s. John and Elizabeth, Sept. 19, 1714.
Henrietta, d. Elijah, jr. and Elizabeth [(Emerson). P. R. 6.], Apr. 5, 1839.
Jane, d. twin, Robert and Jane, June 11, 1774.
John, s. John and Elizabeth, Nov. 16, 1711.
John, s. John and Esther, Apr. 8, 1748.
[Jon. T. C.]athan, s. Jonathan and Elisabeth, Dec. 28, 1693.
[Joseph, s. T. C.] Thomas and Hanah, Apr. 17, 1694.
Joseph, s. Eleazer and Lydia, bp. June 16, 1751. P. R. 4.
Joseph, s. Zachariah and Sarah, Feb. 11, 1761.
Joseph, s. Elijah and Molly, [(Howard). P. R. 26.], Jan. 1, 1801.
Josiah, s. Josiah, May 5, 1691. CT. R.
Josiah, s. Zachery and Sary, May 8, 1734.
Josiah, s. Josiah and Lydia, June 9, 1767.
Josiah, s. Josiah and Sibyl, Dec. 15, 1801.
Lettis, d. twin, Robert and Jane, Oct. 18, 17[torn. bef. 1774.].
Luce, d. Jonathan and Elesebeth, Apr. 6, 1712.

RICHARDSON, Lucy, d. Zachariah and Sarah, Nov. 11, 1742.
Lucy, d. Oliver and Cloe, Jan. 27, 1801.
Lydia, d. Zachary and Sarah, May 17, 1729.
Lydia, d. Eleazer and Lydia, May 10, 1749.
Lydia, d. Josiah and Lydia, Dec. 7, 1763.
Marcy, d. Zachariah anod Sarah, Aug. 5, 1759.
Mary, d. Jonathan and Elesibeth, June 26, 16 [torn. 169-. T. C. 1699?].
Mary, d. John and Elizabeth, July 11, 1705.
Mary, d. John, jr. and Easter, May 15, 1742.
Mary, d. Eleazer and Lydia, Aug. 14, 1765.
Mary, d. twin, Robert and Jane, Oct. 17, 17[torn. bef. 1774.].
Mary, d. Elijah and Molly [(Howard). P. R. 26.], Aug. 14, 1809.
Mary Elisabeth, d. Elijah, jr. and Elisabeth [(Emerson.) P. R. 6.], Mar. 6, 1837.
Mary Jane, d. Francis and Mary, Aug. 21, 1825.
Mercy, d. Zachary and Sary, July 15, 1724.
[Me. T. C.]rsi, d. Josiah [and Mercy. CT. R.], Jan. 9, 168[torn. 1690. T. C.].
Olef, d. Jonathan and Elizabath, June 29, 1706.
Olive, d. Josiah and Lydia, June 7, 1765.
Oliver, s. Eleazer and Lidia, Mar. 17, 1759.
Parish, s. Robert and Debarah, Dec. 18, 1724.
Paul, s. Josiah and Lydia, June 14, 1762.
Phebe, d. Robert and Deborah, Feb. 2, 1719.
Rachel, d. Eleazer and Lydia, June 14, 1751.
Rachell, d. Sam[ue]ll and Rachell, Apr. 14, 1704.
Rebecca, d. John and Esther, Aug. 19, 1753.
[R]obbart, s. Josiah and Marcye, Oct. 2, 1693.
Robert, s. Zacheriah and Sary, Feb. 3, 1756.
Robert, s. twin, Robert and Jane, June 11, 1774.
Robert, s. Oliver and Cloe, Jan. 22, 1804.
Rufus E., s. Elijah and Elizabeth (Emerson), Oct. 29, 1835. P. R. 6.
Samuel, s. Eleazer and Lydia, Sept. 14, 1756.
Samuel, s. Elijah and Mary [(Howard). P. R. 26.], May 4, 1802.
Samuel Augustus, s. Samuel and Sarah, Dec. 7, 1837.
Sam[ue]ll, s. Sam[ue]ll and Rachell, Apr. 17, 1709.
Sarah, d. John and Elisibath, Aug. 5, 1696.
Sarah, d. John and Esther, Apr. 28, 1740.
Sarah, d. Eleazer and Lydia, Oct. 4, 1753.
Sarah, d. Zachariah and Sarah, Dec. 29, 1757.
Sary, d. Samuell and Rachell, June 16, 1706.
Sary, d. Zachary and Sary, Oct. 13, 1719.

RICHARDSON, Sary, d. Zacheriah and Sary, Mar. 15, 1763.
Sibel, d. Zachariah, jr. and Sarah, Jan. 19, 1770.
Sibyl, d. Josiah, jr. and Sibyl, Oct. 1, 1799.
Silas, s. Josiah and Lidia, Dec. 27, 1773. [bp. Jan. 10, 1773. C. R. 1.]
Simeon, s. Josiah and Lydia, Sept. 24, 1768.
Sophia, d. Josiah, jr. and Sibyl, July 14, 1794.
Susana, d. Samuell and Rachell, Dec. 15, 1712.
Susann, d. Oliver and Chloa, Jan. 5, 1792.
Sybill, d. John and Easther, May 19, 1744.
Tabatha, d. John and Easther, June 10, 1746.
Thankfull, d. Jonathan and Elizabeth, Aug. 16, 1709.
William, s. Josiah and Mercy, Sept. 19, 170[1. T. C.].
William George, s. George and Assenath, Nov. 7, 1825.
Zachariah, s. Zachariah and Sarah, Feb. 19, 1721-2.
Zachariah, s. Zachariah, jr. and Hannah [deceased. C. R. 1.], Feb. 22, 1754.
Zacheriah, s. Josiah and Lidia, Oct. 6, 1777.
[torn], d. Josiah and Rememberans, Sept. [torn.] 3, 1677.

RICHARDSUN (see also Richardson), Benjamin, s. Thomas and Hanah, Mar. 30, 1696.

RICHARSON (see also Richardson), Remembrance, d. Josiah and Remembrance, Apr. 29, 1684.
———, d. Thomas and Hannah, Dec. 3, 1684.

RICHERDSON (see also Richardson), Elizibeth, d. John and Easter, Mar. 2, 1738.
Mary, d. Zachery and Sarah, Feb. 20, 1730-31.
Rebeckeh, d. Zacheriah and Sarah, Feb. 16, 1735.
Silas, s. John and Easter, Aug. 21, 1734.

RICHERSON (see also Richardson), Febee, d. James and Brigett, Jan. 10, 1669.
John, s. Josiah and Remembrance, Feb. 14, 1669.

RICHESON (see also Richardson), Ruth, d. James and Brigett, Feb. 16, 1671.
Samuell, s. Josiah and Remembrance, Feb. 21, 1672.
Thomas, s. James and Bridgit, Oct. 26, 1661.

RIDINGS, Alice Jenette, d. Peter, moulder, and Amelia, both b. Bolton, Eng., at North Chelmsford, Jan. 26, 1849.
Amelia Adeline, d. P. and A., Oct. 23, 1837.
Edward, s. Peter and Amelia, Nov. 28, 1840.

RIDINGS, Eliza Harriott, d. Peter and Amelia, Feb. 8, 1843.
Hannah, d. Peter and Amelia, Mar. 15, 1835.
Joseph Healy, s. Peter and Amelia, Oct. 27, 1838.
Maria J., d. Peter, moulder, and Amelia, at North Chelmsford, Oct. 19, 1847.
Ruth Ann, d. Peter, moulder, and Amelia, at North Chelmsford, Apr. 22, 1845.
William Henry, s. Peter and Amelia, June 15, 1833.

RIGHT (see also Wright), Thomas, s. John and Hanah, Sept. 27, 1707.

RIPLEY, Frederic K., s. Lewis, machinist, and Sophia, at North Chelmsford, June 18, 1846.

RITCHARDSON (see also Richardson), Elisabeth, d. James and Bridget, Sept. 27, 1665.
Elizebath, d. John and Elizebath, Mar. 12, 16[95. T. C.].
Esekell, s. James and Bridget, Sept. 3, 1667.
Jonathan, s. Josiah and Rememberanse, Oct. 8, 1667.
Josiah, s. Josiah and Rememberance, May 18, 1665.
Lidyah, d. Jonathan and Elizebeth, July 14, 170 [torn. 1702?].

RITCHARDSUN (see also Richardson), Zaceriah, s. Josiah and Mercy, Feb. —, 16[95-6. T. C.].

RITCHERDSON (see also Richardson), Dorothy, d. Beenjamen and Uness, Mar. 5, 1726-7.

RITCHESON (see also Richardson), James, s. Ja[mes and Bridget. T. C.], Nov. [24. T. C.; 1663. CT. R.].
Mare, d. Josiah and Remembrans, Apr. 14, 1662.
Sarah, d. Josiah and Rememberans, Mar. 25, 1659-60.

ROBBENS (see also Robbins), Ephraim, s. Jonas and Mary, Sept. 1, 1758.
Isaac, s. Jonathan and Elisabeth, Apr. 4, 1776.

ROBBINS (see also Robbens, Robens, Robines, Robins), Azubah, d. Jonas and Mary, Apr. 25, 1749.
Benjamin O., s. James, farmer, and Elzina, at Baptist Corner, May 31, 1837.
Betty, d. Jonathan and Elizabeth, bp. Feb. 27, 1774. C. R. 1.
Elesabeth, d. John and Dorothy, Aug. 29, 1700.
Elizabeth, d. John and Susanna, Mar. 7, 1740-41.
Ellenner, d. Jonas and Mary, Apr. 2, 1747.

ROBBINS, Elzina E., d. James, farmer, and Elzina, at Baptist Corner, Dec. 10, 1832.
Esther, d. Thomas and Sarah, July 16, 1723.
Hanah, d. Thomas and Sarah, Feb. 17, 1718.
Isaac, s. Jonathan and Elizabeth, bp. Feb. 2, 1772. c. r. 1.
James, s. James and Phena, Oct. 28, 1805.
James R., s. James, farmer, and Elzina, at Baptist Corner, Jan. 27, 1834.
Jane, d. Sam[ue]ll and Dorethy, Sept. 11, 1703.
John, s. Benjamin and Hanah, Sept. 15, 1727.
John, s. Jonas and Mary, Feb. 4, 1744-5.
John, s. John and Susanna, Mar. 28, 1748.
Jonas, s. Jonas and Mary, Jan. 26, 1740-41.
Jonathan, s. John and Susanna, June 21, 1750.
Luke, s. Jonathan and Elizabeth, bp. May 17, 1778. c. r. 1
Lydia, d. Jonas and Mary, July 3, 1751.
Martha Mori, d. James and Phena, Mar. 22, 1813.
Mary, d. Jonas and Mary, Oct. 22, 1742.
Mary Brown, d. James and Phena, Sept. 16, 1811.
Mercy, d. John and Susanna, Mar. 1, 1744-5. [bp. Feb. 11, 1744. c. r. 1.]
Nancy, d. James and Phena, Sept. 27, 1803.
Olive, d. John and Susanna, Nov. 25, 1745.
Phillip, s. Thomas and Sarrah, Feb. 24, 1724-5.
Sarah, d. John and Dorotha, Oct. 25, 1704.
Sarah, d. Benjamin and Hannah, Jan. 7, 1723-4.
Sarah, d. John and Sarah, Nov. 11, 1779.
Susan, d. Moses and Sarah, Apr. 2, 1810.
Zachariah, s. Benjamin and Hanah, July 6, 1720.
Zacheus Wright, s. James and Phena, Jan. 14, 1808.

ROBENS (see also Robbins), Sarah Ann, d. Moses and Sarah, Nov. 10, 1807.

ROBIE (see also Roby), Benjamin, s. John and Hannah, Nov. 9, 1715.
Hannah, d. John and Hannah, May 27, 1717.
Mary, d. John and Hannah, Feb. 22, 1719-20.
Samuel, s. John and Hannah, Jan. 9, 1713-14.
Sarai, d. John and Hanah, June 21, 1721.

ROBINES (see also Robbins), Philip, s. George and Mary, Jan. 29, 1670. [June 29. ct. r.]
Samuell, s. George, Jan. 2, 1679.

ROBINS (see also Robbins), Abegell, d. Samuell and Dorithy, July 19, 1708.
Benjamin, s. George and Alles, May 30, 1684.
Benjamin, s. Benjamin and Hanah, Mar. 8, 1708.
Elen, d. John and Dorithy, Dec. 17, 1707.
Eliazer, s. George and Allie [torn.] 12 [torn. 1682?].
John, s. John and Dorithy, Mar. 23, 1710.
John, s. John and Sarah, Oct. 4, 1777.
Jonas, s. John and Dorithy, July 3, 1714.
Jonathan, s. twin, George and Allis, Nov. 19, 1686.
Jonathan, s. twin, Benjamin and Hanah, Apr. 5, 1717.
Joseph, s. twin, George and Allis, Nov. 19, 1686.
Joseph, s. John and Dorithy, Sept. 20 [torn. 170-. T. C. 1702?].
Joseph, s. Benjamin and Hanah, Jan. 30, 1711.
Joseph, s. twin, Benjamin and Hanah, Apr. 5, 1717.
Joseph, s. Jonas and Mary, May 17, 1756.
Leah, d. Thomas and Lidia, Apr. 25, 1718.
Lidiah, d. Thomas and Lidiah, Jan. 23, 1715-16.
Luce, d. John and Dorithy, Feb. 22, 1712.
Lucy, d. Jonas and Mary, Oct. 9, 1753.
Marcy, d. John and Dorithy, Mar. 21, 1717-18.
Mary, d. Georg and Mary, Sept. 1, 1667.
Mary, d. Samuell and Dor[o]thy, Dec. 27, 1705.
Mary, d. Thomas and Sary, Feb. 16, 1720-21.
Rebeckah, d. Jonas and Mary, Sept. 27, 1760.
Sarah, d. Jonas and Mary, Jan. 30, 1738-9.
Sarah, d. John and Susanna, Mar. 19, 1753.
Sary, d. Thomas and Sary, Feb. 11, 1715-16.
Susanah, d. John and Susanah, Jan. 1, 1737-8.
Thankfull, d. Thomas and Lidiah, Apr. 21, 1714.
Thomas, s. George and Mary, Oct. 27, 1687. CT. R.
Thomas, s. Thomas and Sary, Feb. 12, 1715.
Thomas, s. Thomas and Sary, July 16, 1717.

ROBINSON, Anna, d. James, June 10, 1671. CT. R.
Elisebeth Ann, d. A., bp. Aug. 1, 1830. C. R. 3.

ROBY (see also Robie), Lydia, d. John and Esther, Apr. 1, 1772.

ROFE (see also Roff), Daniell, s. Daniell and Mary, Dec. 6, 1686.
[torn], ch. [Da]niell [torn], 1678.
[torn], ch. Daniell [torn. 1679-80?].

ROFF (see also Rofe), Rebekah, d. Danell and Marie, Oct. 4, 1692.

ROWE, Frank Anderson, s. Franklin, machinist, and Sylvia A., at Middlesex Village, June 18, 1846.
Luella Augusta, d. Franklin, machinist, and Sylvia, at North Chelmsford, Dec. 27, 1847.

SAMPSON, Alvah James, s. adopted, Seth P., mason, b. Fitchburg, and Rhoda, b. Ryegate, Vt., true son James C. and Abigail H. Taisey, at North Chelmsford, Oct. 30, 1849.
Leora Frances, d. Albert, stone-cutter, b. Braintree, and Leora, b. Tyngsborough, at North Chelmsford, Nov. 23, 1848.

SANBORN, George L., s. Leonard C., scythe maker, and Sarah E., at Worsted Factory, Oct. 13, 1844.
Hellen Frances, d. John M., machinist, and Fanny J., at North Chelmsford, Dec. 12, 1844.

SAVOY, Charles Henry, s. Joseph, farmer, b. Canada, and Sarah, b. Gloucestershire, Eng., at North Chelmsford, Oct. 8, 1848.
William, s. Joseph, machinist, and Sarah, at Factory Village, Oct. 4, 1846.

SAWIN, John, s. ———, bp. Aug. 1, 1830. C. R. 3.
Lucy A., d. ———, bp. Aug. 1, 1830. C. R. 3.

SAWTELL, Cynthia, d. Solomon and Olive, June 14, 1809.
Sherebiah Fletcher, s. Solomon and Olive, Apr. 23, 1811.

SAWYER, George Washington, s. Jerome, trader, and Adeline, at North Chelmsford, June 25, 1847.

SCAMMELL, Elmira Jane, d. Lisley and Elmira Jane, June 18, 1832.

SHAW, Elisha Hermon, s. Elisha, moulder, and Mercy M., at North Chelmsford, Sept. 29, 1847.
Emma Atwood, d. Elisha and Emily, Oct. 12, 1841.
Martha Maria, d. Elisha, moulder, and M. Maria, at North Chelmsford, Aug. 6, 1845.
Morgianna, d. Elisha, moulder, and Emily, at Furnace Village, June 21, 1843. [June 20. dup.]
———, s. Elisha, moulder, b. Middleborough, and Mercy Maria, b. Reading, at North Chelmsford, Sept. 5, 1849.

SHEAD (see also Shed), Ebenezer, s. Zachariah and Hannah, July 10, 1753.
Ebenezer, s. Ebenezer and Mary, Feb. 19, 1781.
Jonathan, s. Samuell and Elisabeth, Sept. 16, 1696.
Marie, d. Samewell and Elisabeth, Jan. 8, 1694-5.
Mary, d. Ebenezer and Mary, Feb. 12, 1783.
Sameuell, s. Sameuel and Elisabeth, June 30, 1690. [June 3. CT. R.]

SHED (see also Shead, Shedd, Sheed), Amos, s. Capt. John and Mary, Apr. 18, 1803.
George Maddison, s. Eben[eze]r and Lucy, Jan. 9, 1809.
John Spaulding, s. Capt. John and Mary, July 30, 1817.
Jonathan, s. Zachariah and Hannah, bp. June 27, 1756. C. R. 1.
Mary A. Byam, d. Amos and Mary, Aug. 8, 1842.
Mary Elizabeth, d. Capt. John and Mary, Apr. 29, 1808.
Samuel, s. Capt. John and Mary, Aug. 27, 1810.
Zachariah, s. Ebenezer and Mary, Feb. 17, 1785.
Zacheriah, s. Zacheriah and Hannah, bp. Dec. 28, 1746. C. R. 1.

SHEDD (see also Shed), Benjamin, s. Zachariah and Hanah, Aug. 25, 1724.
Hannah, d. Zachariah and Hannah, Aug. 20, 1744.
Lydia, d. Zachariah and Hannah, Dec. 10, 1750.
Noah, s. Zachariah and Hannah, June 12, 1748.
Zachariah, s. Zachariah and Hannah, Aug. 27, 1720.

SHEED (see also Shed), Franklin, s. Capt. Ebenezer and Lucy, May 25, 1800.
Lucy, d. Capt. Ebenezer and Lucy, Dec. 11, 1793.
Mary Blood, d. Capt. Ebenezer and Lucy, Oct. 4, 1795.
Sarah, d. Sam[ue]ll and Elesibeth, Oct. 28, 170[0. T. C.].
Susanna, d. Capt. Ebenezer and Lucy, Dec. 11, 1797.

SHERMAN, Samuel, s. Joseph, bp. Nov. 7, 1813. C. R. 1.
Thomas Thaxter, s. Joseph, bp. May 16, 1813. C. R. 1.

SHIPLEY (see also Shiply), John, s. John, bp. 1: 12 m: 1656, a. abt. 19 y. P. R. 1.
Lidia, d. John, bp. 1: 12 m: 1656, a. abt. 15 y. P. R. 1.
Nathaniel, s. John, bp. 1: 12 m: 1656, a. abt. 17 y. P. R. 1.

SHIPLY (see also Shipley), ——, d. John and Susanah, Mar. 15, 1682.

CHELMSFORD BIRTHS 139

SHORES, Emma Jane, d. Luther W., carpenter, and Clarissa, at North Chelmsford, Sept. 23, 1844.
Martha Ann, d. John, carpenter, and Anna, at North Chelmsford, Sept. 2, 1845.

SILVER, Abba Ann, d. Harvey and Abigail, Oct. 14, 1838.
Edward Harvey, s. Harvey, machinist, and Abby, at North Chelmsford, Nov. 12, 1847.
Ellen Maria, d. Hervy and Abigail, Sept. 16, 1840.
Mary Alvira, d. Hervy, machinist, and Abby, at Furnace Village, Sept. 14, 1843.

SIMONDS, Jonathan, s. Josiah and Mary, July 9, 1774.
Joseph Farwell, s. Abel and Elizabeth Lydia Thurston Farwell, Oct. 5, 1828.
Josiah, s. Josiah and Mary, Oct. 7, 1772.
Polle, d. Josiah and Mary, Aug. 27, 1776.
Rachell, d. Joseph and Rachell, July 6, 1714.
Sallee, d. Josiah and Mary, Sept. 18, 1778.
Sheppard, s. Josiah and Mary, Nov. 18, 1780.
Sukee, d. Josiah and Mary, Mar. 6, 1783.

SLICER, Mary Elizabeth, d. Alexander and Betsey E., Apr. 25, 1839.

SMALL, John, s. Simeon and Lydia, bp. Nov. 10, 1782. c. r. 1.
Samuel, s. Simeon and Lydia, bp. Nov. 10, 1782. c. r. 1.
Simeon, s. Simeon and Lydia, bp. Nov. 10, 1782. c. r. 1.
Tommas, s. Simeon and Lydia, bp. May 9, 1784. c. r. 1.

SMITH, Abigail, d. Jesse and Fanny [(Warren). p. r. 16.], Jan. 24, 1825.
Allen Griffin, s. Jacob B. and Mary A., Feb. 20, 1841.
Jesse, June 19, 1781. p. r. 16.
Jesse, s. Jesse and Francis [(Warren). p. r. 16.], Dec. 16, 1817.
John, s. Jesse and Francis, Jan. 5, 1819.
John Henry, s. Jesse and Fanny [(Warren). p. r. 16.], Jan. 5, 1819.
Joseph Warren, s. Jesse and Francis [(Warren). p. r. 16.], Jan. 11, 1821.
Mary Woodberry, d. Jesse and Francis [(Warren). p. r. 16.], Oct. 23, 1816.
Mathew Adams, s. Jacob Burnam, laborer, and Mary Ann, July 8, 1843.

SMITH, Porter Judson, s. John C., machinist, b. Pelham, N. H., and Mary, b. Canton, at North Chelmsford, Sept. 22, 1848.
Rebecca, d. Jesse and Fanny [(Warren). P. R. 16.], Jan. 22, 1823.
Rebecca Frances, d. Jesse and Fanny [(Warren). P. R. 16.], May 10, 1827.

SNOW, Elesabeth, d. John and Sarah, Oct. 6 [torn. 1701?].
Hannah, d. John and Sarah, Jan. 20, 1704.
Hannah, d. Jonathan and Esther, Mar. 19, 1742-3.
James, s. Joshua and Lowis, June 15, 1773.
Jonathan, s. John and Sary, Sept. 2, 1711.
Jonathan, s. Jonathan and Easter, Mar. 4, 1730-31.
Jonathan, s. Joshua and Lois, May 16, 1762.
Jonathan, s. Jonathan and Sarah, Aug. 31, 1786.
Joshua, s. Jonathan and Easter, July 12, 1738.
Levy, s. Joshua and Loes, July 9, 1766.
Loes, d. Joshua and Loes, Feb. 5, 1771.
Lucy, d. Jonathan and Easther, July 14, 1745.
Lucy, d. Jonathan and Sarah, Mar. 31, 1795.
Nancey, d. Lt. Jonathan and Sarah, May 9, 1797.
Parker, s. Jonathan and Sarah, Nov. 7, 1792.
Parker, s. Lt. Jonathan and Sarah, Jan. 6, 1800.
Polly, d. Jonathan and Sarah, Apr. 4, 1791.
Samuel, s. Jonathan and Easter, Apr. 15, 1736.
Sarah, d. twin, Joshua and Lois, Jan. 5, 1764.
Sarai, d. Jonathan and Esther, Feb. 9, 1740-41.
Thankful, d. twin, Joshua and Lois, Jan. 5, 1764.
Thomas, s. Daniel and Mary, Feb. 16, 1730-31.
William, s. Jonathan and Easther, Aug. 12, 1733.

SPALDEN (see also Spaulding), Dorete, d. Edward and Pricillah, Apr. 3, 1664.
Ebeneser, s. Edward and Margreat, Jan. 13, 1683.
Edward, s. John and Hanah, Sept. 16, 1663.
Hanah, d. John and Hanah, Apr. 28, 1666.
Jonathan, s. John and Anna, Aug. 7, 1688. CT. R.
Joseph, s. Joseph [torn. 1672?].
Josiah, s. Edw[ar]d and Mary, Jan. 13, 1686. CT. R.
Nathaniel, s. Joseph and Mercy, Feb. 24, 1687. CT. R.
[torn. Unis. CT. R.], d. John and Hanah, July [torn], 1661. [July 27. CT. R.]
William, s. Andrew and Hannah, Aug. 3, 1688. CT. R.

SPALDIN (see also Spaulding), Benjamin, s. Benjamin and Olive, July 6, 1685.

CHELMSFORD BIRTHS 141

SPALDIN, Benjamin, s. Edward and Mery, July 20, 1696.
Benoni, s. Edward [torn. 1679-80?].
Edward, s. Edward and Mary, 3: 12 m: 1684.
Jonathan, s. John and Mary, Nov. 11, 1705.
Mary, d. Joseph and Mary, Jan. 29, 1706.
Rachell, d. Andrew and Hannah, Sept. 26, 1685.
Samuell, s. John and Anne, Aug 5., 1686.
Unis, d. Joseph and Mercy, Feb. 14, 1685.

SPALDING (see also Spaulding), Abel, s. Dea. John and Lucy, Oct. 28, 1797.
Adaline Augusta, d. John, bp. June 16, 1823. C. R. 1.
Alpheus, s. Lt. Alpheus and Patty, Mar. 31, 1816.
Ana, d. Joseph, Oct. 20, 1708.
Andrew, s. Edward, bp. 1: 12 m: 1656, a. 4 y. 19: 9 m: 1656. P. R. 1.
Ann Augusta, d. Capt. [Lt. C. R. 1.] Sherebiah and Releaf, Dec. 29, 1818.
Ann P., d. Capt. Sherebeah and Releaf, Mar. 23, 1812.
Asaph Fletcher, s. Ira and Joanna, May 2, 1804.
Augustus Edwards, s. Otis and Elizabeth, June 23, 1818.
Benjamin, s. Edward, bp. 1: 12 m: 1656, a. 14 y. 4: 2 m: 1656. P. R. 1.
Benjamin, s. Henry, 3d and Jemime, June 7, 1818.
Betsy A[nn. C. R. 1.], d. Henry, 3d and Jemima, Dec. 19, 1808.
Charles Barbour, s. Jonathan and Mary Ann, Oct. 21, 1832.
Cintha, d. Lt. Alpheus and Patty, Jan. 9, 1820.
Deborah, d. John and Hanna, 12: 9 m: 1670.
Dinah, d. Edward, bp. 1: 12 m: 1656, a. 7 y. 14: 1 m: 1656. P. R. 1.
Edward, s. Edward, bp. 1: 12 m: 1656, a. abt. 21 y. P. R. 1.
Edward, s. Benjamin and Olive, June 18, 1672.
Edward, s. Simeon, 2d and Rhoda, Mar. 27, 1821.
Elbridge Gerry, s. Lt. Sherebiah and Relief, Feb. 9, 1811.
Elbridge P., s. Capt. [Lt. C. R. 1.] Sherebiah and Rileaf, Apr. 24, 1814.
Elisabeth, d. Benjamin and Olive, Mar. 22, 1680.
Ellen A[delaide. P. R. 18.], d. Isaiah Byam, wheelwright, and Mary A[nn (Richardson). P. R. 18.], at Baptist Village, Oct. 17, 1846. [1847. P. R. 18.]
Ellen Lucinda, d. Jonathan, farmer, and Mary Ann, May 21, 1842.
Ephraim, s. Ephraim and Lidia, Dec. 14, 1809.
Ephraim P[arkhurst. C. R. 1.], s. Henry, 3d and Jemima, Nov. 23, 1813.
Esther, d. Timothy and Rebeckah, Dec. 8, 1705.

SPALDING, Francis, s. Simeon, 2d and Rhoda B., Mar. 26, 1824.
George Augustus, s. Varnum, farmer, and Susan, at Mill Row, Mar. 27, 1848.
George Ephraim, s. Jonathan, farmer, and Mary Ann, Aug. 31, 1844.
Hanah, d. John and Mary, Feb. 7, 1709.
Hannah, d. John and Ane, Aug. 25, 1684.
Hannah A[dams. C. R. 1.], d. Andrew and Ruth, Oct. 8, 1799. P. R. 23.
Harriet, d. Henry, jr. and Lidia, June 28, 1804.
Henry, s. Henry, jr. and Lidia, Oct. 18, 1806.
Henry, s. Ephraim P. and Nancy B., Sept. 6, 1836.
Henry Clay, s. Varnum, farmer, and Susan, at Mill Row, Jan. 9, 1844.
Jacob, s. Edward and Mary, May 14, 1696.
Jeptha, s. Zebulon, jr. and Molly, May 30, 1791.
Joel, s. Henry, 3d and Jemima, Feb. 2, 1816.
Johanna, d. Andrue and Hana, Oct. 8, 1689-90.
John, s. Edward, bp. 1 : 12 m : 1656, a. abt. 23 y. P. R. 1.
John, s. John and Hanah, 15 : 12 m : 1659.
John Barker, s. Eph[rai]m P. and Nancy B., Sept. 11, 1841.
Joseph, s. Edward, bp. 1 : 12 m : 1656, a. 10 y. 25 : 8 m : 1656. P. R. 1.
Josiah, s. Andrew, Jan. 3, 1706.
Julia Anne, d. Noah and Nancy, bp. June 27, 1802. C. R. 1.
Julia Maria, d. Abel, farmer, and Harriott, at Mill Row, Sept. 6, 1847.
Lidia, d. Henry, jr. and Lidia, Jan. 26, 1792.
Louisa Augusta, d. Sherebiah, farmer, and Lurena Augusta, at Mill Row, July 4, 1844.
Lowisa, d. Lt. Sherebiah and Releif, Dec. 11, 1805.
Lucinda, d. Ephraim P. and Nancy B., Apr. 18, 1839.
Lucretia, d. Isaiah and Martha (Byam), Sept. 10, 1815. P. R. 19.
Lucy Abigal, d. Otis and Elizabeth, July 2, 1820.
Lydia, d. Ephraim and Lydia, Oct. 23, 1811.
Lydia Ann, d. Jona[than] and Mary Ann, Dec. 22, 1834.
Lydia Wright, d. Lt. Sherebiah and Relief, Sept. 27, 1807.
Marah, d. Jessy and Elizabeth, Oct. 10, 1808.
Marcus Morton, s. Sherebiah, jr. and Lurena A., Sept. 26, 1841.
Marcus Morton, s. twin, Sherebiah, jr., farmer, and Lurena A., at Mill Row, May 21, 1847.
Martha Ellen, d. Varnum, farmer, and Susan Augusta, at Mill Row, Jan. 10, 1846.

SPALDING, Mary, d. Zebulon, jr. and Molly, Apr. 22, 1796.
Mary, d. Lt. Sherebiah and Releif, Oct. 12, 1803.
Mary, d. Henry, 3d and Jemima, Jan. 24, 1812.
Mary Elizabeth, d. Otis and Elizabeth, bp. Sept. 4, 1826. C. R. 1.
Mary Parker, d. Jonathan and Mary Ann, Dec. 3, 1839.
Morton Marcus, s. twin, Sherebiah, jr., farmer, and Lurena A., at Mill Row, May 21, 1847.
Nathaniel Hutchenson, s. Dea. John and Mary, July 11, 1805.
Owen, s. Zebulon, jr. and Molly, May 21, 1798.
Patty, d. Lt. Alpheus and Patty, Oct. 5, 1817.
Patty Elvira, d. Isaiah and Martha (Byam), Mar. 24, 1814. P. R. 19.
Permilia, d. Ira and Joanna, Feb. 26, 1810.
Phebe, d. Andrew and Ruth, Nov. 3, 1797. P. R. 23.
Philip Parker, s. Noah and Nancy, bp. June 23, 1805. C. R. 1.
Phinias, s. Edward and Lidiah, Apr. 3, 1706.
Relief, d. Sherebiah and Relief, bp. June 27, 1819. C. R. 1.
Rhoda, d. Henry, 3d and Jemima, Jan. 24, 1810.
Sarrah, d. Benjamin and Olive, Jan. 4, 1669.
Sherebiah, s. Lt. Sherebiah and Relief, July 21, 1809.
Thomas Jefferson, s. Zebulon, jr. and Molly, Sept. 18, 1801.
Varnum, s. Dea. John and Mary, Apr. 16, 1808.
William Milton, s. Sherebiah and Relief, Aug. 26, 1820.
William Plinney, s. Noah, 2d and Hannah, Nov. 1, 1823.
William Wallace, s. Sherebiah, 2d and Lurena Augusta, May 4, 1839.
——, s. Varnum, farmer, and Susan A., b. Stoddard, N. H., Sept. 8, 1849.

SPALDYNG (see also Spaulding), Deborah, d. Edward and Prisilah, Sept. 12, 1667.
Samuell, s. John and Hanah, Mar. 6, 1668.

SPARKS, Abiell, d. Henry and Martha, ——. [1686.]
Deliveranc, s. Henery and Martha, Mar. 8, 1690.

SPAULDEN (see also Spaulding), Leonard, s. Timo[thy], jr., bp. Nov. 3, 1728. C. R. 4.

SPAULDIN (see also Spaulding), Ezekiell, s. Edward and Mary, Sept. 8, 1706.
James, s. Andrew and Abigill, Oct. 27, 1714.
Job, s. John and Mary, Oct. 19, 1714.
Josaph, s. Josaph and Mary, Apr. 16, 1697.

SPAULDINE (see also Spaulding), Edward, s. Edward and Prisilah, Aug. 18, 1674.

SPAULDING (see also Spalden, Spaldin, Spalding, Spaldyng, Spaulden, Spauldin, Spauldine, Spauldinge, Spauldyng, Spolding), Aaron, s. Jonathan [jr. P. R. 4.] and Mary, Jan. 23, 1764.
Abel, s. Simion and Sarah, Sept. 2, 1737.
Abel, s. Abel and Mary, June 19, 1768.
Abel, s. Benjamin and Patty, bp. Nov. 23, 1777. C. R. 1.
Abigail, d. Jacob and Susannah, Aug. 31, 1735.
Abigail, d. Henry and Marah, bp. June 28, 1752. C. R. 1.
Abigail, d. twin, Simeon and Abigail, Mar. 15, 1759.
Abigail, d. Joseph and Abigail, Nov. 12, 1788.
Abigail, d. Azariah and Lucey, Jan. 11, 1789.
Abigail, d. Alpheus and Patty, Sept. 8, 1825.
Abigal, d. David and Phebe, Feb. 25, 1757.
Abigall, d. twin, Andrew and Abagall, July 8, 1712.
Abijah, s. Lt. John and Rachil, Nov. 12, 1759.
Abraham Andreas [Andrews. C. R. 1.], s. Joseph, Aug. 8, **1793**.
Almira Augusta, d. Robert and Joanna, Mar. 4, 1827.
Alpheus, s. Joseph and Abigail, Sept. 30, 1791.
Amos, s. Thomas and Mary, Dec. 17, 1750.
Amos, s. John, 3d and Lucy, Dec. 28, 1789.
Andrew, s. Andrew and Hannah, Mar. 25, 1678.
Andrew, s. Andrew and Hannah, Jan. 6, 1728-9.
Andrew, s. David and Phebe, Feb. 10, 1761.
Anna, d. Ebenezer and Anna, Nov. 30, 1731.
Anna, d. Lt. John and Phebe, Nov. 17, 1745.
Anna, d. Robert and Hasadiah, June 28, 1771.
Anna, d. John and Joanna, of Limerick [now Stoddard. P. R. 4.], bp. Nov. 29, 1778. C. R. 1.
Anna, d. Zebulun and Lidia, June 20, 1782.
Anna, d. Andrew and Ruth, July 10, 1785.
Anna, d. Ira and Joanna, Mar. 29, 1807.
Artemas, s. twin, Robert and Asadiah, Feb. 18, 1759.
Asa, s. Henry and Mary, June 15, 1794.
Ashbel, s. Stephen and Easter, Apr. 27, 1763.
Asher, s. Robart and Hasadiah, June 22, 1765.
Augustus Herbert, s. Eri and Almira, May 11, 1836.
Azariah, s. Simeon and Abigail, Feb. 2, 1757.
Benjamin, s. Andrew and Abigail, Jan. 7, 1719-20.
Benjamin, s. Lenord and Elizebath, Feb. 5, 1738-9.
Benjamin, s. Jacob and Susanna, Jan. 6, 1740-41.
Benjamin, s. Jonathan and Mary, Aug. 26, 1756.
Benjamin, s. Henry and Marah, bp. July 17, 1757. C. R. 1.

SPAULDING, Benjamin, s. Benjamin and Mary, Aug. 20, 1765.
Benjamin, s. Benjamin and Patty, late of Ashby, bp. Aug. 2, 1772. C. R. 1.
Benjamin, s. Dea. John and Lucy, May 22, 1795.
Benjamin, s. Ira and Joanna, Dec. 21, 1799.
Bennony, s. Andrew and Hannah, Feb. 6, 1691. [1690. CT. R.]
Bettey, d. Jonathan, 3d and Mary, Jan. 4, 1770.
Betty, d. Lt. John and Phebe, Apr. 16, 1744.
Betty, d. Henery, jr. and Mary, Mar. 28, 1779.
Bridget, d. Ebenezer and Anna, Dec. 25, 1709.
Bridget, d. Timothy and Rebe[cc]ah, Nov. 12, 1718.
Bridget, d. David and Phebe, Mar. 11, 1748-9. [Aug. 20, 1748. P. R. 23.]
Charles, s. Ira and Joanna, Jan. 8, 1803.
Claricy, d. Henry and Jemime, Feb. 28, 1802.
Daniel, s. Cornet Henry and Marah, June 21, 1746.
Daniel, s. Daniel and Hannah [now of Merrimack. P. R. 4.], bp. Feb. 25, 1770. C. R. 1.
David, s. Andrew and Abigail, Sept. 28, 1717.
David, s. David and Phebe, May 19, 1755.
David, s. David and Phebe, Feb. 25, 1757. P. R. 23.
David, s. Andrew and Ruth, Jan. 15, 1796.
Deborah, d. Timothy and Rebecah, Nov. 29, 1707.
Deborah, d. David and Phebe, Jan. 17, 1739.
Dinah, d. John and Ana, Jan. 29, 1693.
Dolly, d. Zebulon, jr. and Lydia, Oct. 12, 1777.
Easter, d. Thomas and Mary, Dec. 5, 1734.
Ebenezer, s. Joseph and Mary, "about the beginning of July," 1701.
Edward, s. Ebenezer and Hana, Mar. 8, 1707-8.
Eleazer, s. Henery and Elizabeth, May 29, 1717.
Eli, s. Peter and Lucy, Mar. 25, 1771.
Eliazer, s. Jacob and Susana, Nov. 12, 1728.
Elijah, s. Henery, jr. and Mary, Sept. 29, 1783.
Elizabath, d. Jesse and Elizabath, Apr. 7, 1796.
Elizabeth, d. Thomas and Mary, Jan. 29, 1731-2.
Elizabeth, d. Leonard and Elizabeth, Dec. 29, 1740.
Elizabeth, d. Henry and Susanna, Aug. 24, 1750.
Elizabeth, d. Benjamin and Patty, late of Ashby, bp. Aug. 2, 1772. C. R. 1.
Ephraim, s. Edward and Mary, Apr. 3, 17[torn. 1701?].
Ephraim, s. Andrew and Abagill, Aug. 8, 1708.
Ephraim, s. Jona[than] and Mary, Nov. 13, 1762.
Ephraim, s. Jonathan, 3d and Mary, Feb. 6, 1766.
Esther, d. Ebenezer and Ana, Feb. 22, 1721-2.
Esther, d. Zebulun and Mary, Apr. 7, 177[faded.].

146   CHELMSFORD BIRTHS

SPAULDING, Esther, d. Benjamin and Mary, Jan. 28, 1790.
Experience, d. Ebenezer and Anna, Mar. 22, 1711.
Gedeon, s. Edward and Lidya, June 12, 1724.
George, s. Alpheus and Patty, Sept. 25, 1830.
George Washington, s. Robert and Joanna, Apr. 12, 1825.
Hannah, d. Thomas and Mary, Oct. 31, 1745.
Hannah, d. John, jr. and Hannah, Aug. 15, 1766.
Hariot Rebecca, d. Joanna, bp. [after Oct. 5, 1828.] C. R. 3.
Harriot Elisibeth, d. Isaiah and Martha (Byam), July 5, 1826. P. R. 19.
Hasadia, d. Robart and Hasadiah, May 22, 1763.
Haskel, s. Simeon and Olive, Jan. 28, 1788.
Hellen Faustina, d. Sherebiah, jr. and Lurena Augusta, July 23, 1837.
Henry, s. Andrew and Hannah, Nov. 2, 1680.
Henry, s. Henry and Mary, Mar. 24, 1729-30.
Henry, s. Henry and Susannah, Jan. 15, 1753.
Henry, s. John and Hannah, May 25, 1764.
Henry, s. Zebulun and Lydia, Oct. 10, 1772.
Henry, s. Henery, jr. and Mary, Nov. 20, 1776.
Henry, s. Henry, 3d and Jemima, June 25, 1805.
Hosea, s. Henry and Mary, Sept. 20, 1798.
Ira, s. Benjamin and Mary, June 17, 1773.
Ira, s. Ira and Joanna, May 17, 1801.
Isaac, s. Andrew and Abagill, Oct. 28, 1710.
Isaack, s. Edward and Marai, Sept. 27, 1693.
Isaiah, s. Edward and Lidiah, Dec. 1, 1709.
Isaiah, s. Henry and Mary, Aug. 15, 1792.
Isaiah Byam, s. Isaiah and Patty (Byam), Apr. 20, 1818. P. R. 18.
Jacob, s. Jacob and Susanah, May 3, 1727.
Jacob, s. Benjamin and Mary, Dec. 13, 1767.
James, s. John and Lucy, June 10, 1793.
Jemime, d. Benja[min] and Mary, Aug. 11, 1778.
Jephthah, s. Simeon and Abigail, Nov. 10, 1754.
Jeremiah, s. Benjamin and Mary, July 30, 1775.
Jerusha, d. Jacob and Elizebeth, Dec. 18, 1757.
Jesse, s. Jacob and Susanna, Sept. 14, 1747.
Jesse, s. Job and Lydia, Dec. 30, 1748.
Jesse, s. Lt. John and Rachel, Mar. 12, 1763.
Jesse, s. Jesse and Elizbath, Mar. 30, 1799.
Joanna, d. Ephraim and Lidia, Oct. 4, 1737.
Joanna, d. Simeon and Sarah, Aug. 4, 1744.
Job, s. Job and Lidya, May 1, 1737.
Joel, s. Simeon and Sarah, Mar. 12, 1742-3.
Joel, s. Henry and Mary, June 23, 1796.

CHELMSFORD BIRTHS 147

SPAULDING, Johanah, d. twin, Andrew and Abagall, July 8, 1712.
Johannah, d. Andrew and Hannah, Oct. 8, 1689.
Johannah, d. Jacob and Suasanna, Mar. 29, 1739.
John, s. Andrew and Hannah, Aug. 20, 1682.
John, s. Joseph and Elizabeth, June 12, 1704.
John, s. John and Mary, Feb. 7, 1724-5.
John, s. Lt. John and Phebe, July 18, 1747.
John, s. John and Hannah, June 8, 1762.
John, s. John, 3d and Lucy, July 20, 1786.
John, s. Micah and Mary, bp. Dec. 30, 1787. C. R. 1.
John, s. Jesse and Elizabath, Aug. 16, 1793.
John Varnum, s. Joanna, bp. [after Oct. 5, 1828.] C. R. 3.
Jonas, s. John and Phebe, Feb. 29, 1735-6.
Jonas, s. Job and Lydia, Mar. 31, 1751.
Jonas, s. Job and Lydia, Jan. 1, 1756.
Jonas, s. twin, Robert and Asadiah, Feb. 19, 1759.
Jonathan, s. Jonathan and Sarah, Jan. 13, 1733.
Jonathan, s. Ep[h]raim and Lidy, Apr. 17, 1734.
Jonathan, s. Jacob and Elizebeth, Dec. 20, 1753.
Jonathan, s. Daniel and Hannah, now of Merrimack, bp. Nov. 24, 1771. C. R. 1.
Jonathan, s. Ephraim and Lidia, Sept. 22, 1806.
Joseph, s. John and Hanah, Oct. 22, 1673.
Joseph, s. John and Phebe, Nov. 23, 1728.
Joseph, s. Jacob and Susanah, May 1, 1737.
Joseph, s. Job and Lydia, Oct. 22, 1739.
Joseph, s. Robert and Hesediah, Apr. 18, 1756.
Joseph, s. Jonathan and Mary, Dec. 26, 1757.
Joseph, s. Joseph and Abigail, June 17, 1784.
Joseph Osgood, s. Alpheus and Patty, Oct. 1, 1827.
Josiah, s. Timothy and Rebecah, Sept. 26, 1712.
Lenord, s. Henery and Elizabeth, Dec. 1, 1713.
Leonard, s. Benjamin and Patty, late of Ashby, bp. Aug. 2, 1772. C. R. 1.
Levi, s. Jonathan and Sarah, June 9, 1739.
Levina, d. Robert and Hasadiah, June 10, 1768.
Levy, s. Stephen and Esther, July 5, 1767.
Lidia, d. Jonathan and Mary, Aug. 14, 1778.
Lidiah, d. Joseph and Mary, July 1, 1708.
Lidiah, d. Edward and Lidiah, Nov. 7, 1718.
Lot, s. John and Lidia, Sept. 24, 1737.
Lucanda [Lucinda. C. R. 1.], d. Henry, 3d and Jemima, May 22, 1803.
Lucy, d. Peter and Lucy, Mar. 13, 1764.
Lucy, d. John, 3d and Lucy, July 8, 1788.

CHELMSFORD BIRTHS

SPAULDING, Lucy, d. Jesse and Elisabeth, Sept. 25, 1802.
Lucy Ann, d. Robert and Joanna, Sept. 10, 1821.
Luse, d. Timothy and Rebeca, Apr. 27, 1716.
Luse, d. Job and Lydia, Jan. 14, 1761.
Lydia, d. Ephraim and Lydia, Nov. 22, 1731.
Lydia, d. Job and Lydia, Mar. 22, 1741-2.
Lydia, d. Robart and Hasadia, Mar. 3, 1761.
Lydia, d. Zebulun and Lydia, Jan. 31, 1768.
Lydia, d. Ephraim and Lydia, Sept. 4, 1808.
Maria Sheldon, d. Isaiah Byam and Mary Ann (Richardson), Dec. 14, 1848. P. R. 18.
Marie, d. Josiph and Marcy [Mary. CT. R.], Feb. 27, 1691-2. [Feb. 23. CT. R.]
Martha, d. Micah and Mary, Jan. 31, 1790.
Martha Maria, d. Robert and Joanna, Apr. 27, 1823.
Mary, d. Edward and Mary, July 23 [1695. T. C.].
Mary, d. Andrew and Hanah, Dec. 5, 169[5. T. C.].
Mary, d. John and Mary, Jan. 19, 1708.
Mary, d. John and Mary, Apr. 7, 1722.
Mary, d. Ebenezer and Anna, May 4, 1724.
Mary, d. Henry and Mary, June 15, 1724.
Mary, d. Thomas and Mary, Apr. 5, 1733.
Mary, d. Henry and Mary, Oct. 14, 1739.
Mary, d. Job and Lydia, Aug. 26, 1744.
Mary, d. Cornet Henry and Marah, Feb. 10, 1748-9.
Mary, d. Jonathan and Mary, bp. Dec. 29, 1754. C. R. 1.
Mary, d. Jonathan and Mary, Mar. 10, 1768.
Mary, d. Benjamin and Mary, July 5, 1769.
Mary, d. John and Hannah, Mar. 16, 1772.
Mary, d. Zebulun, jr. and Lydia, May 22, 1774.
Mary, d. Zebulun and Mary, Sept. [torn. 1774?].
Mary, d. Henry and Mary, bp. Mar. 19, 1775. C. R. 1.
Mary, d. Ira and Joanna, Sept. 8, 1798.
Mary Elizabeth, d. Capt. Otis and Elizabeth, May 10, 1823.
Matathias, s. twin, Micah and Mary, May 14, 1796.
Mattathias, s. Cornet Simeon and Abigal, June 25, 1769.
Micah, s. Simeon and Abigal, Nov. 6, 1752.
Micah, s. Micah and Mary, bp. Apr. 11, 1779. C. R. 1.
Molle, d. Job and Lydia, Nov. 3, 1746.
Nabby, d. Andrew and Ruth, Dec. 2, 1788.
Nabby Adams, d. Jesse and Elizbath, Sept. 7, 1797.
Noah, s. Simeon and Abigail, Feb. 4, 1771.
Noah, s. twin, Micah and Mary, May 14, 1796.
Olever, s. Timothy and Rebeckah, Apr. 21, 1710.
Olive, d. John and Phebe, May 15, 1742.
Olive, d. Jacob and Susanna, Aug. 13, 1745.

CHELMSFORD BIRTHS 149

Spaulding, Olive, d. Jonathan and Sarah, Sept. 18, 1747.
Olive, d. Zebulun, jr. and Lydia, Jan. 6, 1776.
Olive, d. Zebulun and Lidia, July 31, 1780.
Oliver, s. Jonathan and Sarah, Apr. 27, 1736.
Oliver, s. John, jr. and Hannah, Dec. 29, 1768.
Oliver, s. Jeptha and Rebeckah, July 27, 1783.
Orpha, d. Simeon and Olive, Sept. 12, 1785.
Otis, s. Azariah and Lucy, May 16, 1793.
Parker, s. Jesse and Elizabeth, Dec. 6, 1800.
Patte, d. Stephen and Esther, Oct. 15, 1775.
Patty, d. Benjamin and Patty, late of Ashby, bp. Aug. 2, 1772. c. r. 1.
Persis, d. Jacob and Elizebeth, Dec. 16, 1755.
Peter, s. John and Pheebe, May 26, 1734.
Phebe, d. Edward and Liddia, Aug. 13, 1721.
Phebe, d. John and Phebe, Oct. 21, 1737.
Phebe, d. David and Phebe, July 12, 1746. [July 10. p. r. 23.]
Phebe, d. Peter and Lucy, July 3, 1775.
Philip, s. David and Phebe, Mar. 31, 1743.
Philip, s. Simeon and Abigail, June 4, 1762.
Phinehus Wright, s. Zebulun and Lidia, Jan. 13, 1784.
Polle, d. Micah and Mary, July 22, 1780.
Polly, d. Andrew and Ruth, Apr. 20, 1792.
Prescott, s. Jeptha and Rebeckah, Jan. 23, 1780.
Priscila, d. Edward and Lidah, Jan. 24, 1713.
Rachel, d. Jacob and Susana, June 22, 1732.
Rachel, d. Leonard and Eliza[be]th, bp. Nov. 14, 1742. c. r. 1.
Rachel, d. Jonathan and Sarah, bp. May 6, 1744. c. r. 1.
Rachel, d. Jesse and Elisabeth, Jan. 11, 1807.
Rachell, d. Joseph and Mary, Sept. 9, 1710.
Rachil, d. Jonathan and Sarah, May 15, 1745.
Ratchel, d. Andrew and Hannah, Sept. 25, 1686.
Rebecca, d. Cornet Simeon and Abigal, May 11, 1764.
Rebecca, d. Benjamin and Patty, late of Ashby, bp. Aug. 2, 1772. c. r. 1.
Rebecka, d. John and Phebe, Feb. 12, 1739-40.
Rebeckah, d. Henry and Mary, June 29, 1790.
Rebeckah, d. Jesse and Elizabath, Oct. 3, 1794.
Rewben, s. Ebenezer and Anna, July 26, 1728.
Robert, s. John and Phebe, Jan. 28, 1729-30.
Robert, s. David and Phebe, Mar. 12, 1740-41.
Robert, s. David and Phebe, Nov. 29, 1750.
Robert, s. Robert and Hesediah, July 28, 1757.
Ruben, s. Ebenezer and Anna, Mar. 27, 1715.
Rufus, s. Micah and Mary, July 29, 1794.
Ruth, d. John and Pheebe, Aug. 28, 1732.

SPAULDING, Ruth, d. Andrew and Ruth, May 26, 1794.
Sally, d. Benja[min] and Mary, Jan. 31, 1783.
Sally, d. Jesse and Elisabeth, Mar. 24, 1805.
Sally, d. Ira and Joanna, Mar. 6, 1806.
Sampson, s. John and Hannah, Mar. 1, 1775.
Samson, s. John and Mary, June 7, 1711.
Samuel, s. Henry and Lucy, Jan. 31, 1726-7.
Samuel, s. Jonathan and Sarah, Mar. 3, 1736-7.
Sarah, d. Edward and Presila [torn. 1671?].
Sarah, d. Ebenezer and Anna, Nov. 27, 1719.
Sarah, d. Henery and Lucy, June 10, 1734.
Sarah, d. Henery and Mary, Feb. 6, 1734-5.
Sarah, d. Simeon and Sarah, Nov. 22, 1739.
Sarah, d. Job and Lydia, Apr. 8, 1753.
Sarah, d. David and Phebe, Aug. 6, 1759.
Sarah, d. Zebulun and Lydia, June 25, 1771.
Sarah, d. Jonathan and Mary, July 27, 1776.
Sarah, d. Henry, 3d and Mary, Sept. 3, 1786.
Sary, d. Andrew and Abigail, June 9, 1723.
Sebal, d. Jacob and Susannah, Jan. 19, 1742-3.
Sedney, s. Micah and Mary, Nov. 14, 1798.
Sephrona, d. Ira and Joanna, Apr. 20, 1797.
Sewel, s. Jesse and Elisabeth, Mar 7, 1804.
Sherebiah, s. Zebulun, jr. and Lidia, Feb. 4, 1779.
Sibble, d. Henry and Mary, July 9, 1788.
Sibel, d. David and Phebe, Aug. 10, 1753.
Sibyll, d. Ephraim and Lydia, Jan. 31, 1739.
Silas, s. Jonathan and Sarah, Nov. 5, 1741. [Nov. 4. dup.]
Silas, s. Simeon and Sarah, Oct. 30, 1746.
Simeon, s. twin, Simeon and Abigail, Mar. 15, 1759.
Simeon, s. Micah and Mary, Dec. 9, 1785.
Simon, s. Joseph and Elizab[e]th, Aug. 4, 1713.
Simon, s. Jonathan and Mary, Feb. 4, 1772.
Solomon Henry, s. Isaiah and Martha (Byam), Mar. 4, 1836.
    P. R. 19.
Sophia, d. Micah and Mary, June 22, 1792.
Stephen, s. Ebenezer and Hanah, May 28, 1717.
Stephen, s. John and Phebe, Apr. 20, 1731.
Stephen, s. Stephen and Esther, Aug. 12, 1772.
Stephen Hodgman, s. Joseph and Abigail, Aug. 4, 1786.
Supply, s. Abel and Mary, Sept. 16, 1773.
Susana, d. Jacob and Susana, Sept. 22, 1730.
Susanah, d. Joseph and Mary, Sept. 12 [1695. T. C.].
Susanna, d. Benja[min] and Mary, Mar. 8, 1781.
Sybbel, d. Jonathan and Mary, May 8, 1780.
Sybill, d. Thomas and Mary, Feb. 14, 1748-9.

CHELMSFORD BIRTHS

SPAULDING, Thankful, d. Leonard and Elizabeth, bp. Oct. 21, 1744. C. R. 1.
Thankfull, d. Timothy and Rebeckah, Mar. 19, 1720-21.
Thankfull, d. Henry and Mary [Marah. C. R. 1.], Dec. 3, 1761.
Thomas, s. Henery and Elizabeth, July 30, 1707.
Thomas, s. Thomas and Mary, Aug. 28, 1737.
Thomas, s. Cornet Henry and Marah, Nov. 24, 1750.
Thomas, s. Zebulun and Mary, Dec. 27, 1775.
Timothy, s. Timothy and Rebecka, Dec. 18, 1700.
Timothy, s. Abel and Mary, Sept. 1, 1778.
Timothy, s. Azariah and Lucy, Aug. 17, 1786. [bp. Aug. 21, 1785. C. R. 1.]
Tryphena, d. Isaiah and Martha (Byam), Feb. 7, 1821. P. R. 19.
Willam, s. Henry and Elizabet[h], Mar. 17, 1711.
Willard, s. Lt. John and Phebe, July 10, 1750.
William, s. John and Ann, Nov. 14, 169[5. T. C.].
William, s. Edward and Lidya, Feb. 28, 17[00. T. C.].
William, s. Lt. Jonathan and Mary, Sept. 30, 1759.
William, s. Micah and Mary, July 22, 1782.
William, s. Samuel and Lefe, June 19, 1795.
William Barron, s. Azeriah and Lucy, Nov. 24, 1783.
Zacceus, s. Edward and Lidyah, Feb. 15, 17[02. T. C.].
Zachariah, s. Jonathan and Mary, Sept. [torn. bp. Sept. 18, 1774. C. R. 1.].
Zacheus, s. William and Esther, of Westford, bp. July 9, 1780. C. R. 1.
Zebulon, s. Thomas and Mary, Nov. 12, 1741.
Zebulon, s. Cornet Henry and Marah, Mar. 2, 1743-4. [bp. Feb. 11. C. R. 1.]
Zebulon, s. Zebulon, jr. and Lydia, Apr. 9, 1770.

SPAULDINGE (see also Spaulding), Deborah, d. twin, John and Ann [Annah. CT. R.], Aug. 12, 1690. [Aug. 19. CT. R.]
Eleasor, s. twin, John and Anah, Aug. 13, 1690. [Aug. 19. CT. R.]

SPAULDYNG (see also Spaulding), Andrew, s. Andrew and Abbigal, Dec. 8, 1701.
Elesabeth, d. Joseph and Elesabeth, Jan. 17, 170[1.].
Ester, d. Lt. Edward and Margret, Feb. 11, 1700.
Hennery, s. twin, Andrew and Abbigall, Sept. 6, 1703.
Hennery, s. Hennery and Elesibeth, Nov. 22, 1704.
Jacob, s. twin, Andrew and Abbigall, Sept. 6, 1703.
John, s. Joseph and Mary, Apr. 17, 1699.

SPAULDING, Jonas, s. Sam[ue]ll and Marah, Aug. 15, [torn. 170-. T. C. 1700?].
Jonathan, s. Edward and Mary, Apr. 15, 1704.
Mercy, d. Joseph and Mary, Oct. 20, 1703.
Rebecka, d. Timothy and Rebecka, Oct. 31, 1703.
Samuell, s. Sam[u]ell and Mary, June 4, 1699.
Thomas, s. Josiph and Marcy [Mary. CT. R.], Apr. 2, 1690.
Zachariah, s. Samuell and Mary [Nov. T. C.] 3, 1703.

SPOLDING (see also Spaulding), Elesabath, d. Edward and Mary, Aug. 15, 1698.

SPRAGUE, Daniel Reed, s. Abigail, bp. Aug. 3, 1828. C. R. 3.
Ellen, d. Horace, farmer, b. Hudson, N. H., and Lucinda, b. Lowell, Nov. 8, 1849.
Langden Wilson, s. Abigail, bp. Aug. 3, 1828. C. R. 3.
Thomas Stoneman, s. Abigail, bp. Aug. 3, 1828. C. R. 3.

STACEY, John, s. William and Deborah, bp. Nov. 15, 1767. C. R. 1.
William, s. William and Deborah, Mar. 18, 1763.

STARRETT (see also Sterrett), John, s. Henry, moulder, and Ann, at North Chelmsford, Sept. 11, 1845.

STEARNS, Mary Hall, d. Ashael and Fran[c]is Wentworth, ―― 25, 1802.

STEAVENS (see also Stevens), Deborah, d. Samuel and Ruth, Apr. 12, 1745.
Easther, d. Henry and Deborah, Jan. 14, 1743-4.
Hanah, d. Richard and Hannah, Aug. 20, 1700.
Heniry, s. John and Sarah, Oct. 4, 1700.
Jonathan, s. Henry and Deborah, Oct. 5, 1745.
Parker, s. Samuel, jr. and Tabathy, June 20, 1770.

STEEVENS (see also Stevens), Eliazer, s. Henery and Deborah, Apr. 29, 1731.
Hannah, d. Samuel and Ruth, June 22, 1737.
Samuel, s. Samuel and Ruth, Nov. 14, 1733.

STEPHENS (see also Stevens), Elisabeth, d. John and Elisabeth, Feb. 8, 1665.
Ephriam, s. John and Sary, May 21, 1710.
Prewdence, d. John and Sarah, Apr. 28, 1716.

STERRETT (see also Starrett), Jane Noble, d. Henry, moulder, and Ann, at Furnace Village, Feb. 21, 1844.

STEVENS (see also Steavens, Steevens, Stephens), Abel, s. Simeon and Elisabeth, Apr. 24, 1775.
Abigail Ann, d. Joseph and Harriot F., Mar. 18, 1835.
Abigal, d. John and Sarah, Aug. 13, 17[torn. 1702?].
Almaria, d. Samson and Phebe, Feb. 3, 1810.
Andrew Chamberlain, s. twin, Asa, farmer, and Harriett, Feb. 24, 1844.
Asa, s. Samson and Pheby, Aug. 16, 1807.
Benjamin Meril, s. Samson and Phebe, Feb. 9, 1813.
Bill Wright, s. Simeon and Elizebeth, Feb. 18, 1768.
Caleb, s. Caleb and Elezebeth, Mar. 1, 1771.
Charlotte A., d. Jabez, farmer, and Seviah, Oct. [30. different ink.], 1847.
Daniel, s. Henry and Deborah, May 7, 1737.
Deborah, d. John and Sarah, Jan. 2, 1698-9.
Deborah, d. Henery and Deborah, Jan. 21, 1728-9.
Deliveranc, d. Richard and Hanah, Jan. 20, 1705.
Elizebeth, d. John and Sarah, Apr. 16, 1697.
Elizebeth, d. Calip and Elizebeth, Oct. 30, 1769.
Elizebeth, d. Simeon and Elizebeth, Feb. 29, 1772.
Emily [Amela. C. R. 1.], d. Capt. Samuel and Betty, **Feb. 19, 1802.**
Ephraim, s. Henery and Deborah, Apr. 20, 1728.
Ephraim Asa, s. Asa and Harriot, Mar. 24, 1833.
Esther, d. John and Sary, July 23, 1712.
Hannah, d. Samuel and Tabathy, Mar. 21, 1775.
Harriet, d. Samson and Phebe, Sept. 13, 1815.
Harriot Emily, d. Joseph and Harriot F., Apr. 28, 1838.
Harriott Maria, d. Asa and Harriot, Oct. 1, 1836.
Henry, s. Henry and Deborah, Sept. 10, 1724.
Jeptha, s. Samuel, jr. and Tabatha, Feb. 15, 1777.
Jesse, s. Samuel, jr. and Tabatha, Mar. 14, 1764.
Jesse, s. Jesse, bp. Feb. 14, 1796. C. R. 1.
Joanna, d. Simeon and Joanna, Dec. 16, 1757.
John, s. John and Sary, Sept. 16, 1706.
John, s. Henry and Deborah, Sept. 5, 1739.
Jonathan, s. Jonathan and Thankfull, Mar. 10, 1794.
[Jo. T. C.]seph, s. John, Mar. 24, 1679.
Joseph Edwin, s. Joseph and Hariot F., July 18, 1836.
Leucy, d. Jonathan and Thankfull, Oct. 9, 1781.
Lidiah, d. Richard and Hanah, Nov. 1, 1716.
Mary, d. John and Elisabeth [torn. 1672?].
Mary, d. Ritchard and Hannah, May 19, 1702.

154 CHELMSFORD BIRTHS

STEVENS, Merrill, s. Asa and Harriet, Nov. 5, **1834**.
Molley, d. Samuel, jr. and Tabatha, Jan. 19, 1780.
Peter, s. Asa and Harriot, Nov. 27, 1840.
Phebe, d. Samson and Phebe, Feb. 28, 1792.
Porter, s. Asa and Harriott, Sept. 21, 1838.
Rachel, d. Capt. Samuel and Betty, Jan. 11, 1804.
Rachil, d. Samuel and Tabathy, Jan. 28, 1773.
Rebeckah, d. Simeon and Joanna, Oct. 25, 1762.
Rebeckah, d. Simeon and Elisabeth, May 6, 1781.
Richard, s. John and Elisabeth, Sept. 26, 1674.
Ruth, d. Samwel and Ruth, Jan. 5, 1731-2.
Ruth, d. Samuel and Tabatha, Mar. 6, 1766.
Sally, d. Samson and Phebe, June 2, 1799.
Sampson, s. Simeon and Elizebeth, June 11, 1769.
Samson, s. Samson and Phebe, May 7, 1795.
Samuel, s. Samuel, jr. and Tabathy, Apr. 2, 1768.
Samuel Parker, s. Capt. Samuel and Betty, Oct. 5, 1810.
Samuell, s. Richard and Hana, Mar. 30, 1708.
[S. T. C.]ara, d. John and Sara, Feb. 19, 1693-4.
Sarah, d. Henry and Deborah, Sept. 13, 1733.
Sarah, d. Simeon and Elizabeth, bp. Sept. 7, 1777. C. R. 1.
Sarah Phebe, d. twin, Asa, farmer, and Harriett, Feb. 24, **1844**.
Sary, d. Richard and Hanah, Apr. 8, 1713.
Sibbil, d. Samson and Phebe, Mar. 12, 1801.
Simeon, s. Simeon and Elizabeth, June 15, 1765.
Simeon, s. Simeon and Elisabeth, Apr. 12, 1784.
Simeon, s. Samson and Pheby, Apr. 3, 1803.
Simeon, s. Samson and Phebe, July 30, 1805.
Simmion, s. Samuel and Ruth, Nov. 1, 1735.
Solomon, s. Samuel and Tabatha, Apr. 25, 1762.
Sophia, d. Capt. Samuel and Bettey, May 29, 1796.
Susanna, d. Samson and Phebe, Dec. 12, 1796.
Thankfull, d. John and Sary, Apr. 2, 1714.
Thankfull, d. Jonathan and Thankfull, Aug. 9, 1779.

STICKLEMORE, John Joseph, s. ——, bp. Oct. —, 1811. C. R. 1.

STODARD (see also Stoddard), Rebeck[ah], d. Samson and Elezebath, Nov. 4, 1716.
Will[ia]m, s. Samson and Elezebath, May 4, 1712.

STODDARD (see also Stodard), Benjamin, s. Samson and Elizabeth, Dec. 28, 1713.
Elizabeth, d. Samson and Elizabeth, Dec. 14, 1710.
Elizabeth, d. Sampson and Elizabeth, Feb. 12, 1741-2.

CHELMSFORD BIRTHS 155

STODDARD, John s. Sampson and Elizabeth, July 23, 1739.
John Vryling, s. Maj. Sampson and Margrett, Aug. 28, 1745.
Sampson, s. Sampson and Elizabeth, Mar. 12, 1740-41.
Samson, s. Samson and Elizabeth, Mar 21, 1709.
Sarah, d. Sampson and Margaret, Oct. 27, 1752.
Vryling, s. Maj. Sampson and Margret, Dec. 22, 1746.
William, s. Col. Sampson and Margret, May 9, 1749.

STRATTON, Frances, s. Ichabod and Elizabeth, Dec. 8, 1716.
Ichabod, s. Richard and Naomi, Dec. 1, 1688. [1687. CT. R.]
Ichabod, s. Ichabod and Elizabeth, Jan. 11, 1721-2.
Isaac, s. Ichabod and Elezebeth, July 11, 1715.
John, s. Ichobad and Elizabeth, Sept. 11, 1710.
Naomy, d. Ichabod and Elizabeth, Feb. 6, 1718-19.
Richard, s. Ichabod and Elizabeth, June 21, 1712.

SWALLOW (see also Swalo, Swalow), Elizabeth, d. Jonathan and Hanah, July 29, 1729.
Ephraim, s. Jonathan and Hannah, June 13, 1745.
Hanah, d. Jonathan and Hanah, Feb. 11, 1730-31.
Hannah, d. Ambros and Sarah, Jan. 18, 170[3. T. C.].
Jonathan, s. Jonathan and Hanah, May 7, 1734.
Jonathan, s. Jonathan and Hannah, Mar. 24, 1739-40.
Joseph, s. Ambros and Mary, Mar. 16, 1679.
Mary, d. Ambros and Sarah, Feb. 8, 1700.
Mary, d. Jonathan and Hannah, Nov. 11, 1736.
Phebe, d. Jonathan and Hannah, Aug. 9, 1742.
Sarah, d. Amberous and Sarah, July 23, 1698.

SWALO (see also Swallow), John, s. Ambros and Mary, Nov. 19, 1671.
John, s. Ambros and Sary, Aug. 12, 1709.
Jonathan, s. Ambras and Sary, Sept. 11, 1706.
Joseph, s. Ambros and Sary, June 21, 1714.

SWALOW (see also Swallow), Ambros, s. Ambros and Mary, Sept. 8, 1669. [June 8. CT. R.]
Benjamin, s. Ambras and Mary, Nov. 9, 1683.

SWEETSER, Charles Dupee, s. Charles, farmer, and Mary, at Mill Row, Dec. 10, 1844.
Mary Adams, d. Charles, farmer, and Mary, at Mill Row, Sept. 4, 1843.
——, s. Charles, farmer, and Mary, at Mill Row, Mar. 4, 1848.

SWETT, Anna Maria, d. Charles and Anna (Babcock), Oct. 25, 1831. P. R. 30.
Charles Eben, s. Charles and Anna (Babcock), Mar. 12, 1839. P. R. 30.
Harriet Newell Howard, d. Charles and Anna (Babcock), July 10, 1841. P. R. 30.
Henrietta, d. William, lumber merchant, and Belinda, at North Chelmsford, Jan. 20, 1847.
Jane Elizabeth, d. P. and P., bp. Dec. 2, 1832. C. R. 3.
John French, s. Charles and Anna (Babcock), Nov. 29, 1829. P. R. 30.
John Henry, s. P. and P., bp. ——, 1834. C. R. 3.
Martha Ella, d. W[illia]m, miller, b. Bedford, N. H., and Belinda, b. Tyngsborough, at North Chelmsford, Dec. 30, 1849.
Sarah Emeline, d. Charles and Anna (Babcock), July 1, 1836. P. R. 30.

SWETTMAN, Ezekiel, s. Thomas and Mary, Oct. 6, 1725.

TAFT, Phillip W., s. Phillip and Mary W., May 22, 1840.
Russell H., s. Phillip and Mary W., July 20, 1838.

TAINTER, Lydia Ann, d. Lewis, hatter, and Lucinda, at Middlesex Village, Aug. 20, 1843.

TALBOTT (see also Talbut), Petter, s. Petter and Mary, Jan. 1, 1684.

TALBUT (see also Talbott), Elizabeth, d. Peter and Mary, Jan. 13, 1686. CT. R.

TAY, Charlotte, d. Benj[ami]n and Hannah, Nov. 16, 1833.
John Ives, s. Benj[ami]n and Hannah, Feb. 1, 1831.

TAYLOR, John, s. John, jr., bp. at Dracut, May 12, 1765. P. R. 4.

TEMPLE, Joel, s. Ebenezer and Hepzibah, July 31, 1749.
John, s. John and Sary, Oct. 7, 1756.
Phebe, d. Ebenezer and Hepsebe, Oct. 1, 1754.

THOMPSON (see also Tompson), Anna, d. Symon, bp. 1: 12 m: 1656, a. 1 y. 30: 5 m: 1656. P. R. 1.
James, s. Symon, bp. 1: 12 m: 1656, a. 7 y. 15: 1 m: 1656. P. R. 1.

CHELMSFORD BIRTHS 157

THOMPSON, James Munrow, s. Capt. Luke and Betsy, Apr. 18, 1820. [bp. Sept. 12, 1819. C. R. 1.]
Mary, d. Symon, bp. 1: 12 m: 1656, a. 5 y. 9: 11 m: 1656. P. R. 1.
Mary Elizabeth, d. Capt. Luke and Betsy, July 5, 1819.
Sarah, d. Symon, bp. 1: 12 m: 1656, a. 10 y. 25: 12 m: 1656. P. R. 1.

THOREAU, Sophia Elizabeth, d. John and Scynthia, bp. Sept. 27, 1819. C. R. 1.

TILLER, Isaac, s. John and Sarai, Dec. 20, 1719.

TOMPSON (see also Thompson), James, s. Hugh and Mary, July 17, 1723.

TORREY, Hellen Maria, d. Joseph G., moulder, and Nancy, at North Chelmsford, May 9, 1844.

TOWNSEND, Elizabeth, d. Eben[ezer], bp. Dec. 29, 1728. C. R. 4.

TRAINER, James, s. Edward, laborer, and Catherine, at North Chelmsford, Apr. 13, 1848.

TRULL, Alpheus Nesmith, s. Levi, manufacturer, b. Andover, and Nancy, b. Milford, N. H., June 6, 1849.
Margaret, d. Levi, mechanic, and Nancy, at Worsted Mills, Apr. 24, 1846.

TUCKER, John, s. John and Eunice, Nov. 21, 1747.
Martha, d. John and Eunice, Mar. 26, 1750.

TURNER, Mary Elizabeth, d. John, farmer and moulder, and Julia, Aug. 18, 1846.

TWISS, James, s. John and Sarah, Nov. 11, 1773.
Joseph, s. Benja[min] and Phebe, July 2, 1793.
Mehitabel, d. John and Sarah, Oct. 14, 1775.
Page, s. Benja[min] and Abigail, Apr. 16, 1796.

TYLER, Mary Elizabeth, d. Nathan and Mary A[nn. C. R. 1.], Sept. 9, 1841.
Samuel, June 14, 1803. P. R. 12.
William Otis, s. William, farmer, and Mary Ann, b. Ludlow, Vt., at Middlesex Village, Nov. 11, 1849.

TYNG, John, s. Willam and Luce, Jan. 25, 1705.
Mary, d. Willam and Lucy, Oct. 25, 1706.
Sarah, d. Willam and Lucy, Mar. 11, 1702.

UNDERWOOD, Ame, d. Joseph and Susanah, Oct. 16, 1717.
Aquilla, s. Aquilla and Margret, Dec. 6, 1723.
Aquilla, s. William, bp. 1 : 12 m : 1656, a. abt. 8 y. P. R. 1.
Asa Webster, s. Eliza Ann, bp. Oct. 5, 1828. C. R. 3.
Benjamin, s. John and Mary, of Westford, bp. July 7, 1782. C. R. 1.
Deborah, d. William, bp. 1 : 12 m : 1656, a. abt. 4 y. P. R. 1.
Jeptha, s. Phineas and Rebecca, bp. Feb. 22, 1784. C. R. 1.
John, s. Joseph and Susannah, Sept. 15, 1727.
Jonathan, s. Joseph and Susanah, Jan. 22, 1716.
Joseph, s. Phinehus and Rebeckah, May 4, 1782. [bp. Apr. 14. C. R. 1.]
Mary, d. Aquilla and Margret, Nov. 26, 1724.
Mathias, s. Eliza Ann, bp. Oct. 5, 1828. C. R. 3.
Phineas, s. Joseph and Susanah, Jan. 30, 1721-2.
Phinehas, s. Phinehas and Rebeckah, Nov. 11, 1778.
Priscilla, d. William, bp. 1 : 12 m : 1656, a. abt. 10 y. P. R. 1.
Rebeckah, d. Phinehus and Rebeckah, June 22, 1780.
Remembrance, d. William, bp. 1 : 12 m : 1656, a. abt. 15 y. P. R. 1.
Ruth, d. Joseph and Susana, Jan. 2, 1719-20.
Samuel, s. Will[ia]m, Feb. 14, 1655. CT. R.
Samuel, s. William, bp. 1 : 12 m : 1656, a. 1 y. in 1 m : 1657. P. R. 1.
Samuel, s. Aquila and Margret, Feb. 1, 1722-3.
Sarah, d. William, bp. 1 : 12 m : 1656, a. abt. 14 y. P. R. 1.
William, s. Aquila, bp. Jan. 5, 1729. C. R. 4.

UPHAM, Franklin Munroe, s. Ezra A., butcher, and Almira, Sept. 10, 1846.
Laura Jane, d. Ezra A., butcher, b. Wilton, N. H., and Almira, b. Marshfield, Vt., Sept. 5, 1848.
Luther Clement, s. Clement, butcher, b. Wilton, N. H., and Elmira, b. Meredith, N. H., Nov. 8, 1848.
Malintha, d. Clement, butcher, and Almira W., June 28, 1844.

VANCE, George William, s. W[illia]m and Margaret, Nov. 18, 1840.
Glendi, d. William and Margaret, Dec. 10, 1839.
Margaret Glendera, d. William, moulder, and Margaret, at North Chelmsford, May 26, 1843.

CHELMSFORD BIRTHS

VARNUM, Johanah, d. Thomas and Ruth, Mar. 5, 1699.
John, s. Samuell and Sary, Oct. 15, 1[669. T. C.].
Joseph, s. Samuell and Sary, Mar. 15, 1[672-3. T. C.].
Mary, d. Thomas and Joanna, June 3[torn. 1701?].
Naomi, d. Dr. Ebenezer and Lucy, Mar. 12, 1793.
Sarah, d. Joseph and Ruth, Dec. 14, 1698.

VIRGEN (see also Virgin), Marsy, d. Richard and Francies, Feb. —, 1705.

VIRGIN (see also Virgen, Voirgen). Ebenezer, s. Ritchard and Frances, Apr. 2, 1702.
Elisibath, d. Richard and Frensis, Feb. 4, 1696-7.

VOCE (see also Vose), Josiah, jr., s. Josiah and Mary, Aug. 6, 1815.
Louisa, d. Josiah and Mary, Feb. 26, 1818.
Milley, d. Josiah and Mary, Sept. 7, 1820.

VOIRGEN (see also Virgin), Wiljam, s. Rickard and Frances, Jan. 23, 1698-9.

VOSE (see also Voce), Hannah Maria, d. Josiah and Mary, Dec. 8, 1825.
Lucinda, d. Josiah and Mary, Sept. 15, 1829.
William Merion, s. Josiah and Mary, May 5, 1823.

WADDELL (see also Wadell), Rose, d. John and Mary, 22: 8 m: 1670.
William, s. John and Mary, Dec. 28, 1[672. T. C.].

WADELL (see also Waddell), Mary, d. John and Mary, Aug. 1, 1668.

WAITE, Mercy, d. Elizabeth, alias Betty Virgin, bp. Nov. 2, 1746. C. R. 1.

WALDO (see also Waldow, Walldou), Daniel, s. Dan[ie]ll and Susannah, Mar. 25, 1692. CT. R.
Esther, d. Daniell and Susanah, Jan. 3, 1698.
Marah, d. Daniel and Susanah, Feb. 10, 1695-6.

WALDOW (see also Waldo), Beethia, d. Danill and Susanah, Aug. 20, 1688.
[John. T. C.], s. John and Rebeckah, May 19, 1678.

WALKER, Abbott, s. Benjamin and Abial, July 24, 1770.
Abigail, d. Zechariah and Martha, bp. Feb. 11, 1744. C. R. 1.
Alpheus, s. David and Lydia, Sept. 25, 1814.
Andrew, s. John and Lidiah, Nov. 25, 1691.
Charles, s. David and Lydia, Dec. 15, 1817.
David, s. David and Elizabath, Dec. 21, 1787.
Edwad, s. John and Lidiah, Jan. 9, 1688.
Elizabath, d. David and Elizabath, Apr. 18, 1786.
Elizabeth, d. John and Lidiah, Sept. 12, 1706.
Ephraim, s. Benjamin and Abial, July 22, 1772.
Hanah, d. John and Hanah, Apr. 11, 1696.
Hannah, d. Samson and Thankful, bp. Feb. 16, 1777. C. R. 1.
Isaac, s. Zacheus and Patty, bp. Aug. 16, 1772. C. R. 1.
John, s. John and Lidiah, Aug. 9, 1686.
Josepeh, s. John and Leydyah, Aug. 11, 1698.
[Lydi. T. C.]a, d. John and Lidia, Feb. 4, 1693-4.
Mary, d. Zechariah and Martha, bp. Apr. 25, 1742. C. R. 1.
Rhoda, d. Benjamin and Abial, Apr. 12, 1774.
Richard, s. John and Lidya, June 14, [torn. 170-. T. C. 1703?].
Sarah, d. John and Lidya, Feb. 23, 1701.
Thankful, d. Samson and Thankful, bp. June 20, 1773. C. R. 1.

WALLDOU (see also Waldo), [Re. T. C.]beca, d. Daniell and Susana, Feb. 5, 1693-4.

WARD, Bridget, d. Patrick, moulder, and Ellen, at North Chelmsford, Feb. 1, 1845.
Henry, s. James W., ware dresser, and Ann, both b. Ireland, at North Chelmsford, Sept. 1, 1849.
James H., s. Patric, moulder, and Ellen, at North Chelmsford, Aug. 22, 1847.
Mary Adeline, d. Jonathan W., farmer, and Mary G., Sept. 9, 1843.
Mary Elizabeth, d. Patrick R., moulder, and Catharine, at North Chelmsford, Jan. 1, 1848.
Thomas Anthony, s. Patric R., moulder, b. Monaghan Co., Ireland, and Catharine, b. "Cressy Co.," Ireland, June 3, 1849.

WARDEN, George Allen, s. Allen, stone-cutter, b. Chesterfield, N. H., and Hannah, b. Tyngsborough, at North Chelmsford, Sept. 6, 1849.
——, d. Allen, stone-cutter, and Hannah, at North Chelmsford, Jan. 20, 1847.

WARIN (see also Warren), Elisabeth, d. Jacob and Sarah, June 7, 1693.
Ep[h]raim, s. Ephraim and Easter, Dec. 16, 1731.
John, s. Ephraim and Easter, Sept. 14, 1733.
Mary, d. Joseph and Tabitha, Apr. 16, 1736.
Sarah, d. Jacob and Marah, Mar. 3, 1689.
Sarah, d. Joseph and Tabithah, July 30, 1733.

WARINE (see also Warren), Jacob, s. Jacob and Sarah, July 13, 1691.

WARING (see also Warren), Ephariam, s. Joseph and Ruth, Dec. 6, 1707.
John, s. Joseph and Ruth, July 25, 1714.
Ruth, d. Joseph and Ruth, Aug. 23, 1711.

WARREN (see also Warin, Warine, Waring, Warrin, Warring, Worin, Worrin), Abigail, d. Dea. John and Elizebeth, Oct. 27, 1758.
Abigail, d. Lt. Joseph and Rebeckah, Aug. 11, 1795.
Abigal, d. Benjamin and Izebel, May 16, 1765.
Adaline, d. Isaac, jr. and Ann, Aug. 23, 1806.
Alonzo [Lorinzo. C. R. 1.] Lamson, s. Isaac, jr. and Ann, Apr. 11, 1803.
Amos Carlton, s. Ephraim and Esther [(Carlton). P. R. 7.], Aug. 10, 1834.
Ann, d. Isaac, jr. and Ann, Apr. 17, 1800.
Anne, d. Isaac and Lidia, May 31, 1782.
Arther, s. Arther and Abigaill, 2 : 9 m : 166[8. T. C.].
Benj[a]min, s. Benjamin and Izebell, Mar. 12, 1758.
Easter, d. Ephraim and Easter, Apr. 27, 1735.
Edwin Henchman, s. Ephraim and Esther [(Carlton). P. R. 7.], Apr. 7, 1824.
Efraime, s. Jacob, 24 : 4 m : 1680.
Elisabeth, d. Jacob and Mary, Mar. 3, 1674.
Eliza Ann, d. Ephraim and Esther [(Carlton). P. R. 7.], Dec. 19, 1827.
Elizebeth, d. Ephraim and Easter, May 25, 1741.
Elizebeth, d. Lt. Isaac and Lidia, June 27, 1779.
Ephraim, s. Ephraim and Mary, Apr. 8, 1759.
Ephraim, s. Jeremiah and Rachel [S. P. R. 7.], Jan. 5, 1793.
Ephrim, s. Ephrim and Abigal, Apr. 5, 1702.
Faricy [Fanny. C. R. 1.], d. Lt. Joseph and Rebeckah, July 17, 1791.
Henchman, s. Dea. John and Elizabeth, Dec. 21, 1752. [bp. Dec. 22, 1751. C. R. 1.]

WARREN, Isaac, s. Ephriam and Esther, Jan. 30, 1737.
Isaac, s. Isaac and Lydia, Apr. 11, 1774.
Isaac, s. Isaac and Lydia, bp. Jan. 19, 1777. C. R. 1.
Izebell, d. Benjamin and Izebell, Oct. 15, 1754.
Jacob, s. Jacob and Mary, bp. 8 : 12 m : 1673. P. R. 1.
Jacob, s. Ephraim and Esther, bp. Mar. 29, 1747. C. R. 1.
Jeduthun, s. Joseph and Joanna, Nov. 24, 1756.
Joanna, d. Joseph and Joanna, Apr. 6, 1753.
Joanna, d. Jeremiah and Rachel [S. P. R. 7.], Sept. 10, 1790.
Jonas, s. Thomas and Esther, Aug. 28, 1729.
Jonathan, s. Isabell, bp. June 27, 1779. C. R. 1.
Joseph, s. Jacob and Mary, 25 : 8 m : 1670.
Joseph, s. Ephraim and Mary, Mar. 4, 1761.
Joseph, s. Joseph and Sarah, Dec. 7, 1769.
Joseph, s. Joseph and Mary, Aug. 17, 1800.
Josiah, s. Ephraim and Easter, Apr. 27, 1745.
Lucy, d. John and Elizabeth, Sept. 30, 1749.
Lydia, d. Ephraim and Easter, Jan. 1, 1738.
Lydia, d. Isaac and Lydia, July 2, 1766.
Martha C., d. Ephraim and Esther (Carlton), Mar. 27, 1838. P. R. 7.
Mary, d. John and Elizabeth, July 4, 1747.
Mary, d. Joseph and Mary, May 2, 1795.
Mirriam, d. Joseph and Mary, Feb. 20, 1802.
Moses, s. Ephraim and Mary, Dec. 8, 1755.
Oliver, s. Thomas and Esther, Jan. 4, 1732-3.
Oliver, s. Ephraim and Mary [Marah. C. R. 1.], July 2, 1763.
Polley, d. Isaac and Lydia, Nov. 12, 1771.
Polly, d. Jeduthan and Joanna, bp. Jan. 16, 1780. C. R. 1.
Rachel, d. Jeremiah and Rachel [S. P. R. 7.], May 17, 1795.
Rebeckah, d. Dea. John and Elizebeth, Sept. 17, 1754.
Rebeckah, d. Lt. Joseph and Rebeckah, Mar. 12, 1786.
Rebecker, d. Benjamin and Izebell, Feb. 14, 1773.
Rizpah, d. Joseph and Mary, July 11, 1798.
Ruth, d. Joseph and Tabitha, Sept. 4, 1741.
Ruth, d. Ephraim and Esther, bp. July 9, 1749. C. R. 1.
Sarah, d. Benjamin and Izebell, Sept. 28, 1767.
Sarah, d. Isaac and Lydia, July 17, 1769.
Sary, d. Joseph and Mary, June 8, 1796.
Sibbel, d. Jeremiah and Rachel [S. P. R. 7.], Apr. 24, 1797.
Silas, s. Ephraim and Esther, bp. Oct. 13, 1751. C. R. 1.
Siles, s. Ephraim and Mary, Dec. 8, 1757.
Tabatha, d. Benjamin and Isabel, Jan. 21, 1763.
Tabitha, d. Joseph and Tabitha, June 10, 1727.
Thomas, s. Thomas and Easther, May 6, 1727.
Thomas, s. Ephraim and Easter, Apr. 5, 1743.

WARREN, Timothy, s. John and Elizebeth, Dec. 15, 1756.
William, s. Isaac, jr. and Ann, Mar. 12, 1805.

WARRIN (see also Warren), Benjamin, s. Joseph and Tabitha, Aug. 30, 1729.
Elizabeth, d. John and Elizabeth, Jan. 27, 1744-5.
Jeremiah, s. Joseph and Joanna, Feb. 23, 1763.
Joseph, s. Joseph and Tabitha, Aug. 24, 1724.

WARRING (see also Warren), Jacob, s. Joseph and Ruth, Dec. 13, 1700.
Joseph, s. Joseph and Ruth, Apr. 5, 1699.
Thomas, s. Joseph and Ruth, Mar. 5, 1704.

WATSON, Charles Henry, s. J. M., machinist, and Mary L., at North Chelmsford, Mar. 24, 1846.
Frank Roland, s. Jones M., machinist, b. Fayette, Me., and Mary L., b. Vermont, May 24, 1849.
Harriott A., d. Humphrey S. and Harriott A., July 15, 1839.

WEBBER, Josiah K., s. Josiah and Hannah, Oct. 17, 1819.
Mary, d. Josiah and Hannah, May 9, 1815.
William, s. Josiah and Hannah, July 21, 1817.

WEBSTER, Angeline Mandana, d. Eli F. and Roxanna, Oct. 28, 1835.
Callista Antoinette, d. Eli F. and Roxanna, Jan. 20, 1831.
Emily Cordelia, d. Eli F. and Roxana, Feb. 4, 1838.
Granville Sylvester, s. E. F. and Roxanna, Nov. 27, 1833.
Hellen Georgiana, d. Eli F. and Roxanna, Feb. 25, 1841.

WENDELL, Henry, s. Jacob and Lery, bp. Feb. 26, 1769. C. R. 1.
Jacob, s. Jacob and Lory, bp. Mar. 11, 1764. C. R. 1.
Susanna, d. Jacob and Lory, bp. June 15, 1766. C. R. 1.

WENTWORTH, Ann Maria, d. Abraham W. and Dorcas, Nov. 11, 1838.
Julia Maria, d. James M., farmer, b. Ossipee, N. H., and Elizabeth, b. South Reading, Oct. 25, 1849.
Mary Jane, d. Abraham W. and Dorcas, Aug. 1, 1840.

WEYMOUTH, Abby D., d. Converse L., laborer, and Betsey A., Sept. 1, 1845.
Charles Henry, s. Converse L., laborer [farmer. dup.], and Betsey A., Sept. 13, 1846.

WHEELER (see also Wheler), Reuben, s. James and Priscilla, bp. Apr. 19, 1778. C. R. 1.

WHELER (see also Wheeler), Sary, d. Richard and Sary, June 2, 1714.

WHETNEY (see also Whitney), Abagall, d. Joseph and Rebackah, Mar. 5, 1707.
Benjamin, s. Joseph and Rebecca, Mar. 18, 1723-4.
Daniel, s. Joseph and Rebeca, May 20, 1726.

WHIPPLE, Catharine Amanda, d. Oliver M. and Sophronia, May 14, 1823.

WHITEMORE (see also Whittemore), Abraham, s. Sister Butterfeild [formerly Whitemore], bp. in his minority, 8: 5 m: 1666. P. R. 1.
Joel Jefferson, s. Gideon, bp. Aug. 15, 1830. C. R. 3.
Mary Richardson, d. Gideon, bp. Aug. 15, 1830. C. R. 3.
Pelatiah, s. Sister Butterfeild [formerly Whitemore], bp. in his minority, 8: 5 m: 1666. P. R. 1.
Samuel, s. Sister Butterfeild [formerly Whitemore], bp. in his minority, 8: 5 m: 1666. P. R. 1.
W[illia]m Derby, s. Gideon, bp. Aug. 15, 1830. C. R. 3.

WHITING (see also Whitting), Jonathan, s. James, of Chester, and Hepzibah, Apr. 13, 1722.

WHITNEY (see also Whetney, Whittney), Benjamin, s. Josiah, and Miriam, Nov. 20, 1718.
Daniel, s. Daniel and Hannah, Oct. 18, 1751.
Elener, d. Josiah and Miriam, Apr. 2, 1727.
Esther, d. Phineas, bp. at Harvard, Nov. 13, 1768. P. R. 4.
Eunice, d. Josiah and Miriam, Nov. 5, 1707.
Hannah, d. Daniel and Hannah, Sept. 16, 1746. [bp. Nov. 24, 1745. C. R. 1.]
Jonathan, s. Daniel and Hannah, Sept. 3, 1749.
Josiah, s. Josiah and Miriam, Jan. 26, 1714-15.
Martha, d. Josiah and Miriam, June 10, 1712.
Mary, d. Daniel and Hannah, May 31, 1747.
Meriam, d. Josiah and Miriam, Aug. 9, 1721.
Peter, s. Josiah and Miriam, Feb. 17,1724-5.
Rebackah, d. Joseph and Rebeckah, Dec. 6, 1718.
Sary, d. Daniel and Hannah, Apr. 15, 1762.

CHELMSFORD BIRTHS 165

WHITTEMORE (see also Whitemore), Lydia Ann, d. James, wheelwright, and Susan H., at Furnace Village, Oct. 2, 1843.
Susan Adeline, d. James, wheelwright, and Susan H., at North Chelmsford, May 16, 1847.
Susan Theadine, d. James, wheelwright, and Susan H., at North Chelmsford, May 12, 1845.

WHITTING (see also Whiting), Elizabeth, d. James and Hepzibah, Dec. 12, 1719.

WHITTNEY (see also Whitney), Daniel, s. Daniel and Hannah, Dec. 22, 1758.
Rebeckah, d. Daniel and Hannah, May 2, 1759.
Thankfull, d. Daniel and Hannah, Nov. 8, 1753.

WIGGIN, Francelia Maria, d. Nathaniel, machinist, and Lidia P., at North Chelmsford, May 8, 1846.
Francis Marshall, s. True, farmer, and Martha, May 10, 1843.
Mary Louisa, d. True, farmer, and Martha, at Concord River Neck, Feb. 7, 1845.

WILBUR, Shepherd Blake, s. Gardner and Elizabeth Ann, Mar. 13, 1840.

WILLARD, Steven, s. Thomas, Mar. 15, 1670-71. CT. R.

WILLIAMS, Dolley, d. Simeon, bp. at Dracut, May 12, 1765. P. R. 4.
Henry Church, s. Seth and Phebe H., May 31, 1837.
Horatio Leach, s. Seth and P. H., May 7, 1842.
Ruel, s. Seth and Phebe H., July 17, 1835.

WILLOUGHBY, Zelotus, s. John, scythe maker, and Emeline, at Providence, R. I., June 11, 1847.

WILSON, Amelia, d. Simeon and Joanna, Oct. 3, 1794.
Ephraim, s. Samuel and Hannah, Dec. 20, 1759.
Esther, d. Samuel and Hannah, June 14, 1767.
George Richardson, s. George, bp. July 8, 1829. C. R. 1.
Hannah, d. Samuel and Hannah, Feb. 8, 1762.
John, s. Simeon and Joanna, Apr. 9, 1797.
Jonathan, s. Samuel and Hannah, June 29, 1764.
Lydia, d. Samuel and Hannah, June 1, 1773.
Mary, d. Samuel and Hannah, Apr. 25, 1756.
Samuel, s. Samuel and Hannah, June 6, 1754.

WILSON, Sarah, d. Samuel and Hannah, Feb. 19, 1758.
Susan M., d. Charles, machinist, and Mahitabel, at Chesterfield, N. H., Aug. 26, 1846.
——, s. Daniel J., blacksmith, and Jane W., at North Chelmsford, Sept. 28, 1846.

WINN, Mary Ann, d. Rodney, shoemaker, b. Amherst, N. H., and Elizabeth, b. Medford, Nov. 12, 1849.

WITHERELL, Melville H., s. Hiram D., manufacturer, b. Chazy, N. Y., and Jenette, b. Silverlake, Pa., at North Chelmsford, May 3, 1848.

WITHINGTON, Seth, s. Edward and Lydia, Dec. 3, 1812.

WOOD (see also Woods), Benjamin, s. Benjamin and Elisebeth, Jan. 25, 1756.
Elizebeth, d. Benja[min] and Elizebeth, Aug. 24, 1758.
Grace, d. Benjamin and Elisebeth, July 17, 1765.
Hannah, d. Benjamin and Elizebeth, Dec. 6, 1760.
Leaffe, d. twin, Benjamin and Elisebeth, Feb. 20, 1768.
Lucy, d. twin, Benjamin and Elisebeth, Feb. 20, 1768.
Mary, d. Benjamin and Elisebeth, Aug. 23, 1762.
Thomas, s. Simeon and Sarah, Dec. 26, 1757.

WOODHEAD (see also Woodward), Brigett, d. William and Mary, Apr. 3, 1669.
[E]lisabeth, d. William and Mary, Dec. 28, 1674.

WOODS (see also Wood), Benja[min] Franklin, s. Isaac, stone-cutter, b. Francestown, N. H., and Mary.M., b. Washington, N. H., at North Chelmsford, Dec. 27, 1848.
Elizabeth, d. Samuel and Mary, Feb. 13, 1720-21.
Lidy, d. Samuel and Mary, Jan. 21, 1733.
Mary, d. Samuel and Mary, July 29, 1718.
Naomie, d. William and Naomi [of Acton. P. R. 4.], May 18, 1759.
Sarah, d. Samwel and Mary, Mar. 8, 1730.

WOODWARD (see also Woodhead), Amelia Mallisia, d. Geo[rge] W., miller, and Eliza A., at North Chelmsford, May 27, 1844.
Charles Henry, s. Geo[rge] W., miller, and Eliza A., at North Chelmsford, Jan. 24, 1847.
Horace George, s. Geo[rge] W., miller, and Eliza Ann, at North Chelmsford, Aug. 31, 1845.

WORCESTER, Benj[amin] Farnum, s. Osgood and Phebe, bp. Apr. 12, 1801. c. r. 1.
George, s. Osgood, bp. Apr. 11, 1807. c. r. 1.
George, s. Osgood, bp. Sept. 4, 1808. c. r. 1.
George Francis, s. George and Margaret J., Aug. 12, 1835.
Jacob Osgood, s. Osgood and Phebe, bp. Mar. 20, 1803. c. r. 1.
Mary Caroline Victoria, d. George and Margaret Jane, Sept. 7, 1841.
Nancy Attilia, d. George and Margaret J., Feb. 10, 1838.
Phebe Jane, d. George and Margaret Jane, Oct. 29, 1833.
Philip, s. Osgood, bp. Sept. 1, 1805. c. r. 1.
Samuel, s. Osgood and Phebe, bp. bet. May 25, and June 8, 1800. c. r. 1.

WORIN (see also Warren), David, s. Jacob and Sarah, Apr. 4, 1696.

WORRIN (see also Warren), Elisibath, d. Josaph and Ruth, Dec. 9, 1696.

WRIGHT (see also Right, Wrighte), Abigail, d. Zach[eus] and Abigail, bp. Oct. 29, 1815. c. r. 1.
Abigaill, d. John and Abigaill, June 23, 1668.
Abigal, d. Ebenezer and Hannah, Dec. 12, 16[torn. 169-. t. c. 1699?].
Adelaid Putnam, d. Calvin T., farmer, and Martha, at South Chelmsford, Sept. 7, 1846.
Calvin Thomas, s. Capt. Zach[eus], bp. June 7, 1819. c. r. 1.
Caroline A., d. Calvin T., farmer, and Martha H., July 28, 1844.
Deborah, d. Joseph and Deborah, July 29, 1703.
Ebenazar, s. Ebenazar and Hanah, Mar. 5, 1705.
[Ebene. t. c.]sar, s. John and Mari, Dec. 17, 1693.
Ebeneser, s. John and Abigal, Nov. 11, 1665.
Edward, s. John and Mary, May 13, 1695.
Eliza, d. Zacheus, bp. Dec. 4, 1803. c. r. 1.
Elizabeth, d. Thomas and Mary, of Westford, bp. June 17, 1781. c. r. 1. [a. 2 y. or under. p. r. 4.]
Elizebeth, d. Ebenezer and Hannah, June 7, 1702.
Ephraim, s. Jacob and Abgaill, Feb. 7, 1725-6.
Esther, d. Henry and Esther, May 3, 1726.
Hanah, d. Ebenezer and Hanah, June 22, 1697.
Hannah, d. John and Hannah, June 2, 1704.
Hannah, d. Caleb and Elizabeth, bp. July 3, 1768. c. r. 1.
Heniry, s. John and Mary, Jan. 10, 17[00. t. c.].
Jacob, s. John and Abigall, July 2, 1667.

WRIGHT, Jacob, s. John and Mary, Jan. 21, 1698.
Jacob, s. Jacob and Abigail, Apr. 2, 1719.
James Maddison, s. Capt. Zaccheas and Nabby, Jan. 25, 1809.
Joel Barrett, s. Zach[e]us and Nabby, Aug. 7, 1800.
John, s. John and Abigall, June 10, 1662.
John, s. twin, John and Mary, Oct. 23, 1[torn. 1701?].
John, s. Joseph and Deborah, Sept. 5, 1706.
Jonathan, s. Joseph and Deborah, Oct. 24 [torn. 170-. T. C. 1701?].
Joseph, s. John and Abagell, Oct. 15, 1663. [Oct. 14. CT. R.]
Joseph, s. Joseph and Deborah, Jan. 31, 1700.
Josiah, s. John and Abigaill, Mar. 10, 1674.
Lediah, d. Ebenezer and Hanah, Apr. 19, 1708.
Lidiah, d. John and Abigaill, Nov. 23, 1686.
Lucy, d. Capt. Zaccheas and Nabby, June 4, 1807.
Mary, d. twin, John and Mary, Oct. 23, 1[torn. 1701?].
Mary, d. Jacob and Abigil, Feb. 4, 1727-8.
Mary, d. Ebenezer and Deborah, Aug. 20, 1729.
Mary, d. Thomas and Mary, of Westford, bp. Nov. 11, 1781. C. R. 1.
Molly, d. Daniel and Mary, Aug. 5, 1765.
Moses, s. Capt. Zaccheas and Nabby, Oct. 10, 1812.
Nabby, d. Zach[eu]s and Nabby, bp. Apr. 28, 1805. C. R. 1.
Phebe, d. Henry and Esther, Nov. 20, 1728.
Prisilah, d. John and Abigaill, Dec. 3, 1671.
Rufus, s. Capt. Zaccheas and Nabby, Aug. 26, 1810.
Ruth, d. Ebenazer and Hanah, June 19, 1715.
Samuell, s. John and Abigaill, 11: 5 m: 1683.
Sarah, d. Thomas and Mary, of Westford, bp. June 17, 1781. C. R. 1. [a. abt. 4 y. P. R. 4.]
Zacheus, s. Capt. Z. and Abigail, bp. Oct. 16, 1817. C. R. 1.
[torn], d. John and Abigaill, Nov. 21, 1678.

WRIGHTE (see also Wright), John, s. John and Marah, Jan. 2 [torn. Jan. 24, 1692. T. C.].

WYER, Esther, d. Jaremiah and Esther, July 30, 1784.
Jeremiah, s. Jeremiah and Esther, Mar. 20, 1781.
Stephen, s. Jarimiah and Esther, Sept. 1, 1787.

WYMAN, Bridgett, d. Benjamin and Bridgett, Dec. 27, 1729.
Edward, s. Dr. Rufus and Ann, July 18, 1816.
Jeffries, s. Dr. Rufus and Ann, Aug. 11, 1814.
Merrill, s. Dr. Rufus and Ann, July 25, 1812.
Reuben, s. Benjamin and Bridget, Sept. 28, 1727.
Rufus, s. Dr. Rufus and Ann, Dec. 15, 1810.
Sarah Austin, d. Josiah A., farmer, and Ruth, July 3, 1843.

CHELMSFORD BIRTHS

SURNAMES MISSING.

[torn]y, d. Thomas and Mary [torn. 1679-80?].
[torn], Febee, d. Solomon and Fran[ces. torn. 1679-80?].
[torn], Henry, s. Andr[torn. 1680?].
[torn], Jonathan, s. Jonathan [torn. 1672?].
[torn], Samuell, s. Joseph and Marth[a], Dec. 30, 1679.
[torn], d. Samuell and Hannah [torn. 1679?].

NEGROES

Boston, ch. under care of Simeon Moors, bp. Sept. 20, 1767. c. r. 1.
Cato, ch. under care of Henry [and Sarah. p. r. 4.] Prockter, bp. Oct. 12, 1766. c. r. 1.
David, boy under the care of Jerahmeel Bowers, bp. Aug. 10, 1746. c. r. 1.
Dinah, girl under care of Joseph Peirce, bp. Sept. 29, 1745. c. r. 1.
Dinah, girl belonging to Joseph Moors, bp. June 19, 1757. c. r. 1.
Moses, mulatto boy belonging to Henry Spaulding, bp. July 21, 1751. c. r. 1.
Phillis, child belonging to Joseph Mooers, bp. Oct. 29, 1752. c. r. 1.
Prince, boy under the care of Dea. Ep[hrai]m Spaulding, bp. Apr. 14, 1745. c. r. 1.
Rose, ch. under care of Sam[ue]ll Adams, bp. Oct. 15, 1758. c. r. 1.
Silva, ch. under care of Benja[min] Byam, bp. Sept. 15, 1765. c. r. 1.
Tony, under care of Nath[anie]ll Butterfield, bp. Sept. 5, 1762. c. r. 1.

CHELMSFORD MARRIAGES

TO THE END OF THE YEAR 1849

ABBOT (see also Abbott), Bridget, and Benjamin Reed, Dec. 17, 1807.*
Caleb, and Mercy Fletcher, Nov. 4, 1806.*
Jonas, and Betsy Parker, Jan. 18, 1807.*
Martha, and Anthony Baker, Oct. 12, 1823.*
Nehemiah, Dr. [of Andover. int.], and Joanna Parker, Dec. 7, 1748.*
William, and Bridget Spaulding, Dec. 28, 1769.*

ABBOTT (see also Abbot, Abbutt), Jeremiah, and Sally Farror, May 30, 1801.*
Joanna, Mrs., and Rev. [Ebenezer. int.] Bridge, at Billerica, —— 29, 1792. [June 12, 1790. int.; May 19, 1791. P. R. 4.]*
Judith, of Billerica, and Levi Felton, int. Sept. 12, 1824.
Rebecca, of Billerica, and Richard Boyanton, Oct. 29, 1761.
Rufus K., of Lawrence, and Nancy J. Parker, int. Dec. 1, 1849.

ABBUTT (see also Abbott), John, jr., of Westford, and Lucy Proctor, int. July 8, 1769.

ACHROYD, Alice, wid., of Dracut, a. 38 y., d. Isaac and Elizabeth Britton, and Thomas H. Standring, widr., of Lowell, a. 39 y., finisher of flannels, s. James and Sarah, Mar. 3, 1849. [Mar. 8. C. R. 3.]

ADAMES (see also Adams), Samuell, and Ester [Hester. CT. R.] Sparhawk, May 7, 1668.
Susannah, and Daniell Walldow, 20: 9 m: 1683.

ADAMS (see also Adames, Addams), Abel, and Olive Richardson of Westford, at Westford, July 22, 1771.*

*Intention also recorded.

CHELMSFORD MARRIAGES

ADAMS, Abel, and Rebeckah Parker, Nov. 29, 1798.*
Abi, and Solomon Byam, at Westford, Mar. 13, 1791.*
Abial C., and Elisabeth H. Gilchrist of Andover, int. Oct. 27, 1847.
Abigail, of Fitchburg, and Jonas Marshal, int. Dec. 29, 1779.
Abigail, and Hildreth P. Dutton, Dec. 22, 1842.*
Abigaill, and John Larned of Sutton, int. Mar. 3, 1732-3.
Almira, of Waltham, and Samuel S. Fisher, int. Dec. 11, 1825.
Benjamin, and Mary Parker, at Charlestown, Dec. 18, 1707.
Benjamin, and Abigail Parker, Apr. 6, 1721.*
Benjamin, and Olive Richardson, int. Oct. 27, 1723.
Benjamin, and Mary Foster, Nov. 21, 1769.*
Benjamin, and Hannah Spaulding, Jan. 14, 1787.*
Benjamin, and Eliza Ann Bond of Watertown, int. Nov. 20, 1831.
Benjamin, and Adeline Bond of Watertown, int. Dec. 7, 1837.
Benj[ami]n F., and Frances C. Leighton of Westford, int. Apr. 23, 1840.
Betsy, of Jaffrey, N. H., and Jonathan Parker, 4th, int. May 10, 1817.
Charles, and Nancy Robbins, Nov. 30, 1826.*
Charles H[enry. int.], of Boston, a. 22 y., trader, s. Charles and Nancy, and Ann R. Byam, a. 22 y., d. Henry and Ann R., Nov. 29, 1849.*
Civonia, of Westford, and James R. Davis, at Westford, May 25, 1837.*
Dorathy, and Hezikiah Kemp of Groton, int. Jan. —, 1737-8.
Elizabeth, and John Cumins, at Charlestown, Oct. 3, 1705.
Elizabeth [Mrs. int.], and Samuel Perham, Mar. 9, 1769.*
Elizabeth, and Otis Spalding, Feb. 2, 1815.*
Ephraim [late of Stoddard, N. H., now resident in Chelmsford. int.], and Betty Pierce, Mar. 6, 1777.*
Ephraim, and Tabatha Parker, Dec. 30, 1813.*
Esther, and Thomas Warren, int. May 8, 1725.
Esther, and Henry Wright, int. Dec. 19, 1725.
Esther, and Jonas Farmer, Dec. 24, 1739.*
Esther, and Josiah Spaulding [of Westford. int.], Nov. 25, 1760.*
Esther, and Elijah Proctor, at Charlestown, Dec. 31, 1766.*
Esther, and Azariah Harris [of Dunstable, N. H. int.], May 22, 1794.*
Frances, and Thomas Baker [of Johnson, Vt. int.], Feb. 28, 1828.*
Hannah, and Oliver Pierce, July 14, 1741.*

*Intention also recorded.

CHELMSFORD MARRIAGES 173

ADAMS, Hannah, and Isaac Adams, Nov. 30, 1797.*
Hannah, and Daniel Richardson of Tyngsborough, Nov. 23, 1826.*
Hannah M[aria. int.], and Edwin S. Byam, Apr. 14, 1833.*
Henry, and Rebekah Byam, Mar. 18, 1810.*
Isaac, and Hannah Adams, Nov. 30, 1797.*
Jesse, and Betty Frost, May 4, 1773.*
Joel, and Catharine Mary Gibson, Aug. 13, 1809.*
John, and Sarah Adams, Mar. 22, 1743.*
John, and Esther Perham, Nov. 24, 1743.*
John [3d. int.], and Molly Parker, Dec. 14, 1769.*
John [3d. int.], and Mary Lock, Dec. 8, 1772.*
John, and Lidia Adams, Feb. 1, 1781.
John [jr. int.], and Elizabeth B. Clark, ——, 1816. [May 28. C. R. 1.]*
Jonathan, and Leah Goold, Aug. 29, 1681.
Jonathan, and Esther Spaulding, June 8, 1769.*
Joseph, and Mary Stratton, int. Sept. 18, 1720.
Joseph [jr. int.], and Lydia Fletcher, Mar. 2, 1748.*
Joseph [jr. int.], and Lucy Blodget, Oct. 17, 1782.*
Joseph, and Dorcas Osgood, Nov. 22, 1804.*
Joseph, and Mehitabel Manning, ——, 1810. [Apr. 25. C. R. 1.]*
Joseph, and Mary Holmes Crane, July —, 1817. P. R. 24.
Joseph, 2d, and Dorothy Perham, int. Feb. 1, 1838.
Lidia, and John Adams, Feb. 1, 1781.
Lucina M[ehitable. int.], and Solomon Parkhurst, Nov. 15, 1832.*
Lucy, and Amos Byam, Oct. 29, 1807.*
Lucy Ann, and Dudley B. Emerson of Warner, N. H., Mar. 1, 1838.*
Lydia, and Thomas Robbins, at Concord, Aug. 6, 1713.
Lydia, and Isaac Warren, May 20, 1762.*
Lydia, and Ephraim Cumings [jr. of Westford. int.], Nov. 25, 1773.*
Lydia K., of Lowell, and David Warren, int. July 1, 1832.
Marah, and Henry Spaulding, Apr. 27, 1743.*
Maria Juliet, and Dr. John C. Bartlett, Oct. 9, 1834.*
Mary, and Sam[ue]ll Web of Braintree, Dec. 16, 1686. CT. R.
Mary, and John Bates, int. Apr. 26, 1717.
Mary, and Isaac Barron, int. Feb. 28, 1724-5.
Mary, and Thomas Spaulding, int. Mar. 13, 1730-31.
Mary, and John Nutten of Westford, at Westford, Dec. 1, 1747.*

*Intention also recorded.

ADAMS, Mary, and Jonas Barrat [of Merrimack, N. H. int.], Nov. 19, 1751.*
Mary, of Pepperell, and Mathew Griffin, June 18, 1777.
Mary, and Phinehas Chamberlin, Mar. 30, 1784.
Mary, and Joseph Foster, at Westford, Sept. 24, 1789.*
Mary, and Elias Sweetser, ———, 1811. [Feb. 27. C. R. 1.]*
Mary, d. W[illia]m, and Daniel Richardson of Tyngsborough [attorney-at-law. C. R. 1.], Apr. 2, 1816.*
Mary, and Charles Sweetser, int. June 24, 1843.
Nabba, of Jaffrey, and Jessa Spaulding, int. Dec. 26, 1789.
Olive, Mrs., and Capt. John Colborn of Dracut, int. Jan. 12, 1744-5.
Olive, and [Lt. C. R. 1.] Abraham Prescott [of Westford. int.], Nov. 13, 1801.*
Olive, and Charles Davis, July 11, 1830.*
Oliver, and Rachel Procter, Dec. 2, 1756.*
Oliver, of Rindge, N. H., and Betty Marshall, int. Sept. 22, 1798.
Otis, and Abigail O. Reed [of Westford. int.], Apr. 4, 1822. P. R. 5.*
Otis, jr., a. 23 y., farmer, s. Otis and Abigail, and Caroline S[ophia. P. R. 28.] Glover, a. 21 y., d. Joel, Nov. 15, 1849.*
Palatiah, and Zubiah Holt [of Reading. int.], Oct. 14, 1773.*
Pallatiah, and Lydia Fletcher, at Charlestown, June 8, 1711.
Patty, Mrs., and Henry Coburn [jr. C. R. 1.], ———, 1811. [May 6. C. R. 1.]*
Rachell, and Isaac Hildreth, int. Mar. 1, 1724-5.
Rachil, and Benjamin Prescut of Jaffrey, N. H., int. Apr. 3, 1775.
Rebecca, and Joseph Dutton of Westford, at Westford, Nov. 6, 1735.
Rebecca, and William Fletcher [of Temple, N. H. int.], Feb. 19, 1782.*
Rebecca, Mrs., and Benjamin S. Tucker, Apr. 18, 1838. C. R. 1.*
Rebeccah [d. W[illia]m. C. R. 1.], and Francis Perkins of Fitchburg, Nov. 15, 1821.*
Rebeckah, d. Samuell, and John Walldo, s. Cornelias, Mar. —, 16 [torn. 1673-4?].
Robert, and Rachel Wheeler, Dec. 10, 1778. [Dec. 9. P. R. 4.]*
Rufus, a. 29 y., instructor, s. Isaac and Hannah, and Jane G. Coxe, a. 23 y., d. William and Rachel, Aug. 2, 1846.*
Salathial, and Susanna Procter, June 5, 1804.*

*Intention also recorded.

ADAMS, Salathial, and Sarah Parker, Feb. 10, 1808.*
Salathiel, and Betsy Chamberlin of Westford, Dec. 18, 1831.
Sallithial, and Sarah Richardson, int. July 25, 1778.
Sally, and Matthew Griffin, ———, 1810. [Nov. 30. C. R. 1.]*
Samuel, of Westford, and Elizabeth Butterfeild, at Westford, Oct. 28, 1728. [Oct. 31. C. R. 4.]*
Samuel, and Esther Fletcher of Westford, at Westford, Aug. 28, 1734.*
Samuel, and Esther Emerson, Dec. 15, 1746.*
Samuel, and Thankfull Chamberlin, Aug. 30, 1770.*
Samuel [jr. int.], and Lucy Putnam, Oct. 29, 1772.*
Samuel, jr., and Sally Kidder of Carlisle, at Concord, Sept. 5, 1780.*
Samuel, jr., and Betsy Webber, int. Dec. 8, 1805.
Samuel, jr., and Dorcas Hale of Carlisle, int. July 29, 1809.
Sarah, and John Adams, Mar. 22, 1743.*
Sarah, and Moses Estabrooks, Dec. 22, 1768.*
Sarah, and John Harwood, Mar. 16, 1774.*
Sarah, and Aaron Chamberlin [jr. int.], Nov. 15, 1781.*
Sarah, and Charles H. Allen of Andover, int. July 30, 1836.
Sarah Ann, and William Lamb, Apr. 7, 1825.*
Sary, and Ephraim Chandler, int. June 15, 1724.
Stephen, and Patty Butterfield, ———, 1805. [Dec. 22. C. R. 1.]*
Susanna, and Thomas Haggit [of Andover. int.], Mar. 12, 1745.*
Thankful, and Aaron Chamberlain, Feb. 14, 1751. [1750-51. P. R. 4.]*
Thomas, and Elizibeth Minat, int. Nov. 5, 1737.
Thomas, and Esther Perry of Westford, at Westford, Mar. 15, 1781.*
Thomas J., and Clara A. Holt of Merrimack, N. H., Oct. 10, 1848.
Timothy, and Dorethy Chamberlin, Aug. 11, 1699.
Timothy, and Joanna Keyes of Westford, at Westford, Sept. 18, 1781.*
William, and Elizabeth Richardson, Feb. 23, 1758.*
William, and Polle Roby of Dunstable, N. H., int. Oct. 31, 1785.

ADDAMS (see also Adams), Jonas, and Rebeckah Spaulding of Billerica, at Billerica, Aug. 4, 1740.

ADVERD, Experience, d. Henry, of Scituate, and Abraham Biam, s. George, June 18, 1672.

*Intention also recorded.

CHELMSFORD MARRIAGES

AIR (see also Ayer), Martha, and Hugh Cargill, both residents in Chelmsford, int. July 8, 1775.

ALDIN, David, of Lowell, a. 25 y., machinist, s. David and Susan, and Nancy W. Scott of Lowell, a. 27 y., d. Abijah and Nancy, Oct. 18, 1845.

ALEXANDER, Hannah, and Daniel Putnum, Feb. 22, 1798.*
James [of Merrimack, N. H. int.], and Joanna Farmer, Aug. 4, 1775.*
Samuel S., of Windham, N. H., a. 27 y., farmer, s. David and Abba, and Clarissa Holden of Tyngsborough, a. 21 y., d. Silas and Polly, Feb. 3, 1847.

ALLEN, Charles H., of Andover, and Sarah Adams, int. July 30, 1836.
Henry C., and Mary E. Holmes of Nashville, N. H., int. May 13, 1848.
John P., and Susan York, both of Westford, Nov. 21, 1847. c. r. 3.
Wilkes, Rev., and Mary Morrill of Boston, Nov. 20, 1805. c. r. 1.*

AMES, Eliza, and Selah R. Arms of Windham, Vt., int. Feb. 12, 1825.
George, of Dracut, and Mary Ann Marshall, Sept. 19, 1839.*
Nathan [of Groton. int.], and Lydia Goodhue, Apr. 10, 1788.*
Nathan, and [Mrs. int.] Phebe Tyler, Oct. 28, 1797.*

ANDERSON, John, and Lydia Dix of Townsend, int. Mar. 13, 1831.

ANDREWS, Edmund [of Concord. int.], and Millecent Barrat, Dec. 1, 1768.*
Eliza, and Matthias Parkhurst [both of Lowell. c. r. 1.], Jan. 28, 1828. [Jan. 10. c. r. 1.]
Ephraim, and Louiza Currier, June 12, 1825.*
Issachar [of Concord. int.], and Rebecca Hodgman, Apr. 20, 1768.*
Issacher [of Billerica. int.], and Betsy Hodgman, ———, 1805. [Sept. 8. c. r. 1.]*

ANGER, Benjamin [Angier, of Charlestown. c. r. 1.], and Tabatha Blood, Mar. 24, 1805.*

*Intention also recorded.

ANSERT, Julia, of Dracut, and Bradley Varnum, int. Dec. 13, 1806.

APPLETON, James P., of Fitchburg, and Harriet N. Toothaker, int. Oct. 2, 1846.

ARMS, Selah R., of Windham, Vt., and Eliza Ames, int. Feb. 12, 1825.

ATWOOD, Joshua [of Westford. int.], and Esther Chamberlain, Mar. 7, 1758.*
Joshua, of Templeton, and Martha Barrett, at Templeton, Mar. 29, 1780.*

AUSTIN, Adeline, of Andover, and Zaccheus Fletcher, int. Nov. 23, 1823.
Daniel F., and Martha McGrath of Nashua, N. H., int. Oct. 22, 1840.
Deborah, of Methuen, and Reuben Hamblet, at Methuen, Nov. 8, 1759.*

AVERY, Sally, and Joshua Stone [of Concord. int.], Nov. 26, 1789.*

AVRIL, Mary, and Henry Laws [of Billerica. int.], June 4, 1809.*

AYER (see also Air, Ayers), Phineas, and Betsy Corlis of Haverhill, int. Aug. 1, 1812.

AYERS (see also Ayer), Hiram, and Sophia Griffin, Oct. 2, 1828.*

BAAUL (see also Ball), Jeremiah, of Townsend, and Hannah Fletcher, int. Apr. 15, 1765.

BABCOCK, Ann, and Charles Swett, Sept. 3, 1829.*

BACHELLER, Eliza J., Mrs., and Eben[ezer] P. Blood, int. Feb. 5, 1848.

BADGER, Obediah, and Maria Cutler of Burlington, int. Apr. 1, 1827.

*Intention also recorded.

BAILEY (see also Bayley), George O., a. 25 y., stone-cutter, s. Joseph and Laura, and Mary Ann Woods, a. 21 y., d. Isaac and Mary, Sept. 7, 1848.*
Otis, and Sophia Marshall of Lunenburg, int. Mar. 23, 1821.

BAKE (see also Bauke), Hannah, and Joseph Parker, Nov. 19, 1683.

BAKER, Anthony, and Martha Abbot, Oct. 12, 1823.*
Joseph, of Woburn, and Hanna Bauk, at Woburn, Oct. 4, 1686.
Thomas [of Johnson, Vt. int.], and Frances Adams, Feb. 28, 1828.*

BALCOM, Almira, and Joseph Willoughby, int. Jan. 6, 1826.

BALDWIN, Cyrus, Lt., and Elizabeth Varnum of Dracut, at Dracut, Apr. 28, 1799.*
David, of Billerica, and Ruhamah Davis, at Billerica, July 12, 1792.*
John [jr., of Billerica. int.], and Elizabeth Parkhurst, Feb. 21, 1758.*
Rhoda, and Isaac B. Cowdry of Lowell, Nov. 2, 1837.*
Samuel, of Dracut, and Mary Dane, Feb. 1, 1816.*
Sarah, and John Esty of Billerica, June 21, 1840.*
Thomas [of Cavendish, Vt. int.], and Betcey [Elizbath. int.] Davis, Jan. 3, 1797.*

BALES, Samuel B., of Wilton, N. H., a. 27 y., blacksmith, s. John and Milly, and Olive Blanchard of Milford, N. H., a. 25 y., d. Luther and Mary, Nov. 26, 1846.

BALKE, see Bauke.

BALL (see also Baaul), Abigail, and James Kidder, int. May 30, 1752.
Abner, and Sarah Farrar of Concord, int. Sept. 14, 1823.
Bathsheba, of Townsend, and Hezekiah Winn, at Townsend, Nov. —, 1791.*
John, of Concord, and Anna Blazedil, int. Aug. 2, 1746.
Olive, and Reuben Cory, at Concord, Dec. 6, 1757.*
Phebe, resident in Chelmsford, and Amos Kidder, int. Sept. 22, 1752.

*Intention also recorded.

CHELMSFORD MARRIAGES 179

BALL, Sarah, of Concord, and Samuel Fletcher, at Concord, June 7, 1699.
Susanna, and Joseph Haywood, at Townsend, Dec. 16, 1788.*

BALLARD (see also Bollard), Sally, and William B. Fletcher, Oct. 21, 1804.*
Samuel F., and Sarah Ann Sargeant of Lowell, int. Oct. 27, 1839.

BANCROF (see also Bancroft), Stowell, and Martha D. Trough of Mount Vernon, N. H., int. June 12, 1825.

BANCROFT (see also Bancrof), Cloa, of Tyngsborough, and Oliver Richardson, at Tyngsborough, Mar. 31, 1791.*
Edmund [of Pepperell. int.], and [Mrs. int.] Rachel Barron, Apr. 12, 1757.*
Elizabeth, of Dunstable, and Ezra Thompson, June 19, 1755.
Isaac, and Hannah Haywood, Dec. 12, 1813.*
Luther, of Pepperell, and Anna Fletcher, int. Jan. 1, 1803.
Mary Dandridge, of Tyngsborough, and Jonathan Barron, at Tyngsborough, Nov. 19, 1795.*
Rebecca, of Tyngsborough, and Samuel Howard, at Tyngsborough, June 6, 1790.
Stowell, and Mary Heywood, Dec. 3, 1822.*
Susanna, of Tyngsborough, and David Howe Williston [of Tunbridge, Vt. dup.], Jan. 26, 1796.

BANNISTER, Louisa, and James Y. Smith, int. Mar. 6, 1836.

BARAT (see also Barrett), Dorithy, and Samuel Robins, Mar. 4, 1701-2.

BARBER, Charles H., and Lucinda Spaulding, Feb. 8, 1826. [Feb. 10. c. R. 1.]
Charles H. [N. c. R. 1.], and Mary Spaulding [d. Henry, deceased. c. R. 1.], Nov. 26, 1829.*

BARD, see Bearde.

BARDEN, Lettice W., of Lowell, and Azariah Proctor, 3d, int. Oct. 14, 1832.
Zelphia F., and Reuben K. Hardy, Dec. 16, 1833.

*Intention also recorded.

BARETT (see also Barrett), Hannah, and Jonathan Bowers, May 17, 1699.
Joseph, and Martha Goole, d. Francis and Rose, 17: 7 m: 1672.
Margreat, and Edward Spaldin, 22: 9 m: 1681.
Mehetable, d. Thomas and Francis, and Samuell Goole of Dunstable, Mar. 17, 1684.

BARGES (see also Burgess), Mary, of Westford, and Lemuel Lawrance, int. Sept. 21, 1811.

BARIT (see also Barrett), Benjamin, and Hanah Goo[faded], d. Elizabeth, June 18, 1705.
Ebenezer, and Abigil Wallker, int. Sept. 14, 1728.
Joseph, and Abigal Hildreth, Dec. 15, 1696.
Mary, and John Spalding, Feb. 6, 1705.
Rebeca, and Walter Power of Concord, Dec. 16, 1696.
Sarah, and Isaac Spaulding, int. Aug. 4, 1733.

BARITT (see also Barrett), Ephraim, and Rachil Shedd, int. June 9, 1733.

BARKER, Asa, and Sally Foster of Westford, at Carlisle, Sept. 18, 1794.*
Asa, and Nancy Jones, Sept. 7, 1808.*
Elizabeth, of Tyngsborough, and Ebenezer Hall, int. Oct. 17, 1840.
Lidia, and Samuel Healy, both of Tyngsborough, Oct. 10, 1804.
Mary, of Hillsborough, N. H., and Justus Pike, int. Apr. 27, 1823.
Mary, Mrs. [wid. int.], and Jacob Kidder, Nov. 6, 1839.*
Phebe, and Sampson Stevens, May 24, 1791.*
Priscilla, see Parker, Priscilla.

BARNES (see also Barns), Harriet, and James Flood [Floyd. int.], July 17, 1825. C. R. 5.*

BARNET, Susanna, of Londonderry, and James Melvin, int. Jan. 7, 1807.

BARNS (see also Barnes), Lucy C., of Bedford, N. H., and Henry E. Boswith, int. July 18, 1839.
Thomas, and Mary Fletcher of Westford, int. Mar. 13, 1772.

*Intention also recorded.

BARON (see also Barron), Moses, and Mary Richardson, Feb. 2, 1697-8.

BAROS, Joshaue, and Mary Chemberling, July 24, 1696.

BARR, John [of Reading. int.], and Sally Moors, May 20, 1819.*

BARRAT (see also Barrett), Benjamin, and Olive Keyes, Nov. 24, 1760.*
Hannah, and Zacheriah Shed, Nov. 24, 1743.*
Jonas [of Merrimack, N. H. int.], and Mary Adams, Nov. 19, 1751.*
Jonathan [jr. int.], and Abigail Rayment, Mar. 28, 1771.*
Joseph, and Sarah Martin, Oct. 13, 1743.*
Lucy, and David Parker, Mar. 14, 1758.*
Martha, and Zacheus [Zechariah. c. r. 1. and int.] Walker, Dec. 23, 1741.*
Mary, and Noah Emery [of Townsend. int.], Dec. 22, 1743.*
Millecent, and Edmund Andrews [of Concord. int.], Dec. 1, 1768.*
Moses [of Nottingham. int.], and Hannah Procter, Nov. 11, 1742.*
Nath[anie]ll, and Martha Wheeler [of Acton. int.], Nov. 30, 1748.*
Patty, and Benjamin Spaulding, Nov. 29, 1764. [Nov. 27. p. r. 4.]*
Rebecca, and William Lock ["of Monadnick No four," N. H. int.], Feb. 10, 1773.*
Sarah, and Oliver Parker, Jan. 22, 1767.*
Simeon, and Ruth Wright [of Westford. int.], Apr. 11, 1776.*
Thaddeus, and Hannah Meers, Feb. 5, 1789.*

BARRATT (see also Barrett), Elizabeth, and John Heald [of Acton. int.], July 18, 1745.*
Phineus [of Stoddard, N. H. int.], and Polly Herrick, Jan. 15, 1812.*

BARRET (see also Barrett), Abigaill, and Ezekiell Keyes, int. Sept. 30, 1722.
Betty, and Nathan Crosby [jr. int.], June 21, 1764.*
Christopher, and Mary Clark, Sept. 6, 1764.*
John, and Margaret Parker, at Charlestown, Nov. 29, 1705.
Joseph, of Killingly, and Mercy Procter, int. Apr. 12, 1746.

*Intention also recorded.

BARRET, Margret, and Ebenezer Robbins, —— [1701 or 1702?].
Martha, d. Thomas, and Henry Sparks of Exeter, July 10, 1676.
Mary, and George Robbins, Jan. 21, 1686. CT. R.
Rachel, and Nathaniel Langley [Longley. int.], Sept. 14, 1757.*
Sarah, and Ambrose Swallow, at Woburn, Dec. 8, 1696.
Sarah, and Georg Glazier of Lancaster, Dec. 17, 1700.
Sarah, and Daniel Foster, int. Oct. 22, 1749.
Thomas, and Rachel Burdge, May 20, 1714.

BARRETT (see also Barat, Barett, Barit, Baritt, Barrat, Barratt, Barret, Barrit, Barritt, Barrot), Anna, and John Swallow, Jan. 3, 1692-3. CT. R.
Benjamin, and Hannah Foster, at Charlestown, June 18, 1705.
Benjamin [of Killingly. int.], and Thankful Procter, Sept. 23, 1746.*
Hannah, Mrs., and Joel Parkhurst, Nov. 10, 1829.*
John, s. John, and Dorathy Proctor, Dec. 18, 1679.
John, and Martha Heald of Acton, at Concord, May 24, 1738.*
[J]onathan, and Sarah Stevens [torn] 17, ——. [1676?]
Joseph, and Mary Taylor of Concord, at Concord, Mar. 24, 1714.
Josiah, and Mary Dill of Concord, at Concord, Feb. 20, 1749.
Lidiah, d. John, and James Harwood, Apr. 11, 1678.
Martha, and Joshua Atwood of Templeton, at Templeton, Mar. 29, 1780.*
Mary, and Nathan[ie]ll Cokar of Sudbury, Oct. 10, 1693. CT. R.
Moses, s. Thomas, and Anna Smith, d. John, of Dorchester, Sept. 10, 1684.
Moses, and Hannah Wyman, int. Nov. 21, 1824.
Samuell, s. John, and Sarah Buttrik, d. Will[iam], of Concord, Feb. 21, 1683.
Thomas R., of Billerica, a. 35 y., trader, s. Stephen and Olive, of Billerica, and Mahala Brown of Billerica, a. 25 y., d. Elisha and Mary, of Billerica, Sept. 23, 1844.

BARRIT (see also Barrett), Benjamin, and Sarah Chamberlin, Sept. 3, 1786.*
Joel, and Elizebeth Burg, Jan. 31, 1781-2.*
Lucy, and Ebenezer Wright of Narragansett, No. 6, int. Aug. 18, 1758.
Molley, and Stephen Barrit [of Winchendon. int.], Dec. 13, 1780.*

*Intention also recorded.

BARRIT, Stephen [of Winchendon. int.], and Molley Barrit, Dec. 13, 1780.*
Zacheus [of Templeton, N. H. int.], and Rebeckah Burge, May 2, 1780.*

BARRITT (see also Barrett), Sary, and John Cragin of Acton, int. Sept. 27, 1755.

BARRON (see also Baron), Charl[e]s, and Abigail Foster, int. Oct. 17, 1761.
Elias, of Carlisle, and Patty Chamberlin, Sept. 10, 1822.*
Elisabeth, and Samuel French of Billerica, at Billerica, July 7, 1755. [Mar. 19, 1742-3. int.]*
Elizabeth, and Silas Pierce, Apr. 12, 1774.*
Hanah, and Thomas Procter, int. Dec. 23, 1722.
Isaac, and Mary Adams, int. Feb. 28, 1724-5.
John, of Dracut, and Hannah Richardson, int. Apr. 23, 1721.
Jonathan, and Rebeckah Prescot of Concord, int. Aug. 9, 1724.
Jonathan, and Rachel Howard, Oct. 19, 1749.*
Jonathan, and Mary Dandridge Bancroft of Tyngsborough, at Tyngsborough, Nov. 19, 1795.*
Lucy, and Azeriah Spaulding, Sept. 24, 1782.*
Martha, of Dracut, and James Stevens, int. Feb. 15, 1817.
Mary, Mrs., and Col. Tho[ma]s How of Marlborough, int. Nov. 7, 1724.
Mary, Mrs., and Col. Joseph Varnum of Dracut, int. Dec. 17, 1743.
Mary, and Isaac Stokes [of Boston. int.], Aug. 2, 1779.*
Moses, and Lucy Parker, int. Nov. 26, 1732.
Oliver, and Abigail Procter, July 30, 1755.*
Rachel [Mrs. int.], and Edmund Bancroft [of Pepperell. int.], Apr. 12, 1757.*
Rebecca [Mrs. P. R. 4.], and Col. Oliver Wilder [of Lancaster. int.], Aug. 2, 1749.*
Rebecca, and Jepthah Spaulding, July 14, 1779.*
Samuel, and Sarah Fasset [of Bedford. int.], May 23, 1744.*
Samuell, and Mary Sterns of Billerica, May 28, 1705.
Sam[ue]ll, and Sarah Howard, int. Nov. 22, 1730.
Sary, and Zebediah Richardson of Woburn, int. Dec. 20, 1755.
Susanna, and Benjamin Chamberlain [3d. int.], Mar. 21, 1758.*
William, of Amherst, N. H., and Hannah Parker, int. July 15, 1767.

*Intention also recorded.

BARROT (see also Barrett), Martha [H. int.], and Micajah Parkhurst, Apr. 6, 1818.*
Reuben, and Sarah Fletcher, at Woburn, June 19, 1751.*

BARRY, William, of Boston, and Lucinda Pierce, int. Sept. 27, 1845.

BARSTOW, Thomas, and Sarah M. Winn of Hudson, N. H., int. Feb. 1,1835.

BARTLETT, John C., Dr., and Maria Juliet Adams, Oct. 9, 1834.*

BARTON, Martha, and John Harwood, both of Boston, Nov. 20, 1679.

BATEMAN, Abigail, and Stephen Peirce, Apr. 12, 1814.*
Betsy, and Adams Fletcher, int. Apr. 11, 1806.
Charlotte, and Ezekiel Byam, Feb. 15, 1818.*
Hannah, and Ezra Fletcher [of Westford. int.], Oct. 30, 1800.*
Lydia, and Steven Cory of Groton, ——, 1816. [Apr. 14. c. r. 1.]*
Sally, and Nathan Buttrick, Apr. 20, 1820.*

BATES (see also Batties), Bettey, and Isaac Chamberlin, June 13, 1782.*
Betty, and Ephraim Blood, int. Jan. 15, 1731-2.
Debborah, and Jonathan Fletcher, int. Nov. 8, 1719.
Edward, and Mary Snow, int. Feb. 7, 1719-20.
Hannah, and William Read, int. Feb. 7, 1719-20.
John, and Mary Adams, int. Apr. 26, 1717.
Jonathan, and Abigail Howard, int. Apr. 20, 1745. (Apr. 23, banns forbidden by Joanna Parker.)
Lydia, and William Fletcher [jr. int.], Jan. 25, 1774.*
Lydiah, and Samuel Cotten, July 22, 1695.
Mary, and Joseph Spaulding of Groton, int. Mar. 25, 1727.
Robert, and Lydia Spaulding, Apr. 19, 1748.*
Sybel, and Samuel Marshall, June 4, 1780.

BATHRICK, Jonathan, of Leicester, and Rachel Cory, int. Feb. 18, 1748-9.

*Intention also recorded.

BATS (see also Batties), Elisabeth, and Jonathan Richardson, Nov. 8, 1692.
John, and Mary Farwell, Dec. 22, 1665.
Sarah, and Benjamin Buterfild, Feb. 16, 1697.

BATTIES (see also Bates, Bats, Battyes, Betties, Betty, Bettyes), Robert, and Hannah Perrey, int. Mar. 29, 1766.

BATTYES (see also Batties), Andrew, and Mary Tucker, Dec. 24, 1739.*

BAUK (see also Bauke), Hanna, and Joseph Baker of Woburn, at Woburn, Oct. 4, 1686.

BAUKE (see also Bake, Bauk), Sarah, and John Graves of Hatfield, 25: 8 br: 1686. CT. R.

BAYLEY (see also Bailey), Serah B., and Achsah Jones, both of Lowell, Dec. 31, 1840. C. R. 3.

BEAN, Eldad P., and Sarah Sweetser of Westford, at Westford, Nov. 28, 1839.*

BEARD (see also Bearde), Daniel, of Billerica, and Rebecca Clark, int. Nov. 10, 1804.

BEARDE (see also Beard), John [Bard. int.], of Billerica, and Abigail Kemp, at Billerica, Nov. 16, 1769.*

BELNAP, Hanah, and David Chambers, int. Oct. 24, 1780.

BENNET, Zephaniah, and Polly R. Woodward of Tyngsborough, int. Mar. 16, 1830.

BETTIES (see also Batties), Andrew, jr., and Rebecca Farmer of Westford, at Westford, Dec. 6, 1765.*

BETTY (see also Batties), Andrey [Andrew. C. R. 1.], and Mary Johnston, Feb. 23, 1758.*

BETTYES (see also Batties), William, and Olive Corey, at Westford, June 9, 1785.*

*Intention also recorded.

BIAM (see also Byam), Abraham, s. George, and Experience Adver[d. T. C.], d. Henry, of Scituate, June 18, 1672.

BIDGBY (see also Bixby), Deborah, and Henry Stevens, int. June 15, 1724.

BIRCK, Hermonis, and Margaret Herrin, int. Nov. 9, 1816.

BIRD, Henry M., a. 22 y., moulder, s. Jacob P. and Nancy T., and Olive Caryl, a. 21 y., d. John and Lucy, Nov. 19, 1846.*

BIXBY (see also Bidgby), Thomas, and Phebe Spaulding, int. May 7, 1743.

BLACKWELL, Emily, of Lowell, and Elisha Record, int. July 24, 1846.

BLADGET (see also Blodget), Thomas, and Mary Druse of Groton, July 8, 1696.
William, and Mary Worin, June 14, 1696.

BLAISDELL (see also Blaisdill, Blasdel, Blazedell, Blazedil), Adeline F., of Campton, N. H. [of Lowell. C. R. 3.], a. 20 y., d. Moses and Abba, and Warren Damon, jr., widr., of Lowell, a. 28 y., machinist, s. Warren and Nancy, Oct. 30, 1847.
Dorothy, and Joseph Duren [of Billerica. int.], Sept. 6, 1823.*
Mary, and Jonathan Stedman [of Cambridge. int.], June 10, 1742.*
Sarah, and Joseph Haywood, Oct. 30, 1745.*

BLAISDILL (see also Blaisdell), John, and Mary Sawyer of Newbury, at Newbury, Aug. 5, 1756.*

BLAKE, Lois, of Franklin, and Samuel Fechem, int. July 17, 1819.

BLANCHARD, Abigail, and John Bloget, int. July 14, 1723.
Asa, and Sybel Peirce, May 1, 1800.
Caled, of Andover, and Lucy Goold, int. May 21, 1787.
Elizabeth, and Joseph Parker, Jan. 7, 1802.*
Joshua [of Hollis. int.], and Sarah Burge, Dec. 23, 1747.*
Josiah, and Rachel Clemmons of Dracut, int. Mar. 6, 1807.

*Intention also recorded.

CHELMSFORD MARRIAGES

BLANCHARD, Olive, of Milford, N. H., a. 25 y., d. Luther and Mary, and Samuel B. Bales of Winton, N. H., a. 27 y., blacksmith, s. John and Milly, Nov. 26, 1846.
Rebecca, and Elijah Mansfield [of Lynn. int.], May 18, 1769.*
Sarah, and Robert Usher, both of Dunstable, Jan. 23, 1693-4. CT. R.
Sarah, and John Byham, Sept. 12, 1758.*
Susanna, of Carlisle, and David Carlton, int. Oct. 17, 1819.
Tabitha, and Thomas Blodget, at Concord, Apr. 21, 1719.
Thomas [jr., of Dunstable. int.], and Dorcas Dutton, Sept. 24, 1751.*
William, of Hollis, N. H., and Martha Walker, int. July 20, 1751.
[torn], d. ——, and [torn], July 22, 1679.

BLASDEL (see also Blaisdell), Henry, and Lidia Parker, int. Sept. 27, 1719.

BLAZEDELL (see also Blaisdell), Aaron, and Olive Byam, Nov. 29, 1787.*
Lydia, and Samuel Sims [of Dracut. int.], Nov. 22, 1786.*

BLAZEDIL (see also Blaisdell), Anna, and John Ball of Concord, int. Aug. 2, 1746.

BLODGET (see also Bladget, Blodgett, Bloged, Bloget, Blogget, Bloggett), Benjamin [late of Litchfield, N. H. int.], and Susanna McLain, Jan. 14, 1762.*
Elizabeth, and John Hill, June 22, 1711.
Elizabeth, and Benjamin Parker [jr. int.], Jan. 3, 1750. [1749-50. P. R. 4.]*
Esther, and Lenord Foster, int. Oct. 21, 1758.
Esther, and John Robie, Aug. 15, 1771.*
Hannah, and Zachariah Richardson [jr. int.], Oct. 9, 1753.*
Jacob, of Tyngsborough, and Susan Blodget [d. Ezra. C. R. 1.], Feb. 19, 1818.*
Lucy, and Joseph Adams [jr. int.], Oct. 17, 1782.*
Lydia, and John Meads, Nov. 24, 1774.*
Mary, and William Fletcher, Dec. 31, 1747.*
Nancy, of Merrimack, N. H., and John Hunt, int. Apr. 3, 1820.
Nathaniel, and Elizebeth Warren, July 17, 1695.
Oliver, and Rebecca Butterfield, June 15, 1756.*

*Intention also recorded.

BLODGET, Rufus M. [of Tyngsborough. int.], and Hannah Kidder, May 23, 1827.*
Sibel, and Asa Hodgman, Nov. 28, 1782.*
Simeon, and Lydia Spaulding, Oct. 8, 1751.*
Simeon, and Molly Dunn, Dec. 19, 1786.*
Susan [d. Ezra. c. R. 1.], and Jacob Blodget of Tyngsborough, Feb. 19, 1818.*
Thomas, and Tabitha Blanchard, at Concord, Apr. 21, 1719.
Zebulon, Lt., of Dunstable, and Mary Richardson, at Dracut, May 30, 1793.*
——, of Dunstable, and Francis Richardson, int. Apr. 27, 1823.

BLODGETT (see also Blodget), Frederick W., and Betsy B. Johnson of Groton, int. May 4, 1837.

BLOGED (see also Blodget), Daniell, and Mare [Butterfield. CT. R.], Sept. 15, 1653.

BLOGET (see also Blodget), Elizabeth, and Zachariah Spaulding, int. June 9, 1723.
Elizabeth, and Joshua Fletcher, int. Nov. 9, 1723.
Jacob, and Mary Richardson, int. Dec. 19, 1724.
John, and Abigail Blanchard, int. July 14, 1723.
Mary, and Andrew Foster, int. Feb. 25, 1721-2.
Mary, and Henry Spaulding, int. May 19, 1723.

BLOGGET (see also Blodget), Benjamin, and Elizabeth Fletcher of Westford, at Westford, Feb. 14, 1733.*
Sarai, and Ebenezer Parkhurst, int. Oct. 15, 1721.
William, and Elizabeth Wright, int. Dec. 10, 1721.

BLOGGETT (see also Blodget), Benjamin, s. Daniell, and Mary Pellat, d. Thomas, of Concord, Feb. 14, 1683.
Daniell, and Sarah Underwod, d. William, Mar. 10, 1669.
Thomas, and Mary Perkis, d. Joseph, 29: 4 m: 1683.

BLOOD, Abel, and Betsy Davis, June 14, 1826.
Benjamin, 3d, and Susannah Jewett of Hollis, N. H., int. Mar. 4, 1826.
Benjamin, jr., and Jane S. Wood, Feb. 26, 1832.
Benj[ami]n, jr., and Betsey A. Robinson, July 15, 1841.*
Benjamin, jr., widr., a. 43 y., box maker, s. Benja[min] and Mary T., and Eliza Davis, a. 35 y., d. Deliveranc and Eliza, Apr. 2, 1849.*
Betty, and Joshua Davis [jr. of Billerica. int.], May 25, 1769.*

*Intention also recorded.

CHELMSFORD MARRIAGES 189

BLOOD, Charles [Lt. int.], and Betsy Dunn, Aug. 5, 1822. [Aug. 15. C. R. 1.]*
Charles A., and Sarah M. Clark of Lowell, int. Feb. 17, 1848.
Darkhas, and Robert Mear, int. Nov. 10, 1788.
Eben[ezer] P., and Mrs. Eliza J. Bacheller, int. Feb. 5, 1848.
Eliza Jane [of North Chelmsford. C. R. 3.], a. 22 y., d. Charles and Betsey, and David P. Clark [of North Chelmsford. C. R. 3.], a. 24 y., moulder, s. Jona[than] and Sarah, Jan. 31, 1848.*
Elizabeth, and Thomas Goodhue, July 30, 1801.
Ephraim, and Betty Bates, int. Jan. 15, 1731-2.
Esther, of Carlisle, and Jonathan Shed, at Carlisle, Dec. 13, 1781.*
Harriot, of Carlisle, and Abel Spalding, int. Feb. 2, 1823.
Joseph, and Sarah W. Clark of Lowell, int. Aug. 3, 1838.
Josiah, of Hollis, N. H., and Sary Haywood, int. Sept. 25, 1755.
Josiah [of Westford. int.], and Tabitha Corey, July 2, 1767.*
Josiah, and Hannah Smith of Shirley, at Shirley, May 21, 1799.*
Luther, and Martha Woodward, int. Jan. 21, 1837.
Molly, and William Daverson [Davidson. C. R. 1.], Nov. 19, 1795.*
Nathan, and Catharine F. Wellman, int. Apr. 7, 1833.
Nathaniel, and Hannah ——, June 13, 1670. CT. R.
Oliver, and Sally Dunn, Oct. 24, 1808.*
Priscella, a. 23 y., and William Patterson, musician, s. W[illia]m, Mar. 21, 1847.*
Robert, sr., of Concord, and Hannah Parker, at Concord, Jan. 8, 1690.
Sarah, d. Robertt, and Daniell Coborn, June 18, 1685.
Stephen, Capt., of Carlisle, and Mehitable Tuttle, at Carlisle, May 10, 1798.*
Tabatha, and Benjamin Anger [Angier of Charlestown. C. R. 1.], Mar. 24, 1805.*

BLUNT, Harriet F., of Eden, Me., and Haskell Spalding, int. Aug. 22, 1824.
William, and Elisabeth Bollard, d. William, of Andover, Nov. 11, 1668.

BODWELL, Elizabeth, of Methuen, and Jonathan Jones, int. Mar. 15, 1823.

*Intention also recorded.

BOLLARD (see also Ballard), Ane, of Andover, and John Spalden, 20: 7 m: 1681.
Elisabeth, d. William, of Andover, and William Blunt, Nov. 11, 1668.
Lidiah, d. William, of Andover, and Joseph Buterfeild, 12: 3 m: 1674. [2 m. dup.]

BOLTON, Mary, and Hector M. Page, Dec. 16, 1838.*

BOND, Adeline, of Watertown, and Benjamin Adams, int. Dec. 7, 1837.
Eliza Ann, of Watertown, and Benjamin Adams, int. Nov. 20, 1831.
Jane, of Watertown, and Francis Bush, int. Oct. 5, 1828.

BONNER, Martha, and Benjamin P. Hutchins of Carlisle, June 4, 1843.*

BORNE, James, and Mary Proctor, d. Robertt and Jane, Apr. 3, 1685.

BOSWITH (see also Bosworth), Henry E., and Lucy C. Barns of Bedford, N. H., int. July 18, 1839.

BOSWORTH (see also Boswith), Geo[rge] W., of North Chelmsford, and Amy Cram of Lyndeborough, N. H., int. Feb. 4, 1847.

BOWERS, Abiah, of Dracut, and Asaph Spaulding, int. Feb. 12, 1807.
Alpheus, and Julia Augusta Parkhurst, Dec. 1, 1831.*
Ann, and Artemas Holden, int. Sept. 21, 1823.
Betcey, of Greenfield, N. H., and Joshua Davis, int. Dec. 8, 1796.
Betty, and Stephen Pierce, Feb. 26, 1745.*
Betty, and William Corlis of Salem, int. June 18, 1776.
Francis [of Greenfield, N. H. int.], and Rachel Harwood, Dec. 6, 1797.*
Hannah, and Simeon Comings of Merrimack, N. H., int. June 18, 1763.
Hannah, and Micah Phillips [jr. int.], at Dracut, Mar. 28, 1793.*
Hannah, and Benjamin Pierce of Woburn, at Woburn, Apr. 3, 1793. [1693?]

*Intention also recorded.

BOWERS, Irene, and Charles V[arnum. c. r. 1.] Harwood [Howard. int. and c. r. 1.], Dec. 29, 1826.*
James, and Hannah Tayler of Dunstable, int. Nov. 23, 1823.
Jerahmeel, jr., and Elizabeth Shedd of Billerica, int. June 4, 1748.
Jerahmell, and Elisabeth Farley of Billerica, at Billerica, Mar. 17, 1735-6.*
Jonas [Jonathan. int.], and Mary Grimes of Billerica, at Watertown, June 7, 1726.*
Jonathan, and Hannah Barett, May 17, 1699.
Jonathan, and Anna Coburn, Apr. 6, 1824.*
Joseph, and Rhoda Butterfield, Apr. 1, 1804. [1803. p. r. 11.]*
Joseph, of Lowell, and Almaria Stevens, int. Nov. 6, 1830.
Louisa G., and James A. Hay, int. July 28, 1822.
Lucy, and Oliver Coleburn of Dunstable, int. Apr. 6, 1734.
Luke, and Anna Pratt, at Dracut, Mar. 20, 1787.*
Mary A., of Merrimack, N. H., and Amos Adams Byam, int. Feb. 24, 1833.
Mary G., and George Stark of Bedford, N. H., int. Oct. 26, 1848.
Micajah, and Mary Roby of Dunstable, N. H., int. May 26, 1822.
Micajah [of Lowell. int.], and Lucinda [J. int.] Spalding, Dec. 3, 1835.*
Olive, and Willard Marshall, Dec. 28, 1795.*
Oliver, and [Mrs. int.] Elizabeth Pierce, Jan. 3, 1769.*
Philip, and Mary Kidder of Billerica, int. Apr. 4, 1809.
Sarah, and Mial Mooars, at Dracut, Jan. 24, 1793.*
Sewall, and Sylvia P. Fisher of Lowell, int. Nov. 6, 1847.
Susan B., and Christopher Roby, Aug. 31, 1843.*
William, and Hannah Kidder of Billerica, at Billerica, Jan. 1, 1761.*

BOWLES, Julia C., Mrs., and Francis Snow of Wilmington, int. July 22, 1848.

BOYANTON (see also Boynton), Augusta, of Carlisle, a. 23 y., d. Samuel and Sarah S., and John Carlton of Lowell, a. 25 y., mason, s. David, Jan. 11, 1849.
Richard, and Rebecca Abbott of Billerica, Oct. 29, 1761.

BOYDEN, Horatio, and Harriet Sprage of Billerica, int. Mar. 17, 1822.

*Intention also recorded.

BOYNTON (see also Boyanton), Nathaniel, and Hannah Perham of Dunstable, int. Jan. 24, 1719-20.

BRACKETT, Mary, d. John, of Billerica, and Edward Spaldin, s. John, Nov. 27, 1683.

BRADLEY (see also Bradly), Anna [Mrs., now resident in Chelmsford. int.], and James Dunn, May 27, 1777.*
Foster, and Phebe Stevens, Feb. 14, 1810.*

BRADLY (see also Bradley), Peleg, Dr., of Dracut, and Louisa Whitemore, June 26, 1817.*

BRADT, Ann Eliza [of the glass factory. c. r. 1.], and Asa Underwood, Feb. 15, 1822.*
Barnabas N., and Joanna C. Butterfield, int. Dec. 25, 1831.

BRANNON, George, and Joanna Ivory, int. Apr. 29, 1843.

BRIDGE, Betcey, and Benja[min] Fiske, Apr. 12, 1798.*
Ebenezer, Rev., and Mrs. Sarah Stoddard, int. Oct. 24, 1741.
Ebenezer, Col. [jr. int.], and Mary Mountfort of Boston, at Boston, Jan. 25, 1787. p. r. 4.*
[Ebenezer. int.], Rev., and Mrs. Joanna Abbott, at Billerica, —— 29, 1792. [June 12, 1790. int.; May 19, 1791. p. r. 4.]*
Lucretia [Mrs. int.], and Dr. Walter Hastings, Apr. 10, 1777.*
Mary [Mrs. int.], and Timothy Winn [jr. of Woburn. int.], June 4, 1772.*
Sarah, and Rev. Henry Cummings [of Billerica. int.], Sept. 19, 1791. p. r. 4.*
William, and Rachel Minot, Feb. 13, 1776.*
William Stoddard, and Mary Pitts of Tyngsborough, int. Sept. 7, 1811.

BRIGGS, Sarah, and Caleb Torroy, both residents in Chelmsford, int. Sept. 9, 1801.

BRITTON, Jared B., and Keziah Dean of Easton, int. Feb. 24, 1838.

BROOKS, Daniel, of Westford, and Lois Snow, at Westford, Nov. 16, 1797.*
Daniel, of Lowell, and Caroline Butterfield, int. May 12, 1833.

*Intention also recorded.

CHELMSFORD MARRIAGES 193

BROWN (see also Browne), Ann, of Weare, N. H., and Aaron Hall, int. Nov. 18, 1842.
Betsy [B. int.], and Joseph Chamberlain [2d. int.], May 12, 1822.*
Eli, and Mary Ann Sumner of Spencer, int. Sept. 19, 1825.
Hannah E., of Lowell, a. 18 y., d. George and Betsey, and Charles H. Hall of Lowell, a. 19 y., shoemaker, s. Stephen and Lydia, May 31, 1846.
James, and Mary Winch, both of Tyngsborough, Sept. 28, 1806.
Jerusha, of Concord, and Artemos Holden, int. Feb. 17, 1810.
Mahala, of Billerica, a. 25 y., d. Elisha and Mary, of Billerica, and Thomas R. Barrett of Billerica, a. 35 y., trader, s. Stephen and Olive, of Billerica, Sept. 23, 1844.
Mary, and Sydney Spaulding, Apr. 21, 1831. C. R. 3.
Nathaniel [of Billerica. int.], and Sarah Dutton, ———. [Dec. 3, 1812. C. R. 1.].*
Olive, and George Provancha, Nov. 28, 1843.*
Rachel, of Carlisle, and Zaccheus Wright Parker, Nov. 28, 1825.*
Samuel, and Lucy Tayler, July 23, 1798.*
Thomas, of Billerica, and Sarah Stevens, int. Sept. 13, 1774.

BROWNE (see also Brown), Dinnah, and Ebinezer Davis of Concord, Feb. 14, 1700.
Eliazer, and Dinah Spaulding, Feb. 9, 1674.
John, of Reading, and [Mrs. dup.] Annah Fiske, May 30, 1677.
Mary, and William Woodhead, June 21, 1669.
Rebeccah, of Billerica, and Jonas Dutton, int. Dec. 16, 1752.

BRUCE, Sophia F. A., a. 28 y., and Edward Reader, widr., a. 36 y., clerk, Nov. 6, 1847.*

BRYANT, Barnabas H., and Sarah S. Hatch of East Bridgewater, int. Sept. 3, 1826.
Elizabeth, of Lynn, and Joseph Emerson, at Lynn, Sept. 20, 1768.*

BURBANK, Jonathan, and Lucend[a] Wilson of Nottingham West, N. H., int. Nov. 11, 1822.
Samuel, and Harriet Rogers of Billerica, int. Nov. 16, 1828.

*Intention also recorded.

BURDEN, Hanna, of Malden, and Edmond Chambrlin, June 22, 1670.

BURDGE (see also Burge), Eliza, and Nicolas Sprake of Billerica, int. Sept. 3, 1721.
Josiah, and Susana Jaquesh of Bradford, int. July 17, 1725.
Rachel, and Thomas Barret, May 20, 1714.

BURG (see also Burge), Elizebeth, and Joel Barrit, Jan. 31, 1781-2.*
Susanah, and William Chandler of Billerica, int. June 16, 1716.

BURGE (see also Burdge, Burg), David, and Rebecca Shed of Billerica, at Billerica, Mar. 13, 1757.*
Esther, and Nathaniel Taylor of Concord, at Concord, Jan. 20, 1762.*
Hannah, and Thomas Dutton of Billerica, at Charlestown, Jan. 3, 1711.
John, late of Weymouth, and Mare Larned, June 9, 1662.
John, and Grisell Gurny, July 3, 1667.
John, sr., and Jane Gurne of Dorchester, Sept. 6, 1677.
John, and Triall Thare, d. Sidrack, of Braintree, Sept. 19, 1677.
John, and Sarah Taylor of Concord, at Concord, June 27, 1717.
Josiah [of Townsend. int.], and Tabitha Warren, Feb. 7, 1751. [1750-51. P. R. 4.]*
Lucy, and Abraham Talor of Concord, int. July 4, 1772.
Lydia, and Daniel Taylor [jr. of Townsend. int.], Feb. 4, 1756.*
Rebeckah, and Zacheus Barrit [of Templeton, N. H. int.], May 2, 1780.*
Rebeka, and Joseph Whitnee, at Charlestown, May 26, 1706.
Sarah, and Joshua Blanchard [of Hollis. int.], Dec. 23, 1747.*

BURGESS (see also Barges), James C., of Boston, and Susan Amanda Procter, int. Apr. 30, 1833.

BURNHAM, John A., and Mehitable Jenness of Haverhill, int. July 4, 1824.

BURROWS, Mary Ann, of Waltham, and Paul Hills, int. Aug. 10, 1823.

*Intention also recorded.

BUSH, Francis, and Elvira Peirce of Waltham, int. Dec. 2, 1824.
Francis, and Jane Bond of Watertown, int. Oct. 5, 1828.

BUTERFEILD (see also Butterfield), Joseph, and Lidiah Bollard, d. William, of Andover, 12: 3 m: 1674. [2 m. dup.]
Nathaniel, and Abigail Hunt of Billerica, int. Oct. —, 1733.
Rachel, and Jonathan Parker, int. Dec. 20, 1734.

BUTERFIELD (see also Butterfield), Ann, and John Davis, Dec. 19, 1716.

BUTERFILD (see also Butterfield), Benjamin, and Sarah Bats, Feb. 16, 1697.
Daborah, and William Longly, Feb. 16, 1697.
Josaph, and Eunes Hale, Jan. 21, 1696-7.
Nathaniell, and Sarah Flatcher, Jan. 18, 1697-8.

BUTLER, Betsy, Mrs., and Sprake Livingston, Apr. 2, 1836.*
Nancy, of Pelham, N. H., and Jonathan Gould, int. Oct. 3, 1824.
Sarah, and William S. Pierce of Lowell, int. Mar. 14, 1840.

BUTMAN, Bridget, of Tyngsborough, and Silas Peirce, int. Aug. 25, 1800.
Willard L., of Tewksbury, and Mary Dunn, int. July 4, 1830.

BUTTEFIELD (see also Butterfield), Rebecca, and Benja[min] Byam, Dec. 20, 1796.*

BUTTERFEELD (see also Butterfield), Mary, and Sameuell Spolding, June 30, 1698.

BUTTERFEILD (see also Butterfield), Anna, and Isaiah Foster, Nov. 8, 1743.*
Benjamin, and Hanah Whitemore, June 3, 1663.
David, and Kezia Shettleworth of Renton, int. Apr. 3, 1731.
Easther, and Joseph Moors, int. June 21, 1731.
Elizabeth, and Samuel Adams of Westford, at Westford, Oct. 28, 1728. [Oct. 31. c. r. 4.]*
Esther, and Lot Spaulding [of Hollis, N. H. int.], June 27, 1765.*
Jeremiah, and Mary Farrar, Nov. 22, 1764.*
Joana, and Jonathan Parker, int. Oct. 21, 1737.
Jonathan, and Mary Dicson, at Cambridge, June 12, 1667.

*Intention also recorded.

BUTTERFEILD, Laura, and Josiah W. Goward, May 20, 1841.*
Nathaniel, and Deborah Underwood, Dec. 31, 1668. CT. R.
Rhoda, and J. B. Wheeler of Lowell, June 24, 1841.*
Robert, of Westford, and Joanna Parker, at Westford, Feb. 24, 1752.*

BUTTERFIELD (see also Buterfeild, Buterfield, Buterfild, Buttefield, Butterfeeld Butterfield), Abigail, and Henry Parkhurst, May 31, 1831.*
Anna, and Silas Furbush, Mar. 22, 1798.*
Benjamin, and Kezia Pattison, int. July 7, 1723.
Benjamin [jr. int.], of Westford, and Susanna Spaulding, at Westford, Sept. 26, 1748.*
Benjamin, and Olive Procter, Dec. 6, 1758.*
Benjamin [jr. int.], and Sarah Chamberlain, May 13, 1779.*
Bridget, and Jonathan Parkhurst, June 28, 1748.*
Caroline, and Daniel Brooks of Lowell, int. May 12, 1833.
Ebenezer [jr., of Dunstable. int.], and Elizabeth Emmery, Jan. 12, 1762. P. R. 4.*
Elezabeth, and Adam Gould, int. Jan. 25, 1729-30.
Esther, and Ebenezer Frost [jr. int.], Feb. 25, 1766.*
Eunice, and Benjamin Richardson, int. Mar. 27, 1720.
Hannah, and Thomas Tomson of Woburn, Dec. 12, 1700.
Hannah, and George Dane, May 18, 1825.*
Joanna, and Dennis McLain, Dec. 29, 1762.*
Joanna C., and Barnabas N. Bradt, int. Dec. 25, 1831.
John, and Anna Hildreth, int. Dec. 10, 1721.
John, of Groton, and Mary Read, int. Dec. 24, 1727.
John, and Rebecca Kendal, June 15, 1791.*
Jonathan, and Tabatha Butterfield, int. Feb. 15, 1745-6.
Jonathan, and Lydia Procter, Mar. 27, 1751. [Mar. 28. P. R. 4.]*
Joseph, and Dorothy Heild, int. May 14, 1727.
Joseph, and Almira Cheever of Lowell, July 31, 1836.*
Julia Ann, and Hezekiah Parkhurst, Nov. 9, 1826.*
Laura, and [Ens. C. R. 1.] Ira Fry, June 7, 1825.*
Lenord, of Dunstable, and Johannah Parker, int. Feb. 25, 1764.
Louiza, and Owen Emerson, jr., Oct. 16, 1823.*
Lowel, and Hannah Smith [of Dracut. int.], Jan. 20, 1820.*
Lucy [d. Capt. J. C. R. 1.], and Dr. Stillman Spalding [of Lexington. int.], May 13, 1819.*
Lydia, and Ephraim Spaulding, int. Mar. 31, 1730.
Mare, and Daniell Bloged, Sept. 15, 1653.

*Intention also recorded.

CHELMSFORD MARRIAGES 197

BUTTERFIELD, Martha, of Westford, and Enoch Cleveland jr., int. Jan. 27, 1753.
Martha, and Nathan Buttrick [jr. int.], May 1, 1842.*
Mary, and Ephraim Hildreth, int. Jan. 5, 1722-3.
Mary, and David Fletcher of Westford, int. Nov. 30, 1742.
Mary Ann, and William Tyler, int. Nov. 29, 1848.
Nath[anie]l, and Allis Cowdery, Oct. 31, 1748.*
Nathaniel, and Elezebeth Cambell of Tewksbury, int. June 24, 1757.
Olive, and Simeon Spaulding [jr. int.], Dec. 21, 1784.*
Patty, and Stephen Adams, ———, 1805. [Dec. 22. C. R. 1.]*
Phebe, and James Dutton, int. Sept. 5, 1725.
Polly, and Isaac Kent, int. Oct. 21, 1810.
Rachall, and Thomas Colburn of Dunstable, int. Nov. 1, 1740.
Ralph, and Jemime Marshall, ———, 1810. [July 15. C. R. 1.]*
Rebecca, and Oliver Blodget, June 15, 1756.*
Rhoda, and Joseph Bowers, Apr. 1, 1804. [1803. P. R. 11.]*
Samuel, and Tabitha Butterfield of Westford, at Westford, May 7, 1730.*
Samuel, and Mary McLane, Aug. 11, 1772.*
Samuel, and Hannah Peirce, Aug. 12, 1798.*
Samuell, and Hannah Spauldyng, July 2, 1703.
Sam[ue]ll, and Rachell Spauldyng, Dec. 7, 1703.
Sarah, and Thomas Heild, int. Oct. 28, 1725.
Sarah, and Thomas Danforth [of Billerica. int.], Oct. 16, 1744.*
Sarah, and Henry Procter, May 22, 1760.*
Sarah, and Jacob Manning [of Billerica. int.], June 2, 1763.*
Sarah, and Richard Whitney, Mar. 26, 1767.*
Sarah, and Hezekiah Coburn [jr. of Dracut. int.], July 29, 1804.*
Sarai, and David Carver of Canterbury, int. Jan. 14, 1721-2.
Silas [of Stoddard, N. H. int.], and Lucinda Fletcher, ———, 1816. [June 25. C. R. 1.]*
Sivil S. [Sybil. C. R. 1.], d. Capt. Benjamin, and Lt. Jonathan Tyler, s. Nathan, Apr. 4, 1816.*
Stephen, and Mary Ann Parkhurst of Amherst, N. H., int. Aug. 19, 1832.
Susan A., of Lowell, and Varnum Spalding, int. Mar. 14, 1840.
Tabatha, and Jonathan Butterfield, int. Feb. 15, 1745-6.
Tabitha, of Westford, and Samuel Butterfield, at Westford, May 7, 1730.*
William, and Bathsheba Shephard of Concord, int. May 21, 1727.

*Intention also recorded.

CHELMSFORD MARRIAGES

BUTTERFIELD, William, and Lydia Kidder, July 30, 1761.*

BUTTERICK (see also Buttrick), Mary, of Dunstable, N. H., and William Cogswell, ——, 1812. [Sept. 5. C. R. 1.]

BUTTERS, Sally, of Westford, and Ranson Read, int. June 26, 1825.
Sally, of Westford, and Orin Read, int. Sept. 19, 1825.

BUTTRICK (see also Butterick, Buttrik), Abigail, of Concord, and Dea. Aaron Chamberlain, at Concord, June 5, 1792.*
Abner W., of Lowell, and Hannah S. Parkhurst, int. Sept. 20, 1835.
Betsy, and Andrew Parkhurst, int. Sept. 7, 1805.
Ephraim, and Lydia Ford, int. Dec. 22, 1802.
Ephraim, and Mahitabal Emerson, Oct. 11, 1804.*
John A., of Lowell, and Martha Parkhurst, Sept. 13, 1841.*
Nathan, and Sally Bateman, Apr. 20, 1820.*
Nathan, and Thankful Augusta Green of Carlisle, int. May 27, 1837.
Nathan [jr. int.], and Martha Butterfield, May 1, 1842.*

BUTTRIK (see also Buttrick), Sarah, d. Will[iam], of Concord, and Samuell Barrett, s. John, Feb. 21, 1683.

BYAM (see also Biam, Byam), Abraham, and wid. Sarah Ong, 22: 11 m: 1689.
Amos, and Sarah Peirce, Jan. 24, 1780.*
Amos, and Lucy Adams, Oct. 29, 1807.*
Amos, and Elizabeth Hildreth of Westford, int. Jan. 9, 1832.
Amos Adams, and Mary A. Bowers of Merrimack, N. H., int. Feb. 24, 1833.
Ann R., a. 22 y., d. Henry and Ann R., and Charles H[enry. int.] Adams of Boston, a. 22 y., trader, s. Charles and Nancy, Nov. 29, 1849.*
Asaph, Dr., of Westford, and Polly Spalding [d. Andrew. C. R. 1.], May 8, 1817.*
Benja[min], and Rebecca Buttefield, Dec. 20, 1796.*
Benjamin [Ens. int.], and Lidia Parker, Dec. 26, 1811.*
Betsy P., and Benjamin Dudley of Weston, Oct. 14, 1824.*
Clarissa Ann, and Jacob Leach of Boston, Nov. 26, 1829.*
Edwin S., and Hannah M[aria. int.] Adams, Apr. 14, 1833.*
Ezekiel, and Charlotte Bateman, Feb. 15, 1818.*
Henry, and Relief Spaulding, Oct. 28, 1824.*

*Intention also recorded.

BYAM, John, jr., and Sarah Haywood, Nov. 28, 1784.*
Josiah, and Sophronia Flagg [of Littleton. int.], Apr. 17, 1823.*
Josiah, and Sarah Hardy, Dec. 28, 1841.*
Laura, and Samuel White of Tyngsborough, Dec. 28, 1837.*
Lucy, and Jonas Dunn, May 10, 1808.*
Lucy Marinda, and Joseph Richardson, Apr. 4, 1833.*
Marcus D., and Rebecca Chamberlin, Dec. 16, 1832.*
Marcus D., and Mary Proctor, Sept. 26, 1839.*
Martha Ann, a. 16 y., d. Ezekiel and Charlotte, and Otis B. Dudley, a. 19 y., blacksmith, s. Benjamin and Martha P., Aug. 13, 1846.*
Mary, and Moses Procter, int. —— [1738?].
Mary, and John Shed, June 17, 1802. C. R. 1.*
Mary, and Samuel E. Foster, Mar. 15, 1804.*
Mary, and Parker Chamberlain, Sept. 14, 1826.*
Olive, and Aaron Blazedell, Nov. 29, 1787.*
Patty, and Isaiah Spalding, int. Aug. 28, 1813.
Rebeckah, and Nathaniel Foster, Feb. —, 1784.*
Rebekah, and Henry Adams, Mar. 18, 1810.*
Rufus, and Eunice A. Greggory of Weston, int. May 10, 1843.
Sarah, and Jessa Hawood [Haywood. C. R. 1. and int.], Nov. 28, 1782.*
Sarah, Mrs., and Oliver Parkhurst, ——, 1806. [June 3. C. R. 1.]*
Simeon [a. 62 y. C. R. 1.], and Thankful Reed [a. 42 y. C. R. 1.], Nov. 13, 1828.*
Solomon, and Abi Adams, at Westford, Mar. 13, 1791.*
Sophronia Ann, and W[illia]m P. Cook, both of Lowell, Oct. 27, 1842. C. R. 3.
Stillman, and Mary Ann Carpenter, Sept. 6, 1840.*
Susanna, and Supply Read, June 7, 1781.*
Thankfull, and Dean Carlton [of Acworth, N. H. int.], Sept. —, 1785.*
Tryphene, and James Haywood [of Paris, N. Y. int.], June 19, 1814.*
Willard, and Polly [Mary. int.] Osburn, May 28, 1815.*
William, and Rebeckah Herrick, Feb. 27, 1795.*
William A., and Mercy M. Parker, int. Feb. 16, 1841.

BYHAM (see also Byam), Abraham, and Hannah Robie, int. Aug. 21, 1726.
Benjamin, and Mary Keyes, Dec. 11, 1760.*
Dorcas, and Ebenezer Harris [jr. int.], Nov. 14, 1754.*

*Intention also recorded.

BYHAM, Henry, and Lucy Fletcher, Apr. 12, 1742.*
Isaac, and Mary Cowdrey, int. Apr. 4, 1725.
Jacob, and Sarai Hildreth, int. Jan. 1, 1720-21.
Joanna, and Moses Graves, Dec. 17, 1750.*
John, and Sarah Blanchard, Sept. 12, 1758.*
Mary, and David Welch [both residents in Chelmsford. c. r. 1.], Jan. 24, 1750. [1749-50. p. r. 4.]*

CADY (see also Cadye), Nichalos, s. Nichalas, of Groton, and Patience Redland, d. William, of Groton, Mar. 20, 1685.

CADYE (see also Cady), Daniell, and Mary Greene, both of Groton, July 6, 1683.

CAFFERTAY, Ellen, and William Phipps, int. July 19, 1846.

CALDWELL, Mary [of the glass factory. c. r. 1.], and William Hall, May 16, 1821.*

CALL, William D., and Elisa Jane Fullerton, both of Lowell, Feb. 25, 1841. c. r. 1.

CALLEY, Rebeckah, and Phillip Hoseller, int. June 13, 1818.

CAMBELL, Elezebeth, of Tewksbury, and Nathaniel Butterfield, int. June 24, 1757.

CANFIELD, Lydia, and Abel Webster, both of Lowell, July 28, 1839. c. r. 1.

CARBEE, Sarah, a. 19 y., d. Joel, and David S. Simonds, a. 24 y., stone-cutter, s. William, Feb. 29, 1848.*

CARGILL, Hugh, and Martha Air, both residents in Chelmsford, int. July 8, 1775.

CARKIN, Isaac W., and Mahala Ann Coburn, both of North Chelmsford, int. Mar. 17, 1846.
Lucy A., and John H. Farr, int. Mar. 23, 1847.
Maria, and Alonzo Grow, int. Nov. 2, 1848.

CARLETON (see also Carlton), Sarah, of Boscawen, and Samuel Fox Wood, int. July 5, 1807.

*Intention also recorded.

CHELMSFORD MARRIAGES 201

CARLTON (see also Carleton), Abigail, and Jonas [James. int.] Keyes of Westford, at Westford, Nov. 28, 1799.*
David, and Susanna Blanchard of Carlisle, int. Oct. 17, 1819.
David, and Dorothy Pollard of Nottingham West, N. H., int. Jan. 2, 1825.
David, and Sarah Pollard, Sept. 2, 1827.*
Dean [of Acworth, N. H. int.], and Thankfull Byam, Sept. —, 1785.*
Ebenezer, and Rebecca Malcom, both of Alexandria, N. H., Jan. 3, 1784.
Esther [of Billerica. int.], and Ephraim Warren, Oct. 25, 1821. P. R. 7.*
Hannah, of Billerica, and Thomas Laws, Feb. 10, 1761.
John, of Lowell, a. 25 y., mason, s. David, and Augusta Boyanton of Carlisle, a. 23 y., d. Samuel and Sarah S., Jan. 11, 1849.
Martha, of Billerica, and Joseph Warren, jr., Feb. 25, 1836.*
Nathan, of Billerica, and Abigail Spaulding, at Billerica, Nov. 5, 1776.*
Sally, and Abel Ruggs, Dec. 12, 1820.*
Senea, and James Goodhue of Westford, int. May 17, 1803.

CARNS, Polly [Mrs. C. R. 1.], and Samuel Pitts, Apr. 3, 1797.*

CARPENTER, Mary Ann, and Stillman Byam, Sept. 6, 1840.*

CARR, Joseph R., and Lydia W. Spaulding, ——. [Oct. 26, 1828. int.]*

CARRER (see also Currier), John [Cirrier, of New Concord, N. H. int.], and Bridget Chamberlin, Feb. 7, 1793.*

CARROLL, see Caryl.

CARTER, Jeremiah, and Rhoda Marshall, Nov. 29, 1827. [Dec. 9. C. R. 1.]*
Mardany D. [Mrs. int.], and Solomon Harwood, Apr. 9, 1843.*

CARVER, David, of Canterbury, and Sarai Butterfield, int. Jan. 14, 1721-2.
Sary, and Ritcherd Hilldrith, int. Apr. 20, 1728.

CARY, Peter, and Mary Ann Winship, int. June 15, 1823.

*Intention also recorded.

CARYL, Nancy, and Joseph G. Torrey, Jan. 12, 1843.*
Olive, a. 21 y., d. John and Lucy, and Henry M. Bird, a. 22 y., moulder, s. Jacob P. and Nancy T., Nov. 19, 1846.*

CASS, Rectina M., and Charles H. Clifford, int. Sept. 22, 1838.

CHADBOURNE, Benjamin, widr., of Standish, Me., a. 55 y., trader, s. Joseph, and Clarissa Howard, a. 45 y., d. Jacob, Dec. 29, 1846. [Dec. 28. c. r. 3.]*

CHAFFEE, Abigail, and William Rowell, Feb. 23, 1841.*

CHAIMBERLIN (see also Chamberlin), Lydia, and Isaac Pattin of Bedford, Sept. 16, 1760.*

CHAMBERLAIN (see also Chamberlin), Aaron, and Thankful Adams, Feb. 14, 1751. [1750-51. p. r. 4.]*
Aaron, Dea., and Abigail Buttrick of Concord, at Concord, June 5, 1792.*
Aaron [Dea. int.], and [Mrs. int.] Mary Parker of Barre, at Barre, Nov. 24, 1796.*
Abia, and Jonathan Shattuck [3d of Pepperell. int.], Mar. 2, 1769.*
Abigail, and James Pollard of Westford, at Westford, Dec. 17, 1734.*
Abigail, and Hezekiah Thorndike, June 1, 1779.*
Benjamin [3d. int.], and Susanna Barron, Mar. 21, 1758.*
Benj[ami]n [4th. int.], and Susan [Susanna. c. r. 1. and int.] McLain, May 7, 1761.*
Benj[ami]n, and Aseneth Manning, Mar. 18, 1819.*
Elizabeth, and Ezekiel Proctor of Westford, at Concord, Oct. 24, 1734.*
Esther, and Joshua Atwood [of Westford. int.], Mar. 7, 1758.*
Jacob, and Lydia Richardson, May 21, 1761.*
Jane, and John Reed, at Charlestown, Jan. 10, 1706-7.
John, Lt., of Grand Isle, Vt., and Susanna Heywood, int. Feb. 13, 1820.
Joseph, and Elizabeth Stevens, int. Nov. 8, 1719.
Joseph [2d. int.], and Betsy [B. int.] Brown, May 12, 1822.*
Loammi, widr. [of North Chelmsford. c. r. 3.], a. 35 y., stonecutter, s. Rob[er]t B. and Lydia, and Augusta A. Osgood of Westford, a. 21 y., b. Westford, d. Jacob and Patty, Dec. 5, 1848.*

*Intention also recorded.

CHAMBERLAIN, Lydia, and Benj[amin] Procter, int. Feb. 4, 1727-8.
Martha H., and Calvin T. Wright, int. Nov. 19, 1842.
Mary, and Josiah Fletcher, Jan. 16, 1746.*
Mary, of Billerica, and Charles Hans, Jan. 8, 1761.
Mary, and Micah Spaulding, Apr. 23, 1778.*
Mary, and Joseph Spalding, Dec. 1, 1808.*
Parker, and Mary Byam, Sept. 14, 1826.*
Peggy [Margaret, of Billerica. int.], and Joseph Kemp, at Concord, Dec. 20, 1720.*
Phineas, and Sybil Hildreth, July 23, 1776.*
Phineas [of Westford. int.], and Mary Parker, Nov. 2, 1826.*
Rebecca, and James Woodward [of Reading. int.], June 10, 1760.*
Robbart B., and Lydia Haley of Tyngsborough, int. Nov. 21, 1812.
Samuel, and Rebecca Whitcomb of Lancaster, at Lancaster, Jan. 2, 1722-3.*
Samuel, and Eunice Farrar of Concord, at Concord, Dec. 1, 1796.*
Samuel, of Merrimack, N. H., and Charlotte Dunn [d. James. C. R. 1.], Oct. 12, 1818.*
Sarah, and William Martin, Apr. 6, 1742.*
Sarah, and Benjamin Butterfield [jr. int.], May 13, 1779.*
Thomas, and Elisabeth Hall, Jan. 9, 1690. CT. R.
Thomas, and Abigail Hildrick, at Concord, June 10, 1713.

CHAMBERLIN (see also Chaimberlin, Chamberlain, Chamberline, Chambrlin, Chemberling), Aaron [jr. int.], and Sarah Adams, Nov. 15, 1781.*
Benjamin, and Mary Parker, int. May 27, 1722.
Benjamin, and Esther Fasset of Westford, at Westford, Jan. 27, 1732.*
Betsey, d. Capt. Isaac, and Luke Thompson, Nov. 16, 1815.*
Betsy, of Westford, and Salathiel Adams, Dec. 18, 1831.
Bridget, and John Carrer [Cirrier of New Concord, N. H. int.], Feb. 7, 1793.*
Dorethy, and Timothy Adams, Aug. 11, 1699.
Elizabeth, and Daniel Davise of Canterbury, int. Feb. 14, 1724-5.
Ephraim [of Westford. int.], and Sarah Harwood, Nov. 26, 1801.*
Harriet, of Westford, and Asa Stevens, Apr. 23, 1832.*
Ira, and Sarah Spaulding, int. Mar. 12, 1808.

*Intention also recorded.

CHAMBERLIN, Isaac, and Bettey Bates, June 13, 1782.*
Isaac, Capt., and Sally Parker, June 14, 1803.*
Isaac, jr., and Olive Ilesly [of Lunenburg. int.], Dec. 29, 1814.*
Jacob, and Mary Warren of Littleton, int. Mar. 29, 1755.
Jacob, and Ruth Hall [of Westford. int.], Feb. 8, 1780.*
Jacob [jr. int.], and Judath [Judah. C. R. 1.] Laws, May 28, 1794.*
Joanna, and Peter Tayler, Sept. 18, 1807.*
Joseph, and Mary Parker, Dec. 22, 1796.*
Jos[eph, 2d. int.; jr. C. R. 1.], and Martha Putnam, Feb. 26, 1829.*
Lydia, and Joshua Sarnders, Mar. 14, 1785. [Feb. 20. dup.; Mar. 24. C. R. 1.; Mar. 7. int.]*
Lydia, and Nathaniel Goodhue of Merrimack, int. Feb. 19, 1787.
Lydia, and John Farmer, int. Nov. 10, 1787.
Olive, and Joshua Hunt [of Tewksbury. int.], Nov. 20, 1794.*
Patty, and Elias Barron of Carlisle, Sept. 10, 1822.*
Phinehas, and Mary Adams, Mar. 30, 1784.
Phinehas [of Bedford. int.], and Darkes Varnum, Feb. 21, 1797.*
Rebecca, and Marcus D. Byam, Dec. 16, 1832.*
Samuel, and Elizabeth Spaulding, int. Sept. 17, 1721.
Sarah, and Benjamin Barrit, Sept. 3, 1786.*
Thankfull, and Samuel Adams, Aug. 30, 1770.*
Thomas, and Mary Parker, Apr. 17, 1674.

CHAMBERLINE (see also Chamberlin), Thomas, and Sarah Proctor, Aug. [10, 1666. T. C.].

CHAMBERS, David, and Hanah Belnap, int. Oct. 24, 1780.
Joseph, and Mary Davis of Concord, at Concord, Feb. 17, 1795.*
William, and Rachil Lovjoy, Oct. 15, 1782.*

CHAMBRLIN (see also Chamberlin), Edmond, and Hanna Burden of Malden, June 22, 1670.

CHANDLER, Abigail B., of Merrimack, N. H., and Charles Follansbee, int. June 4, 1836.
Ephraim, and Sary Adams, int. June 15, 1724.
Henry, of Enfield, and Hannah Foster, int. Sept. 14, 1723.

*Intention also recorded.

CHANDLER, Isaac [of Westford. int.], and Betty Procter, Nov. 1, 1759. [Oct. 31. P. R. 4.]*
Nyrhe [of Billerica. int.], and Edwin Josselyn, Dec. 3, 1835. P. R. 10.*
Roger [of New Ipswich, N. H. int.], and Lydia Marshall, ———, 1796. [Jan. 2. int.]*
Samuel, and Sally Jaquith of Dracut, at Dracut, Apr. 21, 1796.*
William, of Andover, and Brigett Richardson, Oct. [torn], 1679.
William, of Billerica, and Susanah Burg, int. June 16, 1716.

CHASE, Jacob, of West Richmond, N. Y., and Lucy Richardson, Oct. 19, 1830.*
John, and Eliza Webber of Lowell, int. Apr. 15, 1827.
Rebeckah, of Littleton, and Thomas Warin, int. ——— [1735 or 1736.].
Thomas Legget, and Hannah F. Parker [d. Eben[eze]r. C. R. 1.], Nov. 12, 1825. [Nov. 22. C. R. 1.]

CHEEVER (see also Chevar, Chever), Almira, of Lowell, and Joseph Butterfield, July 31, 1836.*

CHEMBERLING (see also Chamberlin), Mary, and Joshaue Baros, July 24, 1696.

CHESTER, Silas, of Billerica, and Affable Felstead, int. Sept. 10, 1826.

CHEVAR (see also Cheever), Moses, jr., and Rachel Harris of Dracut, int. Aug. 8, 1815.

CHEVER (see also Cheever), Adaline [D. C. R. 1.], and Philo S. Shaw, Nov. 10, 1829.
John, and Mary Ann Homes Shipley of Londonderry, N. H., int. Feb. 19, 1826.
Mary, and Samuel Hamblet of Dracut, int. Dec. 26, 1812.

CHILDS, William T., of Groton, a. 23 y., blacksmith, s. Calvin and Sally, and Mary Jane Hartwell, a. 18 y., d. Nathan and Sally, Aug. 4, 1844.*

CHURCH, Cornelius, and Sarah ———, June 14, 1670. CT. R.

*Intention also recorded.

CLAFLIN, Eliza J., of Boston, and James King, int. Jan. 13, 1849.
Sarah A. [of North Chelmsford. c. r. 3.], a. 18 y., d. Alfred, and Frederic W. Howe of Windsor, Vt., a. 25 y., machinist, s. Frederic, Dec. 16, 1847.*

CLAPP, Samuel [of Merrimack, N. H. int.], and Lucy Dunn, ―――, 1812. [Nov. 4. c. r. 1.]*

CLARK (see also Clerk), Cornelius, of Cambridge, and Abigail Wright, Sept. 2, 1822.
David, of Lowell, and Harriet N. [M. int.] Wilson of Middlesex Village, May 16, 1839.*
David P. [of North Chelmsford. c. r. 3.], a. 24 y., moulder, s. Jona[than] and Sarah, and Eliza Jane Blood [of North Chelmsford. c. r. 3.], a. 22 y., d. Charles and Betsey, Jan. 31, 1848.*
Deborah, of Lyndeborough, and Isaiah Parker, int. Oct. 31, 1801.
Elesibeth, and John Hancok of North Cambridge, Dec. 11, 1700.
Elizabeth B., and John Adams [jr. int.], ―――, 1816. [May 28. c. r. 1.]*
Hannah, and Thomas Marshall [jr. int.], Feb. 28, 1775.*
Hannah D., and George F. Gilmore of Pittsburg, Pa., Mar. 7, 1843.*
Isaac, and Bridget Reading, Dec. 1, 1768.*
Joel, of Stanstead, Lower Canada, and Salla Stevens, int. Nov. 26, 1820.
Jonas, and Ann Frie of Andover, at Andover, Dec. 8, 1741.*
Jonas, and Dolly Hunt of Tewksbury [both of Tewksbury. c. r. 1.], ―――, 1806. [Apr. 10. c. r. 1.]
Josiah, of Dracut, and Phebe Wyman, int. Aug. 21, 1825.
Lucy, and William Tyng of Dunstable, Sept. 19, 1700.
Lucy, and Jonathan Richardson [of Dracut. int.], Dec. 4, 1746.*
Mary, and Ephraim Hildreth, jr. of Dracut, at Dracut, Feb. 11, 1735-6.
Mary, and Christopher Barret, Sept. 6, 1764.*
Rebecca, and Daniel Beard of Billerica, int. Nov. 10, 1804.
Sarah M., of Lowell, and Charles A. Blood, int. Feb. 17, 1848.
Sarah W., of Lowell, and Joseph Blood, int. Aug. 3, 1838.
Thomas, and Lydia Fletcher, July 25, 1765.*

*Intention also recorded.

CLEAVELAND (see also Cleveland), Enoch, jr., and Martha Butterfield of Westford, int. Jan. 27, 1753.

CLEMMENT, Clarissa, and James Coburn, 2d, both of Dracut, Jan. 20, 1820. C. R. 1.

CLEMMONS, Rachel, of Dracut, and Josiah Blanchard, int. Mar. 6, 1807.

CLERK (see also Clark), Elisabeth, and Thomas Fletcher, int. Jan. 3, 1742-3.

CLEVELAND (see also Cleaveland), Johanah, and Josiph Keyes, May 28, 1690.
Samuell, s. Moses, of Woburn, and Jane Keies, d. Solomon, May 17, 1680.
Samuell, and Perses Hildreth, d. Richard, May 23, 1682.

CLIFFORD, Charles H., and Rectina M. Cass, int. Sept. 22, 1838.
Mary L., and Jonas M. Watson, int. Dec. 21, 1844.

COBORN (see also Colburn), Daniell, and Sarah Blood, d. Robertt, June 18, 1685.
[Ezra Colburn. dup.], s. Edward, and Hannah Varnam, d. Samuell, 22: 9 m: 1681.
Hannah [Colburn. int.], d. Edward, and Thomas Richarson, "all" of Dracut, Sept. 28, 1682.
[John. dup.], s. Edward [of Dracut. dup.], and Susanah Read of Salem [Mar. 10. dup.; Mar. 18. T. C.], 1671.
Thomas [Colburn. dup.], s. Edward, of Dracut, and Hannah Rouf, Aug. 6, 1672.
Thomas [Colburn. dup.], and Mary Richardson, d. Josiah, 17: 9 m: 1681.

COBURN (see also Colburn), Amos, of Dracut, and Mary Parkhurst, int. July 4, 1761.
Anna, and Jonatha Bowers, Apr. 6, 1824.*
Deborah, and John Emery, Jan. 9, 1786.*
Deborah, and Aaron Goodhue, both of Dracut, July 20, 1815. C. R. 1.
Elizabeth, of Dracut, and John T. Spafford, int. Aug. 1, 1824.
Hannah, and Micajah Mears, July 29, 1802.*

*Intention also recorded.

COBURN, Henry [jr. C. R. 1.], and Mrs. Patty Adams, ——, 1811. [May 6. C. R. 1.]*
Hezekiah [jr., of Dracut. int.], and Sarah Butterfield, July 29, 1804.*
James, 2d, and Clarissa Clemment, both of Dracut, Jan. 20, 1820. C. R 1.
James B., and Betsey C. Jones, int. Nov. 2, 1844.
John [Colborn. int.], jr., of Dracut, and Sarah Richardson, at Dracut, Feb. 12, 1767.*
Mahala Ann, and Isaac W. Carkin, both of North Chelmsford, int. Mar. 17, 1846.
Mercy [Mary. CT. R.; of Dracut. C. R. 1.], and John Parker, Feb. 20, 1785.
Mercy [of Dracut. C. R. 1.], and Nathaniel Coburn, June 7, 1787.
Nathaniel, and Mercy Coburn [of Dracut. C. R. 1.], June 7, 1787.
Rhoda, of Dracut, and Henry Fletcher, int. Nov. 6, 1825.
Sally I. [T. C. R. 1.], and Samuel Willard, Feb. 10, 1825.*
Sarah, and Capt. Phineus Whiting, Apr. 13, 1817.*
Stephen A., widr., of Lowell, a. 33 y., farmer, s. Henry and Patty, and Gralia [Gratia. int.] Ann Parker, a. 27 y., d. Jona[than] and Betsey, June 22, 1848.*
Thomas, and Lucy Fletcher, ——, 1812. [Dec. 3. C. R. 1.]*

COFEN, Maria, see Coton, Maria.

COFFEN, Charles [of Brunswick. int.], and Dorcas Parker, Sept. 29, 1801.*

COGSWELL, Adam H., and Mary White, Mar. 13, 1823.*
Martha E[lizabeth. int.], and Milton S[pafford. int.] Morse of Winchendon, Oct. 16, 1834.*
Mary, wid. [of Lowell. int.], and Samuel Davis, Nov. 15, 1830.*
Rebeckah, of Westford, and Joel Mansfield, int. Apr. 2, 1814.
Thomas, and Hannah L. Inglee of Marblehead, int. Apr. 1, 1827.
William, and Mary Butterick of Dunstable, N. H., ——, 1812. [Sept. 5. C. R. 1.]

COKAR, Nathan[ie]ll, of Sudbury, and Mary Barrett, Oct. 10, 1693. CT. R.

*Intention also recorded.

COLBORN (see also Colburn), Hanah, and Joseph Farwel, Jan. 23, 1695-6.
Hannah, of Dracut, and William Foster, int. Sept. 15, 1744.
John, Capt., of Dracut, and Mrs. Olive Adams, int. Jan. 12, 1744-5.
Samuel, of Dracut, and Mary Richardson, int. June 30, 1716.

COLBURN (see also Coborn, Coburn, Colborn, Coleburn), Dorcas, of Milford, N. H., and Abraham W. Wentworth, int. Sept. 3, 1837.
Elesibeth, and Joseph Spauldyng, Apr. 10, 1700.
Ezra, of Dracut, and Thankfull Richardson, int. Feb. 25, 1732-3.
Joel, and Fanny E. George of Lowell, June 15, 1843.*
Mary L., and Willard M. Kennon, Nov. 17, 1842.*
Silas, and Esther Keyes, Dec. 1, 1768.*
Susanna, of Dracut, and Stephen Fletcher, int. Aug. 1, 1741.
Thomas, of Dunstable, and Rachall Butterfield, int. Nov. 1, 1740.

COLE, John, and Polly Richardson of Dracut, int. Dec. 29, 1794.

COLEBURN (see also Colburn), Deborah, of Dracut, and John Richerdson, int. Jan. 4, 1734-5.
Jacob, of Dracut, and Sary Perham, int. Nov. 28, 1737.
Oliver, of Dunstable, and Lucy Bowers, int. Apr. 6, 1734.

COLLINS, Nancy, of Merrimack, N. H., and John McKeever, int. Aug. 13, 1826.

COMINGS (see also Cummings), Eleazer, of Dunstable, and Rachel Procter, int. Oct. 26, 1729.
Isaac, of Dunstable, and Elizabeth Perham, int. Jan. 5, 1722-3.
Josiah, of Dunstable, and Miriam Procter, int. Nov. 26, 1732.
Simeon, of Merrimack, N. H., and Hannah Bowers, int. June 18, 1763.
William, of Tyngsborough, and Rebeckah Richardson, int. Oct. 6, 1798.

COMMINGS (see also Cummings), Sarrah, of Dunstable, d. John, and Sam[ue]ll French, Dec. 28, 1682.

COMMINS (see also Cummings), Nathaniell, of Dunstable, and Abigall Parkhurst, Apr. 14, 1697.

*Intention also recorded.

CONN, Thomas [of Charlestown. int.], and Sally Whiting, Mar. 8, 1801.*

CONNER, Frederick C., of Lowell, and Mary Jane Roper, int. Oct. 2, 1840.

COOK (see also Cooke), John, Capt., of Claremont, N. H., and [Mrs. int.] Molly Proctor, at Westford, Apr. 27, 1797.*
Lucinda P., of Westford, and William Laws, jr., int. Apr. 12, 1815.
W[illia]m P., and Sophronia Ann Byam, both of Lowell, Oct. 27, 1842. c. R. 3.

COOKE (see also Cook), Andrew, and Feebe Loven, d. John, both of Dunstable, July 24, 1685.

COOLIDGE, Alexander, of Natick, and Lydia Leighton of Westford, June 11, 1823.
Clarissa, of Antrim, N. H., and Benjamin Spalding, 2d, int. Mar. 9, 1840.

COOMBS, Lydia, of Vinalhaven, Me., and John Spaulding, 3d, int. Sept. 23, 1827.

COOMER, Betsey, and Albert N. Dustin, both of Lowell, Mar. 28, 1838. c. R. 1.

COOPER, Mare [Caper. CT. R.], and Joseph Gillson, Nov. 10, 1661. [Nov. 18. CT. R.]

COREY (see also Cory), Abiel, and William Parker [jr. int.], Sept. 27, 1764.*
Betty, and Ebenezer Dowse [of Billerica. int.], June 18, 1755.*
Eleazer, and Rachel Galusha, Oct. 28, 1742.*
Elizabeth [Long. dup.], and [Daniel. dup.] Shattuck [of Hollis, at Dracut. dup.], Nov. 14, 1793. [Nov. 13. dup.]*
Esther, and Moses Estabrooks [of Dunstable. int.], June 5, 1744.*
Joanna, and Jonas Kemp of Westford, at Westford, Sept. 12, 1769.*
Lois, and John Mansfield, Sept. 23, 1760.*
Mary, of Winchendon, and Stephen Pierce, int. Jan. 2, 1831.
Olive, and William Bettyes, at Westford, June 9, 1785.*

*Intention also recorded.

CHELMSFORD MARRIAGES 211

COREY, Rebecca, and Joel Spaulding, Apr. 25, 1791.*
Ruth, and James Dutton [jr. int.], Nov. 1, 1754.*
Sarah, and Charles Furbush [of Andover. int.], Apr. 1, 1755.*
Solomon, and Rebecca Pierce, Dec. 22, 1767.*
Tabitha, and Josiah Blood [of Westford. int.], July 2, 1767.*
Thomas, and Abigal Golle [Goole. CT. R.], Sept. 19, 1665.

CORLIS (see also Corliss), Betsy, of Haverhill, and Phineas Ayer, int. Aug. 1, 1812.
William, of Salem, and Betty Bowers, int. June 18, 1776.

CORLISS (see also Corlis), John L. [of Haverhill, N. H. int.], and Sally Ford, Feb. 22, 1805. [Jan. 22. C. R. 1.]*

CORY (see also Corey), Ezra, and Phebe Parker, at Westford, May 3, 1798.*
Hanah, and Jonathan Swalow, int. Aug. 10, 1728.
Hannah, and Oliver Cory, int. Oct. 22, 1749.
John, and Ruth Keyes, int. Mar. 9, 1722-3.
Jonathan, and Sarah Russell of Concord, at Concord, Dec. 12, 1699.
Lucy, and William Mansfield, Apr. 16, 1787.*
Lydia, and Willard Mansfield, int. June 23, 1788.
Mary, and Simeon Farmer, int. Sept. 12, 1764.
Oliver, and Hannah Cory, int. Oct. 22, 1749.
Phebe, see Gould, Phebe.
Prissilla, and David Rumrill of Westford, int. July 25, 1765.
Rachel, and Jonathan Bathrick of Leicester, int. Feb. 18, 1748-9.
Rebeckah, and Jonathan Fletcher, May —, 1784.
Reuben, and Olive Ball, at Concord, Dec. 6, 1757.*
Sarah, and Asa Procter, Nov. 16, 1782. [Nov. 26. C. R. 1.]
Steven, of Groton, and Lydia Bateman, ——, 1816. [Apr. 14. C. R. 1.]*

COTON (see also Cotton), Maria [Cofen. CT. R.], and Sameuell Fletcher, jr., June 7, 1692.

COTTEN (see also Cotton), Mary, of Concord, and Samuell Flecher, Sept. 3, 1684.
Samuel, and Lydiah Bates, July 22, 1695.

COTTLE, Joseph [jr. C. R. 1.], of Windham, N. H., and Mary Lincoln, Mar. 30, 1819.*

*Intention also recorded.

COTTON (see also Coton, Cotten), Lydia, and Samuel Procter, int. Mar. 15, 1723-4.

COWDERY (see also Cowdry), Allis, and Nath[anie]l Butterfield, Oct. 31, 1748.*
Samuel, and Elizebeth Robins, int. Sept. 18, 1762.

COWDREY (see also Cowdry), Mary, and Isaac Byham, int. Apr. 4, 1725.
Mathias, and Susanah Sherin of Boxford, int. Feb. 14, 1724-5.

COWDRY (see also Cowdery, Cowdrey), Isaac B., of Lowell, and Rhoda Baldwin, Nov. 2, 1837.*
Mial P., and Mary Crosby, int. Sept. 9, 1808.
Nathaniel [of Westford. int.], and Rebecca Parker, Mar. 11, 1773.*
Silas H. P., and Catharine P. Johnson of Westford, int. Oct. 29, 1832.

COWEN, John, and [Mrs. c. r. 1.] Susanna Peirce, ——, 1812. [Nov. 2. int.]*

COXE, Jane G., a. 23 y., d. William and Rachel, and Rufus Adams, a. 29 y., instructor, s. Isaac and Hannah, Aug. 2, 1846.*

CRAFT, Ephraim, of Roxbury, and Hannah Re[ad. t. c.], May 15, 1699.

CRAGGIN (see also Cragin), Benjamin, and Mercy Robbins, Nov. 27, 1766.*

CRAGIN (see also Craggin), John, of Acton, and Sary Barritt, int. Sept. 27, 1755.

CRAINE (see also Crane), Nancy P., of South Reading, a. 23 y., d. James and Lydia, and Daniel S. Stevens of South Reading, a. 21 y., carpenter, s. Jonathan and Sare, Oct. 5, 1848.

CRAM, Amy, of Lyndeborough, N. H., and Geo[rge] W. Bosworth of North Chelmsford, int. Feb. 4, 1847.
Rhoda E., of Lowell, a. 27 y., d. Gideon and Anna, and Eben Palmer, widr., of Lowell, a. 40 y., carpenter, s. Asa and Mary, Oct. 6, 1847.

*Intention also recorded.

CRANE (see also Craine), Mary Holmes, and Joseph Adams, July —, 1817. P. R. 24.

CRISPE, Marcy, and Roberd Paris, Apr. 11, 1667.

CRITCHET, Benoni, and Rebecca Hoostler [Hostsler. int.], Dec. 22, 1825.*

CROCKETT, Earlsworth, of North Chelmsford, a. 23 y., manufacturer, s. John and Phebe, and Elizabeth Holden of Tyngsborough, a. 23 y., d. Silas and Polly, of Tyngsborough, Dec. 25, 1845.*

CROMELL, Seaborne, and Roberd Paris, May 22, 1663.

CROOKER, [Hezekiah B., of Boston. int.], and Ann Putnam, Nov. 8, 1838. C. R. 1.*

CROSBY, Anna, and Joseph Foster [of Billerica. int.], Dec. 5, 1819.*
Benjamin, and Mary Parrot of Westford, at Westford, Jan. 1, 1767.*
Clarissa, and Charles P. Kidder of Westford, Sept. 20, 1841.*
Hannah [of Billerica. int.], and Phinehas Kidder, Nov. 20, 1784.*
Joel [of Ipswich, N. H. int.], and Hannah Stevens, Mar. 30, 1763.*
John, and Polly White of Ipswich, at Ipswich, May 1, 1783.*
Lydia, of Carlisle, and John Sterns, at Westford, Aug. 27, 1789.*
Mary, and Mial P. Cowdry, int. Sept. 9, 1808.
Nathan, jr., of Billerica, and Hannah Martin, at Billerica, June 4, 1735.*
Nathan [jr. int.], and Betty Barret, June 21, 1764.*
Porter, and Sally S. Dexter, Apr. 1, 1841.*
Rachel [of Carlisle. int.], and Asa Mansfield, Jan. 7, 1801.*
Simon, and Mrs. Deborah Hagget of Andover, at Andover, Feb. 23, 1775.*
Thomas [of Billerica. int.], and Anna Parker, at Billerica, —— [June 27, 1724. int.].*

CROSS, Nathan, and Mary Parkhurst, int. Sept. 26, 1725.
Nathan, of Dunstable, and Sarah Stevens, int. Oct. 15, 1727.

*Intention also recorded.

CROUCH, Arther, and Elisabeth Underwod of Watertown, 21: 3 m: 168[2. dup.].

CUMINGS (see also Cummings), Ephraim [jr., of Westford. int.], and Lydia Adams, Nov. 25, 1773.*
Henry, Rev. [of Billerica. int.], and Sarah Bridge, Sept. 19, 1791. P. R. 4.*
Nathaniel, and Rebecca Wilson of Billerica, int. May 27, 1774.

CUMINS (see also Cummings), John, and Elizabeth Adams, at Charlestown, Oct. 3, 1705.

CUMMINGS (see also Comings, Commings, Commins, Cumings, Cumins, Cummins), Elizabeth, and James Hildreth, at Concord, Nov. 26, 1724.*
John [of Dunstable. int.], and Sarah Howard, Oct. 3, 1776.*
Mary [Mrs., of Westford. int.], and Lt. Jonathan Harwood, Apr. 4, 1776.*
Mary, and Joseph B. Pierce, at North Chelmsford, Apr. 7, 1840.*

CUMMINS (see also Cummings), Aseneth, of Andover, and George Richardson, int. Feb. 14, 1823.
Samuel [of Westford. int.], and Sarah Spalding, Dec. 1, 1741.*

CURRIER (see also Carrer), Louiza, and Ephraim Andrews, June 12, 1825.*

CUSHING, Sarah, and Henry Quesey of Tyngsborough, Apr. 18, 1843.*

CUTLER, Charles, and Lydia Pierce, Feb. 16, 1822. [Feb. 14. C. R. 1.]*
Gershom, of West Cambridge, and Polly Richardson, int. Nov. 16, 1834.
Maria, of Burlington, and Obediah Badger, int. Apr. 1, 1827.

DADMUN, Nathan P., and Martha Laws of Peterborough, N. H., int. Aug. 26, 1843.

DAKIN, Elizabeth, of Concord, and Amos Proctor, at Concord, Oct. 25, 1798.*

DALLON, John C. [Dalton. C. R. 1. and int.], Dr., and Julia Ann Spalding, Feb. 21, 1822.*

*Intention also recorded.

CHELMSFORD MARRIAGES 215

DAMON, Nathaniel, and Mary H. Parker of Lowell, int. Sept. 10, 1826.
Warren, jr., widr., of Lowell, a. 28 y., machinist, s. Warren and Nancy, and Adeline F. Blaisdell of Campton, N. H. [of Lowell. c. r. 3.], a. 20 y., d. Moses and Abba, Oct. 30, 1847.

DANE, Abiah Moors, and Reuben Wright, jr. of Westford, int. Mar. 23, 1834.
Allice, and Asa Procter, int. Oct. 29, 1808.
George, and Hannah Butterfield, May 18, 1825.*
Mary, and Samuel Baldwin of Dracut, Feb. 1, 1816.*
Mary M., of Andover, and Charles H. Goodrich, int. Sept. 22, 1837.
Sophia, and John Elliott of Beverly, int. Mar. 19, 1826.

DANFORTH, Asa, and Abigail Pollard of Billerica, at Billerica, Mar. 14, 1781.*
David, and Elizabeth Pierce, Dec. 7, 1775.*
Jonathan, jr., of Billerica, and Rebecka Parker, at Billerica, 27: 4 m: 1682.
Mary, d. Jonathan, of Billerica, and John Parker, —— [1678?].
Patty, and Zacheus Walker, Oct. 29, 1771.*
Sarah, of Tyngsborough, and Samuel Richardson, Jan. 1, 1835. p. r. 26.*
Thomas [of Billerica. int.], and Sarah Butterfield, Oct. 16, 1744.*

DAVERSON (see also Davidson), William [Davidson. c. r. 1.], and Molly Blood, Nov. 12, 1795.*

DAVIDSON (see also Daverson, Davison), Francis [Daverson. int.], and Rebecca Richardson, Mar. 11, 1779.*
William, of Tewksbury, and Mary Gamil, int. Jan. —, 1738-9.

DAVIS (see also Davise), Anna, and John Smith, Feb. 4, 1747.*
Benjamin [of Billerica. int.], and Mary Mann, Apr. 2, 1778.*
Betcey [Elizbath. int.], and Thomas Baldwin [of Cavendish, Vt. int.], Jan. 3, 1797.*
Betsy, and Abel Blood, June 14, 1826.
Charles, and Olive Adams, July 11, 1830.*
Ebinezer, of Concord, and Dinnah Browne, Feb. 14, 1700.
Eliazer, of Concord, and Mary Perham, int. Apr. 20, 1728.

*Intention also recorded.

DAVIS, Elisabeth [wid. c. R. 1.], and Eli Parker, June 13, 1808.*
Eliza, a. 35 y., d. Deliveranc and Eliza, and Benjamin Blood, jr., widr., a. 43 y., box maker, s. Benja[min] and Mary T., Apr. 2, 1849.*
Eunice, and Moses Parker, at Billerica, Jan. 5, 1797.*
Harriett M., of Dracut, and John N. Park, int. Apr. 22, 1848.
Isaiah, and Mary Warn, int. Dec. 27, 1817.
James R., and Civonia Adams of Westford, at Westford, May 25, 1837.*
John, and Ann Buterfield, Dec. 19, 1716.
John, and Elizabeth Skinner of Westford, at Westford, Feb. 7, 1749.*
John, and Elizabath Herrick, Feb. 19, 1795.*
John L., a. 23 y., scythe maker, s. James and Betsey, and Delia G. Ward, a. 23 y., operative, d. Aaron and Sally, July 15, 1845.*
Johnson, and Sabra Moors, Aug. 25, 1796.*
Johnson, and Betty Fletcher, at Dracut, Apr. 29, 1798.*
Joshua [jr., of Billerica. int.], and Betty Blood, May 25, 1769.*
Joshua, and [Mrs. int.] Kath[e]rine Simpkins [resident in Chelmsford. int.], Sept. 19, 1776.*
Joshua, and Betcey Bowers of Greenfield, N. H., int. Dec. 8, 1796.
Lucy, and Daniel Mullin, int. Jan. 6, 1840.
Mary, and Simeon Fletcher, int. Aug. 6, 1748.
Mary, of Concord, and Joseph Chambers, at Concord, Feb. 17, 1795.*
Polley, and Asher Spaulding of New Boston, N. H., int. Dec. 11, 1796.
Polly, and Jonathan Richardson, jr., int. Nov. 14, 1806.
Rebecca, and Robert Tayler [of Tewksbury. int.], Oct. 17, 1786.*
Ruhamah, and David Baldwin of Billerica, at Billerica, July 12, 1792.*
Sally, and Isaac Stevens [of Richmond, Va. int.], Sept. 11, 1803.*
Samuel, and Phebe Spaulding, Nov. 8, 1798.*
Samuel, and wid. Mary Cogswell [of Lowell. int.], Nov. 15, 1830.*
Sarah C., of Tyngsborough, and Josiah C. Merriam, int. Apr. 29, 1844.
Susanna, and Moses Hall [Hale. int.] of Dracut, at Dracut, Mar. 26, 1769. [Mar. 6, 1789. int.]*

*Intention also recorded.

DAVISE (see also Davis), Daniel, of Canterbury, and Elizabeth Chamberlin, int. Feb. 14, 1724-5.

DAVISON (see also Davidson), John, and Salome Peck of Westmoreland, N. H., int. June 13, 1840.

DAY, Patty, of Nelson, N. H., and Benjamin Spalding, int. Sept. 7, 1822.

DEAN (see also Deans), John B., and Jane M. Wheeler of Newburyport, int. Oct. 16, 1825.
Keziah, of Easton, and Jared B. Britton, int. Feb. 24, 1838.

DEANS (see also Dean), Betsey H., Mrs., of Easton, and Joseph E. Heywood, int. Aug. 22, 1845.

DELL (see also Dill), Peter [Dill. dup.], and Thankes Sheperd, d. Ralph and Thankes, of Concord, 13: 10 m: 1669.

DeWITTE, Park, of Methuen, and Harriet Reed of Westford, May 21, 1828.

DEXTER, Bartlett W., and Mercy F. Jones of Dracut, int. Jan. 12, 1834.
Sally S., and Porter Crosby, Apr. 1, 1841.*

DICSON, Mary, and Jonathan Butterfeild, at Cambridge, June 12, 1667.

DIDSON (see also Ditson), Thankful, of Dunstable, and Benjamin Small, June 21, 1781.

DILL (see also Dell), Mary, and Roburd Robins, both of Groton, Mar. 27, 1697.
Mary, of Concord, and Josiah Barrett, at Concord, Feb. 20, 1749.

DITSON (see also Didson), Josiah, and Naoma Varnum, Mar. 30, 1809.*
Lydia, and John Spalding, jr., Apr. 21, 1814.*
Samuel, of Lowell, a. 24 y., teamster, s. John and Charlotte, and Nancy H. Rollins of Lowell, a. 27 y., d. Joseph and Elizabeth, Jan. 20, 1849.

*Intention also recorded.

DIX, Joel, and Priscilla Parker [Barker. C. R. 1.], of Tyngsborough, ——, 1811. [May 1. C. R. 1.]*
Lydia, of Townsend, and John Anderson, int. Mar. 13, 1831.

DODGE, George, and Eliza Oliver of Malden, int. Nov. 7, 1824.
Nancy, of Groton, and John W. Watkins, int. Dec. 19, 1830.
Sally, of New Boston, N. H., and Capt. Jonathan Spalding, int. Feb. 13, 1819.

DONLEY, Margarett, of Boston, a. 22 y., d. James and Catherine W., and Stephen Parker, a. 23 y., farmer, s. Thaddeus and Lydia, Apr. 24, 1847.

DOUGLASS, Roswell, and Addeline Warren, May 26, 1831.

DOWNING, Mary, of Boston, and John Tucker, int. Aug. 9, 1746.

DOWS (see also Dowse), Benjamin, jr., of Billerica, and Rebeckah Marshall, int. Mar. 11, 1789.

DOWSE (see also Dows), Ebenezer [of Billerica. int.], and Betty Corey, June 18, 1755.*

DRAKE, Hannah, and Hiram L. McGlauthlia, Aug. 15, 1841.*
John, of Easton, and Mrs. Martha T. Newcomb of Boston, Apr. 8, 1845. C. R. 3.
Lucius M., of Winchester, Conn., and Harriott L. Knecttle, June 14, 1843.*
Nahum M., and Lucy Heyward of Easton, int. May 18, 1844.
Sally, a. 23 y., d. Jona[than] and Hannah, and Benj[ami]n B. Ware of Franklin, a. 23 y., manufacturer, s. W[illia]m and Betsey, Nov. 13, 1844.*
Salome, and Elon Lothrop, both of Easton, June 25, 1840. C. R. 3.

DREW, Daniel, of Woburn, and Pamela Spalding, int. Sept. 21, 1842.

DRUSE, Mary, of Groton, and Thomas Bladget, July 8, 1696.

*Intention also recorded.

CHELMSFORD MARRIAGES 219

DUDLEY, Benjamin, of Weston, and Betsy P. Byam, Oct. 14, 1824.*
Benjamin, Dea., and Martha H. Parkhurst, June 28, 1838.*
Elizabeth A., and Rufus D. Spalding of Newport, N. H., int. Oct. 16, 1846.
Mary A., of Lowell, a. 19 y., d. James and Sarah, and Lewis T. Howland [of North Chelmsford. c. r. 3.], a. 20 y., moulder, s. Lewis and Pamelia, Nov. 24, 1847.*
Otis B., a. 19 y., blacksmith, s. Benjamin and Martha P., and Martha Ann Byam, a. 16 y., d. Ezekiel and Charlotte, Aug. 13, 1846.*

DULIHANTY, Hannah, of Boston, and Patrick Welsh, int. Oct. 19, 1823.

DUNN, Betsy, and Joel Mansfield, ———, 1812. [Nov. 16. c. r. 1.]*
Betsy, and [Lt. int.] Charles Blood, Aug. 5, 1822. [Aug. 15. c. r. 1.]*
Betty, and Jonas Pierce, Dec. 7, 1775.*
Center, and Mary Stone of Harvard, int. Apr. 2, 1836.
Charity L., and Abigail F. Parker of Bedford, N. H., int. Apr. 24, 1837.
Charlotte [d. James. c. r. 1.], and Samuel Chamberlain of Merrimack, N. H., Oct. 12, 1818.*
James, and [Mrs. int.] Anna Bradley [now resident in Chelmsford. int.], May 27, 1777.*
James, jr., and Rachel Lund of Merrimack, N. H., int. Nov. 22, 1777.
John, and Hannah Peirce, Feb. 27, 1772.*
John, jr., and Polly Dunn of Dunstable, int. Nov. 19, 1796.
Jonas, and Lucy Byam, May 10, 1808.*
Joseph, and Mary Pierce, Jan. 29, 1765.*
Joseph, and Lucinda McIntire, int. Sept. 4, 1836.
Leafa, and Samuel Dunn of Dunstable, int. Sept. 23, 1795.
Levi, of Stafford [Stoddard. int.], N. H., and Betsy Spaulding, Nov. 30, 1834.*
Lucy, and Samuel Clapp [of Merrimack, N. H. int.], ———, 1812. [Nov. 4. c. r. 1.]*
Martha, of Dunstable, and William Dunn, int. Nov. 22, 1784.
Mary, and Willard L. Butman of Tewksbury, int. July 4, 1830.
Molly, and Simeon Blodget, Dec. 19, 1786.*
Polly, of Dunstable, and John Dunn, jr., int. Nov. 19, 1796.
Rachel, and Jonathan Hay of Merrimack, int. Dec. 8, 1807.

*Intention also recorded.

DUNN, Rebeckah, and Phineas Underwood, int. Jan. 10, 1777.
Roxanna, and Eli F. Webster, July 4, 1830.*
Sally, and Oliver Blood, Oct. 24, 1808.*
Samuel, of Dunstable, and Leafa Dunn, int. Sept. 23, 1795.
Samuel, and Charlotte Keyes of Westford, int. Nov. 30, 1823.
Sibbel, and Zebediah Keyes, int. Aug. 21, 1802.
William, and Martha Dunn of Dunstable, int. Nov. 22, 1784.

DUPEE, Charles H., of West Cambridge, a. 24 y., carpenter, s. W[illia]m and Catharine, and Louisa Hutchins, a. 22 y., d. Oliver and Hannah, Nov. 18, 1847.*
George B., of Westford, and Hannah M. Hutchins, Nov. 30, 1843.*

DURANT (see also Durent, Durrant, Durunt), Abraham, jr., of Billerica, and Lydia Goold [both residents in Chelmsford. int.], at Billerica, Nov. 1, 1764.*
Jacob, and Mercy Farrar, Feb. 23, 1769.*
Leafe, of Carlisle, and Samuel Spalding, at Carlisle, Jan. 21, 1790.*
Olive, and Abel Keyes, Aug. 3, 1768.*
Phebe, and Daniel Stevens, Dec. 12, 1765.*
Sybil, and Jonas Robbins [jr. int.], Feb. 28, 1764.*

DUREN, Azubah, and Ebenezer Whittier, Dec. 2, 1824.*
Elizabeth, of Billerica, and John Foster, int. Mar. 16, 1722-3.
Joseph [of Billerica. int.], and Dorothy Blaisdell, Sept. 6, 1823.*
Willard, jr., of Carlisle, and Mary B. Merrell, Feb. 11, 1836.*

DURENT (see also Durant), Sylvester, and Betsy Warren, ——, 1806. [Feb. 27. C. R. 1.]*

DURGIN, Savina, and Horace Vinton of Oxford, int. Apr. 25, 1841.

DURRANT (see also Durant), John, and Ruth Fletcher of Westford, int. Feb. 12, 1763.
Reuben [Duren, of Billerica. int.], and Mary Goold, Jan. 11, 1770.*

DURUNT (see also Durant), Elizabeth, and Leonerd Spaulding, int. Dec. 18, 1737.

*Intention also recorded.

DUSTIN, Albert N., and Betsey Coomer, both of Lowell, Mar. 28, 1838. C. R. 1.
Diantha E., a. 29 y., d. Nathaniel and Gerusha, and William Fletcher, 3d, a. 26 y., farmer, s. William, jr. and Orpha, Apr. 22, 1845.*

DUTTON, Anna, of Bedford, and Samuel Parkhurst, int. Nov. 8, 1817.
David, and Hannah Wright of Westford, int. May 8, 1802.
Dorcas, and Thomas Blanchard [jr. of Dunstable. int.], Sept. 24, 1751.*
Dorcas, and William C. Smith of Westford [both of Westford. int.], Mar. 20, 1823.*
Elbridge, and Laura Maria Wright of Westford, at Westford, Jan. 23, 1840.*
Hannah, of Billerica, and William Parker [jr. int.], at Billerica, Mar. 30, 1773.*
Hannah, and Zadack P. Hastings [of Westford. int.], Mar. 26, 1829.*
Hildreth P., and Abigail Adams, Dec. 22, 1842.*
James, and Phebe Butterfield, int. Sept. 5, 1725.
James [jr. int.], and Edith Robbins, Sept. 24, 1751.*
James [jr. int.], and Ruth Corey, Nov. 1, 1754.*
John, and Elizabeth Spaulding, Jan. 14, 1779.
John, and Anna Hutchins of Carlisle, int. Feb. 12, 1802.
Jonas, and Rebeccah Browne of Billerica, int. Dec. 16, 1752.
Joseph, of Westford, and Rebecca Adams, at Westford, Nov. 6, 1735.
Laura A[nn. int.], and Varnum Spaulding, Dec. 15, 1831.*
Mary, and Jacob Farmer, Dec. 28, 1748.*
Sarah, and Nathaniel Brown [of Billerica. int.], ———, 1812. [Dec. 3. C. R. 1.]*
Thomas, of Billerica, and Hannah Burge, at Charlestown, Jan. 3, 1711.

EABERT, George M., and Louisa Weaver, int. Oct. 10, 1843.

EASTABROOKS (see also Esterbrook), Thomas, of Dunstable, and Prudence Shedd, int. Oct. 8, 1743.

EASTE (see also Esty), Lot, and Mary F. Winn of Hudson, N. H., int. Feb. 26, 1832.

EASTERBROOKS (see also Esterbrook), Sally, and John Glode, int. Sept. 21, 1823.

*Intention also recorded.

EASTMAN, Sally, and Thomas Goudy, both of Lowell, Sept. 16, 1832. c. r. 1.

EATON, Elizabeth, of Lowell, a. 28 y., dressmaker, d. John G. and Sarah, and Edson H. Hemmingway of Lowell, a. 25 y., carpenter, s. Jonathan and Sylvia, June 15, 1847.
John, and Sybil Spaulding, Apr. 26, 1774.*
John, of Boston, and Susanna Emerson, int. Nov. 10, 1833.
Maria, of Andover, Vt., and Joseph Reed, int. Jan. 17, 1836.

EDGARTON, Abigail, of Shirley, and Rowland Johnson, int. June 8, 1834.

EDSON, Theodore, and Rebecca Jane Parker of Boston, int. Nov. 14, 1824.

EDWARDS, Isaiah, of Salem, and Harriett N. Howard, Dec. 16, 1841.*
Moses, and Mary Eliza Tasker of Loudon, N. H., Apr. 19, 1843.*
Nathan B., of North Chelmsford, a. 25 y., physician, b. Westford, s. Peter and Martha B., of Westford, and Maria H. Fletcher, a. 26 y., d. Gardner and Frances, Oct. 30, 1845.*

ELLIOT (see also Elliott), John [of Boston. int.], and Lucy Spaulding, Jan. 22, 1807.*

ELLIOTT (see also Elliot), Caroline, of Manchester, N. H., and John H. Killom, int. Aug. 27, 1845.
Ebenezer, of Beverly, and Susan B. Littlehale, int. Mar. 26, 1831.
John, of Beverly, and Sophia Dane, int. Mar. 19, 1826.

EMERSON (see also Emmerson), Daniel, of Lexington, and Joanna Warren, Apr. 10, 1814.*
Dudley B., of Warner, N. H., and Lucy Ann Adams, Mar. 1, 1838.*
Edward, and Rabacah Waldo, Jan. 27, 1697-8.
Elizabeth, and Elijah Richardson, Nov. 29, 1832. p. r. 6.*
Esther, and Samuel Adams, Dec. 15, 1746.*
Franklin, and Rebecca Kittridge, Aug. 23, 1835.*
James M., and Mrs. Louisa Warner of Harvard, int. Nov. 22, 1843.

*Intention also recorded.

EMERSON, John B., widr., of Lowell, a. 28 y., laborer, and
Mary Jane Stratton, a. 26 y., d. Barnard and Charlotte,
Sept. 29, 1845.*
John M[ussey. C. R. 1.; of Waltham. int.], and Rebecca Hodgman, Oct. 22, 1827.*
Joseph, and Elizabeth Bryant of Lynn, at Lynn, Sept. 20, 1768.*
Joseph, and Ruth Warren, Apr. 26, 1774.*
Mahitabal, and Ephraim Buttrick, Oct. 11, 1804.*
Mary [d. Dea. O. C. R. 1.], and Oliver Farmer [jr. int.] of Billerica, Feb. 17, 1819.*
Mary, and Rodney McAllister, June 17, 1834.*
Obadiah [of Haverhill. int.], and Esther Parker, Mar. 22, 1744.*
Owen, and Mary Spaulding, Nov. 19, 1795.*
Owen, jr., and Louiza Butterfield, Oct. 16, 1823.*
Parker, and Rebecca Pollord [now resident in Westford. int.], May 16, 1771.*
Susanna, and John Eaton of Boston, int. Nov. 10, 1833.

EMERY (see also Emmery), Anthony, and Abigail Leavitt of Hampton, int. Apr. —, 1738.
Ebenezer, and Agnis Procter [of Westford. int.], Jan. 16, 1769.*
Elizabeth, of Townsend, and Jonathan Robbins, at Townsend, July 10, 1771.*
John, and Deborah Coburn, Jan. 9, 1786.*
Mary, and Thomas Stearns of Littleton, int. Sept. 2, 1750.
Noah [of Townsend. int.], and Mary Barrat, Dec. 22, 1743.*
Samuel, and Mary Green, May 31, 1774.*
Thankfull, and Jonathan Spaulding [of Carlisle. int.], June 20, 1781.*

EMMERSON (see also Emerson), Charles ["of Fishersfield, N. H." int.], and Remembrance Powers, Oct. 14, 1777.*

EMMERY (see also Emery), Elizabeth, and Ebenezer Butterfield [jr. of Dunstable. int.], Jan. 12, 1762. P. R. 4.*
John, and Mary Munroe [of Concord. int.], Apr. 24, 1745.*
Sarah, and James Haywood, Apr. 11, 1751. [Apr. 12. P. R. 4.]*
Zachariah [of Acton. int.], and Thankful Foster, June 26, 1744.*
Zecheriah, and Rebecca Reddington of Topsfield, at Ipswich, May 20, 1733.*

*Intention also recorded.

ESTABROOKS (see also Esterbrook), Aaron, and Hannah Haywood, July 21, 1756.*
Esther, and David Kidder, Feb. 20, 1751. [1750-51. P. R. 4.]*
Moses [of Dunstable. int.], and Esther Corey, June 5, 1744.*
Moses, and Sarah Adams, Dec. 22, 1768.*

ESTERBROOK (see also Eastabrooks, Easterbrooks, Estabrooks), Joel, of Westford, and Abigal Underwood, int. Feb. 6, 1778.
Matilda A., of Charlestown, and Cyrus Oliver, int. Sept. 4, 1825.

ESTY (see also Easte), John, of Billerica, and Sarah Baldwin, June 21, 1840.*

EVERETT, Abial B., of New London, N. H., a. 24 y., scythe maker, s. Jonathan and Apphia, and Harriett E. Spalding, a. 22 y., d. Isaiah and Patty, Nov. 24, 1848.*

EVERS, William Robinson, and Naomi Weaver, int. Dec. 18, 1848.

FALKNER (see also Faulkner), Hannah, of Andover, and William Martin, at Andover, July 19, 1741.*

FAREWELL (see also Farwell), Elisabeth, and John Richardson, Jan. 31, 1693-4. CT. R.

FARLEY, Elisabeth, of Billerica, and Jerahmell Bowers, at Billerica, Mar. 17, 1735-6.*

FARMER, Benjamin, and Rebecca Minot, June 9, 1742.*
Benjamin, and Lydia [Richardson. int.] Mears, Nov. 8, 1827.*
Elizabeth, and Abner Herrick, Dec. 14, 1775.*
Isabella [of Billerica. int.], and Benjamin Warren, Jan. 10, 1754.*
Jacob, and Mary Dutton, Dec. 28, 1748.*
Jesse, and Experience Laken [of Dunstable. int.], Feb. 20, 1800.*
Joanna, and James Alexander [of Merrimack, N. H. int.], Aug. 4, 1775.*
John, and Lydia Chamberlin, int. Nov. 10, 1787.
John [of Billerica. int.], and Mary Ann Kimball, Oct. 6, 1823.*

*Intention also recorded.

FARMER, Jonas, and Esther Adams, Dec. 24, 1739.*
Jonas, and Anna Russ, June 24, 1776.*
Mary, and Aaron Maynard, Jan. 12, 1823.
Mary N., of Tewksbury, and William Hamblett, int. Apr. 15, 1848.
Mary S., and Alfred Shepard, June 18, 1843.*
Oliver [jr. int.], of Billerica, and Mary Emerson [d. Dea. O. c. r. 1.], Feb. 17, 1819.*
Rebecca, of Westford, and Andrew Batties, jr., at Westford, Dec. 6, 1765.*
Sarah, and Thomas Pathio, Dec. 18, 1821.
Simeon, and Mary Cory, int. Sept. 12, 1764.
Simeon, and Abigail Mears, int. June 10, 1827.
Susanna, of Tewksbury, and Charles Macklain, int. Aug. 1, 1740.

FARNSWORTH (see also Farnworth), Roxany, and Luther Hartwell of Shirley, Nov. 5, 1836.*
William, and Catherine Haskell, int. Apr. 6, 1816.

FARNUM, Phebe, of Andover, and Osgood Worcester, at Andover, Dec. 27, 1798.*
Stephen, of Wilton, N. H., and Keziah Skidmoor, int. Feb. 12, 1765.

FARNWORTH (see also Farnsworth), Ephraim, of Groton, and Deborah Stevens, int. Apr. 11, 1725.

FARR, John H., and Lucy A. Carkin, int. Mar. 23, 1847.
Levi, and Polly Pierce [d. Capt. Jonas. c. r. 1.], Sept. 14, 1818.*
Mary, Mrs., and John W. Underwood, June 12, 1825.*

FARRAR (see also Farrer, Farror), Eliza H., and George Harton [Harlow. int.], Nov. 29, 1827. c. r. 1.*
Eunice, of Concord, and Samuel Chamberlain, at Concord, Dec. 1, 1796.*
Hannah, of Concord, and David Proctor, at Concord, Dec. 31, 1730.
John, and Lydia Richardson, at Westford, Jan. 24, 1788.
John, and Mary Parker, Dec. 29, 1836.*
Mary, and Jeremiah Butterfeild, Nov. 22, 1764.*
Mercy, and Jacob Durant, Feb. 23, 1769.*
Nathaniel, and [Mrs. int.] Rachel Fletcher, Nov. 16, 1773.*
Sarah, of Concord, and Abner Ball, int. Sept. 14, 1823.

*Intention also recorded.

FARRER (see also Farrar), Deborah, and Jonathan Read [Rood. C. R. 1.], June 27, 1781.
Joseph, and Deborah Richardson, int. Mar. 7, 1742-3.
Nathaniel, and Lidia Spaulding, Jan. 1, 1805.*
Oliver, and Elisabeth Taylor, Nov. 26, 1807.*

FARRINGTON, Maria D., of Andover, Me., and Milo Pierce, at Nashville, N. H., Nov. 18, 1849.

FARROR (see also Farrar), Sally, and Jeremiah Abbott, May 30, 1801.*

FARWEL (see also Farwell), Joseph, and Hanah Colborn, Jan. 23, 1695-6.

FARWELL (see also Farewell, Farwel, Ferwell), Asa T., and Mary Ann Keyes, July 22, 1839.*
Betty, of Dunstable, and Benjamin Marshall, May 14, 1754.
Elizabeth L. T., and Abel Simonds, int. Nov. 4, 1827.
Hannah, d. Joseph, and Samuell Wood, s. Samuell, of Groton, Dec. 30, 1685.
Hannah T., and Sumner Hale, int. Oct. 2, 1839.
Henry, and Susanah Ritchardsun, Jan. 23, 1695-6.
Isaac, of Dunstable, and Sarah Howard, int. May 15, 1726.
John T., and Mersylvia Todd of New Ipswich, N. H., int. Jan. 24, 1830.
Joseph, and Hanah Larned [torn. Dec. 25, 1666. CT. R.].
Juliet, of Washington, N. H., and Cranmore Wallace, int. Apr. 30, 1827.
Mahitabel, and William R. Lincoln of Boston, Dec. 25, 1839.*
Mary, and John Bats, Dec. 22, 1665.
Olive, d. Henry, and Benjamin Spalding, s. Edward, Oct. 30, 1668.
Sarah, of Dunstable, and Jonathan Howard, at Charlestown, Sept. 5, 1707.
Thomas T., and Sally Keyes of Pelham, N. H., int. Nov. 6, 1831.

FASSET, Esther, of Westford, and Benjamin Chamberlin, at Westford, Jan. 27, 1732.*
Mary, of Westford, and William Thomson, at Westford, Jan. 18, 1743.*
Sarah [of Bedford. int.], and Samuel Barron, May 23, 1744.*

*Intention also recorded.

FAULKNER (see also Falkner), Luther W., of Billerica, and Martha Prescott Merriam, int. Sept. 24, 1842.

FEARLOW, Ambrose, and Mary Martin, Dec. 2, 1668. CT. R.

FECHEM, Samuel, and Lois Blake of Franklin, int. July 17, 1819.

FELSTEAD, Affable, and Silas Chester of Billerica, int. Sept. 10, 1826.

FELTON, Levi, and Judith Abbott of Billerica, int. Sept. 12, 1824.

FERRIN, Dorothy, Mrs., of Concord, N. H., and Samuel L. Knowles, int. Dec. 9, 1848.

FERWELL (see also Farwell), John, and Elizebeth Hunt [Elizabeth Hunt Smith. C. R. 1.], of Dunstable [at Dunstable. P. R. 4.], Dec. 7, 1784.

FISHER, Fanny J., of Francistown, N. H., and John M. Sanborn, int. Oct. 28, 1843.
Mary, wid., and Joseph Rousoe, int. June 3, 1842.
Moses B., and Persis A. Varnum of Dracut, int. Mar. 3, 1843.
Samuel S., and Almira Adams of Waltham, int. Dec. 11, 1825.
Sylvia P., of Lowell, and Sewall Bowers, int. Nov. 6, 1847.

FISK (see also Fiske), Noah, and Mercy Goold, June 16, 1686. CT. R.

FISKE (see also Fisk), Annah [Mrs. dup.], and John Browne of Reading, May 30, 1677.
Benja[min], and Betcey Bridge, Apr. 12, 1798.*
John, and Lidiah Fletcher, 27: 1 m: 1666.
John [Rev. P. R. 1.], and Elisabeth Hinchman [Hincksman, wid. Edmund. P. R. 1.], Aug. 1, 167[2. T. C.].

FITCH, Joseph, of Boston, and Lydia Read, Dec. 5, 1822.*
Samuel [of Acton. int.], and Abiel Walker, Apr. 23, 1778.*

FITCHGERLS, Hannah [Fitz Gerald. C. R. 1.], and Thomas Nelson, July 14, 1782.

*Intention also recorded.

FLAGG, Sophronia [of Littleton. int.], and Josiah Byam, Apr. 17, 1823.*

FLANDERS, Lucy B., of Warner, N. H., and James M. Hammon, int. Jan. 9, 1831.
William S., and Mary S. Searle of Methuen, int. Nov. 30, 1839.

FLATCHER (see also Fletcher), Hanah, and Ebinezer Wright, May 14, 1697.
Sarah, and Nathaniell Buterfild, Jan. 18, 1697-8.

FLECHER (see also Fletcher), Ester, d. William and Isack Parker, Apr. 11, 1681.
Joshuah, s. William, and Grisill Jewell, May 4, 1668.
Lydea, and John Perram, Dec. 27, 1692. CT. R.
Mary, d. Ens. William, and Thomas Parker, Oct. 21, 1678.
Samuell, and Hannah Foster, d. Samuell, —— 16, ——. [1677?]
Samuell, and Mary Cotten of Concord, Sept. 3, 1684.
William, s. W[illia]m, and Sarah Richardson, d. Josiah, Sept. 19, 1677.

FLETCHER (see also Flatcher, Flecher), Aaron, and Sally Neef, Dec. 16, 1806.*
Abel, of Westford, and Sukey [Susanna. int.] Richardson, Dec. 28, 1820.*
Adams, and Betsy Bateman, int. Apr. 11, 1806.
Andrew, and Lydia Howard, May 14, 1746.*
Andrew, and Elizabeth Parker, May 5, 1748.*
Andrew, and Mary Holt, July 4, 1774.*
Anna, and Luther Bancroft of Pepperell, int. Jan. 1, 1803.
Benjamin [jr. int.], and Hannah Parker, Jan. 29, 1767.*
Benjamin, and Rachil Spaulding, Dec. 4, 1770.*
Benjamin, and Anna Spaulding [d. Lt. John. P. R. 4.], Oct. 21, 1779.*
Benjamin, Capt. [a. 77 y. C. R. 1.], and Mrs. Sarah Wilson [a. 55 y. C. R. 1.], Jan. 30, 1823.*
Benjamin, jr., and Sarah M. Wright, May 27, 1842.*
Betsy, and Stephen Spaulding, ——, 1806. [Jan. 9. C. R. 1.]*
Betsy, of Westford, and Calvin Howard, int. Mar. 26, 1826.
Betty, and Johnson Davis, at Dracut, Apr. 29, 1798.*
Charles [of Wilton. int.], and Sarah Fletcher, June 6, 1780.*

*Intention also recorded.

CHELMSFORD MARRIAGES 229

FLETCHER, Daniel [Capt. int.], and Charlotte Roby [of Dunstable, N. H. int.], Dec. 30, 1824.*
David, of Westford, and Mary Butterfield, int. Nov. 30, 1742.
David [jr., of Westford. int.], and Joanna Stevens, Nov. 17, 1774.*
David [of Westford. int.], and Ann Warren [d. Isaac. C. R. 1.], Dec. 2, 1819.*
Elizabeth, and Joseph Keyes, int. Feb. 28, 1719-20.
Elizabeth, and Samuel Hartwell of Concord, at Concord, Feb. 6, 1723-4.*
Elizabeth, of Westford, and Benjamin Blogget, at Westford, Feb. 14, 1733.*
Elizabeth, and Jacob Spaulding [jr. int.], Apr. 24, 1753.*
Elzina, and James Robbins, jr., Mar. 11, 1832.
Ester, and Stephen Perce, Feb. 5, 1707.
Esther, of Westford, and Samuel Adams, at Westford, Aug. 28, 1734.*
Ezra [of Westford. int.], and Hannah Bateman, Oct. 30, 1800.*
Fanny G., of Westford, and Gardner Fletcher, int. Mar. 10, 1815.
Gardner, and Fanny G. Fletcher of Westford, int. Mar. 10, 1815.
Hannah, and Jeremiah Baaul of Townsend, int. Apr. 15, 1765.
Hannah, and Ebenezer Parker, at Westford, May 29, 1787.*
Hannah [d. Maj. Joseph. C. R. 1.], and [Lt. int.] Josiah Fletcher, 3d, Oct. 13, 1818.*
Henry, and Sarah Spaulding, Apr. 12, 1753.*
Henry, and Remembrance Foster, June 6, 1776.*
Henry, and Marriam Smith of Princeton, int. Jan. 26, 1805.
Henry, and Huldah Spalding of Carlisle, int. July 17, 1810.
Henry, and Rhoda Coburn of Dracut, int. Nov. 6, 1825.
James K., and Charlotte Turner of Walpole, int. Sept. 19, 1825.
James T., of Topsfield, a. 22 y., blacksmith, s. Leonard and Lucinda, and Mary A. Lane of Lowell, a. 22 y., d. Jonathan and Hannah, Aug. 27, 1846. [Aug. 1. C. R. 3.]
Joanna, and Joseph Warren [jr. int.], Apr. 15, 1752.*
Joanna, and Benjamin Melvin, Feb. 27, 1777.*
Joanna [of Westford. int.], and Ira Spaulding, Oct. 19, 1795.*
John, of Concord, and Sarah Kidder, at Concord, Sept. 12, 1751.*
John, 2d, and Dolly Johnson, int. Apr. 20, 1822.
Jonas, and Elizabeth Robbins, int. Nov. 8, 1722.

*Intention also recorded.

FLETCHER, Jonathan, and Debborah Bates, int. Nov. 8, 1719.
Jonathan [jr., of Westford. int.], and Sarah Spaulding, Jan. 22, 1761.*
Jonathan, and Rebeckah Cory, May —, 1784.
Jonathan, and Polly Varnum of Dracut, int. Nov. 29, 1809.
Jonathan T., and Joanna French of Lowell, Apr. 22, 1840.*
Joseph, and Lucy Proctor, at Westford, Nov. 17, 1791.*
Joseph, jr., of Amherst, N. H., and Shuah H. Fletcher, Jan. 21, 1826.*
Joshua, and Doretha Halde, Mar. 3, 1701.
Joshua, and Elizabeth Bloget, int. Nov. 9, 1723.
Joshuah, and Sarah Wily, July 18, 1682.
Josiah, and Mary Chamberlain, Jan. 16, 1746.*
Josiah [3d. int.], and Mary [Marcy. int.] Richardson, Oct. 16, 1781.*
Josiah [3d. int.], and Zilpah Procter [d. Dan[ie]ll. P. R. 4.], Apr. 9, 1789.*
Josiah [Capt. int.], and Lucy Nourse of Ipswich, at Ipswich, Mar. 7, 1792.*
Josiah, 3d [Lt. int.], and Hannah Fletcher [d. Maj. Joseph. C. R. 1.], Oct. 13, 1818.*
Josiah, Cornet, and Joanna Spalding of Merrimack, N. H., int. Feb. 26, 1820.
Levi, and Phebe Holt, int. Jan. 11, 1790.
Lidiah, and John Fiske, 27: 1 m: 1666.
Lovel, and Prudence Spalding, Apr. 18, 1819.*
Lucinda, and Silas Butterfield [of Stoddard. N. H. int], ———, 1816. [June 25. C. R. 1.]*
Lucy, and William Prockter, int. July 9, 1733.
Lucy, and Henry Byham, Apr. 12, 1742.*
Lucy, and William French of Hollis, int. June 28, 1776.
Lucy [of Westford. int.], and John Spaulding, 3d, Jan. 26, 1786.*
Lucy, and Thomas Coburn, ———, 1812. [Dec. 3. C. R. 1.]*
Lucy W., and Abel Stevens, both of Westford, June 22, 1828.
Lydia, and Pallatiah Adams, at Charlestown, June 8, 1711.
Lydia, and Joseph Adams [jr. int.], Mar. 2, 1748.*
Lydia, and Thomas Clark, July 25, 1765.*
Maria H., a. 26 y., d. Gardner and Frances, and Nathan B. Edwards of North Chelmsford, a. 25 y., physician, b. Westford, s. Peter and Martha B., of Westford, Oct. 30, 1845.*
Mary, wid., and John Spauldyng, Nov. 18, 1700.
Mary, and William Fletcher, Dec. 10, 1701.

*Intention also recorded.

FLETCHER, Mary, of Westford, and Josiah Spaulden, at Westford, July 2, 1733.
Mary, and Jonathan Spaulding, Mar. 21, 1754.*
Mary [d. Josiah. P. R. 4.], and Zebulun Spaulding, Nov. 21, 1771. [Oct. 21. P. R. 4.]*
Mary, of Westford, and Thomas Barns, int. Mar. 13, 1772.
Mary [of Westford. int.], and Henry Spaulding [jr. int.], Nov. 17, 1774.*
Mary C., and [Capt. C. R. 1.] David Pulsifer [jr. int.] of Salem, June 7, 1825.*
Mary Jane, a. 32 y., d. W[illia]m and Orpah, and Levi Sherwin, widr., of Townsend, a. 33 y., farmer, s. Levi and Hannah, Oct. 16, 1849.*
Mary P., of Tyngsborough, and John A. Pierce, int. Nov. 14, 1824.
Mercy, and Caleb Abbot, Nov. 4, 1806.*
Moses, and Susanah Hildrith of Dracut, int. Oct. 19, 1803.
Oliver [jr. int.], and Tabitha Richardson, at Charlestown, Feb. 25, 1766.*
Oliver, and [Mrs. int.] Grace Weld of Roxbury, at Roxbury, Nov. 13, 1766.*
Patty, and Jabez Hatch Weld of Plymouth [New Plymouth. int.], N. H., at Billerica, Jan. 21, 1793.*
Paul, and Deliverance Stevens, at Charlestown, Apr. 12, 1705.
Phebe, and Joseph Hildreth, int. Mar. 29, 1720.
Polly, and Andrew Wille of Nottingham East, N. H., int. Nov. 29, 1794.
Rachel, and Jacob Howard, Feb. 6, 1745.*
Rachel [Mrs. int.], and Nathaniel Farrar, Nov. 16, 1773.*
Remembrance, and Levi Pierce, Jan. 3, 1776.*
Remembrance, and Jonathan Parker, Apr. 19, 1792.*
Robert, and Remembrance Foster, int. Oct. 25, 1742.
Robert, and Sarah Foster, Mar. 28, 1771.*
Ruth, of Westford, and John Durrant, int. Feb. 12, 1763.
Sally, and Marcus Peckins, Aug. 12, 1810.*
Sally [of Westford. int.], and Sewall Parkhurst, Feb. 7, 1828.*
Sameuell, jr., and Marie Coton [Cofen. CT. R.], June 7, 1692.
Samewell, and Marget Hailstoane, Oct. 14, 1659.
Samuel, and Sarah Ball of Concord, at Concord, June 7, 1699.
Samuel, and Elizabeth Proctor, at Concord, Dec. 20, 1705.
Samuel, jr., and Mary Lawrence of Littleton, at Westford, Sept. 17, 1729.*
Samuel, and Deborah Stevens, June 24, 1761.*

*Intention also recorded.

FLETCHER, Samuel, jr., and Buler Hathron of Temple, N. H., int. July 25, 1786.
Samuell, s. William, and Hannah Whealer, d. George, of Concord, July 5, 1[torn. 1673?].
Sarah, and Tho[mas] Reed, at Charlestown, Mar. 14, 1709.
Sarah, and Jerimiah Miller, int. Nov. 6, 1725. (Nov. 8, banns forbidden by Hannah Fletcher.)
Sarah, and Reuben Barrot, at Woburn, June 19, 1751.*
Sarah, and John Robbens [jr. int.], Oct. 1, 1771.*
Sarah [Mrs. int.], and Obadiah Sawtell [of Shirley. int.], Sept. 13, 1774.*
Sarah, and Daniel Kenney [of Wilton, N. H. int.], May 16, 1780.*
Sarah, and Charles Fletcher [of Wilton. int.], June 6, 1780.*
Sarah, of Tyngsborough, and Dean Holt, int. Oct. 28, 1832.
Sarah Jane, of New Boston, N. H., and Leonard C. Sanborn, int. Apr. 11, 1846.
Shuah H., and Joseph Fletcher, jr. of Amherst, N. H., Jan. 21, 1826.*
Simeon, and Mary Davis, int. Aug. 6, 1748.
Stephen, and Susanna Colburn of Dracut, int. Aug. 1, 1741.
Susanna, and Simon Parker, at Westford, July 5, 1791.*
Sybel, and Zacheus Fletcher, Sept. 18, 1794.*
Tabitha, and Cotton Proctor, Nov. 6, 1745.*
Thankful, and Eliazer Rice of Marlborough, at Concord, Dec. 8, 1720.*
Thankful, and Ebenezer Shed [of Billerica. int.], Mar. 30, 1758. [May 30. dup.]*
Thomas, and Elisabeth Clerk, int. Jan. 3, 1742-3.
Timothy, and Mary Prescott of Concord, int. Oct. 5, 1729.
Timothy, of Westford, and Bridget Richardson, int. Feb. 15, 1745-6.
Willard, and Abigail Hadley of Westford, Dec. 26, 1775.
Willard [jr., of Westford. int.], and Sally Spaulding, Apr. 18, 1808.*
William, and Mary Fletcher, Dec. 10, 1701.
William, and Mary Foster, int. May 26, 1716.
William, and Mary Powers, int. Oct. 18, 1724.
William, and Mary Blodget, Dec. 31, 1747.*
William [jr. int.], and Lydia Bates, Jan. 25, 1774.*
William, and Lucy [(Robbins). P. R. 4.] Hildreth, Nov. 10, 1778.*
William [of Temple, N. H. int.], and Rebecca Adams, Feb. 19, 1782.*

*Intention also recorded.

FLETCHER, William [Capt. int.], and Orpha Spalding, ———, 1813. [Mar. 23. C. R. 1.]*
William, sr., and Polly Osgood, June 18, 1818.*
William, 3d, a. 26 y., farmer, s. William, jr. and Orpha, and Diantha E. Dustin, a. 29 y., d. Nathaniel and Gerusha, Apr. 22, 1845.*
William B., and Sally Ballard, Oct. 21, 1804.*
Zaccheus, and Adeline Austin of Andover, int. Nov. 23, 1823.
Zacheus, and Sybel Fletcher, Sept. 18, 1794.*

FLINT, Polly [Patty. dup.; of Tewksbury. int.], and Abel Marshall [s. Sam[ue]l. P. R. 4.], Mar. 11, 1788.*
Sally, and Joel Hodgeman of Carlisle, int. Oct. 8, 1807.
Thomas, and Betsy Keyes of Westford, int. Sept. 6, 1806.
Thomas Grenville, and Anna Spaulding, May 13, 1834.*

FLOOD (see also Floyd), James [Floyd. int.], and Harriet Barnes, July 17, 1825. C. R. 5.*

FLOYD (see also Flood), Clarisa, of Woburn, and Benjamin Livingston, int. Jan. 6, 1822.

FLYNN, Priscilla, wid., a. 38 y., d. Ezekiel and Betsey A. Wentworth, and Elhanan Winchester, widr., a. 43 y., farmer, s. Charles and Liberty, Aug. 1, 1847.*

FOLLANSBEE, Charles, and Abigail B. Chandler of Merrimack, N. H., int. June 4, 1836.

FORD, Elisha, and Sally Perham, May 7, 1807.*
Lydia, and Ephraim Buttrick, int. Dec. 22, 1802.
Sally, and John L. Corliss [of Haverhill, N. H. int.], Feb. 22, 1805. [Jan. 22. C. R. 1.]*

FOSTER, Abigail, and Charl[e]s Barron, int. Oct. 17, 1761.
Andrew, and Mary Bloget, int. Feb. 25, 1721-2.
Anna, and Willard Parker, Feb. 11, 1766.*
Bridget, and Jacob Marshall [of Lunenburg. int.], Mar. 28, 1805.*
Daniel, and Sarah Barret, int. Oct. 22, 1749.
Dolly, of Wilmington, and Elnathan Glood, int. Jan. 1, 1803.
Ebenezer, and Sarah Parker, Nov. 3, 1743.*
Ebenezer, and Ruth Merril, Dec. 11, 1766.*
Ebenezer, and Hannah Foster, Nov. 8, 1768.*

*Intention also recorded.

FOSTER, Edward, and Phebe Peirce, Jan 23, 1772.*
Elizabeth, and Abel French of Billerica, int. Mar. 15, 1817.
Ely, s. Samuell, and Judeth Keies, d. Solomon, 17: 8 m: 1680.
Hannah, d. Samuell, and Samuell Flecher, —— 16, ——. [1677?]
Hannah, and Benjamin Barrett, at Charlestown, June 18, 1705.
Hannah, and Henry Chandler of Enfield, int. Sept. 14, 1723.
Hannah, and Ebenezer Foster, Nov. 8, 1768.*
Hannah, and William Wood, Apr. 20, 1800.*
Isaiah, and Anna Butterfeild, Nov. 8, 1743.*
Jacob, and Elizabeth Frost, int. Nov. 8, 1802.
Jean, and John Senter, at Woburn, Apr. 8, 1717.
John, and Elizabeth Duren of Billerica, int. Mar. 16, 1722-3.
Jonathan, of Tewksbury, and Mrs. Olive Harwood, int. Feb. 22, 1777.
Jonathan, and Sarah Parker, Mar. 7, 1799.*
Joseph, and Thankfull Wallker, int. Apr. 21, 1733.
Joseph, and Mary Adams, at Westford, Sept. 24, 1789.*
Joseph [of Billerica. int.], and Anna Crosby, Dec. 5, 1819.*
Josiah [late of Winchester. int.], and Sarah Procter, Apr. 2, 1761.*
Lenord, and Esther Blodget, int. Oct. 21, 1758.
Lidya, and Nathaniel Langley, int. Mar. 11, 1721-2.
Louisa W., and John A. Griffin, both of Lowell, June 18, 1843. C. R. 3.
Lydia, and Jonathan Richardson, Oct. 6, 1772.*
Martha, and Silas Parker, Sept. 4, 1788.*
Martha, Mrs., and Capt. Zaccheus Wright, July 5, 1829.
Mary, and William Fletcher, int. May 26, 1716.
Mary, and Benjamin Adams, Nov. 21, 1769.*
Mary, Mrs., and James Osbourn, ——, 1811. [May 26. C. R. 1.]*
Moses, of Dunstable, N. H., and Abigal F. Hunting, June 20, 1822.*
Nathaniel, and Francis Lovejoy of Andover, at Charlestown, Apr. 29, 1701.
Nathaniel, and Rebeckah Byam, Feb. —, 1784.*
Obadiah, and Mary Goodhue, at Westford, July 15, 1790.*
Rebecca, and Simeon Proctor, Mar. 12, 1754.*
Remembrance, and Robert Fletcher, int. Oct. 25, 1742.
Remembrance, and Henry Fletcher, June 6, 1776.*
Robert, and Mary Read of Dunstable, int. Sept. 4, 1762.
Robert, and Betsy Sprague of Malden, int. July 20, 1805.

*Intention also recorded.

CHELMSFORD MARRIAGES 235

FOSTER, Sally, of Westford, and Asa Barker, at Carlisle, Sept. 18, 1794.*
Samuel E., and Mary Byam, Mar. 15, 1804.*
Samuel E., and Mary C. Parker of Lowell, int. Sept. 28, 1828.
Samuell, s. Samuell, and Sarah Keies, d. Solomon, May 28, 1678.
Sarah, and William Parker, Apr. 3, 1751.*
Sarah [Mrs. int.], and John Senter [of Londonderry, N. H. int.], Sept. 20, 1768. [Sept. 21. P. R. 4.]*
Sarah, and Robert Fletcher, Mar. 28, 1771.*
Sarah, and John Keyes, int. May 24, 1781.
Thankful, and Zachariah Emmery [of Acton. int.], June 26, 1744.*
Thankful, and Jonathan Stevens, Dec. 30, 1777.*
William, and Hannah Colborn of Dracut, int. Sept. 15, 1744.

FOWLE, Mary, of Temple, N. H., and Zebulon Parker, jr., int. Apr. 9, 1819.

FREDERICK, George, and Rhoda Read of Westford, at Westford, Mar. 18, 1788.*

FREELAND, John, and Mary Kemp, Jan. 12, 1796.*

FREEMAN, Thomas N., of Cambridge, a. 24 y., house-wright, s. Tho[ma]s W. and Deborah F., and Lydia F. Glidden of Cambridge, a. 21 y., d. Andrew and Sarah, Mar. 28, 1846. [Mar. 22. C. R. 3.]

FRENCH, Abel, of Billerica, and Elizabeth Foster, int. Mar. 15, 1817.
Candace, of Southwick, and Foster Stevens, int. Dec. 12, 1824.
Joanna, of Lowell, and Jonathan T. Fletcher, Apr. 22, 1840.*
Mary B., and Joseph Sanderson of Cambridgeport, Aug. 2, 1841.*
Samuel, of Billerica, and Elisabeth Barry, at Billerica, July 7, 1755. [Mar. 19, 1742-3. int.]*
Sam[ue]ll, and Sarrah Commings of Dunstable, d. John, Dec. 28, 1682.
Sarah, of Dunstable, and Ebenezer Pakhust, int. Dec. ——, 1733.
Thomas T., of Manchester, N. H., and Sarah J. Peirce of Lexington, May 3, 1840. C. R. 3.

*Intention also recorded.

FRENCH, William, of Billerica, and Tabitha Pearce, int. Apr.
——, 1736.
William, of Hollis, and Lucy Fletcher, int. June 28, 1776.

FRIE (see also Frye), Ann, of Andover, and Jonas Clark, at Andover, Dec. 8, 1741.*

FROST, Asa, and Rhoda Trull of Billerica, at Billerica, July 25, 1790.*
Betty, and Jesse Adams, May 4, 1773.*
Charles A., and Harriet Merrell of Lowell, int. Aug. 9, 1835.
Ebenezer [jr. int.], and Esther Butterfield, Feb. 25, 1766.*
Ebenezer [jr. int.], and Olive Trull of Billerica, at Billerica, Apr. 15, 1794.*
Elizabeth, and Jacob Foster, int. Nov. 8, 1802.
Esther [of Billerica. int.], and Samuel Marshall, Jan. 2, 1755.*
Hannah, and Thomas Marshall, Feb. 22, 1753.*
Jesse, and Joanna Spaulding, May 6, 1760.*
Olive, of Tyngsborough, and Benjamin Peirce, int. Oct. 6, 1816.
Rebecca, of Watertown, and Charles Williams, int. Apr. 12, 1829.
Salathiel, and Pamilla Wilson, Nov. 11, 1828.
Sarah, and Joseph Marshall, Jan. 10, 1758.*
Sarah, wid., resident in Chelmsford, and Abel Russell of Westford, at Westford, Nov. 1, 1781.
Sarah, and S[t]ephen Kenney [of Nottingham West, N. H. int.], Apr. 14, 1796.*
William, of Billerica, and Molly Spaulding, at Billerica, June 14, 1775.*

FRY (see also Frye), Ira [Ens. c. r. 1.], and Laura Butterfield, June 7, 1825.*
Timothy, and Sophia Spaulding [of Dunstable, N. H. int.], Dec. 12, 1823.*

FRYE (see also Frie, Fry), John, and Cynthia Phelps of Wilton, N. H., int. Mar. 13, 1831.
Ruth H., of Lowell, and Josiah A. Wyman, int. June 20, 1840.

FULLER, Lucy Ann, of Amherst, N. H., and John Trask Ray, int. May 8, 1825.

FULLERTON, Elisa Jane, and William D. Call, both of Lowell, Feb. 25, 1841. c. r. 1.

*Intention also recorded.

FURBER, Andrew, and Ann McDaniel of Danvers, int. Aug. 4, 1841.
Geo[rge] D., a. 30 y., tailor, s. William and Polly, of Belfast, Me., and Ann Maria Parker, a. 25 y., d. Jonathan and Hannah, July 22, 1847.*

FURBUSH, Charles [of Andover. int.], and Sarah Corey, Apr. 1, 1755.*
Silas, and Anna Butterfield, Mar. 22, 1798.*

GALUSHA (see also Galusiah), Rachel, and Eleazer Corey, Oct. 28, 1742.*

GALUSIAH (see also Galusha), Daniel, and Hannah Goold, d. Frances, Oct. 10, 1676.

GAMIL (see also Gammel), Mary, and William Davidson of Tewksbury, int. Jan. —, 1738-9.

GAMMEL (see also Gamil), Eleziabeth, and William Patten of Litchfield, int. Nov. 11, 1739.
William [of Concord. int.], and Thankful Keyes, June 17, 1777.*

GARFIELD, Moses B., of Concord, and Elizabeth Gordon Merriam, int. Sept. 24, 1842.

GEBLER, William, and Cedora [Cedona. int.] Hirsch, June 11, 1829. c. r. 3.*

GEER, Frederick S., of Pembroke, N. H., and Louisa D. Wilson, int. Aug. 28, 1841.

GEORGE, Fanny E., of Lowell, and Joel Colburn, June 15, 1843.*

GIBSON, Catharine Mary, and Joel Adams, Aug. 13, 1809.*
James, and Lydia Merrill of Windham, N. H., int. Dec. 20, 1835.

GIDDINGS, George W., and Harriot E. Montague, int. Mar. 24, 1837.

GILCHRIST, Elisabeth H., of Andover, and Abial C. Adams, int. Oct. 27, 1847.

*Intention also recorded.

GILLSON (see also Gilson), Joseph, and Mare Cooper [Caper. CT. R.], Nov. 10, 1661. [Nov. 18. CT. R.]

GILMORE, George F., of Pittsburg, Pa., and Hannah D. Clark, Mar. 7, 1843.*

GILSON (see also Gillson), Sarah, of Groton, and Jonathan Kemp, at Concord, Nov. 19, 1718.

GLAZIER, Georg, of Lancaster, and Sarah Barret, Dec. 17, 1700.

GLEZEN, Hannah, of Upton, and Samuel Temple, int. Sept. 25, 1751.

GLIDDEN, Lydia F., of Cambridge, a. 21 y., d. Andrew and Sarah, and Thomas N. Freeman of Cambridge, a. 24 y., house-wright, s. Tho[ma]s W. and Deborah F., Mar. 28, 1846. [Mar. 22. C. R. 3.]

GLINES, Elizabeth B., of Lowell, and Orin Parckard, at North Chelmsford, Apr. 29, 1841.*

GLODE (see also Glood), John, and Esther Powars, at Charlestown, Mar. 15, 1770.*
John, and Sally Easterbrooks, int. Sept. 21, 1823.
Sally, and Andrew McEntire of Wilton, int. Dec. 12, 1807.

GLOOD (see also Glode), Elnathan, and Dolly Foster of Wilmington, int. Jan. 1, 1803.
Esther, and James Wille, Dec. 31, 1795.*
Nancy, and John Vincent, ——, 1812. [June 10. C. R. 1.]*
William, and Sally Spaulding, Apr. 29, 1794.*

GLOVER, Caroline S[ophia. P. R. 28.], a. 21 y., d. Joel, and Otis Adams, jr., a. 23 y., farmer, s. Otis and Abigail, Nov. 15, 1849.*

GLYNN, Hannah, and Samuel Roby, Apr. 2, 1805.*

GOLLE (see also Gould), Abigal [Goole. CT. R.], and Thomas Corey, Sept. 19, 1665.

*Intention also recorded.

GOODHUE, Aaron, and Deborah Coburn, both of Dracut, July 20, 1815. C. R. 1.
James, of Westford, and Senea Carlton, int. May 17, 1803.
Lydia, and Nathan Ames [of Groton. int.], Apr. 10, 1788.*
Mary, and Obadiah Foster, at Westford, July 15, 1790.*
Nathaniel, of Merrimack, and Lydia Chamberlin, int. Feb. 19, 1787.
Sarah, and Silas Peirce, Dec. 28, 1797.*
Thomas, and Elizabeth Blood, July 30, 1801.

GOODRICH, Charles H., and Mary M. Dane of Andover, int. Sept. 22, 1837.
Charles Whitting, of Norwich, Vt., and Anna Pierce, int. Feb. 15, 1811.

GOODWIN, William, and Sarah Peabody of Newport, N. H., int. May 8, 1825.

GOOFE, John, of Boston, and Hanah Parrish [torn. 1699?].

GOOLD (see also Gould), Abijah, and Sarah Spaulding, Oct. 29, 1766.*
Benjamin, and Sarai Parkhurst, int. Oct. 15, 1721.
Ebenezer, and Olive Parker, Jan. 22, 1751. [1750-51. P. R. 4.]*
Ebenezer [jr. int.], and Anna Lane of Bedford, at Bedford, May 20, 1779.*
Hannah, d. Frances, and Daniel Galusiah, Oct. 10, 1676.
Leah, and Jonathan Adams, Aug. 29, 1681.
Lucy, and Caled Blanchard of Andover, int. May 21, 1787.
Lydia, and Abraham Durant, jr. of Billerica [both residents in Chelmsford. int.], at Billerica, Nov. 1, 1764.*
Mary, and Reuben Durrant [Duren of Billerica. int.], Jan. 11, 1770.*
Mercy, and Noah Fisk, June 16, 1686. CT. R.
Nathaniel [of Ipswich, N. H. int.], and Hannah Shed, Nov. 20, 1766.*
Reuben, and Deborah Spaulding, Mar. 10, 1762.*
Reuben, and Martha Phillips, Mar. 23, 1790.*
Sarah [Mrs. int.], and Moses Graves, Aug. 11, 1767.*
Sarah, and Ebenezer Hill [of Merrimack, N. H. int.], May 25, 1772.*
Simeon, and Elizabeth Pike, June 19, 1760. [June 18. P. R. 4.]*

*Intention also recorded.

GOOLE (see also Gould), Mare, and John Waddell, Dec. 25, 1[66. T. C.]6.
Martha, d. Francis and Rose, and Joseph Barett, 17: 7 m: 1672.
Samuell, of Dunstable, and Mehetable Barett, d. Thomas and Francis, Mar. 17, 1684.

GOO[faded], Hanah, d. Elizabeth, and Benjamin Barit, June 18, 1705.

GORDON, Rebecca, now resident in Chelmsford, and Daniel Rand of Cambridge, int. Feb. 24, 1776.

GOUDY, Thomas, and Sally Eastman, both of Lowell, Sept. 16, 1832. C. R. 1.

GOULD (see also Golle, Goold, Goole), Adam, and Elezabeth Butterfield, int. Jan. 25, 1729-30.
Adam, and Jemima Skidmore of Methuen, at Methuen, Feb. 23, 1758.*
Dana, and Mary Harris of Merrimack, N. H., int. Mar. 30, 1828.
Ebenezer, Dea., and Lowes Snow, Dec. 28, 1797.*
Joanna [P. int.], and Ichabod G. Kimball, Dec. 5, 1821.*
John, and Sarah Hartwell of Concord, at Concord, Apr. 16, 1717.
Jonathan, and Nancy Butler of Pelham, N. H., int. Oct. 3, 1824.
Mary, of Dunstable, and Solomon Pollard, June 27, 1775.
Phebe, and Bill Wright Stevens, at Westford, Nov. 29, 1792.*
Phebe [Cory. int.], and Jeduthan Parker, at Westford, Jan. 1, 1793.*
Sally, and Samuel Procter, jr., int. Apr. 11, 1793.
Sally, and Henry Lawrance [of Boston. int.], Feb. 18, 1809.*

GOULDING, John, and Aseneth Haskell of Templeton, int. Sept. 30, 1814.

GOVE, Betsy, of Merrimack, N. H., and James Howard, int. July 25, 1824.

GOWARD, Josiah W., and Laura Butterfeild, May 20, 1841.*
Zephaniah, and Martha A. Newcomb of Mansfield, int. Apr. 8, 1841.

*Intention also recorded.

GRAHAM, Joseph, and Eliza Ann Wheeler of Tewksbury, int. Nov. 15, 1823.

GRANT, Thomas, "a Transient person" [resident of Massachusetts. int.], and Rachel Upton, at Dracut, Mar. 20, 1786.*
William H., and Caroline S. Plaisted of Jefferson, N. H., int. Nov. 23, 1847.

GRAVES, John, of Hatfield, and Sarah Bauke, 25: 8 br: 1686. CT. R.
Moses, and Edee Robbins, int. Mar. 26, 1749.
Moses, and Joanna Byham, Dec. 17, 1750.*
Moses, and [Mrs. int.] Sarah Goold, Aug. 11, 1767.*

GREELE (see also Greeley), Nancy Holland, of Wilton, and Oliver Scripture, int. Nov. 3, 1809.

GREELEY (see also Greele), Sarah, of Nottingham West, N. H., and Daniel Hadan, int. Nov. 21, 1800.

GREEN (see also Greene), John, and Lucy Procter, int. Dec. —, 1808.
Mary, and Samuel Emery, May 31, 1774.*
Thankful Augusta, of Carlisle, and Nathan Buttrick, int. May 27, 1837.

GREENE (see also Green), Marv, and Daniell Cadye, both of Groton, July 6, 168₃.

GREENLEAF, Daniel E. [G. int.], and Rebecca Proctor, Apr. 21, 1833.*

GREGGORY, Eunice A., of Weston, and Rufus Byam, int. May 10, 1843.

GREY, Mary, "sometime of Late" resident in Chelmsford, and James Hallett of Cambridge, int. Jan. 3, 1732-3.

GRIFFIN, [Elizabeth S., of Westford. int.], and Asaph Mansfield, Apr. 9, 1840. P. R. 21.*
John A., and Louisa W. Foster, both of Lowell, June 18, 1843. C. R. 3.
Mary A., of Westford, and Jacob B. Smith, at Westford, Mar. 12, 1840.*

*Intention also recorded.

GRIFFIN, Mathew, and Mary Adams of Pepperell, June 18, 1777.
Matthew, and Sally Adams, ———, 1810. [Nov. 30. c. r. 1.]*
Phebe, of Dracut, and Abel Lincoln, int. Dec. 4, 1818.
Sophia, and Hiram Ayers, Oct. 2, 1828.*

GRIMES, Mary, of Billerica, and Jonas [Jonathan. int.] Bowers, at Watertown, June 7, 1726.*

GROW, Alonzo, and Maria Carkin, int. Nov. 2, 1848.

GUILD, Nathan, widr., a. 45 y., farmer, s. John and Olive, and Eunice Russell, a. 35 y., d. Abner and Sarah, Apr. 21, 1845.*

GURNE (see also Gurny), Jane, of Dorchester, and John Burge, sr., Sept. 6, 1677.

GURNY (see also Gurne), Grisell, and John Burge, July 3, 1667.

HADAN, Daniel, and Sarah Greeley of Nottingham West, N. H., int. Nov. 21, 1800.

HADLEY, Abigail, of Westford, and Willard Fletcher, Dec. 26, 1775.
Belinda P., a. 22 y., b. Middlesex Village, d. Sam[ue]l P. and Belinda, and Paul Hill of Lowell, a. 29 y., overseer in factory, b. Billerica, s. John and Sarah A., of Billerica, Oct. 9, 1845.*
Ebenezer [of Westford. int.], and Abigail Spaulding, June 11, 1753.*
Ebenezer, of Lowell, and Philena Morse, int. Oct. 14, 1837.
Samuel, and Lucy Read of Hollis, N. H., int. Sept. 8, 1822.

HAGGET (see also Haggit), Deborah, Mrs., of Andover, and Simon Crosby, at Andover, Feb. 23, 1775.*

HAGGIT (see also Hagget), Thomas [of Andover. int.], and Susanna Adams, Mar. 12, 1745.*

HAILSTOANE, Marget, and Samewell Fletcher, Oct. 14, 1659.

*Intention also recorded.

HALD (see also Heald), Hannah, and Richard Stevens, Nov. 15, 1699.

HALDE (see also Heald), Doretha, and Joshua Fletcher, Mar. 3, 1701.

HALE, Dorcas, of Carlisle, and Samuel Adams, jr., int. July 29, 1809.
Eunes, and Joseph Buterfild, Jan. 21, 1696-7.
Harriot, d. Moses, and Nathaniel Stevens of Andover, Nov. 7, 1815.*
Lydia, d. Moses, and Moses Tyler, s. Joseph, of Tewksbury, Dec. 26, 1815.*
Sophronia, and Oliver M. Whipple, Apr. 4, 1820. [1821. C. R. 1; Mar. 18, 1821. int.]*
Sukey, and Salathial Maning, Dec. 13, 1807.*
Sumner, and Hannah T. Farwell, int. Oct. 2, 1839.

HALEY (see also Healey), Lydia, of Tyngsborough, and Robbart B. Chamberlain, int. Nov. 21, 1812.

HALKERSTON, Margarett, Mrs., of Boston, and Rev. Sampson Stoddard, int. Jan. 1, 1726-7.

HALL (see also Halle), Aaron, and Ann Brown of Weare, N. H., int. Nov. 18, 1842.
Asenath J. [L. int.], of Billerica, and Simeon B. Proctor, May 21, 1840.*
Charles H., of Lowell, a. 19 y., shoemaker, s. Stephen and Lydia, and Hannah E. Brown of Lowell, a. 18 y., d. George and Betsey, May 31, 1846.
Cynthia, and Reuel Pierce, int. Jan. 29, 1826.
Darius, and Sarah Ann Vincent, July 4, 1830.*
Ebenezer, and Elizabeth Barker of Tyngsborough, int. Oct. 17, 1840.
Elijah, and Mrs. Hannah P. Kent, Nov. 22, 1842.*
Elisabeth, and Thomas Chamberlain, Jan. 9, 1690. CT. R.
Moses [Hale. int.], of Dracut, and Susanna Davis, at Dracut, Mar. 26, 1769. [Mar 6, 1789. int.]*
Ruth [of Westford. int.], and Jacob Chamberlin, Feb. 8, 1780.*
Thomas, of Salisbury, a. 22 y., wool sorter, s. Thomas and Lucy, of Farnumsville, and Sarah Townsend of Amesbury, a. 22 y., d. W[illia]m and Sarah, of Amesbury, May 10, 1847.

*Intention also recorded.

HALL, William, and Mary Caldwell [of the glass factory. C. R. 1.], May 16, 1821.*

HALLE (see also Hall), Hannah, and John Spalden, May 18, 1658.

HALLETT, James, of Cambridge, and Mary Grey, "sometime of Late" resident in Chelmsford, int. Jan. 3, 1732-3.
John A., a. 24 y., carpenter, b. New Brunswick, s. John and Gertrude, and Sarah Parkhurst, a. 23 y., d. John and Celia, Jan. 18, 1849.*

HAMBLET (see also Hamblett), Reuben, and Deborah Austin of Methuen, at Methuen, Nov. 8, 1759.*
Samuel, of Dracut, and Mary Chever, int. Dec. 26, 1812.

HAMBLETT (see also Hamblet), William, and Mary N. Farmer of Tewksbury, int. Apr. 15, 1848.

HAMMON, James M., and Lucy B. Flanders of Warner, N. H., int. Jan. 9, 1831.

HANCOK, John, of North Cambridge, and Elesibeth Clark, Dec. 11, 1700.

HANDLEY, Russell, and Lucy Y. Martin, Dec. 30, 1838.*

HANS, Charles, and Mary Chamberlain of Billerica, Jan. 8, 1761.

HANSON, Thomas [Harrison. C. R. 1.], and Elizabeth Manning, ——, 1811. [May 28. C. R. 1.]*

HARDY, Bethiah, of Nottingham West, N. H., and Benjamin Procter, int. June 20, 1761.
Caroline, and Jonas L. Parker, Feb. 28, 1836.
Reuben K., and Zelphia F. Barden, Dec. 16, 1833.
Sarah, and Josiah Byam, Dec. 28, 1841.*
Susan, and Charles Hyde, Oct. 16, 1841.*
Zachariah, of Tewksbury, and Prudence Stevens, int. Jan. 27, 1750-51.

*Intention also recorded.

HARMAN, Moses M., of Lowell, a. 22 y., house carpenter, s. Moses and Betsey, and Adeline E. Noble of Lowell, a. 20 y., d. Nathan and Mary, Feb. 28, 1847.

HARRINGTON, Philena I., and Zebadiah Holt, int. Nov. 11, 1833.

HARRIS, Azariah [of Dunstable, N. H. int.], and Esther Adams, May 22, 1794.*
Ebenezer, and Elizabeth Spaulding, int. Nov. 13, 1720.
Ebenezer [jr. int.], and Dorcus Byham, Nov. 14, 1754.*
John D., and Maria Libbey, at Lowell, Jan. 1, 1838.*
Julia, and John Shaw, int. Oct. 17, 1846.
Mary, of Merrimack, N. H., and Dana Gould, int. Mar. 30, 1828.
Rachel, of Dracut, and Moses Chevar, jr., int. Aug. 8, 1815.

HART, Harriot, and Benjamin Ives Ober, Jan. 24, 1816.*

HARTON, George [Harlow. int.], and Eliza H. Farrar, Nov. 29, 1827. C. R. 1.*

HARTWELL, Betsey, of Carlisle, and Ruben Parker, int. May 21, 1810.
Joseph, jr., of Bedford, and Sarah Skinner, int. June 1, 1751.
Lucy, of Carlisle, and Capt. Ebenezer Shead, at Carlisle, May 16, 1793.*
Luther, of Shirley, and Roxany Farnsworth, Nov. 5, 1836.*
Mary Jane, a. 18 y., d. Nathan and Sally, and William T. Childs of Groton, a. 23 y., blacksmith, s. Calvin and Sally, Aug. 4, 1844.*
Samuel, of Concord, and Elizabeth Fletcher, at Concord, Feb. 6, 1723-4.*
Sarah, of Concord, and John Gould, at Concord, Apr. 16, 1717.
Sarah E., of Littleton, and Leonard C. Sanborn, int. Sept. 14, 1837.
Silas, of Carlisle, and Sally Keyes, int. Jan. 18, 1802.

HARVEL, John, and Hester [Easter. int.] Proctor of Concord, at Concord, Apr. 25, 1734.*

HARVY, Elsey, of Dracut, and Antoni Hilbert, int. Sept. 17, 1820.

*Intention also recorded.

HARWOOD (see also Howard), Abigail, of Dunstable, and Jacob Hildreth, int. Oct. 18, 1730.
Anna, and Asa Hodgman [of Carlisle. c. R. 1.], Oct. 7, 1829.
Betsy, and Francis B. Woods, June 23, 1825.*
Charles V[arnum Howard. c. R. 1.], and Irene Bowers, Dec. 29, 1826.*
Hannah, and Peter Procter, int. Apr. 10, 1720.
James, and Lidiah Barrett, d. John, Apr. 11, 1678.
Joanna, and Simeon Stevens, Feb. 22, 1757.*
John, and Martha Barton, both of Boston, Nov. 20, 1679.
John, and Sarah Adams, Mar. 16, 1774.*
Jonath[a]n, and Joanna Spaulding, int. Apr. 3, 1731.
Jonathan, and Mary Parker, int. Mar. 18, 1737-8.
Jonathan [jr. int.], and Olive Spaulding, Oct. 28, 1762.*
Jonathan, Lt., and Mrs. Lucy Proctor, int. Aug. 20, 1768.
Jonathan, Lt., and [Mrs. int.] Mary Cummings [of Westford. int.], Apr. 4, 1776.*
Jonathan, and Mary Parker of Carlisle, int. Feb. 3, 1810.
Mary, and Jonathan Snow, Mar. 25, 1756.*
Mary Ann, and Jonathan Spaulding, Apr. 29, 1831.*
Molly, and Reuben Parker, Jan. 27, 1801.*
Nathanil, and Rachel Peirce, May 6, 1784.*
Olive, Mrs., and Jonathan Foster of Tewksbury, int. Feb. 22, 1777.
Rachel, and Francis Bowers [of Greenfield, N. H. int.], Dec. 6, 1797.*
Rachell, and Stephen Peirce, int. Dec. 1, 1722.
Rufus, and Marianne Stevens of Mount Vernon, N. H., int. Feb. 4, 1843.
Rufus, and Sarah C. Moody of Lowell, int. Sept. 6, 1845.
Sarah, and Ephraim Chamberlin [of Westford. int.], Nov. 26, 1801.*
Solomon, and [Mrs. int.] Mardany D. Carter, Apr. 9, 1843.*
Susanah, and John Robins, int. May 1, 1736.

HASKELL, Aseneth, of Templeton, and John Goulding, int. Sept. 30, 1814.
Catherine, and William Farnsworth, int. Apr. 6, 1816.
Ezekiel [of Lancaster. int.], and Rebecca Howard, Sept. 26, 1759.*

HASSELTON, Amy, of Billerica, and Henry Richardson, at Billerica, Feb. 20, 1732-3.*

*Intention also recorded.

HASTING (see also Hastings), Elmira [of Woburn. C. R. 1.], and Reuben Parker, "published in Woburn," Dec. 12, 1815.

HASTINGS (see also Hasting), Walter, Dr., and [Mrs. int.] Lucretia Bridge, Apr. 10, 1777.*
Zadack P. [of Westford. int.], and Hannah Dutton, Mar. 26, 1829.*

HATCH, Sarah S., of East Bridgewater, and Barnabas H. Bryant, int. Sept. 3, 1826.

HATHRON, Buler, of Temple, N. H., and Samuel Fletcher, jr., int. July 25, 1786.

HAWARD (see also Hayward), Benjamin [Hayward. CT. R.; Howard. C. R. 1.], and Sarah Worster, Dec. 20, 1785.*
Sarah [Hayward. CT. R.], and Bengamin Parker, Jan. 14, 1690-91.

HAWOOD (see also Heywood), Benja[min], [Haywood. C. R. 1.], and Hannah Robbins, Jan. 21, 1783.*
Jessa [Haywood. C. R. 1. and int.], and Sarah Byam, Nov. 28, 1782.*

HAY, James A., and Louise G. Bowers, int. July 28, 1822.
Jonathan, of Merrimack, and Rachel Dunn, int. Dec. 8, 1807.

HAYDEN, Hannah, of Harvard, and John Peckens, jr., int. Dec. 15, 1822.

HAYES, Aaron, and Pheby Wood, int. Dec. 1, 1808.

HAYWARD (see also Haward, Heyward), Abigal, of Acton, and William Levingstone, int. Feb. 10, 1810.

HAYWOOD (see also Heywood), Betsy, and John Wright [of Westford. int.], Oct. 28, 1819.*
Hannah, and Aaron Estabrooks, July 21, 1756.*
Hannah, and Isaac Bancroft, Dec. 12, 1813.*
James, and Sarah Emmery, Apr. 11, 1751. [Apr. 12. P. R. 4.]*
James [of Paris, N. Y. int.], and Tryphene Byam, June 19, 1814.*
Jonathan [Ens. Jonathan Harwood. int.], and [Mrs. int.] Judeth Reed of Woburn, at Woburn, May 2, 1759.*

*Intention also recorded.

HAYWOOD, Joseph, and Sarah Blaisdell, Oct. 30, 1745.*
Joseph, and Susanna Ball, at Townsend, Dec. 16, 1788.*
Sarah, and John Byam, jr., Nov. 28, 1784.*
Sary, and Josiah Blood of Hollis, N. H., int. Sept. 25, 1755.

HEALD (see also Hald, Halde, Heild), Israel [Hail, of Acton. int.], and Susanna Robbins, Dec. 30, 1760.*
John [of Acton. int.], and Elizabeth Barratt, July 18, 1745.*
Martha, of Acton, and John Barrett, at Concord, May 24, 1738.*
Mary, of Acton, and Jonas Robbins, at Concord, May 24, 1738.*
Phebe [Hale. int.], of Westford, and Benjamin Twist, at Westford, Apr. 17, 1792.*
Sarah, of Acton, and Jonas Hildreth, int. Nov. 10, 1744.

HEALEY (see also Haley, Healy), Lorinda, and Artemas Parker, jr., int. Sept. 27, 1829.

HEALY (see also Healey), Mary W., and Isaac Woods, Aug. 8, 1826.*
Samuel, and Lidia Barker, both of Tyngsborough, Oct. 10, 1804.

HEILD (see also Heald), Dorothy, and Joseph Butterfield, int. May 14, 1727.
Ephraim, of Townsend, and Elanor Robbins, int. Feb. 25, 1732-3.
John [of Stow. int.], and Mercy Robbins, June 28, 1743.*
Thomas, and Sarah Butterfield, int. Oct. 28, 1725.

HELDERETH (see also Hildreth), James, and Marget [Ward. CT. R.], at Dorchester, June 1, 1659.

HELDRETH (see also Hildreth), Elizabeth, and Ickabod Stratton, Oct. 13, 1709.

HELLDRETH (see also Hildreth), Margret, and Isarell Procter, Jan. 10, 1689.

HEMMINGWAY, Edson H., of Lowell, a. 25 y., carpenter, s. Jonathan and Sylvia, and Elizabeth Eaton of Lowell, a. 28 y., dressmaker, d. John G. and Sarah, June 15, 1847.

*Intention also recorded.

HERICK (see also Herrick), B[e]thyah, of Concord, and Timothy Spaulding, int. Sept. 28, 1728.

HERRICK (see also Herick), Abner, and Elizabeth Farmer, Dec. 14, 1775.*
Elisabeth, and Benjamin Parkhurst, jr., Apr. 11, 1805.*
Elisha, of Morristown, Vt., and Bethiah Libby, Jan. 20, 1842.*
Elizabath, and John Davis, Feb. 19, 1795.*
Polly, and Phineus Barratt [of Stoddard, N. H. int.], Jan. 15, 1812.*
Rebeckah, and William Byam, Feb. 27, 1795.*
Samuel, and Mary Spaulding, Jan. 22, 1795.*

HERRIN (see also Herring), Margaret, and Hermonis Birck, int. Nov. 9, 1816.

HERRING (see also Herrin), Jane, and William Nolin, int. May 22, 1813.

HERWOOD (see also Howard), Thomas, of Dunstable, and Abigil Whitney, int. Jan. 4, 1729.

HEYWARD (see also Hayward), Lucy, of Easton, and Nahum M. Drake, int. May 18, 1844.

HEYWOOD (see also Hawood, Haywood), Benjamin, and Esther Richardson, Feb. 28, 1833.*
Joseph, and Fidelia Reed, Sept. 3, 1820.*
Joseph E., and Mrs. Betsey H. Deans of Easton, int. Aug. 22, 1845.
Mary, and Stowell Bancroft, Dec. 3, 1822.*
Susanna, and Lt. John Chamberlain of Grand Isle, Vt., int. Feb. 13, 1820.

HIDE (see also Hyde), W[illia]m, and Eliza [P. int.] Hovey, Mar. 30, 1829.*

HILBERT, Antoni, and Elsey Harvy of Dracut, int. Sept. 17, 1820.

HILDRETCH (see also Hildreth), Sarah, and John Robbens, 3d, int. Sept. 12, 1771.

*Intention also recorded.

HILDRETH (see also Heldereth, Heldreth, Helldreth, Hildretch, Hildrick, Hildrith, Hilldereth, Hilldrith), Abigail, and Zacheus Wright [of Westford. int.], Feb. —, 1799.*
Abigaill, d. Richard, and Moses Parker, June 19, 1684.
Abigal, and Joseph Barit, Dec. 15, 1696.
Anna, and John Butterfield, int. Dec. 10, 1721.
Dorcas, and Simeon Wright of Westford, at Westford, Oct. 31, 1738.*
Dorithy, and John Robbins, Nov. 30, 169[torn. 1699.].
Ebenezer, and Sarai Swallow, int. Dec. 13, 1719.
Elizebeth, of Westford, and Amos Byam, int. Jan. 9, 1832.
Emely, of Westford, and Elisha Shaw, int. May 15, 1840.
Ephraim, and Mary Butterfield, int. Jan. 5, 1722-3.
Ephraim, jr., of Dracut, and Mary Clark, at Dracut, Feb. 11, 1735-6.
Ezekiel [of Westford. int.], and Lucy Robbins, Sept. 28, 1774.*
Hannah, and Daniel Whitney, Feb. 6, 1745.*
Hannah E., and Leavitt R. Joslyn [of Boston. int.], Oct. 25, 1832.*
Isaac, and Rachell Adams, int. Mar. 1, 1724-5.
Isaac, jr., of Nichewaug, and Esther Snow, int. Oct. 22, 1749.
Isack, and Elisabeth Willson of Woburn, Nov. 12, 1685. [July 24. CT. R.]
Jacob, and Abigail Harwood of Dunstable, int. Oct. 18, 1730.
James, and Dorothy Prescot of Concord, int. Dec. 20, 1721.
James, and Elizabeth Cummings, at Concord, Nov. 26, 1724.*
James, and Lidya Wright, int. Aug. 13, 1727.
Jonas, and Sarah Heald of Acton, int. Nov. 10, 1744.
Jonas, and Mary Parlin [of Concord. int.], Jan. 18, 1749.*
Jonas, and Sarah Procter, Dec. 27, 1759.*
Jonathan, and Hannah Spaulding, int. Dec. 5, 1725.
Jonathan, and Hannah Spalding, at Concord, June 13, 1738.*
Jonathan [jr. int.], and Mary Robbins, Jan. 25, 1749.*
Joseph, and Abigaill Willson, at Woburn, 25: 12 m: 1683.
Joseph, and Phebe Fletcher, int. Mar. 29, 1720.
Lois [of Westford. int.], and Joshua Snow, Apr. 28, 1761.*
Lucy [(Robbins). P. R. 4.], and William Fletcher, Nov. 10, 1778.*
Mary Martha [Martha M. int.], and Joel C. Witherell, June 15, 1823.*

*Intention also recorded.

HILDRETH, Mercy M., a. 16 y., b. Westford, d. Moses and
    Eliza, and Ezekiel L. Shurtleff, a. 24 y., cabinet turner,
    b. Westford, s. Caleb W. and Susan, Dec. 26, 1848.*
Perses, d. Richard, and Samuell Cleveland, May 23, 1682.
Rachel, and [Capt. C. R. 1.] James Pitts, Dec. 24, 1808.*
Sally, of Dracut, and John Pierce, at Dracut, Jan. 8, 1795.*
Sampson, and Lydia Parlin of Concord, at Concord, Feb. 25, 1752.*
Samuel [of Westford. int.], and Sarah Procter, Mar. 14, 1753.*
Sarah C., and Josiah F. Perry of Boston, int. Dec. 27, 1835.
Sarai, and Jacob Byham, int. Jan. 1, 1720-21.
Sybil, and Phineas Chamberlain, July 23, 1776.*
William, and Susan Palmer [Parmenter. int.], Jan. 25, 1827.*

HILDRICK (see also Hildreth), Abigail, and Thomas Chamberlain, at Concord, June 10, 1713.

HILDRITH (see also Hildreth), Susanah, of Dracut, and Moses Fletcher, int. Oct. 19, 1803.
Susanna, of Tyngsborough, and Jonas Peirce, jr., int. May 4, 1805.

HILL (see also Hills), Ebenezer, of Nichewaug, and Sarah Wheeler, int. Dec. —, 1738.
Ebenezer [of Merrimack, N. H. int.], and Sarah Goold, May 25, 1772.*
John, and Elizabeth Blodget, June 22, 1711.
Paul, of Lowell, a. 29 y., overseer in factory, b. Billerica, s. John and Sarah A., of Billerica, and Belinda P. Hadley, a. 22 y., b. Middlesex Village, d. Sam[ue]l P. and Belinda, Oct. 9, 1845.*
Susana, of Billerica, and Daniel Procter, int. Sept. 17, 1727.

HILLDERETH (see also Hildreth), Elisabeth, and John Stephens, Dec. 15, 1664.
Mary, and Jacob Warrin, June 21, 1667.

HILLDRITH (see also Hildreth), Ritcherd, and Sary Carver, int. Apr. 20, 1728.

HILLS (see also Hill), Franklin M., of Amherst, N. H., a. 25 y., carpenter, s. Moses and Sally, of Amherst, N. H., and Martha S. Parkhurst, a. 22 y., d. J. K. and Ruth, Dec. 26, 1844.*
Paul, and Mary Ann Burrows of Waltham, int. Aug. 10, 1823.

*Intention also recorded.

HILTON, Sophia, of Lunenburg, and Hilliard E. Woodward, int. Oct. 11, 1829.

HINCHMAN (see also Hincksman), Elisabeth [Hinksman, wid. Edmund. P. R. 1.], and [Rev. int.] John Fiske, Aug. 1, 167[2. T. C.].

HINCKSMAN (see also Hinchman), Briget, and James Ritcheson, Nov. 28, 1660.

HINKLEY, Stephen [of Gorham, Me. C. R. 1.], and Sophrona Shed, Nov. 8, 1829.

HIRSCH, Cedora [Cedona. int.], and William Gebler, June 11, 1829. C. R. 3.*
Charles F., and Isabel Maria Jameson, int. Jan. 26, 1834.
Friderick, and Caroline Starrett of New Boston, N. H., int. Apr. 14, 1837.
Henrietta A., a. 22 y., b. Middlesex Village, d. Hannah, and Ephraim S. Moore, a. 22 y., mason, s. Joseph and Mary, May 24, 1844.*
William E., and Frances Ann Willard of Lowell, int. June 9, 1833.

HOAR, Laura, and Nathaniel Wright, int. Feb. 6, 1820.

HOBART, Jeremiah, and Rebecca Saunders of Groton, Mar. 4, 1776.

HOBSON, John, and Sarah Varnum, d. Samuel, at Rowley, Dec. 4, 1679.

HODGEMAN (see also Hodgman), Joel, of Carlisle, and Sally Flint, int. Oct. 8, 1807.

HODGMAN (see also Hodgeman), Abigail, and Joseph Spaulding, Feb. 19, 1784.*
Asa, and Sibel Blodget, Nov. 28, 1782.*
Asa [jr. int.; Lt. C. R. 1.], and Sally Spaulding [d. Job. C. R. 1.], Jan. 28, 1824.*
Asa [of Carlisle. C. R. 1.], and Anna Harwood, Oct. 7, 1829.
Benjamin [of Concord. int.], and Lydia Walker, Nov. 24, 1743.*

*Intention also recorded.

CHELMSFORD MARRIAGES

HODGMAN, Betsy, and Issacher Andrews [of Billerica. int.], ——, 1805. [Sept. 8. C. R. 1.]*
Elizabeth, and Jesse Marshall, Nov. 16, 1779.
Esther, and Ephraim Wesson [Willson. int.], at Concord, Apr. 13, 1780.*
Hannah, and Stephen Webber, Nov. 28, 1825.*
John, and Rebecca Parker, Apr. 3, 1823.*
Lucy, and Azariah Procter, ——, 1806. [Feb. 16. C. R. 1.]*
Lydia, and Edward Withington, ——, 1812. [Aug. 20. C. R. 1.]*
Mary Adams, and Joseph Hutchenson [of Carlisle. int.], Oct. 9, 1806.*
Rebecca, and Issachar Andrews [of Concord. int.], Apr. 20, 1768.*
Rebecca, and John M[ussey. C. R. 1.] Emerson [of Waltham. int.], Oct. 22, 1827.*
Sarah, of Carlisle, and Gilman Hunter, int. Feb. 15, 1845.
Stephen, of Merrimack, N. H., and Hannah Wright, int. Nov. 27, 1776.
Sybil, and Jonas [R. int.] Proctor [of Tyngsborough. int.], Nov. 14, 1809.*

HOLDEN, Artemas, and Ann Bowers, int. Sept. 21, 1823.
Artemos, and Jerusha Brown of Concord, int. Feb. 17, 1810.
Clarissa, of Tyngsborough, a. 21 y., d. Silas and Polly, and Samuel S. Alexander of Windham, N. H., a. 27 y., farmer, s. David and Abba, Feb. 3, 1847.
Elizabeth, of Tyngsborough, a. 23 y., d. Silas and Polly, of Tyngsborough, and Earlsworth Crockett of North Chelmsford, a. 23 y., manufacturer, s. John and Phebe, Dec. 25, 1845.*

HOLLIS, Nancy, of Woburn, and Joseph Peirce, int. Apr. 5, 1805.

HOLMAN, Mary Ann, of Douglass, and Samuel Austin Waters, int. Nov. 2, 1834.

HOLMES, Jane [Jean. int.], of Charlestown, and John Page, at Charlestown, Mar. 5, 1760.*
Jason F., and Hannah L. Round of Foster, R. I., int. Aug. 2, 1846.
Mary E., of Nashville, N. H., and Henry C. Allen, int. May 13, 1848.

*Intention also recorded.

HOLT, Clara A., of Merrimack, N. H., and Thomas J. Adams, Oct. 10, 1848.
Dean, and Sarah Fletcher of Tyngsborough, int. Oct. 28, 1832.
Mary, and Andrew Fletcher, July 4, 1774.*
Phebe, and Levi Fletcher, int. Jan. 11, 1790.
Polley, and Solomon Hunt of Tewksbury, int. Mar. 15, 1794.
Zebadiah, and Philena I. Harrington, int. Nov. 11, 1833.
Zubiah [of Reading. int.], and Palatiah Adams, Oct. 14, 1773.*

HOOSTLER (see also Hoseller), Rebecca [Hoetsler. int.], and Benoni Critchet, Dec. 22, 1825.*

HOPKINGS, Samuel, Rev., of Hadley, and Mrs. Margrit Stoddard, int. Sept. 14, 1776.

HORTON, David, and Abigail [K. int.] Morgan, July 12, 1829. C. R. 3.*

HOSELLER (see also Hoostler), Philip, and Rebeckah Calley, int. June 13, 1818.

HOSMER, Abiel, and Sarah Whittemore Upton of Dunstable, int. Nov. 29, 1835.
Joel [of Wilmington, Vt. int.], and Betsy Walker, ———, 1813. [Feb. 13. C. R. 1.]*

HOVEY, Eliza [P. int.], and W[illia]m Hide, Mar. 30, 1829.*
Rhoda B., of Dracut, and Simeon Spalding, jr., int. Apr. 16, 1816.
Samuel [of Rowley. int.], and Lydia Langley, May 24, 1757.*

HOW (see also Howe), Tho[ma]s, Col., of Marlborough, and Mrs. Mary Barron, int. Nov. 7, 1724.
Winthrop, and Lydia Hunting, int. June 30, 1822.

HOWARD (see also Harwood, Herwood), Abigail, and Jonathan Bates, int. Apr. 20, 1745. (Apr. 23, banns forbidden by Joanna Parker.)
Ann K., of West Bridgewater, and Hiram White, int. Dec. 25, 1831.
Benjamin, and Mrs. Martha Poor of Andover, at Andover, Jan. 12, 1748.*
Calvin, and Betsy Fletcher of Westford, int. Mar. 26, 1826.

*Intention also recorded.

CHELMSFORD MARRIAGES 255

HOWARD, Caroline, of Dracut, and Joseph B. Varnum of Newbury, Nov. 17, 1846. C. R. 3.
Clarissa, a. 45 y., d. Jacob, and Benjamin Chadbourne, widr., of Standish, Me., a. 55 y., trader, s. Joseph, Dec. 29, 1846. [Dec. 28. C. R. 3.]*
Eleziabeth, and John Warren, int. Feb. 23, 1739.
Elizabeth [wid. dup.], of Charlestown [of Newton. dup. and int.], and [Capt. dup.] Jonathan Richardson, at Charlestown, May 18, 1724.*
Harriett N., and Isaiah Edwards of Salem, Dec. 16, 1841.*
Jacob, and Rachel Fletcher, Feb. 6, 1745.*
Jacob, jr., and Rachel Varnum of Dracut, at Dracut, May 1, 1796.*
James, and Betsy Gove of Merrimack, N. H., int. July 25, 1824.
Jonathan, and Sarah Farwell of Dunstable, at Charlestown, Sept. 5, 1707.
Jonathan, and Susanna Row of Marblehead, int. Feb. 18, 1743-4.
Jonathan, and Charlottee Roby of Dunstable, N. H., int. Jan. 29, 1796.
Lydia, and Andrew Fletcher, May 14, 1746.*
Lydia, and Jonathan Manning [jr. int.], Feb. 23, 1802.*
Martha, and Jonathan Manning of Billerica, at Billerica, Mar. 17, 1774.*
Mary, and Amos Richardson of Pelham, N. H., int. Jan. 10, 1756.
Mary, and Timothy Manning of Billerica, at Billerica, June 13, 1776.
Molley, and Elijah Richardson, Mar. 11, 1800. C. R. 1.*
Nathaniel, and Hannah Stevens [of Dunstable. int.], Mar. 29, 1798.*
Olive, and Thomas Read, jr. of Westford, int. Feb. 21, 1746-7.
Rachel, and Jonathan Barron, Oct. 19, 1749.*
Ratchel, and Samuel Ritchardsun, Jan. 27, 1702-3.
Rebecca, and Ezekiel Haskell [of Lancaster. int.], Sept. 26, 1759.*
Samuel, and Mary Snow, Dec. 14, 1758.*
Samuel, and Rebecca Bancroft of Tyngsborough, at Tyngsborough, June 6, 1790.
Sarah, and Isaac Farwell of Dunstable, int. May 15, 1726.
Sarah, and Sam[ue]ll Barron, int. Nov. 22, 1730.
Sarah, and John Cummings [of Dunstable. int.], Oct. 3, 1776.*
Timothy, and Sarah Spaulding, at Westford, July 15, 1788.*

*Intention also recorded.

HOWE (see also How), Frederic W., of Windsor, Vt., a. 25 y., machinist, s. Frederic, and Sarah A. Claflin [of North Chelmsford. C. R. 3.], a. 18 y., d. Alfred, Dec. 16, 1847.*
Mary, of Topsfield, and Aaron Hubbard, at Topsfield, June 1, 1733.*

HOWLAND, Lewis T. [of North Chelmsford. C. R. 3.], a. 20 y., moulder, s. Lewis and Pamelia, and Mary A. Dudley of Lowell, a. 19 y., d. James and Sarah, Nov. 24, 1847.*

HOYT, Collings, of Grafton, N. H., and Sabra Moors [d. wid. Miel. C. R. 1.], Oct. 17, 1820.*
Eunice, and William Morse [of Dunstable. int.], Nov. 7, 1824. [Nov. 17. C. R. 1.]*

HUBBARD, Aaron, and Mary Howe of Topsfield, at Topsfield, June 1, 1733.*
John, and Sally Robinson, Sept. 2, 1830.

HUDDLETON, Maria, of Lowell, and Willard Proctor, int. Mar. 25, 1832.

HUNT, Abigail, of Billerica, and Nathaniel Buterfeild, int. Oct. —, 1733.
Ann, of Billerica, and Oliver Pierce, at Billerica, Mar. 21, 1733-4.*
Asenath, of Marlborough, and Joseph Sherman, int. Apr. 29, 1809.
Dolly, of Tewksbury, and Jonas Clark [both of Tewksbury. C. R. 1.], ——, 1806. [Apr. 10. C. R. 1.]
Eliphalet, and Persis Wilson of Bradford, Vt., int. Apr. 12, 1838.
Elizebeth [Elizabeth Hunt Smith. C. R. 1.], of Dunstable, and John Ferwell [at Dunstable. P. R. 4.], Dec. 7, 1784.
Harriet B., of Tewksbury, and Rufus Spalding, int. Mar. 10, 1822.
Jane, of Lowell, and John Sweet, int. Apr. 25, 1830.
John, and Nancy Blodget of Merrimack, N. H., int. Apr. 3, 1820.
Joshua [of Tewksbury: int.], and Olive Chamberlin, Nov. 20, 1794.*
Joshua, jr., and Lucia Todd of Rindge, N. H., int. Dec. 29, 1822.

*Intention also recorded.

HUNT, Lydia, Mrs., of Tewksbury, and Thomas Marshall, int. Nov. 17, 1769.
Mary, and John Swett, int. June 9, 1837.
Mary Ann, a. 40 y., d. Joshua and Olive, and Eli Parker, widr., a. 57 y., farmer, s. W[illia]m and Lucy, June 18, 1844.*
Neomy, and Frances Wever, int. July 5, 1817.
Paul, and Betty Parkhurst, at Westford, Nov. 19, 1789.*
Samuel, and Naome [Nancy. int.] Wilson, Aug. 7, 1798.*
Sarah, and Daniel K. Kimball, int. Apr. 17, 1831.
Solomon, of Tewksbury, and Polley Holt, int. Mar. 15, 1794.
Solomon, and Phebe Lyon of Windham, N. H., int. Sept. 2, 1821.
Susan, of Dunstable, N. H., and Charles Melvin, int. Jan. 11, 1824.
Thaddeus W., and Ann S. Thompson, at Marlborough, Jan. 3, 1838.*

HUNTER, Gilman, and Sarah Hodgman of Carlisle, int. Feb. 15, 1845.
Joel, and Lucy Read of Westford, int. July 13, 1809.

HUNTING, Abigal F., and Moses Foster of Dunstable, N. H., June 20, 1822.*
Lydia, and Winthrop How, int. June 30, 1822.
Nancy, and Philip Tyler [of Tewksbury. int.], May 3, 1821.*

HUNTINGTON, Martha, of Boston, a. 22 y., d. John and Martha, and Charles Smith of Boston, a. 31 y., carpenter, s. Seth and Wealthy, Oct. 5, 1847.

HUSSEY, Hannah J. [of North Chelmsford. c. r. 3.], a. 19 y., d. Benjamin and Phebe, and John R. Smith [of North Chelmsford. c. r. 3.], a. 21 y., moulder, s. Ransom and Nancy, Oct. 7, 1847.*

HUSTON, Catharine, and Joseph Stow [of Concord. int.], Dec. 3, 1778.*

HUTCHENSON (see also Hutchinson), Eliza, of Andover, and Benjamin Melvin, jr., int. Sept. 4, 1825.
Joseph [of Carlisle. int.], and Mary Adams Hodgman, Oct. 9, 1806.*

*Intention also recorded.

HUTCHERSON (see also Hutchinson), Mary, of Carlisle, and Dea. John Spaulding, int. Nov. 20, 1802.

HUTCHINS, Anna, of Carlisle, and John Dutton, int. Feb. 12, 1802.
Benjamin P., of Carlisle, and [Mrs. c. r. 1.] Phebe Spalding [d. Andrew. c. r. 1.], Apr. 23, 1820.*
Benjamin P., of Carlisle, and Martha Bonner, June 4, 1843.*
Dorothy, and Amos Taylor [of Walpole, N. H. int.], Feb. 19, 1778.*
Hannah M., and George B. Dupee of Westford, Nov. 30, 1843.*
Louisa, a. 22 y., d. Oliver and Hannah, and Charles H. Dupee of West Cambridge, a. 24 y., carpenter, s. W[illia]m and Catharine, Nov. 18, 1847.*
Oliver, of Carlisle, and Hannah [A. int.] Spalding [d. Andrew. c: r. 1.], Feb. 20, 1823.*
Samuel [of Temple, N. H. int.], and Olive Robbens, May 20, 1773.*
Sarah, and John Temple [of Acton. int.], Apr. 21, 1756.*
Thomas, of Carlisle, and Abigail Spalding [d. Andrew. c. r. 1.], Nov. 27, 1821.*

HUTCHINSON (see also Hutchenson, Hutcherson), Betty [Molly. int.], of Bedford, and Samuel Parkhurst, at Bedford, Feb. 12, 1788.*
Nathaniel [jr. int.], of Carlisle, and Thankful Snow, at Carlisle, July 14, 1785.*

HYDE (see also Hide), Charles, and Susan Hardy, Oct. 16, 1841.*

ILESLY, Olive [of Lunenburg. int.], and Isaac Chamberlin, jr., Dec. 29, 1814.*

INGLEE, Hannah L., of Marblehead, and Thomas Cogswell, int. Apr. 1, 1827.

IVORY, Joanna, and George Brannon, int. Apr. 29, 1843.

JAMESON, Isabel Maria, and Charles F. Hirsch, int. Jan. 26, 1834.

*Intention also recorded.

JAQUES (see also Jaquesh, Jaquith), Nathan, of Tewksbury, and Thankful Thorndike, June 25, 1818.*

JAQUESH (see also Jaques), Susana, of Bradford, and Josiah Burdge, int. July 17, 1725.

JAQUITH (see also Jaques), Sally, of Dracut, and Samuel Chandler, at Dracut, Apr. 21, 1796.*

JEFES, Hanah, d. Henry, of Billerica, and Andrew Spalding, Apr. 30, 1674.

JEFFRAY, John [Jeppoye. int.], a. 22 y., woolstapler, s. Joseph and Mary, and Harriett Sherwood of Lowell, a. 20 y., d. Henry and Charlotte, Nov. 30, 1844.*

JENKINS, Mary A. D., of Boston, and Benjamin J. Spalding, int. Nov. 25, 1848.

JENNESS, Mehitable, of Haverhill, and John A. Burnham, int. July 4, 1824.

JEWEL (see also Jewell), John, and Margret Parrot of Westford, int. Oct. 20, 1764.

JEWELL (see also Jewel), Grisill, and Joshuah Flecher, s. William, May 4, 1668.
Mercy, and Joseph Spalding, Dec. 9, 1670.

JEWETT, John, and Susan Sweet of Newburyport, int. Jan. 8, 1826.
Susannah, of Hollis, N. H., and Benjamin Blood, 3d, int. Mar. 4, 1826.

JOHNSON, Betsy B., of Groton, and Frederick W. Blodgett, int. May 4, 1837.
Catharine P., of Westford, and Silas H. P. Cowdry, int. Oct. 29, 1832.
Dolly, and John Fletcher, 2d, int. Apr. 20, 1822.
Elizabeth R., and John Parkhurst, 2d, int. June 29, 1844.
Hasadiah, of Southborough, and Robert Spaulding, int. Mar. 15, 1755.
Horace, and Mary Ann McConnihie of Merrimack, N. H., int. Aug. 25, 1838.

*Intention also recorded.

JOHNSON, John W., and Ann D. Philbrick of Lowell, int. Nov. 2, 1848.
Mary, and Aaron Whitney, jr. of Harvard, June 1, 1836.*
Molly, and Zebulon Parker, int. Mar. 1, 1812.
Rowland, and Abigail Edgarton of Shirley, int. June 8, 1834.

JOHNSTON, Mary, and Andrey [Andrew. c. r. 1:] Betty, Feb. 23, 1758.*

JONES, Aaron, and Lidia Jones of Acton, int. Sept. 22, 1803.
Abigail, of Acton, and Archebald McFarlin, int. Feb. 18, 1803.
Abigail, of Hillsborough, N. H., and Hervy Silver, int. Dec. 3, 1837.
Achsah, and Serah B. Bayley, both of Lowell, Dec. 31, 1840. c. r. 3.
Archible R., and Lucy Ann Shurtliff, Aug. 8, 1841.*
Betsey C., and James B. Coburn, int. Nov. 2, 1844.
Betsy, of Lowell, and Alexander Slicer, int. Jan. 17, 1836.
Charles P., of North Chelmsford, a. 26 y., machinist, s. Samuel and Mary, and Lydia P. [T. int.] Nason of Lowell [of Elliot, Me. int.], a. 27 y., d. Samuel and Mary, Nov. 20, 1845.*
Eunis, of Boston, and Ebenezer Spaulding, int. Dec. 29, 1800.
Isaac, and Hannah C. Wheeler of Nashville, N. H., int. June 27, 1846.
Jonathan, and Elizabeth Bodwell of Methuen, int. Mar. 15, 1823.
Lidia, of Acton, and Aaron Jones, int. Sept. 22, 1803.
Mercy F., of Dracut, and Bartlett W. Dexter, int. Jan. 12, 1834.
Nancy, and Asa Barker, Sept. 7, 1808.*
Rachel, and John Peckins, jr., int. July 19, 1846.
William, a. 25 y., blacksmith, s. Joshua and Betsey, and Caroline S. Wheeler, a. 17 y., d. Eli and Abigail, Feb. 4, 1847.*

JOSLYN (see also Josselyn), Leavitt R. [of Boston. int.], and Hannah E. Hildreth, Oct. 25, 1832.*

JOSSELYN (see also Joslyn), Edwin, and Nyrhe Chandler [of Billerica. int.], Dec. 3, 1835. p. r. 10.*

KEDDER (see also Kidder), John, and Lidiah Parker, d. Abraham and Rose, Dec. 3, 1684. [Sept. ct. r.]

KEEMP (see also Kemp), Josiah, and Sarah Parrot, int. July 1, 1758.

*Intention also recorded.

KEIES (see also Keyes), Jane, d. Solomon, and Samuell Cleveland, s. Moses, of Woburn, May 17, 1680.
Judeth, d. Solomon, and Ely Foster, s. Samuell, 17: 8 m: 1680.
Sarah, d. Solomon, and Samuell Foster, s. Samuell, May 28, 1678.

KEIYS (see also Keyes), Anna, and Peter Power of Dunstable, int. Apr. 20, 1728.

KELLEY, Clarissa Goves, and Reuben Parker, 2d, Mar. 20, 1828.*

KEMP (see also Keemp, Keymp), A[bel. int.] Hartwell, of Westford, and Susan Shurtleff, Dec. 25, 1840.*
Abigail, and John Bearde [Bard. int.] of Billerica, at Billerica, Nov. 16, 1769.*
Benjamin, and Judith Reed [of Woburn. int.], May 5, 1761.*
Hezikiah, of Groton, and Dorathy Adams, int. Jan. —, 1737-8.
Jonas, of Westford, and Joanna Corey, at Westford, Sept. 12, 1769.*
Jonathan, and Sarah Gilson of Groton, at Concord, Nov. 19, 1718.
Joseph, and Peggy [Margaret. int.] Chamberlain [of Billerica. int.], at Concord, Dec. 20, 1720.*
Mary, and John Freeland, Jan. 12, 1796.*
Mehetabel, and Moses Keyse, June 27, 1693. CT. R.
Olive, and Willard Peirce, Mar. 23, 1780.*

KENDAL (see also Kendall), Rebecca, and John Butterfield, June 15, 1791.*

KENDALL (see also Kendal), Lucy Ann, of Tyngsborough, and George F. Tuttle, at Tyngsborough, Jan. 4, 1839.*
Maria L., of Tyngsborough, and Benj[amin] E. Parkhurst, Aug. 2, 1840.*

KENNEY (see also Kenny), Daniel [of Wilton, N. H. int.], and Sarah Fletcher, May 16, 1780.*
Lucy, of Millbury, and Dexter Wood, int. Sept. 11, 1825.
S[t]ephen [of Nottingham West, N. H. int.], and Sarah Frost, Apr. 14, 1796.*

*Intention also recorded.

KENNON, Sarah A., of Worcester, and Charles H. Sherwin, int. Mar. 1, 1847.
Willard M., and Mary L. Colburn, Nov. 17, 1842.*

KENNY (see also Kenney), Sarah, and Loamma Sanders of Billerica, int. Oct. 4, 1806.

KENT, Hannah P., Mrs., and Elijah Hall, Nov. 22, 1842.*
Isaac, and Polly Butterfield, int. Oct. 21, 1810.

KEYES (see also Keies, Keiys, Keyse, Kyess), Abel, and Olive Durant, Aug. 3, 1768.*
Abigal, and Jonathan Keymp, int. Nov. 17, 1744.
Betsy, of Westford, and Thomas Flint, int. Sept. 6, 1806.
Charlotte, of Westford, and Samuel Dunn, int. Nov. 30, 1823.
Daniel [of Westford. int.], and Abigail Procter, Sept. 19, 1754.*
Elizabeth, and David Satle of Groton, int. Mar. 1, 1723-4.
Ephraim, and Rebeckah Townsend of Billerica, at Billerica, July 11, 1751.*
Esther, and Silas Colburn, Dec. 1, 1768.*
Ezekiell, and Abigaill Barret, int. Sept. 30, 1722.
Henry, and Ruth More, int. May 7, 1727.
Joanah, and Thomas Kidder, Dec. 31, 1716.
Joanna, of Westford, and Timothy Adams, at Westford, Sept. 18, 1781.*
John, and Sarah Foster, int. May 24, 1781.
Jonas, and Elizabeth Townsend [of Billerica. int.], Apr. 21, 1756.*
Jonas [James. int.], of Westford, and Abigail Carlton, at Westford, Nov. 28, 1799.*
Joseph, and Elizabeth Fletcher, int. Feb. 28, 1719-20.
Josiph, and Johanah Cleveland, May 28, 1690.
Lucy, and Daniel Lawrance, ———, 1806. [Mar. 30. c. r. 1.]*
Mary, and Christopher Osgood of Billerica, at Billerica, June 1, 1711.
Mary, and Benjamin Byham, Dec. 11, 1760.*
Mary Ann, and Asa T. Farwell, July 22, 1839.*
Moses, and Susanna Stratton of Concord, at Concord, July 4, 1718.
Olive, and Benjamin Barrat, Nov. 24, 1760.*
Phebe, and John Spaulding, int. Dec. 3, 1727.
Ruth, and John Cory, int. Mar. 9, 1722-3.
Sally, and Silas Hartwell of Carlisle, int. Jan. 18, 1802.

*Intention also recorded.

CHELMSFORD MARRIAGES 263

KEYES, Sally, of Pelham, N. H., and Thomas T. Farwell, int. Nov. 6, 1831.
Thankful, and William Gammel [of Concord. int.], June 17, 1777.*
Uriah, and Hannah Livingstone, Nov. 24, 1774.*
Zebediah, and Sibbel Dunn, int. Aug. 21, 1802.

KEYMP (see also Kemp), Jonathan, and Abigal Keyes, int. Nov. 17, 1744.

KEYSE (see also Keyes), Moses, and Mehetabel Kemp, June 27, 1693. CT. R.

KIDDER (see also Kedder, Kider), Amos, and Phebe Ball, resident in Chelmsford, int. Sept. 22, 1752.
Amos, and Mercy Nutting of Groton, at Groton, Oct. 3, 1774.*
Ann, of Billerica, and William Underwood, Mar. 17, 1684-5.
Charles P., of Westford, and Clarissa Crosby, Sept. 20, 1841.*
David, and Esther Estabrooks, Feb. 20, 1751. [1750-51. P. R. 4.]*
Ebenezer, and Esther Willson [of Carlisle. int.], Nov. 23, 1786.*
Elizabeth, and Jonathan Powers of Littleton, int. Dec. 5, 1725.
Esther, and Jeremiah Wier [of Concord. int.], Apr. 6, 1775.*
Hannah, of Billerica, and William Bowers, at Billerica, Jan. 1, 1761.*
Hannah, and Rufus M. Blodget [of Tyngsborough. int.], May 23, 1827.*
Jacob, and Mrs. Mary Barker [wid. int.], Nov. 6, 1839.*
James, and Abigail Whitcombe, int. Apr. 26, 1729.
James, and Abigail Ball, int. May 30, 1752.
Lydia, and William Butterfield, July 30, 1761.*
Mary, of Billerica, and Philip Bow[e]rs, int. Apr. 4, 1809.
Mary Ann, of Tyngsborough, and Daniel Tuck, int. Feb. 15, 1818.
Phinehas, and Hannah Crosby [of Billerica. int.], Nov. 20, 1784.*
Sally, of Carlisle, and Samuel Adams, jr., at Concord, Sept. 5, 1780.*
Samuel [of Charlestown. C. R. 1.], and Hannah P. Roggers of Tewksbury, ———, 1806. [Mar. 31. C. R. 1.]
Sarah, and John Fletcher of Concord, at Concord, Sept. 12, 1751.*
Thomas, and Joanah Keyes, Dec. 31, 1716.

*Intention also recorded.

KIDDER, William D., and Caroline C. Shipley of Townsend, int. Mar. 13, 1825.
Zimri, and Mary Swan of Tyngsborough, int. Oct. 10, 1824.

KIDER (see also Kidder), Joseph, and Hanah Procter, int. May 8, 1720.

KILLOM, John H., and Caroline Elliott of Manchester, N. H., int. Aug. 27, 1845.

KIMBALL, Daniel K., and Sarah Hunt, int. Apr. 17, 1831.
Hiram, and Sabrina Steele of Dunstable, N. H., at Tyngsborough, July 30, 1835.
Ichabod G., and Joanna [P. int.] Gould, Dec. 5, 1821.*
Margeret Jane, of Goffstown, N. H., and George Worcester, int. Sept. 2, 1832.
Mary Ann, and John Farmer [of Billerica. int.], Oct. 6, 1823.*
Prescott, and Mary Spaulding of Wilton, N. H., int. Mar. 23, 1828.
William, and Mary Tuttel, Apr. 10, 1796.*

KING, E[l]izebeth, of Littleton, and Josiah Parkhurst, int. Feb. 24, 1758.
James, and Eliza J. Claflin of Boston, int. Jan. 13, 1849.
Samuel, Dr., and Hannah Richardson, Sept. 3, 1751.*

KITTRIDGE, Albert G., and Melvina D. Mead, May 5, 1843.*
Rebecca, and Franklin Emerson, Aug. 23, 1835.*

KNECTTLE, Harriott L., and Lucius M. Drake of Winchester, Conn., June 14, 1843.*
Mary Ann, and James Smith of Lowell, int. Mar. 10, 1839.

KNOWLES, Mary J. C., a. 19 y., d. Samuel L., and Horace D. Sanborn of Dracut, a. 25 y., carpenter, s. John and Lydia, int. Aug. 24, 1849.
Phebe C., and Charles G. Watson of Somersworth, N. H., int. Nov. 8, 1845.
Samuel L., and Mrs. Dorothy Ferrin of Concord, N. H., int. Dec. 9, 1848.

KYESS (see also Keyes), Stephen, and Anne Robin, Mar. 7, 1706.

*Intention also recorded.

LAKEN, Experience [of Dunstable. int.], and Jesse Farmer, Feb. 20, 1800.*

LAMB, William, and Sarah Ann Adams, Apr. 7, 1825.*

LAMSON, Lois, of Mt. Vernon, N. H., and Joseph Marshall, int. Sept. 2, 1836.
Sally [Anny. int.; Anna. C. R. 1.], and Isaac Warren, jr., July 28, 1799.*
Sarah, and Otis Marshall, int. Oct. 5, 1834.
William, and Sarah Starret of New Boston, N. H., int. May 10, 1835.

LANCY, Samuel, and Elizebeth Peirce, int. Sept. 8, 1783.

LANDLEE (see also Langley), Mary, and Robert Perce, int. June 13, 1731.

LANE, Anna, of Bedford, and Ebenezer Goold [jr. int.], at Bedford, May 20, 1779.*
Mary A., of Lowell, a. 22 y., d. Jonathan and Hannah, and James T. Fletcher of Topsfield, a. 22 y., blacksmith, s. Leonard and Lucinda, Aug. 27, 1846. [Aug. 1. C. R. 3.]
Sarah, wid., of Bedford, and Benjamin Parker, at Bedford, July 14, 1791.*

LANGLEY (see also Landlee), Lydia, and Samuel Hovey [of Rowley. int.], May 24, 1757.*
Naomi, and William Woods [late of Groton. int.], Feb. 9, 1757.*
Nathaniel, and Lidya Foster, int. Mar. 11, 1721-2.
Nathaniel [Longley. int.], and Rachel Barret, Sept. 14, 1757.*

LARCOM (see also Larkom), Jonathan, and Harriott Obear, Mar. 30, 1841.*

LARKOM (see also Larcom), Hannah, and Benj[amin] Tay [of Salem. int.], Apr. 13, 1830.*

LARNED, Hanah, and Joseph Farwell [torn. Dec. 25, 1666. CT. R.].
John, of Sutton, and Abigaill Adams, int. Mar. 3, 1732-3.
Mare, and John Burge, late of Weymouth, June 9, 1662.

*Intention also recorded.

LAUGHTON, Hannah, and Henry Shepard [of Dunstable. int.], Aug. 6, 1776.*

LAWRANCE (see also Lawrence), Daniel, and Lucy Keyes, ———, 1806. [Mar. 30. C. R. 1.]*
Henry [of Boston. int.], and Sally Gould, Feb. 18, 1809.*
Joseph, and Ledea ———, Mar. 13, 1670-71. CT. R.
Lemuel, and Mary Barges of Westford, int. Sept. 21, 1811.

LAWRENCE (see also Lawrance), Mary, of Littleton, and Samuel Fletcher, jr., at Westford, Sept. 17, 1729.*

LAWS, Abigail, and William Laws [of Sharon, N. H. C. R. 1; of Clarendon, N. H. int.], Sept. 9, 1804.*
Henry [of Billerica. int.], and Mary Avril, June 4, 1809.*
John, of Billerica, and Sarah Spalding, at Billerica, Dec. 29, 1774.*
Judath [Judah. C. R. 1.], and Jacob Chamberlin [jr. int.], May 28, 1794.*
Martha, of Peterborough, N. H., and Nathan P. Dadmun, int. Aug. 26, 1843.
Sears C., and Mary Shed, Mar. 29, 1818.*
Thomas, and Hannah Carlton of Billerica, Feb. 10, 1761.
William [of Sharon, N. H. C. R. 1; of Clarendon, N. H. int.], and Abigail Laws, Sept. 9, 1804.*
William, jr., and Lucinda P. Cook of Westford, int. Apr. 12, 1815.

LAWSON, David [of Petersham. int.], and Hannah Snow, Dec. 13, 1763.*

LEACH, Caroline Ann, Mrs., and Elias Warner of Harvard, int. Sept. 12, 1845.
Jacob, of Boston, and Clarissa Ann Byam, Nov. 26, 1829.*

LEAKING, William [Lakin. dup.], s. William, of Groton, and Elisabeth Robison, d. Jam[e]s, of Groton, Jan. 4, 1685.

LEAVITT, Abigail, of Hampton, and Anthony Emery, int. Apr. —, 1738.

LEE, Elvira, of Waltham, and John Peck, int. Oct. 23, 1831.

*Intention also recorded.

LEIGHTON, Frances C., of Westford, and Benj[ami]n F. Adams, int. Apr. 23, 1840.
Lydia, of Westford, and Alexander Coolidge of Natick, June 11, 1823.
Reuben M., of Westford, and Abigail Wright, Apr. 19, 1838.*

LEONARD, see Larned.

LEPENE, Andrew J., and Harriett H. Parker, int. May 6, 1846.

LEVESTON (see also Livingston), John, and Eunice Shed of Billerica, at Charlestown, Nov. 29, 1705.

LEVESTONE (see also Livingston), Sarah, of Billerica, and Samuel Lufkin, at Billerica, Dec. 19, 1786.*

LEVINGSTON (see also Livingston), Charlotte, and David Sterns, int. Sept. 29, 1822.

LEVINGSTONE (see also Livingston), William, and Abigal Hayward of Acton, int. Feb. 10, 1810.

LEWIS, Asenath, of Lowell, and Samuel P. Perham, int. July 20, 1844.
Samuel, and Bette Parker of Billerica, at Billerica, June 3, 1773.*

LIBBEY (see also Libby), Maria, and John D. Harris, at Lowell, Jan. 1, 1838.*

LIBBY (see also Libbey), Bethiah, and Elisha Herrick of Morristown, Vt., Jan. 20, 1842.*

LINCOLN, Abel, and Phebe Griffin of Dracut, int. Dec. 4, 1818.
Martha E[lizabeth. int.], of Westford, a. 23 y., d. Daniel and Martha, and Elisha Shaw, widr., a. 29 y., moulder, s. Sam[ue]l and Lydia, July 4, 1844.*
Mary, and Peter Marshall, Nov. 29, 1801.*
Mary, and Joseph Cottle [jr. c. r. 1.] of Windham, N. H., Mar. 30, 1819.*
Mercy M[aria. int.], a. 21 y., d. Daniel and Martha, and Elisha Shaw, widr., a. 29 y., moulder, s. Samuel and Lydia, Oct. 1, 1844.*

*Intention also recorded.

LINCOLN, Otis, and Hannah Witherell of Taunton, int. Sept. 13, 1829.
William R., of Boston, and Mahitabel Farwell, Dec. 25, 1839.*

LINDSEY, Nathaniel, a. 28 y., shoemaker, s. Richard and Louis, and Rhoda Parker, a. 25 y., d. Jona[than] and Betsey, Feb. 22, 1848.*

LISCOM, Abigail, and William Zanes, int. Aug. 24, 1834.

LITTLEALE (see also Littlehale), Hannah, of Dracut, and Silas Peirce, int. Oct. 25, 1806.

LITTLEHALE (see also Littleale), Elizabeth, of Dunstable, and Asa Underwood, May 15, 1777.
Susan B., and Ebenezer Elliott of Beverly, int. Mar. 26, 1831.
Susan J., and Charles H. Sanger, Mar. 23, 1828.*

LIVERMORE, Martha, d. John, of Watertown, and Abraham Parker, 15: 5 m: 1682.

LIVINGSTON (see also Leveston, Levestone, Levingston, Levingstone, Livingstone), Abigail, and Ephraim Osgood, Dec. 15, 1799.*
Benjamin, and Clarisa Floyd of Woburn, int. Jan. 6, 1822.
Sprake, and Abigail Pierce, Mar. 27, 1827.*
Sprake, and Mrs. Betsy Butler, Apr. 2, 1836.*

LIVINGSTONE (see also Livingston), Hannah, and Uriah Keyes, Nov. 24, 1774.*
Larkin, and Susan Munroe of Lexington, int. Nov. 4, 1821.

LLOYD, Charlotte Eliza Hayson [Nayson, of the factory. C. R. 1.], and Thomas Newell, Oct. 24, 1824.*

LOCK, Mary, and John Adams [3d. int.], Dec. 8, 1772.*
William ["of Monadnick No. four," N. H. int.], and Rebecca Barrat, Feb. 10, 1773.*

LONGLY, William, and Daborah Buterfild, Feb. 16, 1697.

LOTHROP, Elon, and Salome Drake, both of Easton, June 25, 1840. C. R. 3.

*Intention also recorded.

LOVEJOY (see also Lovjoy), Abigail, of Pepperell, and Jonas Powers, int. Apr. 7, 1825.
Betsy, of Amherst, N. H., and Edmand Swett, int. Feb. 8, 1824.
Francis, of Andover, and Nathaniel Foster, at Charlestown, Apr. 29, 1701.
Naomi, of Andover, and Richard Stratton, Jan. 6, 1686. CT. R.

LOVEN, Feebe, d. John, and Andrew Cooke, both of Dunstable, July 24, 1685.

LOVJOY (see also Lovejoy), Rachil, and William Chambers, Oct. 15, 1782.*

LOWELL, John, of Boston, and Mrs. Rebecca Tyng of Dunstable, Jan. 27, 1778.

LUFKIN, Samuel, and Sarah Levestone of Billerica, at Billerica, Dec. 19, 1786.*

LUN (see also Lund), Elesebeth, and Henry Spaulding, —— [1701 or 1702?].

LUND (see also Lun), Mary, of Milford, N. H., and Ignatius Tyler, int. Nov. 10, 1833.
Rachel, of Merrimack, N. H., and James Dunn, jr., int. Nov. 22, 1777.

LYON, Phebe, of Windham, N. H., and Solomon Hunt, int. Sept. 2, 1821.

McALLISTER, Rodney, and Mary Emerson, June 17, 1834.*

McCLARY, Hannah, of Cambridge, and Varnum Spalding, int. Feb. 13, 1819.

McCONNIHIE, Mary Ann, of Merrimack, N. H., and Horace Johnson, int. Aug. 25, 1838.

McCOY, John, and Margaret Sullivan, int. May 26, 1845.

McDANIEL, Ann, of Danvers, and Andrew Furber, int. Aug. 4, 1841.

*Intention also recorded.

McENTIRE (see also McIntire), Andrew, of Wilton, and Sally Glode, int. Dec. 12, 1807.

McFARLIN, Archebald, and Abigail Jones of Acton, int. Feb. 18, 1803.

McGLAUTHLIA, Hiram L., and Hannah Drake, Aug. 15, 1841.*

McGRATH, Martha, of Nashua, N. H., and Daniel F. Austin, int. Oct. 22, 1840.

McINTERE (see also McIntire), Rebecca, and Isaac N. Senter of Lowell, Mar. 25, 1830.*

McINTIRE (see also McEntire, McIntere), George W., and Eliza Raynor of Lowell, int. Oct. 3, 1848.
Lucinda, and Joseph Dunn, int. Sept. 4, 1836.
Mary A., of Lowell, and Charles Weaver, int. July 30, 1846.
Rebecca, wid. [a. 50 y. c. r. 1.], and Andrew Spaulding [a. 70 y. c. r. 1.], Nov. 7, 1830.*

McKEEVER, John, and Nancy Collins of Merrimack, N. H., int. Aug. 13, 1826.

MACKENEY (see also Makiney), John, and Sarah Parot, int. Dec. 31, 1737.

MACKLAIN (see also McLain), Charles, and Susanna Farmer of Tewksbury, int. Aug. 1, 1740.

McLAIN (see also Macklain, McLane), Dennis, and Joanna Butterfield, Dec. 29, 1762.*
Susan [Susanna. c. r. 1. and int.], and Benj[ami]n Chamberlain [4th. int.], May 7, 1761.*
Susanna, and Benjamin Blodget [late of Litchfield, N. H. int.], Jan. 14, 1762.*

McLANE (see also McLain), Mary, and Samuel Butterfield, Aug. 11, 1772.*

McLENNA, William, and Deborah Woods of Boston, int. Feb. 24, 1822.

*Intention also recorded.

CHELMSFORD MARRIAGES 271

McMURPHY, Mary, and Benjamin Parker, int. Nov. 25, 1838. (Nov. 27, Aaron Fletcher guardian of Benjamin Parker objected to any further proceedings in the case.)

McQUSTON, William, of Litchfield, and Anna Parker, int. Mar. 6, 1799.

MAKINEY (see also Mackeney), Sarah, and Joseph Temple [of Westford. int.], at Concord, June 6, 1744.*

MALCOM, Rebecca, and Ebenezer Carlton, both of Alexandria, N. H., Jan. 3, 1784.

MANING (see also Manning), Salathial, and Sukey Hale, Dec. 13, 1807.*
Surviah [of Billerica. c. r. 1.], and John Parkhurst, Feb. 26, 1805.*

MANN, Mary, and Benjamin Davis [of Billerica. int.], Apr. 2, 1778.*

MANNING (see also Maning), Asa, of Billerica, and Olive Spaulding, int. May 20, 1803.
Asenath, and Benj[ami]n Chamberlain, Mar. 18, 1819.*
Elizabeth, and Thomas Hanson [Harrison. c. r. 1.], ——, 1811. [May 28. c. r. 1.]*
Jacob [of Billerica. int.], and Sarah Butterfield, June 2, 1763.*
Jonathan, of Billerica, and Martha Howard, at Billerica, Mar. 17, 1774.*
Jonathan [jr. int.], and Lydia Howard, Feb. 23, 1802.*
Joseph, Maj., and Julia M. Parker, Oct. 16, 1828.*
Martha, and Ephraim Walker, Jan. 4, 1801.
Mehitabel, and Joseph Adams, ——, 1810. [Apr. 25. c. r. 1.]*
Soloman, and Lucy Webber, ——, 1812. [Aug. 11. c. r. 1.]*
Timothy, of Billerica, and Mary Howard, at Billerica, June 13, 1776.

MANSFEILD (see also Mansfield), Abyal, and John Wheeler of Barre, int. July 30, 1780.
Jeremiah C., and Susan E[lizabeth. int.] Parkhurst, July 13, 1843. [July 11. p. r. 2.]*
Leonard J., and Mary E. Reed of Bedford, Mar. 31, 1842.*

*Intention also recorded.

MANSFIELD (see also Mansfeild), Asa, and Rachel Crosby [of Carlisle. int.], Jan. 7, 1801.*
Asaph, and [Elizabeth S. Griffin of Westford. int.], Apr. 9, 1840. P. R. 21.*
Elijah [of Lynn. int.], and Rebecca Blanchard, May 18, 1769.*
Joel, and Betsy Dunn, ——, 1812. [Nov. 16. C. R. 1.]*
Joel, and Rebeckah Cogswell of Westford, int. Apr. 2, 1814
John, and Lois Corey, Sept. 23, 1760.*
John, and Lucy Woods [now residing in Carlisle. int.], Jan. 23, 1798.*
Rachel, and Stephen Wilson, at Westford, Mar. 13, 1791.*
Sarah, and Elikim Reed, Nov. 28, 1784.*
Willard, and Lydia Cory, int. June 23, 1788.
William, and Lucy Cory, Apr. 16, 1787.*

MANSOR, Aaron [of Pembroke. int.], and Rebecca Warren, Dec. 29, 1807.*

MARBLE, Eliza, of Dracut, and Jonathan Morse, int. Nov. 30, 1823.

MARCH, Mariah B., of Londonderry, N. H., and Jeremiah B. Webb, int. Sept. 14, 1834.

MARCY (see also Masse), Lydia, and Silas Richardson of Westford, at Westford, Oct. 30, 1797.*

MARDEN, Mary Jane, of Concord, N. H., and Charles M. Templeton, int. May 10, 1845.

MARSHAL (see also Marshall), Jonas, and Abigail Adams of Fitchburg, int. Dec. 29, 1779.

MARSHALL (see also Marshal), Abel, and Polly [Patty. dup.] Flint [of Tewksbury. int.], Mar. 11, 1788.*
Abel, and Patty Pierce, int. Jan. 13, 1810.
Benjamin, and Betty Farwell of Dunstable, May 14, 1754.
Betty, and Oliver Adams of Rindge, N. H., int. Sept. 22, 1798.
Eliza A., and George Marshall of Lowell, int. July 8, 1836.
Esther, and William Mears, June 8, 1784.
George, of Lowell, and Eliza A. Marshall, int. July 8, 1836.
Hannah, and Stephen Pierce [jr. int.], July 30, 1778.*
Jacob, and Pattey Richardson of Tewksbury, int. May 12, 1788.

*Intention also recorded.

CHELMSFORD MARRIAGES 273

MARSHALL, Jacob [of Lunenburg. int.], and Bridget Foster, Mar, 28, 1805.*
James, and Joanna Peirce, June 16, 1785.*
James, jr., and Sarah Skinner of Bedford, int. Mar. 5, 1816.
Jemime, and Ralph Butterfield, ——, 1810. [July 15. C. R. 1.]*
Jesse, and Elizabeth Hodgman, Nov. 16, 1779.
Jesse [of Rindge. C. R. 1.], and Sally Mears, Jan. 22, 1807.*
Jonas [Dr. int.], and Mary Parker of Groton, at Groton, Feb. 10, 1768.*
Joseph, and Sarah Frost, Jan. 10, 1758.*
Joseph, and Susanna Walker, June 24, 1766.*
Joseph, and Lois Lamson of Mount Vernon, N. H., int. Sept. 2, 1836.
Joshua, and Esther Mores, Apr. 13, 1780.*
Lydia, and Roger Chandler [of New Ipswich, N. H. int.], ——, 1796. [Jan. 2. int.]*
Martha, and True Wiggin of Lexington, int. Mar. 17, 1839.
Mary, and John Spaulding [of Tewksbury. int.], Nov. 23, 1801.*
Mary Ann, and George Ames of Dracut, Sept. 19, 1839.*
Otis, and Sarah Lamson, int. Oct. 5, 1834.
Peter, and Mary Lincoln, Nov. 29, 1801.*
Rebeckah, and Benjamin Dows, jr. of Billerica, int. Mar. 11, 1789.
Rhoda, and Jeremiah Carter, Nov. 29, 1827. [Dec. 9. C. R. 1.]*
Richard [jr. int.], of Tyngsborough, and Lucretia Spalding, May 14, 1840.*
Sally, of Nottingham West, N. H., and Reuben Melven, int. May 31, 1794.
Samuel, and Esther Frost [of Billerica. int.], Jan. 2, 1755.*
Samuel, and Sybel Bates, June 4, 1780.
Sibel, and Samuel Moore [jr. of Bedford, N. H. int.], ——, 1812. [May 12. C. R. 1.]*
Sophia, of Lunenburg, and Otis Bailey, int. Mar. 23, 1821.
Susan, of Danvers, and Jesse Moores, int. Jan. 20, 1818.
Thomas, and Hannah Frost, Feb. 22, 1753.*
Thomas, and Mrs. Lydia Hunt of Tewksbury, int. Nov. 17, 1769.
Thomas [jr. int.], and Hannah Clark, Feb. 28, 1775.*
Thomas, and Mary N. Wiggin of Lowell, May 24, 1835.*
Thomas, and Ann F. Spalding of Tewksbury, int. Feb. 13, 1843.
Willard, and Olive Bowers, Dec. 28, 1795.*

*Intention also recorded.

MARTIN, Amos, and Judith Thorndick of Tewksbury, int. May 12, 1775.
Asa, and Mary Rogers of Andover, at Andover, Jan. 12, 1748-9.*
Franklin, of Lowell, a. 27 y., hawker and pedler, s. Thomas, and Matilda C. Pickering, a. 35 y., d. W[illia]m S. and Abigail, int. Sept. 16, 1849.
Hannah, and Nathan Crosby, jr. of Billerica, at Billerica, June 4, 1735.*
Hannah, and Peter Read, Apr. 13, 1779.*
Jane, of Tewksbury, and William Spaulding, int. Jan. 23, 1741-2.
Lucy Y., and Russell Handley, Dec. 30, 1838.*
Mary, and Ambrose Fearlow, Dec. 2, 1668. CT. R.
Sarah, and Joseph Barrat, Oct. 13, 1743.*
William, and Hannah Falkner of Andover, at Andover, July 19, 1741.*
William, and Sarah Chamberlain, Apr. 6, 1742.*
William, and Ruth Patch, Jan. 2, 1752.*

MASON, Isaac, and Sarah A. P. Young, int. Jan. 28, 1837.

MASSE (see also Marcy), Mary [of Dracut. int.], and John Parry [Perry. int.], July 11, 1754.*

MATHES, Margaret, and John Parrott, at Concord, June 14, 1744.*

MAYNARD, Aaron, and Mary Farmer, Jan. 12, 1823.

MEAD (see also Meads), John, and Mary Wheeler of Sudbury, int. Apr. 20, 1823.
Melvina D., and Albert G. Kittridge, May 5, 1843.*

MEADS (see also Mead), John, and Lydia Blodget, Nov. 24, 1774.*

MEAR (see also Mears), Robert, and Darkhas Blood, int. Nov. 10, 1788.

MEARS (see also Mear, Meers), Abigail, and Simeon Farmer, int. June 10, 1827.
Jeremiah [of Danvers. int.], and Mary Smith, ———. [Feb. 27, 1813. C. R. 1.]*

*Intention also recorded.

MEARS, John, and Sally Parker, at Dracut, Feb. 1, 1792.*
Lydia [Richardson. int.], and Benjamin Farmer, Nov. 8, 1827.*
Micajah, and Hannah Coburn, July 29, 1802.*
Rebecca [K. int.], and William Mears, jr. of Westford, Feb. 8, 1826.*
Sally, and Jesse Marshall [of Rindge. c. r. 1.], Jan. 22, 1807.*
William, and Esther Marshall, June 8, 1784.
William, jr., of Westford, and Rebecca [K. int.] Mears, Feb. 8, 1826.*

MEERS (see also Mears), Hannah, and Thaddeus Barrat, Feb. 5, 1789.*

MELVEN (see also Melvin), G[e]org, and Nabby Stickney of Tewksbury, int. Oct. 9, 1793.
Reuben, and Sally Marshall of Nottingham West, N. H., int. May 31, 1794.

MELVIN (see also Melven), Benjamin, and Joanna Fletcher, Feb. 27, 1777.*
Benjamin, jr., and Eliza Hutchenson of Andover, int. Sept. 4, 1825.
Charles, and Susan Hunt of Dunstable, N. H., int. Jan. 11, 1824.
James, and Susanna Barnet of Londonderry, int. Jan. 7, 1807.
Martha, and Zenas Stetson, Oct. 30, 1835.*
Rufus, and Eunice Smith Warren of Plymouth, int. Sept. 5, 1824.

MERRELL (see also Merrill), Harriet, of Lowell, and Charles A. Frost, int. Aug. 9, 1835.
Mary B., and Willard Duren, jr. of Carlisle, Feb. 11, 1836.*

MERRIAM (see also Miriam), Elizabeth Gordon, and Moses B. Garfield of Concord, int. Sept. 24, 1842.
Josiah C., and Sarah C. Davis of Tyngsborough, int. Apr. 29, 1844.
Martha Prescott, and Luther W. Faulkner of Billerica, int. Sept. 24, 1842.

MERRIL (see also Merrill), Ruth, and Ebenezer Foster, Dec. 11, 1766.*

*Intention also recorded.

MERRILL (see also Merrell, Merril), Elizabeth, of Methuen, and Benjamin Pierce, at Methuen, ———. [Aug. 2, 1746. int.]*
Enoch, and Adeline E. Parker of Merrimack, N. H., int. May 18, 1828.
Lydia, of Windham, N. H., and James Gibson, int. Dec. 20, 1835.

MESSER, Mary, of Lowell, and George W. Wyman, int. Sept. 18, 1841.
Richard, and Sally Spaulding, Nov. 19, 1829.*

MILLER, Jerimiah, and Sarah Fletcher, int. Nov. 6, 1725. (Nov. 8, banns forbidden by Hannah Fletcher.)
Naoma, and Nathaniel H. Shed, int. Aug. 5, 1821.

MINAT (see also Minot), Elizebeth, and Thomas Adams, int. Nov. 5, 1737.

MINOT (see also Minat, Minott), Anna, and Philip Robbins of Westford, int. June 24, 1750.
John, and Rachel Spaulding, June 27, 1753.*
Rachel, and William Bridge, Feb. 13, 1776.*
Rebecca, and Benjamin Farmer, June 9, 1742.*

MINOTT (see also Minot), Jonathan, and Esther Proctor of Westford, at Westford, Mar. 6, 1746.*

MIRIAM (see also Merriam), John, of Concord, and Sarah Spalden, Feb. 16, 1692-3. CT. R.

MOAR (see also Moore), Asa [of Andover. int.], and Eunice Thomas, Apr. 23, 1765.*

MONTAGUE, Harriot E., and George W. Giddings, int. Mar. 24, 1837.

MONTEETH, Robert, and Sarah A. Stockbridge, both of Lowell, Mar. 5, 1848. C. R. 3.

MOOARS (see also Moore), Mial, and Sarah Bowers, at Dracut, Jan. 24, 1793.*

MOODY, Abigail, Mrs., and William Sweetser of Lowell, int. June 28, 1835.
Sarah C., of Lowell, and Rufus Harwood, int. Sept. 6, 1845.

*Intention also recorded.

MOOR (see also Moore), William [of Charlestown. int.], and Sally Varnum, Oct. 20, 1799.*

MOORE (see also Moar, Mooars, Moor, Moores, Moors, More, Mores), Charles, and Laura Ann Moore, int. Feb. 17, 1838.
Dorinda, and Jotham M. Stevens, int. Dec. 21, 1834.
Ephraim S., a. 22 y., mason, s. Joseph and Mary, and Henrietta A. Hirsch, a. 22 y., b. Middlesex Village, d. Hannah, May 24, 1844.*
Eunice T., of Dunstable, N. H., and Allen Robinson, int. Dec. 2, 1827.
Laura Ann, and Charles Moore, int. Feb. 17, 1838.
Lucian, of Rutland, and Azubah Robbins Pelsue, Mar. 28, 1831.
Roxanna, and Sewell Parker of Cavendish, Vt., int. Oct. 13, 1833.
Samuel [jr., of Bedford, N. H. int.], and Sibel Marshall, ———, 1812. [May 12. C. R. 1.]*
Samuel M., and Mary Smith of Gilmanton, N. H., int. Apr. 24, 1825.

MOORES (see also Moore), Jesse, and Susan Marshall of Danvers, int. Jan. 20, 1818.
Larken, and Rachel Osgood of Dracut, int. Nov. —, 1801.
Simeon, and Joannah Thorndicke of Tewksbury, int. Nov. 29, 1755.

MOORS (see also Moore), Charlotte, and Abijah Smith [of Dracut. int.], Nov. 11, 1819.*
Joanna, and Jeduthan Warren, July 22, 1779.*
Joseph, and Easther Butterfeild, int. June 21, 1731.
Lucr[e]tia, and Jason Sanders [of Grafton, N. H. int.], Nov. 6, 1811.*
Pamelia, and Jonathan Smith, Nov. 25, 1825.*
Sabra, and Johnson Davis, Aug. 25, 1796.*
Sabra [d. wid. Miel. C. R. 1.], and Collings Hoyt of Grafton, N. H., Oct. 17, 1820.*
Sally, and John Barr [of Reading. int.], May 20, 1819.*
Simeon, and Betsy Parker, Dec. 6, 1820.*

MORE (see also Moore), Ruth, and Henry Keyes, int. May 7, 1727.

*Intention also recorded.

MORES (see also Moore), Esther, and Joshua Marshall, Apr. 13, 1780.*

MORGAN, Abigail [K. int.], and David Horton, July 12, 1829. C. R. 3.*
Henry, of Westford, and Hannah Whitney, at Westford, Aug. 25, 1768.*

MORRELL (see also Morrill), Ann, of Boston, and Rufas Wyman, int. Nov. 25, 1809.
Clarissa A., of Gilmanton, N. H., and Simon F. Staunton, int. Sept. 6, 1844.

MORRILL (see also Morrell), Mary, of Boston, and Rev. Wilkes Allen, Nov. 20, 1805. C. R. 1.*

MORSE, Elmira, of Lowell, and Ezra Abbott Upham, int. Mar. 12, 1836.
Jonathan, and Eliza Marble of Dracut, int. Nov. 30, 1823.
Milton S[pafford. int.], of Winchendon, and Martha E[lizabeth. int.] Cogswell, Oct. 16, 1834.*
Philena, and Ebenezer Hadley of Lowell, int. Oct. 14, 1837.
Seneca P., of North Chelmsford, and Cordelia A. Poole of West Bridgewater, int. Nov. 8, 1845.
Stephen, and Sophia Stearns of Waltham, int. Sept. 1, 1823.
William [of Dunstable. int.], and Eunice Hoyt, Nov. 7, 1824. [Nov. 17. C. R. 1.]*

MOUNTFORT (see also Mounthforth), Mary, of Boston, and Col. Ebenezer Bridge [jr. int.], at Boston, Jan. 25, 1787. P. R. 4.*

MOUNTHFORTH (see also Mountfort), Betcy, and Thomas Pitts, int. May 1, 1802.

MULLIN, Daniel, and Lucy Davis, int. Jan. 6, 1840.

MUNROE, Mary [of Concord. int.], and John Emmery, Apr. 24, 1745.*
Susan, of Lexington, and Larkin Livingstone, int. Nov. 4, 1821.
Thaddeus, of Hillsborough, N. H., and Hannah Richardson, at Concord, Feb. 17, 1780.*

*Intention also recorded.

MURFEY, Mary, and Ferdinanda Prichtte [both of the factory. C. R. 1.], Oct. 6, 1817.*

MUZZY, John, and Relief A. Smith of New Ipswich, N. H., int. Apr. 3, 1825.

NASON, Lydia P. [T. int.], of Lowell [of Elliot, Me. int.], a. 27 y., d. Samuel and Mary, and Charles P. Jones of North Chelmsford, a. 26 y., machinist, s. Samuel and Mary, Nov. 20, 1845.*

NEEF, Sally, and Aaron Fletcher, Dec. 16, 1806.*

NELSON, Nancy, of Easton, and Erastus Packard, int. Nov. 29, 1839.
Thomas, and Hannah Fitchgerls [Fitz Gerald. C. R. 1.], July 14, 1782.

NEWCOMB, Martha A., of Mansfield, and Zephaniah Goward, int. Apr. 8, 1841.
Martha T., Mrs., of Boston, and John Drake of Easton, Apr. 8, 1845. C. R. 3.

NEWELL (see also Nuel), Thomas, and Charlotte Eliza Hayson [Nayson. C. R. 1.] Lloyd [of the factory. C. R. 1.], Oct. 24, 1824.*

NICHOLS, Daniel [of Reading. int.], and Susanna Spaulding, Dec. 1, 1760.*

NOBLE, Adeline E., of Lowell, a. 20 y., d. Nathan and Mary, and Moses M. Harman of Lowell, a. 22 y., house carpenter, s. Moses and Betsey, Feb. 28, 1847.

NOLIN, William, and Jane Herring, int. May 22, 1813.

NOURSE, Lucy, of Ipswich, and [Capt. int.] Josiah Fletcher, at Ipswich, Mar. 7, 1792.*

NOYES (see also Noys), Sally, of Amherst, N. H., and David Swett, int. Aug. 15, 1845.

*Intention also recorded.

NOYS (see also Noyes), Abby L., of Windham, N. H., and Moses P. Palmer of North Chelmsford, int. Sept. 15, 1846.

NUEL (see also Newell), Timothy, of Boston, and Mary Philips, int. Oct. 14, 1791.

NUTTEN (see also Nutting), John, of Westford, and Mary Adams, at Westford, Dec. 1, 1747.*

NUTTER, Julia A., and John H. Webster, Nov. 4, 1843.*

NUTTING (see also Nutten), John, of Groton, and Mary Spaulding, int. Mar. 31, 1727.
Louisa, of Westford, and Nathan Pennington, int. Dec. 5, 1824.
Mercy, of Groton, and Amos Kidder, at Groton, Oct. 3, 1774.*
Nancy, and John H. Young, Dec. 18, 1821.*

OBEAR (see also Ober), Benjamin I., and Rebecca Parker, int. Aug. 29, 1830.
Harriott, and Jonathan Larcom, Mar. 30, 1841.*
Tho[ma]s W., and Emely Woods, June 6, 1841.*

OBER (see also Obear), Benjamin Ives, and Harriot Hart, Jan. 24, 1816.*

OLIVER, Cyrus, and Matilda A. Esterbrook of Charlestown, int. Sept. 4, 1825.
Eliza, of Malden, and George Dodge, int. Nov. 7, 1824.

ONG, Sarah, wid., and Abraham Byam, 22: 11 m: 1689.

OSBORN (see also Osbourn, Osburn), Mary Maria, and Francis B. Parker, int. Jan. 31, 1836.
Sarah, and Joel Barrett Wright, Dec. 2, 1824.*

OSBOURN (see also Osborn), James, and Mrs. Mary Foster, ——, 1811. [May 26. c. r. 1.]*

OSBURN (see also Osborn), Polly [Mary. int.], and Willard Byam, May 28, 1815.*

*Intention also recorded.

CHELMSFORD MARRIAGES

OSGOOD (see also Ozgood), Anna, of Tewksbury, and Philip Parker, int. Oct. 22, 1768.
Augusta A., of Westford, a. 21 y., b. Westford, d. Jacob and Patty, and Loammi Chamberlain, widr. [of North Chelmsford. c. r. 3.], a. 35 y., stone-cutter, s. Rob[er]t B. and Lydia, Dec. 5, 1848.*
Christopher, of Billerica, and Mary Keyes, at Billerica, June 1, 1711.
Dolly, and Samuel Perham [jr. int.], Aug. 7, 1777.*
Dorcas, and Joseph Adams, Nov. 22, 1804.*
Ephraim, and Abigail Livingston, Dec. 15, 1799.*
John, of Westford, and wid. Sarah Perham [wid. Sam[ue]l. c. r. 1.], Feb. 18, 1816. [Feb. 1. c. r. 1.]*
Martha, of Westford, and Samuel S. Stevens of Gardner, Nov. 16, 1830.
Patty, of Westford, and Alpheous Spalding, int. Aug. 19, 1815.
Polly, and William Fletcher, sr., June 18, 1818.*
Rachel, of Dracut, and Larken Moores, int. Nov. —, 1801.
Sarah [Mrs. int.], of Billerica, and Joseph Warren [jr. int.], at Billerica, Feb. 23, 1769.*
Sarah, and Jonathan Parker, Dec. 8, 1774.*
Thaddeus [of Methuen. int.], and Tabetha E[lizabeth. int.] Parkhurst [d. wid. Rachel. c. r. 1.], Oct. 1, 1829.*

OZGOOD (see also Osgood), Joseph, of Billerica, and Sarah Peirce, int. July 30, 1748.

PACKARD (see also Parckard), Erastus, and Nancy Nelson of Easton, int. Nov. 29, 1839.
Hezekiah, Rev., and Mary Spring [of Kittery. int.], Nov. 23, 1796.*

PAGE, Hector M., and Mary Bolton, Dec. 16, 1838.*
John, and Jane [Jean. int.] Holmes of Charlestown, at Charlestown, Mar. 5, 1760.*

PAKHUST (see also Parkhurst), Ebenezer, and Sarah French of Dunstable, int. Dec. —, 1733.

PALMER, Eben, widr., of Lowell, a. 40 y., carpenter, s. Asa and Mary, and Rhoda E. Cram of Lowell, a. 27 y., d. Gideon and Anna, Oct. 6, 1847.
Moses P., of North Chelmsford, and Abby L. Noyes of Windham, N. H., int. Sept. 15, 1846.
Susan [Parmenter. int.], and William Hildreth, Jan. 25, 1827.*

*Intention also recorded.

PARCKARD (see also Packard), Orin, and Elizabeth B. Glines of Lowell, at North Chelmsford, Apr. 29, 1841.*

PARIS (see also Parise, Parrish), Roberd, and Seaborne Cromell, May 22, 1663.
Roberd, and Marcy Crispe, Apr. 11, 1667.

PARISE (see also Paris), John, of Groton, and Mary Wattell, d. John, Dec. 29, 1685.

PARK, John N., and Harriett M. Davis of Dracut, int. Apr. 22, 1848.

PARKER (see also Perker), Aaron, jr., of Westford, and Lydia Spaulding, at Westford, June 3, 1766.*
Abigail, and Benjamin Adams, Apr. 6, 1721.*
Abigail F., of Bedford, N. H., and Charity L. Dunn, int. Apr. 24, 1837.
Abraham, and Martha Livermore, d. John, of Watertown, 15: 5 m: 1682.
Adeline E., of Merrimack, N. H., and Enoch Merrill, int. May 18, 1828.
Ann Maria, a. 25 y., d. Jonathan and Hannah, and Geo[rge] D. Furber, a. 30 y., tailor, s. William and Polly, of Belfast, Me., July 22, 1847.*
Anna, and Thomas Crosby [of Billerica. int.], at Billerica, —— [June 27, 1724. int.].*
Anna, and William McQuston of Litchfield, int. Mar. 6, 1799.
Anna, and Noah Spaulding, Dec. 26, 1799.*
Artemas, jr., and Lorinda Healey, int. Sept. 27, 1829.
Artimas, and Sybbel Spaulding, int. Jan. 3, 1807.
Bengamin, and Sarah Haward [Hayward. CT. R.], Jan. 14, 1690-91.
Benjamin, and Elizabeth Warrin, int. Feb. 18, 1721-2.
Benjamin [jr. int.], and Elizabeth Blodget, Jan. 3, 1750. [1749-50. P. R. 4.]*
Benjamin, and Bitty Reed [of Carlisle. int.], Oct. 28, 1784.*
Benjamin, and wid. Sarah Lane of Bedford, at Bedford, July 14, 1791.*
Benjamin, and Mary McMurphy, int. Nov. 25, 1838. (Nov. 27, Aaron Fletcher guardian of Benjamin Parker objected to any further proceedings in the case.)
Betsey, and Capt. John Winning of Billerica, Nov. 19, 1792.*
Betsy, and Jonas Abbot, Jan. 18, 1807.*

*Intention also recorded.

CHELMSFORD MARRIAGES 283

PARKER, Betsy, and Simeon Moors, Dec. 6, 1820.*
Bette, of Billerica, and Samuel Lewis, at Billerica, June 3, 1773.*
Bridget, and Ephraim Pierce, Oct. 2, 1760.*
Daniel [of Reading. int.], and Sarah Richardson, May 2, 1780.*
Daniel, and Abigail Spalding, Jan. 20, 1814.*
David, and Lucy Barrat, Mar. 14, 1758.*
David [of Billerica. int.], and Phebe Swallow, Oct. 4, 1764.*
David, 3d, and Olive Peirce, Oct. 14, 1800.*
Dorcas, and Charles Coffen [of Brunswick. int.], Sept. 29, 1801.*
Dorothy, of Westford, and Peter Read of Littleton, at Westford, Sept. 24, 1772.
Ebenezer, Capt., and Mrs. Ruth Wood of Dracut, int. July 3, 1756.
Ebenezer, and Sarah Richardson, int. Aug. 21, 1783.
Ebenezer, and Hannah Fletcher, at Westford, May 29, 1787.*
Ebenezer, and Rebekah Roby of Dunstable, int. Mar. 27, 1792.
Eli, and [wid. C. R. 1.] Elisabeth Davis, June 13, 1808.*
Eli, widr., a. 57 y., farmer, s. W[illia]m and Lucy, and Mary Ann Hunt, a. 40 y., d. Joshua and Olive, June 18, 1844.*
Eli P., and Nancy B. Pierce, Jan. 16, 1840.*
Elizabeth, and Thomas Wright of Westford, int. Jan. 14, 1732-3.
Elizabeth, of Westford, and Gershom Proctor, at Westford, July 22, 1746.*
Elizabeth, and Andrew Fletcher, May 5, 1748.*
Ephraim, and Sybil Warren, Dec. 23, 1762.*
Ephraim, jr., of Dracut, and Sally Warren, int. Dec. 19, 1803.
Ester, and Jeams Procter, Dec. 3, 1691.
Esther, and Obadiah Emerson [of Haverhill. int.], Mar. 22, 1744.*
Francis B., and Mary Maria Osborn, int. Jan. 31, 1836.
Francis B., and Mary Richardson, Nov. 30, 1837.*
Gralia [Gratia. int.] Ann, a. 27 y., d. Jona[than] and Betsey, and Stephen A. Coburn, widr., of Lowell, a. 33 y., farmer, s. Henry and Patty, June 22, 1848.*
Hannah, and Robert Blood, sr. of Concord, at Concord, Jan. 8, 1690.
Hannah, and Benjamin Fletcher [jr. int.], Jan. 29, 1767.*
Hannah, and William Barron of Amherst, N. H., int. July 15, 1767.
Hannah [Mrs. int.], and James Parkhurst, June 3, 1773.*

*Intention also recorded.

PARKER, Hannah, and Daniel Proctor [jr. int.], May 31, 1774.*
Hannah, and Benjamin Stevens, at Westford, June 1, 1797.*
Hannah, and Samuel Wesson, at Westford, Nov. 28, 1799.*
Hannah, and Noah Spalding, 2d, int. Nov. 24, 1821.
Hannah, and Nathaniel Sweetser, Sept. 20, 1835.*
Hannah F. [d. Eben[eze]r. C. R. 1.], and Thomas Legget Chase, Nov. 12, 1825. [Nov. 22. C. R. 1.]
Harriett H., and Andrew J. Lepene, int. May 6, 1846.
Henry Spaulding, and Polly Warren, Aug. 12, 1798.*
Isaac, and Elizabeth Walker, Mar. 15, 1770.*
Isack, and Ester Flecher, d. William, Apr. 11, 1681.
Isaiah, and Deborah Clark of Lyndeborough, int. Oct. 31, 1801.
James, s. Capt. James, and Mary Parker, d. Abraham, Dec. 11, 1678.
Jeduthan, and Phebe Gould [Cory. int.], at Westford, Jan. 1, 1793.*
Jeptha, and Mary Amanda Spalding of Carlisle, at Boston, Nov. 9, 1843.*
Joanna, and Dr. Nehemiah Abbot [of Andover. int.], Dec. 7, 1748.*
Joanna, and Robert Butterfeild of Westford, at Westford, Feb. 24, 1752.*
Johannah, and Lenord Butterfield of Dunstable, int. Feb. 25, 1764.
John, and Mary Danforth, d. Jonathan, of Billerica, —— [1678?].
John, and Mercy [Mary. CT. R.] Coburn [of Dracut. C. R. 1.], Feb. 20, 1785.
Jonas, and Rebecca Procter, Oct. 8, 1761.*
Jonas L., and Caroline Hardy, Feb. 28, 1836.
Jonathan, and Rachel Buterfeild, int. Dec. 20, 1734.
Jonathan, and Joana Butterfeild, int. Oct. 21, 1737.
Jonathan, and Sarah Osgood, Dec. 8, 1774.*
Jonathan, and Remembrance Fletcher, Apr. 19, 1792.*
Jonathan, 4th, and Betsy Adams of Jaffrey, N. H., int. May 10, 1817.
Joseph, and Hannah Bake, Nov. 19, 1683.
Joseph, and Tabitha Warren, May 13, 1783.*
Joseph, and Elizabeth Blanchard, Jan. 7, 1802.*
Josiah, s. Capt. James, and Elisabeth Saxson, d. Thomas, of Boston, May 8, 1678.
Josiah, and Hannah Parkhurst, int. July 9, 1757.

*Intention also recorded.

PARKER, Julia M., and Maj. Joseph Manning, Oct. 16, 1828.*
Lidia, and Henry Blasdel, int. Sept. 27, 1719.
Lidia, and [Ens. int.] Benjamin Byam, Dec. 26, 1811.*
Lidiah, d. Abraham and Rose, and John Kedder, Dec. 3, 1684.
[Sept. CT. R.]
Lucy, and Moses Barron, int. Nov. 26, 1732.
Lucy, of Carlisle, and Ebinezer Shed, jr., int. Feb. 6, 1808.
Margaret, and John Barret, at Charlestown, Nov. 29, 1705.
Mary, and Thomas Chamberlin, Apr. 17, 1674.
Mary, d. Abraham, and James Parker, s. Capt. James, Dec. 11, 1678.
Mary, and Benjamin Adams, at Charlestown, Dec. 18, 1707.
Mary, and Benjamin Chamberlin, int. May 27, 1722.
Mary, and Jonathan Harwood, int. Mar. 18, 1737-8.
Mary, of Westford, and Oliver Proctor, at Westford, Apr. 10, 1744.*
Mary, and Ephraim Warren [jr. int.], Aug. 7, 1755.*
Mary, and Jonathan Spaulding [3d. int.], Dec. 17, 1761.*
Mary, of Groton, and [Dr. int.] Jonas Marshall, at Groton, Feb. 10, 1768.*
Mary [Mrs. int.], of Barre, and [Dea. int.] Aaron Chamberlain, at Barre, Nov. 24, 1796.*
Mary, and Joseph Chamberlin, Dec. 22, 1796.*
Mary, and Jonathan Perham, June 24, 1800.*
Mary, of Carlisle, and Jonathan Harwood, int. Feb. 3, 1810.
Mary, and Samuel Winchester, May 17, 1825.*
Mary, and Phineas Chamberlain [of Westford. int.], Nov. 2, 1826.*
Mary, and John Farrar, Dec. 29, 1836.*
Mary C., of Lowell, and Samuel E. Foster, int. Sept. 28, 1828.
Mary H., of Lowell, and Nathaniel Damon, int. Sept. 10, 1826.
Mercy M., and William A. Byam, int. Feb. 16, 1841.
Molly, and John Adams [3d. int.], Dec. 14, 1769.*
Moses, and Abigaill Hildreth, d. Richard, June 19, 1684.
Moses, and Eunice Davis, at Billerica, Jan. 5, 1797.*
Nancy J., and Rufus K. Abbott of Lawrence, int. Dec. 1, 1849.
Nathaniel, of Billerica, and Eleanor Robbins, at Billerica, May 9, 1771.*
Obadiah, and Hannah Stevens, int. Dec. 26, 1724.
Obadiah [jr., of Groton. int.], and Ruth Stevens, Oct. 17, 1752.*
Olive, and Ebenezer Goold, Jan. 22, 1751. [1750-51. P. R. 4.]*
Oliver, and Sarah Barrat, Jan. 22, 1767.*

*Intention also recorded.

PARKER, Phebe, and Ezra Cory, at Westford, May 3, 1798.*
Phebe, and Samuel Winchester of Hopkinton, N. H., int. May 12, 1822.
Philip, and Anna Osgood of Tewksbury, int. Oct. 22, 1768.
Polly, and Joel Parkhurst, Jan. 7, 1802.*
Priscilla [Barker. C. R. 1.], of Tyngsborough, and Joel Dix, ——, 1811. [May 1. C. R. 1.]*
Rachel [Mrs. int.], and Lt. John Spaulding, Feb. 26, 1759.*
Rachel, and Zacheus Wright [of Westford. int.], Jan. 5, 1764.*
Rachel, and Elldad Procter, int. Dec. 13, 1791.
Rachel, Mrs., and Jeremy [B. C. R. 1.] Reed [both of Westford. C. R. 1.], Oct. 19, 1828.
Rebecca, and Reuben Senter [of Londonderry, N. H. int.], June 3, 1760.*
Rebecca, and Nathaniel Cowdry [of Westford. int.], Mar. 11, 1773.*
Rebecca, and John Hodgman, Apr. 3, 1823.*
Rebecca, and Benjamin I. Obear, int. Aug. 29, 1830.
Rebecca Jane, of Boston, and Theodore Edson, int. Nov. 14, 1824.
Rebecka, and Jonathan Danforth, jr. of Billerica, at Billerica, 27: 4 m: 1682.
Rebeckah, and Abel Adams, Nov. 29, 1798.*
Rebeckar, and Gershan Procter, int. Dec. 10, 1721.
Reuben, and Molly Harwood, Jan. 27, 1801.*
Reuben, and Elmira Hasting [of Woburn. C. R. 1.], "published in Woburn," Dec. 12, 1815.
Reuben, 2d, and Clarissa Goves Kelley, Mar. 20, 1828.*
Rhoda, a. 25 y., d. Jona[than] and Betsey, and Nathaniel Lindsey, a. 28 y., shoemaker, s. Richard and Louis, Feb. 22, 1848.*
Rhody, of Tyngsborough, and Simeon Richardson, int. Oct. 10, 1807.
Ruben, and Betsey Hartwell of Carlisle, int. May 21, 1810.
Ruth, and Timothy Rogers [of Tewksbury. int.], June 2, 1757.*
Sally, and John Mears, at Dracut, Feb. 1, 1792.*
Sally, and Capt. Isaac Chamberlin, June 14, 1803.*
Samuel, of New Boston, N. H., and Anna P. Procter, June 3, 1823.*
Samuel [of Lowell. int.], and Sarah H. Wood, July 20, 1835.*
Sarah, and Ebenezer Foster, Nov. 3, 1743.*
Sarah [of Carlisle. int.], and Jonathan Snow, Apr. 9, 1786.*

*Intention also recorded.

PARKER, Sarah, and Ashbill Spaulding of Ludlow, Vt., int. Feb. 8, 1798.
Sarah, and Jonathan Foster, Mar. 7, 1799.*
Sarah, and Salathial Adams, Feb. 10, 1808.*
Sewell, of Cavendish, Vt., and Roxanna Moore, int. Oct. 13, 1833.
Silas, and Martha Foster, Sept. 4, 1788.*
Simeon, and Thankful Walker of Carlisle, at Carlisle, Nov. 29, 1789.*
Simon, and Susanna Fletcher, at Westford, July 5, 1791.*
Stephen, a. 23 y., farmer, s. Thaddeus and Lydia, and Margarett Donley of Boston, a. 22 y., d. James and Catherine W., Apr. 24, 1847.
Tabatha, and Ephraim Adams, Dec. 30, 1813.*
Tabitha, d. Jacob, and Steven Peirce, s. Thomas, of Woburn, Nov. 8, 1676. [Nov. 18. dup.]
Tabitha, and Joseph Warrin, int. Feb. 18, 1721-2.
Tabitha, and Samuel Stevens [jr. int.], Jan. 15, 1761.*
Thomas, and Mary Flecher, d. Ens. William, Oct. 21, 1678.
Thomas, of Dracut, and Mrs. Lydia Richardson, int. Jan. 1, 1720-21.
Thomas [of Lexington. int.], and Jane Parrot, Mar. 8, 1750. [1749-50. P. R. 4.]*
Willard, and Anna Foster, Feb. 11, 1766.*
William, and Sarah Foster, Apr. 3, 1751.*
William [jr. int.], and Abiel Corey, Sept. 27, 1764.*
William [jr. int.], and Hannah Dutton of Billerica, at Billerica, Mar. 30, 1773.*
Zaccheus Wright, and Rachel Brown of Carlisle, Nov. 28, 1825.*
Zebulon, and Rachel Richardson [of Dracut. int.], May 31, 1792.*
Zebulon, and Molly Johnson, int. Mar. 1, 1812.
Zebulon, jr., and Mary Fowle of Temple, N. H., int. Apr. 9, 1819.

PARKHURST (see also Pakhust, Parkhust, Parkis, Perkhurst, Perkhust, Perkis), Abigall, and Nathaniell Commins of Dunstable, Apr. 14, 1697.
Adeline, and Elbridge P. Spalding, Nov. 29, 1840.*
Andrew, and Betsy Buttrick, int. Sept. 7, 1805.
Benjamin, and Elizabeth Warren, Jan. 12, 1764.*
Benjamin, jr., and Elisabeth Herrick, Apr. 11, 1805.*

*Intention also recorded.

PARKHURST, Benj[amin] E., and Maria L. Kendall of Tyngsborough, Aug. 2, 1840.*
Betsey, and Ephraim Spaulding, Mar. 15, 1837.*
Betty, and Paul Hunt, at Westford, Nov. 19, 1789.*
Ebenezer, and Sarai Blogget, int. Oct. 15, 1721.
Elizabeth, and John Baldwin [jr. of Billerica. int.], Feb. 21, 1758.*
Ephraim, and Esther Peirce, May 10, 1770. [May 9. P. R. 4.]*
Ephraim, and Sally Procter, May 3, 1807.*
Hannah, and Josiah Parker, int. July 9, 1757.
Hannah S., and Abner W. Buttrick of Lowell, int. Sept. 20, 1835.
Henry, and Lydia Spaulding, Apr. 29, 1802.*
Henry, and Abigail Butterfield, May 31, 1831.*
Hezekiah, and Julia Ann Butterfield, Nov. 9, 1826.*
James, and [Mrs. int.] Hannah Parker, June 3, 1773.*
Joel, and Polly Parker, Jan. 7, 1802.*
Joel, and Mrs. Hannah Barrett, Nov. 10, 1829.*
John, and Surviah Maning [of Billerica. C. R. 1.], Feb. 26, 1805.*
John, 2d, and Elizabeth R. Johnson, int. June 29, 1844.
Jonathan, and Hannah Richardson, int. June 7, 1724.
Jonathan, and Bridget Butterfield, June 28, 1748.*
Josiah, and E[l]izebeth King of Littleton, int. Feb. 24, 1758.
Josiah, and Rachel Stevens, at Westford, May 3, 1792.*
Josiah K[ing. C. R. 1.], and Ruth Spalding, June 2, 1822.*
Julia Augusta, and Alpheus Bowers, Dec. 1, 1831.*
Martha, and John A. Buttrick of Lowell, Sept. 13, 1841.*
Martha H., and Dea. Benjamin Dudley, June 28, 1838.*
Martha S., a. 22 y., d. J. K. and Ruth, and Franklin M. Hills of Amherst, N. H., a. 25 y., carpenter, s. Moses and Sally, of Amherst, N. H., Dec. 26, 1844.*
Mary, and Nathan Cross, int. Sept. 26, 1725.
Mary, of Cavendish, Vt., and Jesse Spaulding, int. Mar. 8, 1829.
Mary Ann, of Amherst, N. H., and Stephen Butterfield, int. Aug. 19, 1832.
Matthias, and Eliza Andrews [both of Lowell. C. R. 1.], Jan. 28, 1828. [Jan. 10. C. R. 1.]
Micajah, and Martha [H. int.] Barrot, Apr. 6, 1818.*
Oliver, and Mrs. Sarah Byam, ——, 1806. [June 3. C. R. 1.]*
Philip, and Mary Spaulding, Mar. 14, 1771.*
Samuel, and Betty [Molly. int.] Hutchinson of Bedford, at Bedford, Feb. 12, 1788.*

*Intention also recorded.

CHELMSFORD MARRIAGES 289

PARKHURST, Samuel, and Anna Dutton of Bedford, int. Nov. 8, 1817.
Sarah, of Dunstable, and Isaac Taylor, Nov. 21, 1776.
Sarah, a. 23 y., d. John and Celia, and John A. Hallett, a. 24 y., carpenter, b. New Brunswick, s. John and Gertrude, Jan. 18, 1849.*
Sarai, and Benjamin Goold, int. Oct. 15, 1721.
Sewall, and Sally Fletcher [of Westford. int.], Feb. 7, 1828.*
Solomon, and Lucina M[ehitable. int.] Adams, Nov. 15, 1832.*
Surviah [M. int.], and Jabez Stevens [of Lowell. int.], Aug. 23, 1831.*
Susan E[lizabeth. int.], and Jeremiah C. Mansfield, July 13, 1843. [July 11. P. R. 21.]*
Tabetha E[lizabeth. int.; d. wid. Rachel. C. R. 1.], and Thaddeus Osgood [of Methuen. int.], Oct. 1, 1829.*

PARKHUST (see also Parkhurst), Hannah, and Robert Redding, int. May 28, 1743.
Mary, and Amos Coburn of Dracut, int. July 4, 1761.
William [of Wilton, N. H. int.], and Anna Peirce, May 4, 1780.*

PARKIS (see also Parkhurst), Joseph, and Rebeckah Read, at Concord, June 26, 1656. [June 24. CT. R.]

PARLIN, Lydia, of Concord, and Sampson Hildreth, at Concord, Feb. 25, 1752.*
Mary [of Concord. int.], and Jonas Hildreth, Jan. 18, 1749.*

PARMENTER, Micah, of Westford, and Mary R. Porter, June 10, 1841.*

PAROT (see also Parrott), Sarah, and John Mackeney, int. Dec. 31, 1737.

PARRISH (see also Paris), Hanah, and John Goofe of Boston [torn. 1699?].

PARROT (see also Parrott), Jane, and Thomas Parker [of Lexington. int.], Mar. 8, 1750. [1749-50. P. R. 4.]*
Margret, of Westford, and John Jewel, int. Oct. 20, 1764.
Mary, of Westford, and Benjamin Crosby, at Westford, Jan. 1, 1767.*
Sarah, and Josiah Keemp, int. July 1, 1758.

*Intention also recorded.

PARROTT (see also Parot, Parrot), John, and Margaret Mathes, at Concord, June 14, 1744.*

PARRY (see also Perry), John [Pery. int.], and Mary Masse [of Dracut. int.], July 11, 1754.*

PATCH, Abigail, and Edward Rayment, Oct. 3, 1751.*
Elizabeth, and Jonas Pierce, Nov. 8, 1838.*
Ruth, and William Martin, Jan. 2, 1752.*

PATHIO, Thomas, and Sarah Farmer, Dec. 18, 1821.

PATTEN (see also Pattin), Betsey, and Stephen Richardson, Feb. 18, 1829. C. R. 3.
William, of Litchfield, and Eleziabeth Gammel, int. Nov. 11, 1739.

PATTERSON (see also Pattison), William, musician, s. W[illia]m, and Priscella Blood, a. 23 y., Mar. 21, 1847.*

PATTIN (see also Patten), Isaac, of Bedford, and Lydia Chaimberlin, Sept. 16, 1760.*

PATTISON (see also Patterson), Kezia, and Benjamin Butterfield, int. July 7, 1723.

PEABODY, Hiram, and Zoa Ann Wyman, Sept. 17, 1843.*
Sarah, of Newport, N. H., and William Goodwin, int. May 8, 1825.

PEACH, Jonathan J., and Phebe Q. Richardson, int. Mar. 16, 1848.

PEACOCK, Harriett, a. 29 y., supposed d. J. P. Merriam, and Franklin Willowby of Milford, N. H., a. 35 y., cooper, s. David, Feb. 24, 1847.*

PEARCE (see also Pierce), Easther, and John Richardson, int. Dec. 15, 1733.
Tabitha, and William French of Billerica, int. Apr. —, 1736.

PEAVEY, Levi L., of Lowell, and Cynthia Spalding, int. Apr. 2, 1840.

*Intention also recorded.

CHELMSFORD MARRIAGES 291

PECK, John, and Elvira Lee of Waltham, int. Oct. 23, 1831.
Salome, of Westmoreland, N. H., and John Davison, int. June 13, 1840.

PECKEN (see also Peckins), Betcy, and Gaus Procter, May 31, 1797.*

PECKENS (see also Peckins), Horace, and Jemima Robbins of Carlisle, int. Apr. 7, 1807.
John, jr., and Hannah Hayden of Harvard, int. Dec. 15, 1822.

PECKINS (see also Pecken, Peckens), John, jr., and Rachel Jones, int. July 19, 1846.
Marcus, and Sally Fletcher, Aug. 12, 1810.*

PEIRCE (see also Pierce), Agness, and Joseph Procter, int. Dec. 1, 1722.
Ann, and David Welch, int. Feb. 3, 1816.
Anna, and William Parkhust [of Wilton, N. H. int.], May 4, 1780.*
Benjamin, and Olive Frost of Tyngsborough, int. Oct. 6, 1816.
Elizebeth, and Samuel Lancy, int. Sept. 8, 1783.
Elvira, of Waltham, and Francis Bush, int. Dec. 2, 1824.
Esther, and Ephraim Parkhurst, May 10, 1770. [May 9. P. R. 4.]*
Esther, and Benjamin Walker [of Fitchburg. int.], Jan. 25, 1786.*
Hannah, and John Dunn, Feb. 27, 1772.*
Hannah, and Samuel Butterfield, Aug. 12, 1798.*
Joanna, and James Marshall, June 16, 1785.*
Jonas, jr., and Susanna Hildrith of Tyngsborough, int. May 4, 1805.
Joseph, and Nancy Hollis of Woburn, int. Apr. 5, 1805.
Lucy, and Stephen Sanders [of Temple, N. H. int.], Nov. 25, 1773.*
Marshall, and Mary Stearns of Tewksbury, int. Aug. 13, 1815.
Mary, and Oliver Perham, Mar. 30, 1784.*
Olive, and David Parker, 3d, Oct. 14, 1800.*
Phebe, and Edward Foster, Jan. 23, 1772.*
Rachel, and Nathanil Harwood, May 6, 1784.*
Remembrance, and William Powers, Nov. 14, 1739.*
Rhoda, and Zachariah Spaulding, Feb. 9, 1802.*
Robert [jr. int.], and Molley Trull, Feb. 21, 1781.*
Ruth, and Andrew Spaulding, May 6, 1783.*

*Intention also recorded.

PEIRCE, Ruth, and John Perkhurst, May 14, 1801.*
Sarah, and Joseph Ozgood of Billerica, int. July 30, 1748.
Sarah, and John Stevens [of Wilton, N. H. int.], Feb. 5, 1770.*
Sarah, and Amos Byam, Jan. 24, 1780.*
Sarah, d. Capt. Jonas, and Timothy Reed, May 16, 1815.*
Sarah J., of Lexington, and Thomas T. French of Manchester, N. H., May 3, 1840. C. R. 3.
Silas, and Lydia Richardson, Dec. 7, 1786.*
Silas, and Sarah Goodhue, Dec. 28, 1797.*
Silas, and Bridget Butman of Tyngsborough, int. Aug. 25, 1800.
Silas, and Hannah Littleale of Dracut, int. Oct. 25, 1806.
Silos, and Lucy Spaulding [of Westford. int.], Mar. 26, 1771.*
Stephen, and Rachell Harwood, int. Dec. 1, 1722.
Stephen, 3d, and Phebe Trull, Dec. 25, 1787.*
Stephen, and Abigail Bateman, Apr. 12, 1814.*
Steven, s. Thomas, of Woburn, and Tabitha Parker, d. Jacob, Nov. 8, 1676. [Nov. 18. dup.]
Susanah, and Jacob Spaulding, int. Dec. 5, 1725.
Susanna [Mrs. C. R. 1.], and John Cowen, —, 1812. [Nov. 2. int.]*
Sybel, and Asa Blanchard, May 1, 1800.
Willard, and Olive Kemp, Mar. 23, 1780.*
William, of Groton, and Sarah Richardson, int. Oct. 7, 1739.

PELLAT, Mary, d. Thomas, of Concord, and Benjamin Bloggett, s. Daniell, Feb. 14, 1683.

PELSUE, Azubah Robbins, and Lucian Moore of Rutland, Mar. 28, 1831.
Oliver, and Betsy Wright, Dec. 1, 1803.*
Sally, and W[illia]m M. Wheeler [of Carlisle. C. R. 1; of Boxborough. int.], Apr. 7, 1817.*
Sukey, and William Shurtliff of Charlestown, int. Dec. 18, 1808.
Suky, and Caleb Shirtliff [of Charlestown. int.], Jan. 1, 1809.*
William, Ens., and Betsy Spaulding, int. Sept. 15, 1804.

PENNINGTON, Nathan, and Louisa Nutting of Westford, int. Dec. 5, 1824.

PERCE (see also Pierce), Anner, and Oliver Perham, May 8, 1787.*
Robert, and Mary Landlee, int. June 13, 1731.
Stephen, and Ester Fletcher, Feb. 5, 1707.

*Intention also recorded.

PERHAM (see also Perram, Perum), Benoni, and Sarah Robbins of Cambridge, at Concord, Dec. 6, 1704.
David, and Reb[e]cah Spalding, Apr. 19, 1809.*
David, jr., and Elutheria W. Wait, at Boston, Apr. 28, 1839. P. R. 15.
Dorothy, and Joseph Adams, 2d, int. Feb. 1, 1838.
Elizabeth, and Isaac Comings of Dunstable, int. Jan. 5, 1722-3.
Esther, and John Adams, Nov. 24, 1743.*
Hannah, of Dunstable, and Nathaniel Boynton, int. Jan. 24, 1719-20.
Jonathan, and Mary Parker, June 24, 1800.*
Lidya, and William Whitney of Groton, Mar. [torn. 1700?].
Lydia, and Eleazer Richardson, Mar. 30, 1748.*
Mary, and Eliazer Davis of Concord, int. Apr. 20, 1728.
Mary Ann, and Nathan Tyler, int. Nov. 3, 1838.
Oliver, and Mary Peirce, Mar. 30, 1784.*
Oliver, and Anner Perce, May 8, 1787.*
Perley P., a. 24 y., milkman, s. Samuel and Nancy, and Emeline A. Spalding, a. 24 y., d. John and Lydia, Oct. 5, 1847.*
Rebecca, and Samuel P. Perham of Wilton, N. H., Sept. 16, 1841.*
Sally, and Elisha Ford, May 7, 1807.*
Samuel, and Sarah Richardson, int. Apr. 11, 1741.
Samuel, and [Mrs. int.] Elizabeth Adams, Mar. 9, 1769.*
Samuel [jr. int.], and Dolly Osgood, Aug. 7, 1777.*
Samuel, and Anna Spaulding, Jan. 8, 1805.*
Samuel, and Sarah Spalding, Nov. 3, 1808.*
Samuel P., of Wilton, N. H., and Rebecca Perham, Sept. 16, 1841.*
Samuel P., and Asenath Lewis of Lowell, int. July 20, 1844.
Sarah, and Samuel Serll of Dunstable, Sept. 26, 1699.
Sarah, wid. [wid. Sam[ue]l. C. R. 1.], and John Osgood of Westford, Feb. 18, 1816. [Feb. 1. C. R. 1.]*
Sary, and Jacob Coleburn of Dracut, int. Nov. 28, 1737.

PERKER (see also Parker), Moses, and Margerit Straton, int. Aug. 3, 1728.

PERKHURST (see also Parkhurst), John, and Ruth Peirce, May 14, 1801.*

PERKHUST (see also Parkhurst), James, and Abigail Spaulding, int. Dec. 25, 1731.

*Intention also recorded.

PERKINS, Francis, of Fitchburg, and Rebeccah Adams [d. W[illia]m. c. r. 1.], Nov. 15, 1821.*
Jesse H. [S. c. r. 3.], and Sarah Young, Nov. 29, 1840.*

PERKIS (see also Parkhurst), Joseph, and Eunice Spaulden, 4: 9 br: 1686. ct. r.
Mary, d. Joseph, and Thomas Bloggett, 29: 4 m: 1683.

PERLEY, John [of Winchendon. int.], and Mary Spaulding, June 23, 1795.*

PERRAM (see also Perham), John, and Lydea Flecher, Dec. 27, 1692. ct. r.

PERREY (see also Perry), Hannah, and Robert Batties, int. Mar. 29, 1766.

PERRIN, Asa, and Caroline Wellington of Waltham, int. Dec. 19, 1824.

PERRY (see also Parry, Perrey), Eliza, of Methuen, and Dr. Charles Toothaker, int. Dec. 13, 1841.
Esther, of Westford, and Thomas Adams, at Westford, Mar. 15, 1781.*
Josiah F., of Boston, and Sarah C. Hildreth, int. Dec. 27, 1835.

PERUM (see also Perham), John, and Lideah Shiple, Dec. 15, 1664.

PHELPS, Cynthia, of Wilton, N. H., and John Frye, int. Mar. 13, 1831.

PHILBRICK, Ann D., of Lowell, and John W. Johnson, int. Nov. 2, 1848.
Jonathan, and Olivia Wyman, both of Lowell, June 18, 1837.

PHILIPS (see also Phillips), Mary, and Timothy Nuel of Boston, int. Oct. 14, 1791.

PHILLIPS (see also Philips), Joseph E., and Patty E. Spaulding, int. July 20, 1834.
Martha, and Reuben Goold, Mar. 23, 1790.*
Micah [jr. int.], and Hannah Bowers, at Dracut, Mar. 28, 1793.*

*Intention also recorded.

CHELMSFORD MARRIAGES 295

PHIPPS, William, and Ellen Caffertay, int. July 19, 1846.

PICKERING, Matilda C., a. 35 y., d. W[illia]m S. and Abigail, and Franklin Martin of Lowell, a. 27 y., hawker and pedler, s. Thomas, int. Sept. 16, 1849.

PIERCE (see also Pearce, Peirce, Perce), Abigail, of Billerica, and Job Spalding, jr., at Billerica, Feb. 17, 1757.*
Abigail, and Sprake Livingston, Mar. 27, 1827.*
Anna, and Charles Whitting Goodrich of Norwich, Vt., int. Feb. 15, 1811.
Benjamin, and Elizabeth Merrill of Methuen, at Methuen, ———. [Aug. 2, 1746. int.].*
Benjamin, of Woburn, and Hannah Bowers, at Woburn, Apr. 3, 1793. [1693?]
Betsy, and [Lt. int.] Daniel Tuck, Feb. 13, 1823.*
Betty, and Ephraim Adams [late of Stoddard, N. H., now resident in Chelmsford. int.], Mar. 6, 1777.*
Elizabeth, and William Pierce, Mar. 19, 1761.*
Elizabeth [Mrs. int.], and Oliver Bowers, Jan. 3, 1769.*
Elizabeth, and David Danforth, Dec. 7, 1775.*
Ephraim, and Bridget Parker, Oct. 2, 1760.*
Hannah, Mrs., and Jonathan Pierce, May 7, 1827.*
John, and Sally Hildreth of Dracut, at Dracut, Jan. 8, 1795.*
John A., and Mary P. Fletcher of Tyngsborough, int. Nov. 14, 1824.
Jonas, and Betty Dunn, Dec. 7, 1775.*
Jonas, and Elizabeth Patch, Nov. 8, 1838.*
Jonathan, and Mrs. Hannah Pierce, May 7, 1827.*
Joseph, and Mary Pierce, Mar. 20, 1744.*
Joseph B., and Mary Cummings, at North Chelmsford, Apr. 7, 1840.*
Lefy, and David Putman, int. Mar. 1, 1781.
Levi, and Remembrance Fletcher, Jan. 3, 1776.*
Lucinda, and William Barry of Boston, int. Sept. 27, 1845.
Lydia, and Charles Cutler, Feb. 16, 1822. [Feb. 14. c. r. 1.]*
Mary, and Joseph Pierce, Mar. 20, 1744.*
Mary, and Joseph Dunn, Jan. 29, 1765.*
Milo, of Lowell, and Mary A. Spalding, Nov. 3, 1842.*
Milo, and Maria D. Farrington of Andover, Me., at Nashville, N. H., Nov. 18, 1849.
Nancy B., and Eli P. Parker, Jan. 16, 1840.*
Olive, and Abijah Spaulding, Dec. 1, 1791.*

*Intention also recorded.

PIERCE, Oliver, and Ann Hunt of Billerica, at Billerica, Mar. 21, 1733-4.*
Oliver, and Hannah Adams, July 14, 1741.*
Oliver [jr. int.], and Deborah Stevens, Dec. 21, 1769.*
Pamela, and Anthony Resch [Rusch, both of the factory. c. r. 1.], July 16, 1817.*
Patty, and Abel Marshall, int. Jan. 13, 1810.
Polly [d. Capt. Jonas. c. r. 1.], and Levi Farr, Sept. 14, 1818.*
Rachel, and Benjamin Procter [jr. int.], Nov. 16, 1757.*
Rebecca, and Solomon Corey, Dec. 22, 1767.*
Reuel, and Cynthia Hall, int. Jan. 29, 1826.
Silas, and Elizabeth Barron, Apr. 12, 1774.*
Stephen, and Betty Bowers, Feb. 26, 1745.*
Stephen [jr. int.], and Hannah Marshall, July 30, 1778.*
Stephen, and Mary Corey of Winchendon, int. Jan. 2, 1831.
Sybil, and Silas Spaulding, June 8, 1775. [June 7. p. r. 4.]*
William, and Elizabeth Pierce, Mar. 19, 1761.*
William S., of Lowell, and Sarah Butler, int. Mar. 14, 1840.

PIKE, Elizabeth, and Simeon Goold, June 19, 1760. [June 18. p. r. 4.]*
James, jr., and Betsey B. Pool, int. Apr. 17, 1839.
Justus, and Mary Barker of Hillsborough, N. H., int. Apr. 27, 1823.

PINNEY, Alden, of Lowell, and Martha [M. int.] Robbins, Dec. 31, 1837.*

PITTS, James [Capt. c. r. 1.], and Rachel Hildreth, Dec. 24, 1808.*
John, Hon., of Boston, and Mrs. Mary Tyng of Dunstable, June 3, 1779.
Mary, of Tyngsborough, and William Stoddard Bridge, int. Sept. 7, 1811.
Mary Ann [of Cambridge. int.], and Ezra Warren, Jan. 6, 1825.*
Samuel, and [Mrs. c. r. 1.] Polly Carns, Apr. 3, 1797.*
Thomas, and Betcy Mounthforth, int. May 1, 1802.

PLAISTED, Caroline S., of Jefferson, N. H., and William H. Grant, int. Nov. 23, 1847.

POLLARD (see also Pollord), Abigail, of Billerica, and Asa Danforth, at Billerica, Mar. 14, 1781.*

*Intention also recorded.

CHELMSFORD MARRIAGES

POLLARD, Dorothy, of Nottingham West, N. H., and David Carlton, int. Jan. 2, 1825.
James, of Westford, and Abigail Chamberlain, at Westford, Dec. 17, 1734.*
Sarah, and David Carlton, Sept. 2, 1827.*
Solomon, and Mary Gould of Dunstable, June 27, 1775.

POLLORD (see also Pollard), Rebecca [now resident in Westford. int.], and Parker Emerson, May 16, 1771.*

POOL (see also Poole), Betsey B., and James Pike, jr., int. Apr. 17, 1839.

POOLE (see also Pool), Cordelia A., of West Bridgewater, and Seneca P. Morse of North Chelmsford, int. Nov. 8, 1845.

POOR, Martha, Mrs., of Andover, and Benjamin Howard, at Andover, Jan. 12, 1748.*

PORTER, Mary R., and Micah Parmenter of Westford, June 10, 1841.*

POWARS (see also Power), Esther, and John Glode, at Charlestown, Mar. 15, 1770.*

POWER (see also Powars, Powers), Betty, and Ebenezer Townsend, jr. of Billerica, int. Dec. 2, 1750.
Peter, of Dunstable, and Anna Keiys, int. Apr. 20, 1728.
Walter, of Concord, and Rebeca Barit, Dec. 16, 1696.

POWERS (see also Power), Jonas, and Abigail Lovejoy of Pepperell, int. Apr. 7, 1825.
Jonathan, of Littleton, and Elizabeth Kidder, int. Dec. 5, 1725.
Mary, d. Walter, of Nashoba, and Joseph Whealer of Nashoba, Mar. 1, 1681.
Mary, and William Fletcher, int. Oct. 18, 1724.
Remembrance, and Charles Emmerson ["of Fishersfield, N. H." int.], Oct. 14, 1777.*
William, and Remembrance Peirce, Nov. 14, 1739.*

*Intention also recorded.

PRATT, Abigail, wid., of Greenfield, N. H., a. 45 y., d. Samuel and Katy Straw, and Geo[rge] W. Sumner, widr., of Hill, N. H., a. 56 y., farmer, s. George and Lydia, Sept. 17, 1848.
Anna, and Luke Bowers, at Dracut, Mar. 20, 1787.*

PRENTIS, Susan, of Lexington, and Edmond Stevens, int. Feb. 24, 1822.

PRESCOT (see also Prescott), Dorothy, of Concord, and James Hildreth, int. Dec. 20, 1721.
Rebeckah, of Concord, and Jonathan Barron, int. Aug. 9, 1724.
Thankfull, of Groton, and Timothy Spaulding, int. May 15, 1726.

PRESCOTT (see also Prescot, Prescut), Abraham [Lt. c. r. 1; of Westford. int.], and Olive Adams, Nov. 13, 1801.*
Eliza Ann, of Groton, and George W. Woodward, int. Mar. 25, 1841.
Jonas, and Esther Spaulding, int. Mar. 6, 1725-6.
Levi T., and Sophia Tittle of Beverly, int. Aug. 3, 1823.
Mary, of Concord, and Timothy Fletcher, int. Oct. 5, 1729.
Polly F., of Westford, and Benjamin Spalding, int. Jan. 17, 1830.

PRESCUT (see also Prescott), Benjamin, of Jaffrey, N. H., and Rachil Adams, int. Apr. 3, 1775.

PRESTON, Erasmus D., and Sarah White of Leicester, int. Aug. 29, 1846.

PRICHTTE, Ferdinanda, and Mary Murfey [both of the factory. c. r. 1.], Oct. 6, 1817.*

PROCKTER (see also Proctor), Azariah, and Azubah Robbens, Feb. 11, 1772.*
William, and Lucy Fletcher, int. July 9, 1733.

PROCTER (see also Proctor), Abigail, and Daniel Keyes [of Westford. int.], Sept. 19, 1754.*
Abigail, and Oliver Barron, July 30, 1755.*
Agnis [of Westford. int.], and Ebenezer Emery, Jan. 16, 1769.*

*Intention also recorded.

CHELMSFORD MARRIAGES 299

PROCTER, Anna P., and Samuel Parker of New Boston, N. H., June 3, 1823.*
Asa, and Sarah Cory, Nov. 16, 1782. [Nov. 26. C. R. 1.]
Asa, and Allice Dane, int. Oct. 29, 1808.
Azariah, and Lucy Hodgman, ———, 1806. [Feb. 16. C. R. 1.]*
Azubah, and Oliver Willard, resident in Chelmsford, Nov. 29, 1792.*
Benj[amin], and Lydia Chamberlain, int. Feb. 4, 1727-8.
Benjamin [jr. int.], and Rachel Pierce, Nov. 16, 1757.*
Benjamin, and Bethiah Hardy of Nottingham West, N. H., int. June 20, 1761.
Betty, and Isaac Chandler [of Westford. int.], Nov. 1, 1759. [Oct. 31. P. R. 4.]*
Daniel, and Susana Hill of Billerica, int. Sept. 17, 1727.
Elizabeth, and Eleazer Spaulding, Oct. 30, 1753.*
Elldad, and Rachel Parker, int. Dec. 13, 1791.
Gaus, and Betcy Pecken, May 31, 1797.*
Gershan, and Rebeckar Parker, int. Dec. 10, 1721.
Gershom, and Sarah Whittaws, July 4, 1690. CT. R.
Hanah, and Joseph Kider, int. May 8, 1720.
Hannah, and Moses Barrat [of Nottingham. int.], Nov. 11, 1742.*
Henry, and Sarah Butterfield, May 22, 1760.*
Isarell, and Margret Helldreth, Jan. 10, 1689.
Jane [Jean. int.], and David Sprague [of Sunderland. int.], Nov. 26, 1767.*
Jeams, and Ester Parker, Dec. 3, 1691.
Jonathan, and Elizabeth Robbins of Stow, int. Feb. 7, 1719-20.
Joseph, and Agness Peirce, int. Dec. 1, 1722.
Lucy, and Henry Spaulding, int. Dec. 5, 1725.
Lucy, and John Green, int. Dec. —, 1808.
Lydia, and Jonathan Butterfield, Mar. 27, 1751. [Mar. 28. P. R. 4.]*
Mary, and Thomas Swetman, int. July 9, 1721.
Mary [of Westford. int.], and William Procter, May 11, 1769.*
Mercy, and Joseph Barret of Killingly, int. Apr. 12, 1746.
Miriam, and Josiah Comings of Dunstable, int. Nov. 26, 1732.
Moses, and Mary Byam, int. ———. [1738?]
Olive, and Benjamin Butterfield, Dec. 6, 1758.*
Peter, and Hannah Harwood, int. Apr. 10, 1720.
Peter [jr. int.], and Molly Putnam, Oct. 19, 1769.*
Rachel, and Eleazer Comings of Dunstable, int. Oct. 26, 1729.
Rachel, and Oliver Adams, Dec. 2, 1756.*

*Intention also recorded.

PROCTER, Rebecca, and Jonas Parker, Oct. 8, 1761.*
Sally, and Ephraim Parkhurst, May 3, 1807.*
Samuel, and Lydia Cotton, int. Mar. 15, 1723-4.
Samuel, jr., and Sally Gould, int. Apr. 11, 1793.
Sarah, and Samuel Hildreth [of Westford. int.], Mar. 14, 1753.*
Sarah, and Jonas Hildreth, Dec. 27, 1759.*
Sarah, and Josiah Foster [late of Winchester. int.], Apr. 2, 1761.*
Sarah, and Moses Robbens [of Carlisle. int.], Mar. 22, 1807.*
Susan Amanda, and James C. Burgess of Boston, int. Apr. 30, 1833.
Susanna, and Daniel Sherwin [of Dunstable. int.], June 3, 1756.*
Susanna, and Salathial Adams, June 5, 1804.*
Thankful, and Benjamin Barrett [of Killingly. int.], Sept. 23, 1746.*
Thomas, and Hanah Barron, int. Dec. 23, 1722.
William, and Mary Procter [of Westford. int.], May 11, 1769.*
Zilpah [d. Dan[ie]ll. P. R. 4.], and Josiah Fletcher [3d. int.], Apr. 9, 1789.*

PROCTOR (see also Prockter, Procter), Alfred, and Harriett E. Taylor of Carlisle, int. Aug. 22, 1846.
Amos, and Elizabeth Dakin of Concord, at Concord, Oct. 25, 1798.*
Asa, and Ama Trull, at Dracut, Apr. 23, 1793.*
Azariah, 3d, and Lettice W. Barden of Lowell, int. Oct. 14, 1832.
Charles, and Genett Way, int. Feb. 17, 1838.
Cotton, and Tabitha Fletcher, Nov. 6, 1745.*
Daniel [jr. int.], and Mary Robbins, Jan. 1, 1767.*
Daniel [jr. int.], and Hannah Parker, May 31, 1774.*
Daniel, of Westford, and Esther Spalding, int. June 1, 1811.
David, and Hannah Farrar of Concord, at Concord, Dec. 31, 1730.
Dorathy, and John Barrett, s. John, Dec. 18, 1679.
Elijah, and Esther Adams, at Charlestown, Dec. 31, 1766.*
Eliza, and Abraham Van Doorn, int. Sept. 19, 1824.
Elizabeth, and Samuel Fletcher, at Concord, Dec. 20, 1705.
Esther, of Westford, and Jonathan Minott, at Westford, Mar. 6, 1746.*

*Intention also recorded.

PROCTOR, Ezekiel, of Westford, and Elizabeth Chamberlain, at Concord, Oct. 24, 1734.*
George, and Ann Maria Whittemore of Groton, int. May 7, 1836.
Gershom, and Elizabeth Parker of Westford, at Westford, July 22, 1746.*
Henry B., and S. Elisabeth Proctor, int. May 5, 1849.
Hester [Easter. int.], of Concord, and John Harvel, at Concord, Apr. 25, 1734.*
Israel, and Sarah Raymond of Concord, at Concord, Sept. 18, 1734.*
Jonas [R., of Tyngsborough. int.], and Sybil Hodgman, Nov. 14, 1809.*
Jonas R., jr., and Fanny Thurlow, int. Mar. 3, 1840.
Lucy, Mrs., and Lt. Jonathan Harwood, int. Aug. 20, 1768.
Lucy, and John Abbutt, jr. of Westford, int. July 8, 1769.
Lucy, and Joseph Fletcher, at Westford, Nov. 17, 1791.*
Lydia, and Henry Spaulding, 3d, at Westford, Dec. 22, 1791.*
Marah [Lydia. int.], and Ephraim Wesen of Wilmington, at Westford, Nov. 16, 1748.*
Mary, d. Robertt and Jane, and James Borne, Apr. 3, 1685.
Mary, and Timothy Read, int. Nov. 13, 1825.
Mary, and Marcus D. Byam, Sept. 26, 1839.*
Molly [Mrs. int.], and Capt. John Cook of Claremont, N. H., at Westford, Apr. 27, 1797.*
Nathan [jr. int.], of Westford, and Lydia Robbins, at Concord, Jan. 9, 1774. [Apr. 23. int.]*
Oliver, and Mary Parker of Westford, at Westford, Apr. 10, 1744.*
Rebecca, and Daniel E. [G. int.] Greenleaf, Apr. 21, 1833.*
S. Elisabeth, and Henry B. Proctor, int. May 5, 1849.
Sarah, and Thomas Chamberline, Aug. [10, 1666. T. C.].
Sibbel, and Joseph Reed of Temple, N. H., at Concord, Nov. 16, 1769.*
Simeon, and Rebecca Foster, Mar. 12, 1754.*
Simeon B., and Asenath J. [L. int.] Hall of Billerica, May 21, 1840.*
Willard, and Maria Huddleton of Lowell, int. Mar. 25, 1832.

PROVANCHA, George, and Olive Brown, Nov. 28, 1843.*

PULSIFER, David [jr. int.; Capt. c. r. l.], of Salem, and Mary C. Fletcher, June 7, 1825.*

*Intention also recorded.

PUTFARK, Catharine M., and Charles F. Syffermann of Malden, int. Oct. 1, 1844.

PUTMAN (see also Putnam), David, and Lefy Pierce, int. Mar. 1, 1781.

PUTNAM (see also Putman, Putnum), Ann, and [Hezekiah B. int.] Crooker [of Boston. int.], Nov. 8, 1838. c. r. 1.*
Betcy, and Abel Stevens, int. Nov. 24, 1801.
Geo[rge] W., of Nashua, N. H., a. 32 y., portrait-painter, b. Salem, s. Joseph and Mary, of Salem, and Julia Amanda Putnam, a. 31 y., d. Joseph and Anna, Aug. 21, 1844.*
Hannah, and Daniel Spaulding, June 8, 1769.*
Israel, and Mary L. Putnam of Salem, int. Sept. 2, 1837.
Julia Amanda, a. 31 y., d. Joseph and Anna, and Geo[rge] W. Putnam of Nashua, N. H., a. 32 y., portrait-painter, b. Salem, s. Joseph and Mary, of Salem, Aug. 21, 1844.*
Lucy, and Samuel Adams [jr. int.], Oct. 29, 1772.*
Martha, and Jos[eph. int.] Chamberlin [2d. int.; jr. c. r. 1.], Feb. 26, 1829.*
Mary L., of Salem, and Israel Putnam, int. Sept. 2, 1837.
Molly, and Peter Procter [jr. int.], Oct. 19, 1769.*
Nabby, of Fitchburg, and Zacheriah [Zacheus. int.] Wright, at Fitchburg, July 8, 1799.*

PUTNUM (see also Putnam), Daniel, and Hannah Alexander, Feb. 22, 1798.*

QUESEY, Henry, of Tyngsborough, and Sarah Cushing, Apr. 18, 1843.*

RAMSDILL, Rebecca, of Hanson, and Marcus Thomas, int. July 14, 1833.

RAND, Daniel, of Cambridge, and Rebecca Gordon, now resident in Chelmsford, int. Feb. 24, 1776.

RAY, John Trask, and Lucy Ann Fuller of Amherst, N. H., int. May 8, 1825.

RAYMENT (see also Raymond), Abigail, and Jonathan Barrat [jr. int.], Mar. 28, 1771.*
Edward, and Abigail Patch, Oct. 3, 1751.*

*Intention also recorded.

CHELMSFORD MARRIAGES 303

RAYMOND (see also Rayment), Lucinda G., of Dunstable, and Josiah R. Reed, int. Apr. 19, 1835.
Paul, and Margaret Ward of Wenham, at Wenham, Mar. 5, 1758.*
Sarah, of Concord, and Israel Proctor, at Concord, Sept. 18, 1734.*

RAYNOR, Eliza, of Lowell, and George W. McIntire, int. Oct. 3, 1848.

READ (see also Reed), Hannah, and Ephraim Craft of Roxbury, May 15, 1699.
John, and Sarah Wilson, Dec. 2, 1779.*
Jonathan [Rood. c. R. 1.], and Deborah Farrer, June 27, 1781.
Joseph, and Leonora Spalding of Cavendish, Vt., int. Oct. 17, 1830.
Lucy, of Westford, and Joel Hunter, int. July 13, 1809.
Lucy, of Hollis, N. H., and Samuel Hadley, int. Sept. 8, 1822.
Lydia, and Joseph Fitch of Boston, Dec. 5, 1822.*
Mary, and John Butterfield of Groton, int. Dec. 24, 1727.
Mary, of Dunstable, and Robert Foster, int. Sept. 4, 1762.
Orin, and Sally Butters of Westford, int. Sept. 19, 1825.
Peter, of Littleton, and Dorothy Parker of Westford, at Westford, Sept. 24, 1772.
Peter, and Hannah Martin, Apr. 13, 1779.*
Ranson, and Sally Butters of Westford, int. June 26, 1825.
Rebeckah, and Joseph Parkis, at Concord, June 26, 1656. [June 24. CT. R.]
Rhoda, of Westford, and George Frederick, at Westford, Mar. 18, 1788.*
Sally, of Westford, and Samuel Sherburn, at Westford, June 24, 1794.*
Supply, and Susanna Byam, June 7, 1781.*
Susanah, of Salem, and [John. dup.] Coborn, s. Edward [of Dracut, Mar. 10. dup.; Mar. 18. T. C.], 1671.
Thomas, jr., of Westford, and Olive Howard, int. Feb. 21, 1746-7.
Timothy, and Mary Proctor, int. Nov. 13, 1825.
William, and Hannah Bates, int. Feb. 7, 1719-20.
William, Capt., of Hollis, N. H., and Bettey Sheed, int. May 11, 1796.

READER, Edward, widr., a. 36 y., clerk, and Sophia F. A. Bruce, a. 28 y., Nov. 6, 1847.*

*Intention also recorded.

READING (see also Redding), Bridget, and Isaac Clark, Dec. 1, 1768.*

RECORD, Elisha, and Emily Blackwell of Lowell, int. July 24, 1846.

REDDING (see also Reading), Robert, and Hannah Parkhust, int. May 28, 1743.

REDDINGTON, Rebecca, of Topsfield, and Zecheriah Emmery, at Ipswich, May 20, 1733.*

REDLAND, Patience, d. William, of Groton, and Nichalos Cady, s. Nichalas, of Groton, Mar. 20, 1685.

REED (see also Read), Abigail O. [of Westford. int.], and Otis Adams, Apr. 4, 1822. p. r. 5.*
Almira [of Westford. int.], and Eben[eze]r Richardson, Apr. 29, 1831.*
Benjamin, and Bridget Abbot, Dec. 17, 1807.*
Bitty [of Carlisle. int.], and Benjamin Parker, Oct. 28, 1784.*
Elikim, and Sarah Mansfield, Nov. 28, 1784.*
Fidelia, and Joseph Heywood, Sept. 3, 1820.*
Harriet, of Westford, and Park DeWitte of Methuen, May 21 1828.
Jeremy [B. c. r. 1.], and Mrs. Rachel Parker [both of Westford. c. r. 1.], Oct. 19, 1828.
John, and Jane Chamberlain, at Charlestown, Jan. 10, 1706-7.
Joseph, of Temple, N. H., and Sibbel Proctor, at Concord, Nov. 16, 1769.*
Joseph, and Maria Eaton of Andover, Vt., int. Jan. 17, 1836.
Josiah R., and Lucinda G. Raymond of Dunstable, int. Apr. 19, 1835.
Judeth [Mrs. int.], of Woburn, and [Ens. int.] Jonathan Haywood [Harwood. int.], at Woburn, May 2, 1759.*
Judith [of Woburn. int.], and Benjamin Kemp, May 5, 1761.*
Mary E., of Bedford, and Leonard J. Mansfeild, Mar. 31, 1842.*
Ransom, and Mary Sprake, Oct. 3, 1825.
Sarah E., and Samuel A. Waters [of Millbury. int.], Dec. 5, 1838.*
Thankful [a. 42 y. c. r. 1.], and Simeon Byam [a. 62 y. c. r. 1.], Nov. 13, 1828.*
Tho[mas], and Sarah Fletcher, at Charlestown, Mar. 14, 1709.
Timothy, and Sarah Peirce, d. Capt. Jonas, May 16, 1815.*

*Intention also recorded.

CHELMSFORD MARRIAGES 305

RELPH, Desiah, and James Taylor, Oct. 26, 1828.

REMME, Fredric, and Nancy Spalding, int. Oct. 5, 1823.

RENNICK, Francis, and Maria [G. int.] Rollins, June 23, 1839.*

RESCH, Anthony [Rusch. C. R. 1.], and Pamela Pierce [both of the factory. C. R. 1.], July 16, 1817.*

RICE, Eliazer, of Marlborough, and Thankful Fletcher, at Concord, Dec. 8, 1720.*
Euclyd, and Mary Vincent, int. Mar. 14, 1835.

RICHARDSON (see also Richarson, Richerdson, Richeson, Ritchardsun, Ritcheson), Amos, of Pelham, N. H., and Mary Howard, int. Jan. 10, 1756.
Benjamin, and Eunice Butterfield, int. Mar. 27, 1720.
Bridget, and Timothy Fletcher of Westford, int. Feb. 15, 1745-6.
Brigett, and William Chandler of Andover, Oct. [torn], 1679.
Daniel, of Tyngsborough [attorney-at-law. C. R. 1.], and Mary Adams, d. W[illia]m, Apr. 2, 1816.*
Daniel, of Tyngsborough, and Hannah Adams, Nov. 23, 1826.*
Deborah, and Joseph Farrer, int. Mar. 7, 1742-3.
Eben[eze]r, and Almira Reed [of Westford. int.], Apr. 29, 1831.*
Eleazer, and Lydia Perham, Mar. 30, 1748.*
Elijah, and Molley Howard, Mar. 11, 1800. C. R. 1.*
Elijah, and Elizabeth Emerson, Nov. 29, 1832. P. R. 6.*
Elizabeth, and William Adams, Feb. 23, 1758.*
Esther, and Stephen Spaulding, Jan. 7, 1762.*
Esther, and Benjamin Heywood, Feb. 28, 1833.*
Francis, and —— Blodget of Dunstable, int. Apr. 27, 1823.
George, and Aseneth Cummins of Andover, int. Feb. 14, 1823.
Hannah, and John Barron of Dracut, int. Apr. 23, 1721.
Hannah, and Jonathan Parkhurst, int. June 7, 1724.
Hannah, and Dr. Samuel King, Sept. 3, 1751.*
Hannah, and Thaddeus Munroe of Hillsborough, N. H., at Concord, Feb. 17, 1780.*
Harriot P. [F. int.], of Lowell, and Joseph Stevens, June 4, 1834.*
Henry, and Amy Hasselton of Billerica, at Billerica, Feb. 20, 1732-3.*

*Intention also recorded.

RICHARDSON, John, and Elisabeth Farewell, Jan. 31, 1693-4. CT. R.
John, and Easther Pearce, int. Dec. 15, 1733.
Jonathan, and Elisabeth Bats, Nov. 8, 1692.
Jonathan [Capt. dup.], and [wid. dup.] Elizabeth Howard of Charlestown [of Newton. dup. and int.], at Charlestown, May 18, 1724.*
Jonathan [of Dracut. int.], and Lucy Clark, Dec. 4, 1746.*
Jonathan, and Lydia Foster, Oct. 6, 1772.*
Jonathan, jr., and Polly Davis, int. Nov. 14, 1806.
Joseph, of Fitchburg, and Ruth Stevens, at Westford, Feb. 14, 1791.*
Joseph, and Lucy Marinda Byam, Apr. 4, 1833.*
Josiah, and Lydia Warren, Dec. 2, 1761. [Dec. 1. P. R. 4.]*
Josiah [jr. int.], and Sibbel Richardson of Dracut, at Dracut, Mar. 2, 1794.*
Lucy, and Peter Spaulding, Feb. 24, 1763.*
Lucy, and Jacob Chase of West Richmond, N. Y., Oct. 19, 1830.*
Lydia, Mrs., and Thomas Parker of Dracut, int. Jan. 1, 1720-21.
Lydia, and Joseph Spaulding, int. Jan. 24, 1756.
Lydia, and Jacob Chamberlain, May 21, 1761.*
Lydia, and Silas Peirce, Dec. 7, 1786.*
Lydia, and John Farrar, at Westford, Jan. 24, 1788.
Lydia, and Alonzo L. Warren, int. Sept. 25, 1837.
Mary, d. Josiah, and Thomas Coborn [Colburn. dup.], 17: 9 m: 1681.
Mary, and Moses Baron, Feb. 2, 1697-8.
Mary, and Samuel Colborn of Dracut, int. June 30, 1716.
Mary, and Jacob Bloget, int. Dec. 19, 1724.
Mary [Marcy. int.], and Josiah Fletcher [3d. int.], Oct. 16, 1781.*
Mary, and Lt. Zebulon Blodget of Dunstable, at Dracut, May 30, 1793.*
Mary, and Francis B. Parker, Nov. 30, 1837.*
Mary Ann, a. 21 y., d. Zacheus and Eliza, and Isaiah B[yam. P. R. 18.] Spalding, a. 28 y., wheelwright, s. Isaiah and Patty [(Byam). P. R. 18.], July 1, 1846.*
Nathaniel, of Townsend, and Elizabeth Stevens, at Townsend, Sept. 15, 1738.
Olive, and Benjamin Adams, int. Oct. 27, 1723.
Olive, of Westford, and Abel Adams, at Westford, July 22, 1771.*

*Intention also recorded.

RICHARDSON, Oliver, and Cloa Bancroft of Tyngsborough, at Tyngsborough, Mar. 31, 1791.*
Pattey, of Tewksbury, and Jacob Marshall, int. May 12, 1788.
Phebe Q., and Jonathan J. Peach, int. Mar. 16, 1848.
Polly, of Dracut, and John Cole, int. Dec. 29, 1794.
Polly, and Gershom Cutler of West Cambridge, int. Nov. 16, 1834.
Rachel [of Dracut. int.], and Zebulon Parker, May 31, 1792.*
Rebecca, and Francis Davidson [Daverson. int.], Mar. 11, 1779.*
Rebeckah, and William Comings of Tyngsborough, int. Oct. 6, 1798.
Robert, and Sybil [Ann. int.] Rider, Apr. 20, 1830.*
Samuel, and Prudance Wood of Dracut, int. Feb. 16, 1795.
Samuel, and Sarah Danforth of Tyngsborough, Jan. 1, 1835. P. R. 26.*
Sarah, d. Josiah, and William Flecher, s. W[illia]m, Sept. 19, 1667.
Sarah, and William Peirce of Groton, int. Oct. 7, 1739.
Sarah, and Samuel Perham, int. Apr. 11, 1741.
Sarah, and John Coburn [Colborn. int.], jr. of Dracut, at Dracut, Feb. 12, 1767.*
Sarah, and Sallithial Adams, int. July 25, 1778.
Sarah, and Daniel Parker [of Reading. int.], May 2, 1780.*
Sarah, and Ebenezer Parker, int. Aug. 21, 1783.
Sibbel, of Dracut, and Josiah Richardson [jr. int.], at Dracut, Mar. 2, 1794.*
Silas, of Westford, and Lydia Marcy, at Westford, Oct. 30, 1797.*
Simeon, and Rhody Parker of Tyngsborough, int. Oct. 10, 1807.
Stephen, and Betsey Patten, Feb. 18, 1829. C. R. 3.
Sukey [Susanna. int.], and Abel Fletcher of Westford, Dec. 28, 1820.*
Susanna, and Henry Spaulding, Nov. 21, 1748.*
Tabitha, and Oliver Fletcher [jr. int.], at Charlestown, Feb. 25, 1766.*
Thankfull, and Ezra Colburn of Dracut, int. Feb. 25, 1732-3.
William, and Lucy Ann Webber of Westford, Oct. 8, 1829.*
Zachariah [jr. int.], and Hannah Blodget, Oct. 9, 1753.*
Zachariah, and Sarah Warren, Apr. 22, 1755.*
Zebediah, of Woburn, and Sary Barron, int. Dec. 20, 1755.

*Intention also recorded.

RICHARSON (see also Richardson), Thomas, and Hannah Coborn [Colburn. int.], d. Edward, all of Dracut, Sept. 28, 1682.

RICHERDSON (see also Richardson), John, and Deborah Coleburn of Dracut, int. Jan. 4, 1734-5.
Josiah, and Experiance Wight of Sudbury, Oct. 23, 1728.*
Lucy, and John Sprake of Charlestown, int. Feb. 18, 1737-8.
Lucy, and John Sprake, jr. of Charlestown, int. Apr. —, 1738.
Sarah, and Jonathan Spaulding, int. Jan. 15, 1731-2.

RICHESON (see also Richardson), Josiah, and Rememberans [Underwood. CT. R.], at Concord, June 6, 1659.

RIDER, Sybil [Ann. int.], and Robert Richardson, Apr. 20, 1830.*

RITCHARDSUN (see also Richardson), Samuel, and Ratchel Howard, Jan. 27, 1702-3.
Susanah, and Henry Farwell, Jan. 23, 1695-6.

RITCHESON (see also Richardson), James, and Briget [Hincksman. CT. R.], Nov. 28, 1660.

ROBBENS (see also Robbins), Azubah, and Azariah Prockter, Feb. 11, 1772.*
John, 3d, and Sarah Hildretch, int. Sept. 12, 1771.
John [jr. int.], and Sarah Fletcher, Oct. 1, 1771.*
Moses [of Carlisle. int.], and Sarah Procter, Mar. 22, 1807.*
Olive, and Samuel Hutchins [of Temple, N. H. int.], May 20, 1773.*

ROBBINS (see also Robbens, Robin, Robins), Ebenezer, and Margret Barret, —— [1701 or 1702?].
Edee, and Moses Graves, int. Mar. 26, 1749.
Edith, and James Dutton [jr. int.], Sept. 24, 1751.*
Elanor, and Ephraim Heild of Townsend, int. Feb. 25, 1732-3.
Eleanor, and Nathaniel Parker of Billerica, at Billerica, May 9, 1771.*
Elizabeth, of Stow, and Jonathan Procter, int. Feb. 7, 1719-20.
Elizabeth, and Jonas Fletcher, int. Nov. 8, 1722.
George, and Mary Barret, Jan. 21, 1686. CT. R.

*Intention also recorded.

CHELMSFORD MARRIAGES   309

ROBBINS, Hannah, and Benja[min] Hawood [Haywood. c. r.
    1.], Jan. 21, 1783.*
James, jr., and Elzina Fletcher, Mar. 11, 1832.
Jemima, of Carlisle, and Horace Peckens, int. Apr. 7, 1807.
John, and Dorithy Hildreth, Nov. 30, 169[torn. 1699.].
Jonas, and Mary Heald of Acton, at Concord, May 24, 1738.*
Jonas [jr. int.], and Sybil Durant, Feb. 28, 1764.*
Jonathan, and Elizabeth Emery of Townsend, at Townsend,
    July 10, 1771.*
Lucy, and Ezekiel Hildreth [of Westford. int.], Sept. 28,
    1774.*
Lydia, and Nathan Proctor [jr. int.] of Westford, at Concord,
    Jan. 9, 1774. [Apr. 23. int.]*
Martha [M. int.], and Alden Pinney of Lowell, Dec. 31,
    1837.*
Mary [of Westford. int.], and Jason Russell, at Concord, Nov.
    6, 1740.*
Mary, and Jonathan Hildreth [jr. int.], Jan. 25, 1749.*
Mary, and Daniel Proctor [jr. int.], Jan. 1, 1767.*
Mercy, and John Heild [of Stow. int.], June 28, 1743.*
Mercy, and Benjamin Craggin, Nov. 27, 1766.*
Nancy, and Charles Adams, Nov. 30, 1826.*
Philip, of Westford, and Anna Minot, int. June 24, 1750.
Sarah, of Cambridge, and Benoni Perham, at Concord, Dec. 6,
    1704.
Sarah, and Simeon Wright [of Ipswich, N. H. int.], Nov. 21,
    1768.*
Susanna, and Israel Heald [Hail, of Acton. int.], Dec. 30,
    1760.*
Thomas, and Lydia Adams, at Concord, Aug. 6, 1713.

ROBIE (see also Roby), Hannah, and Abraham Byham, int.
    Aug. 21, 1726.
John, and Esther Blodget, Aug. 15, 1771.*

ROBIN (see also Robbins), Anne, and Stephen Kyess, Mar. 7,
    1706.

ROBINS (see also Robbins), Elizebeth, and Samuel Cowdrey,
    int. Sept. 18, 1762.
George, of Harvard, and Thankfull Steevens, int. Dec. 25,
    1734.
John, and Susanah Harwood, int. May 1, 1736.
Roburd, and Mary Dill, both of Groton, Mar. 27, 1697.
Samuel, and Dorithy Barat, Mar 4, 1701-2.

*Intention also recorded.

ROBINSON (see also Robison), Allen, and Eunice T. Moore of Dunstable, N. H., int. Dec. 2, 1827.
Betsey A., and Benj[ami]n Blood, jr., July 15, 1841.*
Sally, and John Hubbard, Sept. 2, 1830.

ROBISON (see also Robinson), Elisabeth, d. Jam[e]s, of Groton, and William Leaking [Lakin. dup.], s. William, of Groton, Jan. 4, 1685.

ROBY (see also Robie), Charlotte [of Dunstable, N. H. int.], and [Capt. int.] Daniel Fletcher, Dec. 30, 1824.*
Charlottee, of Dunstable, N. H., and Jonathan Howard, int. Jan. 29, 1796.
Christopher, and Susan B. Bowers, Aug. 31, 1843.*
Mary, of Dunstable, N. H., and Micajah Bowers, int. May 26, 1822.
Polle, of Dunstable, N. H., and William Adams, int. Oct. 31, 1785.
Rebekah, of Dunstable, and Ebenezer Parker, int. Mar. 27, 1792.
Samuel, and Hannah Glynn, Apr. 2, 1805.*
William [of Dunstable, N. H. int.], and Dorothy Spaulding, Feb. 27, 1800.*

ROGERS (see also Roggers), Abigal, and Arther Warin [torn. 1667?].
Harriet, of Billerica, and Samuel Burbank, int. Nov. 16, 1828.
Mary, of Andover, and Asa Martin, at Andover, Jan. 12, 1748-9.*
Timothy [of Tewksbury. int.], and Ruth Parker, June 2, 1757.*

ROGGERS (see also Rogers), Hannah P., of Tewksbury, and Samuel Kidder [of Charlestown. c. r. 1.], ——, 1806. [Mar. 31. c. r. 1.]

ROLLINS, Maria [G. int.], and Francis Rennick, June 23, 1839.*
Nancy H., of Lowell, a. 27 y., d. Joseph and Elizabeth, and Samuel Ditson of Lowell, a. 24 y., teamster, s. John and Charlotte, Jan. 20, 1849.

ROPER, Mary Jane, and Frederick C. Conner of Lowell, int. Oct. 2, 1840.

*Intention also recorded.

CHELMSFORD MARRIAGES 311

ROSS, Sarah, of Lowell, and Daniel S. Wait, Sept. 17, 1843.*

ROUF, Hannah, and Thomas Coborn [Colburn. dup.], s. Edward, of Dracut, Aug. 6, 1672.

ROUND, Hannah L., of Foster, R. I., and Jason F. Holmes, int. Aug. 2, 1846.

ROUSOE, Joseph, and wid. Mary Fisher, int. June 3, 1842.

ROW, Susanna, of Marblehead, and Jonathan Howard, int. Feb. 18, 1743-4.

ROWELL, William, and Abigail Chaffee, Feb. 23, 1841.*

RUGGS, Abel, and Sally Carlton, Dec. 12, 1820.*

RUMRELL (see also Rumrill), Simon, of Enfield, and Mercy Spaulding, int. Oct. 22, 1722.

RUMRILL (see also Rumrell), David, of Westford, and Prissilla Cory, int. July 25, 1765.

RUSS, Anna, and Jonas Farmer, June 24, 1776.*

RUSSEL (see also Russell), Abigail, of Bow, N. H., and Benjamin Twiss, int. Oct. 11, 1794.
William [of Bedford. int.], and Salla Simons, Aug. 17, 1797.*

RUSSELL (see also Russel), Abel, of Westford, and wid. Sarah Frost, resident in Chelmsford, at Westford, Nov. 1, 1781.
Eunice, a. 35 y., d. Abner and Sarah, and Nathan Guild, widr., a. 45 y., farmer, s. John and Olive, Apr. 21, 1845.*
Jason, and Mary Robbins [of Westford. int.], at Concord, Nov. 6, 1740.*
Sarah, of Concord, and Jonathan Cory, at Concord, Dec. 12, 1699.

SALENDIN, John, and Elisabeth Usher, Apr. 4, 1679.

SANBORN, Horace D., of Dracut, a. 25 y., carpenter, s. John and Lydia, and Mary J. C. Knowles, a. 19 y., d. Samuel L., int. Aug. 24, 1849.

*Intention also recorded.

SANBORN, John M., and Fanny J. Fisher of Francistown, N. H., int. Oct. 28, 1843.
Leonard C., and Sarah E. Hartwell of Littleton, int. Sept. 14, 1837.
Leonard C., and Sarah Jane Fletcher of New Boston, N. H., int. Apr. 11, 1846.
Lydia P., of Gilmanton, N. H., and Nathaniel Wiggin, int. Mar. 1, 1843.

SANDERS (see also Saunders), Jason [of Grafton, N. H. int.], and Lucr[e]tia Moors, Nov. 6, 1811.*
Loamma, of Billerica, and Sarah Kenny, int. Oct. 4, 1806.
Stephen [of Temple, N. H. int.], and Lucy Peirce, Nov. 25, 1773.*

SANDERSON, Daniel, and Eliza P. Treat of Waltham, int. July 31, 1825.
Joseph, of Cambridgeport, and Mary B. French, Aug. 2, 1841.*

SANGER, Charles H., and Susan J. Littlehale, Mar. 23, 1828.*

SARGEANT, Sarah Ann, of Lowell, and Samuel F. Ballard, int. Oct. 27, 1839.

SARNDERS (see also Saunders), Joshua, and Lydia Chamberlin, Mar. 14, 1785. œFeb. 20. dup.; Mar. 24. C. R. 1; Mar. 7. int.]*

SATLE, David, of Groton, and Elizabeth Keyes, int. Mar. 1, 1723-4.

SAUNDERS (see also Sanders, Sarnders), Rebecca, of Groton, and Jeremiah Hobart, Mar. 4, 1776.

SAWTELL, Obadiah [of Shirley. int.], and [Mrs. int.] Sarah Fletcher, Sept. 13, 1774.*

SAWYER, Mary, of Newbury, and John Blaisdill, at Newbury, Aug. 5, 1756.*

SAXSON, Elisabeth, d. Thomas, of Boston, and Josiah Parker, s. Capt. James, May 8, 1678.

*Intention also recorded.

SCOTT, Nancy W., of Lowell, a. 27 y., d. Abijah and Nancy, and David Aldin of Lowell, a. 25 y., machinist, s. David and Susan, Oct. 18, 1845.

SCRIPTURE, Oliver, and Nancy Holland Greele of Wilton, int. Nov. 3, 1809.
Samuel, of Groton, and Elizabeth Spaulding, int. Feb. 6, 1723-4.

SEARLE (see also Searls, Serll), Augustus H., and Rebecca Wright [of Westford. int.], Dec. 8, 1831.*
Mary S., of Methuen, and William S. Flanders, int. Nov. 30, 1839.

SEARLS (see also Searle), Samuel [of Dunstable, N. H. int.], and Lydia Stevens, Sept. 16, 1755.*

SENTER, Isaac N., of Lowell, and Rebecca McIntere, Mar. 25, 1830.*
John, and Jean Foster, at Woburn, Apr. 8, 1717.
John [of Londonderry, N. H. int.], and [Mrs. int.] Sarah Foster, Sept. 20, 1768. [Sept. 21. P. R. 4.]*
Mary [of Woburn. int.], and Jesse Spaulding, July 4, 1776.*
Reuben [of Londonderry, N. H. int.], and Rebecca Parker, June 3, 1760.*

SERLL (see also Searle), Samuel, of Dunstable, and Sarah Perham, Sept. 26, 1699.

SEVOIE, Joseph, a. 23 y., farmer, s. Joseph and Clara, and Sarah R. Smith of Lowell, a. 23 y., d. James and Elizabeth, Sept. 23, 1844.*

SHATTUCK, [Daniel, of Hollis. dup.], and Elizabeth Corey [Long, at Dracut. dup.], Nov. 14, 1793. [Nov. 13. dup.]*
Jonathan [3d, of Pepperell. int.], and Abia Chamberlain, Mar. 2, 1769.*
Sophia, of Waltham, and Jefferson Wheeler, int. Jan. 9, 1825.

SHAW, Elisha, and Emely Hildreth of Westford, int. May 15, 1840.
Elisha, widr., a. 29 y., moulder, s. Sam[ue]l and Lydia, and Martha E[lizabeth. int.] Lincoln of Westford, a. 23 y., d. Daniel and Martha, July 4, 1844.*

*Intention also recorded.

SHAW, Elisha, widr., a. 29 y., moulder, s. Samuel and Lydia, and Mercy M[aria. int.] Lincoln, a. 21 y., d. Daniel and Martha, Oct. 1, 1844.*
John, and Julia Harris, int. Oct. 17, 1846.
Philo S., and Adaline [D. c. r. 1.] Chever, Nov. 10, 1829.

SHEAD (see also Shed), Ebenezer, Capt., and Lucy Hartwell of Carlisle, at Carlisle, May 16, 1793.*

SHED (see also Shead, Shedd, Sheed), Amos, and Mary Spaulding, ———. [Nov. 2, 1828. int.]*
Ebenezer [of Billerica. int.], and Thankful Fletcher, Mar. 30, 1758. [May 30. dup.]*
Ebinezer, jr., and Lucy Parker of Carlisle, int. Feb. 6, 1808.
Eunice, of Billerica, and John Leveston, at Charlestown, Nov. 29, 1705.
Hannah, and Nathaniel Goold [of Ipswich, N. H. int.], Nov. 20, 1766.*
Jacob, of Tewksbury, and Susanna Spaulding, int. July 24, 1803.
John, and Mary Byam, June 17, 1802. c. r. 1.*
Jonathan, and Esther Blood of Carlisle, at Carlisle, Dec. 13, 1781.*
Lurena Augusta, of Lowell, and Sherebiah Spalding, jr., Sept. 22, 1836.*
Mary, and Sears C. Laws, Mar. 29, 1818.*
Nathaniel H., and Naoma Miller, int. Aug. 5, 1821.
Rebecca, of Billerica, and David Burge, at Billerica, Mar. 13, 1757.*
Samuel [of Pepperell. int.], and Betty Spaulding, July 18, 1771.*
Sophrona, and Stephen Hinkley [of Gorham, Me. c. r. 1.], Nov. 8, 1829.
Zacheriah, and Hannah Barrat, Nov. 24, 1743.*

SHEDD (see also Shed), Elizabeth, of Billerica, and Jerahmeel Bowers, jr., int. June 4, 1748.
Prudence, and Thomas Eastabrooks of Dunstable, int. Oct. 8, 1743.
Rachil, and Ephraim Baritt, int. June 9, 1733.

SHEED (see also Shed), Bettey, and Capt. William Read of Hollis, N. H., int. May 11, 1796.

*Intention also recorded.

SHEPARD (see also Sheperd, Shephard, Shepherd), **Alfred,** and Mary S. Farmer, June 18, 1843.*
Frances W[intworth. int.], and Asahel Stearns, Apr. 23, 1801.*
Henry [of Dunstable. int.], and Hannah Laughton, Aug. 6, 1776.*

SHEPERD (see also Shepard), Thankes, d. Ralph and Thankes, of Concord, and Peter Dell [Dill. dup.], 13: 10 m: 1669.

SHEPHARD (see also Shepard), Bathsheba, of Concord, and William Butterfield, int. May 21, 1727.

SHEPHERD (see also Shepard), Charles, of Bedford, N. H., and Betsy Wright of Westford, Nov. 2, 1824.

SHERBURN, Samuel, and Sally Read of Westford, at Westford, June 24, 1794.*

SHERIN (see also Sherwin), Susanah, of Boxford, and Mathias Cowdrey, int. Feb. 14, 1724-5.

SHERMAN, Joseph, and Asenath Hunt of Marlborough, int. Apr. 29, 1809.

SHERWIN (see also Sherin), Charles H., and Sarah A. Kennon of Worcester, int. Mar. 1, 1847.
Daniel [of Dunstable. int.], and Susanna Procter, June 3, 1756.*
Levi, widr., of Townsend, a. 33 y., farmer, s. Levi and Hannah, and Mary Jane Fletcher, a. 32 y., d. W[illia]m and Orpah, Oct. 16, 1849.*

SHERWOOD, Harriett, of Lowell, a. 20 y., d. Henry and Charlotte, and John Jeffray [Jeppoye. int.], a. 22 y., wool stapler, s. Joseph and Mary, Nov. 30, 1844.*

SHETTLEWORTH, Kezia, of Renton, and David Butterfeild, int. Apr. 3, 1731.

SHIPLE (see also Shipley), Lideah, and John Perum, Dec. 15, 1664.

*Intention also recorded.

SHIPLEY (see also Shiple, Shiply), Caroline C., of Townsend, and William D. Kidder, int. Mar. 13, 1825.
Mary Ann Homes, of Londonderry, N. H., and John Chever, int. Feb. 19, 1826.

SHIPLY (see also Shipley), John, and Susanah Wheler of Concord, Sept. 23 [1672. dup.].

SHIRTLIFF (see also Shurtliff), Caleb [of Charlestown. int.], and Suky Pelsue, Jan. 1, 1809.*

SHURTLEFF (see also Shurtliff), Ezekiel L., a. 24 y., cabinet turner, b. Westford, s. Caleb W. and Susan, and Mercy M. Hildreth, a. 16 y., b. Westford, d. Moses and Eliza, Dec. 26, 1848.*
Susan, and A[bel. int.] Hartwell Kemp of Westford, Dec. 25, 1840.*

SHURTLIFF (see also Shirtliff, Shurtleffff), Benjamin, and Paulina Stearns of Carlisle, Mar. 22, 1841.*
Lucy Ann, and Archible R. Jones, Aug. 8, 1841.*
William, of Charlestown, and Sukey Pelsue, int. Dec. 18, 1808.

SILVER, Hervy, and Abigail Jones of Hillsborough, N. H., int. Dec. 3, 1837.

SIMONDS (see also Simons), Abel, and Elizabeth L. T. Farwell, int. Nov. 4, 1827.
Abel, and Jane Todd, int. Aug. 12, 1830.
David S., a. 24 y., stone-cutter, s. William, and Sarah Carbee, a. 19 y., d. Joel, Feb. 29, 1848.*

SIMONS (see also Simonds), Salla, and William Russel [of Bedford. int.], Aug. 17, 1797.*

SIMPKINS, Kath[e]rine [Mrs., resident in Chelmsford. int.], and Joshua Davis, Sept. 19, 1776.*

SIMS, Samuel [of Dracut. int.], and Lydia Blazedell, Nov. 22, 1786.*

SKIDMOOR (see also Skidmore), Keziah, and Stephen Farnum of Wilton, N. H., int. Feb. 12, 1765.

*Intention also recorded.

CHELMSFORD MARRIAGES 317

SKIDMORE (see also Skidmoor), Jemima, of Methuen, and Adam Gould, at Methuen, Feb. 23, 1758.*

SKINNER, Elizabeth, of Westford, and John Davis, at Westford, Feb. 7, 1749.*
Sarah, and Joseph Hartwell, jr. of Bedford, int. June 1, 1751.
Sarah, of Bedford, and James Marshall, jr., int. Mar. 5, 1816.

SLICER, Alexander, and Betsy Jones of Lowell, int. Jan. 17, 1836.

SMALL, Benjamin, and Thankful Didson of Dunstable, June 21, 1781.
Roxanna Williams, of New Boston, N. H., and Zenas Small, int. Sept. 2, 1827.
Zenas, and Roxanna Williams Small of New Boston, N. H., int. Sept. 2, 1827.

SMITH, Abijah [of Dracut. int.], and Charlotte Moors, Nov. 11, 1819.*
Anna, d. John, of Dorchester, and Moses Barrett, s. Thomas, Sept. 10, 1684.
Charles, of Boston, a. 31 y., carpenter, s. Seth and Wealthy, and Martha Huntington of Boston, a. 22 y., d. John and Martha, Oct. 5, 1847.
Charles C., of Boston, and Harriet Stevens, int. Sept. 7, 1834.
Charlotte, and Weld Spalding, int. Apr. 17, 1825.
Hannah, of Shirley, and Josiah Blood, at Shirley, May 21, 1799.*
Hannah [of Dracut. int.], and Lowel Butterfield, Jan. 20, 1820.*
Jacob B., and Mary A. Griffin of Westford, at Westford, Mar. 12, 1840.*
James, of Lowell, and Mary Ann Knecttle, int. Mar. 10, 1839.
James Y., and Louisa Bannister, int. Mar. 6, 1836.
Jesse, trader, and Fanny Warren, d. Joseph, deceased, Nov. 22, 1815.*
John, and Anna Davis, Feb. 4, 1747.*
John, and Harriott Wilson of Tyngsborough, int. Mar. 6, 1825.
John R. [of North Chelmsford. c. r. 3.], a. 21 y., moulder, s. Ransom and Nancy, and Hannah J. Hussey [of North Chelmsford. c. r. 3.], a. 19 y., d. Benjamin and Phebe, Oct. 7, 1847.*

*Intention also recorded.

SMITH, Jonathan, and Pamelia Moors, Nov. 25, 1825.*
Marriam, of Princeton, and Henry Fletcher, int. Jan. 26, 1805.
Mary, and Jeremiah Mears [of Danvers. int.], ――. [Feb. 27, 1813. C. R. 1.]*
Mary, of Gilmanton, N. H., and Samuel M. Moore, int. Apr. 24, 1825.
Mary, and Nahum Wetherbee of Andover, int. Apr. 5, 1835.
Relief A., of New Ipswich, N. H., and John Muzzy, int. Apr. 3, 1825.
Sarah A. [of North Chelmsford. C. R. 3.], a. 28 y., d. Benj[ami]n and Sarah, of Woodstock, Vt., and Benj[ami]n F. Spalding [of North Chelmsford. C. R. 3.], a. 27 y., farmer, s. Asahel and Lucinda, of Woodstock, Vt., Nov. 28, 1847.*
Sarah R., of Lowell, a. 23 y., d. James and Elizabeth, and Joseph Sevoie, a. 23 y., farmer, s. Joseph and Clara, Sept 23, 1844.*
William C., of Westford, and Dorcas Dutton [both of Westford. int.], Mar. 20, 1823.*

SNOW, Esther, and Isaac Hildreth, jr. of Nichewaug, int. Oct. 22, 1749.
Francis, of Wilmington, and Mrs. Julia C. Bowles, int. July 22, 1848.
Hannah, and David Lawson [of Petersham. int.], Dec. 13, 1763.*
Joann, of Westford, and Robert Spalding, int. June 25, 1820.
John, of Woburn, and Sarah Stevens, Feb. 13, 1693-4. CT. R.
Jonathan, and Mary Harwood, Mar. 25, 1756.*
Jonathan, and Sarah Parker [of Carlisle. int.], Apr. 9, 1786.*
Joshua, and Lois Hildreth [of Westford. int.], Apr. 28, 1761.*
Julia, of Lowell, and John Turner, int. Sept. 13, 1835.
Lois, and Daniel Brooks of Westford, at Westford, Nov. 16, 1797.*
Lowes, and Dea. Ebenezer Gould, Dec. 28, 1797.*
Mary, and Edward Bates, int. Feb. 7, 1719-20.
Mary, and Samuel Howard, Dec. 14, 1758.*
Sarah, of Woburn, and John Steevens, Jan. 17, 1692-3. CT. R.
Thankful, and Nathaniel Hutchinson [jr. int.], of Carlisle, at Carlisle, July 14, 1785.*

SPAFFORD, John T., and Elizabeth Coburn of Dracut, int. Aug. 1, 1824.

*Intention also recorded.

CHELMSFORD MARRIAGES 319

SPALDEN (see also Spaulding), Edward, and Pricillah Underwad, July 6, 1663.
John, and Hannah Halle, May 18, 1658.
John, and Ane Bollard of Andover, 20: 7 m: 1681.
Sarah, and John Miriam of Concord, Feb. 16, 1692-3. CT. R.

SPALDIN (see also Spaulding), Edward, and Margreat Barett, 22: 9 m: 1681.
Edward, s. John, and Mary Brackett, d. John, of Billerica, Nov. 27, 1683.
Timothy, and Rebeckah Winn of Woburn, at Woburn, Mar. 5, 1700.

SPALDING (see also Spaulding), Abel, and Harriot Blood of Carlisle, int. Feb. 2, 1823.
Abigail, and Daniel Parker, Jan. 20, 1814.*
Abigail [d. Andrew. C. R. 1.], and Thomas Hutchins of Carlisle, Nov. 27, 1821.*
Alpheous, and Patty Osgood of Westford, int. Aug. 19, 1815.
Amos [Capt. int.], and Mary Warren [d. Joseph. C. R. 1.], Sept. 9, 1819.*
Andrew, and Hanah Jefes, d. Henry, of Billerica, Apr. 30, 1674.
Ann F., of Tewksbury, and Thomas Marshall, int. Feb. 13, 1843.
Benjamin, s. Edward, and Olive Farwell, d. Henry, Oct. 30, 1668.
Benjamin, and Patty Day of Nelson, N. H., int. Sept. 7, 1822.
Benjamin, and Polly F. Prescott of Westford, int. Jan. 17, 1830.
Benjamin, 2d, and Clarissa Coolidge of Antrim, N. H., int. Mar. 9, 1840.
Benj[ami]n F. [of North Chelmsford. C. R. 3.], a. 27 y., farmer, s. Asahel and Lucinda, of Woodstock, Vt., and Sarah A. Smith [of North Chelmsford. C. R. 3.], a. 28 y., d. Benj[ami]n and Sarah, of Woodstock, Vt., Nov. 28, 1847.*
Benjamin J., and Mary A. D. Jenkins of Boston, int. Nov. 25, 1848.
Cynthia, and Levi L. Peavey of Lowell, int. Apr. 2, 1840.
Elbridge P., and Adeline Parkhurst, Nov. 29, 1840.*
Elijah, and Abigail Wright, Oct. 28, 1826. C. R. 1.
Emeline, of Peterborough, N. H., and Joel Spalding, Apr. 15, 1838. [Mar. 21, 1839. int.]*

*Intention also recorded.

SPALDING, Emeline A., a. 24 y., d. John and Lydia, and Perley P. Perham, a. 24 y., milkman, s. Samuel and Nancy, Oct. 5, 1847.*
Esther, and Daniel Proctor of Westford, int. June 1, 1811.
Hannah, and Jonathan Hildreth, at Concord, June 13, 1738.*
Hannah [A. int.; d. Andrew. C. R. 1.], and Oliver Hutchins of Carlisle, Feb. 20, 1823.*
Harriett E., a. 22 y., d. Isaiah and Patty, and Abial B. Everett of New London, N. H., a. 24 y., scythe maker, s. Jonathan and Apphia, Nov. 24, 1848.*
Haskell, and Harriet F. Blunt of Eden, Me., int. Aug. 22, 1824.
Huldah, of Carlisle, and Henry Fletcher, int. July 17, 1810.
Ira, jr., and Mahala Swallow, Nov. 3, 1823.*
Isaiah, and Patty Byam, int. Aug. 28, 1813.
Isaiah B[yam. P. R. 18.], a. 28 y., wheelwright, s. Isaiah and Patty [(Byam). P. R. 18.], and Mary Ann Richardson, a. 21 y., d. Zacheus and Eliza, July 1, 1846.*
Joanna, of Merrimack, N. H., and Cornet Josiah Fletcher, int. Feb. 26, 1820.
Job, jr., and Abigail Pierce of Billerica, at Billerica, Feb. 17, 1757.*
Joel, and Emeline Spalding of Peterborough, N. H., Apr. 15, 1838. [Mar. 21, 1839. int.]*
John, and Mary Barit, Feb. 6, 1705.
John, jr., and Lydia Ditson, Apr. 21, 1814.*
Jonathan, Capt., and Sally Dodge of New Boston, N. H., int. Feb. 13, 1819.
Joseph, and Mercy Jewell, Dec. 9, 1670.
Joseph, and Mary Chamberlain, Dec. 1, 1808.*
Joseph, and Mrs. Lucy Varnum [wid. int.], Mar. 28, 1816.*
Julia Ann, and Dr. John C. Dallon [Dalton. C. R. 1 and int.], Feb. 21, 1822.*
Leonora, of Cavendish, Vt., and Joseph Read, int. Oct. 17, 1830.
Lucinda [J. int.], and Micajah Bowers [of Lowell. int.], Dec. 3, 1835.*
Lucretia, and Richard Marshall [jr. int.], of Tyngsborough, May 14, 1840.*
Mary A., and Milo Pierce of Lowell, Nov. 3, 1842.*
Mary Amanda, of Carlisle, and Jeptha Parker, at Boston, Nov. 9, 1843.*
Nancy, and Frederic Remme, int. Oct. 5, 1823.
Noah, 2d, and Hannah Parker, int. Nov. 24, 1821.

*Intention also recorded.

SPALDING, Orpha, and [Capt. int.] William Fletcher, ——, 1813. [Mar. 23. C. R. 1.]*
Otis, and Elizabeth Adams, Feb. 2, 1815.*
Owen, and Eliza Wright of Woburn, int. Apr. 13, 1823.
Pamela, and Daniel Drew of Woburn, int. Sept. 21, 1842.
Phebe [Mrs., d. Andrew. C. R. 1.], and Benjamin P. Hutchins of Carlisle, Apr. 23, 1820.*
Polly [d. Andrew. C. R. 1.], and Dr. Asaph Byam of Westford, May 8, 1817.*
Prudence, and Lovel Fletcher, Apr. 18, 1819.*
Reb[e]cah, and David Perham, Apr. 19, 1809.*
Robert, and Joann Snow of Westford, int. June 25, 1820.
Rufus, and Harriet B. Hunt of Tewksbury, int. Mar. 10, 1822.
Rufus D., of Newport, N. H., and Elizabeth A. Dudley, int. Oct. 16, 1846.
Ruth, and Josiah K[ing. C. R. 1.] Parkhurst, June 2, 1822.*
Samuel, and Leafe Durant of Carlisle, at Carlisle, Jan. 21, 1790.*
Sarah, and Samuel Cummins [of Westford. int.], Dec. 1, 1741.*
Sarah, and John Laws of Billerica, at Billerica, Dec. 29, 1774.*
Sarah, and Samuel Perham, Nov. 3, 1808.*
Sherebiah, jr., and Lurena Augusta Shed of Lowell, Sept. 22, 1836.*
Simeon, jr., and Rhoda B. Hovey of Dracut, int. Apr. 16, 1816.
Simon [Simeon. int.], and Abigail Willson of Woburn, at Woburn, Nov. 13, 1751.*
Stillman, Dr. [of Lexington. int.], and Lucy Butterfield [d. Capt. J. C. R. 1.], May 13, 1819.*
Varnum, and Hannah McClary of Cambridge, int. Feb. 13, 1819.
Varnum, and Susan A. Butterfield of Lowell, int. Mar. 14, 1840.
Weld, and Charlotte Smith, int. Apr. 17, 1825.

SPARHAWK, Ester [Hester. CT. R.], and Samuell Adames, May 7, 1668.

SPARKES (see also Sparks), Frencess, and Richard Virgin of Rehoboth, May 1, 1696.

SPARKS (see also Sparkes), Henry, of Exeter, and Martha Barret, d. Thomas, July 10, 1676.

*Intention also recorded.

SPAULDEN (see also Spaulding), Eunice, and Joseph Perkis, 4: 9 br: 1686. CT. R.
Josiah, and Mary Fletcher of Westford, at Westford, July 2, 1733.

SPAULDING (see also Spalden, Spaldin, Spalding, Spaulden, Spauldyng, Spolding), Abel, and Mary Warren, Apr. 29, 1767.*
Abigail, and James Perkhust, int. Dec. 25, 1731.
Abigail, and Ebenezer Hadley [of Westford. int.], June 11, 1753.*
Abigail, and Nathan Carlton of Billerica, at Billerica, Nov. 5, 1776.*
Abigail, and Joseph Tyler, Jan. 10, 1779.
Abigal [of Carlisle. int.], and Nathaniel Tuttle, Feb. 27, 1788.*
Abijah, and Olive Pierce, Dec. 1, 1791.*
Almira, and Eri Spaulding, int. Feb. 15, 1835.
Andrew, and Abbigall Waring, Feb. 5, 1701.
Andrew, and Hannah Wright, int. Nov. 21, 1725.
Andrew, and Ruth Peirce, May 6, 1783.*
Andrew [a. 70 y. C. R. 1.], and wid. Rebecca McIntire [a. 50 y. C. R. 1.], Nov. 7, 1830.*
Anna [d. Lt. John. P. R. 4.], and Benjamin Fletcher, Oct. 21, 1779.*
Anna, and Thomas Warren, Dec. 20, 1803.*
Anna, and Samuel Perham, Jan. 8, 1805.*
Anna, and Thomas Grenville Flint, May 13, 1834.*
Asaph, and Betcy Tayler of Lancaster, int. Mar. 13, 1801.
Asaph, and Abiah Bowers of Dracut, int. Feb. 12, 1807.
Ashbill, of Ludlow, Vt., and Sarah Parker, int. Feb. 8, 1798.
Asher, of New Boston, N. H., and Polley Davis, int. Dec. 11, 1796.
Azeriah, and Lucy Barron, Sept. 24, 1782.*
Benjamin, of Plainfield, and Abigail Wright, int. Feb. 7, 1719-20. (Feb. 10, banns forbidden by Ephraim Hildreth, jr.)
Benjamin, and Mary Spaulding, May 16, 1764.*
Benjamin, and Patty Barrat, Nov. 29, 1764. [Nov. 27. P. R. 4.]*
Betsy, and Ens. William Pelsue, int. Sept. 15, 1804.
Betsy, and Levi Dunn of Stafford [Stoddard. int.], N. H., Nov. 30, 1834.*
Betty, and Samuel Shed [of Pepperell. int.], July 18, 1771.*

*Intention also recorded.

SPAULDING, Betty, and Samuel Stevens [jr. int.], Feb. 26, 1794. [Feb. 27. C. R. 1.]*
Bridget, and Benjamin Wyman, int. Sept. 18, 1726.
Bridget, and William Abbot, Dec. 28, 1769.*
Daniel, and Hannah Putnam, June 8, 1769.*
Deborah, of Westford, and John Swallow, int. Nov. 16, 1729.
Deborah, and Reuben Goold, Mar. 10, 1762.*
Dinah, and Eliazer Browne, Feb. 9, 1674.
Dorothy, and William Roby [of Dunstable, N. H. int.], Feb. 27, 1800.*
Ebenezer, and Eunis Jones of Boston, int. Dec. 29, 1800.
Eleazer, and Elizabeth Procter, Oct. 30, 1753.*
Elijah M., of Ludlow, Vt. [of "Ludon," Vt. int.], and Lucy Wright, Oct. 29, 1826.*
Elizabeth, and Ebenezer Harris, int. Nov. 13, 1720.
Elizabeth, and Samuel Chamberlin, int. Sept. 17, 1721.
Elizabeth, and Samuel Scripture of Groton, int. Feb. 6, 1723-4.
Elizabeth, and John Dutton, Jan. 14, 1779.
Ephraim, and Lydia Butterfield, int. Mar. 31, 1730.
Ephraim, of Fitchburg, and Lydia Spaulding, at Westford, Apr. 5, 1792.*
Ephraim, and Betsey Parkhurst, Mar. 15, 1837.*
Ephraim P., and Nancy B. Spaulding, int. Oct. 25, 1835.
Eri, and Almira Spaulding, int. Feb. 15, 1835.
Esther, and Jonas Prescott, int. Mar. 6, 1725-6.
Esther, and Jonathan Adams, June 8, 1769.*
Hannah, and Jonathan Hildreth, int. Dec. 5, 1725.
Hannah, and John Spaulding [jr. int.], Sept. 10, 1761.*
Hannah, and Benjamin Adams, Jan. 14, 1787.*
Hazadiah, and Moses Woods of Acton, at Westford, Apr. 16, 1793.*
Henry, and Elesebeth Lun, —— [1701 or 1702?].
Henry, and Mary Bloget, int. May 19, 1723.
Henry, and Lucy Procter, int. Dec. 5, 1725.
Henry, and Marah Adams, Apr. 27, 1743.*
Henry, and Susanna Richardson, Nov. 21, 1748.*
Henry [jr. int.], and Mary Fletcher [of Westford. int.], Nov. 17, 1774.*
Henry, 3d, and Lydia Proctor, at Westford, Dec. 22, 1791.*
Henry, and Jemima Spaulding, Mar. 1, 1801.*
Ira, and Joanna Fletcher [of Westford. int.], Oct. 19, 1795.*
Isaac, and Sarah Barit, int. Aug. 4, 1733.
Jacob, and Susanah Peirce, int. Dec. 5, 1725.
Jacob [jr. int.], and Elizabeth Fletcher, Apr. 24, 1753.*

*Intention also recorded.

SPAULDING, Jemima, and Henry Spaulding, Mar. 1, 1801.*
Jephthah, and Rebecca Barron, July 14, 1779.*
Jessa, and Nabba Adams of Jaffrey, int. Dec. 26, 1789.
Jesse, and Mary Senter [of Woburn. int.], July 4, 1776.*
Jesse, and Betcy Wood, int. Nov. 20, 1792.
Jesse, and Elizabeth Stevens, Nov. 17, 1796.*
Jesse, and Mary Parkhurst of Cavendish, Vt., int. Mar. 8, 1829.
Joanna, and Jonath[a]n Harwood, int. Apr. 3, 1731.
Joanna, and Jesse Frost, May 6, 1760.*
Joel, and Phebe Tylor [Tayler. CT. R.], Mar. 16, 1773.*
Joel, and Rebecca Corey, Apr. 25, 1791.*
John, and Phebe Keyes, int. Dec. 3, 1727.
John, Lt., and [Mrs. int.] Rachel Parker, Feb. 26, 1759.*
John [jr. int.], and Hannah Spaulding, Sept. 10, 1761.*
John [3d. int.], and Joanna Warren, Feb. 13, 1777.*
John, 3d, and Lucy Fletcher [of Westford. int.], Jan. 26, 1786.*
John [of Tewksbury. int.], and Mary Marshall, Nov. 23, 1801.*
John, Dea., and Mary Hutcherson of Carlisle, int. Nov. 20, 1802.
John, 3d, and Lydia Coombs of Vinalhaven, Me., int. Sept. 23, 1827.
Jonathan, and Sarah Richerdson, int. Jan. 15, 1731-2.
Jonathan, and Mary Fletcher, Mar. 21, 1754.*
Jonathan [3d. int.], and Mary Parker, Dec. 17, 1761.*
Jonathan [of Carlisle. int.], and Thankfull Emery, June 20, 1781.*
Jonathan, and Mary Ann Harwood, Apr. 29, 1831.*
Joseph, of Groton, and Mary Bates, int. Mar. 25, 1727.
Joseph, and Lydia Richardson, int. Jan. 24, 1756.
Joseph [of Pepperell. int.], and Phebe Spaulding, Dec. 29, 1761.*
Joseph [jr. int.], and Hannah Stearns of Billerica, at Billerica, May 4, 1779.*
Joseph, and Abigail Hodgman, Feb. 19, 1784.*
Joseph, and Betsey Wood of Dracut, at Dracut, Dec. 25, 1792.
Josiah [of Westford. int.], and Esther Adams, Nov. 25, 1760.*
Leonerd, and Elizebeth Durunt, int. Dec. 18, 1737.
Lidia, and Nathaniel Farrer, Jan. 1, 1805.*
Lot [of Hollis, N. H. int.], and Esther Butterfield, June 27, 1765.*

*Intention also recorded.

SPAULDING, Lucinda, and Charles H. Barber, Feb. 8, 1826. [Feb. 10. C. R. 1.]
Lucy [of Westford. int.], and Silos Peirce, Mar. 26, 1771.*
Lucy, and William Spaulding, at Concord, Apr. 6, 1780.*
Lucy, and Ebenezer Varnum of Tyngsborough [of Bedford. int.], at Tyngsborough, Nov. 29, 1792.*
Lucy, and John Elliot [of Boston. int.], Jan. 22, 1807.*
Lydia, and Robert Bates, Apr. 19, 1748.*
Lydia, and Simeon Blodget, Oct. 8, 1751.*
Lydia, and Aaron Parker, jr. of Westford, at Westford, June 3, 1766.*
Lydia, and Ephraim Spaulding of Fitchburg, at Westford, Apr. 5, 1792.*
Lydia, and Henry Parkhurst, Apr. 29, 1802.*
Lydia W., and Joseph R. Carr, ———. [Oct. 26, 1828. int.]*
Mary, and John Nutting of Groton, int. Mar. 31, 1727.
Mary, and Benjamin Spaulding, May 16, 1764.*
Mary, and Philip Parkhurst, Mar. 14, 1771.*
Mary, of Carlisle, and Joseph Warren, jr., at Carlisle, Feb. 27, 1794.*
Mary, and Samuel Herrick, Jan. 22, 1795.*
Mary, and John Perley [of Winchendon, int.], June 23, 1795.*
Mary, and Owen Emerson, Nov. 19, 1795.*
Mary, of Wilton, N. H., and Prescott Kimball, int. Mar. 23, 1828.
Mary, and Amos Shed, ———. [Nov. 2, 1828. int.]*
Mary [d. Henry, deceased. C. R. 1.], and Charles H. [N. C. R. 1.] Barber, Nov. 26, 1829.*
Mercy, and Simon Rumrell of Enfield, int. Oct. 22, 1722.
Micah, and Mary Chamberlain, Apr. 23, 1778.*
Molly, and William Frost of Billerica, at Billerica, June 14, 1775.*
Molly, and Jesse Stevens of Fitchburg, at Westford, Nov. 25, 1790.*
Molly, and Jonathan Winn, Feb. 8, 1798.*
Nancy B., and Ephraim P. Spaulding, int. Oct. 25, 1835.
Noah, and Anna Parker, Dec. 26, 1799.*
Olive, and Jonathan Harwood [jr. int.], Oct. 28, 1762.*
Olive, and Asa Manning of Billerica, int. May 20, 1803.
Patty, and Phinehas Wood of Dracut, int. Jan. 7, 1802.
Patty E., and Joseph E. Phillips, int. July 20, 1834.
Peter, and Lucy Richardson, Feb. 24, 1763.*
Phebe, and Thomas Bixby, int. May 7, 1743.

*Intention also recorded.

SPAULDING, Phebe, and Joseph Spaulding [of Pepperell. int.], Dec. 29, 1761.*
Phebe, and Samuel Davis, Nov. 8, 1798.*
Phebe, and Joseph Butterfield Varnum [of Dracut. int.], Dec. 28, 1800.*
Rachel, and John Minot, June 27, 1753.*
Rachel, of Billerica, and Jeremiah Warren, at Westford, Oct. 1, 1789.*
Rachil, and Benjamin Fletcher, Dec. 4, 1770.*
Rebecca, and Jonas Varnum [jr. of Pepperell. int.], Dec. 29, 1761.*
Rebeckah, of Billerica, and Jonas Addams, at Billerica, Aug. 4, 1740.
Rebeckah, and Joseph Warren, Mar. 29, 1785.*
Relief, and Henry Byam, Oct. 28, 1824.*
Robert, and Hasadiah Johnson of Southborough, int. Mar. 15, 1755.
Sally, and William Glood, Apr. 29, 1794.*
Sally, and Willard Fletcher [jr. of Westford. int.], Apr. 18, 1808.*
Sally [d. Job. C. R. 1.], and [Lt. C. R. 1.] Asa Hodgman [jr. int.], Jan. 28, 1824.*
Sally, and George W. Willson, Apr. 8, 1826.*
Sally, and Richard Messer, Nov. 19, 1829.*
Samuel, of Merrimack, and Sarah Woods, int. Mar. 17, 1753.
Sarah, and Henry Fletcher, Apr. 12, 1753.*
Sarah, and Jonathan Fletcher [jr. of Westford. int.], Jan. 22, 1761.*
Sarah, and Abijah Goold, Oct. 29, 1766.*
Sarah, and Timothy Howard, at Westford, July 15, 1788.*
Sarah, and Ira Chamberlin, int. Mar. 12, 1808.
Silas, and Sybil Pierce, June 8, 1775. [June 7. P. R. 4.]*
Simeon [jr. int.], and Olive Butterfild, Dec. 21, 1784.*
Sophia [of Dunstable, N. H. int.], and Timothy Fry, Dec. 12, 1823.*
Stephen, and Esther Richardson, Jan. 7, 1762.*
Stephen, and Betsy Fletcher, ——, 1806. [Jan. 9. C. R. 1.]*
Susanna, and Benjamin Butterfield [jr. int.] of Westford, at Westford, Sept. 26, 1748.*
Susanna, and Daniel Nichols [of Reading. int.], Dec. 1, 1760.*
Susanna, and Jacob Shed of Tewksbury, int. July 24, 1803.
Sybbel, and Artimas Parker, int. Jan. 3, 1807.
Sybil, and John Eaton, Apr. 26, 1774.*
Sydney, and Mary Brown, Apr. 21, 1831. C. R. 3.

*Intention also recorded.

SPAULDING, Thomas, and Mary Adams, int. Mar. 13, 1730-31.
Timothy, and Thankfull Prescot of Groton, int. May 15, 1726.
Timothy, and B[e]thyah Herick of Concord, int. Sept. 28, 1728.
Varnum, and Laura A[nn. int.] Dutton, Dec. 15, 1831.*
Willard, and Sarah Stearns of Billerica, at Billerica, Feb. 12, 1789.*
William, and Olive Wincoll, int. Nov. 9, 1729.
William, and Jane Martin of Tewksbury, int. Jan. 23, 1741-2.
William, and Lucy Spaulding, at Concord, Apr. 6, 1780.*
Zachariah, and Elizabeth Bloget, int. June 9, 1723.
Zachariah, and Rhoda Peirce, Feb. 9, 1802.*
Zebulon [jr. int.], and Lydia Wright [of Westford. int.], Feb. 12, 1767.*
Zebulon, jr., and Molly Stevens [Mears. int.], at Westford, Mar. 9, 1791.*
Zebulun, and Mary Fletcher, Nov. 21, 1771. [Oct. 21. p. r. 4.]*

SPAULDYNG (see also Spaulding), Hannah, and Samuell Butterfield, July 2, 1703.
John, and wid. Mary Fletcher, Nov. 18, 1700.
Joseph, and Elesibeth Colburn, Apr. 10, 1700.
Rachell, and Sam[ue]ll Butterfield, Dec. 7, 1703.

SPOFFORD, see Spafford.

SPOLDING (see also Spaulding), Sameuell, and Mary Butterfeeld, June 30, 1698.

SPRAGE (see also Sprague), Harriet, of Billerica, and Horatio Boyden, int. Mar. 17, 1822.

SPRAGUE (see also Sprage, Sprake), Betsy, of Malden, and Robert Foster, int. July 20, 1805.
David [of Sunderland. int.], and Jane [Jean. int.] Procter, Nov. 26, 1767.*
Nancy, of Concord, and John Vincent, int. Apr. 15, 1832.

SPRAKE (see also Sprague), John, of Charlestown, and Lucy Richerdson, int. Feb. 18, 1737-8.
John, jr., of Charlestown, and Lucy Richerdson, int. Apr. —, 1738.

*Intention also recorded.

SPRAKE, Mary, and Ransom Reed, Oct. 3, 1825.
Nicolas, of Billerica, and Eliza Burdge, int. Sept. 3, 1721.

SPRING, Mary [of Kittery. int.], and Rev. Hezekiah Packard, Nov. 23, 1796.*

STACEY, William, and Deborah Varnum, Nov. 11, 1762.*

STANDRING, Thomas H., widr., of Lowell, a. 39 y., finisher of flannels, s. James and Sarah, and Alice Achroyd, wid., of Dracut, a. 38 y., d. Isaac and Elizabeth Britton, Mar. 3, 1849. [Mar. 8. C. R. 3.]

STARK, George, of Bedford, N. H., and Mary G. Bowers, int. Oct. 26, 1848.

STARRET (see also Starrett), Sarah, of New Boston, N. H., and William Lamson, int. May 10, 1835.

STARRETT (see also Starret), Caroline, of New Boston, N. H., and Friderick Hirsch, int. Apr. 14, 1837.

STAUNTON, Simon F., and Clarissa A. Morrell of Gilmanton, N. H., int. Sept. 6, 1844.

STEARN (see also Stearns), Nancy, and Jonathan Wood of Billerica, int. Dec. 24, 1820.

STEARNS (see also Stearn, Sterns), Asahel, and Frances W[intworth. int.] Shepard, Apr. 23, 1801.*
Betty, see Stevens, Betty.
Hannah, of Billerica, and Joseph Spaulding [jr. int.], at Billerica, May 4, 1779.*
Mary, of Tewksbury, and Marshall Peirce, int. Aug. 13, 1815.
Paulina, of Carlisle, and Benjamin Shurtliff, Mar. 22, 1841.*
Sarah, of Billerica, and Willard Spaulding, at Billerica, Feb. 12, 1789.*
Sophia, of Waltham, and Stephen Morse, int. Sept. 1, 1823.
Thomas, of Littleton, and Mary Emery, int. Sept. 2, 1750.

STEDMAN, Jonathan [of Cambridge. int.], and Mary Blaisdell, June 10, 1742.*

*Intention also recorded.

STEELE, Sabrina, of Dunstable, N. H., and Hiram Kimball, at Tyngsborough, July 30, 1835.

STEEVENS (see also Stevens), John, and Sarah Snow of Woburn, Jan. 17, 1692-3. CT. R.
Thankfull, and George Robins of Harvard, int. Dec. 25, 1734.

STEPHENS (see also Stevens), John, and Elizabeth Hilldereth, Dec. 15, 1664.
Marie, and John Wrighte, Apr. 13, 1692.

STERNS (see also Stearns), David, and Charlotte Levingston, int. Sept. 29, 1822.
John, and Lydia Crosby of Carlisle, at Westford, Aug. 27, 1789.*
Mary, of Billerica, and Samuell Barron, May 28, 1705.

STETSON, Almira, of Waltham, and Francis Winch, int. Oct. 31, 1824.
Zenas, and Martha Melvin, Oct. 30, 1835.*

STEVENS (see also Steevens, Stephens), Abel, and Betcy Putnam, int. Nov. 24, 1801.
Abel, and Lucy W. Fletcher, both of Westford, June 22, 1828.
Almaria, and Joseph Bowers of Lowell, int. Nov. 6, 1830.
Asa, and Harriet Chamberlin of Westford, Apr. 23, 1832.*
Benjamin, and Hannah Parker, at Westford, June 1, 1797.*
Betty [Stearns, of Billerica. int.], and David Walker, June 27, 1785.*
Bill Wright, and Phebe Gould, at Westford, Nov. 29, 1792.*
Caleb, and Elisabeth Willson of Billerica, at Billerica, Dec. 1, 1768.*
Daniel, and Phebe Durant, Dec. 12, 1765.*
Daniel S., of South Reading, a. 21 y., carpenter, s. Jonathan and Sare, and Nancy P. Craine of South Reading, a. 23 y., d. James and Lydia, Oct. 5, 1848.
Deborah, and Ephraim Farnworth of Groton, int. Apr. 11, 1725.
Deborah, and Samuel Fletcher, June 24, 1761.*
Deborah, and Oliver Pierce [jr. int.], Dec. 21, 1769.*
Deleverance, and Ebenezer Wright of Westford, at Westford, May 25, 1730.*
Deliverance, and Paul Fletcher, at Charlestown, Apr. 12, 1705.
Edmond, and Susan Prentis of Lexington, int. Feb. 24, 1822.

*Intention also recorded.

STEVENS, Elizabeth, and Joseph Chamberlain, int. Nov. 8, 1719.
Elizabeth, and Nathaniel Richardson of Townsend, at Townsend, Sept. 15, 1738.
Elizabeth, and Jesse Spaulding, Nov. 17, 1796.*
Foster, and Candace French of Southwick, int. Dec. 12, 1824.
George, and Louiza E. Williams of Pepperell, int. July 4, 1824.
Hannah, and Obadiah Parker, int. Dec. 26, 1724.
Hannah, and Joel Crosby [of Ipswich, N. H. int.], Mar. 30, 1763.*
Hannah [of Dunstable. int.], and Nathaniel Howard, Mar. 29, 1798.*
Harriet, and Charles C. Smith of Boston, int. Sept. 7, 1834.
Henry, and Deborah Bidgby, int. June 15, 1724.
Isaac [of Richmond, Va. int.], and Sally Davis, Sept. 11, 1803.*
Jabez [of Lowell. int.], and Surviah [M. int.] Parkhurst, Aug. 23, 1831.*
James, and Martha Barron of Dracut, int. Feb. 15, 1817.
Jesse, of Fitchburg, and Molly Spaulding, at Westford, Nov. 25, 1790.*
Joanna, and David Fletcher [jr. of Westford. int.], Nov. 17, 1774.*
Joanna [Mrs., of the factory. C. R. 1; of Tewksbury. int.], and Humphry Webster, Feb. 15, 1824.*
John [of Wilton, N. H. int.], and Sarah Peirce, Feb. 15, 1770.*
Jonathan, and Thankful Foster, Dec. 30, 1777.*
Joseph, and Harriot P. [F. int.] Richardson of Lowell, June 4, 1834.*
Jotham M., and Dorinda Moore, int. Dec. 21, 1834.
Lydia, and Samuel Searls [of Dunstable, N. H. int.], Sept. 16, 1755.*
Marianne, of Mount Vernon, N. H., and Rufus Harwood, int. Feb. 4, 1843.
Molly [Mears. int.], and Zebulon Spaulding, jr., at Westford, Mar. 9, 1791.*
Nathaniel, of Andover, and Harriot Hale, d. Moses, Nov. 7, 1815.*
Phebe, and Foster Bradley, Feb. 14, 1810.*
Prudence, and Zachariah Hardy of Tewksbury, int. Jan. 27, 1750-51.
Rachel, and Josiah Parkhurst, at Westford, May 3, 1792.*
Rachel, and Edward [L. C. R. 1.] Tyler, Apr. 26, 1832.
Richard, and Hannah Hald, Nov. 15, 1699.

*Intention also recorded.

STEVENS, Ruth, and Obadiah Parker [jr. of Groton. int.], Oct. 17, 1752.*
Ruth, and Joseph Richardson of Fitchburg, at Westford, Feb. 14, 1791.*
Salla, and Joel Clark of Stanstead, Lower Canada, int. Nov. 26, 1820.
Sampson, and Phebe Barker, May 24, 1791.*
Samson, and Polly Woods of Acton, int. May 3, 1817.
Samuel, and Ruth Wright of Westford, at Westford, Mar. 4, 1731.*
Samuel [jr. int.], and Tabitha Parker, Jan. 15, 1761.*
Samuel [jr. int.], and Betty Spaulding, Feb. 26, 1794. [Feb. 27. C. R. 1.]*
Samuel S., of Gardner, and Martha Osgood of Westford, Nov. 16, 1830.
Sarah, and [J]onathan Barrett [torn] 17, [1676.?].
Sarah, and John Snow of Woburn, Feb. 13, 1693-4. CT. R.
Sarah, and Nathan Cross of Dunstable, int. Oct. 15, 1727.
Sarah, and Thomas Brown of Billerica, int. Sept. 13, 1774.
Simeon, and Joanna Harwood, Feb. 22, 1757.*
Simeon, and Elizabeth Wright, July 19, 1764.*
Susan [d. Sampson, deceased. C. R. 1.], and Ezekiel C. Wright of Westford, Mar. 8, 1821.*
Sybel, and Jesse Wright of Westford, int. Dec. 2, 1827.

STICKLEMIRE, George L., and Harriot Woods of Groton, int. Nov. 21, 1830.

STICKNEY, Nabby, of Tewksbury, and G[e]org Melven, int. Oct. 9, 1793.

STOCKBRIDGE, Sarah A., and Robert Monteeth, both of Lowell, Mar. 5, 1848. C. R. 3.

STODDARD, Margrit, Mrs., and Rev. Samuel Hopkings of Hadley, int. Sept. 14, 1776.
Sampson, Rev., and Mrs. Margarett Halkertson of Boston, int. Jan. 1, 1726-7.
Sampson, Maj., and Mrs. Margarett Vryling of Boston, int. Sept. 29, 1744.
Sampson, jr., and Jemima White, "probably of Boston," [of Boston. int.], at Boston, Sept. 20, 1772.*
Sarah, Mrs., and Rev. Ebenezer Bridge, int. Oct. 24, 1741.
Sarah, and Levi Wilder [of Lancaster. int.], Aug. 26, 1779.*

*Intention also recorded.

STOKES, Isaac [of Boston. int.], and Mary Barron, Aug. 2, 1779.*

STONE, Joshua [of Concord. int.], and Sally Avery, Nov. 26, 1789.*
Mary, of Harvard, and Center Dunn, int. Apr. 2, 1836.

STOW, Joseph [of Concord. int.], and Catharine Huston, Dec. 3, 1778.*

STRATON (see also Stratton), Margerit, and Moses Perker, int. Aug. 3, 1728.

STRATTON (see also Straton), Ickabod, and Elizabeth Heldreth, Oct. 13, 1709.
Margrett, and Jonas Whetney of Stow, int. Mar. 13, 1725-6.
Mary, and Joseph Adams, int. Sept. 18, 1720.
Mary Jane, a. 26 y., d. Barnard and Charlotte, and John B. Emerson, widr., of Lowell, a. 28 y., laborer, Sept. 29, 1845.*
Richard, and Naomi Lovejoy of Andover, Jan. 6, 1686. CT. R.
Ruth, and Jacob Warrin, int. Feb. 11, 1721-2.
Susanna, of Concord, and Moses Keyes, at Concord, July 4, 1718.

SULLIVAN, Margaret, and John McCoy, int. May 26, 1845.

SUMNER, Geo[rge] W., widr., of Hill, N. H., a. 56 y., farmer, s. George and Lydia, and Abigail Pratt, wid., of Greenfield, N. H., a. 45 y., d. Samuel and Katy Straw, Sept. 17, 1848.
Mary Ann, of Spencer, and Eli Brown, int. Sept. 19, 1825.

SWALLOW (see also Swalow), Ambrose, and Sarah Barret, at Woburn, Dec. 8, 1696.
Elizabeth, and Benjamin Wood [of Carlisle. int.], Apr. 10, 1755.*
Hannah, and Samuel Wilson [of Concord. int.], Jan. 17, 1754.*
John, and Anna Barrett, Jan. 3, 1692-3. CT. R.
John, and Deborah Spaulding of Westford, int. Nov. 16, 1729.
Mahala, and Ira Spalding, jr., Nov. 3, 1823.*
Phebe, and David Parker [of Billerica. int.], Oct. 4, 1764.*
Sarai, and Ebenezer Hildrith, int. Dec. 13, 1719.

*Intention also recorded.

CHELMSFORD MARRIAGES 333

SWALOW (see also Swallow), Jonathan, and Hanah Cory, int. Aug. 10, 1728.

SWAN, Mary, of Tyngsborough, and Zimri Kidder, int. Oct. 10, 1824.

SWEET (see also Swett), John, and Jane Hunt of Lowell, int. Apr. 25, 1830.
Susan, of Newburyport, and John Jewett, int. Jan. 8, 1826.

SWEETSER, Charles, and Mary Adams, int. June 24, 1843.
Elias, and Mary Adams, ———, 1811. [Feb. 27. c. r. 1.]*
Nathaniel, and Hannah Parker, Sept. 20, 1835.*
Sarah, of Westford, and Eldad P. Bean, at Westford, Nov. 28, 1839.*
William, of Lowell, and Mrs. Abigail Moody, int. June 28, 1835.

SWETMAN, Thomas, and Mary Procter, int. July 9, 1721.

SWETT (see also Sweet), Charles, and Ann Babcock, Sept. 3, 1829.*
David, and Sally Noyes of Amherst, N. H., int. Aug. 15, 1845.
Edmand, and Betsy Lovejoy of Amherst, N. H., int. Feb. 8, 1824.
Edmund, and Elizabeth Tyler, Aug. 12, 1841.*
John, and Mary Hunt, int. June 9, 1837.

SYFFERMANN, Charles F., of Malden, and Catharine M. Putfark, int. Oct. 1, 1844.

TAFT, Philip, and Mary Wheelock of Cumberland, R. I., int. May 3, 1836.

TALOR (see also Taylor), Abraham, of Concord, and Lucy Burge, int. July 4, 1772.

TASKER, Mary Eliza, of Loudon, N. H., and Moses Edwards, Apr. 19, 1843.*

TAY, Benj[amin], [of Salem. int.], and Hannah Larkom, Apr. 13, 1830.*

*Intention also recorded.

CHELMSFORD MARRIAGES

TAYLER (see also Taylor), Betcy, of Lancaster, and Asaph Spaulding, int. Mar. 13, 1801.
Hannah, of Dunstable, and James Bowers, int. Nov. 23, 1823.
Lucy, and Samuel Brown, July 23, 1798.*
Peter, and Joanna Chamberlin, Sept. 18, 1807.*
Robert [of Tewksbury. int.], and Rebecca Davis, Oct. 17, 1786.*

TAYLOR (see also Talor, Tayler), Amos [of Walpole, N. H. int.], and Dorothy Hutchins, Feb. 19, 1778.*
Daniel [jr., of Townsend. int.], and Lydia Burge, Feb. 4, 1756.*
Elisabeth, and Oliver Farrer, Nov. 26, 1807.*
Harriett E., of Carlisle, and Alfred Proctor, int. Aug. 22, 1846.
Isaac, and Sarah Parkhurst of Dunstable, Nov. 21, 1776.
James, and Desiah Relph, Oct. 26, 1828.
Mary, of Concord, and Joseph Barrett, at Concord, Mar. 24, 1714.
Nathaniel, of Concord, and Esther Burge, at Concord, Jan. 20, 1762.*
Sarah, of Concord, and John Burge, at Concord, June 27, 1717.
Sybil, of Dunstable, and Isaac Wright, Oct. 3, 1776.

TEMPLE, John [of Acton. int.], and Sarah Hutchins, Apr. 21, 1756.*
Joseph [of Westford. int.], and Sarah Makiney, at Concord, June 6, 1744.*
Samuel, and Hannah Glezen of Upton, int. Sept. 25, 1751.

TEMPLETON, Charles M., and Mary Jane Marden of Concord, N. H., int. May 10, 1845.

THARE, Triall, d. Sidrack, of Braintree, and John Burge, Sept. 19, 1677.

THOMAS, Eunice [of Middleton. int.], and John Tucker, Oct. 28, 1746.*
Eunice, and Asa Moar [of Andover. int.], Apr. 23, 1765.*
Marcus, and Rebecca Ramsdill of Hanson, int. July 14, 1833.

THOMPSON (see also Thomson, Tomson), Ann S., and Thaddeus W. Hunt, at Marlborough, Jan. 3, 1838.*
Ezra, and Elizabeth Bancroft of Dunstable, June 19, 1755.
Luke, and Betsey Chamberlin, d. Capt. Isaac, Nov. 16, 1815.*

*Intention also recorded.

CHELMSFORD MARRIAGES 335

THOMSON (see also Thompson), William, and Mary Fasset of Westford, at Westford, Jan. 18, 1743.*

THORNDICK (see also Thorndike), Judith, of Tewksbury, and Amos Martin, int. May 12, 1775.

THORNDICKE (see also Thorndike), Joannah, of Tewksbury, and Simeon Moores, int. Nov. 29, 1755.

THORNDIKE (see also Thorndick, Thorndicke), Emily L., and Nathan Witherell of Grand Isle, Vt., Feb. 18, 1838. [Feb. 2, 1839. int.]*
Hezekiah, and Abigail Chamberlain, June 1, 1779.*
Thankful, and Nathan Jaques of Tewksbury, June 25, 1818.*

THURLOW, Fanny, and Jonas R. Proctor, jr., int. Mar. 3, 1840.

TILLSON, Elisha W., and Almira K. Turner of Pembroke, int. Feb. 1, 1829.

TITTLE, Sophia, of Beverly, and Levi T. Prescott, int. Aug. 3, 1823.

TODD, Jane, and Abel Simonds, int. Aug. 12, 1830.
Lucia, of Rindge, N. H., and Joshua Hunt, jr., int. Dec. 29, 1822.
Mersylvia, of New Ipswich, N. H., and John T. Farwell, int. Jan. 24, 1830.

TOMSON (see also Thompson), Thomas, of Woburn, and Hannah Butterfield, Dec. 12, 1700.

TOOTHAKER, Charles, Dr., and Eliza Perry of Methuen, int. Dec. 13, 1841.
Harriett N., and James P. Appleton of Fitchburg, int. Oct. 2, 1846.
Sarah, and Jonathan Whittaker, at Boston, Nov. 15, 1694.

TORREY (see also Torroy), John T., and Maria Watriss of Easton, int. May 24, 1829.
Joseph G., and Nancy Caryl, Jan. 12, 1843.*

*Intention also recorded.

TORROY (see also Torrey), Caleb, and Sarah Briggs, both residents in Chelmsford, int. Sept. 9, 1801.

TOWNSEND, Ebenezer, jr., of Billerica, and Betty Power, int. Dec. 2, 1750.
Elizabeth [of Billerica. int.], and Jonas Keyes, Apr. 21, 1756.*
Rebeckah, of Billerica, and Ephraim Keyes, at Billerica, July 11, 1751.*
Sarah, of Amesbury, a. 22 y., d. W[illia]m and Sarah, of Amesbury, and Thomas Hall of Salisbury, a. 22 y., wool sorter, s. Thomas and Lucy, of Farnumsville, May 10, 1847.

TREAT, Eliza P., of Waltham, and Daniel Sanderson, int. July 31, 1825.

TROUGH, Martha D., of Mount Vernon, N. H., and Stowell Bancroft, int. June 12, 1825.

TRULL, Ama, and Asa Proctor, at Dracut, Apr. 23, 1793.*
Molley, and Robert Peirce [jr. int.], Feb. 21, 1781.*
Olive, of Billerica, and Ebenezer Frost [jr. int.], at Billerica, Apr. 15, 1794.*
Phebe, and Stephen Peirce, 3d, Dec. 25, 1787.*
Rhoda, of Billerica, and Asa Frost, at Billerica, July 25, 1790.*

TUCK, Daniel, and Mary Ann Kidder of Tyngsborough, int. Feb. 15, 1818.
Daniel [Lt. int.], and Betsy Pierce, Feb. 13, 1823.*

TUCKER, Benjamin S., and Mrs. Rebecca Adams, Apr. 18, 1838. c. r. 1.*
John, and Mary Downing of Boston, int. Aug. 9, 1746.
John, and Eunice Thomas [of Middleton. int.], Oct. 28, 1746.*
Mary, and Andrew Battyes, Dec. 24, 1739.*

TURNER, Almira K., of Pembroke, and Elisha W. Tillson, int. Feb. 1, 1829.
Charlotte, of Walpole, and James K. Fletcher, int. Sept. 19, 1825.
John, and Julia Snow of Lowell, int. Sept. 13, 1835.

TUTTEL (see also Tuttle), Mary, and William Kimball, Apr. 10, 1796.*

*Intention also recorded.

TUTTLE (see also Tuttel), George F., and Lucy Ann Kendall of Tyngsborough, at Tyngsborough, Jan. 4, 1839.*
Margret, of Littleton, and Aquila Underwood, int. Feb. 3, 1721-2.
Mehitable, and Capt. Stephen Blood of Carlisle, at Carlisle, May 10, 1798.*
Nathaniel, and Abigal Spaulding [of Carlisle. int.], Feb. 27, 1788.*
Sally, and Jonathan Wilson, ——, 1805. [Nov. 28. C. R. 1.]*

TWISS (see also Twist), Benjamin, and Abigail Russel of Bow, N. H., int. Oct. 11, 1794.

TWIST (see also Twiss), Benjamin, and Phebe Heald [Hale. int.] of Westford, at Westford, Apr. 17, 1792.*

TYLER (see also Tylor), Edward [L. C. R. 1.], and Rachel Stevens, Apr. 26, 1832.
Elizabeth, and Edmund Swett, Aug. 12, 1841.*
Fanny, and Lucius Whipple of Lowell, Apr. 3, 1828.*
Ignatius, and Mary Lund of Milford, N. H., int. Nov. 10, 1833.
Jonathan, Lt., s. Nathan, and Sivil S. [Sybil. C. R. 1.] Butterfield, d. Capt. Benjamin, Apr. 4, 1816.*
Joseph, and Abigail Spaulding, Jan. 10, 1779.
Lucy, Mrs., of Dunstable [grandd. Judge Tyng. P. R. 4.], and Dr. Samuel Whitwell of Boston, Nov. 11, 1783.
Moses, s. Joseph, of Tewksbury, and Lydia Hale, d. Moses, Dec. 26, 1815.*
Nathan, and Polly Wood, at Dracut, July 31, 1788.*
Nathan, and Mary Ann Perham, int. Nov. 3, 1838.
Phebe [Mrs. int.], and Nathan Ames, Oct. 28, 1797.*
Philip [of Tewksbury. int.], and Nancy Hunting, May 3, 1821.*
William, and Mary Ann Butterfield, int. Nov. 29, 1848.

TYLOR (see also Tyler), Phebe [Tayler. CT. R.], and Joel Spaulding, Mar. 16, 1773.*

TYNG, Mary, Mrs., of Dunstable, and Hon. John Pitts of Boston, June 3, 1779.
Rebecca, Mrs., of Dunstable, and John Lowell of Boston, Jan. 27, 1778.
Sarah, Mrs., of Dunstable, and John Winslow of Boston, Sept. 4, 1760.
William, of Dunstable, and Lucy Clark, Sept. 19, 1700.

*Intention also recorded.

UNDERWAD (see also Underwood), Pricillah, and Edward Spalden, July 6, 1663.

UNDERWOD (see also Underwood), Elisabeth, of Watertown, and Arthur Crouch, 21: 3 m: 168[2. dup.].
Sarah, d. William, and Daniell Bloggett, Mar. 10, 1669.
William, and Ann Kidder of Billerica, Mar. 17, 1684-5.

UNDERWOOD (see also Underwad, Underwod), Abigal, and Joel Esterbrook of Westford, int. Feb. 6, 1778.
Aquila, and Margret Tuttle of Littleton, int. Feb. 3, 1721-2.
Asa, and Elizabeth Littlehale of Dunstable, May 15, 1777.
Asa, and Ann Eliza Bradt [of the glass factory. C. R. 1.], Feb. 15, 1822.*
Deborah, and Nathaniel Butterfeild, Dec. 31, 1668. CT. R.
John W., and Mrs. Mary Farr, June 12, 1825.*
Phineas, and Rebeckah Dunn, int. Jan. 10, 1777.
Rememberans, and Josiah Richeson, at Concord, June 6, 1659.

UPHAM, Ezra Abbott, and Elmira Morse of Lowell, int. Mar. 12, 1836.

UPTON, Rachel, and Thomas Grant, "a Transient person" [resident of Massachusetts. int.], at Dracut, Mar. 20, 1786.*
Sarah Whittemore, of Dunstable, and Abiel Hosmer, int. Nov. 29, 1835.

USHER, Elisabeth, and John Salendin, Apr. 4, 1679.
Robert, and Sarah Blanchard, both of Dunstable, Jan. 23, 1693-4. CT. R.

VAN DOORN, Abraham, and Eliza Proctor, int. Sept. 19, 1824.

VARNAM (see also Varnum), Hannah, d. Samuell, and [Ezra. dup.] Coborn [Colburn. dup.], s. Edward, 22: 9 m: 1681.

VARNUM (see also Varnam, Vernun), Bradley, and Julia Ansert of Dracut, int. Dec. 13, 1806.
Darkes, and Phinehas Chamberlin [of Bedford. int.], Feb. 21, 1797.*
Deborah, and William Stacey, Nov. 11, 1762.*
Ebenezer, of Tyngsborough [of Bedford. int.], and Lucy Spaulding, at Tyngsborough, Nov. 29, 1792.*

*Intention also recorded.

CHELMSFORD MARRIAGES

VARNUM, Elizabeth, of Dracut, and Lt. Cyrus Baldwin, at Dracut, Apr. 28, 1799.*
Hannah E., of Dracut, and Albert Viles, int. Jan. 29, 1847.
Jonas [jr., of Pepperell. int.], and Rebecca Spaulding, Dec. 29, 1761.*
Joseph, Col., of Dracut, and Mrs. Mary Barron, int. Dec. 17, 1743.
Joseph B., of Newbury, and Caroline Howard of Dracut, Nov. 17, 1846. C. R. 3.
Joseph Butterfield [of Dracut. int.], and Phebe Spaulding, Dec. 28, 1800.*
Lucy, Mrs. [wid. int.], and Joseph Spalding, Mar. 28, 1816.*
Naoma, and Josiah Ditson, Mar. 30, 1809.*
Persis A., of Dracut, and Moses B. Fisher, int. Mar. 3, 1843.
Polly, of Dracut, and Jonathan Fletcher, int. Nov. 29, 1809.
Rachel, of Dracut, and Jacob Howard, jr., at Dracut, May 1, 1796.*
Sally, and William Moor [of Charlestown. int.], Oct. 20, 1799.*
Sarah, d. Samuel, and John Hobson, at Rowley, Dec. 4, 1679.
Susan H., and James Whittemore, Oct. 28, 1841.*

VERNUN (see also Varnum), Hannah [of Dracut. int.], and Phinehas Whiting, Feb. 5, 1795.*

VICKERS, Irene, of Fall River, and Silas Williams, int. Oct. 16, 1847.

VILES, Albert, and Hannah E. Varnum of Dracut, int. Jan. 29, 1847.

VINCENT, John, and Nancy Glood, ——, 1812. [June 10. C. R. 1.]*
John, and Nancy Sprague of Concord, int. Apr. 15, 1832.
Mary, and Euclyd Rice, int. Mar. 14, 1835.
Sarah Ann, and Darius Hall, July 4, 1830.*

VINTON, Horace, of Oxford, and Savina Durgin, int. Apr. 25, 1841.

VIRGIN, Richard, of Rehoboth, and Frencess Sparkes, May 1, 1696.

VRYLING, Margarett, Mrs., of Boston, and Maj. Sampson Stoddard, int. Sept. 29, 1744.

*Intention also recorded.

WADDELL (see also Wattell), John, and Mare Goole, Dec. 25, 1[66 T. C.]6.

WAIT, Daniel S., and Sarah Ross of Lowell, Sept. 17, 1843.*
Elutheria W., and David Perham, jr., at Boston, Apr. 28, 1839. P. R. 15.

WALDO (see also Walldo, Walldow), Rabacah, and Edward Emerson, Jan. 27, 1697-8.

WALKER (see also Wallker), Abiel, and Samuel Fitch [of Acton. int.], Apr. 23, 1778.*
Benjamin [of Fitchburg. int.], and Esther Peirce, Jan. 25, 1786.*
Betsy, and Joel Hosmer [of Wilmington, Vt. int.], ——, 1813. [Feb. 13. C. R. 1.]*
David, and Betty Stevens [Stearns of Billerica. int.], June 27, 1785.*
Elizabath, and Isaac Parker, Mar. 15, 1770.*
Ephraim, and Martha Manning, Jan. 4, 1801.
Lydia, and Benjamin Hodgman [of Concord. int.], Nov. 24, 1743.*
Martha, and William Blanchard of Hollis, N. H., int. July 20, 1751.
Susanna, and Joseph Marshall, June 24, 1766.*
Thankful, of Carlisle, and Simeon Parker, at Carlisle, Nov. 29, 1789.*
Zacheus [Zechariah. C. R. 1 and int.], and Martha Barrat, Dec. 23, 1741.*
Zacheus, and Patty Danforth, Oct. 29, 1771.*

WALLACE, Cranmore, and Juliet Farwell of Washington, N. H., int. Apr. 30, 1827.

WALLDO (see also Waldo), John, s. Cornelias, and Rebeckah Adams, d. Samuell, Mar. —, 16[torn. 1673-4?].

WALLDOW (see also Waldo), Daniell, and Susannah Adames, 20: 9 m: 1683.

WALLKER (see also Walker), Abigil, and Ebenezer Barit, int. Sept. 14, 1728.
Thankfull, and Joseph Foster, int. Apr. 21, 1733.

*Intention also recorded.

WARD, Delia G., a. 23 y., operative, d. Aaron and Sally, and John L. Davis, a. 23 y., scythe maker, s. James and Betsey, July 15, 1845.*
Margaret, of Wenham, and Paul Raymond, at Wenham, Mar. 5, 1758.*
Marget, and James Heldereth, at Dorchester, June 1, 1659.

WARE, Benj[ami]n B., of Franklin, a. 23 y., manufacturer, s. W[illia]m and Betsey, and Sally Drake, a. 23 y., d. Jona[than] and Hannah, Nov. 13, 1844.*

WARIN (see also Warren), Abigall, and John Wright, May 10, 1661.
Arther, and Abigal Rogers [torn. 1667?].
Thomas, and Rebeckah Chase of Littleton, int. —— [1735 or 1736].

WARING (see also Warren), Abbigall, and Andrew Spaulding, Feb. 5, 1701.

WARN, Mary, and Isaiah Davis, int. Dec. 27, 1817.

WARNER, Elias, of Harvard, and Mrs. Caroline Ann Leach, int. Sept. 12, 1845.
Louisa, Mrs., of Harvard, and James M. Emerson, int. Nov. 22, 1843.

WARREN (see also Warin, Waring, Warrin, Worin), Addeline, and Roswell Douglass, May 26, 1831.
Alonzo L., and Lydia Richardson, int. Sept. 25, 1837.
Ann [d. Isaac. c. r. 1.], and David Fletcher [of Westford. int.], Dec. 2, 1819.*
Benjamin, and Isabella Farmer [of Billerica. int.], Jan. 10, 1754.*
Betsy, and Sylvester Durent, ——, 1806. [Feb. 27. c. r. 1.]*
David, and Lydia K. Adams of Lowell, int. July 1, 1832.
Elizabeth, and Benjamin Parkhurst, Jan. 12, 1764.*
Elizebeth, and Nathaniel Blodget, July 17, 1695.
Ephraim [jr. int.], and Mary Parker, Aug. 7, 1755.*
Ephraim, and Esther Carlton [of Billerica. int.], Oct. 25, 1821. p. r. 7.*
Eunice Smith, of Plymouth, and Rufus Melvin, int. Sept. 5, 1824.
Ezra, and Mary Ann Pitts [of Cambridge. int.], Jan. 6, 1825.*

*Intention also recorded.

WARREN, Fanny, d. Joseph, deceased, and Jesse Smith, trader, Nov. 22, 1815.*
Isaac, and Lydia Adams, May 20, 1762.*
Isaac, jr., and Sally [Anny. int.; Anna. C. R. 1.] Lamson, July 28, 1799.*
Jeduthan, and Joanna Moors, July 22, 1779.*
Jeremiah, and Rachel Spaulding of Billerica, at Westford, Oct. 1, 1789.*
Joanna, and John Spaulding [3d. int.], Feb. 13, 1777.*
Joanna, and Daniel Emerson of Lexington, Apr. 10, 1814.*
John, and Eleziabeth Howard, int. Feb. 23, 1739.
Joseph [jr. int.], and Joanna Fletcher, Apr. 15, 1752.*
Joseph [jr. int.], and [Mrs. int.] Sarah Osgood of Billerica, at Billerica, Feb. 23, 1769.*
Joseph, and Rebeckah Spaulding, Mar. 29, 1785.*
Joseph, jr., and Mary Spaulding of Carlisle, at Carlisle, Feb. 27, 1794.*
Joseph, jr., and Martha Carlton of Billerica, Feb. 25, 1836.*
Lydia, and Josiah Richardson, Dec. 2, 1761. [Dec. 1. P. R. 4.]*
Mary, of Littleton, and Jacob Chamberlin, int. Mar. 29, 1755.
Mary, and Abel Spaulding, Apr. 29, 1767.*
Mary [d. Joseph. C. R. 1.], and [Capt. int.] Amos Spalding, Sept. 9, 1819.*
Polly, and Henry Spaulding Parker, Aug. 12, 1798.*
Rebecca, and Aaron Mansor [of Pembroke. int.], Dec. 29, 1807.*
Ruth, and Joseph Emerson, Apr. 26, 1774.*
Sally, and Ephraim Parker, jr. of Dracut, int. Dec. 19, 1803.
Sarah, and Zachariah Richardson, Apr. 22, 1755.*
Sybil, and Ephraim Parker, Dec. 23, 1762.*
Tabitha, and Josiah Burge [of Townsend. int.], Feb. 7, 1751. [1750-51. P. R. 4.]*
Tabitha, and Joseph Parker, May 13, 1783.*
Thomas, and Esther Adams, int. May 8, 1725.
Thomas, and Anna Spaulding, Dec. 20, 1803.*

WARRIN (see also Warren), Elizabeth, and Benjamin Parker, int. Feb. 18, 1721-2.
Jacob, and Mary Hilldereth, June 21, 1667.
Jacob, and Ruth Stratton, int. Feb. 11, 1721-2.
Joseph, and Tabitha Parker, int. Feb. 18, 1721-2.

WATERS (see also Watriss), Samuel A. [of Millbury. int.], and Sarah E. Reed, Dec. 5, 1838.*

*Intention also recorded.

CHELMSFORD MARRIAGES 343

WATERS, Samuel Austin, and Mary Ann Holman of Douglass, int. Nov. 2, 1834.

WATKINS, John W., and Nancy Dodge of Groton, int. Dec. 19, 1830.

WATRISS (see also Waters), Maria, of Easton, and John T. Torrey, int. May 24, 1829.

WATSON, Charles G., of Somersworth, N. H., and Phebe C. Knowles, int. Nov. 8, 1845.
Jonas M., and Mary L. Clifford, int. Dec. 21, 1844.

WATTELL (see also Waddell), Mary, d. John, and John Parise of Groton, Dec. 29, 1685.

WAY, Genett, and Charles Proctor, int. Feb. 17, 1838.

WEAVER (see also Wever), Charles, and Mary A. McIntire of Lowell, int. July 30, 1846.
Louisa, and George M. Eabert, int. Oct. 10, 1843.
Naomi, and William Robinson Evers, int. Dec. 18, 1848.

WEB (see also Webb), Sam[ue]ll, of Braintree, and Mary Adams, Dec. 16, 1686. CT. R.

WEBB (see also Web), Jeremiah B., and Mariah B. March of Londonderry, N. H., int. Sept. 14, 1834.

WEBBER, Betsy, and Samuel Adams, jr., int. Dec. 8, 1805.
Eliza, of Lowell, and John Chase, int. Apr. 15, 1827.
Lucy, and Soloman Manning, ——, 1812. [Aug. 11. C. R. 1.]*
Lucy Ann, of Westford, and William Richardson, Oct. 8, 1829.*
Stephen, and Hannah Hodgman, Nov. 28, 1825.*

WEBSTER, Abel, and Lydia Canfield, both of Lowell, July 28, 1839. C. R. 1.
Eli F., and Roxanna Dunn, July 4, 1830.*
Humphry, and [Mrs. C. R. 1.] Joanna Stevens [of the factory. C. R. 1; of Tewksbury. int.], Feb. 15, 1824.*
John H., and Julia A. Nutter, Nov. 4, 1843.*

*Intention also recorded.

WELCH (see also Welsh), David, and Mary Byham [both residents in Chelmsford. c. R. 1.], Jan. 24, 1750. [1749-50. p. r. 4.]*
David, and Ann Peirce, int. Feb. 3, 1816.

WELD, Grace [Mrs. int.], of Roxbury, and Oliver Fletcher, at Roxbury, Nov. 13, 1766.*
Jabez Hatch, of Plymouth [New Plymouth. int.], N. H., and Patty Fletcher, at Billerica, Jan. 21, 1793.*

WELLINGTON, Caroline, of Waltham, and Asa Perrin, int. Dec. 19, 1824.

WELLMAN, Catharine F., and Nathan Blood, int. Apr. 7, 1833.
Marietta E., of Lowell, and Isaac Winn, int. Apr. 29, 1832.

WELSH (see also Welch), Patrick, and Hannah Dulihanty of Boston, int. Oct. 19, 1823.

WENTWORTH, Abraham W., and Dorcas Colburn of Milford, N. H., int. Sept. 3, 1837.

WESEN (see also Wesson), Ephraim, of Wilmington, and Marah [Lydia. int.] Proctor, at Westford, Nov. 16, 1748.*

WESSON (see also Wesen), Ephraim [Willson. int.], and Esther Hodgman, at Concord, Apr. 13, 1780.*
Samuel, and Hannah Parker, at Westford, Nov. 28, 1799.*

WETHERBEE, Nahum, of Andover, and Mary Smith, int. Apr. 5, 1835.

WEVER (see also Weaver), Frances, and Neomy Hunt, int. July 5, 1817.

WHEALER (see also Wheeler), Hannah, d. George, of Concord, and Samuell Fletcher, s. William, July 5, 1[torn. 1673?].
Joseph, of Nashoba, and Mary Powers, d. Walter, of Nashoba, Mar. 1, 1681.

*Intention also recorded.

WHEELER (see also Whealer, Wheler), Caroline S., a. 17 y., d. Eli and Abigail, and William Jones, a. 25 y., blacksmith, s. Joshua and Betsey, Feb. 4, 1847.*
Eliza Ann, of Tewksbury, and Joseph Graham, int. Nov. 15, 1823.
Hannah C., of Nashville, N. H., and Isaac Jones, int. June 27, 1846.
J. B., of Lowell, and Rhoda Butterfeild, June 24, 1841.*
Jane M., of Newburyport, and John B. Dean, int. Oct. 16, 1825.
Jefferson, and Sophia Shattuck of Waltham, int. Jan. 9, 1825.
Joanna, of Carlisle, and Simeon Wilson, at Carlisle, June 29, 1790.*
John, of Barre, and Abyal Mansfeild, int. July 30, 1780.
Martha [of Acton. int.], and Nath[anie]ll Barrat, Nov. 30, 1748.*
Mary, of Sudbury, and John Mead, int. Apr. 20, 1823.
Rachel, and Robert Adams, Dec. 10, 1778. [Dec. 9. P. R. 4.]*
Ruth, and Josaph Worin, Mar. 11, 1696.
Sarah, and Ebenezer Hill of Nichewaug, int. Dec. —, 1738.
W[illia]m M. [of Carlisle. C. R. 1; of Boxborough. int.], and Sally Pelsue, Apr. 7, 1817.*

WHEELOCK, Mary, of Cumberland, R. I., and Philip Taft, int. May 3, 1836.

WHELER (see also Wheeler), Susanah, of Concord, and John Shiply, Sept. 23 [1672. dup.].

WHETNEY (see also Whitney), Jonas, of Stow, and Margrett Stratton, int. Mar. 13, 1725-6.

WHIPPLE, Lucius, of Lowell, and Fanny Tyler, Apr. 3, 1828.*
Oliver M., and Sophronia Hale, Apr. 4, 1820. [1821. C. R. 1; Mar. 18, 1821. int.]*

WHITCOMB (see also Whitcombe), Rebecca, of Lancaster, and Samuel Chamberlain, at Lancaster, Jan. 2, 1722-3.*

WHITCOMBE (see also Whitcomb), Abigail, and James Kidder, int. Apr. 26, 1729.

*Intention also recorded.

WHITE (see also Wight), Hiram, and Ann K. Howard of West Bridgewater, int. Dec. 25, 1831.
Jemima, "probably of Boston" [of Boston. int.], and Sampson Stoddard, jr., at Boston, Sept. 20, 1772.*
Mary, and Adam H. Cogswell, Mar. 13, 1823.*
Polly, of Ipswich, and John Crosby, at Ipswich, May 1, 1783.*
Samuel, of Tyngsborough, and Laura Byam, Dec. 28, 1837.*
Sarah, of Leicester, and Erasmus D. Preston, int. Aug. 29, 1846.

WHITEMORE (see also Whittemore), Hanah, and Benjamin Butterfeild, June 3, 1663.
Louisa, and Dr. Peleg Bradly of Dracut, June 26, 1817.*

WHITHERELL (see also Witherell), Joel C., and Mary Martha [Martha M. int.] Hildreth, June 15, 1823.*

WHITING, Phinehas, and Hannah Vernun [of Dracut. int.], Feb. 5, 1795.*
Phineus, Capt., and Sarah Coburn, Apr. 13, 1817.*
Sally, and Thomas Conn [of Charlestown. int.], Mar. 8, 1801.*

WHITNEE (see also Whitney), Joseph, and Rebeka Burge, at Charlestown, May 26, 1706.

WHITNEY (see also Whetney, Whitnee), Aaron, jr., of Harvard, and Mary Johnson, June 1, 1836.*
Abigil, and Thomas Herwood of Dunstable, int. Jan. 4, 1729.
Daniel, and Hannah Hildreth, Feb. 6, 1745.*
Hannah, and Henry Morgan of Westford, at Westford, Aug. 25, 1768.*
Richard, and Sarah Butterfield, Mar. 26, 1767.*
William, of Groton, and Lidya Perham, Mar. [torn. 1700?].

WHITTAKER, Jonathan, and Sarah Toothaker, at Boston, Nov. 15, 1694.

WHITTAWS, Sarah, and Gershom Procter, July 4, 1690. CT. R.

WHITTEMORE (see also Whitemore), Ann Maria, of Groton, and George Proctor, int. May 7, 1836.
James, and Susan H. Varnum, Oct. 28, 1841.*

*Intention also recorded.

CHELMSFORD MARRIAGES 347

WHITTIER, Ebenezer, and Azubah Duren, Dec. 2, 1824.*

WHITWELL, Samuel, Dr., of Boston, and Mrs. Lucy Tyler of Dunstable [grandd. Judge Tyng. P. R. 4.], Nov. 11, 1783.

WIER, Jeremiah [of Concord. int.], and Esther Kidder, Apr. 6, 1775.*

WIGGIN, Mary N., of Lowell, and Thomas Marshall, May 24, 1835.*
Nathaniel, and Lydia P. Sanborn of Gilmanton, N. H., int. Mar. 1, 1843.
True, of Lexington, and Martha Marshall, int. Mar. 17, 1839.

WIGHT (see also White), Experiance, of Sudbury, and Josiah Richerdson, Oct. 23, 1728.*

WILDER, Levi [of Lancaster. int.], and Sarah Stoddard, Aug. 26, 1779.*
Oliver, Col. [of Lancaster. int.], and [Mrs. P. R. 4.] Rebecca Barron, Aug. 2, 1749.*

WILLARD, Frances Ann, of Lowell, and William E. Hirsch, int. June 9, 1833.
Oliver, resident in Chelmsford, and Azubah Procter, Nov. 29, 1792.*
Samuel, and Sally I. [T. C. R. 1.] Coburn, Feb. 10, 1825.*

WILLE (see also Wily), Andrew, of Nottingham East, N. H., and Polly Fletcher, int. Nov. 29, 1794.
James, and Esther Glood, Dec. 31, 1795.*

WILLIAMS, Charles, and Rebecca Frost of Watertown, int. Apr. 12, 1829.
Dency, and Orville Worcester, int. Dec. 26, 1824.
Louiza E., of Pepperell, and George Stevens, int. July 4, 1824.
Lucy, and Jesse Wilson of Anson [Me. int.], Jan. 31, 1810.*
Silas, and Irene Vickers of Fall River, int. Oct. 16, 1847.

WILLISTON, David Howe [of Tunbridge, Vt. dup.], and Susanna Bancroft of Tyngsborough, Jan 26, 1796.

*Intention also recorded.

WILLOUGHBY (see also Willowby), Joseph, and Almira Balcom, int. Jan. 6, 1826.

WILLOWBY (see also Willoughby), Franklin, of Milford, N. H., a. 35 y., cooper, s. David, and Harriett Peacock, a. 29 y., supposed d. J. P. Merriam, Feb. 24, 1847.*

WILLSON (see also Wilson), Abigail, of Woburn, and Simon [Simeon. int.] Spalding, at Woburn, Nov. 13, 1751.*
Abigaill, and Joseph Hildreth, at Woburn, 25 : 12 m : 1683.
Elisabeth, of Woburn, and Isack Hildreth, Nov. 12, 1685. [July 24. CT. R.]
Elisabeth, of Billerica, and Caleb Stevens, at Billerica, Dec. 1, 1768.*
Esther [of Carlisle. int.], and Ebenezer Kidder, Nov. 23, 1786.*
George W., and Sally Spaulding, Apr. 8, 1826.*

WILSON (see also Willson), Harriet N. [M. int.], of Middlesex Village, and David Clark of Lowell, May 16, 1839.*
Harriott, of Tyngsborough, and John Smith, int. Mar. 6, 1825.
Jesse, of Anson [Me. int.], and Lucy Williams, Jan. 31, 1810.*
Jonathan, and Sally Tuttle, ——, 1805. [Nov. 28. C. R. 1.]*
Louisa D., and Frederick S. Geer of Pembroke, N. H., int. Aug. 28, 1841.
Lucend[a], of Nottingham West, N. H., and Jonathan Burbank, int. Nov. 11, 1822.
Naome [Nancy. int.], and Samuel Hunt, Aug. 7, 1798.*
Pamilla, and Salathiel Frost, Nov. 11, 1828.
Persis, of Bradford, Vt., and Eliphalet Hunt, int. Apr. 12, 1838.
Rebecca, of Billerica, and Nathaniel Cumings, int. May 27, 1774.
Samuel [of Concord. int.], and Hannah Swallow, Jan. 17, 1754.*
Sarah, and John Read, Dec. 2, 1779.*
Sarah, Mrs. [a. 55 y. C. R. 1.], and Capt. Benjamin Fletcher [a. 77 y. C. R. 1.], Jan. 30, 1823.*
Simeon, and Joanna Wheeler of Carlisle, at Carlisle, June 29, 1790.*
Stephen, and Rachel Mansfield, at Westford, Mar. 13, 1791.*

WILY (see also Wille), Sarah, and Joshuah Flet[c]her, July 18, 1682.

*Intention also recorded.

WINCH, Francis, and Almira Stetson of Waltham, int. Oct. 31, 1824.
Mary, and James Brown, both of Tyngsborough, Sept. 28, 1806.

WINCHESTER, Elhanan, widr., a. 43 y., farmer, s. Charles and Liberty, and Priscilla Flynn, wid., a. 39 y., d. Ezekiel and Betsey A. Wentworth, Aug. 1, 1847.*
Samuel, of Hopkinton, N. H., and Phebe Parker, int. May 12, 1822.
Samuel, and Mary Parker, May 17, 1825.*

WINCOLL, Olive, and William Spaulding, int. Nov. 9, 1729.

WINN, Hezekiah, and Bathsheba Ball of Townsend, at Townsend, Nov. —, 1791.*
Isaac, and Marietta E. Wellman of Lowell, int. Apr. 29, 1832.
Jonathan, and Molly Spaulding, Feb. 8, 1798.*
Mary F., of Hudson, N. H., and Lot Easte, int. Feb. 26, 1832.
Rebeckah, of Woburn, and Timothy Spaldin, at Woburn, Mar. 5, 1700.
Sarah M., of Hudson, N. H., and Thomas Barstow, int. Feb. 1, 1835.
Timothy [jr., of Woburn. int.], and [Mrs. int.] Mary Bridge, June 4, 1772.*

WINNING, John, Capt., of Billerica, and Betsey Parker, Nov. 19, 1792.*

WINSHIP, Mary Ann, and Peter Cary, int. June 15, 1823.

WINSLOW, John, of Boston, and Mrs. Sarah Tyng of Dunstable, Sept. 4, 1760.

WITHERELL (see also Whitherell), Hannah, of Taunton, and Otis Lincoln, int. Sept. 13, 1829.
Nathan, of Grand Isle, Vt., and Emily L. Thorndike, Feb. 18, 1838. [Feb. 2, 1839. int.]*

WITHINGTON, Edward, and Lydia Hodgman, ——, 1812. [Aug. 20. C. R. 1.]*

*Intention also recorded.

WOOD (see also Woods), Benjamin [of Carlisle. int.], and Elizabeth Swallow, Apr. 10, 1755.*
Betcy, and Jesse Spaulding, int. Nov. 20, 1792.
Betsey, of Dracut, and Joseph Spaulding, at Dracut, Dec. 25, 1792.
Dexter, and Lucy Kenney of Millbury, int. Sept. 11, 1825.
Jane S., and Benjamin Blood, jr., Feb. 26, 1832.
Jonathan, of Billerica, and Nancy Stearn, int. Dec. 24, 1820.
Pheby, and Aaron Hayes, int. Dec. 1, 1808.
Phinehas, of Dracut, and Patty Spaulding, int. Jan. 7, 1802.
Polly, and Nathan Tyler, at Dracut, July 31, 1788.*
Prudance, of Dracut, and Samuel Richardson, int. Feb. 16, 1795.
Ruth, Mrs., of Dracut, and Capt. Ebenezer Parker, int. July 3, 1756.
Samuel Fox, and Sarah Carleton of Boscawen, int. July 5, 1807.
Samuell, s. Samuell, of Groton, and Hannah Farwell, d. Joseph, Dec. 30, 1685.
Sarah H., and Samuel Parker [of Lowell. int.], July 20, 1835.*
William, and Hannah Foster, Apr. 20, 1800.*

WOODHEAD (see also Woodward), William, and Mary Browne, June 21, 1669.

WOODS (see also Wood), Deborah, of Boston, and William McLenna, int. Feb. 24, 1822.
Emely, and Tho[ma]s W. Obear, June 6, 1841.*
Francis B., and Betsy Harwood, June 23, 1825.*
Harriot, of Groton, and George L. Sticklemire, int. Nov. 21, 1830.
Isaac, and Mary W. Healy, Aug. 8, 1826.*
Lucy [now residing in Carlisle. int.], and John Mansfield, Jan. 23, 1798.*
Mary Ann, a. 21 y., d. Isaac and Mary, and George O. Bailey, a. 25 y., stone-cutter, s. Joseph and Laura, Sept. 7, 1848.*
Moses, of Acton, and Hazadiah Spaulding, at Westford, Apr. 16, 1793.*
Polly, of Acton, and Samson Stevens, int. May 3, 1817.
Sarah, and Samuel Spaulding of Merrimack, int. Mar. 17, 1753.
William [late of Groton. int.], and Naomi Langley, Feb. 9, 1757.*

*Intention also recorded.

CHELMSFORD MARRIAGES 351

WOODWARD (see also Woodhead), George W., and Eliza Ann Prescott of Groton, int. Mar. 25, 1841.
Hilliard E., and Sophia Hilton of Lunenburg, int. Oct. 11, 1829.
James [of Reading. int.], and Rebecca Chamberlain, June 10, 1760.*
Martha, and Luther Blood, int. Jan. 21, 1837.
Polly R., of Tyngsborough, and Zephaniah Bennet, int. Mar. 16, 1830.

WORCESTER (see also Worster), George, and Margeret Jane Kimball of Goffstown, N. H., int. Sept. 2, 1832.
Orville, and Dency Williams, int. Dec. 26, 1824.
Osgood, and Phebe Farnum of Andover, at Andover, Dec. 27, 1798.*

WORIN (see also Warren), Josaph, and Ruth Wheeler, Mar. 11, 1696.
Mary, and William Bladget, June 14, 1696.

WORSTER (see also Worcester), Sarah, and Benjamin Haward [Hayward. CT. R.; Howard. C. R. 1.], Dec. 20, 1785.*

WRIGHT (see also Wrighte), Abigail, and Benjamin Spaulding of Plainfield, int. Feb. 7, 1719-20. (Feb. 10, banns forbidden by Ephraim Hildrith, jr.)
Abigail, and Cornelius Clark of Cambridge, Sept. 2, 1822.
Abigail, and Elijah Spalding, Oct. 28, 1826. C. R. 1.
Abigail, and Reuben M. Leighton of Westford, Apr. 19, 1838.*
Betsy, and Oliver Pelsue, Dec. 1, 1803.*
Betsy, of Westford, and Charles Shepherd of Bedford, N. H., Nov. 2, 1824.
Calvin T., and Martha H. Chamberlain, int. Nov. 19, 1842.
Ebenezer, of Westford, and Deleverance Stevens, at Westford, May 25, 1730.*
Ebenezer, of Narragansett, No. 6, and Lucy Barrit, int. Aug. 18, 1758.
Ebinezer, and Hanah Flatcher, May 14, 1697.
Eliza, of Woburn, and Owen Spalding, int. Apr. 13, 1823.
Elizabeth, and William Blogget, int. Dec. 10, 1721.
Elizabeth, and Simeon Stevens, July 19, 1764.*
Ezekiel C., of Westford, and Susan Stevens [d. Sampson, deceased. C. R. 1.], Mar. 8, 1821.*
Hannah, and Andrew Spaulding, int. Nov. 21, 1725.

*Intention also recorded.

WRIGHT, Hannah, and Stephen Hodgman of Merrimack, N. H., int. Nov. 27, 1776.
Hannah, of Westford, and David Dutton, int. May 8, 1802.
Henry, and Esther Adams, int. Dec. 19, 1725.
Isaac, and Sybil Taylor of Dunstable, Oct. 3, 1776.
Jesse, of Westford, and Sybel Stevens, int. Dec. 2, 1827.
Joel Barrett, and Sarah Osborn, Dec. 2, 1824.*
John, and Abigall Warin, May 10, 1661.
John [of Westford. int.], and Betsy Haywood, Oct. 28, 1819.*
Laura Maria, of Westford, and Elbridge Dutton, at Westford, Jan. 23, 1840.*
Lidya, and James Hildreth, int. Aug. 13, 1727.
Lucy, and Elijah M. Spaulding of Ludlow, Vt. [of "Ludon," Vt. int.], Oct. 29, 1826.*
Lydia [of Westford. int.], and Zebulon Spaulding [jr. int.], Feb. 12, 1767.*
Mary, and Washington Wright [of Richmond, Va. int.], Feb. 3, 1825.*
Nathaniel, and Laura Hoar, int. Feb. 6, 1820.
Rebecca [of Westford. int.], and Augustus H. Searle, Dec. 8, 1831.*
Reuben, jr., of Westford, and Abiah Moors Dane, int. Mar. 23, 1834.
Ruth, of Westford, and Samuel Stevens, at Westford, Mar. 4, 1731.*
Ruth [of Westford. int.], and Simeon Barrat, Apr. 11, 1776.*
Sarah M., and Benjamin Fletcher, jr., May 27, 1842.*
Simeon, of Westford, and Dorcas Hildreth, at Westford, Oct. 31, 1738.*
Simeon [of Ipswich, N. H. int.], and Sarah Robbins, Nov. 21, 1768.*
Thomas, of Westford, and Elizabeth Parker, int. Jan. 14, 1732-3.
Washington [of Richmond, Va. int.], and Mary Wright, Feb. 3, 1825.*
Zaccheus, Capt., and Mrs. Martha Foster, July 5, 1829.
Zacheriah [Zacheus. int.], and Nabby Putnam of Fitchburg, at Fitchburg, July 8, 1799.*
Zacheus [of Westford. int.], and Rachel Parker, Jan. 5, 1764.*
Zacheus [of Westford. int.], and Abigail Hildreth, Feb. —, 1799.*

WRIGHTE (see also Wright), John, and Marie Stephens, Apr. 13, 1692.

*Intention also recorded.

WYMAN, Benjamin, and Bridget Spaulding, int. Sept. 18, 1726.
George W., and Mary Messer of Lowell, int. Sept. 18, 1841.
Hannah, and Moses Barrett, int. Nov. 21, 1824.
Josiah A., and Ruth H. Frye of Lowell, int. June 20, 1840.
Olivia, and Jonathan Philbrick, both of Lowell, June 18, 1837.
Phebe, and Josiah Clark of Dracut, int. Aug. 21, 1825.
Rufas, and Ann Morrell of Boston, int. Nov. 25, 1809.
Zoa Ann, and Hiram Peabody, Sept. 17, 1843.*

YORK, Susan, and John P. Allen, both of Westford, Nov. 21, 1847. C. R. 3.

YOUNG, John H., and Nancy Nutting, Dec. 18, 1821.*
Sarah, and Jesse H. [S. C. R. 3.] Perkins, Nov. 29, 1840.*
Sarah A. P., and Isaac Mason, int. Jan. 28, 1837.

ZANES, William, and Abigail Liscom, int. Aug. 24, 1834.

SURNAMES MISSING

——, Hannah, and Nathaniel Blood, June 13, 1670. CT. R.
——, Hannah, d. John [torn], and [torn], [1679?].
——, Ledea, and Joseph Lawrance, Mar. 13, 1670-71. CT. R.
——, Sarah, and Cornelius Church, June 14, 1670. CT. R.
——, and [torn] Blanchard, d. ——, July 22, 1679.

NEGROES

Newel, Cato, and Dinah Tony, Oct. 16, 1782.
Prince, belonging to Lt. W[illia]m Kitteridge of Tewksbury, and Zube, mulatto, belonging to [Dr. dup.] Nehemiah Abbot, Mar. 3, 1772.*
Tony, Dinah, and Cato Newel, Oct. 16, 1782.
Zube, mulatto, belonging to [Dr. dup.] Nehemiah Abbot, and Prince, belonging to Lt. W[illia]m Kitteridge of Tewksbury, Mar. 3, 1772.*

*Intention also recorded.

CHELMSFORD DEATHS

TO THE END OF THE YEAR 1849

ABBOT (see also Abbott), Nehemiah, Dr., bur. July 13, 1785. c. r. 1.
——, Mr., of the glass factory, lately from Tewksbury, Mar. 12, 1821. c. r. 1.

ABBOTT (see also Abbot), Caleb, b. Nov. 10, 1779, d. Dec. 4, 1846. g. r. 1.
Marcy M. R. [Mary Maria. c. r. 1.], d. [Capt. c. r. 1.] Caleb A. and Marcy [typhus fever. c. r. 1.], Aug. 21, 1825, a. 17 y. g. r. 1.
Mercy F., Mrs. [w. Caleb. dup.], Feb. 8, 1834, a. 51 y. g. r. 1.
William Stackpole, grands. Caleb and Mercy, May 6, 1846, a. 17 m. g. r. 1.

ACKROYD, John, b. Bedford, Eng., ship-fever, Mar. 22, 1848, a. 50 y.
William, b. England, ship-fever, Feb. 25, 1848, a. 60 y.

ADAMES (see also Adams), John, s. Dea. Benjamin and Mary, Dec. 16, 1753.
Mary, d. Temothy and Mary, Jan. 29, 1681.
Sarah, d. Samuel and Esthar, Sept. 25, 1754. [a. 3 m. 23 d. g. r. 1.]

ADAMS (see also Adames, Addams), Abel, Capt., Feb. 21, 1792. [a. 46 y. c. r. 1.]
Abel, s. Capt. Salathiel and Sarah, Mar. 10, 1809, a. 8 w. g. r. 1.
Abigail, wid. Dea. Benjamin, July 22, 1771. [a. 86 y. c. r. 1.]
Adeline, b. Watertown, w. Gen. Benjamin, dysentery, Sept. 10, 1849, a. 30 y. 4 m. 21 d.

Benjamin [jr. g. r. 1.], s. Benjamin and Olive, Dec. 18, 1755. [a. 27 y. 9 m. 12 d. g. r. 1.]
Benjamin, Dea., Aug. [13. c. r. 1.], 1762. [a. 83 y. c. r. 1.]

ADAMS, Benj[amin], old age, Sept. 26, 1826, a. 82 y. C. R. 1.
Betsey, w. William, Sept. 19, 1836, a. 40 y. G. R. 2.
Betsy, w. Samuel, jr. [putrid fever. C. R. 1.], Apr. 6, 1807, a. 21 y. 11 m. 15 d.
Bettey, d. Joseph and Abigail, of Fitchburg, June 19, 1782, a. 8 y. 3 m. 14 d. G. R. 1.
Charles Edwin [s. Joel and Catharine Mary, class of 1832 Harvard University. C. R. 1.], Mar. 27, 1833. [Feb. 27, a. 21 y. C. R. 1.]
Dorcas, w. Joseph, Apr. 27, 1838. P. R. 5. [a. 72 y. P. R. 24.]
Dorothy, wid., bur. June 21, 1766, a. 90 y. C. R. 1. [d. June 19. P. R. 4.]
Eben, b. Westford, Oct. 20, 1775, d. at Middlesex Village, Sept. 8, 1836. G. R. 1.
Edee, d. Timothy and Doratha, Apr. 14, 1743.
Eliza [Eliza Ann. G. R. 3.], w. [Gen. G. R. 3.] Benj[a]m[in], May 18, 1835. [a. 30 y. G. R. 3.]
Eliza Jane B[ush. G. R. 3.], d. Col. Benjamin and Eliza [Eliza Ann. G. R. 3.], Aug. 29, 1837. [a. 4 y. 4 m. 23 d. G. R. 3.]
Elizabeth, d. Benjamin and Abigail, Apr. 20, 1742.
Elizibeth, d. Timothy and Dorathy, Apr. 22, 1734.
Ella E., d. Benjamin and Adeline, dysentery, Aug. 24, 1849, a. 2 y. 24 d.
Esther, w. Samuel, Nov. 4, 1745. [a. 32 y. 9 m. 16 d. G. R. 1.]
Esther, d. Sam[ue]ll [and Ester. G. R. 1.], bur. Oct. 6, 1759. C. R. 1. [in her 22d y. G. R. 1.]
Eunice [Cole. G. R. 1.], w. W[illia]m [H. G. R. 1.], jr., mortification, July 27, 1827, a. 20 y. C. R. 1.
Hannah, d. Oliver and Rachel, Aug. 20, 1766, a. 2 y. 4 m. 14 d. G. R. 1.
Hannah, w. Benjamin, Feb. 18, 1849, a. 82 y. 6 m. G. R. 2.
Henery, s. Thomas, Nov. 19, 1709.
Henry Kirkland, s. Joel [and Catharine. G. R. 1.], Sept. 17, 1820, a. 19 m. 17 d.
Horace, s. William and Susannah, July 9, 1838, a. 21 y. G. R. 2.
Isaac, dysentery, Aug. 28, 1829, a. 60 y. C. R. 1. [Aug. 30, 1827. P. R. 27.]
John, bur. May 21, 1759. C. R. 1.
John, bur. Mar. 17, 1791, a. 72 or 73 y. C. R. 1. [d. Mar. 15. P. R. 4; a. 71 y. 6 m. G. R. 2.]
John, Dec. 31, 1820, a. 74 y. C. R. 1.
John, fits, Jan. 22, 1824, a. 35 y. C. R. 1. [Jan. 21. C. R. 2; a. 37 y. G. R. 2.]
John Henry, s. Dea. Joel [and Catharine. G. R. 1.], June 26, 1826, a. 4 y. C. R. 1.

CHELMSFORD DEATHS

ADAMS, John Q., s. William and Betsey, Sept. 20, 1836, a. 3 y. G. R. 2.
John R., lawyer [grad. Harv. Univ. 1818. G. R. 3.], s. W[illia]m and Mary, consumption, June 16, 1848, a. 49 y. [a. 50 y. G. R. 1.]
Jonas, s. Jonas and Rebecka, Feb. 4, 1741-2.
Jonas, s. Lt. Abel and Olive, Sept. 5, 1778, a. 6 y. 6 d. [Sept. 6. G. R. 1.]
Jonas, Jan. 18, 1792. [a. 80 y. C. R. 1.]
Jonas [suddenly, cause unknown. C. R. 1.], s. Capt. Abel, July 28, 1806, a. 17 y.
Jonathan, Nov. 25, 1712.
Jonathan, s. William and Elizebeth [wid. C. R. 1.], May 15, 1767.
Joseph, Capt., Jan. 22, 1717-18. [a. 45 y. G. R. 1.]
Joseph, bur. June 9, 1772, a. 74 y. C. R. 1.
Joseph [apoplexy. C. R. 1.], Sept. 17, 1796. [a. abt. 75 y. C. R. 1; in his 71st y. G. R. 1.]
Joseph, Jan. 17, 1843, a. 84 y.
Josiah Francis, s. W[illia]m, jr. and Sarah S., Feb. 12, 1842. [a. 9 y. 3 m. 21 d. G. R. 3.]
Levi, s. Joseph, jr. and Lidia, May 15, 1753.
Lucy [d. Dea. Benjamin and Abigail. G. R. 1; suddenly. P. R. 4.], bur. May 25, 1782, a. 58 y. C. R. 1. [d. May 24. P. R. 4; in her 56th y. G. R. 1.]
Lucy [d. Lt. Samuel and Sarah. G. R. 2.], consumption, Oct. 14, 1808, a. 14 y. C. R. 1. [Oct. 13, a. 15 y. 7 m. 17 d. G. R. 2.]
Lucy [(Blodget). P. R. 24.], w. Joseph, Oct. 12, 1803, a. 42 y. 2 m. 15 d.
Lydia, d. Pellatiah and Lydia, Dec. 30, 1745. [a. 29 y. 7 m. 4 d. G. R. 1.]
Lydia, wid., bur. Nov. 5, 1766, a. 78 y. C. R. 1. [d. Nov. 4. P. R. 4.]
Lydia, w. [wid. C. R. 1.] Joseph, July 18, 1799, in her 76th y. G. R. 1.
Mahitebal Manning, w. Joseph, at Boston, Apr. 9, 1816. C. R. 1.
Mary, w. Benjamin, Jan. 12, 1715-16.
Mary, wid., bur. Mar. 14, 1778, a. 76 y. C. R. 1.
Mary, w. Benjamin [d. Eben[e]z[er] Foster. P. R. 4.], Sept. 18, 1785. [a. 42 y. 7 m. G. R. 1.]
Mary, Mar. 23, 1836, a. 85 y. P. R. 27.
Mary, b. Dunstable, now Nashua, N. H., wid. William, old age, July 3, 1849, a. 85 y.

ADAMS, Mary E., d. Joseph and Dorothy, scarlatina, Feb. 26, 1847, a. 1 y. 5 m. 11 d.
Molly, w. John, jr., July 2, 1771. P. R. 4.
Moses, Rev., at Acton, Nov. —, 1819, a. 70 y. C. R. 1.
Noris, s. Capt. Salathiel and Sarah, Feb. 1, 1818. [a. 6 w. G. R. 1.]
Olive, d. Oliver and Rachal, May 31, 1773, a. 13 y. 8 m. 3 d. G. R. 1.
Olive, wid. Capt. Abel, Oct. 5, 1819, a. 77 y. G. R. 1.
Pelatiah, sr., Apr. 29, 1725.
Pelatiah, "killed by the enemy Tories & Indians at Chery Valley, upon Mohaw River above Albany, fall," 1778. C. R. 1.
Pellatiah, July 15, 1746. [a. 63 y. 7 m. 29 d. G. R. 1.]
Rebeckah, w. Jonas, Mar. 3, 1781. [a. 58 y. 6 m. 2 d. G. R. 1.]
Rebeckah, d. Joseph and Lydia, Aug. 23, 1789. [Aug. 24. P. R. 4; a. 22 y. C. R. 1.]
Robert, Sept. 19, 1798, a. 47 y. G. R. 2.
Ruth, w. Pellatiah, Sept. 18, 1719.
Salathial, s. Jonas and Rebeckah, Oct. 7, 1778, in his 25th y.
Sally, d. Capt. Timothy and Joanna, Aug. 5, 1793. [a. 1 y. 8 m. 6 d. G. R. 2.]
Samewel, Capt., Jan. 24, 1688-9.
Samuel, s. Capt. Joseph, Sept. 7, 1721.
Samuel, s. Joseph and Mary, Dec. 5, 1738, a. 3 y. 11 m. 25 d. G. R. 1.
Samuel, s. Samuel and Esther, Nov. 4, 1745. [a. 10 y. 1 m. 30 d. G. R. 1.]
Samuel, dropsy in ye head, Dec. 11, 1808, a. 2 y. C. R. 1.
Sam[ue]l [Lt. G. R. 2.], liver complaint, Sept. 3, 1816, a. 62 y. C. R. 1.
Samuell, s. Pelitiah and Ruth, June 29, 1689.
Sarah, w. John, Jan. 3, 1808, a. 84 y. G. R. 2.
Sarah, d. Capt. Salathiel and Sarah, Nov. 14, 1812, a. 6 w. G. R. 1.
Sarah C., d. Charles and Nancy, whooping cough, Mar. 22, 1846, a. 1 y. 4 m.
Sarah Elizabeth, d. William, jr. and Sarah S., Aug. 19, 1838. [a. 4 m. 11 d. G. R. 3.]
Simeon, s. Joseph and Lucy, May 24, 1797. [a. 1 y. 2 d. G. R. 1.]
Susanna, w. Salathiel, fever, Dec. 21, 1806, a. 25 y. C. R. 1. [a. 26 y. G. R. 1.]
Tabitha Maria, d. Ephraim and Tabitha, Oct. 20, 1826. [a. 7 y. C. R. 1.]
Thankful [d. Joseph and Lydia. G. R. 1.], bur. June 15, 1790, a. 35 y. C. R. 1. [d. June 14. P. R. 4.]

CHELMSFORD DEATHS 359

ADAMS, Thomas, July 20, 1688, a. 76 y. CT. R.
Timothy, July 1, 1708.
Timothy, bur. Feb. 27, 1761, a. 83 y. C. R. 1. [d. Feb. 26. P. R. 4.]
Timothy, consumption, Mar. —, 1814, a. 6 y. C. R. 1.
William, Oct. 20, 1766. [Oct. 21. P. R. 4; a. 34 y. 4 m. 12 d. G. R. 1.]
W[illia]m, [a Revolutionary Soldier Under Gen. Benedict Arnold. An eyewitness to the execution of Major Andre. G. R. 1.], fever and old age, Dec. 25, 1843, a. 81 y. 8 m.
William H., at Burlington, Vt., May 22, 1829, a. 28 y. G. R. 1.
W[illia]m Henry, student at college, s. Capt. W[illia]m, consumption, Aug. 4, 1845, a. 21 y.
Zacceus, s. Pellitiah and Liddia, May 17, 1719.
Zacheus, s. Pellitiah and Liddia, Dec. 11, 1714.
——, ch. Jonas, bur. Jan. 1, 1743. C. R. 1.
——, ch. John, bur. Oct. 20, 1746. C. R. 1.
——, ch. Jonas, bur. Feb. 7, 1749. C. R. 1.
——, inf. ch. Jo[seph. P. R. 4.], jr., bur. Apr. 10, 1754. C. R. 1.
——, inf. ch. Jonas, bur. Mar. 19, 1757. C. R. 1.
——, ch. John, bur. Mar. 23, 1757. C. R. 1.
——, inf. ch. Jonas, bur. Apr. 4, 1758. C. R. 1.
——, ch. Will[ia]m, bur. Apr. 10, 1761. C. R. 1.
——, ch. Sam[ue]ll, 3d, bur. Nov. 29, 1773. C. R. 1.
——, w. Sam[ue]ll, 3d, bur. Dec. 1, 1773. C. R. 1.
——, ch. Oliver, bur. Oct. 2, 1777. C. R. 1.
——, inf. ch. Will[ia]m, bur. Oct. 6, 1786. C. R. 1.
——, wid., bur. Oct. 16, 1791. C. R. 1.
——, ch. Joseph and Dolly, July 12, 1847, a. 5 d.
——, s. Gen. Benja[min] and Adeline, dysentery, Sept. 1, 1849, a. 5 d. [Sept. 6. G. R. 3.]

ADDAMS (see also Adams), Abijah, s. Benjamin and Olive, Sept. 14, 1757. [a. 23 y. 5 m. 8 d. G. R. 1.]
Rebekah, w. Samuell [Oct. T. C.; Sept. CT. R.] 8, 1664.
Thomas, s. Tho[mas], 30: 9 m: 16[torn. 1660?].

ALDRIDGE, ——, Mr., of Connecticut, smallpox, Feb. 1, 1824, a. 26 y. C. R. 1.

ALFORD, ——, Col., at Charlestown, Sept. 30, 1761. P. R. 4.

ALLEN, Israel, s. [Rev. G. R. 1.] Wilkes and Mary, Jan. 16, 1815, a. 7 w. C. R. 1.
John Clarke, s. Rev. Wilkes and Mary, grad. Harv. Univ. 1833, d. June 26, 1834. G. R. 1.

ALLEN, Mary, d. Rev. W[ilkes. G. R. 1.] and Mary, cholera infantum, Sept. 9, 1821, a. 3 y. 7 m. C. R. 1.
Sarah, d. Rev. W[ilkes and Mary. G. R. 1.], dysentery, Sept. 18, 1821, a. 18 m. C. R. 1. [Sept. 17. G. R. 1.]
Wilkes, Rev., for 29 y. Pastor of the first Church and society in Chelmsford, b. Shrewsbury, July 10, 1775, grad. Harv. Univ. 1801, Ordained Nov. 16, 1803, Retired Nov. 16, 1832, d. N. Andover, Dec. 2, 1845. G. R. 1.

AMES (see also Eames), Jeremiah, typhus fever [after Dec. 27], 1825, a. 25 y. C. R. 1.
Mary, Apr. "abt." 23, 1826. C. R. 2.
Phebe Amilia, d. N. P., Nov. 5, 1825, a. 17 y. C. R. 1.

ANDREWS, William, Rev., Nov. 18, 1838, a. 28 y. C. R. 1.

ANGEL, W[illia]m H., dislocated neck, accidental, June 8, 1847, a. 23 y.

ANTHONY, ——, inf. ch. Joseph and Mary Ann, July 23, 1847.
——, inf. ch. Joseph and Mary A., May 17, 1848.
——, d. Joseph, watchman, b. Island of Field, Western Isles, and Mary Ann, b. Yorkshire, Eng. [May 1, 1849?].

BAILY, Charles, s. Joseph [and Martha. G. R. 1.], Feb. 16, 1816, a. 15 m. C. R. 1. [Feb. 14. G. R. 1.]
Joseph [s. Joseph and Martha. G. R. 1.], lung fever, Apr. 28, 1808, a. 16 m. C. R. 1. [Apr. 26. G. R. 1.]

BAIRD, Mary [bet. July 12 and Sept. 3.], 1816, a. 87 y. C. R. 1.

BAKER, ——, ch. ——, living at Adams Mills, Dec. 23, 1812, a. 2 y. C. R. 1.

BALDWIN, Charles J., drowned in the canal, May 11, 1811, a 2 1-2 y. C. R. 1.
Cyrus, Dea., June —, 1834, a. 61 y. C. R. 3.
Elizabeth, d. Cyrus, May 27, 1815, a. 2 y. C. R. 1.
Mary F., only ch. Cyrus, bloody fungus on her shoulder and arm, June 18, 1824, a. 21 y. C. R. 1.

BALKE, see Barke.

CHELMSFORD DEATHS 361

BANCROFT, George W., s. ——, Mar. 16, 1804, a. 14 d. c. r. 1.
Isaac, s. Isaac and Hannah, at Lowell, May 17, 1827, a. 15 m. 8 d. G. R. 2.
Mary, w. Stowell, Jan. 3, 1825, a. 28 y. G. R. 2.
——, s. twin, Isaac and Hannah, May 4, 1819. G. R. 2.
——, d. twin, Isaac and Hannah, May 5, 1819. G. R. 2.

BARATT (see also Barrett), Ebenezer, s. Joseph and Abigail, Dec. 22, 1729.

BARBER, Lucinda, w. Charles, Apr. 30, 1826, a. 23 y. C. R. 1.
——, inf. ch. Charles H., Oct. 8, 1830. C. R. 1.

BARETT (see also Barrett), Martha, w. Joseph, May 15, 1698.
[torn], d. Jonathan and Sarah, Jan. 20, 16[torn. 1679 or 1680.].

BARIT (see also Barrett), Abigall, w. Jonathan, Oct. 19, 1706.
Benjamin, Feb. 14, 1705.
Elenar, d. John, June 25, 1706.
Fransis, w. Thomas, May 27, 1694.
John, Lt., May 19, 1706.
Joseph, Dec. 17, 1711.
Josiah, Jan. 27, 1712.

BARITE (see also Barrett), Experinc, Jan. 29, 1694-5.
John, Sept. 5, 1694-5.
Sarah, w. Jonathan, Jan. 11, 1694-5.

BARITT (see also Barrett), Mary, w. Joseph, Nov. 22, 1728.
Ruth, d. Benjamin, Mar. 21, 1734-5.

BARKE, John, 5 : 5 m: 1683.

BARKER, Eliza, Jan. 8, 1837. C. R. 2.
Lydia, wid., Feb. 8, 1823, a. 72 y. C. R. 1. [Feb. 5. C. R. 2.]
Mary, wid., a stranger [late of Boston. P. R. 4.], at Mr. Sam[ue]ll Pitts,' bur. Nov. 25, 1787. C. R. 1. [d. Nov. 24. P. R. 4.]
Samuel, fever, July 10, 1804, a. 6 m. C. R. 1.

BARNES, Nancy B., d. James R. and Ann, June 9, 1824. G. R. 7.

BARRAN (see also Barron), Moses, sr., Apr. 25, 1699.

BARRAT (see also Barrett), Abigail, bur. Nov. 27, 1747. C. R. 1.
Hannah [d. Thomas and Rachel. G. R. 1.], bur. Mar. 19, 1759. C. R. 1. [d. Mar. 17. P. R. 4; a. 28 y. 11 m. G. R. 1.]
Jonathan, bur. Mar. 28, 1743, a. 89 y. C. R. 1.
Joseph, bur. July 22, 1743. C. R. 1.
Lydia, wid. [Jonathan. G. R. 1.], bur. Nov. 18, 1789, a. 96 y. C. R. 1. [Nov. 16, in her 92d y. G. R. 1.]
Rachel, bur. June 2, 1747. C. R. 1.
Rachel, wid. [w. Thomas. G. R. 1.], bur. May 1, 1785, a. 92 y. C. R. 1. [d. Apr. 29. P. R. 4.]
Sarah, d. Samuell and Sary, Dec. 17, 1695.
——, ch. Nath[anie]ll, bur. Jan. 29, 1750. C. R. 1.
——, d. John, bur. Dec. 26, 1751. C. R. 1.
——, ch. Mercy [d. Peter Prockter. P. R. 4.], bur. Nov. 30, 1753. C. R. 1. [d. Nov. 29. P. R. 4.]
——, ch. Oliver, bur. Apr. 24, 1760. C. R. 1.
——, ch. stillborn, Simeon, bur. Feb. 16, 1778. C. R. 1.

BARRATT (see also Barrett), Abigail, w. Joseph, Dec. 30, 1729.
Dorcas, d. Joseph and Abigail, Nov. 10, 1730.
Ebenezer, s. Jona[than], bur. Feb. 1, 1753. C. R. 1. [d. Jan. 30. P. R. 4.]

BARREN (see also Barron), Patty [C., w. Elias. G. R. 2.], Apr. 23, 1837. C. R. 2. [a. 48 y. G. R. 2.]

BARRET (see also Barrett), Benjamin, s. Joseph, Nov. 13, 1745.
Ebenezer, s. Jonathan and Lydia, Feb. 23, 1752, a. 16 y. 11 m. 23 d. G. R. 1.
Elizabeth, Mrs. [w. Joel. G. R. 2.], Jan. 24, 1820, a. 82 y. C. R. 1.
Hannah, wid. Moses, Apr. 6, 1745.
Joel, instantaneous death, cause unknown, June 6, 1805, a. 67 y. C. R. 1. [June 5. G. R. 2.]
Jonathan, Oct. 9, 1773, a. 86 y. 11 m. 14 d. G. R. 1.
Joseph, Apr. 15, 1740.
Lydia, d. Jonathan and Lydia, Feb. 12, 1736-7, in her 18th y. G. R. 1.
Moses, Nov. 28, 1743.
Moses, Oct. 13, 1828. C. R. 3.
Nancy, w. ——, consumption, lately of Nottingham, Sept. 12, 1823, a. 30 y. C. R. 1.
Sarah, d. Thomas and Rachel, Sept. 18, 1747.

BARRETT (see also Baratt, Barett, Barit, Barite, Baritt, Barrat, Barratt, Barret, Barrit, Barritt), Margreat, d. John and Sarah, —: 11 m: 1681.
Margreatt, w. Thomas, July 8, 1681.
Martha, d. Joseph, July 25, 1678.
Thomas, sr., Oct. 6, 1668. CT. R.
——, inf. ch. Nancy, Oct. 14, 1823. C. R. 1.

BARRIT (see also Barrett), Bridget, d. Jonathan and Abigal, Sept. 7, 1702.
John, s. John and Martha, at Lake George, Oct. [15. dup.], 1756.
John, Dr., Dec. 20, 1773. [a. 87 y. C. R. 1.]
Sarrah, w. Jonathan, May 23, 1716. [in her 25th y. G. R. 1.]
Thomas, Dec. 8, 1702.
Thomas, July 9, 1761. [a. 73 or 74 y. C. R. 1; a. 72 y. 4 m. G. R. 1.]

BARRITT (see also Barrett), John, Mar. 18, 1772. [a. 62 y. C. R. 1.]

BARRON (see also Barran, Barren), Abigail, d. Capt. Oliver and Abigail, June 6, 1763, a. 4 y. 4 m. 25 d. G. R. 1.
Abigail, wid. Oliver, old age, Sept. 10, 1820, a. 87 y. C. R. 1.
Benjamin, s. Lt. Jonathan and Rachel [wid. C. R. 1.], Mar. 9, 1756.
Isaa[c], s. Moses and Mary, Sept. 16, 1739. [a. 67 y. 9 m. 16 d. G. R. 1.]
Jane, bur. Nov. 8, 1768. C. R. 1.
John, s. Moses, 13: 11 m: 1677.
Jonathan, Lt., Aug. 23, 1748. [Aug. 20, in his 51st y. G. R. 1.]
Jonathan, s. Jonathan and Rachel, Dec. 18, 1750.
Jonathan, Lt., s. Lt. Jonathan and Rebeckah, "in the Grate Battle" at Lake George, Sept. 8, 1755.
Jonathan, s. Lt. Jonathan and Rachel [wid. C. R. 1.], Jan. 26, 1756.
Jona[than], s. Oliver, brother of Lucy Spalding, at Dunstable, Aug. 12, 1820, a. 54 y. C. R. 1.
Mary, d. Samuel and Mary, Feb. 7, 1719-20.
Mary, w. Samuel, June 25, 1743.
Moses, Capt., Sept. 16, 1719. [a. abt. 50 y. G. R. 1.]
Olive, d. twin, Samuel and Sarah, sister twin, Elizabeth, Nov. 15, 1760, in her 19th y. G. R. 1. [Nov. 16. P. R. 4.]
Oliver, dysentery and old age, Nov. 11, 1809, a. 77 y. C. R. 1.
Samuel, Mar. 15, 1771. [a. 65 y. C. R. 1.]

BARRON, Sam[ue]ll, bur. Nov. 16, 1751, a. 72 y. C. R. 1. [d. Nov. 14. P. R. 4.]
Sarah, w. Ens. Samuel, Feb. 26, 1756.
Sarah, d. Samuel and Sarah, Mar. 17, 1756.
———, ch. Sam[ue]ll, jr., bur. Nov. 5, 1749. C. R. 1.

BARRY, Lucretia Caroline, w. William, Sept. 10, 1843, a. 24 y. G. R. 1.

BARTON, Hannah M., d. James [H. G. R. 3.] and Maria [Marinda. G. R. 3.] P., Apr. 19, 1849, a. 2 y. 25 d.
———, Mr., at the scythe factory, Dec. 29, 1827. C. R. 1.

BATEMAN, Ephraim, s. Lt. John, "killed instantly by a waggon passing over his neck," at West Cambridge, Nov. 12, 1818, in his 15th y. C. R. 1.
John, s. Lt. John and Hannah, Nov. 7, 1803, a. 2 y. 7 m. G. R. 1.
John, Lt., Dec. 22, 1828, a. 71 y. C. R. 1.
Lucy, d. John and Hannah, consumption, May 13, 1847, a. 49 y. 9 m.
Nancy, d. Lt. John, consumption, July 6, 1816, a. 21 y. C. R. 1.
Polley, d. Lt. John and Hannah, Mar. 13, 1798, a. 12 y. G. R. 1.

BATES (see also Battes), Deborah, bur. Mar. 25, 1772, a. 78 y. C. R. 1. [d. Mar. 23. P. R. 4.]
John, sr., Apr. 11, 1722. [a. abt. 80 y. G. R. 1.]
John, jr., May 1, 1722. [a. 53 y. 4 m. 9 d. G. R. 1.]
John [s. John and Deborah. G. R. 1.], May 22, 1724. [in his 17th y. G. R. 1.]
John, d. in ye army at Cambridge, bur. at Cambridge, Dec. 4, 1775. C. R. 1.
Jonathan, May 28, 1764. [a. 55 y. C. R. 1; in his 57th y. G. R. 1.]
Jonathan, s. Jonathan and Abigail [brother John, at Isaac Parker's. P. R. 4.], Mar. 1, 1771.
Lydia [w. Robert. G. R. 1.], old age, July 6, 1806, a. 88 y. C. R. 1. [in her 88th y. G. R. 1.]
Mary, w. John, Mar. 7, 1713-14.
Olive [Miss. G. R. 1.], consumption, Dec. 29, 1810, a. 55 y. C. R. 1. [Dec. 28, in her 59th y. G. R. 1.]
Robert, bur. May 23, 1791, a. 80 y. C. R. 1. [d. May 21. P. R. 4.]
———, wid., old age, Apr. 13, 1806, a. 93 y. C. R. 1.

CHELMSFORD DEATHS

BATTES (see also Bates, Bettey, Betty, Bettyes), Rebeckah, d. John and Mary, July 6, 1682.

BEAN, Sarah E., d. Eldad P. and Sarah S. [typhoid fever. P. R. 2.], Nov. 11, 1849, a. 7 y. G. R. 2.

BETTEY (see also Battes), Mary [wid. Andrew. G. R. 1.], old age, Jan. 27, 1813, a. 93 y. C. R. 1. [Jan. 28. G. R. 1.]
Molley, w. Andrew [bur. Sept. 25. C. R. 1.], 1757. G. R. 1. [d. Sept. 24. P. R. 4.]
——, ch. Andrew and Molley, ——, 1757. G. R. 1.

BETTY (see also Battes), Benjamin, s. And[re]w [fever. P. R. 4.], bur. Sept. 3, 1757. C. R. 1.
James, s. Andrew [fever. P. R. 4.], bur. Sept. 9, 1757. C. R. 1.
John, s. Andrew, bur. June 14, 1744. C. R. 1.
John, "a victim to Rum — once a sensible man & physician," May 5, 1827, a. 75 y. C. R. 1.
Joseph, s. And[re]w [fever. P. R. 4.], bur. Sept. 7, 1757. C. R. 1.

BETTYES (see also Battes), Andrew [Bettey. G. R. 1.], Apr. 26, 1786, a. 73 y. 8 m. 20 d.

BIAM (see also Byam), Exsperience, w. Abraham, 5: 5 m: 1683.
Sary, w. Abraham, Jan. 8, 1717-18.

BIAME (see also Byam), George, May 28, 1680. [May 27. P. R. 31.]

BICKFORD, ——, ch. Jonathan, bur. June 11, 1778. C. R. 1.

BIGSBY (see also Bixby), Thomus, Dec. 5, 1754. [a. 73 y. C. R. 1.]

BIRD, Mary Frances, d. Henry M. and Olive C., dysentery [scarlatina. dup.], June 21, 1849, a. 1 y. 5 m. 19 d.
Sarah Sheldon, d. Charles T. and Sarah H., Aug. 24, 1839. [a. 15 m. C. R. 3.]

BIXBY (see also Bigsby), Sary, d. Thomas and Deborah, Aug. 10, 1714.

BLAISDEL (see also Blaisdell), ——, ch. Will[ia]m, bur. Aug. 18, 1759. C. R. 1.

BLAISDELL (see also Blaisdel, Blasdell, Blesdill), Sarah, old age, Apr. 24, 1815, a. 80 y. C. R. 1.

BLANCHARD, Ann, wid., June 24, 1662.
John, July 23, 1678.
Martha, d. John and Hannah, Nov. 16, 1676.
[torn], —— [bet. 1678 and 1680.].

BLASDELL (see also Blaisdell), ——, wid., pauper, Oct. 20, 1820, a. 61 y. C. R. 1.

BLESDILL (see also Blaisdell), Aceneth, d. Henry and Mary Heald [after 1800], a. 37 y. G. R. 2.
Andrew, s. Henry and Mary Heald [after 1800], a. 32 y. G. R. 2.
Caroline, d. Henry and Mary Heald [after 1788], a. 2 y. G. R. 2.
Hellen, d. Henry and Mary Heald [after 1800], a. 20 y. G. R. 2.
John, s. Henry and Mary Heald [after 1788], a. 11 y. G. R. 2.
Mary Heald, w. Hen[r]y, May 10, 1842, a. 74 y. G. R. 2.
Roxy, d. Henry and Mary Heald [after 1788], a. 3 w. G. R. 2.
Sarah, d. Henry and Mary Heald [after 1800], a. 37 y. G. R. 2.

BLODGET (see also Blodgett, Blodgit, Blogett, Blogged, Blotchet), Benjamin, Apr. 9, 1708.
Betty, d. Simeon and Lidia, Mar. 21, 1778. [a. 10 y. 9 m. 16 d. G. R. 1.]
Ebenezer, s. Lt. William and Elizabeth, Jan. 1, 1733-4. [a. 4 y. 5 m. 14 d. G. R. 1.]
Elizabeth, w. Lt. William, Sept. 11, 1769, a. 67 y. 2 m. 23 d. G. R. 1.
Ephraim, s. Simeon and Lidia, Mar. 9, 1778. [a. 8 y. 4 m. 4 d. G. R. 1.]
Hannah, d. Simeon [and Lydia. G. R. 1; of a short illness. P. R. 4.], bur. Feb. 25, 1778. C. R. 1. [d. Feb. 23. P. R. 4; a. 20 y. 2 m. 13 d. G. R. 1.]
Lydia, w. Simeon, dropsy, bur. Oct. 8, 1801, a. 70 y. C. R. 1. [a. 69 y. G. R. 1.]
Mary, wid., June 8, 1749. [a. 87 y. C. R. 1.]
Nancy, w. Capt. Sewell, Nov. 7, 1820, a. 26 y. C. R. 1.
Nathanel, Oct. 12, 1710, a. 40 y. G. R. 1.
Olive, d. Lt. William and Elizabeth, Sept. 24, 1749. [a. 7 y. 2 m. 27 d. G. R. 1.]

BLODGET, Reuben, s. Lt. William and Elizabeth, Sept. 22, 1749. [a. 12 y. 3 m. 28 d. G. R. 1.]
Ruth, d. Lt. William and Elizabeth, Oct. 15, 1749. [a. 14 y. 7 m. 10 d. G. R. 1.]
Simeon, m., farmer, old age, Jan. 17, 1849, a. 84 y. 9 m.
Will[ia]m, Lt., bur. June 1, 1779, a. 83 y. C. R. 1. [a. 82 y. 2 m. 17 d. G. R. 1.]
William, s. Ezra, suddenly, Sept. 10, 1817, a. 26 y. C. R. 1.
——, inf. ch. Simeon, bur. May 19, 1752. C. R. 1.
——, inf. ch. Oliver, bur. June 22, 1760. C. R. 1.

BLODGETT (see also Blodget), Daniel, 28: 11 m: 1671. P. R. 31.

BLODGIT (see also Blodget), Daniel [Cornet. G. R. 1.], Apr. 14, 1761. [a. 72 y. C. R. 1; in his 72d y. G. R. 1.]

BLOGETT (see also Blodget), Marie, w. Thomas, Sept. 6, 1694. [Sept. 9. dup.]

BLOGGED (see also Blodget), Mare, w. Daniell, Sept. 5, 1666.
Nathaniell, s. Daniell, Oct. [torn. Oct. 27, 1666. CT. R.]

BLOOD (see also Bloud), Ada F., d. Charles S. and Sarah M., Jan. 24, 1849, a. 17 d.
Betsey A., w. Benja[min], jr., childbirth, July 21, 1847.
Elezebeth, w. Ephraim, Dec. 28, 1771. [a. 59 y. C. R. 1; a. 58 y. 7 m. 12 d. G. R. 1.]
Ephraim, bur. Mar. 18, 1775, a. 71 y. C. R. 1. [d. Mar. 16. P. R. 4; a. 72 y. 9 m. 2 d. G. R. 1.]
Lucy, d. Ephraim and Bettey, Dec. 27, 1756.
Tabatha, w. Josiah, July 29, 1796. [bur. Aug. 31. C. R. 1.]
Willard, s. Ephraim and Elizabeth, Jan. 9, 1747-8. [a. 4 y. 7 m. G. R. 1.]
——, inf. ch. Eph[rai]m, bur. Mar. 3, 1752. C. R. 1.
——, inf. ch. Ephraim, bur. May 23, 1755. C. R. 1.
——, s. Josiah, bur. Mar. 28, 1782. C. R. 1.
——, ch. stillborn, Josiah, bur. Feb. 20, 1783. C. R. 1.
——, ch. Aaron, bur. Aug. 2, 1797, a. 9 d. C. R. 1.
——, ch. Benja[min], jr. and Betsey A., July 27, 1847, a. 6 d.

BLOTCHET (see also Blodget), Simeon, old age, Nov. 10, 1804, a. 78 y. C. R. 1.

BLOUD (see also Blood), Richard, s. James, July 8, 1670. CT. R.

BOARDMAN, Sarah W., w. Amos, June 13, 1848, a. 42 y. G. R. 1.

BOWERS, Adelaide, d. Alpheus and Julia, lung fever, bur. Dec. 8, 1841, a. 1 y. C. R. 1.
Benjamin, of Merrimack, bur. May 8, 1781. C. R. 1.
Charles, late of Charlestown [d. at his brother Oliver's. P. R. 4.], bur. Dec. 11, 1770. C. R. 1.
Charles H., Mar. 1 [blot. 13?], 1829, a. 4 y. C. R. 3.
Chloe, w. Philip, enlargement of the liver, Nov. 19, 1807. C. R. 1.
Eben[eze]r, s. Luke, bur. July 18, 1799, a. 9 y. C. R. 1.
Elizabeth, w. Capt. Jerathmell, Mar. 4, 1721, in her 76th y. G. R. 1.
Elizabeth, w. Francis, bur. Aug. 8, 1794. C. R. 1.
Esther, w. Oliver, May 13, 1767. [May 14. P. R. 4.]
Hannah, wid. W[illia]m, Dec. 29, 1815, a. 75 y. C. R. 1. [a. 78 y. dup.]
Jerahmeel, Serg. [palsy. P. R. 4.], July 16, 1764. [July 15. P. R. 4; a. 79 y. C. R. 1.]
Jerath[m]eel, jr., s. Jerathmeel, Dec. 18, 1751.
Jerathmel, s. Jonathan and Hannah, May 7, 1713, a. 15 y. 4 m. G. R. 1.
John Fry, s. Philip and Chloe, bur. July 20, 1799. C. R. 1. [a. 2 y. 7 m. G. R. 1.]
Jonathan, Lt., bur. Sept. 28, 1756. C. R. 1. [d. Sept. 26. P. R. 4; in his 35th y. G. R. 1.]
Joseph A., s. Alpheus and Julia, dysentery, Aug. 16, 1848, a. 3 y.
Luke, dropsy, Aug. 28, 1818, a. 54 y. C. R. 1.
Mary, wid., bur. Oct. 11, 1780, a. 76 y. C. R. 1.
Mary [Miss, old age. C. R. 1.], Feb. 12, 1804. [a. 78 y. C. R. 1.]
Mary, Nov. 27, 1834, a. 34 y. C. R. 3.
Nathaniel, s. Jerathmel and Sarah, Feb. 27, 1726, a. 4 y. 11 m. G. R. 1.
Nathaniel, Apr. 4, 1726.
Samuel, s. [inf. C. R. 1.], Jerathmeel, jr. and Elizabeth, Apr. 1, 1751.
Sarah, w. Jerahmeel, Sept. 19, 1735. [Oct., a. 47 y. G. R. 1.]
William, fell down dead in his field, Nov. 25, 1812, a. 77 y. C. R. 1.

BOWERS, ——, wid. [Jerahmeel. P. R. 4.], bur. Mar. 8, 1771, a. 90 y. C. R. 1. [d. Mar. 7. P. R. 4.]
——, ch. Francis, bur. Sept. 16, 1777. C. R. 1.
——, inf. ch. Francis, bur. Jan. 14, 1781. C. R. 1.
——, s. Philip, Jan. 19, 1807, a. 4 y. C. R. 1.
——, ch. ——, drowned in the canal, Dec. —, 1824. C. R. 1.

BOYDEN, James [after Dec. 27], 1825, a. 34 y. C. R. 1.

BRACKLEY, Julia A., d. John and Lois, Jan. 27, 1849, a. 1 y. 3 m.

BRADSHAW, Sherwood, s. Luke and Charlotte, scarlatina, June 18, 1849, a. 6 y. [June 17. G. R. 3.]

BRADT, Barnabas, fever, May 3, 1828, a. 45 y. C. R. 1. [May 4. C. R. 3; May 1, a. 56 y. G. R. 1.]
Henry, drowned, Oct. 2, 1830, a. 32 y. C. R. 1. [Sept. 30. G. R. 1.]
Margaret, wid. Barnabus, June 25, 1848, a. 78 y. G. R. 1.

BREWER, ——, Mrs., at the glass house, Dec. —, 1831, a. 78 y. C. R. 1. [a. 76 y. C. R. 3.]

BRIDGE, Ebenezer, Rev., "ordained a minister in this Town", May 20, 1741, d. Oct. 1, 1792, in his 77th y. [a. 78 y. G. R. 1.]
Eben[eze]r, s. Rev. E., at Cassenobia, N. Y., Feb. 22, 1814, a. 71 y. C. R. 1.
Elizebeth, d. Rev. Ebenezer and Sary, Mar. 31, 1756. [a. 7 y. 8 m. 20 d. G. R. 1.]
Jerusha, sister Rev. Ebenezer, throat distemper, at Roxbury, Dec. 1, 1753, a. abt. 11 y. P. R. 4.
Joanna, 2d w. Rev. Eben[ezer], old age, Sept. 20, 1810, a. 86 y. C. R. 1.
Katharine, d. Rev. Ebenezer and Sary, Mar. 22, 1756. [Mar. 23, a. 1 y. 1 m. 7 d. G. R. 1.]
Rachel, wid. William, at Boston [at the residence of her son W[illia]m. C. R. 1.], Dec. 14, 1840, a. 86 y. [Dec. 13. C. R. 1.]
Sarah, w. Rev. Ebenezer, 3d d. Rev. Samson Stoddard, 3d pastor, Apr. 9, 1783, a. 64 y. G. R. 1.
W[illia]m, s. Rev. E., old age, July 13, 1826, a. 73 y. C. R. 1.
——, inf. ch. [d. Rev. P. R. 4.] Eben[eze]r, bur. Apr. 5, 1760. C. R. 1. [d. Apr. 4. P. R. 4.]

BRIDGE, ——, w. Eben[eze]r [eldest s. Rev. Ebenezer. P. R. 4.], bur. Sept. 29, 1787. C. R. 1. [d. Sept. 24. P. R. 4.]

BROOKS, Walter, pauper, fit, at the almshouse, Feb. 23, 1842, a. abt. 60 y. C. R. 1.

BROWN, Lucy, d. Samuel and Lucy, Oct. 14, 1802, a. 18 d.
Lucy, w. Samuel, Aug. 17, 1814, a. 36 y. G. R. 2.
Lucy, Mar. 19, 1840. C. R. 2.
Molly, old age, Mar. 7, 1810, a. 84 y. C. R. 1.
Reuben, consumption, Oct. 2, 1815, a. 27 y. C. R. 1.
Samuel, shoemaker, Revolutionary pensioner, old age, Jan. 23, 1846, a. 81 y. [Jan. 22, 1847. G. R. 2.]
Thomas, at Westford, Mar. 21, 1830. C. R. 2.

BRYANT, Henry, s. Henry and Lydia, Dec. 5, 1832.
Lucinda [Miss, late of Hillsborough, N. H. G. R. 1.], Dec. 20, 1830, a. 21 y. C. R. 1. [Dec. 14. G. R. 1.]

BULKLY, Edward, Rev., Jan. 2, 1695-6.

BURDG (see also Burge), John, Nov. 30, 1704.

BURDGE (see also Burge), John, s. John and Sarai, Mar. 12, 1740-41. [a. 21 y. 7 m. 19 d. G. R. 1.]
Joseph, s. John, Aug. 11, 1722.

BURDICK, Pliney, s. John and Phebe, drowned, Sept. 19, 1847, a. 3 y. 6 m.

BURGE (see also Burdg, Burdge), David, bur. June 26, 1776. C. R. 1.
Grisill, w. John [torn. July. CT. R.] 9, [torn. 1669. CT. R.].
[John. T. C.], s. John, 29: 9 m: 1680.
John, bur. Sept. 11, 1761, a. 74 y. C. R. 1. [d. Sept. 9. P. R. 4.]
Mare, w. John, Jan. 9 [torn. Jan. 8, 1663. CT. R.].
Rebecca, d. wid., bur. Nov. 25, 1778. C. R. 1. [d. Nov. 24. P. R 4.]
Rebeckah, d. John and Triall, Jan. 5, 1682.
Samuel, Jan. 25, 1728-9. [in his 82d y. G. R. 5.]
Tryal, Jan. 1, 1736-7.
——, ch. wid., bur. Nov. 2, 1778. C. R. 1.

BURGESS, Carrie, d. James C. and Susan A., May 27, 1849, a. 15 m. G. R. 3.

CHELMSFORD DEATHS 371

BURGESS, William B., machinist, s. Lancey Lot A., consumption, May 22, 1846, a. 35 y.
William Lott, s. William B. and Sarah P., Aug. 25, 1844, a. 7 w. G. R. 1.

BUSH, Elvira, w. ——, hatter, Apr. 18, 1828, a. 24 y. C. R. 1. [a. 29 y. C. R. 3.]

BUTERFEILD (see also Butterfield), Isek, s. Josiph and Lidah, Nov. 4, 1689.

BUTERFELLD (see also Butterfield), Deborah, w. Nathanill, June 25, 1691.

BUTERFIELD (see also Butterfield), Benjamin, jr. [Serg. G. R. 1.], Mar. 31, 1715. [a. 35 y. 1 m. 2 w. G. R. 1.]
Benjamin, sr., July 24, 1715.
Jonathan, Apr. 3, 1673.

BUTERFILD (see also Butterfield), Hannah, w. Benjamin, 19: 3 m: 1677.
——, d. Samuell, 13: 5 m: 1683.

BUTRICK (see also Butterick), ——, w. Ephraim, at Dracut, bur. May 20, 1803. C. R. 1.

BUTTERFEILD (see also Butterfield), Anna, w. Benjamin [torn. May 19. CT. R.], 1661.
Benjamin, s. Benjamin, Feb. [torn. 1662-3?].
Hannah, w. Samuel, Feb. 22, 1728-9.
Sarah, d. John and Anna, Apr. 28, 1738. [a. 12 y. 7 m. 2 d. G. R. 1.]
Sary, w. Nathaniel, June 19, 1734. [June 10. G. R. 1.]

BUTTERFELD (see also Butterfield), Abraham, June 8, 1693.
Mary, w. Jonathan, Apr. 8, 1673.
Mary, w. Samuel, Jan. 25, 1702-3.

BUTTERFIELD (see also Buterfeild, Buterfelld, Buterfield, Buterfild, Butterfeild, Butterfeld), Abigail, wid., bur. Mar. 6, 1773. C. R. 1.
Alles [wid. C. R. 1.], Mar. 6, 1777. [a. abt. 90 y. C. R. 1.]
Anna, d. Benjamin and Olive, Sept. 26, 1775, a. 4 y. 8 m. 1 d. G. R. 1.

BUTTERFIELD, Anna, wid., bur. Feb. 24, 1784, a. 81 y. C. R. 1.
Benjamin, Mar. 2, 1687-8. CT. R.
Benj[amin], old age, Nov. 16, 1811, a. 77 y. C. R. 1.
David, Dec. 3, 1763. [a. 52 y. C. R. 1.]
Emeline, d. Samuel and Hannah, Mar. 20, 1833, a. 13 y. G. R. 1.
Ephraim [s. Capt. John and Anna. G. R. 1.], bur. June 7, 1777. C. R. 1. [a. 36 y. 10 d. G. R. 1.]
Hannah, d. stillborn, Sam[ue]ll and Hannah, Nov. 14, 1704.
Hannah M., d. Stephen, whooping cough, Jan. 17, 1841, a. 9 m. C. R. 1.
Jacob, bur. Jan. 12, 1774. C. R. 1.
Jane, bur. Sept. 14, 1771. C. R. 1. [d. Sept. 13. P. R. 4.]
Joanna, wid. [formerly w. Jonathan Parker. P. R. 4.], bur. Mar. 27, 1791, a. 73 y. C. R. 1.
John, Capt., Jan. 8, 1766. [a. 68 y. C. R. 1.]
John, disease of the heart, Mar. 1, 1840, a. 74 y. C. R. 1.
Jonathan [sr. P. R. 4.], Apr. 17, 1750. [in his 67th y. G. R. 1.]
Keziah, wid., Mar. 17, 1792, a. 80 y. P. R. 4.
Mary, d. Capt. John and Anna, Apr. 20, 1747.
Mary, w. Nathaniel, June 1, 1748.
Mary [d. Samuel and Hannah. G. R. 1.], dysentery, Oct. 4, 1821, a. 12 y. C. R. 1.
Mercy, w. Jonathan, Apr. 25, 1743. [in her 75th y. G. R. 1.]
Nathaniel, Mar. 5, 1748-9. [a. 75 y. C. R. 1.]
Nathaniel, s. Nathaniel and Sary, at Lake George, Oct. —, 1756.
Olive, wid. Benj[amin], Aug. 21, 1826, a. 90 y. C. R. 1.
Ralph, typhus fever, Oct. 10, 1819, a. 32 y. C. R. 1. [Oct. 9. G. R. 6.]
Rebecca, wid. John, old age, Apr. 5, 1847, a. 84 y.
Reuben, s. Benjamin and Olive, Oct. 3, 1775, a. 11 y. 7 m. 23 d. G. R. 1.
Samuel, Jan. 24, 1741-2.
Sam[ue]l [s. Samuel and Hannah. G. R. 1.], worms, Jan. 18, 1805, a. 5 y. C. R. 1.
Sam[ue]ll, s. Sam[ue]ll and Rachell, Dec. 16, 1704.
Samuell, July 30, 1714.
Silous, s. Benjamin and Olive, Sept. 30, 1775, a. 2 y. 5 m. 1 d. G. R. 1.
Susan, fever, at Burlington, Feb. 27, 1813, a. 16 y. C. R. 1.
Tabitha, wid., bur. Feb. 20, 1781, a. 97 or 98 y. C. R. 1.
——, ch. Jona[than], bur. Sept. 23, 1745. C. R. 1.
——, ch. stillborn, Samuel, bur. Aug. 28, 1773. C. R. 1.
——, inf. ch. Sam[ue]ll, bur. Oct. 21, 1774. C. R. 1.
——, ch. stillborn, Sam[ue]ll, bur. Oct. 28, 1779. C. R. 1.

BUTTERFIELD, ——, ch. Sam[ue]ll, bur. Nov. 7, 1784. c. r. 1.
[d. Nov. 6. p. r. 4.]
——, ch. Benja[min], bur. May 15, 1790. c. r. 1.
——, ch. stillborn, John, bur. Sept. 1, 1792. c. r. 1.
——, ch. John, bur. Jan. 3, 1795, a. 10 w. c. r. 1.
——, ch. Samuel and Hannah, bur. Dec. 30, 1798. c. r. 1.

BUTTERICK (see also Butrick), Susan, w. Nathan, lately from Concord, convulsions, Mar. 13, 1817, a. 27 y. c. r. 1.
——, ch. stillborn, Nathan and Susan, Mar. 13, 1817. c. r. 1.

BYAM (see also Biam, Biame, Byham), Abraham [sr. dup.], Dec. 19, 1732.
Abraham, May 23, 1774. [a. 94 y. c. r. 1.]
Easther, Feb. 14, 1775.
Eunice [A. g. r. 3.] G[regory. g. r. 3.], b. Weston, w. Rufus, inflammation after parturition, May 22, 1845, a. 26 y. 9 m.
Henry, s. Henry and Lucy [throat distemper. p. r. 4.], June 22, 1756.
Henry, s. Henry, Sept. 3, 1828, a. 3 y. c. r. 1.
Isaac, bur. Jan. 22, 1778, a. 87 y. c. r. 1. [d. Jan. 21. p. r. 4.]
James, s. Henry and Lucy, June 10, 1756. [June 9. p. r. 4.]
James, s. John and Sarah, Jan. 3, 1766.
John, old age, July 3, 1813, a. 82 y. c. r. 1.
John Bateman, s. Ezekiel, Mar. 24, 1827, a. 4 y. c. r. 1.
Lucy, d. Henry and Lucy, Dec. 10, 1775.
Lucy, old age, Jan. 29, 1809, a. 88 y. c. r. 1.
Lucy [(Adams). p. r. 24.], w. Amos, Mar. 18, 1831, a. 45 y. c. r. 1.
Lydia, wid. Benjamin, cancer, Aug. 11, 1848, a. 79 y.
Mary, w. Isaac, May 4, 1760. [May 5. p. r. 4.]
Mary, old age, Apr. 16, 1828, a. 89 y. c. r. 1.
Nancy Bateman, d. Ezekiel, Aug. 26, 1828, a. 3 y. c. r. 1.
Oliver, s. Henry and Lucey [suddenly. p. r. 4.], Aug. 25, 1763.
Rebeckah C[hamberlain. p. r. 13.], w. Marcus D., Aug. 24, 1838, a. 33 y. g. r. 2.
Rebekah, w. Ens. Benjamin [worms. c. r. 1.], May 18, 1811. [a. 43 y. c. r. 1; a. 42 y. g. r. 1.]
Rufus, Oct. 2, 1845, a. 29 y. 23 d. g. r. 3.
Rufus G., s. Rufus and Eunice [A. g. r. 3.] G., May 17, 1845, a. 2 d.
Samuel, s. Isaac, Feb. 20, 1729-30.
Solomon, Jan. 16, 1834. c. r. 2. [a. 62 y. 8 m. p. r. 27.]
Sophronia, w. Josiah, Sept. 11, 1843, a. 43 y. g. r. 2.

BYAM, Susanna, wid. George, Aug. 21, 1687. CT. R.
Tabitha, d. Abraham and Mary, May 15, 1729.
Willard, s. Henry and Lucy, Oct. 10, 1776.
——, d. John, bur. July 27, 1775. C. R. 1.
——, two chn. Josiah, dysentery, July —, 1829. C. R. 1.

BYHAM (see also Byam), Amos, bur. Oct. 24, 1792. C. R. 1. [a. 38 y. G. R. 1.]
Experience, Sept. 14, 1741.
George, Jan. 12, 1739-40.
Henry, bur. Mar. 8, 1784, a. 63 y. C. R. 1.
Jacob, bur. Dec. 26, 1754. C. R. 1. [d. Dec. 24. P. R. 4.]
Jemima, Jan. 26, 1738-9.
Mary, w. Abraham, Nov. 14, 1725.
Mary, bur. Mar. 16, 1781. C. R. 1.
Sarah, d. Jacob, Jan. 10, 1723-4.
——, ch. Jacob, jr., bur. May 29, 1748. C. R. 1.
——, s. Jacob, jr., bur. Aug. 24, 1752. C. R. 1.
——, w. Ab[ra]h[a]m, bur. Nov. 5, 1766, a. 77 y. C. R. 1. [d. Nov. 3. P. R. 4.]
——, ch. John, bur. Feb. 16, 1775. C. R. 1.

CALDWELL (see also Colwell), John, old age, Feb. 25, 1825, a. 85 y. C. R. 1.
[Latitia. G. R. 1.], w. John, Aug. 21, 1819, a. 74 y. C. R. 1. [a. 79 y. G. R. 1.]

CAMPBELL, ——, ch. W[illia]m, bur. at Tewksbury, June 1, 1773. C. R. 1.
——, ch. William, bur. Sept. 23, 1775. C. R. 1.
——, ch. William, bur. Oct. 3, 1775. C. R. 1.

CARKIN, Joseph, lately from Vermont, glass blower, typhus fever, Nov. 26, 1820, a. 23 y. C. R. 1.

CARLETON (see also Carlton), John, s. John, fever, May 11, 1821, a. 25 y. C. R. 1.
Sarah, w. John, Oct. 30, 1825, a. 53 y. C. R. 1. [Oct. 25, a. 55 y. G. R. 1.]
Susanna, w. David, consumption, Oct. 4, 1823, a. 27 y. C. R. 1. [a. 26 y. G. R. 1.]
——, ch. Dean, bur. Feb. 21, 1791. C. R. 1.

CARLTON (see also Carleton), Amos, Aug. 7, 1833, a. 67 y. P. R. 7.

CHELMSFORD DEATHS 375

CARLTON, Daniel, s. Amos and Esther (Manning), Jan. 20, 1836, a. 29 y. P. R. 7.
David, May 14, 1848, a. 53 y. G. R. 1.
Dorothy, w. David, Nov. 31, 1825, a. 23 y. C. R. 1. [Nov. 30. G. R. 1.]
Esther (Manning), w. Amos, Jan. 21, 1823, a. 56 y. P. R. 7.
George, Aug. 3, 1843, a. 31 y. G. R. 1.
John, Sept. 15, 1846, a. 85 y. G. R. 1.
Mary J., d. David and Sarah, June 17, 1849, a. 16 y. 4 m. G. R. 1.
Sarah, w. David, intemperance, Sept. 14, 1845, a. 41 y.

CARLTOTLER, P., drowned in the canal, Aug. 15, 1813, a. 5 y. C. R. 1.

CARR, Joseph, s. Samuel and Maria, drowned, May 29, 1847, a. 8 y. 6 m.

CHAIMBERLEN (see also Chamberlin), Elizebeth, w. [wid. C. R. 1.] Joseph, Mar. 2, 1770. [a. 74 y. C. R. 1.]
Thomas, s. Benjamin and Esther, Nov. 13, 1757.

CHAIMBERLIN (see also Chamberlin), Abigail, w. Capt. Samul, May 15, 1760. [a. 77 y. C. R. 1; May 16, a. 76 y. 4 m. 10 d. G. R. 1.]
Samuel, Capt., Apr. 12, 1767. [a. 87 y. C. R. 1.]

CHAMBELIN (see also Chamberlin), Anna, d. Sam[ue]ll and Anna, Mar. 19, 1717.
Mary, w. Edmond, 6: 10 m: 16[torn. 1669. CT. R.].
Sam[ue]ll, s. Sam[ue]ll and Anne, Dec. 29, 1711.

CHAMBERLAIN (see also Chamberlin), Asunith, w. Benj[amin], June 23, 1828, a. 37 y. C. R. 1.
Benja[min], bur. Oct. 12, 1771, a. 67 y. C. R. 1. [d. Oct. 11. P. R. 4.]
Benjamin [jr. P. R. 4.], bur. Mar. 28, 1780. C. R. 1. [d. Mar. 27. P. R. 4.]
Caroline, Mar. 10, 1825, a. 5 w. G. R. 1.
Eleanor, d. Joseph, bur. Oct. 26, 1747. C. R. 1.
Harriet M., d. Isaac and Olive, very suddenly, at Portsmouth, May 22, 1821, a. 4 y. 23 d. G. R. 1.
Joseph [s. Jacob. P. R. 4.], bur. Dec. 4, 1787. C. R. 1. [d. Dec. 3. P. R. 4.]
Joseph, consumption, Dec. 20, 1830, a. 57 y. C. R. 1. [Dec. 19. G. R. 1.]

CHAMBERLAIN, Mary, wid., bur. Nov. 10, 1766, a. 69 y. C. R. 1.
[d. Nov. 8. P. R. 4.]
Mary, wid. Phinehas, Oct. 3, 1824, a. 77 y. C. R. 1.
Mary, w. Joseph, Oct. 20, 1845, a. 78 y. G. R. 1.
Nathaniel [s. Dea. P. R. 4.], bur. June 3, 1790. C. R. 1. [d. June 1. P. R. 4.]
Olive, d. Joseph, bur. Oct. 31, 1747. C. R. 1.
Phinehas, July 5, 1813, a. 68 y. C. R. 1. [July 4, a. 67 y. G. R. 1.]
Sally, wid. [w. Capt. G. R. 1.] Isaac, Jan. 12, 1840, a. 71 y. C. R. 1.
Sybil, bur. May 7, 1783. C. R. 1.
——, ch. Benja[min], jr., bur. Feb. 14, 1744. C. R. 1.
——, ch. Joseph, bur. Oct. 20, 1747. C. R. 1.
——, w. Benj[amin], jr., bur. Aug. 10, 1753. C. R. 1. [d. Aug. 9. P. R. 4.]
——, ch. stillborn, Aaron, bur. May 28, 1766. C. R. 1.
——, inf. ch. Aaron, bur. Apr. 6, 1767. C. R. 1.
——, ch. Benja[min], jr., bur. Dec. 29, 1768. C. R. 1.
——, ch. Ben[jamin], jr., bur. Jan. 23, 1769. C. R. 1.
——, inf. ch. Phineas, bur. Feb. 28, 1777. C. R. 1.
——, ch. Benjamin, bur. July 29, 1778. C. R. 1.
——, ch. Benja[min], bur. Aug. 12, 1778. C. R. 1.
——, inf. ch. Benja[min], bur. Apr. 23, 1782. C. R. 1.
——, ch. Benja[min], bur. June 14, 1783. C. R. 1.
——, s. Dea., bur. Sept. 22, 1783. C. R. 1.
——, w. Dea., bur. Apr. 3, 1790, a. 60 y. C. R. 1. [d. Apr. 2. P. R. 4.]
——, w. Jacob, bur. Aug. 15, 1792. C. R. 1.

CHAMBERLIN (see also Chaimberlen, Chaimberlin, Chambelin, Chamberlain, Chamberline, Chamberlyne, Chambrlin, Chambrling), Aaron [Dea. dup.], old age, Sept. 27, 1815, a. 90 y. C. R. 1.
Abigail, d. ——, very sudden, bur. Nov. 20, 1795. C. R. 1.
Anne, w. Samuell, Apr. 21, 1720. [in her 29th y. G. R. 1.]
Benjamin, Ens., Apr. 30, 1763. [a. 68 y. C. R. 1.]
Benjamin, "commonly Known by the name of the Lawyer," Dec. 26, 1812, a. 79 y. C. R. 1.
Benj[ami]n Franklin, s. Jacob, bur. Nov. 3, 1801, a. 8 m. C. R. 1.
Bettey, w. Isaac, July 12, 1795, in her 40th y. G. R. 1.
Clarissa, consumption, Apr. —, 1811, a. 14 y. C. R. 1.
Elisabeth, w. Thomas, jr., June 13, 1699.
Elizabeth, July 18, 1722.
Hannah, consumption, Mar. 25, 1805, a. 26 y. C. R. 1.

CHAMBERLIN, Ichabod, s. Capt. Isaac [and Sarah. G. R. 1.], Apr. 4, 1807, a. 2 m. 1 d. [a. 3 m. C. R. 1; in his 3d m. G. R. 1.]
Isaac, Dec. 29, 1827, a. 72 y. C. R. 1. [Dec. 18. G. R. 1.]
Isaac, Mar. 28, 1834, in his 46th y. G. R. 1.
Jacob, bur. Feb. 11, 1800, a. 71 y. C. R. 1. [Feb. 9, a. 73 y. G. R. 1.]
Jan [Jane. C. R. 1.], d. Capt. Samuel and Abigail, Aug. 8, 1754.
Joseph, Nov. 16, 1755.
Joseph, jr. [3d. G. R. 2.], Sept. 25, 1828, a. 30 y. C. R. 1. [Sept. 23. G. R. 2.]
Josiah B., s. Parker and Mary, Mar. 1, 1838, a. 1 y. 9 m. G. R. 2.
Judith, w. Jacob, bur. July 11, 1801, a. 24 y. C. R. 1. [in her 26th y. G. R. 1.]
Judith, d. Jacob, bur. Nov. 23, 1801, a. abt. 2 y. C. R. 1.
Lucy, d. Joseph and Elizebeth, Sept. 25, 1755.
Lucy Elizabeth, d. Joseph, 3d and Betsy, Jan. 7, 1827, a. 2 m. 9 d. G. R. 2.
Lydia, w. Jacob, May 31, 1775. [a. 46 y. 2 d. G. R. 1.]
Lydia Ann, June 17, 1832, a. 3 y. C. R. 1.
Mari, w. Thomas, sr., Feb. 7, 1692. [Feb. 8, a. 88 y. C. R. 1.]
Moriah J., d. Isaac and Olive [croup. C. R. 1.], Nov. 27, 1821, a. 2 y. 3 d. G. R. 1.
Rebecka, d. Phinehas and Rebecka, Jan. 9, 1773, a. 2 y. 4 m. 11 d. G. R. 1.
Rebekah, w. Phinehas, Aug. 12, 1775, in her 30th y. G. R. 1.
Rebekah, 2d d. Phinehas and Rebekah, Aug. 31, 1775, a. 2 m. 7 d. G. R. 1.
Sally, d. Aaron, Aug. [22?], 1821, a. 30 y. C. R. 1.
Samuel, Feb. 8, 1721-2.
Samuel, Feb. 16, 1745, a. 30 y. 7 m. G. R. 1.
Susanna, w. Benjamin, Oct. 7, 1801, a. 63 y. G. R. 1.
Thomas, Mar. 28, 1727.

CHAMBERLINE (see also Chamberlin), Annah, w. Thomas, Dec. 20, 1669. CT. R.

CHAMBERLYNE (see also Chamberlin), Elizebath, d. Sam[ue]ll and Elizebath, Nov. 13, 1694.

CHAMBERS, Dolly, in derangement, Aug. 21, 1822, a. 22 y. C. R. 1.
Joseph, cancer and dysentery, Sept. 5, 1809, a. 55 y. C. R. 1.
——, wid., bur. Sept. 27, 1775. C. R. 1.
——, ch. W[illia]m, bur. Oct. 4, 1785. C. R. 1.

CHAMBRLIN (see also Chamberlin), Eleizear, s. Samuell and Ana, Apr. 18, 1719.
Samuell, s. Sam[ue]ll and Ana, Apr. 3, 1719.

CHAMBRLING (see also Chamberlin), Eleiezer, s. Joseph, Dec. 9, 1717.
Susanah, w. Joseph, Dec. 2, 1717. [in her 26th y. G. R. 1.]

CHANDLER, Abigail Ann, d. Roger and Lydia, Oct. 9, 1825, a. 8 y. G. R. 1. [Oct. 8. C. R. 1.]
John, Rev., minister in Billerica from 1747 to 1760, Nov. 10, 1762. C. R. 1. [a. 39 y. P. R. 4.]

CHASE, Alfred K., s. A. J. and S. E. W., Oct. 12, 1846, a. 1 y. 5 m. G. R. 3.
Arabine, d. Mary J., a foreigner, cause unknown, Nov. 30, 1848, a. 2 m.
Sarah, w. John, Sept. 21, 1825, a. 36 y. G. R. 6.
[Sherburne. G. R. 1.], of Litchfield [N. H. G. R. 1.], died from effects of explosion in powder mill, Dec. 8, 1820. C. R. 1. [Dec. 7. G. R. 1.]

CHIVERS, ——, lockjaw, Aug. 4, 1812, a. 16 y. C. R. 1.

CLARK (see also Clarke, Clerk), Bridget, w. Isaac, bur. May 14, 1795. C. R. 1.
Edward A., s. Carlos C. and Emily G., Mar. 2, 1846, a. 6 y. G. R. 3.
Elizabeth, crazy, bur. Jan. 31, 1794, a. abt. 70 y. C. R. 1.
Elizabeth, d. Lt. Jonas and Elizabeth, ——. G. R. 1. [17—.]
Elizebeth, w. Col. Jonas, Apr. 27, 1767. [a. 74 y. C. R. 1; a. 76 y. P. R. 4.]
Frances M., d. Carlos C. and Emily G., Mar. 7, 1841, a. 3 y. G. R. 3.
Henry D., s. David and Harriet, Jan. 18, 1844, a. 2 y. 4 m. G. R. 3.
Isaac, widr., consumption, Feb. 4, 1804, a. 59 y. C. R. 1.
Jonas [Col. G. R. 1.], bur. May 1, 1770, a. 86 y. C. R. 1. [d. Apr. 28. P. R. 4; in his 86th y. G. R. 1.]
Mary, w. Thomas, Dec. 2, 1700. [Dec. 3, a. 53 y. G. R. 1.]
Mary Ella, d. Rev. Benja[min] F. and Mahitable [A. G. R. 3.], dysentery, July 17, 1849, a. 1 y. 8 m.
Mary Jane, d. David and Harriet, June 14, 1848, a. 2 y. 7 m. G. R. 3.
Sarah, d. Isaac, bur. Mar. 28, 1787. C. R. 1.

CLARK, Thomas, minister of Chelmsford [2d pastor, ordained in 1698. C. R. 1.], Dec. 7, 1704. [in his 52d y. G. R. 1.]
Timothy, bur. Apr. 17, 1790. C. R. 1. [d. Apr. 16. P. R. 4; in his 64th y. G. R. 1.]
——, eldest s. Col. [bef. May 22], 1753. P. R. 4.
——, ch. Isaac, bur. Apr. 25, 1793. C. R. 1.

CLARKE (see also Clark), [Adrian. G. R. 1.], "ch. Mrs., d. [sister?] Mrs. Dickerson and a resident of Buffalo, N. Y." [grands. Benjamin and Amey Prescott. G. R. 1.], May —, 1839. C. R. 1. [a. 9 m. G. R. 1.]
Isaac, jr., bur. Aug. 28, 1802. C. R. 1.

CLEAVELANDE (see also Cleveland), Jonathan, s. Josiah and Mary, Apr. 5, 1698.

CLERK (see also Clark), Mary, d. Jonas and Elizabeth, June 25, 1711.

CLEVELAND (see also Cleavelande), Jane, w. Samuell, Nov. 14, 1681.

COBORN (see also Colburn), John, Jan. 31, 1694-5.
Jonathan, Dec. 6, 1693.
Simon, July 31, 1694.

COBURN (see also Colburn), Henry, old age, May 21, 1829, a. 84 y. C. R. 1.
Olive, Mrs., of Dracut, on a visit at Mr. Henry Coburn's, suddenly, Aug. 3, 1819, a. 94 y. C. R. 1.
Rachel [Colburn. C. R. 1.], w. Dea. Thomas, Aug. —, 1763. [Aug. 18. P. R. 4; a. 79 y. C. R. 1.]
Ralph, s. Henry, jr., sore throat, Oct. 3, 1822, a. 2 y. C. R. 1.
Ralph Butterfield, s. Henry, Sept. 10, 1825, a. 2 y. C. R. 1.
Sarah, palsy, Sept. [bet. 2 and 22], 1826, a. 71 y. C. R. 1.
——, ch. Henry, Oct. 20, 1826, a. 1 y. 1 m. C. R. 1.

COCHRAN, Oscar A. [Oscar A. D. C. R. 3.], s. W[illia]m K. and Lydia, cholera infantum, Sept. 22, 1844, a. 1 y. 10 m.

COFFIN, Dorcas, wid. Dr. Charles, Nov. 16, 1836, a. 57 y. G. R. 1.

COLBORN (see also Colburn), Simon, s. Daniall and Sarah, June 26, 1695.

COLBURN (see also Coborn, Coburn, Colborn), Edward, Corp., Feb. 17, 1700.
Josiah, bur. Apr. 9, 1790. c. r. 1.
——, inf. ch. Timo[thy], of Dracut, d. at house of Jona[than] Bates, bur. May 21, 1752. c. r. 1.

COLBY, ——, Mrs., bur. Feb. 2 or 3, 1841. c. r. 3.

COLE, ——, w. John, bur. at Dracut, June 26, 1795. c. r. 1.

COLLER, Mary, d. stillborn, Nathanel and Mary, May 19, 1695.

COLWELL (see also Caldwell), ——, ch. ——, at the glass house, Jan. 23, 1816, a. 1 y. c. r. 1.

COMINGS (see also Cummings), Abraham [soldier, lately returned from Nova Scotia. p. r. 4.], s. Eleazer and Rachel, May 13, 1756.
Ebenezer, s. Dea. John, Mar. 5, 1726-7.

CONNETTLE (see also Knecttle), Ann [P. Knecttle, d. John R. and Harriett. g. r. 1.], Aug. 8, 1831, a. 9 m. c. r. 1. [Aug. 10, a. 7 m. g. r. 1.]
Daniel [B. Knecttle, s. John R. and Harriett. g. r. 1.], at the glass house, Aug. 1, 1831, a. 3 y. c. r. 1. [a. 2 y. g. r. 1.]

COREY (see also Cory), Ephraim, Sept. 16, 1741.
Olive, wid., July 3, 1805.

CORRY (see also Cory), Amme [Anne. ct. r.], d. Thomas and Abigaill, Apr. 29, 1686.

CORY (see also Corey, Corry), Eleazer, bur. Oct. 14, 1746. c. r. 1.
Elizabeth [at wid. Perham's. p. r. 4.], bur. Feb. 2, 1789. c. r. 1. [d. Jan. 30. p. r. 4.]
Esther, wid., bur. Dec. 11, 1775, a. 75 y. c. r. 1.
Hannah, wid., Dec. 13, 1746.
Han[na]h, wid., bur. June 14, 1769. c. r. 1. [d. June 13. p. r. 4.]
John, Nov. 15, 1747. [a. 81 y. c. r. 1.]
John, Jan. 28, 1753. [Feb. 8. p. r. 4.]
Josiah, s. Josiah, Oct. 10, 1738.
Josiah, Nov. 29, 1769. [Nov. 30. p. r. 4; a. 72 y. c. r. 1.]
Mary, old age, July [bet. 4 and 12], 1805, a. 80 y. c. r. 1.

CORY, Nathanill, s. Thomas and Abigaill, 22 : 10 m: 1674.
Oliver, bur. Jan. 30, 1769. C. R. 1. [d. Jan. 28. P. R. 4.]
Phinehas, s. Josiah, Sept. 28, 1738.
Reuben, bur. Mar. 10, 1774. C. R. 1.
Ruth, w. John, May 11, 1752.
Simeon, s. Ephraim and Hannah, at Lake George, Sept. —, 1756.
Solomon, June 2, 1772.
Willaird, s. John and Ruth, Nov. 30, 1739.
———, wid., bur: June 13, 1770. C. R. 1. [d. June 12. P. R. 4.]
———, ch. Hannah, bur. Mar. 19, 1790. C. R. 1. [bur. Mar. 20. P. R. 4.]

COTTON, Thomas, Sept. 30, 1687. CT. R.

COWDERY (see also Cowdry), Sam[ue]ll, bur. May 7, 1742. C. R. 1.

COWDRY (see also Cowdery), David, s. wid. Allis Butterfield, drowned in Souhegan River, Mar. 25, 1752. P. R. 4.
Matthias, Oct. 15, 1739, a. 41 y. 9 d. G. R. 1.

CROSBY, Almira, ch. illegitimate, Susannah, fever, Jan. 27, 1849, a. 6 m.
Hannah, bur. Dec. 31, 1770. C. R. 1.
Mary, Dec. 11, 1827. C. R. 2.
———, s. Nathan, jr., bur. Dec. 1, 1770. C. R. 1. [d. Nov. 29. P. R. 4.]
———, ch. Nathan, bur. Mar. 21, 1774. C. R. 1.
———, w. Simon, bur. Aug. 18, 1774. C. R. 1.

CROUCH, Elizabeth, July 20, 1722.

CUMMINGS (see also Comings), Henry, Rev. Dr., at Billerica, Sept. 6, 1823, in his 84th y. and 61st of his ministry. C. R. 1.

CURTIS (see also Curtiss), James, Feb. 27, 1848, a. 40 y. G. R. 4.

CURTISS (see also Curtis), Albert, s. James and Jane, May 9, 1847, a. 4 m. [May 8. G. R. 4.]

CUTLER, ———, ch. Charles, Oct. 15, 1825, a. 1 y. C. R. 1.

DADMUN, Betsey [w. Joseph. G. R. 2.], Sept. 6, 1839. C. R. 2. [a. 63 y. G. R. 2.]

DAKIN, —— [at ye Neck, at ye house of Josiah Fletcher. P. R. 4.], bur. Feb. 1, 1790, a. 94 y. C. R. 1. [d. Mar. 2, bur. at Dracut. P. R. 4.]

DALTON, John C., s. Dr. J. C., Oct. 17, 1824, a. 1 y. 3 m. C. R. 1.

DANE (see also Danes), [Alice. G. R. 6.], w. Joseph, consumption, Apr. 18, 1823, a. 68 y. C. R. 1. [Apr. 17, a. 64 y. G. R. 6.]
Dorcas, consumption, Jan. 26, 1828, a. 30 y. C. R. 1.
——, ch. ——, at Pawtucket, Aug. 24, 1823. C. R. 1.

DANES (see also Dane), Mehitabel, Nov. 16, 1833. C. R. 2.

DANIELS, ——, inf. ch. ——, Sept. 29, 1829. C. R. 3.

DAVICE (see also Davis), Experianc, d. Sam[ue]ll and Hanah, Dec. 11, 1707.
Stephen, s. Sam[ue]ll and Hanah, Feb. 28, 1711.

DAVIDSON, ——, w. Francis, bur. Dec. 31, 1779. C. R. 1.

DAVIS (see also Davice, Daviss), Bettey, w. Joshua [only d. Ephraim and Betty Blood. G. R. 1.], Dec. 3, 1769. [a. 22 y. 8 m. 15 d. G. R. 1.]
Elisha, s. Moses and Lydia, Sept. 18, 1775, a. 1 y. 4 m. 7 d. G. R. 1.
Elizabeth, 2d w. Joshua, Sept. 11, 1775, a. 30 y. 4 m. 7 d. G. R. 1.
Harriet, d. Johnson, quinsy, Dec. 12, 1810, a. 7 y. C. R. 1.
Johnson, Oct. 7, 1826, a. 56 y. G. R. 1.
Joshua, bur. Feb. 15, 1792, a. 49 y. C. R. 1. [Feb. 11, in his 49th y. G. R. 1.]
Joshua, consumption, Feb. 3, 1805, a. 34 y. C. R. 1.
Moses, fever, June 20, 1806, a. 66 y. C. R. 1. [June 21, a. 65 y. G. R. 1.]
Otis, inf. s. Josh[u]a and Eliza[beth], bur. June 16, 1800. C. R. 1.
Phebe, w. Sam[ue]l, Sept. 18, 1828, a. 52 y. C. R. 1.
Sabra, w. Johnson, bur. Dec. 27, 1796, a. 19 y. C. R. 1.
Sally, wid., bur. Sept. 21, 1801. C. R. 1.

DAVIS, Sarah Chardon Pitts, d. Sam[ue]l Pitts, at Belgrade, Me., May 12, 1834, a. 49 y.
Thomas, bur. Jan. 14, 1788. C. R. 1. [a. 40 y. G. R. 1.]
——, ch. Reuben, bur. Feb. 18, 1788. C. R. 1.
——, inf. ch. Reuben, bur. Sept. 10, 1790. C. R. 1.
——, ch. Abijah and Sally, both deceased, bur. Sept. 1, 1803. C. R. 1.

DAVISS (see also Davis), Anna, w. John, Jan. 30, 1747-8.

DEARDEN, Martha, w. Simon, b. 1782, d. ——, 1848. G. R. 1.
Simon, b. 1780, d. ——, 1845. G. R. 1.
William Ferriday, s. W[illia]m and Sarah F., b. 1843, d. ——, 1845. G. R. 1.

DEMERS, Louis, laborer, b. Quebec, L. C., cause unknown, Aug. 23, 1849, a. 23 y.

DICKENSON, Henry Ware, grands. Benjamin and Amey Prescott, Mar. 7, 1839, a. 9 1-2 m. G. R. 1. [Apr. —. C. R. 1.]

DIGGS, ——, ch. ——, bur. at Dunstable, Oct. 14, 1778. C. R. 1.

DILL, Peter, Aug. 13, 1692.

DITSON, Bridget, w. Seth, July 31, 1837, a. 79 y. G. R. 1.
Josiah, s. Josiah, Oct. 13, 1819, a. 3 y. C. R. 1.
Josiah Varnum, s. Josiah, quinsy, July 17, 1810, a. 4 m. C. R. 1.
——, Mr. [after Nov. 6], 1822, a. 60 y. C. R. 1.

DODGE, Rebecca, Nov. 4, 1825, a. 66 y. C. R. 1.

DRAKE, Ann Maria, d. Nathaniel [jr. C. R. 3.] and Susanah, July 7, 1844, a. 19 d. [July 25, a. 1 m. 19 d. G. R. 3.]
Susannah, b. Easton, w. Nathaniel [jr. C. R. 3], measles, June 24, 1844, a. 26 y. 9 m.

DRAPER, Josaph, Dec. 25, 1696.

DUDLEY (see also Dudly), Abi, Jan. 2, 1839. C. R. 2.
Martha Amanda, d. Otis B. and Martha, lung fever, May 12, 1848, a. 1 y. 6 m.

DUDLY (see also Dudley), Betsey [P., w. Dea. Benj[amin]. G. R. 2.], Nov. 28, 1837. C. R. 2. [a. 34 y. P. R. 27.]

DUNN, Betsey, d. James and Rachel, May 23, 1813.
Betty, d. Joseph and Mary, Aug. 23, 1778, a. 7 y. 9 d. G. R. 1.
Center, m., farmer, s. James and Rachel, pulmonary, intemperance, Jan. 23, 1849, a. 47 y.
Elizabeth, w. James, July 18, 1774, a. 58 y. 8 m. 4 d. G. R. 1.
James, bur. Apr. 19, 1803, a. 88 y. C. R. 1.
James, jr., s. James and Betsey [lung fever. C. R. 1.], Nov. 16, 1820. [a. 69 y. C. R. 1.]
John, dropsy, Apr. 19, 1805, a. 70 y. C. R. 1.
Jonas, s. Benjamin and Phebe, Dec. 31, 1773. [a. 5 y. 11 m. 19 d. G. R. 1.]
Joseph, Dec. 21, 1778, a. 41 y. 7 m. 10 d. G. R. 1.
Loammi, s. James and Rachel [at Litchfield, bur. with military honors being a member of the Rifle Company. C. R. 1.], Oct. 30, 1820. [a. 25 y. C. R. 1.]
Mary, wid., Oct. 11, 1822, a. 81 y. C. R. 1.
Mary, wid. John, Dec. 16, 1825, a. 43 y. C. R. 1.
Polly, d. James and Rachel, May 30, 1781.
Rachel, b. Merrimack, N. H., wid. James, old age, July 3, 1849, a. 89 y.
Relief, wid., dropsy, Apr. 6, 1818, a. 51 y. C. R. 1.
Robert, s. John, jr., bur. Aug. 30, 1803. C. R. 1.
Roxana R., d. Center and Mary, fever, Nov. 7, 1846, a. 7 y.
Sam[ue]l, delirium tremens, May 4, 1832, a. 35 y. C. R. 1.
Samuel C., Jan. 27, 1829, a. 1 y. C. R. 3.
Sarah [d. James, suddenly, at Phineus Underwood's, her brother-in-law. P. R. 4.], bur. June 15, 1781. C. R. 1. [d. June 14. P. R. 4.]
William, bur. July 12, 1785. C. R. 1. [d. July 11. P. R. 4.]
William, "brother of Betsey Mansfield, died at his sister's in Merrimak," fever, Mar. —, 1813, a. 28 y. C. R. 1.
William, s. James and Rachel, May 3, 1813.
———, ch. John, bur. Aug. 13, 1778. C. R. 1.
———, ch. John, bur. Apr. 20, 1782. C. R. 1. [d. Apr. 19. P. R. 4.]
———, w. James, bur. Mar. 9, 1802, a. 78 y. C. R. 1.
———, ch. John, jr., bur. May 2, 1803. C. R. 1.
———, ch. Sam[ue]l, Mar. —, 1831, a. 1 1-2 y. C. R. 1.

DURANT (see also Durrent), Benj[amin], scald, Mar. 16, 1808, a. 10 m. C. R. 1.
Cyrus, s. William and L. [Maria. G. R. 1.], scarlatina, Jan. 25, 1847, a. 7 y. 12 d.

DUREN, Isaac, May 28, 1835. C. R. 2.

DURGIN, Betsey, w. Silas, Mar. 12, 1844, a. 59 y. G. R. 3.
Celesta, b. New York, consumption, Oct. 12, 1847, a. 25 y.
Lomira A., w. Joseph H., consumption, Dec. 3, 1846, a. 25 y.
  [Dec. 23. G. R. 3.]
Silas, May 14, 1847, a. 62 y.

DURRENT (see also Durant), Benja[min], s. Benja[min] and
  Mary, Aug. 10, 1755.

DUTTEN (see also Dutton), James, July 12, 1755. [July 11.
  P. R. 4; a. 90 y. C. R. 1.]
James, s. James and Phebe, at Lake George, Oct. —, 1756.
Phebe, wid., bur. Mar. 1, 1759, a. 69 y. C. R. 1. [d. Feb. 28.
  P. R. 4.]
——, s. Alexander, Jan. 11, 1841, a. 6 m. C. R. 1.
——, d. A. P. [H. P. G. R. 1.], Apr. 10, 1841, a. 2 w. C. R. 1.

DUTTON (see also Dutten), Abigail, d. James and Ruth [wid.
  C. R. 1.], Dec. 17, 1773.
Edy, w. Ja[me]s, jr., Apr. 17, 1753. P. R. 4.
Elizabeth J. [J. B. G. R. 1.], Mrs. [w. H. P. G. R. 1.], consumption, Dec. 15, 1841, a. 26 y. C. R. 1.
Esther, d. James and Phebe, Jan. 22, 1750-51.
Hannah, w. David, apoplexy, Mar. 13, 1846, a. 69 y. [a. 70 y.
  G. R. 1.]
Jonas, Oct. 24, 1760.
Jonas, bur. Oct. 1, 1776. C. R. 1. [d. Sept. 29. P. R. 4.]
Levy, s. David and Hannah, Apr. 15, 1808.
Lucretia Williams, d. Parker and Lucretia B., Mar. 1, 1843,
  a. 1 y. G. R. 3.
Lucretia Woodbridge, d. Parker and Lucretia B., Feb. 5, 1839,
  a. 19 y. G. R. 3.
Mary, w. James, Feb. 9, 1724, in her 53d y. G. R. 1.
R., found dead in the field, Dec. 18, 1814, a. 17 y. C. R. 1.
Rebeca, cancer, Feb. 25, 1810, a. 54 y. C. R. 1.
Rebecca, wid., bur. Apr. 29, 1802, a. 80 y. C. R. 1.
——, ch. Mary, bur. Aug. 17, 1747. C. R. 1.
——, ch. wid. Ruth, bur. Nov. 2, 1757. C. R. 1.
——, wid., cancer, Mar. 3, 1809, a. 75 y. C. R. 1.
——, Mr., of Tewksbury, murdered, found in the Merrimac
  River below the falls, Oct. 17, 1822, a. 60 y. C. R. 1.

EAMES (see also Ames), ——, ch. Nathan and Phebe, bur.
  Oct. 26, 1800. C. R. 1.

EASTABROOKS (see also Estabrooks), Moses, consumption, Sept. 20, 1810, a. 58 y. C. R. 1.

EASTERBROOK (see also Estabrooks), Ester, wid., Aug. 26, 1825, a. 80 y. C. R. 1.

EBERT, Charles H., s. G. M. and Louisa, June 15, 1845, a. 11 m. G. R. 3.
George Edward [s. G. M. and Eva. G. R. 3.], Sept. 3, 1848, a. 12 y. 3 m.

EDWARDS, George Henry, s. Nathan B. and Maria H. F[letcher. G. R. 3.], dropsy on the brain, Oct. 19, 1849, a. 1 y. 9 m.
Harriet A., d. Isaiah and Harriet N. Howard, Apr. 25, 1846, a. 1 y. 11 m. G. R. 3.

ELIOT, Ann, wid., an old School Dame, bur. Apr. 23, 1780, a. 91 y. C. R. 1. [d. Apr. 22. P. R. 4.]

ELLIS, Laroy, s. Benja[min] and Mahala, Apr. 5, 1849, a. 1 y. 2 m.

EMERSON (see also Emmerson), Bryant, farmer, s. Dea. Owen and Mary, consumption, Nov. 5, 1846, a. 46 y.
Charles H., s. adopted, Thomas and Betsey Saunders, Mar. 9, 1844, a. 4 y. G. R. 3.
Elizabeth, w. Joseph, Oct. 23, 1773, a. 23 y. 11 m. 13 d. G. R. 1.
Elizabeth, d. Joseph and Ruth, Nov. 19, 1782, in her 4th y. G. R. 1.
Franklin, s. Dea. Owen [intemperance. C. R. 1.], Nov. 29, 1841. [Nov. 30, a. 35 y. C. R. 1.]
Hannah Eliza, d. Bryant and Hannah [A. G. R. 1.], Aug. 31, 1837. [a. 1 y. 2 m. 22 d. P. R. 3.]
Joanna (Warren), Mrs., Apr. 14, 1834, a. 43 y. P. R. 7.
John, s. Joseph and Elizabeth, July 10, 1772, a. 5 m. 3 d. G. R. 1.
John, s. Owen, Sept. 10, 1825, a. 13 m. C. R. 1.
John O., engineer, s. Owen and Louisa B., fever, Nov. 24, 1846, a. 20 y. [Nov. 23. G. R. 1.]
Joseph, Rev., of Pepperell, Oct. 29, 1775. C. R. 1.
Joseph, Capt., bur. Nov. 26, 1792. C. R. 1. [Nov. 22, a. 46 y. 2 d. G. R. 1.]
Joseph L., s. Owen and Louisa B., b. Aug. 4, 1824, d. Sept. 7, 1825. G. R. 1.

CHELMSFORD DEATHS 387

EMERSON, Mary Rebecca, d. Owen and Loiza [Louisa B. G. R. 1.], epilepsy, Jan. 5, 1840, a. 12 y. C. R. 1.
Owen, Dea., June 19, 1836. [June 11, a. 63 y. C. R. 1.]
Owen Spalding, s. Franklin, Nov. 27, 1840, a. 1 y. C. R. 1.
Rufus, s. Dea. Owen and Mary, Nov. 18, 1835.
Ruth, wid., consumption, Feb. 8, 1804, a. 62 y. C. R. 1. [Feb. 7, a. 59 y. G. R. 1.]

EMERY (see also Emmery), James, s. Zacheriah, "in the Grate Battle" at Lake George [at Fort Edward. P. R. 4.], Sept. 8, 1755.
Noah, s. Zachariah and Sary, July 18, 1718.
Noah, bur. Feb. 13, 1747. C. R. 1.
Sarah, w. Zachary, Oct. 8, 1732.
Thankful, w. Zachariah, Aug. 31, 1785, in her 75th y. G. R. 1.
Thankfull, d. Zachariah and Thankfull, Oct. 9, 1751.
Thomas, s. Dr. Anthony and Abigail, Aug. 18, 1747.
——, ch. stillborn, Zach., bur. June 20, 1746. C. R. 1.
——, ch. wid. Mary, bur. June 2, 1747. C. R. 1.
——, ch. stillborn, Zach., bur. Sept. 12, 1747. C. R. 1.
——, ch. Samuel, bur. Mar. 23, 1778. C. R. 1.

EMMERSON (see also Emerson), Obadiah, bur. Jan. 13, 1746. C. R. 1.
William, Rev., of Concord, Chaplain in ye Army at Ticonderoga, ——, 1776. C. R. 1.

EMMERY (see also Emery), Zechariah, Aug. 30, 1776. [a. 86 or 87 y. C. R. 1; in his 86th y. G. R. 1.]

ESTABROOKS (see also Eastabrooks, Easterbrook), John, Feb. 11, 1821, a. 40 y. C. R. 1.
——, ch. Moses, bur. Feb. 20, 1746. C. R. 1.
——, inf. ch. Moses, bur. Jan. 16, 1779. C. R. 1.

ESTY, Mary Abigail, d. John and Sarah B., Apr. 30, 1847, a. 3 y. G. R. 1.

EVERETT, John, see Weebe, John.

FALKNER, Sarah, d. Timothy and Deborah, Aug. 27, 1740.

FARLEY, ——, ch. Timo[thy], bur. Oct. 29, 1758. C. R. 1.

FARMER, Charlotte, wid. Elijah, July 26, 1826, a. 45 y. C. R. 1. [July 27. G. R. 1.]

FARMER, Elijah, consumption, Feb. 2, 1826, a. 50 y. C. R. 1.
[Feb. 3. G. R. 1.]
John, ———, 1814. C. R. 1.
Jonas, May 5, 1801.
Sampson, "non com" [after Nov. 4], 1823, a. 60 y. C. R. 1.
Simeon, Jan. 25, 1822, a. 87 y. C. R. 1.
———, inf. ch. Jonas, bur. Mar. 21, 1764. C. R. 1.
———, ch. Simeon, bur. Dec. 9, 1765. C. R. 1.
———, w. Jonas, bur. Apr. 11, 1775. C. R. 1.
———, w. Simeon, bur. Oct. 15, 1781. C. R. 1.

FARNUM, Pamela, Nov. 20, 1827, a. 59 y. C. R. 1.

FARR, Levi [consumption. C. R. 1.], Jan. 19, 1821. [a. 72 y. C. R. 1.]
———, Mr., of Fitchburg, mortally wounded by the explosion of the powder mill, June 6, 1821. C. R. 1.

FARRAR, Deborah [w. Joseph. G. R. 1.], in a fit, very sudden, June 31, 1808, a. 81 y. C. R. 1. [June 30. G. R. 1.]
Elizabeth, w. John, Mar. 5, 1844, a. 70 y. G. R. 1.
John, lung fever, Jan. 22, 1830, a. 62 y. C. R. 1.
Jonas, consumption, June 5, 1806, a. 45 y. C. R. 1. [in his 45th y. G. R. 1.]
Joseph, numb palsy, bur. Apr. 22, 1797. C. R. 1. [Apr. 20, in his 79th y. G. R. 1.]
Joseph, bur. Aug. 1, 1799, a. 21 y. C. R. 1.
Petre, widr., consumption, Mar. 7, 1804, a. 39 y. C. R. 1. [Mar. 5, in his 36th y. G. R. 1.]

FARWELL, Henry [torn. suddenly. P. R. 1; Aug. 1, 1670. CT. R.].
Ollive, wid. Henre, Mar. 1, 1691-2.
———, Mrs., Nov. 26, 1828. C. R. 3.

FAVER, Reuben, trader, Sept. 6, 1830, a. 38 y. C. R. 1.

FISH, Mary J., d. John B. and Mary, Mar. 17, 1849, a. 7 m.

FISHER, George Abbot, s. John and Lucy, Oct. 7, 1814.
John Adams, s. John and Lucy, Apr. 19, 1814.
John T., s. John and Lucy, Oct. 11, 1823, a. 8 y. G. R. 6.

FISK (see also Fiske), Eliza, d. Benj[amin] and Betsy, Mar. 12, 1804, a. 1 d. C. R. 1.
John, Aug. 29, 1687. CT. R.

FISKE (see also Fisk), Ann, w. [Rev. P. R. 1.] John, 14: 12 m: 1671.
Chloe, bur. Oct. 26, 1801, a. 19 y. C. R. 1.
John, pastor, ———. [1st pastor of church in Chelmsford, b. St. James, Suffolk Co., Eng. C. R. 1; b. South Elmham, Suffolk Co., Eng., ab't 1601. In 1637 he came to New England. In 1644 he gathered a church at Wenham, and continued as its pastor until 1656 when he removed with the greater part of his church to Chelmsford where he ministered both as pastor and physician, d. Jan. 14, 1676, a. 76 y. G. R. 1.]
John Minot, counsellor-at-law, intemperance, Aug. 16, 1841, a. 43 y. C. R. 1.
Jonathan, consumption, Mar. 18, 1812, a. 33 y. C. R. 1.

FITCH, Hannah, w. Sam[ue]l, d. at Andover, bur. May 21, 1795. C. R. 1.

FITZGERALD, James, bur. Aug. 9, 1781. C. R. 1. [d. Aug. 9. P. R. 4.]
———, Mr., of Fitchburg, mortally wounded by the explosion of the powder mill, June 6, 1821. C. R. 1.

FLATCHER (see also Fletcher), Hanah, w. Samuell, Dec. 11, 1697.
Samuell, Serg., Dec. 9, 1697. [a. 65 y. G. R. 1.]
Samuell, s. Samuell and Mary, Feb. 11, 1698. [Feb. 1, 1697, a. 11 d. G. R. 1.]

FLECHER (see also Fletcher), Grisell, w. Joshuah, 17: 1 m: 1682.
Hannah, w. Samuell, 11: 6 m: 168[3. T. C.].
Thomis, s. Sameuell and Mary, Mar. 3, 1698. [Apr. 3, a. 4 y. 10 m. G. R. 1.]
William [Ens. T. C.], Nov. 6, 1677.
William, s. Joshuah, 6: 1 m: 1682.

FLETCHER (see also Flatcher, Flecher), Aaron, nervous fever, bur. July 22, 1801, a. 22 y. C. R. 1.
Andrew [s. Josiah and Joanna. G. R. 1.], Apr. 23, 1759. [a. 37 y. 6 m. 24 d. G. R. 1.]
Andrew, bur. Apr. 4, 1792. C. R. 1. [d. Apr. 2, a. abt. 40 y. P. R. 4.]
Andrew, July 15, 1811.
Anna, w. Capt. Benjamin [after Nov. 6], 1822, a. 73 y. C. R. 1.

FLETCHER, Benjamin, s. Andrew and Elizabeth [wid. C. R. 1.], July 25, 1764. [a. 4 y. 8 m. 26 d. G. R. 1.]
Benjamin, bur. Dec. 24, 1772. C. R. 1. [d. Dec. 23. P. R. 4; in his 57th y. G. R. 1.]
Benjamin, s. Aaron and Sally, Sept. 29, 1810, a. 3 y. 8 d. G. R. 1.
Benjamin, m., farmer, s. Benjamin, Sept. 23, 1844, a. 41 y.
Benjamin Chamberlin, s. Maj. Joseph and Lucy, Nov. 23, 1815. [Nov. 24, a. 4 m. C. R. 1.]
Betsy, w. Adams, typhus fever, Dec. 5, 1811, a. 28 y. C. R. 1. [Dec. 4. G. R. 1.]
Deborah, wid., old age, Feb. 8, 1804, a. 75 y. C. R. 1.
Edward, s. Robert and Remembrance, Sept. 28, 1746.
Elizabeth, wid. Joshua, jr., Mar. 8, 1741-2.
Elizabeth, d. Andrew and Elizabeth [wid. C. R. 1.], July 30, 1764. [a. 11 y. 4 m. 16 d. G. R. 1.]
Elizabeth, wid., bur. Nov. 29, 1782. C. R. 1.
Ephraim, s. Samuel and Deborah, Nov. 7, 1763. [a. 3 m. P. R. 2.]
Esther, d. Joshua and Elizabeth, Oct. 27, 1737, a. 11 y. 1 m. 13 d. G. R. 1.
Ezekiel [H. G. R. 1.], Dr., s. W[illia]m, typhus fever, Aug. 15, 1817, a. 31 y. C. R. 1.
Franklin, instantly, by a wagon, Sept. 30, 1810, a. 3 y. C. R. 1.
Grace, wid. Oliver, at Plymouth, Vt., Aug. 10, 1818, a. 85 y. C. R. 1.
Hannah, w. Lt. Benja[min], Sept. 26, 1778. [in her 30th y. G. R. 1.]
Hannah, w. Josiah, June 9, 1836, a. 41 y. 9 m. G. R. 1.
Henry, s. Josiah and Joanna, June 1, 1764. [a. 35 y. 16 d. G. R. 1.]
Henry, slain in Battle at Stillwater, Feb. 3, 1780.
Isaac, Dec. 15, 1772. [a. 81 y. C. R. 1.]
Jacob, s. Sam[ue]ll, Feb. 15, 1716.
Jemima, d. William and Lydia, Sept. 24, 1779, a. 3 y. 10 m. G. R. 1.
Jeptha, s. Lt. Benja[min] and Hannah, Sept. 26, 1778. [in his 4th y. G. R. 1.]
Joana, wid. [w. Josiah. G. R. 1.], bur. Oct. 3, 1768, a. 80 y. C. R. 1. [d. Oct. 1. P. R. 4; in her 79th y. G. R. 1.]
Joanna, d. Josiah and Joanna, Apr. 13, 1718, a. 2 y. 7 m. G. R. 1.
John, s. Capt. Benj[amin], apoplectic fit, July 22, 1830, a. 48 y. C. R. 1.
John Adams, s. Maj. Joseph and Lucy, Feb. 14, 1817.

CHELMSFORD DEATHS 391

FLETCHER, Jonathan, s. Lt. William and Mary, Nov. 14, 1739, a. 18 y. 3 m. 22 d. G. R. 1.
Jonathan, s. Andrew and Elizabeth [wid. C. R. 1.], Aug. 9, 1764. [a. 8 y. 10 m. 9 d. G. R. 1.]
Joseph M., Oct. 1, 1828. G. R. 1.
Joshua, Nov. 21, 1713. [Nov. 22. P. R. 31.]
Joshua, Sept. 15, 1727, a. 26 y. 4 m. 1- d. G. R. 1.
Joshua, s. Joshua and Elizabeth, Nov. 5, 1737, a. 13 y. 3 m. 26 d. G. R. 1.
Josiah, Jan. 30, 1760. [a. 73 y. G. R. 1.]
Josiah, bur. July 20, 1802, a. 83 y. C. R. 1. [July 18, 1803. G. R. 1.]
Lucy, w. W[illia]m, hydrocephalus, Dec. 20, 1814, a. 61 y. C. R. 1. [Dec. 19. G. R. 1.]
Lucy, w. Cornet Josiah, consumption, Sept. 30, 1818, a. 51 y. C. R. 1.
Lydia, w. Andrew, Feb. 9, 1746-7. [a. 24 y. 4 d. G. R. 1.]
Lydia, d. Thomas and Mary, Nov. —, 1770, a. 5 y. 4 m. 13 d. G. R. 1. [bur. Nov. 30. C. R. 1.]
[Lydia. G. R. 1.], w. Will[ia]m, bur. Jan. 20, 1779. C. R. 1. [Jan. 8, a. 28 y. 8 m. 16 d. G. R. 1.]
Lydya, wid., Oct. 12, 1704.
Marah, wid., old age, Feb. 20, 1806, a. 75 y. C. R. 1.
Marriam, w. Henry, June 19, 1806, a. 30 y. [a. 31 y. C. R. 1.]
Mary, w. Samuell, Jan. 30, 1705. [a. 28 y. G. R. 1.]
Mary, w. William, Dec. 13, 1721. [a. 39 y. G. R. 1.]
Mary, wid. [w. Lt. William. G. R. 1; mother Benja[min]. P. R. 4.], bur. Feb. 25, 1768, a. 84 y. C. R. 1. [d. Feb. 23. P. R. 4.]
Mary, d. Lt. Benja[min] and Hannah, Oct. 3, 1778. [in her 9th y. G. R. 1.]
Mary, w. Josiah, June 9, 1781, a. 58 y. G. R. 1.
Mary A. Johnson, w. Moses, b. —— 1806, d. June 27, 1839. G. R. 3.
Membrance, w. Robert, Feb. 13, 1778. [in her 59th y. G. R. 1.]
Oliver [Justice, apoplexy. P. R. 4.], Nov. 30, 1771. [a. 64 y. C. R. 1; in his 63d y. G. R. 1.]
Oliver, in a state of derangement, July 12, 1825, a. 30 y. C. R. 1.
Orpha, w. William, jr., very suddenly, Feb. 24, 1839. C. R. 1.
Paull, s. William and Lidiah, Aug. 9, 1676.
Perciss, w. Isaac, Sept. 5, 1747.
Polley, b. Dracut, wid. W[illia]m, sr., dysentery, Oct. 6, 1849, a. 70 y.
Rebeckah, d. Lt. Benja[min] and Hannah, Sept. 24, 1778.
Robert, bur. Mar. 8, 1781, a. 68 y. C. R. 1.

FLETCHER, Sampson, s. William [and Mary. G. R. 1.], Mar. 6, 1721-2. [1720-21, a. 2 y. 1 m. G. R. 1.]
Samuel, s. Sam[uel], of Temple, bur. Dec. 4, 1795, a. 8 y. C. R. 1.
Samuel, bur. Dec. 16, 1802, a. 76 y. C. R. 1.
Samuell, Jan. 24, 1705. [1704-5. P. R. 31; a. 40 y. 6 m. G. R. 1.]
Samuell, s. Samuell, Feb. 26, 1716.
Sarah, w. Sam[ue]ll, d. Joseph Mariam of Concord, Apr. 29, 1703.
Sarah, d. Joshua and Doretha, May 18, 1704.
Sarah, d. Thomas and Mary, Aug. 20, 1758. [a. 1 m. 24 d. G. R. 1.]
Sarah, d. Lt. Benja[min] and Hannah, Oct. 5, 1778. [in her 6th y. G. R. 1.]
Solomon, Dec. 10, 1811, a. 42 y. C. R. 1.
Stephen, bur. Dec. 8, 1767, a. 55 y. C. R. 1. [d. Dec. 6. P. R. 4.]
Susa, d. William and Lucy, Feb. 10, 1785, a. 6 y. 5 m. 19 d. G. R. 1. [Feb. 11. P. R. 4.]
Susanna, wid. Steven, old age, Oct. 18, 1817, a. 96 y. C. R. 1.
Sybil, w. Zacheus, bur. June 8, 1796. C. R. 1.
Tabitha, wid. William, Feb. 6, 1741-2. [in her 52d y. G. R. 1.]
Tabitha, for many years blind, July 14, 1820, a. 69 y. C. R. 1.
Thomas, s. Thomas and Mary, July 4, 1764, a. 3 y. 4 m. 29 d. G. R. 1.
Thomas, Aug. 7, 1771. [a. 60 y. C. R. 1.]
Timothy, Mar. 2, 1705.
Varnum, typhus fever, Nov. 6, 1825, a. 12 y. C. R. 1.
William, Lt., May 23, 1712, a. 55 y. 4 m. G. R. 1.
William, Serg., Jan. 27, 1741-2. [a. 52 y. 10 m. G. R. 1.]
William, Lt., Mar. 21, 1743-4. [in his 71st y. G. R. 1.]
William, bur. Feb. 10, 1777. C. R. 1.
William, farmer, old age, June 18, 1845, a. 90 y. 6 m.
William, widr., farmer, s. William, consumption, Dec. 15, 1846, a. 65 y.
——, inf. ch. Sime[on], bur. Nov. 18, 1748. C. R. 1.
——, ch. Stephen, bur. Feb. 9, 1750. C. R. 1.
——, s. Will[ia]m, bur. Oct. 25, 1751. C. R. 1.
——, ch. stillborn, Stephen, bur. June 26, 1754. C. R. 1.
——, ch. stillborn, Stephen, bur. Aug. 18, 1755. C. R. 1.
——, s. Steph[e]n, bur. Oct. 7, 1756. C. R. 1.
——, ch. Will[ia]m, bur. Aug. 15, 1757. C. R. 1.
——, inf. ch. Robert, bur. Mar. 30, 1759. C. R. 1.
——, inf. ch. stillborn, Stephen, bur. Apr. 27, 1759. C. R. 1.
——, inf. ch. stillborn, Robert, bur. Jan. 31, 1761. C. R. 1.

FLETCHER, ——, ch. Stephen, bur. Oct. 20, 1764. C. R. 1.
——, ch. Stephen, bur. Oct. 29, 1764. C. R. 1.
——, ch. William, bur. Jan. 17, 1765. C. R. 1.
——, ch. Benja[min], bur. Aug. 10, 1772. C. R. 1. [d. Aug. 8. P. R. 4.]
——, ch. William, bur. Sept. 25, 1778. C. R. 1.
——, ch. Will[ia]m, bur. Feb. 12, 1786. C. R. 1.
——, w. Josiah, jr., bur. Dec. 6, 1786. C. R. 1. [d. Dec. 3, P. R. 4.]
——, ch. stillborn, Andrew, bur. Dec. 22, 1786. C. R. 1.
——, inf. ch. Capt. Ben[jamin], bur. Mar. 27, 1787. C. R. 1.
——, inf. ch. Lt. Josi[a]h, bur. Apr. 17, 1790. C. R. 1.
——, ch. W[illia]m Benjamin, Feb. 16, 1816, a. 15 m. C. R. 1.
——, w. Andrew, jr., Nov. 24, 1846. C. R. 3.

FLINT, Luther, consumption, July 10, 1810, a. 23 y. C. R. 1.

FORD, Eben[eze]r, s. John, drowned, bur. July 18, 1796, a. 7 y. C. R. 1.
Iekeli, s. Elisha, dropsy in the head, Mar. 28, 1812, a. 1 1-2 y. C. R. 1.
John, a Revolutionary patriot, Nov. 6, 1822, a. 82 y. C. R. 1.
Sam[ue]l Perham, s. Elisha, "killed by a waggon passing over his head," May 18, 1822, a. 7 y. C. R. 1.
Sarah, w. Elisha, consumption, Nov. 22, 1815, a. 31 y. C. R. 1.
——, ch. John, bur. July 4, 1774. C. R. 1.
——, ch. John, bur. Apr. 20, 1790. C. R. 1.
——, Mrs., palsy, Dec. 29, 1804, a. 60 y. C. R. 1.
——, two chn. Elisha, Sept. 18, 1809. C. R. 1.
——, ch. Capt. Elisha, Nov. 14, 1812. C. R. 1.

FORSTER (see also Foster), Elizabeth, w. James, consumption, Aug. 15, 1824, a. 44 y. C. R. 1.

FOSTER (see also Forster), Aaron, s. William and Hannah, Nov. 4, 1753. [a. 2 y. 9 m. 8 d. G. R. 1.]
Abigail, w. J[o]nathan, Jan. 8, 1759.
Abraham, s. Samuell and Ester, Dec. 7, 1671.
Andrew, s. Samuell and Ester, Dec. 20, 1671.
Andrew, s. Samuell and Ester, Aug. 13, 1676.
[Anna. G. R. 1.], w. Isaiah, bur. May 26, 1786, a. 64 y. C. R. 1. [d. May 25. P. R. 4; in her 63d y. G. R. 1.]
Benj[amin], Lt., "killed by lightening," Aug. 2, 1819. C. R. 1.
Benony, s. Joseph and Thankfull, Feb. 7, 1733-4.
Betsey, Miss, May —, 1839. C. R. 1.

FOSTER, Bridget, d. wid. Rem[embrance], bur. Mar. 23, 1752. C. R. 1. [d. Mar. 20. P. R. 4.]
Ebenezer, s. Edward and Rebeckah, May 13, 1756. [a. 65 y. C. R. 1.]
Ebenezer, Jan. 1, 1763.
Eb[ene]z[er], s. in-law W[illia]m, in the army [bef. Nov. 5], 1777. P. R. 4.
Edmund, Rev., Mar. 28, 1826, in the ministry 45 y. C. R. 1.
Edward, "by faling into the sawmil," Feb. 22, 1715-16. [a. abt. 39 y. G. R. 1.]
Edward, Lt., s. Samuell and Sarah, July 12, 1740. [1741, a. 51 y. 5 m. 13 d. G. R. 1.]
Eli, Jan. 24, 1717-18. P. R. 31.
Eliza[beth], wid. [Jonathan. P. R. 4.], bur. Feb. 10, 1759, a. 85 y. C. R. 1. [d. Feb. 9. P. R. 4.]
Elizabeth, bur. Jan. 20, 1770, a. 67 y. C. R. 1. [d. Jan. 18. P. R. 4.]
Ester, w. Samuel, Apr. 16, 1702. [a. 70 y. G. R. 1.]
Hammond, s. Jacob and Elizabeth, "drowned by the mother!! who was acquitted by the court," June 8, 1809, a. 4 m. C. R. 1.
Hannah, wid. [w. William. G. R. 1.], bur. July 4, 1795, a. 72 y. C. R. 1. [July 3, a. 71 y. G. R. 1.
Hannah, wid., Mar. 25, 1803. C. R. 1.
Hannah, dropsy in the chest, Feb. 14, 1844, a. 63 y. C. R. 1.
Isa[iah], jr., bur. Dec. 26, 1776. C. R. 1. [in his 77th y. G. R. 1.]
Isaiah, Nov. 17, 1803.
Jacob, s. Robert and Mary, Sept. 8, 1791.
Jacob, decline, bur. Mar. 6, 1801, a. 53 y. C. R. 1.
Jacob, laborer, at almshouse, suicide by drowning, June 9, 1845, a. 73 y.
Jerusha, d. Jacob, Feb. 6, 1815, a. 4 y. C. R. 1.
John, s. Samuell and Ester, Dec. 13, 1671.
Jonathan, Jan. 5, 1755. [a. 83 y. C. R. 1.]
Joseph, May 4, 1741.
Josiph, s. Sameuell and Sarah, Dec. 15, 1688.
Leonard, s. w. of Zach[ariah] Emery, at Louisburg [bef. July 25], 1759. P. R. 4.
Lidia, w. Ebenezer, Mar. 19, 1736-7. [a. 38 y. 6 m. G. R. 1.]
Lydia, d. Ebenezer and Lydia, Nov. 8, 1745. [a. 22 y. 11 m. 22 d. G. R. 1.]
Martha Davis, d. Levi, dropsy in the head, Oct. 12, 1817, a. 1 y. C. R. 1.
Mary, bur. Feb. 1, 1773. C. R. 1.

CHELMSFORD DEATHS

FOSTER, Mary, wid. [Eben[eze]r. G. R. 1.], June 23, 1787. [a. 88 y. C. R. 1.]
Mary, wid., jaundice, July 18, 1820, a. 78 y. C. R. 1.
Naomy, d. Nathaniel and Francis, June 10, 1728.
Noah, s. William and Hannah, slain in battle near Saratoga [at Stillwater. G. R. 1.], Oct. 7, 1777, a. 20 y. 1 m. 10 d.
Rebeckah, w. Edward, Oct. 30, 1722, a. abt. 6[- y. G. R. 1; a. abt. 62 y. P. R. 2.]
Rebeckah, Dec. 8, 1722.
Remembrance, wid., bur. May 18, 1752. C. R. 1. [d. May 17. P. R. 1.]
Reuben, brother Isa[iah], jr., smallpox, at Concord, Nov. —, 1776. C. R. 1.
Robert, s. Joseph and Thankfull, Apr. 14, 1737.
Robert, May 30, 1782.
Ruth, d. Ely, Dec. 23, 1704.
Sameuell, s. Sameuell and Sarah, Dec. 17, 1698.
Samuel, Serg., July 21, 1730.
Samuel, s. Edward and Rememberance, fever, in the army at Schenectady, Feb. 28, 1756.
Samuel, cramp, July 23, 1804, a. 27 y. C. R. 1.
Samu[e]ll, Dea., July 10, 1702. [a. 83 y. G. R. 1.]
Sam[ue]ll, s. Samuell and Sary, Feb. 18, 1717-18.
Sarah, w. Samuel, Jan. 27, 1718, in her 63d y. G. R. 1.
Simeon, s. Ebenezer and Lydia, Feb. [6, 1826, a. 2 m. 4 d. P. R. 2.]. G. R. 1.
Sollomon, s. Ely and Judah, Nov. 20, 1700.
William, s. William and Hannah, Feb. 20, 1749-50. [a. 4 y. 5 m. 8 d. G. R. 1.]
William, s. William and Hannah, July 3, 1756. [a. 1 y. 2 m. 5 d. G. R. 1.]
William, bur. Mar. 14, 1786, a. 69 y. C. R. 1. [d. Mar. 12. P. R. 4.]
——, ch. wid. Thank[ful], bur. May 30, 1742. C. R. 1.
——, ch. stillborn, Eben[eze]r, bur. Oct. 31, 1767. C. R. 1.
——, w. Eben[eze]r, bur. Nov. 14, 1767. C. R. 1. [d. Nov. 12. P. R. 4.]
——, Mr., old man, bur. [bet. Sept. 27 and Dec. 5], 1803. C. R. 1.
——, ch. Levi, dropsy of the head, Feb. 19, 1825, a. 6 y. C. R. 1.

FREELAND, John, bur. Jan. 21, 1801, a. 61 y. C. R. 1. [Jan. 17, in his 61st y. G. R. 1.]
Mary [wid. John. G. R. 1.], consumption, Sept. [9. G. R. 1.], 1826, a. 77 y. C. R. 1. [a. 76 y. G. R. 1.]

FROST, Asa, s. Ebenezer and Hannah, Oct. 2, 1758.
Ebenezer, bur. Feb. 12, 1772, a. 70 y. c. r. 1.
Ebenezer, old age, Dec. 12, 1812, a. 80 y. c. r. 1.
Esther, wid. Eben[eze]r, Sept. 19, 1824, a. 88 y. c. r. 1.
G[i]lbridge, ch. wid. Asa, Mar. 4, 1816, a. 8 y. c. r. 1.
Hannah, wid., bur. Oct. 12, 1781, a. 79 y. c. r. 1.
——, d. Eben[eze]r, bur. Nov. 20, 1779. c. r. 1.
——, ch. Ebenezer, bur. Oct. 22, 1784. c. r. 1.
——, d. Ebenezer, bur. Nov. 8, 1784. c. r. 1.

FULLER, Ellen L., d. Cha[rle]s A. W. and Emily, Aug. 28, 1848, a. 3 y. 3 m. 23 d. g. r. 2.
Julia M., d. Cha[rle]s A. W. and Emily, Aug. 21, 1848, a. 4 y. 11 m. 18 d. g. r. 2.

GALUSHA (see also Golushaw), ——, wid., bur. May 1, 1749. c. r. 1.
——, wid., bur. May 17, 1790, a. 78 or 79 y. c. r. 1.

GEORGE, Benjamin Franklin, s. W[illia]m W. and Judith, Aug. 6, 1825, a. 3 y. g. r. 6.

GIBSON, Ichabod, Dr., cancer, May 10, 1810, a. 43 y. c. r. 1.

GIDLY, Henry, Oct. 22, 1678.

GILMON, Emeline, d. William and Emeline, drowned, June 2, 1849, a. 1 y. 9 m.
William, m., hatter, intemperance, fell down stairs and broke his skull, June 1, 1849, a. 50 y.

GLASS, Mary [a stranger. c. r. 1.], late of Boston, Dec. 9, 1743.

GLEASON, Alpheus, s. Alpheus and Cornelia, June 12, 1848, a. 13 m. g. r. 3.
——, ch. Alpheus and Polly, Sept. 12, 1847, a. 1 m.
——, inf. ch. Alpheus and Cornelia, Sept. 12, 1848, a. 7 d. g. r. 3.

GLOAD (see also Glode), William, laborer, fever, Feb. 6, 1847, a. 78 y.

GLODE (see also Gload), Easter, fever and decline, Sept. 23, 1810, a. 58 y. c. r. 1.
John, Sept. 20, 1824, a. 70 y. c. r. 1.
Sally, w. John, Oct. 3, 1824, a. 40 y. c. r. 1.

CHELMSFORD DEATHS 397

GLYN, Simeon, dysentery, July 4, 1805. C. R. 1.

GOLUSHAW (see also Galusha), Nathaniel, s. Sam[ue]ll and Easter, Mar. 18, 1745.

GOODE (see also Gould), John, s. Francis and Roas, A[pr. T. C.] 20, 1660.

GOOLD (see also Gould), Benjamin [apoplexy. P. R. 4.], Dec. 28, 1765. [a. 70 y. 2 m. 15 d. G. R. 1.]
Easter, d. [inf. C. R. 1.] Benjamin, jr., Apr. —, 1763. [bur. Apr. 26. C. R. 1.]
Eben [Eben[eze]r. dup.], a Dea. 35 y., taught the first singing school in town, Apr. 6, 1816, a. 90 y. 36 d. C. R. 1.
Joseph Phillips [Philip. G. R. 1.], s. Reuben and Patty, bur. Feb. 23, 1795. C. R. 1. [a. 6 m. 6 d. G. R. 1.]
Mary, d. Benjamin and Sarah, Nov. 8, 1736. [a. 5 y. 9 m. 26 d. G. R. 1.]
Mary [Mrs. G. R. 1.], bur. Aug. 6, 1769, a. 88 y. C. R. 1. [a. 77 y. 7 m. G. R. 1.]
Mehitibel, w. Samuel, Oct. 3, 1733.
Olive [d. Dea. Eben[ezer] and Olive. G. R. 1.], bur. Mar. 7, 1792, a. 41 y. C. R. 1. [d. Mar. 5. P. R. 4; a. 40 y. 4 m. 3 d. G. R. 1.]
Samuel, Oct. 27, 1747.
Samuell, s. Sam[ue]ll and Mehetabel, May 6, 1704.
Rachel, d. Ebenezer and Olive, Dec. 4, 1754, a. 1 y. 9 m. 4 d. G. R. 1.
Rachell, d. Francis and Rose, Feb. 12, 1674.
Ruth [d. Dea. Ebenezer and Olive. G. R. 1.], bur. Apr. 20, 1785. C. R. 1. [d. Apr. 17. P. R. 4; a. 22 y. 6 m. 14 d. G. R. 1.]
——, w. Adam, jr., bur. Oct. 23, 1756. C. R. 1. [d. Oct. 22. P. R. 4.]
——, ch. stillborn, Eben[eze]r, bur. Dec. 10, 1756. C. R. 1.
——, youngest s. Benjamin, s. Dea., bur. July 12, 1787. P. R. 4.
——, ch. Benjamin, bur. Sept. 16, 1791. C. R. 1.

GOOLE (see also Gould), Francis, Mar. 27, 1676.

GORDIE, John, of the glass factory, consumption, Dec. 3, 1810, a. 27 y. C. R. 1.

GOULD (see also Goode, Goold, Goole), Benjamin [jr. C. R. 1.], s. Benjamin and Sarah, Mar. 18, 1741-2. [a. 18 y. 7 m. 11 d. G. R. 1.]

GOULD, Benja[min], pleurisy fever, Feb. 14, 1813, a. 54 y. C. R. 1. [a. 56 y. G. R. 1.]
Deborough, fever, Jan. 1, 1810, a. 70 y. C. R. 1. [a. 80 y. dup.]
Ebenezar, onlv s. Benj[amin], deceased, wound received by carriage passing over his breast, at Savannah, Ga., Sept. —, 1819, a. 25 y. C. R. 1.
Lois, ——, 1824. C. R. 1.
Martha, wid. Reuben, old age, Jan. 4, 1849, a. 81 y.
Mary, d. Benj[amin], deceased, dysentery, Aug. 20, 1825, a. 29 y. C. R. 1.
Nancy [d. Benjamin and Sarah. G. R. 1.], dysentery, at Boston, Sept. 5, 1815, a. 17 y. C. R. 1.
Olive, w. Dea. Ebenezer, Oct. 6, 1790. [a. 59 y. 3 m. 13 d. G. R. 1.]
Polly, for 16 y. in a state of idiotism from fits, Nov. 4, 1823, a. 33 y. C. R. 1.
Reuben, fever and old age, June 14, 1809, a. 74 y. C. R. 1.
Reuben, nervous fever, Feb. 5, 1813, a. 48 y. C. R. 1.
Ruth [Miss. G. R. 1.], at Boston [Mar. 23. G. R. 1.], 1831, a. 39 y. C. R. 1.
Sarah [w. Benjamin. G. R. 1.], lung fever and lethargy, Feb. 12, 1813, a. 57 y. C. R. 1. [Feb. 11. G. R. 1.]

GOWARD, Josiah W., Sept. 6, 1845, a. 35 y. G. R. 3.

GRAINGER, ——, wid., from Billerica, bur. Mar. 14, 1757. C. R. 1.

GRAVES, Anna, w. Moses, Feb. 9, 1747-8.
Moses, Mar. 10, 1771. [a. 76 y. C. R. 1.]
Sarah, wid. [Moses, formerly wid. Benja[min] Goold. G. R. 1.], bur. Apr. 6, 1793, a. 89 y. C. R. 1. [a. 90 y. G. R. 1.]
——, w. Moses, bur. Sept. 14, 1766. C. R. 1. [a. 48 y. P. R. 4.]

GRAY, Catharine, w. Peter, Sept. 20, 1822, a. 41 y. G. R. 1.

GREEN, Amos, m., farmer, pleurisy, Jan. 26, 1849, a. 52 y.
Louisa, w. Amos, disease of the heart, Mar. 16, 1847, a. 40 y.

HALE, Joshua, s. Moses and Lydia, Aug. 2, 1805, a. 1 d. C. R. 1.
Moses, of Lowell, Apr. 5, 1828, a. 63 y. C. R. 1.
Willard, Rev., of Westford, Mar. 19, 1779, a. 76 y. and in the 52d y. of his ministry. C. R. 1.
——, inf. ch. Moses, bur. [bet. Apr. 22 and May 30], 1797. C. R. 1.

HALL, Daniel, hydrocephalus, Jan. 19, 1821, a. 5 y. c. r. 1.
Esther A., d. Darius and Mary Ann [Sarah A. G. R. 1.], scarlatina, May 3, 1847, a. 3 y. 6 d.
Frederic Udall, s. Harrisson and Esther [S. G. R. 3.], Oct. 8, 1847, a. 2 y. 6 m.
John Adams, s. Darius and Sarah Ann, Jan. 11, 1843. [Jan. 10, a. 4 m. G. R. 1.]
Mary Ann [Mary M. G. R. 3.], d. Harrison and Esther [S. G. R. 3.], consumption, Sept. 19, 1849, a. 2 y.
——, ch. ——, of M[iddlesex] Village, bur. Dec. 6, 1841. c. r. 3.
——, Mrs., bur. Dec. 3, 1841. c. r. 3.

HANCOCK, ——, Bishop, of Lexington, suddenly, Dec. 5, 1752, a. 82 y. and in the 54th y. of his ministry. c. r. 1.

HARAD (see also Harwood), John, Oct. 29, 1697.

HARDEY, ——, w. John [bet. Feb. 6 and Mar. 4], 1826, a. 53 y. c. r. 1.

HARPER, Israel D., formerly of New Hampton, N. H., oldest s. John and Sarah, Dec. 19, 1832, a. 22 y. 2 m. G. R. 1.

HARRINGTON, Rufus, putrid fever, at Boston, Oct. 18, 1807, a. 17 y. c. r. 1.
Sarah, w. Timothy, May 26, 1845, a. 92 y. G. R. 1.
Timothy, Dr., had honors of Cambridge University in 1776, bur. Feb. 28, 1802, a. 48 y. c. r. 1. [Feb. 26, a. 49 y. G. R. 1.]

HARRIS, Tho[ma]s, s. Eben[eze]r, bur. Aug. 19, 1749. c. r. 1.
William, s. Eben[eze]r, bur. Aug. 19, 1749. c. r. 1.

HARTWELL, Elizabeth, wid., Oct. 4, 1732.

HARWOD (see also Harwood), Abigal, d. James and Lidyah, Dec. 1, 1695.

HARWOOD (see also Harad, Harwod), Esther, in a season of insanity hung herself, bur. May 30, 1797. c. r. 1.
Joana, w. Jonathan, May 10, 1737, in her 25th y.
John, jr., liver complaint, Aug. 24, 1826, a. 50 y. c. r. 1.
John, by suicide with a rope, Apr. 16, 1830, a. 77 y. c. r. 1.
Jonathan, jr., bur. Mar. 11, 1769. c. r. 1. [d. Mar. 10. p. r. 4.]

HARWOOD, Jona[than], Lt., bur. June 18, 1783, a. 73 y. C. R. 1.
Judeth, w. Lt. Jonathan, Sept. 15, 1766, a. 46 y. 6 m. 15 d. G. R. 1. [Sept. 11. P. R. 4.]
Lucy, w. Lt. Jonathan, June 14, 1774, in her 65th y. G. R. 1.
Mary, w. Jonathan, Dec. 27, 1754, in her 37th y. G. R. 1. [Dec. 29. P. R. 4.]
Mary, wid., bur. Oct. 10, 1758, a. 85 y. C. R. 1.
Nath[anie]l, of a decline, bur. Aug. 1, 1796. C. R. 1. [a. 36 y. G. R. 1.]
Nath[anie]ll, bur. Aug. 31, 1751, a. 82 y. C. R. 1. [d. Aug. 30. P. R. 4.]
Sarah [w. John. G. R. 1.], derangement, Mar. 4, 1827, a. 74 y. C. R. 1.
——, inf. ch. Jona[than], bur. Aug. 10, 1747. C. R. 1.
——, s. Ens. Jona[than], in the army, at Crown Point [bef. Aug. 28], 1760. P. R. 4.
——, ch. Jona[than], jr., bur. July 29, 1768. C. R. 1.
——, ch. stillborn, John, bur. Oct. 12, 1786. C. R. 1.

HASTINGS, Walter, Dr., A. M., bur. Dec. 2, 1782, a. 30 y. C. R. 1.

HAWARD (see also Howard), Marah, d. Nathanile, Nov. 28, 1689.

HAY, Hannah [Mrs. G. R. 1.], fever, Apr. 10, 1830, a. 55 y. C. R. 1. [Apr. 12. G. R. 1.]
James, "a native of Scotland for 16 years employed at the Glass factory as an engraver & worker of stone," Mar. 15, 1826, a. 52 y. C. R. 1. [Mar. 26. G. R. 1.]

HAYDEN, Daniel Flagg, s. Daniel and Sarah, Nov. 6, 1803, a. 7 m. G. R. 1.
Granville [G., s. Daniel and Sarah. G. R. 1.], lung fever, Mar. 21, 1806, a. 5 y. C. R. 1.
Sally Maria [d. Daniel and Sarah. G. R. 1.], convulsions, Jan. 22, 1806, a. 1 y. 5 m. C. R. 1.

HAYNES, Amanda L., d. Ch[arles] B. and Lucy, dropsy on the brain, July 19, 1845, a. 9 m.
Lucy, w. Ch[arles] B., consumption, Nov. 29, 1845, a. 27 y.
Susanna, Mrs., of Boston, old age, died at her nieces Mrs. Noars, Oct. 29, 1817, a. 80 y. C. R. 1.

HAYWOOD (see also Heywood), Benjamin, Jan. 4, 1763. [a. 80 y. c. R. 1.]
Jesse, s. James and Sary, Aug. 30, 1755.
——, ch. Joseph, bur. July 20, 1746. C. R. 1.
——, d. Ja[me]s, bur. Oct. 16, 1752. C. R. 1.
——, inf. ch. Joseph, bur. Dec. 14, 1758. C. R. 1.
——, ch. James, bur. Mar. 10, 1759. C. R. 1.
——, w. Benja[min], bur. Apr. 7, 1759, a. 70 y. C. R. 1. [d. Apr. 6. P. R. 4.]
——, ch. Joseph, Sept. [bet. 2 and 22], 1826, a. 18 m. C. R. 1.

HEALD, Lydia, at a very great age, at Pepperell, "autumn", 1823. C. R. 2.
Mary, Mar. 7, 1835, a. 87 y. C. R. 2.

HEARRICK (see also Herrick), Sarah, d. [inf. C. R. 1.] Abner and Elizebeth, May 30, 1785.

HEILEY, Henry [Hyler, a stranger. C. R. 1; of Stow, at Isaac Kent's. P. R. 4.], Apr. 20, 1771.

HELDRETH (see also Hildreth), Abigall, d. Josiph and Abigell, May 25, 1688. [May 5. CT. R.]
Benjamin, s. Joseph, Feb. 2, 1706.
Ebenezer, s. Richard and Darkes, May 4, 1712.
Jonas, s. Richard, Dec. 16, 1716.
Joseph, Jan. 28, 1706.
Thomas, s. Epharim, Oct. 7, 1707.
Thomas, Nov. 19, 1708.

HENCHMAN (see also Hinchman), Nathaniel Hurd, of Boston, May 29, 1826, a. 48 y. G. R. 1.

HENNON, Sarah Ann, Miss, Oct. —, 1849. C. R. 3.

HERRICK (see also Hearrick), Abner, mortification in his leg, Aug. 4, 1806, a. 55 y. C. R. 1.
Eliz[a]bath, w. Abner, Nov. 4, 1789. [Nov. 5. P. R. 4; a. 44 y. 7 m. 4 d. G. R. 1.]
Patty [Martha. C. R. 1.], d. Abner [and Elizabeth. G. R. 1; throat distemper. C. R. 1.], Apr. 29, 1796. [a. 13 y. 3 d. G. R. 1.]

HERVEY, ——, Mrs. [after Nov. 6], 1822, a. 73 y. C. R. 1.

HEYWOOD (see also Haywood), James, s. [inf. C. R. 1.] James and Sarah, Jan. 22, 1770.
James, Nov. 6, 1791, a. 66 y. 10 m. 15 d. G. R. 2.
Joseph, s. Joseph and Sarah, June 28, 1749.
Joseph, Sept. 1, 1805, a. 45 y. G. R. 2.
Sarah, w. James, Mar. 31, 1802, a. 75 y. G. R. 2.
Sarah, Miss, Feb. 17, 1837, a. 37 y. G. R. 2.
Susanna, w. Joseph, Oct. 9, 1833, a. 73 y. G. R. 2.
——, Mr., consumption, ——, 1806, a. 60 y. C. R. 1.

HIBBARD, Deborah, July 3, 1830. C. R. 3.
Eli H., s. Eli and Laura, Dec. 18, 1843, a. 9 m. G. R. 3.
Eli H., s. Eli and Laura, Sept. 7, 1846, a. 3 y. 9 m. [a. 19 m. G. R. 3.]

HICKS, ——, wid. [formerly of Charlestown. P. R. 4.], bur. Oct. 17, 1784. C. R. 1.

HILDRETCH (see also Hildreth), Hannah [(Spalding). P. R. 4.], wid. Lt. Jonathan [sister Lt. Spaulding. P. R. 4.], Nov. 4, 1758.
Jonathan, s. Lt. Jonathan and Hannah [wid. C. R. 1.], Nov. 4, 1758.

HILDRETH (see also Heldreth, Hildretch, Hildrith, Hilldereth, Hilldreath, Hilldreth, Hilldrith), Dorcas, w. Richard, May 10, 1727. [in her 48th y. G. R. 1.]
Elisabeth, wid. Richard, Aug. 3, 1693.
Elizabeth, wid. Isaac, Jan. 4, 1742-3.
Esther, d. Isaac and Esther, Aug. 9, 1754.
Isaac, sr., Apr. 15, 1730.
Isaac, of Petersham [at his mother Snow's. P. R. 4.], bur. May 31, 1764. C. R. 1. [d. May 30. P. R. 4.]
James, s. James, —— [1682-3?].
James [Thomas. T. C.; James. P. R. 31.], Lt., Apr. 14, 1695.
John [s. Richard and Dorcas. G. R. 1.], Mar. 17, 1723-4. [Mar. 10, in his 21st y. G. R. 1.]
Jonas, Apr. 17, 1770.
Jona[than], Lt., bur. Mar. 19, 1752. C. R. 1. [d. Mar. 17. P. R. 4.]
Joseph, s. Joseph and Abigail, May 24, 1688. CT. R.
Leonard, s. Lt. Jonathan and Hannah, May 1, 1745.
Margret, w. Lt. Jeams, "last of" Aug., 1693.
Mary, w. Jonas, Sept. 25, 1757. [a. 33 y. 1 m. 9 d. G. R. 1.]
Rachall, d. Isaa[c] and Rachall, Mar. 18, 1739.
Richard, s. Joseph and Abigail, May 26, 1688. CT. R.

HILDRETH, Richard, Feb. 23, 1692-3. [a. 88 y. G. R. 1.]
Richard [Ens. G. R. 1.], bur. Apr. 28, 1760, a. 83 y. C. R. 1.
    [d. Apr. 26. P. R. 4; in his 83d y. G. R. 1.]
Samuel, s. Richard, June 1, 1727.
Sarah, d. James, ———, 1682.
Sarah, d. Eben[eze]r and Sarah, Apr. 12, 1721.
Sarah, w. Jonas, Nov. 11, 1746. [a. 24 y. 9 m. 9 d. G. R. 1.]
Susan, w. William [at the almshouse. C. R. 1.], Nov. 4, 1841, a. 44 y. G. R. 1.
Thomas, see Hildreth, James.
———, d. Dorithy, Aug. 17, 1697.
———, ch. Jona[than], bur. Sept. 26, 1747. C. R. 1.
———, ch. Sampson, bur. Jan. 12, 1754. C. R. 1. [d. Jan. 11. P. R. 4.]
———, ch. Sampson, of Harvard, upon a visit in this town, bur. Sept. 13, 1756. C. R. 1.
———, w. Rich[ar]d, bur. Sept. 24, 1759, a. 84 y. C. R. 1. [d. Sept. 22. P. R. 4.]
———, wid. [at Capt. Butterfield's P. R. 4.], bur. Apr. 8, 1760, a. 95 y. C. R. 1. [d. Apr. 7. P. R. 4.]
———, ch. Joseph, bur. Nov. 22, 1764. C. R. 1.

HILDRITH (see also Hildreth), Hannah, w. Jonathan, May 16, 1737. [a. 24 y. 7 m. 9 d. G. R. 1.]
Leah, d. Isaac and Rachil, Aug. 15, 1733.
Mary, d. Jonathan and Hanah, Dec. 15, 1737.
Sary, w. Richerd, Apr. 5, 1735, in her 58th y.

HILL, Eliza[beth], wid. [at her nephew Eph[rai]m Warren's. P. R. 4.], bur. Jan. 23, 1754, a. 80 y. C. R. 1. [d. Jan. 21. P. R. 4.]
Jane [Jean. G. R. 1.], Nov. 15, 1711. [a. 30 y. 11 m. G. R. 1.]
Jonathan, Mar. 24, 1711. [1710-11, a. 36 y. G. R. 1.]
Lidya, wid., Jan. 13, 1729-30.
Nathaniell, Cornet, May 14, 1706. [a. 64 y. G. R. 1.]
Rachell, bur. Sept. 13, 1779. C. R. 1.
———, d. John, of Billerica, bur. May 16, 1761. P. R. 4.

HILLDERETH (see also Hildreth), Elisabeth, d. James and Margre[t], June 27, 1666.
Thomas, s. Richard and Elisabeth, May 28, 16[62. T. C.].

HILLDREATH (see also Hildreth), Elizabeth, d. Joseph and Abigail, Sept. ——. G. R. 1. [Sept. 4, 1716, in her 14th y. P. R. 2.]

HILLDREATH, John, s. Joseph and Abigail, Mar. 17, 1714-15, in his 17th y. G. R. 1.

HILLDRETH (see also Hildreth), James, s. Ephriem and An, Dec. 11, 1696.

HILLDRITH (see also Hildreth), Elizibeth, w. James, Feb. 18, 1726-7. [in her 21st y. G. R. 1.]
Ep[h]raim, at Westford, Apr. 5, 1731.

HINCHMAN (see also Henchman, Hincksman), Elesibeth, wid., Oct. 17, 1704.
Thomas, Maj., July 18, 1703. [July 17, a. 74 y. G. R. 1.]

HINCKSMAN (see also Hinchman), Edmond, Oct. 27 [torn. 1668. CT. R.].

HIRSCH (see also Hursch), Francis G., Feb. 13, 1847, a. 28 y. 9 m. 4 d. G. R. 1.
Lewis, by a fall from a chaise, Mar. 6, 1830, a. 18 y. C. R. 1.

HOAR, Mary, w. Silas, apoplexy, Apr. 30, 1822, a. 62 y. C. R. 1.

HOBBS, James, Rev., of Pelham, June 20, 1765. C. R. 1.

HODGES, Benjamin F. [jr. G. R. 1.], s. Benj[amin] F. and Julia A., scarlatina, Jan. 31, 1847, a. 9 y.
Charles H., s. Benja[min] F. and Julia [A. G. R. 1.], [spasms. P. R. 3.], Oct. 5, 1844, a. 5 d. [Oct. 5, 1846. G. R. 1.]
Hannah A., d. B. F. and J. A., b. Sept. 25, 1844, d. Sept. 25, 1845. G. R. 1.

HODGMAN, Dorathy [w. Josiah. G. R. 1.], old age, May 13, 1811, a. 89 y. C. R. 1. [a. 91 y. G. R. 1.]
Dorothy, Apr. 15, 1831, a. 78 y. C. R. 1.
Josiah, bur. Feb. 26, 1801, a. 80 y. C. R. 1.
Lucy [d. Josiah and Dorothy. G. R. 1.], bur. Mar. 28, 1785. C. R. 1. [d. Mar. 26. P. R. 4; a. 21 y. 1 m. 1 d. G. R. 1.]
Sybyl, old age, Jan. 5, 1844, a. 85 y. C. R. 1.

HOLDEN, [Jerusha. G. R. 6.], w. Artemas, Mar. 8, 1821, a. 37 y. C. R. 1. [a. 38 y. G. R. 6.]

HOLLIS, David, Dec. 31, 1831, a. 77 y. C. R. 1.
Mary, w. [David. G. R. 1.], July 4, 1826, a. 71 y. C. R. 1. [a. 72 y. G. R. 1.]

HOLMES, Diama, wid. Isaac, at the almshouse, old age, Jan. 22, 1841, a. 81 y. C. R. 1.
Lucia B., Oct. 12, 1828, a. 26 y. C. R. 3.
Luia B., Dec. 22, 1828. C. R. 1.

HORN, Henrietta, d. Martin N. and Lydia, Oct. 27, 1818, a. 5 y. 27 d. G. R. 6.

HOSMER, John Horatio,* s. Benjamin, jr. and Permelia, July 17, 1827, a. 19 m. G. R. 1.
William Wallace, s. Benjamin and Permelia, Jan. 8, 1829, a. 22 m. G. R. 1.

HOW, Mary, Mrs. [wid. Thomas, of Marlborough. G. R. 1.], May 7, 1741. [in her 73d y. G. R. 1.]

HOWARD (see also Haward), Abigal, d. Jacob and Rachel, Aug. 5, 1764. [a. 7 y. 1 m. 8 d. G. R. 1.]
Benjamin [jr. C. R, 1.], s. Benjamin and Mary [brother Mrs. Barron. P. R. 4.], May 16, 1754. [a. 30 y. 3 m. 10 d. G. R. 1.]
Benjamin [very suddenly. P. R. 4.], Jan. 19, 1760. [a. 69 y. C. R. 1; a. 68 y. 9 m. G. R. 1.]
Hannah, d. [Lt. G. R. 1.] Nathaniel and Hannah, Sept. 26, 1803, a. 4 y. 8 m. 26 d.
Jacob, Mar. 26, 1798, a. 78 y. 5 m. G. R. 1. [a. 79 y. C. R. 1.]
Joanna, d. Jacob and Rachel, Aug. 3, 1764. [a. 9 y. 8 m. 7 d. G. R. 1.]
Jonathan, Apr. 9, 1708.
Jonathan [suddenly. P. R. 4.], bur. Sept. 15, 1758, a. 77 y. C. R. 1. [d. Sept. 14. P. R. 4.]
Lowell, s. [Lt. G. R. 1.] Nathaniel and Hannah, Sept. 21, 1803, a. 1 y. 2 m. 2 d.
Lydia, d. Benjamin and Martha [wid. C. R. 1.], Aug. 14, 1764. [Aug. 15, a. 10 y. 4 m. 7 d. G. R. 1.]
Martha, wid. [Benjamin. G. R. 1.], bur. Apr. 30, 1793, a. 80 y. C. R. 1. [Apr. 27. G. R. 1.]
Mary, w. Benj[amin], Jan. 27, 1741-2. [in her 47th y. G. R. 1.]
Mary, d. Samuel and Mary, Oct. 21, 1764. [a. 3 y. 4 m. 16 d. G. R. 1.]
Mary, w. Samuel [old age. C. R. 1.], Dec. 5, 1812, a. 79 y. 10 m. 19 d.

CHELMSFORD DEATHS

HOWARD, Nathaniel, s. Benjamin and Mary, Jan. 29, 1741-2. [in his 22d y. G. R. 1.]
Nath[anie]l, inflammation of the bowels, Nov. 14, 1831, a. 60 y. C. R. 1.
Nathaniell [sr. G. R. 1.], Jan. 24, 1709. [Jan. 21, 1709-10, a. abt. 67 y. C. R. 1.]
Rachael [w. Jacob. G. R. 1.], old age, July 25, 1814, a. 92 y. C. R. 1. [July 24, a. 90 y. G. R. 1.]
Rachael [Mrs. G. R. 1.], old age, Oct. 22, 1818, a. 76 y. C. R. 1. [a. 73 y. G. R. 1.]
Samuel, s. Samuel and Mary, Sept. 15, 1764. [a. 1 y. 4 m. 19 d. G. R. 1.]
Samuel [jr. C. R. 1.], of Tyngsborough [s. Samuel and Mary. G. R. 1.], Mar. 14, 1790, a. 22 y. [a. 22 y. 11 m. 14 d. G. R. 1.]
Samuel [old age. C. R. 1.], July 7, 1816, a. 84 y. 10 m. 27 d.
Samuel, ———, 1816, a. 55 y. C. R. 1.
Sarah, w. Jonathan, Oct. 6, 1736. [in her 54th y. G. R. 1.]
Sarah, Mrs., Sept. 26, 1737.
Sarah, wid. Nath[a]n[ie]l, Sept. 26, 1739, in her 85th y. G. R. 1.
Sarah Elizabeth, b. Harvard, d. Dr. Levi and Lydia J., diarrhoea, Sept. 17, 1849, a. 1 y. 6 m. 20 d.
Timothy, s. Benjamin and Mary [at Halifax, N. S. P. R. 4.], Dec. 30, 1749.
Willard, Jan. 1, 1837, a. 90 y. G. R. 1.
———, Mr., of Hillsborough, N. H., mortally wounded by the explosion of the powder mill, June 6, 1821. C. R. 1.

HUNT, Joshua, Apr. 27, 1843, a. 72 y. G. R. 1.

HUNTER, Charles W., s. William and Jane, convulsions, July 1, 1846, a. 11 m. 11 d.
Jane S., w. William, consumption, Sept. 22, 1846, a. 22 y.
William Collier, s. William and Mary, Sept. 4, 1849, a. 9 d. G. R. 1.

HURSCH (see also Hirsch), Francis [G. G. R. 1.], intemperance, Oct. 25, 1829, a. 50 y. C. R. 1. [Oct. 23, a. 45 y. G. R. 1.]
Joseph, from Germany, blower at the glass factory, dropsy, Aug. 24, 1823, a. 42 y. C. R. 1. [Aug. 27. G. R. 1.]

HUTCHENS (see also Hutchins), Eliakim, s. Samuel and Marcy, May 17, 1756.
Samuel, May 17, 1755.

HUTCHINS (see also Hutchens), Andrew, bur. Dec. 14, 1757. C. R. 1. [d. Dec. 13. P. R. 4.]
Anna, wid., June 8, 1819, a. 86 y. G. R. 2.
Hannah, Mar. 28, 1838. C. R. 2.
Marcy, wid. Samuel, May 3, 1796, a. 85 y. G. R. 2.
Phebe [(Spalding). P. R. 23; w. Benjamin P. G. R. 2.], Jan. 4, 1842. C. R. 2. [a. 44 y. G. R. 2.]
Simon, s. Abram and Betsey, Oct. 27, 1838, a. 4 w. 6 d. G. R. 2.
Solomon, s. Dea. Eliakim and Mary, Feb. 28, 1813, a. 1 y. G. R. 2.
Thomas, Oct. 15, 1807, a. 78 y. G. R. 2.
——, ch. Sam[ue]ll, bur. Nov. 27, 1752. C. R. 1.
——, inf. twin chn. Thomas, bur. Feb. 18, 1771. C. R. 1.
——, inf. ch. Tho[ma]s, bur. Dec. 26, 1774. C. R. 1.

HYDE, ——, ch. ——, "a Seperate Speaker at ye South End," bur. Feb. 28, 1754. C. R. 1.
——, ch. ——, "a Seperate Speaker at ye South End," bur. Mar. 12, 1754. C. R. 1.

ILSLEY, William, Nov. 24, 1829, a. 18 y. C. R. 3.

IVES, John [of Sudbury. G. R. 1.], killed by explosion in powder mill, Dec. 6, 1820, a. 25 y. C. R. 1. [Dec. 5. G. R. 1.]

JACOBS, ——, Mrs., consumption, June 20, 1810, a. 23 y. C. R. 1.

JEFFS, ——, ch. Simeon, organic affection, July 19, 1817, a. 2 y. C. R. 1.

JEWELL, ——, Miss, at the workhouse, Aug. 27, 1825, a. 65 y. C. R. 1.

JOHNSON, Abigail P., w. Rowland, May 26, 1837.
Abram, Oct. 2, 1819, a. 50 y. G. R. 6.

JONES, Lydia T., w. Charles P., Dec. 1, 1848, a. 29 y.
Thomas, Rev., of Woburn Precinct, Mar. 13, 1774. C. R. 1.
Thomas [leprosy or consumption. C. R. 1.], Apr. 5, 1805, a. 27 y. 3 m.

JOSSELYN, Albert W[arren. P. R. 10.], s. Edwin and Nyrhe [(Chandler). P. R. 10.], Aug. 4, 1843, a. 10 m. 16 d. G. R. 3.
Eliza A[nn. P. R. 10.], d. Edwin and Nyrhe [(Chandler). P. R. 10.], Sept. 27, 1840, a. 18 d. G. R. 3.

KEIES (see also Keyes), Ruth, d. Solomon, Mar. 31, 1671.

KEMP (see also Kempe), Abigail, at Bedford, Sept. 14, 1824. c. r. 2.
Mary, bur. July 13, 1744. c. r. 1.
——, ch. John, bur. Nov. 14, 1747. c. r. 1.
——, "old Mr.", brought from Billerica, bur. Apr. 3, 1752. c. r. 1.
——, inf. ch. Jona[than], jr., bur. June 16, 1753. c. r. 1.
——, ch. Josiah, from Billerica, bur. May 20, 1754. c. r. 1.

KEMPE (see also Kemp), Ann, w. Edward, Apr. 17 [torn. 1666. ct. r.].
Edward [Dec. ct. r.] 17, [torn. 1668. ct. r.].

KENDALL, ——, inf. ch. Joel, on a Journey, at John Butterfield's, Jan. 3, 1792. p. r. 4.

KENT, ——, inf. ch. Isaac, bur. May 8, 1762. c. r. 1.
——, wid., bur. June 14, 1770, a. 81 y. c. r. 1. [d. June 13. p. r. 4.]

KEYES (see also Keies, Keys, Kyes), Abigail, wid., at the almshouse, Feb. 5, 1840, a. 75 y. c. r. 1.
Annes, d. Zachariah and Dinah [wid. c. r. 1.], July 11, 1768.
Ezekiel, Dec. 5, 1742.
Hellen Maria, d. Marcus and Maria, Aug. 25, 1847, a. 2 y. 6 m.
Jane [unm. p. r. 4.], bur. Oct. 18, 1772, a. 80 y. c. r. 1.
Joanna, consumption, July 23, 1828, a. 75 y. c. r. 1.
Mehetab[e]l, wid., bur. Apr. 16, 1768, a. 97 y. c. r. 1. [d. Apr. 14. p. r. 4.]
Moses, Jan. 14, 1746-7.
Sarah, bur. Sept. 29, 1742. c. r. 1.
Solomon, Serg., Mar. 28, 1702.
Solomon, smallpox, bur. Apr. —, 1777. c. r. 1.
Stephen, Feb. 6, 1714.
Sybil, bur. Mar. 14, 1776. c. r. 1.
Zachariah ["one of ye rangers in Reduction of Quebeck." p. r. 4.], Dec. 21, 1759.
Zebediah, Nov. 4, 1758.
Zebediah, a young lad [of Billerica, s. wid. Mary. p. r. 4.], smallpox, bur. "near his late fathers house in ye Neck," Dec. 26, 1760. c. r. 1. [d. Dec. 24. p. r. 4.]
Zebelon, s. Zachariah and Dinah, Feb. 26, 1752.
——, ch. Zach., bur. Feb. 14, 1752. c. r. 1.
——, ch. Ep[hrai]m, bur. Apr. 1, 1754. c. r. 1.

KEYES, ——, d. Daniel, bur. Aug. 6, 1775. C. R. 1.
——, inf. ch. Uriah, bur. Dec. 7, 1776. C. R. 1.
——, inf. ch. Uriah, bur. Oct. 6, 1777. C. R. 1.
——, ch. Abel, bur. Sept. 13, 1778. C. R. 1.
——, inf. ch. John, bur. Aug. 6, 1781. C. R. 1.

KEYS (see also Keyes), Daniel, Oct. 31, 1797. C. R. 1.
Hanah, d. Soloman and Mary, Feb. 17, 1698.
Sarah, d. Abel and Olive, Oct. 18, 1769.
Sarah, w. David, drowned, Sept. 3, 1806, a. 50 y. C. R. 1.

KIDDER (see also Kider), Elizebeth, d. James and Sary, Apr. 29, 1756.
Hannah, bur. Oct. 31, 1748. C. R. 1.
Isaac, s. John and Mary, Nov. 23, 1742.
James, sr., Dec. 15, 1732.
James, s. James and Abigail, Dec. 21, 1732.
John, Aug. 28, 1762. [a. 75 y. C. R. 1.]
Jonas, s. John, Dec. 25, 1738.
Joseph, Rev., at Dunstable, N. H., Sept. 6, 1818, a. 77 y. C. R. 1.
Lidia, d. John, Oct. 31, 1738.
Marah [Mary. C. R. 1.], d. John and Mary, Sept. 12, 1742.
Marah, wid., bur. Aug. 30, 1778, a. 84 y. C. R. 1.
Phebe, w. Amos, Oct. 13, 1759.
Sarah, w. James, Apr. 16, 1749.
Sary, d. James and Sary, Apr. 11, 1756.
Thomas, Sept. 22, 1729, in his 39th y. G. R. 5.
——, ch. twin, James and Sarah, bur. Apr. 15, 1749. C. R. 1.
——, inf. ch. James, bur. Apr. 15, 1749. C. R. 1.
——, ch. James, bur. May 18, 1749. C. R. 1.
——, wid., bur. Mar. 10, 1752, a. 86 y. C. R. 1. [d. Mar. 9. P. R. 4.]
——, ch. David, bur. May 27, 1755. C. R. 1.
——, inf. ch. Amos, bur. June 1, 1756. C. R. 1.
——, ch. stillborn, Dav[i]d, bur. Sept. 3, 1765. C. R. 1.
——, ch. stillborn, David, bur. Dec. 22, 1769. C. R. 1.
——, inf. ch. Eben[eze]r, bur. Mar. 17, 1787. C. R. 1.

KIDER (see also Kidder), Isaiah, s. Thomas and Joanna, Oct. 19, 1728. [in his 8th m. G. R. 5.]
Jonathan, s. John, Apr. 27, 1728.
Rachil, d. John and Mary, Nov. 27, 1728.

KIMBALL, Hannah, Mar. 9, 1841, a. 45 y. G. R. 1.
Sally, w. Samuel, Jan. 19, 1845, a. 65 y. G. R. 3.

KING, Hannah, d. Dr. Samuel and Hannah, Feb. 19, 1754.
——, d. Dr. Sam[ue]ll, bur. July 27, 1758. C. R. 1.
——, brother of Mrs. Williams, died in ye Southern Army, bef. June 12, 1781. P. R. 4.

KITTREDGE, Cullen F., m., machinist, b. Littleton, s. Dr. Paul and Rebecca, consumption, Jan. 2, 1845, a. 32 y. 10 m.
Dorcas Melvina, d. F. M. and A. M., Sept. 12, 1840, a. 3 y. G. R. 1.
Forestus Darwin, s. Paul and Rebbecca, Apr. 29, 1828, a. 14 y. 2 m. 27 d. G. R. 1.
Henry Mead, s. F. M. and T. Almira [A. M. G. R. 1.], Feb. 13, 1843. [Feb. 8, a. 8 d. G. R. 1.]
Paul, physician, b. Tewksbury, s. Benj[ami]n, apoplexy, Aug. 10, 1845, a. 61 y. [Aug. 9. G. R. 1.]
——, two inf. daughters, Paul and Rebbecca, Feb. 20, 1821. G. R. 1.

KNECTTLE (see also Connettle), Harmon, s. John and Satira, dysentery, Sept. 30, 1848, a. 4 m.

KNOWLES, Elizabeth C., w. Sam[ue]l L., dropsy, May 31, 1848, a. 51 y.

KNOWLTON, ——, young ch. ——, of Westford, Oct. 1, 1839. C. R. 1.

KYES (see also Keyes), Mary, w. Soloman, Feb. 29, 1708.

LAMB, Adolphus, dysentery, Sept. 14, 1825, a. 19 y. C. R. 1.

LANDRY, Simon, Frenchman, bur. Dec. 2, 1760. C. R. 1.
——, ch. Joseph, a French neutral, bur. Aug. 13, 1759. C. R. 1.

LANE, ——, Mrs., old age, at workhouse, Aug. 8, 1832, a. 92 y. C. R. 1.

LANGLEE (see also Longley), William [jr. C. R. 1.], s. Nathaniel and Lydia, Aug. 4, 1752.

LARCOM, Benj[amin] F., s. Jonathan and Harriett [O. G. R. 1.], pulmonary, Apr. 22, 1846, a. 5 y. [Apr. 23, a. 5 m. G. R. 1.]

LAREY, John Miles, s. Capt. John and Joanna, of Lincoln, Sept. 18, 1831, a. 21 y. G. R. 1.

LARKIN, ——, w. Peter, bur. Nov. 26, 1774. C. R. 1.

LARNED, Isake [sr. CT. R.], h. Mare, Nov. 29, 1657. [Dec. 4. CT. R.; 8: 10 m: P. R. 1.]

LAWES (see also Laws), Archelaus, s. William, bur. Feb. 21, 1796, a. 3 y. C. R. 1.

LAWS (see also Lawes), Mary, d. Cears, Apr. 17, 1820, a. 2 y. C. R. 1.
Patty, d. William and Sarah, bur. July 10, 1794, a. 10 y. C. R. 1.
W[illia]m, ossification and dropsy, Aug. 1, 1823, a. 77 y. C. R. 1.
——, w. William, bur. [bet. Sept. 27 and Dec. 5], 1803. C. R. 1.

LEVINGSTON (see also Livingston), Abigail [w. Seth. G. R. 1.], Dec. 1, 1819, a. 66 y. C. R. 1. [Nov. 24, a. 64 y. G. R. 1.]
Abigail, w. Sprake, childbirth, Feb. 13, 1830, a. 38 y. C. R. 1. [Feb. 12. G. R. 1.]
Benjamin [at his brother Seth's. P. R. 4.], bur. June 11, 1789. C. R. 1.
Seth, consumption, May 23, 1809, a. 56 y. C. R. 1.

LINCOLN, Albert H., s. Isaac L. and Mary A., Oct. 4, 1840, a. 8 m. G. R. 3. [a. 7 m. C. R. 3.]
Levi R., a stranger from Boston, consumption, July 22, 1839, a. 40 y. C. R. 1.
Mary Ella, d. Isaac L. and Mary A., Dec. 13, 1841, a. 15 m. G. R. 3.

LINDSEY, Nathaniel, m., shoemaker, b. Marblehead, dysentery, Aug. 11, 1849, a. 29 y.

LITCHFIELD, Paul, Rev., Nov. 3, 1827, a. 76 y. and 46th y. of his ministry. C. R. 1.

LITTLEHALE, Richard [Dea. dup.], May 16, 1841. C. R. 3.
Susan [Mrs. dup.], Sept. 5, 1841. C. R. 3.

LIVERMORE, Grase, Mrs. [w. John. G. R. 1.], Jan. 12, 1690. [Jan. 14, a. 75 y. G. R. 1.]

LIVINGSTON (see also Levingston), William, s. W[illia]m, Dec. 26, 1810, a. 1 d. C. R. 1.
——, inf. ch. Sprake and Abigail, Feb. 12, 1830. G. R. 1.

LOCK, ——, ch. Daniel, bur. Oct. 18, 1749. C. R. 1.
——, ch. Daniel [a seperate Baptist. P. R. 4.], bur. Mar. 5, 1766. C. R. 1.

LONGLEY (see also Langlee), Deborah [Langley. C. R. 1.], wid. William, May 27, 1761. [a. 92 or 93 y. C. R. 1.]
Lydia [Langley. C. R. 1.], w. Nathaniel, Oct. 20, 1755. [Oct. 21. P. R. 4.]
Mary [Langley. C. R. 1.], d. Nathaniel and Lydia, Aug. 1, 1755.
Nathaniel, s. Nathaniel and Lydia, at Lake George, Oct. —, 1756.
Nathaniel [Langley. C. R. 1.], Nov. 18, 1773.
William [Langley. C. R. 1.], June 15, 1755. [a. 85 y. C. R. 1.]

LORD, Hannah, d. Robert and Ann, dysentery, July 14, 1849, a. 3 m.
Samuel, foreigner [from Rochdale, Eng. G. R. 3.], cause unknown, Feb. 3, 1847, a. 68 y.

LUFKIN, Hannah, smallpox, bur. Apr. 30, 1777. C. R. 1.
——, smallpox, bur. Apr. —, 1777. C. R. 1.
——, inf. ch. Mr., "who with his family were passing thro town to Westford, died at Mr. Benj Levingston's," Oct. 15, 1823. C. R. 1.

LYON, Ebenezer [jr. C. R. 1.], s. Ebenezer [soldier lately returned from Nova Scotia. P. R. 4.], May 13, 1756.

McCLARRAN, ——, ch. ——, a Scotch prisoner, a highlander, bur. Jan. 28, 1777. C. R. 1.

McCLENCH, ——, ch. John, bur. Apr. 22, 1746. C. R. 1.

McCLINING, John [McClennings, in consequence of drinking a quart of brandy. C. R. 1.], Apr. 25, 1798.

McCLUSKY, Dennis, s. Pattrick and Elizabeth, Dec. 27, 1840.

MACFARLAIN (see also McFarlin), Abigail, w. Archibald, Mar. 4, 1821, a. 36 y. C. R. 1.
Mary, dysentery, July 12, 1805, a. 1 y. C. R. 1.

McFARLIN (see also Macfarlain), Clarisa, d. Archibald and Abigail, July 7, 1821, a. 3 y. G. R. 6.
Susan, d. Archibald and Abigail, Mar. 18, 1821, a. 15 m. G. R. 6.

McGLAUTHLIA, ——, d. Hiram L., moulder, b. Pembroke, N. H., and Hannah, b. Easton, at North Chelmsford, [Sept. 13, 1849?].

McINTIRE (see also McIntyre), Eda, d. Jacob and Rebekah, Aug. 20, 1833, a. 24 y. G. R. 2.
Nathaniel T., s. Jacob and Rebekah, Nov. 12, 1829, a. 18 y. G. R. 2.
——, ch. Amos B. and Mary A., Aug. 26, 1847, a. 2 y. 5 m. 8 d.

McINTYRE (see also McIntire), Levi, s. Warren, of Middlesex Village, cholera infantum, Aug. 19, 1840, a. 1 y. C. R. 1.

McKAVOR, Mary, b. Canada, typhoid fever, Aug. 27, 1847, a. 20 y.

MCLAIN, Charl[e]s, Dec. 17, 1758.

McQUESTION, Ann [Mrs., formerly w. Phillip Parker. G. R. 1.], Sept. 6, 1825, a. 77 y. C. R. 1. [Sept. 3. G. R. 1.]

MANNING, Asa, widr., farmer, s. Timothy, consumption, Mar. 27, 1845, a. 64 y.
Benjamin, s. Jonathan and Martha, Sept. 2, 1793, a. 15 y. 6 d. G. R. 1.
George Josiah, s. Joseph and Julia, Sept. 18, 1836. [a. 8 m. G. R. 1.]
Jona[than], fever and old age, Apr. 6, 1828, a. 78 y. C. R. 1. [Apr. 8. G. R. 1.]
Lydia, Miss, neuralgia, May 4, 1841, a. 59 y. C. R. 1.
Martha, w. Jona[than], lethargy, Nov. 10, 1809, a. 59 y. C. R. 1.
Mary, d. Timothy and Mary, Dec. 23, 1787. [a. 5 y. G. R. 1.]
Mary, w. Timothy, Feb. 27, 183[6, a. 87 y. G. R. 1.].
Nath[anie]l, died in the U. S. Service, Sept. 19, 1814, a. 30 v. G. R. 1.

MANNING, Salathiel, Oct. 7, 1828, a. 48 y. G. R. 1.
Timothy, Mar. 11, 1836. [a. 84 y. G. R. 1.]
———, inf. ch. Jona[than], bur. Apr. 29, 1785. C. R. 1.

MANSFIELD, Asaph, consumption, June 10, 1812, a. 32 y. C. R. 1.
Betsey, w. Joel, internal mortification, Mar. 22, 1813. C. R. 1.
George W., Sept. 18, 1836, in his 21st y. P. R. 21.
Joel, consumption, Feb. 25, 1813, a. 28 y. C. R. 1.
Joel, consumption, June 31, 1826, a. 39 y. C. R. 1. [June 30. P. R. 21.]
John, old age, Aug. 25, 1814, a. 80 y. C. R. 1.
Mary J., May 5, 1839, in her 17th y. P. R. 21.
———, ch. John, bur. Jan. 27, 1763. C. R. 1.

MANSUR, Mary Frances, b. 1828, d. ———, 1834. G. R. 1.

MARCHALL (see also Marshall), Hannah, w. Thomas, Dec. 9, 1770, a. 38 y. G. R. 1.
John, June 20, 1771, a. 2 y. G. R. 1.
Thomas, May 25, 1799, a. 70 y. G. R. 1.

MARSHALL (see also Marchall), Aaron, s. Samuel and Esther, Aug. 9, 1771.
Anna, lingering decline, Sept. 20, 1807, a. 18 y. C. R. 1.
Esther, w. Sam[ue]l, Sept. 23, 1812, a. 81 y. C. R. 1.
Fordyce, inflammation on the brain, Nov. 23, 1815, a. 19 y. C. R. 1.
George L., s. George and Eliza, cause unknown, June 26, 1847, a. 4 m. 2 d.
Hannah, w. Thomas, Dec. 27, 1767.
James, Sept. 2, 1826, a. 66 y. C. R. 1. [Sept. 6. G. R. 1.]
John, s. Dr. Jonas and Mary [smallpox. C. R. 1.], Dec. 25, 1776. [a. 12 d. G. R. 2.]
Joseph A., Apr. 24, 1833, a. 29 y. G. R. 1.
Levi, s. James [and Joanna. G. R. 1.], killed by explosion in powder mill, Dec. 6, 1820, a. 26 y. C. R. 1. [Dec. 5. G. R. 1.]
Loring, at Lowell, Apr. 23, 1845, a. 37 y. G. R. 1.
Lydia, wid. [w. Thomas. G. R. 1.], speechless 2 y., bur. May 23, 1801. C. R. 1. [May 25, a. 66 y. G. R. 1.]
Lydia Chandler, d. Petre [and Mary. G. R. 1.], worms, Dec. 26, 1809, a. 4 y. C. R. 1. [a. 3 y. G. R. 1.]
Mary, w. Dr. Jonas [smallpox. C. R. 1.], Dec. 17, 1776. [a. 38 y. 10 m. G. R. 2.]

CHELMSFORD DEATHS 415

MARSHALL, Mary, d. James [and Joanna. G. R. 1.], fever, at Bradford, Feb. 11, 1816, a. 24 y. C. R. 1.
Mary Ann, d. Thomas and Ann F., infantile, bur. Concord River, Sept. 15, 1846, a. 2 m.
Mary N., w. Thomas, Mar. 25, 1837, a. 29 y. G. R. 1.
Nathaniel, s. James [and Joanna. G. R. 1.], brother of Levi, died from effects of explosion in powder mill, Dec. 6, 1820, a. 22 y. C. R. 1. [Dec. 7, a. 23 y. G. R. 1.]
Otis, Aug. 29, 1837, a. 30 y. G. R. 1.
Peter, Apr. 5, 1828, a. 52 y. C. R. 1. [Apr. 3, a. 55 y. G. R. 1.]
Ruth, bur. Oct. 11, 1801, a. 22 y. C. R. 1. [Sept. 27, a. 20 y. G. R. 1.]
Sam[ue]l [jr. dup.], ulcers upon the lungs, Nov. 11, 1818, a. 64 y. C. R. 1.
Sibil, d. Dr. Jonas and Mary [smallpox. C. R. 1.], Dec. 16, 1776. [a. 1 y. 2 m. 7 d. G. R. 2.]
Thomas, very suddenly, bur. May 25, 1800. C. R. 1.
———, w. Joseph, bur. Nov. 8, 1765. C. R. 1. [d. Nov. 7. P. R. 4.]
———, ch. Tho[ma]s [drowned in a well, Apr. 2. P. R. 4.], bur. Apr. 3, 1766. C. R. 1.
———, inf. ch. Tho[ma]s, bur. Sept. 25, 1771. C. R. 1.
———, ch. stillborn, Samuel, bur. Feb. 4, 1772. C. R. 1.
———, inf. ch. Tho[ma]s, jr., bur. June 16, 1775. C. R. 1.
———, d. "wife of Jonas Marshall," bur. June 20, 1782. C. R. 1.
———, ch. Isaac, bur. Sept. 12, 1788. C. R. 1.
———, ch. Joshua, bur. Sept. 1, 1792. C. R. 1.
———, ch. Joshua, bur. June 12, 1793. C. R. 1.
———, s. James and Joanna, Sept. 6, 1804, a. 6 h. C. R. 1.

MARTAIN (see also Martin), William, May 11, 1760. [May 12. P. R. 4; a. 69 y. C. R. 1.]

MARTIN (see also Martain), Patty [d. Asa, at Josiah Symonds'. P. R. 4.], bur. Jan. 30, 1788. C. R. 1.
William, s. William and Elizabeth, "in his majesties Servis," at Cape Breton, Nov. 13, 1745.
———, w. W[illia]m, bur. Feb. 28, 1743. C. R. 1.
———, ch. Asa, bur. Nov. 29, 1765. C. R. 1.

MAYNARD, Elizabeth, d. Aaron and Mary, dropsy in the head, May 26, 1826, a. 2 y. C. R. 1.

MEAD (see also Meads), ———, inf. ch. John, bur. Jan. 25, 1775. C. R. 1.

MEADS (see also Mead), Lidia, w. John [d. Sim[eo]n Blodget, late of Lyndeborough, childbed. P. R. 4.], June 24, 1776.
Lidia, d. John and Lidia [grandch. Simeon Blodget. C. R. 1.], Apr. 5, 1778. [a. 1 y. 9 m. 21 d. G. R. 1.]

MEARS (see also Meers), Dorcas, pauper, d. Robert and Dorcas, dysentery, at the almshouse, Aug. 21, 1849, a. 59 y.
Dorcas, wid. W[illia]m, old age, Nov. 30, 1849, a. 82 y.
Loisa, d. Micajah, hydrocephalus, Nov. 15, 1809, a. 2 m. C. R. 1.
Micajah, quinsy, Apr. 30, 1806, a. 10 w. C. R. 1.
Rebecca, w. W[illia]m, of Westford, d. Robert Mears, Apr. 20, 1827. C. R. 1.
Robert, at the almshouse, Feb. 12, 1843.

MEERS (see also Mears), ———, ch. John, bur. Aug. 31, 1775. C. R. 1.

MELLEN, Elizabeth J., d. Robert and Deborah, Oct. 10, 1844, a. 20 y.

MELVIN, Abiah, colic, May 29, 1818, a. 35 y. C. R. 1.
Fletcher, brother of Abiah, consumption, June 6, 1818, a. 40 y. C. R. 1.
———, ch. Benjamin, bur. Apr. 26, 1781. C. R. 1.
———, inf. ch. Benja[min], bur. May 8, 1784. C. R. 1.
———, inf. ch. Benja[min], bur. Apr. 2, 1785. C. R. 1.

MERIDETH, William, who died in the Mexican War, ———, [1846-48.]. G. R. 4.

MINOT, Eliza[beth], wid. [Lt. Jonathan. G. R. 1.], bur. May 9, 1772, a. 80 y. C. R. 1. [May 7, in her 80th y. G. R. 1.]
John, dropsy, Sept. 16, 1809, a. 80 y. C. R. 1.
Jonath[a]n, Lt., bur. July 24, 1770, a. 81 y. C. R. 1. [July 23. G. R. 1.]
Rachael, old age, Dec. 31, 1812, a. 80 y. C. R. 1.
———, w. Sam[ue]ll, from Westford, bur. Oct. 22, 1752. C. R. 1.

MOARS (see also Moore), Esther, w. Lt. Joseph, Nov. 18, 1773. [a. 70 y. C. R. 1; Nov. 17. G. R. 1.]
Joseph, Lt., July 5, 1775. [a. 74 y. C. R. 1; a. 71 y. 4 m. 1 d. G. R. 1.]

MONTAGUE, James, s. James, dysentery, Sept. 22, 1825, a. 19 m. C. R. 1.

MOODY, Mary Ann, consumption, Aug. 9, 1846, a. 21 y.

MOOR (see also Moore), George Henry, s. Thomas and Laura W., Apr. 1, 1841, a. 14 m. G. R. 1.

MOORE (see also Moars, Moor, Moors), Charles, nephew Capt. P. Whiting, inflammation on the brain, Apr. 18, 1823, a. 18 y. C. R. 1.
Laura W., w. Thomas, Feb. 22, 1842, a. 45 y. G. R. 1.
Lewis, s. Eph[rai]m S. and Henrietta, dysentery, Aug. 31, 1847, a. 1 y. 4 m.
Susan, Mar. —, 1824, a. 23 y. C. R. 1.

MOORS (see also Moore), Charlotte, very suddenly, at Litchfield, June 12, 1793. C. R. 1.
Hannah, dysentery, July 30, 1808, a. 2 y. C. R. 1.
Joanna, old age and fever, Oct. 13, 1815, a. 78 y. C. R. 1.
Joseph, consumption, Aug. 23, 1814, a. 56 y. C. R. 1.
Miel, organic affection of the heart, Sept. 6, 1814, a. 50 y. C. R. 1.
Rachel, w. Larkin, Apr. 8, 1820, a. 49 y. C. R. 1.
Sarah, wid. Miel, consumption, Sept. 25, 1822, a. 56 y. C. R. 1.
Simeon [s. Lt. Joseph. G. R. 1.], bur. Dec. 22, 1781. C. R. 1. [a. 49 y. 2 d. G. R. 1.]
——, inf ch. Simeon, bur. Feb. 28, 1775. C. R. 1.
——, inf. ch. Simeon, bur. Feb. 2, 1776. C. R. 1.
——, ch. Simeon, Dec. —, 1824. C. R. 1.

MOTTLEY, Charles, s. Capt. Joseph and Mehetabel [wid. C. R. 1.], Oct. 2, 1778, in his 9th y. G. R. 1.
Joseph, Capt., June 13, 1777, a. 52 y. G. R. 1.

MOULTON, William H., s. W[illia]m B. and Jane F., Nov. 9, 1840, a. 7 d. G. R. 3.

MUNGER, Nancy R., w. Harvey, Jan. 17, 1846, a. 38 y. G. R. 3.

MURPHY, ——, Mr., pauper, old age and paralysis, at the almshouse, Aug. 3, 1839, a. supposed to be 90 y. C. R. 1.

MYRICK, Horace Allen, s. Freeman H. and Eliza, consumption, Sept. 8, 1849, a. 1 y. 10 m. [Sept. 5. G. R. 3.]

NAYLOR, Ann, b. England, d. John, chronic diarrhoea, Aug. 31, 1849, a. 1 y. 3 m.

NICHOLS, Daniel, Nov. 20, 1768. [a. 61 y. 3 m. 10 d. G. R. 1.]
Susanna, w. Daniel [old age. C. R. 1.], Oct. 11, 1806, a. 91 y. G. R. 1. [a. 92 y. C. R. 1.]
——, s. Capt., of Reading, drowned in Souhegan River, Mar. 25, 1752. P. R. 4.
——, s. W[illia]m Edward, spinner, b. Hillsborough, N. H., and Elizaeth B., b. Tyngsborough [Dec. 30, 1849?].

NOYCE, Isaac [of Andover. C. R. 1; at Cape. Barrons. P. R. 4.], Dec. 31, 1762.

NUT, Mr., of Tyngsborough, very suddenly, at W[illia]m Adams', July 13, 1825. C. R. 1.

NUTTING, Josiah, s. John, Dec. 10, 1658.
Mary, Mrs., d. Timo[thy] Adams, bur. at Westford, May 16, 1751. P. R. 4.

OBER (see also Obier), Charles [T. G. R. 1.], s. Tho[ma]s W. and Emily, dysentery, Oct. 3, 1848, a. 4 y.

OBIER (see also Ober), Harriet [H. G. R. 1.], w. Benj[amin J. G. R. 1.], June 22, 1830, a. 40 y. C. R. 1. [June 21, a. 38 y. G. R. 1.]

OSBORN (see also Osburn), Abigail, wid. Samuel, Jan. 29, 1838, a. 83 y. G. R. 1.

OSBURN (see also Osborn), James, intemperance, Sept. [bet. 2 and 22], 1826, a. 41 y. C. R. 1.
Sarah Abigail, d. James, Oct. 14, 1819, a. 18 m. C. R. 1.

OSGOOD, Laura Maria, d. Tho[ma]s T. and Laura [of the Factory Vil[lage]. C. R. 3.], Dec. 27, 1840. [Dec. 28, a. 7 m. C. R. 3.]
——, Mr., Apr. —, 1829. C. R. 3.

PACKARD, William, s. Rev. Hez[ekia]h, member of junior class in Bowdoin College, Jan. 28, 1834, a. 18 y. G. R. 1.

PAGE, Francis B., s. Hector M. and Mary Bolton, Aug. 29, 1841, a. 11 m. G. R. 3.
Martha B., d. Hector M. and Mary Bolton, b. 1840, d. June 16, 1846. G. R. 3.

PARIS (see also Parish), Seaborne, w. Roberd, Sept. 28, 1664.

PARISH (see also Paris), Hannah, June 8, 1671, a. abt. 2 y. CT. R.

PARKER, Abby, d. Daniel and Abby, consumption, Sept. 27, 1849, a. 33 y.
Abiel, w. W[illia]m, decline, bur. Aug. 2, 1801. C. R. 1.
Abraham, sr., Aug. 12, 1685.
Anah, d. Joseph and Margit [torn. 1662?].
Anna, d. Philip and Anna, Sept. 17, 1775, a. 5 y. 6 m. 14 d. G. R. 1.
Anna [d. Willard and Anna. G. R. 1.], bur. Sept. 9, 1788, a. 22 y. C. R. 1. [d. Sept. 7. P. R. 4.]
Anna, wid. Willard, old age, Sept. 8, 1832, a. 88 y. C. R. 1. [Sept. 7. G. R. 1.]
Benjamin, sr. [Ens. dup.], Apr. 14, 1742.
Benjamin, Lt., May 23, 1771. [a. 72 y. C. R. 1.]
Benjamin, s. Joseph and Tabitha (Warren), Aug. 10, 1787. P. R. 8.
Benj[ami]n, bur. Feb. 19, 1801, a. nearly 78 y. C. R. 1.
Benjamin, Nov. 30, 1848, a. 74 y. G. R. 1.
Benoni, Aug. 18, 1694. [Aug. 28. dup.]
Betsey, bur. July 4, 1799, a. 20 y. C. R. 1.
Charlott, d. Eben[eze]r and Rebecca, Nov. 28, 1804. [a. 2 y. 10 m. G. R. 1.]
Clarise, d. Ebenezer and Rebecca, Jan. 16, 1803. [a. 3 y. 2 m. 16 d. G. R. 1.]
Clarrisee, d. Ebenezer and Rebekah [worms. C. R. 1.], Sept. 15, 1806. [a. 2 y. 5 m. 7 d. G. R. 1.]
Clifton, s. Jepthah and M[ary. G. R. 1.] Amanda, croup, July 7, 1848, a. 1 y. 8 m. 11 d.
David, Lt. [old age. C. R. 1.], Jan. 11, 1811. [a. 80 y. C. R. 1.]
Dorcus, d. Philip and Anna, Sept. 27, 1775, a. 1 y. 24 d. G. R. 1.
Ebenezer [jr. C. R. 1.], s. Capt. Ebenezer and Elizabeth, Nov. 29, 1745. [a. 25 y. G. R. 1.]
Ebenezer, s. William and Sary, Jan. 3, 1756.
Ebenezer, Capt., Dec. 24, 1773. [a. 83 y. C. R. 1.]
Ebenezer, old age, Sept. 25, 1843, a. 83 y.
Elizabeth, w. Jo[h]n, Sept. 23, 1709. [a. 33 y. G. R. 1.]
Elizabeth, w. Lt. Benjamin, Dec. 30, 1765. [Dec. 19, a. 69 y. 1 m. 10 d. G. R. 1.]
Elizabeth, d. Lt. Isaac and Elizabeth, Aug. 30, 1775, a. 4 y. 8 m. 5 d. G. R. 1.
Elizabeth, w. Benjamin, Apr. 17, 1787, a. 64 y. 6 m. 13 d. G. R. 1. [Apr. 18. P. R. 4.]
Elizabeth, Feb. 20, 1829. C. R. 2.

PARKER, Elizabeth [B. G. R. 1.], Mrs. [w. Eli. G. R. 1.], formerly Davis, June 17, 1832, a. 62 y. C. R. 1. [a. 61 y. G. R. 1.]
Elizebeth [an aged maid. P. R. 4.], July 10, 1758. [a. 78 y. C. R. 1.]
Ephraim, found dead in his house, Nov. 27, 1840. C. R. 1.
Granville, s. Reuben, Jan. 11, 1811, a. 1 m. C. R. 1.
Hannah, d. Lt. Isaac and Elizabeth, Aug. 28, 1775, a. 1 y. 9 d. G. R. 1.
Hannah, w. Ebenezer, Oct. 22, 1790. [a. 23 y. 11 m. 4 d. G. R. 1.]
Henry S., rupture of a blood vessel, at almshouse, June 12, 1845, a. 73 y.
Isaac, Feb. 22, 1688-9. P. R. 31.
Isaac, s. John and Rebecka, Feb. 17, 1741-2.
Jacob, s. John and Rebeckah, "in the Grate Battle," at Lake George, Sept. 8, 1755.
Jeduthan, s. Jeduthan and Phebe, Apr. 6, 1795, a. 1 y. 3 m.
Jepthah, m., farmer, s. Ebenezer and Rebecca, erysipelas, July 25, 1848, a. 58 y.
John, s. Joseph, Oct. 8, 166[0. T. C.].
John, Corp., Apr. 14, 1699.
John, sr., Feb. 20, 1741-2. [in his 60th y. G. R. 1.]
John, s. John and Hannah, Sept. 2, 1744. [a. 7 m. 7 d. G. R. 1.]
John, Lt., Mar. 18, 1763. [Mar. 17, a. 51 y. 2 m. 5 d. G. R. 1.]
John, s. Ebenezer and Hannah, consumption, Oct. 3, 1847, a. 59 y.
Jonathan, s. John and Rebecca, Nov. 14, 1745.
Jonathan, Nov. 14, 1769. [a. 60 y. C. R. 1.]
Jona[than], palsy, May 20, 1818, a. 69 y. C. R. 1.
Joseph, Capt., Apr. 29, 1738, a. 44 y. 1 m. 9 d. G. R. 1.
Joseph, deaf and dumb, old age, Nov. 8, 1806, a. 78 y. C. R. 1.
Joseph, s. Moses and Sarah, paralysis and apoplexy, Jan. 19, 1840, a. 77 y. C. R. 1.
Josiah, s. John, Jan. 20, 1698.
Loiza, d. Thadeus, Feb. 26, 1825, a. 51 y. C. R. 1.
Lucy, w. [wid. C. R. 1.], David, Dec. 23, 1829, a. 91 y. G. R. 1.
Martha, of Carlisle, consumption, Sept. 30, 1804. C. R. 1.
Mary, w. Reuben, Sept. 5, 1803, a. 28 y. G. R. 1. [a. 29 y. C. R. 1.]
Mary, of Carlisle, cancer, July 9, 1814, a. 70 y. C. R. 1.
Mary Ann [Ann Mari. G. R. 1.], d. Jona[than], [3d and Hannah. G. R. 1.], Apr. 2, 1814, a. 9 m. C. R. 1.
Moses, jr., "kild wt thunder", July 28, 1702.
Moses, Oct. 12, 1732.

PARKER, Moses, Col. [Lt. Col. C. R. 1.], at Boston [wounded at Charlestown June 17, carried captive to Boston, where he died of his wound in prison. C. R. 1.], July 4, 1775. [a. 44 y. C. R. 1.]
Moses, at the almshouse, bleeding internally, Mar. 12, 1840, a. 56 y. C. R. 1.
Oliver, bur. Jan. 6, 1786. C. R. 1.
Philip, bur. June 27, 1791, a. 58 y. C. R. 1. [June 25, 1790. G. R. 1.]
Rachel, d. Jacob and Rachel, Sept. 10, 1746, a. 4 y. 5 m. 6 d. G. R. 1.
Rachel [w. Jonathan. G. R. 1.], bur. Apr. 7, 1797, a. 88 y. C. R. 1.
Rachel, w. Zebulon [consumption. C. R. 1.], Feb. 16, 1811. [Feb. 18, a. 45 y. C. R. 1.]
Rebecca, wid. [Capt. Joseph. G. R. 1.], bur. Jan. 5, 1791, a. 88 y. C. R. 1. [Jan. 1, in her 88th y. G. R. 1.]
Rebecca, d. Eben, July 25, 1831, a. 37 y. C. R. 1.
Rebecca, wid. Ebenezer, old age, Dec. 20, 1844.
Rebecka, wid. John, sr., Feb. 21, 1741-2. [in her 53d y. G. R. 1.]
Rebeckah, d. John [and Rebeckah. G. R. 1.], Dec. 12, 1724. [a. 5 y. 6 m. G. R. 1.]
Rebeckah, d. John and Hannah, Jan. 17, 1736, a. 14 m. G. R. 1.
Rebeckah, d. William [jr. C. R. 1.] and Hannah, Sept. 13, 1778.
Remembrance [w. Jonathan. G. R. 1.], Apr. 17, 1831, a. 78 y. C. R. 1.
Reuben, s. Willard and Anna [fell into a kettle of hot water. P. R. 4.], Sept. 7, 1783, a. 3 y. 4 m. 7 d. G. R. 1. [bur. Sept. 28. C. R. 1.]
Rhoda, cancer, Nov. 11, 1819, in her 33d y. C. R. 1.
Roase, wid. Abraham, Nov. 30, 1691.
Rufus, s. Joseph and Tabithy [(Warren). P. R. 8.], Nov. 7, 1798.
Samuel, s. Abraham and Mathew, Apr. 29, 1700.
Sarah, d. Joseph and Rebeca, Feb. 14, 1729-30. [a. 7 y. 10 m. 8 d. P. R. 2.]
Sarah, w. Benjamin, June 18, 1741.
Sarah, d. Lt. Benjamin and Elizebeth, Apr. 30, 1771. [a. 35 y. 7 m. 6 d. G. R. 1.]
Sarah, w. Jonathan, May 19, 1784, in her 31st y. G. R. 1.
Sarah, wid., bur. May 4, 1788. C. R. 1. [d. May 1. P. R. 4.]
Sarah, wid. Col. Moses, Mar. 10, 1817, a. 80 y. C. R. 1. [a. 82 y. dup.]

PARKER, Thomas, s. Thomas and Mary, July 7, 168[4. T. C.;
July 10. CT. R.]
Thomas, s. Ebenezer, Feb. 24, 1720-21.
Thomas, Sept. 12, 1757. [a. 71 y. C. R. 1.]
Thomas, Rev., of Dracut, Mar. 18, 1765, a. 64 y. C. R. 1.
Thomis, Serg., May 8, 1698.
Willard, jr. [eldest s. Willard. P. R. 4; and Anna. G. R. 1.],
drowned [in the Merrimac River, May 20. P. R. 4.], bur.
May 23, 1788. [a. 15 y. 10 m. 29 d. G. R. 1.]
Willard [cold. C. R. 1.], Apr. 4, 1808. [a. 66 y. C. R. 1; a. 65 y.
G. R. 1.]
William, s. John and Rebecakh, Jan. 27, 1739.
William, bur. June 12, 1772. C. R. 1. [d. June 10. P. R. 4.]
Will[ia]m, Feb. 3, 1822, a. 81 y. C. R. 1.
——, ch. Jacob, bur. Nov. 29, 1744. C. R. 1.
——, w. Eb[eneze]r, bur. Sept. 7, 1754. C. R. 1.
——, inf. ch. Hannah [d. Jona[than]. P. R. 4.], bur. June 22,
1767. C. R. 1.
——, ch. [d. P. R. 4.] twin, Isaac, bur. Dec. 26, 1770. C. R. 1.
[a. abt. 1 d. P. R. 4.]
——, ch. stillborn, Philip, bur. Dec. 21, 1771. C. R. 1.
——, ch. William, bur. May 8, 1775. C. R. 1.
——, ch. Col. Moses, deceased, bur. Sept. 2, 1775. C. R. 1.
——, inf. ch. twin, William, bur. Sept. 10, 1776. C. R. 1.
——, ch. Col. Moses, deceased, bur. Oct. 7, 1776. C. R. 1.
——, ch. stillborn, Philip, bur. Nov. 15, 1781. C. R. 1.
——, ch. Phillip, bur. Apr. 13, 1791. C. R. 1.
——, inf. ch. Jonathan, bur. Mar. 21, 1795. C. R. 1.
——, ch. Moses, bur. Mar. 3, 1801, a. 10 m. C. R. 1.
——, ch. Zebulon, July 27, 1805, a. 8 h. C. R. 1.
——, w. Dr., so called, dropsy, May 25, 1817, a. 60 y. C. R. 1.
——, ch. Lydia, an idiot, infantile, at the almshouse, Dec. 30,
1845, a. 21 d.

PARKHURST (see also Parkhust), Abigail, w. James, July 29,
1772. [a. 60 y. C. R. 1.]
Abigail, d. Dea. Benja[min] and Elisabeth,. Nov. 10, 1784,
a. 19 y. 11 m. 20 d. G. R. 1. [Nov. 8. P. R. 4.]
Abraham, s. wid. John [s. John and Surviah M. P. R. 3.], ty-
phus fever, Aug. 31, 1840, a. 27 y. C. R. 1.
Amos, farmer, s. Andrew and Betsey, dysentery, Oct. 11, 1848,
a. 36 y.
Andrew, s. James and Abigal, Nov. 10, 1753, a. 10 y. 6 m. 19 d.
G. R. 1. [Nov. 9. P. R. 4.]
Andrew, July 26, 1834, a. 63 y. G. R. 1.

CHELMSFORD DEATHS 423

PARKHURST, Benj[amin] [Dea. dup.], "41 years an officer in the Church," dropsy, June 24, 1812, a. 71 y. C. R. 1.
Benj[amin], Feb. 11, 1820, a. 47 y. C. R. 1.
Betsey, w. Sam[ue]l, fever and bleeding, Jan. 29, 1817, a. 57 y. C. R. 1.
Betsy [d. Samuel and Betty. G. R. 1.], consumption, Oct. 13, 1811, a. 15 y. C. R. 1.
Elisabeth, d. Dea. Benjamin and Elisabeth, Dec. 6, 1787, a. 18 y. 9 m. 6 d. G. R. 1. [Dec. 7. P. R. 4.]
Eliz[abeth], wid. Dea. Benj[amin], May 20, 1822, a. 81 y. C. R. 1.
Ephraim, Sept. 5, 1822, a. 76 y. C. R. 1.
Hannah, w. James, formerly w. Lt. John Parker, Feb. 5, 1781, a. 66 y. 5 m. 4 d. G. R. 1.
James, Jan. 18, 1796, a. 88 y. 2 m. 12 d. G. R. 1.
Joel, s. Joel and Hannah, Oct. 6, 1841, a. 1 y. G. R. 1.
John, paralytic affection, Aug. 29, 1830, a. 55 y. C. R. 1. [Aug. 28. G. R. 1.]
Josiah, d. Wilton, bur. at Wilton, Oct. 13, 1778. C. R. 1.
Josiah, Dea., Dec. 31, 1818, a. 56 y. [Dec. 30. C. R. 1.]
Julia Louisa, d. Rev. John and Celia, Nov. 11, 1840. [a. 4 m. 24 d. P. R. 3.]
Louisa, w. Amos, Mar. 16, 1847, a. 40 y. G. R. 1.
Maria, d. Rev. John, Aug. 29, 1843, a. 22 y.
Mary, w. Ebenezer, Oct. 28, 1732.
Mary, wid. Philip, Mar. 4, 1826, a. 77 y. C. R. 1. [Mar. 6. G. R. 1.]
Micajah, bleeding at the nose, Jan. 8, 1832, a. 38 y. C. R. 1.
Oliver, brother Josiah, Sept. 5, 1835, a. 68 y. G. R. 1.
Philip, "of a large excressence," Dec. 13, 1810, a. 65 y. C. R. 1. [Dec. 14, a. 66 y. G. R. 1.]
Rachel, d. Josiah and Rachel, Sept. 20, 1801. [a. 2 1-2 y. C. R. 1.]
Ruth [P. G. R. 1.], w. John, Jan. 1, 1804, a. 31 y. C. R. 1. [Dec. 30, 1803, a. 30 y. G. R. 1.]
Samuel, s. S[amuel. G. R. 1.] and Susannah [Betty. G. R. 1.], very suddenly, bur. Jan. 19, 1802, a. 2 y. 8 m. C. R. 1. [Jan. 16. G. R. 1.]
Samuel, m., farmer, old age, Jan. 15, 1849, a. 89 y.
Sarah Ann, d. Ephraim, July 18, 1810, a. 3 y. C. R. 1.
Silas, s. Andrew [and Betsy. G. R. 1.], Sept. 19, 1810, a. 2 y. C. R. 1.
Sukey, Mar. 26, 1832, a. 58 y. C. R. 1.
Susannah, d. Sam[ue]l and Susannah [Betty. G. R. 1.], bur. June 26, 1794, a. 3 y. 3 m. C. R. 1.
——, ch. Ja[me]s, bur. Mar. 4, 1742. C. R. 1.

PARKHURST, ——, w. Eben[eze]r, bur. Mar. 25, 1742. C. R. 1.
——, ch. twin, stillborn, James [and Abigail. P. R. 4.], bur. July 3, 1754. C. R. 1.
——, ch. twin, James [and Abigail. P. R. 4.], bur. July 26, 1754. C. R. 1.
——, inf. ch. Philip, bur. Jan. 3, 1772. C. R. 1.
——, d. Philip, bur. Aug. 21, 1782. C. R. 1.
——, wid., bur. Apr. 18, 1790, a. 61 y. C. R. 1. [d. Apr. 16. P. R. 4.]
——, ch. Philip, bur. Aug. 28, 1791. C. R. 1.

PARKHUST (see also Parkhurst), Abigail, d. James and Abigail, Feb. 17, 1736-7. [a. 2 y. 2 m. 12 d. G. R. 1.]
Benjamin, s. James and Abigail, Feb. 17, 1736-7. [a. 4 y. 3 m. 11 d. G. R. 1.]
Ebenezer, Nov. 9, 1745.
Hanah, d. Josaph and Eunis, Aug. 8, 1697.
James, s. James and Abigail, Feb. 22, 1738-9.
Jonathan, Mar. 25, 1737. [a. 55 y. 3 m. 23 d. G. R. 1.]
Joseph, Nov. 30, 1709.
Sarah, d. James and Abigail, Mar. 2, 1730-31.
——, ch. Philip, bur. Sept. 15, 1791. C. R. 1.

PARLIN, Elizabeth, Apr. 15, 1837. C. R. 2.

PARROT, John, Nov. 20, 1756.
——, wid., bur. Feb. 22, 1775. C. R. 1.

PATCH, Isaac, Oct. ——, 1841. C. R. 2.
Phebe, Jan. "about the 10th," 1843. C. R. 2.

PATIN (see also Pattin), Oliver, s. Isaac and Lydia [at his Father Chamberlain's. P. R. 4.], May 13, 1763. [May 12, a. 3 m. 18 d. G. R. 1.]

PATTIN (see also Patin), Lydia, w. Isaac, Feb. 3, 1763. [Feb. 4. P. R. 4; in her 24th y. G. R. 1.]

PEARCE (see also Pierce), Stephen, sr., June 10, 1733. [a. 82 y. G. R. 1.]

PECKENS (see also Peckins), Abigail, w. Rev. John, Dec. 15, 1835, a. 75 y. G. R. 2.
Hannah, w. John, jr., Aug. 31, 1841, a. 74 y. G. R. 2.
John [Rev. G. R. 2.], b. Middleborough, farmer, formerly pastor of the Baptist Church, old age, July 30, 1846, a. 91 y.

PECKINS (see also Peckens), Abigail [d. Rev. John and Abagil. G. R. 2.], internal obstruction, Oct. 24, 1830, a. 44 y. C. R. 1. [Oct. 27. G. R. 2.]
Horace, widr., farmer, s. Rev. John, intemperance, Feb. 20, 1849, a. 67 y.
——, w. Horace, June 1, 1824, a. 40 y. C. R. 1.

PEIRCE (see also Pierce), Abigail, w. Steven, Sept. [bet. 2 and 22], 1826, a. 35 y. C. R. 1.
Benjamin, June 16, 1764.
Benj[ami]n, s. Steven, bur. Feb. 6, 1796, a. 5 y. C. R. 1.
Bradley, s. William and Elizabeth, Aug. 30, 1775, a. 3 y. 3 m. 25 d. G. R. 1.
Elizabath, w. Silas, Mar. 23, 1786.
Ephraim [very suddenly, by overwhelming intemperance. C. R. 1.], Mar. 6, 1798.
Esther, wid. [Dea. P. R. 4.], bur. Sept. 21, 1767, a. 82 y. C. R. 1. [d. Sept. 20. P. R. 4.]
Joseph, June 14, 1796. [bur. June 12, a. 74 y. C. R. 1; in his 74th y. G. R. 1.]
Lucy, w. Silas, July 31, 1773.
Lydia, w. Silas, Mar. 4, 1796. [a. 47 y. C. R. 1.]
Marshall, June 2, 1839. C. R. 1.
Mary, w. Robert, June 5, 1761. [a. 52 y. 3 m. 22 d. G. R. 1.]
Mary, d. Silas and Lucy, Mar. 4, 1773.
Mary [Sarah. C. R. 1.], w. Silas, May 31, 1799.
Mary [w. Joseph. G. R. 1.], old age, Nov. 1, 1807, a. 85 y. C. R. 1. [Nov. 5. G. R. 1.]
Oliver, bur. Nov. 27, 1784, a. 75 y. C. R. 1. [d. Nov. 25. P. R. 4.]
Rebeckah, d. Oliver and Deborah, Nov. 18, 1789, a. 9 y. 10 m. 18 d. G. R. 1.
Robert, bur. Apr. 2, 1789, a. 81 y. C. R. 1. [d. Apr. 1. P. R. 4.]
Sarah, d. Dea. Steaphen and Esther, Jan. 19, 1745-6.
Stephen, Dea., Sept. 9, 1749. [a. 71 y. C. R. 1; in his 70th y. G. R. 1.]
Stephen, bur. Dec. 8, 1798, in his 85th y. C. R. 1.
Susy [Miss. G. R. 1.], bur. Dec. 12, 1775. C. R. 1. [a. 21 y. 1 m. G. R. 1.]
Tabitha, wid., Jan. 31, 1741-2.
William [suddenly. P. R. 4.], bur. June 7, 1782. C. R. 1. [d. June 6. P. R. 4.]
——, ch. Eph[rai]m, bur. June 5, 1766. C. R. 1. [a. 2 d. P. R. 4.]
——, ch. stillborn, Oliver, jr., bur. Jan. 25, 1772. C. R. 1.
——, inf. ch. twin, Robert, bur. Dec. 1, 1781. C. R. 1.
——, ch. twin, stillborn, Robert, bur. Dec. 1, 1781. C. R. 1.

CHELMSFORD DEATHS

PEIRCE, ——, w. Stephen, bur. Nov. 30, 1786. C. R. 1. [d. Nov. 29. P. R. 4.]
——, inf. ch. Stephen, jr., bur. July 5, 1789. C. R. 1.
——, inf. ch. Robert, bur. July 11, 1789. C. R. 1.
——, inf. ch. Robert, bur. June 12, 1790. C. R. 1.
——, ch. Silas and Sarah, bur. June 1, 1799. C. R. 1.

PELSUE, Betsey, wid. Ens. William, malignant fever, Oct. 9, 1808, a. 29 y. [a. 30. y. G. R. 2.]
William, Ens., malignant fever, Oct. 2, 1808, a. 34 y. [a. 35 y. G. R. 2.]
William, s. Ens. William and Betsy, malignant fever, Oct. 4, 1808, a. 3 y. [a. 4 y. G. R. 2.]

PERHAM (see also Perrum), Anna, w. Sam[ue]l, putrid fever, Oct. 28, 1807. C. R. 1. [Oct. 29, a. 22 y. G. R. 1.]
Benoni, Cornet, Mar. 14, 1724, a. 48 y. G. R. 1.
Benoni, s. Samuel and Sarah, Feb. 10, 1774. [a. 23 y. 10 m. 27 d. G. R. 1.]
David, May 23, 1841, a. 57 y. G. R. 1.
Dolly, consumption, Sept. 3, 1807, a. 49 y. C. R. 1.
Edwin P., s. Samuel P. and Rebecca [(Perham). P. R. 14.], Dec. 1, 1843, a. 1 y. 3 m. 10 d. G. R. 1.
Eliz[a]beth, d. Jonathan and Mary [consumption. C. R. 1.], Sept. 9, 1807. [Sept. 8, a. 18 m. C. R. 1; Sept. 2. G. R. 1.]
Elizabeth, Mrs. [w. Samuel. G. R. 1; wid., old age. C. R. 1.], Dec. 24, 1820, in her 83d y. [a. 83 y. G. R. 1.]
Gonathan, s. Goseph and Dorithy, Mar. 21, 1706-7.
Hannah, d. Benoni and Sarah, Aug. [broken], 1736, in her 19th y. G. R. 1.
Joel, s. David and Rebecca S., Jan. 9, 1839, a. 18 y. 8 m. 8 d. G. R. 1.
John [s. Samuel and Sarah. G. R. 1.], fever, Sept. 22, 1815, a. 5 y. C. R. 1. [Sept. 16, a. 4 y. 6 m. G. R. 1.]
Jonathan, s. Benoni and Sarah, Apr. 7, 1724, in his 13th y. G. R. 1.
Jona[than], [s. Samuel and Elizabeth. G. R. 1.], hung himself, July 28, 1827, a. 51 y. C. R. 1. [a. 52 y. G. R. 1.]
Lidia, w. John, June 21, 1710. [June 20. dup.; June 26, in her 67th y. G. R. 1.]
Mary, d. Samuel and Sarah, Nov. 28, 1745.
Mary, w. Jonathan, Apr. 16, 1836, a. 61 y. G. R. 1.
Rebecca, w. Samuel P., Jan. 9, 1844, a. 26 y. 4 m. 1 d. G. R. 1.
Rebecca S., wid. David, consumption, July 30, 1847, a. 57 y.
Samuel, s. Samuel and Sary, Mar. 7, 1756.

PERHAM, Samuel, jr., bur. Mar. 5, 1788. C. R. 1. [a. 31 y. 6 m. 8 d. G. R. 1.]
Samuel, suddenly, bur. May 24, 1794, a. 78 y. C. R. 1. [May 20. G. R. 1.]
Samuel [consumption. C. R. 1.], Jan. 13, 1812, a. 32 y. 2 m. 15 d.
Sarah, wid. [Benoni. G. R. 1.], Feb. 22, 1741-2. [in her 65th y. G. R. 1.]
Sarah, d. Samuel and Sarah, Aug. 16, 1747.
Sarah, d. Samuel and Sarah, July 1, 1749.
Sarah, w. Samuel, Apr. 28, 1767. [a. 47 y. 6 m. 16 d. G. R. 1.]
——, ch. Sam[ue]ll, bur. Oct. 13, 1746. C. R. 1.
——, ch. Sam[ue]ll, bur. July 21, 1753. C. R. 1. [d. July 20. P. R. 4.]
——, w. Oliver [suddenly. P. R. 4.], bur. Jan. 16, 1785. C. R. 1.
——, inf. ch. Oliv[e]r, bur. Jan. 28, 1785. C. R. 1.

PERRUM (see also Perham), John, Jan. 23, 1720-21. [Jan. 21, a. 88 y. G. R. 1.]

PHILIPS (see also Phillips), ——, ch. stillborn, Micah, bur. Mar. 9, 1795. C. R. 1.

PHILLIP (see also Phillips), ——, ch. stillborn, —— ["a new commer into Town." P. R. 4.], bur. Jan. 2, 1792. C. R. 1.

PHILLIPS (see also Philips, Phillip), William, b. Hudson, N. H., Oct. 5, 1848, a. 40 y.

PIERCE (see also Pearce, Peirce), Betsy, w. Jonas, Mar. 4, 1821, a. 76 y. C. R. 1.
Betty [Bridget. G. R. 1.], 5th w. Silas, disorder on the liver, June 12, 1805, a. 59 y. C. R. 1.
Bridget, wid., Oct. 9, 1822, a. 89 y. C. R. 1.
Cynthia A. [F G. R. 3.], d. Ruel and Cynthia [W. G. R. 3.], Aug. 2, 1848, a. 1 y. 7 m.
Deborah, w. Oliver, Oct. 27, 1837, a. 92 y. 6 m. G. R. 1.
George D., s. George and Ruhannah W., May 13, 1839, a. 10 m. 6 d. G. R. 1.
George D., s. George and Ruhannah W., Aug. 28, 1847, a. 5 m. 16 d. G. R. 1.
Hannah, Mrs. [w. Stephen. G. R. 1.], Oct. 15, 1825, a. 70 y. C. R. 1. [Sept. 27. G. R. 1.]
Harriet E., d. Reuel and Cynthia W., Dec. 2, 1848, a. 18 m. G. R. 3.

PIERCE, Henry C., s. Jonathan and Hannah, Feb. 2, 1834, a. 5 m. G. R. 1.
Jacob, d. Westford, bur. Sept. 26, 1749. C. R. 1.
Jesse [s. Stephen and Hannah. G. R. 1.], sudden, intemperance, July 5, 1820. [June 20, a. 30 y. G. R. 1.]
John, s. Stephen and Hannah, ———, 1824, a. 41 y. G. R. 1. [a. 40 y. C. R. 1.]
Jonas, jr., nervous fever, May 3, 1810, a. 30 y. C. R. 1.
Lucinda, dysentery, Oct. 2, 1826, a. 6 y. C. R. 1.
Mary [Miss. G. R. 1.], lethargy, Oct. 27, 1826, a. 71 y. C. R. 1. [Oct. 28. G. R. 1.]
Mary A., w. Milo, Jan. 28, 1849, a. 25 y. G. R. 1.
Oliver, s. Capt. Jonas, Apr. 19, 1817, a. 27 y. C. R. 1.
Oliver, fit, Jan. 22, 1821, a. 79 y. C. R. 1. [Jan. 21. G. R. 1.]
Rachel, wid. Jacob, d. Westford, bur. Feb. 26, 1754. C. R. 1.
Silas, old age, Apr. 14, 1828, a. 84 y. C. R. 1. [1827. dup.]
Stephen, intoxication, Mar. 28, 1812, a. 52 y. C. R. 1.
Steven, Apr. 15, 1826, a. 72 y. C. R. 1. [Apr. 16. G. R. 1.]
Wallace W., s. Joseph B. and Mary B., Feb. 6, 1844, a. 3 m. G. R. 3.

PIKE, Franklin [Frank M. G. R. 3.], s. James and Betsey B., inflammation of the heart, May 3, 1847, a. 6 y. 3 m.

PILSBURY, ———, Mr., fell 75 feet from the gable end of one of the factories, into the wheel pit, Dec. —, 1824, a. 42 y. C. R. 1.

PITTS, Elizabeth, w. Thomas, at Cambridge, Aug. 14, 1843, a. 64 y.
James, Capt., hemmorhage of lungs, with dropsy in heart, Dec. 19, 1843, a. 66 y. C. R. 1.
Joanna [w. Samuel. C. R. 1.], Apr. 5, 1796, a. 45 y.
John, s. Sam[ue]l, at Belgrade, Nov. 9, 1834, a. 52 y.
Mary Bachelder, 2d w. Sam[ue]l, at Belgrade, Apr. 10, 1824, a. 57 y.
Rachel Hildreth, w. James, Feb. 22, 1836, a. 60 y.
Sam[ue]l [dropsy. C. R. 1.], Mar. 6, 1805, a. 59 y.
Sam[ue]l, s. Sam[ue]l, at New Orleans, June 13, 1818, a. 27 y.
Thomas, s. Sam[ue]l, at Cambridge, Sept. 5, 1836, a. 57 y.
William Lindall, s. Sam[ue]l, at St. Augustine, Fla., Oct. 24, 1821, a. 32 y.

POLLARD, Charles D., s. Dawson [and Julia Ann. G. R. 4.],
July 19, 1848, a. 1 y. 4 m. 5 d. [a. 14 m. 5 d. G. R. 4.]
——, ch. Jonathan, bur. at Billerica, June 24, 1765. P. R. 4.
——, wid., late of Billerica [at her son Isa[ia]h Abbott's.
P. R. 4.], bur. Sept. 22, 1785, a. 75 y. C. R. 1. [d. Sept. 20.
P. R. 4.]

POWER (see also Powers), ——, d. John, shoemaker, b. Limerick, Ireland, and Bridgett, b. Monaghan Co., Ireland, at North Chelmsford [Dec. 29, 1849?].

POWERS (see also Power), Lois, bur. Dec. 18, 1746. C. R. 1.
Lydia, d. William and Remembrance, Jan. 3, 1745-6.
William, s. William and Remembrance, Sept. 12, 1742.

PRATT, Warren Hamilton, s. John R. and Lydia, Oct. 27, 1835. [Oct. 25, 1838, a. 4 y. 6 m. G. R. 1.]
William H., inf. s. Oliver R. and Mary A., Sept. 2, 1844. G. R. 3.

PRENTICE (see also Prentiss), Sarah, old age and mortification, Mar. 29, 1805, a. 75 y. C. R. 1.

PRENTISS (see also Prentice), ——, Mr., of Middlesex Village, suddenly, Aug. 23 or 24, 1840, a. abt. 50 y. C. R. 3.
——, Mrs., bur. June ——, 1841. C. R. 3.

PRESCOTT, Benjamin, May 22, 1833, in his 64th y. G. R. 1.
——, ch. Levi, Feb. 10, 1825. C. R. 1.
——, ch. Levi, Oct. 28, 1825, a. 1 y. 6 m. C. R. 1.

PROCKTER (see also Proctor), Charls, s. Sam[ue]ll and Sary, Oct. 28, 1710.
Daniel, s. Daniel and Susanah, Nov. 23, 1728.
Easter, d. Peter, May 17, 1707.
Gershom, Nov. 8, 1714, a. 66 y. 6 m. G. R. 1.
Gershom [sr. G. R. 1.], bur. Oct. 19, 1774, a. 84 y. C. R. 1. [a. 81 y. 5 m. 23 d. G. R. 1.]
Hannah, wid. [Peter. P. R. 4.], bur. Oct. 2, 1781, a. 81 y. C. R. 1. [d. Sept. 30. P. R. 4.]
Miriam, wid., bur. Jan. 20, 1767, a. 99 y. C. R. 1. [d. Jan. 19. P. R. 4.]
Samuel, bur. Oct. 8, 1764, a. 68 y. C. R. 1. [d. Oct. 6. P. R. 4.]
——, ch. Israel, bur. Jan. 2, 1752. C. R. 1.
——, s. Benja[min], bur. Feb. 28, 1758. C. R. 1. [d. Feb. 26. P. R. 4.]

PROCKTER, ——, w. Benjamin, bur. Apr. 16, 1759. C. R. 1. [d. Apr. 14. P. R. 4.]
——, s. Tim[oth]y, bur. July 18, 1768. C. R. 1.
——, wid., of Westford, brought from Billerica, bur. Apr. 27, 1785. C. R. 1.
——, w. Asa, bur. Apr. 5, 1790. C. R. 1.

PROCTER (see also Proctor), Asubah, w. [Capt. G. R. 1.] Azariah, Dec. 28, 1826, a. 77 y. C. R. 1. [Dec. 29. G. R. 1.]
Azariah, Capt., Nov. 11, 1832, a. 83 y. G. R. 1.
Azariah, Nov. 21, 1838, a. 57 y. G. R. 1.
Daniel, Lt. [jr. P. R. 13.], fever, bur. Dec. 5, 1803, a. 59 y. C. R. 1.
Daniel, typhus fever, Sept. 12, 1822, a. 38 y. C. R. 1.
Edwin, s. Azariah and Lucy, Mar. 12, 1833, a. 2 y. 6 m. G. R. 1.
Elijah, Lt., old age, Apr. 14, 1819, a. 80 y. C. R. 1.
Ephraim, s. wid. Dan[ie]l, July 6, 1826, a. 4 y. C. R. 1.
Ester, w. Jeames, Dec. 6, 1693.
Genett W., w. Charles, Oct. 25, 1840, a. 23 y. G. R. 1.
Gershom [jr. C. R. 1.], s. Gershom and Rebecka [fever. P. R. 4.], Feb. 7, 1750-51. [a. 27 y. 10 m. 8 d. G. R. 1.]
Hosea, of Westford, Mar. 6, 1796, a. 19 y.
Hyram, s. Azariah and Azubah, Sept. 8, 1775, a. 3 y. 5 m. 8 d. G. R. 1.
Isaac, s. Peter and Hannah, Oct. "at the Half Moon," 1756.
Israel, June 9, 1755. [a. 46 y. 8 m. 5 d. G. R. 1.]
Joanna, d. Cornet Daniel and Susanna, Sept. 23, 1749.
Jonas R., July 2, 1843, a. 57 y. G. R. 1.
Levie, s. William and Lucy, Nov. 19, 1755. [a. 15 y. 2 m. 19 d. G. R. 1.]
Lidia, w. David, formerly of Acton, Apr. 13, 1796. [a. 88 y. C. R. 1.]
Lucy, d. William and Lucy, Nov. 21, 1755. [a. 7 y. 8 m. 24 d. G. R. 1.]
Lydia, w. Samuel, Feb. 10, 1763. [Feb. 11. P. R. 4.]
Mary, w. Peter, Oct. 12, 1724.
Mary, d. Benjamin and Lydia, Oct. 4, 1747.
Mary, d. Israel and Sarah, Jan. 2, 1750-51.
Meriam, d. Benjamin and Lydia, Oct. 6, 1747.
Moly, d. Azariah and Azubah, Aug. 30, 1775, a. 1 y. 9 m. 2 d. G. R. 1.
Peter [suddenly, at work in his field. P. R. 4.], June 15, 1792. [a. 56 y. C. R. 1; a. 55 y. 4 m. G. R. 1.]
Rebekah, w. [wid. C. R. 1.] Gershom, Apr. 16, 1776, a. 79 y. 1 m. 16 d. G. R. 1.

PROCTER, Robord, Apr. 28, 1697.
Sarah, d. Sameuel and Sarah, May 11, 1694.
Sarah, d. Daniel and Susannah, Feb. 10, 1736-7.
Sarah, wid. Samuel, Jan. 17, 1757. [a. 85 y. C. R. 1.]
Susanah, d. Daniel and Susanah, Sept. 19, 1734.
Susannah, wid. [Capt. Daniel. G. R. 1.], Nov. 26, 1785. [a. 81 y. C. R. 1.]
Uriah, s. Daniel and Susanna, Jan. 28, 1741-2.
William, s. William and Lucy, Sept. 10, 1738. [a. 3 y. 10 m. 11 d. G. R. 1.]
William, Oct. 13, 1767. [Oct. 14. P. R. 4; a. 63 y. 1 m. 3 d. G. R. 1.]
———, w. Levi, dysentery, Oct. 29, 1817, a. 69 y. C. R. 1.

PROCTOR (see also Prockter, Procter), Asa, s. Simeon and Rebeckah, July 16, 1768.
Benj[ami]n, asthma, bur. Aug. 3, 1794, a. 90 y. C. R. 1.
Bethiah, w. Benjamin [old age. C. R. 1.], Jan. 3, 1812, a. 96 y. [Jan. 2, a. 97 y. C. R. 1.]
Daniel, Capt., Jan. 28, 1775. [a. 68 y. C. R. 1 ; a. 69 y. 1 m. 17 d. G. R. 1.]
Eldad, dropsy in chest, May 22, 1811, a. 42 y. C. R. 1.
Ester, d. [Lt. P. R. 4.] Daniel and Susanna, Nov. 10, 1757.
Esther, w. Elijah, drowned herself in a well in a deranged state of mind, Apr. 6, 1808, a. 59 y. C. R. 1.
Hannah [wid. Lt. Daniel. G. R. 1; Daniel, jr. P. R. 13.], Apr. 10, 1837. C. R. 1. [Apr. 11, a. 92 y. G. R. 1.]
Lideah, d. Roberd and Jane, Aug. 13, 1661.
Mary, w. Samuel and Lydia, Nov. 6, 1795, a. 63 y. G. R. 2.
Mary L., d. S. B. and A. J. H. P., b. Sept. 20, 1845, d. Dec. 20, 1846. G. R. 1.
Mary [R. P. R. 13.], w. Daniel [jr. C. R. 1.], Mar. 3, 1773. [in her 31st y. G. R. 1.]
Mathew, s. Daniel and Betsey, Aug. 31, 1835, a. 2 y. G. R. 1.
Milo Jefferson, s. Jonas R. and Sybil [H. G. R. 1.], Mar. 12, 1834. [a. 2 y. 5 m. G. R. 1.]
Molly, dysentery, July 30, 1806, a. 29 y. C. R. 1.
Peter, Feb. 20, 1772. [a. 78 y. C. R. 1.]
Rufus Pecken, s. Gaius and Betsy, Oct. 11, 1800, a. 18 m. 6 d. G. R. 2.
Samuel, Oct. 5, 1799, a. 73 y. G. R. 2.
Samuell, s. Robert and Jane, Apr. 12, 1740. [a. 74 y. 6 m. 27 d. G. R. 1.]
Sybil Mariah, d. Jonas R. and Sybil, Feb. 27, 1819. [a. 18 m. C. R. 1.]

PULSIFER, Mary C. [w. Capt. David, of Salem. G. R. 1.], d. Capt. Josiah and Zilpah Fletcher, suddenly, at Salem, Apr. 7, 1826, a. 20 y. C. R. 1.
Mary F., Sept. 22, 1826, a. 6 m. C. R. 1.

PUTNAM, David, bur. June 23, 1785. C. R. 1. [d. June 21. P. R. 4.]
Hannah [w. Jonathan. G. R. 1.], old age, May 15, 1826, a. 95 y. C. R. 1.
Hannah W., d. Israel and Mary L., infantile, Sept. 24, 1845, a. 22 d.
Israel, bur. Feb. 25, 1800, a. 78 y. C. R. 1. [in his 77th y. G. R. 1.]
Jonathan, bur. Dec. 11, 1784. C. R. 1. [d. Dec. 9. P. R. 4; in his 58th y. G. R. 1.]
Jonathan [s. Jonathan and Hannah. G. R. 1.], bur. June 6, 1790. C. R. 1. [d. June 4. P. R. 4; a. 27 y. 2 d. G. R. 1.]
Polley [Patty. C. R. 1.], d. Jona[tha]n and Hannah, June 29, 1785, a. 16 y. 1 m. 1 d. G. R. 1.
——, ch. Jonathan, bur. Apr. 15, 1769. C. R. 1.
——, ch. John, Mar. 11, 1806, a. 24 h. C. R. 1.

RANGER, ——, ch. Nath[aniel]ll, bur. Jan. 4, 1744. C. R. 1.

READ (see also Reed), Elezebeth, d. Thomas and Sary, Dec. 11, 1711.
Sarah, w. Timo[thy], d. Capt. Jonas Pierce, Aug. 22, 1821, a. 37 y. C. R. 1.
Thomas, s. John, Mar. 12, 1727-8.

READING (see also Redding, Reeding, Ridings), Robert, bur. Jan. 21, 1797, a. 85 y. C. R. 1.

REDDING (see also Reading), Sarah, d. Robert and Hannah, Aug. 22, 1748.

REED (see also Read), Andrew J[ackson. C. R. 1.], s. Joseph and Maria, cholera infantum, Sept. 25, 1844, a. 6 m. 10 d.
Caroline A., d. Joseph and Maria, Feb. 26, 1843, a. 3 y. 3 m. G. R. 1.
Jacob, bur. May 6, 1794, a. 77 y. C. R. 1.
Leonora, w. Joseph, June 13, 1835, a. 26 y. G. R. 1.
Leonora S., d. Joseph and Leonora, Feb. 20, 1832, a. 2 m. G. R. 1.
Lucy, wid., old age, Oct. 23, 1804, a. 84 y. C. R. 1.
Lucy E., d. Joseph and Maria, Aug. 25, 1841, a. 3 m. G. R. 1.

CHELMSFORD DEATHS 433

REED, Martima, d. Joseph and Maria, infantile, Sept. 3, 1845, a. 24 d.
Mary Ann, d. Timo[thy], by her clothes accidentally taking fire, Oct. 12, 1826, a. 9 y. C. R. 1.
Merriam, b. Littleton or Acton, w. Willard, consumption, Nov. 29, 1846, a. 70 y.
Mortimer, s. Joseph and Maria, Sept. 2, 1845, a. 1 m. G. R. 1.
Olive, Dec. 29, 1827, a. 78 y. C. R. 1.
Roxy, consumption, Sept. 22, 1826, a. 26 y. C. R. 1.
William, s. [in-law] Henry Spaulding, at Litchfield, Jan. —, 1769. P. R. 4.
Zachary T., s. Joseph and Maria, dysentery, Aug. 27, 1848, a. 7 m. 3 d. [Aug. 26. G. R. 1.]
——, ch. Jacob, bur. Sept. 13, 1757. C. R. 1. [d. Sept. 11. P. R. 4.]
——, Mrs., formerly of Westford, consumption, Feb. —, 1828. C. R. 1.

REEDING (see also Reading), Hannah, w. Robert [formerly w. Jonathan Parkhurst. G. R. 1.], Sept. 24, 1768. [a. 64 y. 4 m. 17 d. G. R. 1.]

RICE, Mary, a transient person, b. Canada, dysentery, Sept. 4, 1849, a. 52 y.

RICH, ——, ch. Elisha, Baptist teacher and blacksmith, bur. near Baptist meeting house, South End, Oct. 5, 1774. C. R. 1.
——, d. Robert, jr., bur. June 30, 1775. C. R. 1.

RICHARDSON (see also Ritchardsun), Abby Ann, d. Capt. Sylvester, Aug. 25, 1824, a. 9 y. 1 m. 9 d. G. R. 1.
Almah [Mar. 4. P. R. 2.], 1844. G. R. 1. [a. 28 y. P. R. 2.]
Alva Howard, s. Elijah [and Molly. G. R. 1.], Aug. 26, 1810, a. 4 y. C. R. 1. [a. 3 y. 7 m. 19 d. G. R. 1.]
Asa [Edwin. G. R. 1.], s. George and Asenath, disease of the heart, Mar. 9, 1846, a. 9 y. 9 m. [Mar. 10. G. R. 1.]
Benony, s. Josiah and Lidia, Oct. 7, 1777.
Chloe, w. Oliver, Jan. 17, 1807, a. 38 y. C. R. 1.
Eleazer [consumption. P. R. 4.], bur. Aug. 16, 1776, a. 58 y. C. R. 1.
Elizabeth, Mrs. [w. Capt. Jonathan. G. R. 1.], May 9, 1722. [in her 51st y. G. R. 1.]
Elizabeth, w. John, Mar. 13, 1728-9.
Emerson, s. Elijah, jr. and Elisabeth, Nov. 21, 1835.

RICHARDSON, Esther, d. Josiah and Lydia, Jan. 24, 1787. [Jan. 25, 1788, a. 16 y. G. R. 1.]
Esther, d. Josiah, Sept. 27, 1799, a. 1 y. 9 m.
Esther, wid., bur. Sept. 2, 1803, a. 93 y. C. R. 1.
Ezekell, Nov. 27, 1696. [a. 29 y. G. R. 1.]
Hannah, w. Zachariah, jr., Mar. 10, 1754. [a. 22 y. 1 m. 20 d. G. R. 1.]
Hannah, d. Robert and Jan[e], June 28, 1775, a. 11 y. 1 m. 15 d. G. R. 1.
Hannah [d. Zachariah and Sarah. G. R. 1.], bur. Feb. 20, 1784. C. R. 1. [a. 19 y. G. R. 1.]
John, Sept. 13, 1746.
John, suddenly, Aug. 28, 1764. [a. 52 y. 9 m. 27 d. G. R. 1.]
Jonathan, Capt., bur. Feb. 21, 1753. C. R. 1. [d. Feb. 18. P. R. 1.]
Jona[than], found dead, May 8, 1753. P. R. 4.
Jonathan, fever, Mar. 20, 1813, a. 68 y. C. R. 1.
Joseph, h. Lucy M. (Byam), Feb. 24, 1848, a. 47 y. P. R. 26.
Josiah, Lt., Oct. 17, 1711. [Sept. 17. P. R. 31; in his 47th y. G. R. 1.]
Josiah, bur. Apr. 16, 1801, a. 67 y. C. R. 1.
Josiah, consumption, May 8, 1822, a. 55 y. C. R. 1.
Lydia, wid. Eleazer [at Westford. C. R. 1.], Feb. 21, 1797, a. 74 y. G. R. 1.
Lydia, wid. [Josiah. G. R. 1.], Oct. 13, 1822, a. 84 y. C. R. 1. [Oct. 15. G. R. 1.]
Mary [(Howard). P. R. 4.], wid. [Amos, of Pelham. G. R. 1.], bur. Apr. 2, 1791, a. 70 y. C. R. 1. [d. Apr. 1. P. R. 4; in her 76th y. G. R. 1.]
Mercy, d. Capt. Zachariah and Sarah, Jan. 19, 1745-6. [in her 22d y. G. R. 1.]
Olive, d. Josiah and Lydia, Apr. 28, 1769.
Oliver, May 18, 1816, a. 57 y. C. R. 1. [May 17, a. 58 y. G. R. 1.]
Paul, "Idiotical occasion'd by convulsion fits which attended him thro life," bur. Apr. 2, 1799, a. 36 y. C. R. 1.
Rachal, d. [2d d. P. R. 4.] Elezer and Lydia, Oct. 21, 1760, a. 9 y. 4 m. 18 d. G. R. 1. [Oct. 22. P. R. 4.]
Rach[e]l, w. Samuel, Feb. 26, 1727, a. abt. 45 y. G. R. 1.
Rebecca, bur. Dec. 19, 1803, a. 9 y. C. R. 1.
Rememberance, w. Capt. Josiah, Feb. 20, 1718-19, in her 79th y. G. R. 1.
Robert, bur. Nov. 4, 1799, a. 44 y. C. R. 1.
Robert, delirium induced by intemperance, Apr. 7, 1841, a. 37 y. C. R. 1.
Rufus E., s. Elijah and Elizabeth (Emerson), Nov. 22, 1835. P. R. 6.

RICHARDSON, Ruth, d. James and Brigett, Dec. 6, 1674.
Sam[ue]l, s. Sam[ue]l and Rachel, Feb. 18, 1727, a. abt. 19 y.
G. R. 1.
Samuel, Apr. 23, 1754. [a. 81 y. C. R. 1; a. 82 y. 1 m. 19 d.
G. R. 1.]
Samuel, s. Elijah and Molly, Apr. 30, 1838. [a. 36 y. P. R. 26.]
Sarah, d. Zachariah [jr. C. R. 1.] and Sarah, Jan. 10, 1760.
Sarah [d. Zachariah and Sarah. G. R. 1.], bur. Apr. 11, 1784.
C. R. 1. [a. 21 y. G. R. 1.]
Sarah, wid. [Zachariah, jr. G. R. 1.], bur. July 4, 1785. C. R. 1.
[a. 52 y. G. R. 1.]
Sarah, w. [wid. C. R. 1.] Capt. Zacheriah, Aug. 11, 1788. [a. 87
y. C. R. 1; a. 78 y. G. R. 1.]
Simeon, consumption, May 10, 1811, a. 41 y. C. R. 1.
Sophia, d. Josiah, Dec. 18, 1803, a. 9 y. 5 m. 4 d.
Sybil [d. Zachariah and Sarah. G. R. 1.], of a decline, bur. Dec.
14, 1798, a. 28 y. C. R. 1. [a. 29 y. G. R. 1.]
Sybil, wid. Josiah, July 27, 1827, a. 58 y. C. R. 1. [June 20, a.
54 y. G. R. 1.]
Sybil, May 21, 1831, a. 31 y. 7 m. 21 d. G. R. 1.
Thomas, s. Ezekiell and Mary, May 6, 1698. [a. abt. 8 y.
G. R. 1.]
Thomas, Feb. 10, 1699-1700.
Zachariah [jr. C. R. 1.], May 20, 1773. [a. 51 y. 2 m. 18 d.
G. R. 1.]
Zachariah, jr. [s. Zechariah and Hannah. G. R. 1.], bur. Sept.
8, 1775. C. R. 1. [Sept. 7, a. 21 y. 6 m. 16 d. G. R. 1.]
Zach[aria]h, Capt., bur. Mar. 23, 1776, a. 80 y. C. R. 1.
——, s. Henry, of Pelham, burnt, at Pelham [bef. Oct. 28,
1750.]. P. R. 4.
——, w. Capt. Jona[than], bur. Jan. 24, 1752, a. abt. 80 y.
C. R. 1. [d. Jan. 22. P. R. 4.]
——, ch. Jonath[a]n, bur. Sept. 29, 1783. C. R. 1.
——, d. Jona[than], bur. Sept. 6, 1786. C. R. 1.
——, ch. Jona[than], bur. Apr. 23, 1790. C. R. 1.

RICHMOND, Abby Ann, d. Capt. Sylvester, Aug. 25, 1824,
a. 9 y. 1 m. 9 d. G. R. 1. [Aug. 26. C. R. 1.]

RIDINGS (see also Reading), Maria Jenette, d. Peter and
Amelia, Mar. 12, 1848, a. 4 m. 21 d.

RIGHT (see also Wright), John, Oct. 14, 1730.

RIMMER, Ann Prudence [Remme. G. R. 1.], d. [Frederic and
Nancy. G. R. 1.], Aug. 28, 1829, a. 10 m. C. R. 1. [Aug.
30. G. R. 1.]

RIPLEY, Isabell, d. Lewis and Sophia, Jan. 24, 1846, a. 2 y. 8 m. G. R. 3.

RITCHARDSUN (see also Richardson), Josiah, Capt., July 22, 1695. [June 22. P. R. 31; a. 61 y. G. R. 1.]

ROBBINS (see also Robines, Robins), James, May 15, 1835, a. 56 y. G. R. 1.
John, bur. Sept. 6, 1775, a. 65 y. C. R. 1.
Jonas, Ens., Feb. 25, 1775. [a. 61 y. 7 m. 22 d. G. R. 1.]
Joseph, s. Ens. Jonas and Mary, Feb. 18, 1775. [a. 18 y. 9 m. 2 d. G. R. 1.]
Moses [s. Geo[rge]. P. R. 4.], under care of Sam[ue]ll Adams, bur. Dec. 31, 1751. C. R. 1. [d. Dec. 30. P. R. 4.]
Zaccheus W., Sept. 17, 1837, a. 30 y. G. R. 1.

ROBINES (see also Robbins), Mary, w. George, 24: 7 m: 1672.

ROBINS (see also Robbins), Allis, w. George, Nov. 25, 1686.
Betty, d. Jonathan and Elizabeth, Sept. 1, 1775, a. 1 y. 8 m. 12 d. G. R. 1.
Dorathy, w. Serg. John, Apr. 19, 1757. [Apr. 20. P. R. 4; a. 83 y. C. R. 1.]
Isaac, s. Jonathan and Elizabeth, Aug. 28, 1775, a. 3 y. 9 m. 28 d. G. R. 1.
John, ———, 1762. [Aug. 10. P. R. 4; a. 89 y. C. R. 1.]
Joseph, s. John, Mar. 27, 1707.
Sary, d. John and Dorothy, June 26, 1728.
Susannah, w. John, Aug. 28, 1775, in her 63d y. G. R. 1.
———, ch. Moses, dysentery, Oct. 20, 1817, a. 2 y. C. R. 1.

ROBINSON, Elizabeth Ann, ———, 1831, a. 10 m. C. R. 3.

ROBY, Benjamin, s. John and Hanah, June 3, 1733.
John, Mar. 22, 1723-4.

ROFE, [torn], June 4, 1678.

ROGERS (see also Roggers), Daniel, Rev., of Littleton, "58 y. minister of sd Town," Nov. 22, 1782, a. 76 y. C. R. 1.

ROGGERS (see also Rogers), Henry B., Col., of Boston, consumption, June 12, 1823, a. 42 y. C. R. 1.

ROPER, Andrew, s. Joel and Nancy Ellis, Aug. 29, 1837, a. 20 y. G. R. 3.
Sarah Jane, d. Joel and Nancy Ellis, Feb. 9, 1826, a. 6 y. G. R. 3.

ROUSE, John, s. Capt., of Boston [grands. Capt. Jona[than] Richardson's wife. P. R. 4.], "being upon a Visit At Mr. Bates'," bur. Jan. 8, 1751. C. R. 1. [d. Jan. 4. P. R. 4.]

RUGGLES, Sam[ue]ll, Rev., of Billerica, Mar. 1, 1748-9, a. 67 y. and in the 41st y. of his ministry. C. R. 1.

RUSCH, Allois, from Germany, glass blower, Feb. 20, 1825, a. 25 y. C. R. 1. [Feb. 19, a. 23 y. G. R. 1.]

RUSSELL, Martha Truell, w. Abbott, b. 1808, d. —, 1846. G. R. 1.
Nelson Abbott, s. Abbott and Martha Truell, b. 1842, d. —, 1846. G. R. 1.

SANBORN, Arthur L., s. Leonard C. and Sarah E., Mar. —, 1845, a. 5 d. [May 10, a. 5 m. G. R. 3.]
Sarah E. H., Mrs. [w. Leonard C. C. R. 3.], June 6, 1845. C. R. 3. [a. 34 y. G. R. 3.]

SANDERS, Joanna, wid., bur. Apr. 5, 1792. C. R. 1.

SANGER, Charles H., s. Charles H. and Hannah J., Oct. 13, 1832, a. 3 y. 6 m. G. R. 1.

SARGENT, James F., drowned in Concord River, June 19, 1824. C. R. 1.

SAWTELL, Obadiah, Capt., Apr. 18, 1819, a. 86 y. C. R. 1.

SAWYER, ——, inf. ch. ——, Nov. 21, 1828. C. R. 1.

SCALES, Stephen [A. M., graduate of Harvard College. G. R. 1; some while tutor at Harvard College and now lawyer, apoplectic seizure after measles. P. R. 4.], Nov. 5, 1772. [a. 31 y. C. R. 1.]

SCRIPTURE, Elizabeth, wid., bur. Apr. 17, 1781, a. 98 y. 4 m. C. R. 1.

SEARLE, Abigail, May 6, 1833, a. 27 y. G. R. 2.
Uriah A., s. Augustus H. and Rebecah, Dec. 29, 1833, a. 1 y. G. R. 2.

SEMPLE, John A., s. John and Caroline, Feb. 23, 1836, a. 3 y. 6 m. G. R. 1.

SHAW, Emily, w. Elisha, Sept. 30, 1843, a. 26 y. G. R. 3.
Martha E., b. Reading, w. Elisha, inflammation of the stomach, July 20, 1844, a. 24 y.

SHED (see also Shedd, Sheed), Ebenezer, Capt., Mar. 1, 1829, a. 75 y. 9 m. G. R. 1.
George, intemperance, Feb. —, 1828, a. 42 y. C. R. 1.
Lucy, w. Capt. Ebenezer, Feb. 2, 1849, a. 86 y. 3 m. G. R. 1.
Lydia, d. Zechariah and Hannah, Dec. 28, 1775, in her 24th y. G. R. 1.
Mary, w. [Lt. G. R. 1.] Eb[e]nezer, Aug. 3, 1785. [a. 28 y. 3 m. 27 d. G. R. 1.]
Mary [(Byam). P. R. 25.], w. John, Sept. 3, 1830, a. 48 y. C. R. 1.
Mary Elizabeth, d. Capt. John [and Mary. G. R. 1.], Aug. 2, 1818, a. 10 y. C. R. 1. [Aug. 3. G. R. 1.]
Noah, s. Zachariah and Hannah, Sept. 10, 1772, a. 24 y. 2 m. 10 d. G. R. 1.
Polly, d. Eben and Lucy, bur. May 9, 1794, a. 11 y. C. R. 1.
Sam[ue]l, s. Capt. John [and Mary. G. R. 1.], May 2, 1829, a. 19 y. C. R. 1.
Zachariah, Feb. 2, 1784. [a. 63 y. G. R. 1.]
——, ch. Zach[ariah], bur. Jan. 22, 1747. C. R. 1.
——, wid., burnt, Oct. [bet. 18 and 28], 1807, a. 75 y. C. R. 1.

SHEDD (see also Shed), Amos [h. Mary. P. R. 3.], Aug. 7, 1842, a. 39 y. G. R. 1.
Ebenezer, Feb. 21, 1815, a. 34 y. G. R. 1.
John, Mar. —, 1848, a. 74 y. P. R. 25.
Mary S., d. Amos and Mary S., Aug. 28, 1838, a. 3 m. G. R. 1. [a. 3 y. P. R. 3.]
——, inf. ch. Amos and Mary S. [after Oct. 8, 1842.] G. R. 1.

SHEED (see also Shed), Hannah, July 4, 1758.

SHEPARD, Mary [S. G. R. 1.], w. Alfred, consumption, June 7, 1845, a. 21 y.
——, s. John and Betsey, b. "Hinefield," Eng., dysentery, Sept. 4, 1849, a. 1 y. 1 m. 11 d.

SHEPLEY (see also Sheply), John, Sept. 10, 1678.

SHEPLY (see also Shepley), Ane, w. John, July 11, 1685. [July 13. CT. R.]

SHERBURN, Sally, w. Samuel, fever, Sept. 23, 1804, a. 28 y. C. R. 1.

SHIRTLIFF, ——, ch. ——, Jan. 20, 1820, a. 2 y. C. R. 1.

SHORES, Ansel S., s. Luther W. and Clarissa M., Mar. 25, 1844, a. 16 m. 8 d. G. R. 3.
Wesley H., s. Luther W. and Clarissa M., Oct. 27, 1846, a. 3 m. 21 d. G. R. 3.

SIMONDS (see also Simons), Eliz[abeth] L. T. [w. Abel. G. R. 2; Mary, Mrs., d. Dea. Farewell. C. R. 1.], Sept. 28, 1829. C. R. 2. [a. 21 y. G. R. 2; Sept. 29, a. 22 y. C. R. 1.]

SIMONS (see also Simonds), Josiah, dropsy and mortification, Nov. 26, 1809, a. 61 y. C. R. 1.

SMITH, Agnes, w. Alexander, Sept. 10, 1728.
Alexander, father of Heugh and Alexander, Oct. 14, 1728.
Anna, b. England, ship-fever, Aug. 24, 1847, a. 25 y.
Edward, late of Charlestown, May 6, 1836, a. 25 y. G. R. 1.
Elisha [Capt. G. R. 3.], b. Sanbornton, N. H., lung fever, Aug. 26, 1847, a. 55 y. [a. 52 y. G. R. 3.]
Jesse, s. Jesse and Francis [(Warren). P. R. 16.], Dec. 17, 1817. [a. 1 d. C. R. 1.]
Jesse, m., merchant, dysentery, Aug. 23, 1848, a. 67 y.
Louisa Bannister, w. J. Y., June 3, 1837, a. 21 y. G. R. 1.
Mary Woodbury, d. Jesse and Fanny [(Warren). P. R. 16.], June 27, 1835.
Rebecca, d. Jesse and Fanny [(Warren). P. R. 16.], May 29, 1826. [May 26, a. 3 1-2 y. C. R. 1.]

SNOW, Elizabath, d. John and Sary, Apr. 30, 1705.
Esther, wid., Aug. 3, 1776. [a. 73 y. C. R. 1.]
Jonathan [jr. C. R. 1.], s. Jonathan and Ester, July 15, 1757.
Jonathan, Apr. 18, 1762. [Apr. 19. P. R. 4.]
Joshua, Mar. 17, 1783. [a. 44 y. 8 m. 5 d. G. R. 1.]
Parker, s. Lt. Jonathan and Sarah, Jan. 28, 1796. [a. 4 y. C. R. 1; a. 3 y. 2 m. 21 d. G. R. 1.]
Samuel, s. Jonathan, Oct. 22, 1738.

SNOW, Sarah [d. Jona[than]. P. R. 4.], bur. May 12, 1758.
C. R. 1. [d. May 11. P. R. 4.]
Sarah, d. Joshua and Loes, "and twin with Thankfull," Jan.
20, 1776. [a. 12 y. 15 d. G. R. 1.]
William, s. Jonathan and Ester [fever, at Hollis. P. R. 4.],
Aug. 12, 1757.
——, inf. ch. Jona[than], soon after birth, Apr. 8, 1751.
P. R. 4.
——, ch. stillborn, Joshua, bur. May 13, 1768. C. R. 1.

SPALDEN (see also Spaulding), ——, d. Joseph, 1: 2 m:
1683.

SPALDIN (see also Spaulding), Hannah, d. Andrew and Hannah, Mar. 10, 1677.

SPALDING (see also Spaulding), Abigail, Mrs. [w. Joseph.
G. R. 1.], dropsy and consumption, Aug. 11, 1805, a. 45 y.
C. R. 1. [Aug. 10. G. R. 1.]
Abigail, consumption, Oct. 23, 1808, a. 19 y. C. R. 1.
Abigail, ossification of the heart, June 20, 1812, a. 88 y. C. R. 1.
Albert, consumption, Sept. 29, 1832, a. 29 y. C. R. 1.
Andrew, suddenly, Sept. 18, 1840, a. 79 y. C. R. 1.
Ann Augusta, d. Capt. Sherebiah, throat distemper, Nov. 19,
1821, a. 3 y. C. R. 1.
Asaph [F. G. R. 1.], fever, Aug. 15, 1827, a. 23 y. C. R. 1.
[Aug. 13. G. R. 1.]
Azariah, Sept. 13, 1821, a. 65 y. C. R. 1.
Betsey [Elizabeth. G. R. 1.], w. Jesse, 3 w. after childbirth,
bur. May 2, 1796. C. R. 1. [a. 29 y. G. R. 1.]
Betsy A[nn. C. R. 1.], d. Henry, 3d and Jemima, Apr. 2, 1809.
[Apr. 3, a. 3 m. C. R. 1.]
Clarissa, d. Simeon and Olive, very sudden, bur. July 19, 1801,
a. 8 [or] 9 y. C. R. 1. [July 14, a. 8 y. G. R. 1.]
Clarissa, d. Henry, 3d and Jemima, Dec. 30, 1814. [a. 13 y.
C. R. 1.]
Ebenezer, jr., Nov. 17, 1832, a. 26 y. G. R. 1.
Ebenezer, m., farmer, formerly cooper, dropsy, Apr. 14, 1845,
a. 75 y. 7 m.
Edward, Feb. 26, 1669. CT. R.
Edward, s. Simeon, 2d and Rhoda B., drowned, May 30, 1825,
a. 4 y. G. R. 6.
Elbridge Gerry, s. Lt. Sherebiah and Relief, Mar. 22, 1811.
Elijah, s. Dea. John and Lucy, July 29, 1800, a. 16 d. G. R. 2.
Elizabeth, wid. Jesse, slow fever, Sept. 19, 1812, a. 40 y. C. R.
1. [a. 41 y. G. R. 1.]

CHELMSFORD DEATHS 441

SPALDING, Elizabeth, d. Jesse, deceased [and Elizabeth. G. R. 1], hanged herself by a skein of yarn, in the house of Joseph Spalding, Apr. 10, 1815, a. 19 y. C. R. 1.
Ellen L., d. Jonathan and Mary Ann, croup, Oct. 9, 1846, a. 4 y. 4 m. 18 d.
Ephraim, typhus fever, Feb. 4, 1826, a. 60 y. C. R. 1.
Esther, cancer for 25 y., Dec. 10, 1808, a. 74 y. C. R. 1.
Eunice, b. Hingham, wid. [w. G. R. 1.] Ebenezer, found dead in bed, May 7, 1849, a. 80 y.
Francis [W. G. R. 2.], s. Benj[amin] and Mary [Polly F. G. R. 2.], brain fever, Feb. 6, 1849, a. 15 y. [Feb. 4, a. 14 y. G. R. 2.]
Hannah, d. Dea. John and Lucy, Oct. 28, 1801, a. 1 y. 3 m. 15 d. G. R. 2.
Hazadiah, jaundice, Mar. 11, 1806, a. 75 y. C. R. 1.
Henry, 3d, typhus fever, Dec. 27, 1825, a. 49 y. C. R. 1.
Henry [jr. dup.], s. H., deceased, Mar. 30, 1829, a. 24 y. C. R. 1.
Henry, June 30, 1832, a. 80 y. C. R. 1. [June 29, a. 79 y. G. R. 2.]
Ira, Sept. 19, 1829, a. 56 y. C. R. 1. [Sept. 18. G. R. 2.]
Job, dropsy, Oct. 1, 1806, a. 70 y. C. R. 1.
Joel, old age, July 25, 1823, a. 81 y. C. R. 1. [July 26. G. R. 6.]
John, old age, Oct. 10, 1805, a. 80 y. C. R. 1. [Oct. 12. G. R. 2.]
John, shoemaker, s. Robert, deceased, scarlet fever, July 12, 1816, a. 21 y. C. R. 1.
John, s. [Capt. C. R. 1.] Jonathan and Sarah, Feb. 9, 1825, a. 16 m. 20 d. G. R. 6.
John, jr. [2d. G. R. 1.], fever, Oct. 25, 1830, a. 44 y. C. R. 1. [Oct. 27. G. R. 1.]
John, Nov. 15, 1834, a. 33 y. C. R. 3.
Jona[than], dropsy, Dec. 15, 1809, a. 75 y. C. R. 1. [Dec. 16. G. R. 1.]
Joseph, "fired the first gun on Bunker Hill & Killed Pitcarne." Aug. 6, 1820, a. 67 y. C. R. 1. [July 31, a. 64 y. G. R. 1.]
Lavina, consumption, Oct. 14, 1808, a. 40 y. C. R. 1.
Lidia, d. Henry, jr. and Lidia, May 5, 1793.
Loisa, d. Capt. Sherebiah, throat distemper, Dec. 6, 1821, a. 16 y. C. R. 1.
Louisa A., d. Sherebiah, 2d and Lurena, scarlatina, Feb. 16, 1847, a. 2 y. 6 m. 11 d.
Lucinda, d. Ephraim P., dysentery, Oct. 1, 1840, a. 18 m. C. R. 1.
Lucy, w. Dea. John, Mar. 20, 1802, a. 40 y. G. R. 2.
Lucy, w. Azariah, d. Oliver Barron, gall-stones, July 19, 1820, a. 56 y. C. R. 1.

SPALDING, Lydia, ——, 1806, a. 92 y. C. R. 1.
Lydia, d. Ephraim, Apr. 2, 1828, a. 17 y. C. R. 1.
Lydia, Nov. 1, 1829, a. 84 y. C. R. 1.
Marcus M., s. Sherebiah, jr. and Lurena, scarlatina, Mar. 20, 1847, a. 5 y.
Martha, d. Alpheus and Martha, consumption, Feb. 10, 1848, a. 30 y.
Mary, wid. Jona[than], Jan. 3, 1817, a. 78 y. C. R. 1.
Mary, w. Henry, Dec. 20, 1820, a. 74 y. C. R. 1. [a. 64 y. G. R. 2.]
Mary, wid. Benj[amin], Sept. 23, 1825, a. 81 y. C. R. 1.
Mary, b. Carlisle, wid. Dea. John, old age, July 7, 1846, a. 80 y.
Mary Ann, d. Dea. John [and Mary. G. R. 2.], throat distemper, Oct. —, 1821, a. 10 y. C. R. 1. [Nov. 10. G. R. 2.]
Micah, instantly, Apr. 22, 1830, a. 78 y. C. R. 1.
Nath[anie]l [s. Job and Sarah. G. R. 1.], lung fever, Feb. 12, 1829, a. 38 y. C. R. 1.
Noah, Dea., widr., farmer, disease of the heart, May 9, 1849, a. 78 y.
Olive, w. Simion, fever, Sept. 3, 1813, a. 52 y. C. R. 1.
Phebe Tyler, b. Mar. 23, 1750, d. Feb. 12, 1780. G. R. 6.
Phillip P., unm., farmer, s. Dea. Noah and Nancy, consumption, Feb. 4, 1849, a. 44 y.
Rachel [wid. Lt. John. G. R. 1.], bur. Apr. 13, 1797, a. 72 y. C. R. 1.
Rebecca, 2d w. Andrew, Nov. 27, 1844. P. R. 23.
Rhoda, d. Henry, 3d and Jemima, Apr. 4, 1813. [Apr. 3, a. 4 y. C. R. 1.]
Ruth, w. Andrew, Sept. 4, 1828, a. 72 y. C. R. 1.
Sarah, fever, very sudden, Jan. 3, 1816, a. 38 y. C. R. 1.
Sarah, w. Job, Oct. 7, 1830, a. 69 y. C. R. 1. [Oct. 5. G. R. 1.]
Simeon, pleurisy fever, May 11, 1841, a. 82 y. C. R. 1.
Steven, Feb. 6, 1826, a. 53 y. C. R. 1. [Feb. 5. G. R. 4.]
William, fever, at sea, ——, 1804, a. 20 y. C. R. 1.
Zebulon [fever. C. R. 1.], Feb. 26, 1816. [a. 72 y. C. R. 1.]
——, ch. stillborn, Job, bur. [bet. Feb. 24 and Apr. 7], 1797. C. R. 1.
——, w. Job, bur. Mar. 4, 1802, a. 68 y. C. R. 1.
——, ch. Sherebiah, Nov. 5, 1812, a. 7 m. C. R. 1.
——, w. Benj[amin], Sept. 19, 1829, a. 32 y. C. R. 1.

SPARKES (see also Sparks), Martha, Feb. 28, 1697.

SPARKS (see also Sparkes), Henri, July 16, 1694.
——, s. Henry, 6: 5 m: 1683.

SPAULDING (see also Spalden, Spaldin, Spalding, Spauldyng, Spolding), Abigail, d. [Dea. P. R. 4.] And[re]w, jr. [of Westford; grandd. Dea. P. R. 4.], d. "at Old Dea. Spaulding he having taken her to live with him," bur. Nov. 20, 1749. C. R. 1.
Abigail, wid. Dea. Andrew, May 12, 1768. [a. 85 y. C. R. 1.]
Abraham A., Sept. 8, 1836, a. 43 y. G. R. 1.
Amas, s. Thomas and Mary, Oct. 1, 1753.
Andrew, Dea., May 5, 1713. [a. 59 y. 5 m. G. R. 1.]
Andrew, Dea., Nov. 7, 1753. [a. 75 y. C. R. 1; in his 75th y. G. R. 1.]
Asa, s. Henry and Mary, Feb. 14, 1796. [a. 1 y. 8 m. G. R. 2.]
Benjamin, s. Dea. Andro [and Abigail. G. R. 1.], Dec. 13, 1737, in his 18th y.
Benjamin, s. Jonathan and Mary, Oct. —, 1756. [bur. Oct. 21. C. R. 1.]
Benjamin [jr. P. R. 4.], s. Benjamin [jr. C. R. 1.] and Mary, July 5, 1784.
Benjamin [lingering decline. C. R. 1.], Aug. 5, 1806. [a. 65 y. C. R. 1.]
Benony, of Billerica, Dec. 17, 1752.
Bridget, d. Timothy and Rebecka, Dec. 5, 1720.
David [jr. C. R. 1.], s. David and Phebe [smallpox, in ye army near Ticonderoga. C. R. 1.], Aug. 28, 1776.
David, Nov. 9, 1793. [1794. P. R. 23; a. 77 y. C. R. 1.]
David, s. Andrew and Ruth, Feb. 24, 1798. [Feb. 23, a. 2 y. 1 m. 9 d. G. R. 1; a. 2 1-2 y. C. R. 1.]
Edward, Lt., Jan. 10, 1707-8. [a. 73 y. G. R. 1.]
Edward, bur. Nov. 26, 1761, a. 87 y. C. R. 1. [d. Nov. 25. P. R. 4.]
Elbridge A., s. Elbridge P. and Adeline P., Sept. 2, 1842, a. 11 m. G. R. 1.
Elijah, s. Henry and Mary, Oct. 14, 1798. [a. 15 y. G. R. 2.]
Eliza[beth], wid. [mother of Simeon. P. R. 4.], bur. Jan. 3, 1759, a. 79 y. C. R. 1. [d. Jan. 2. P. R. 4.]
Elizibeth, d. Thomas and Mary, Sept. 16, 1736.
Ephraim, s. [inf. C. R. 1.] Jonathan [3d. C. R. 1.] and Mary, Dec. 8, 1762.
Ephraim, Dea., Dec. 26, 1791. [Dec. 20. G. R. 1; a. 83 y. C. R. 1.]
Ester, d. Lt. Edward and Margret, Nov. 30, 1700.
Esther, d. Thomas and Mary, Sept. 19, 1753.
Esther, d. Leonard, deceased, bur. Dec. 13, 1772. C. R. 1. [d. Dec. 11, a. abt. 18 y. P. R. 4.]
Esther [(Perham). P. R. 4.], w. [wid. C. R. 1.] Josiah, Jan. 21, 1790. [a. 76 y. G. R. 1.]

SPAULDING, Gideon, bur. Feb. 7, 1783, a. 58 y. C. R. 1.
Hanah, w. John, Aug. 14, 1689.
Hannah, wid. Dea. Andrew, Jan. 21, 1729-30. [in her 77th y. G. R. 1.]
Hannah, d. Thomas and Mary, May 5, 1754.
Hannah, wid., July 17, 1814, a. 83 y. G. R. 2.
Henery, s. [only s. G. R. 1.] Henry and Mary, Jan. 22, 1737-8. [Jan. 23, in his 8th y. G. R. 1.]
Henry, Apr. 5, 1718, a. 38 y. 5 m. 3 d. G. R. 1.
Henry, Apr. 4, 1720.
Henry, s. [Dea. P. R. 4.] Andrew, jr. [of Westford. P. R. 4.], "at Old Dea. Spaulding's [at his grandfathers Dea. Spaulding. P. R. 4.], he having taken him to live with him," bur. Sept. 16, 1749. C. R. 1. [d. Sept. 19. P. R. 4.]
Henry, Oct. 2, 1754, in his 52d y. G. R. 1.
Henry [jr. C. R. 1.], s. [Cornet. G. R. 1.] Henry and Lucy, Feb. 3, 1760. [a. 23 y. 3 m. 16 d. G. R. 1.]
Henry, s. Zebulun, jr. and Lydia, Apr. 26, 1776. [a. 3 y. 6 m. 16 d. G. R. 1.]
Henry, Cornet, Apr. 29, 1792. [a. 88 y. C. R. 1.]
Henry, Apr. 25, 1827, a. 63 y. G. R. 2.
Isaac W., b. Billerica, s. Jacob and Mary A., of Billerica, Feb. 1, 1839, a. 17 m. P. R. 3.
Isaiah, bur. Dec. 12, 1786. C. R. 1. [d. Dec. 9. P. R. 4.]
Isaiah, brother of Lydia Bates, Nov. 27, 1787, a. 77 y. wanting 2 d. G. R. 1.
Jacob, Mar. 4, 1776. [a. 70 y. C. R. 1.]
Jane, bur. Mar. 31, 1743. C. R. 1.
Jesse, s. Jacob and Susanna, Oct. 8, 1749.
Jesse [low spirits and debility. C. R. 1.], May —, 1808. [May 16, a. 45 y. C. R. 1; May 15. G. R. 1.]
Joana, d. Ephraim and Lidia, Oct. 19, 1737.
Joanna, d. Simeon and Sarah, Aug. 24, 1747, a. 3 y. 20 d.
Joanna [F., w. Ira. G. R. 2.], Apr. 5, 1840. C. R. 2. [a. 67 y. G. R. 2.]
Job, a Revolutionary pensioner, b. Mar. —, 1762, d. Nov. 15, 1835. G. R. 1.
John, sr., Oct. 3, 1721.
John, Mar. 7, 1760. [a. 78 y. C. R. 1.]
John, Lt., bur. May 6, 1791, a. 87 y. C. R. 1. [d. May 4, in his 87th y. G. R. 1.]
John, Dea., Sept. 13, 1835, a. 73 y. G. R. 2.
Jonas, s. Job and Lidia, Sept. 5, 1753. [Sept. 6. P. R. 4.]
Jonas, s. Lt. John and Phebe [in ye war. P. R. 4.], Oct. 26, 1758.
Jonas, Apr. 30, 1833, a. 74 y. G. R. 1.

CHELMSFORD DEATHS 445

SPAULDING, Joseph, Mar. 12, 1728. [a. 54 y. G. R. 1.]
Joseph, s. Lt. John and Phebe, Apr. 5, 1756.
Joseph Osgood, s. [Capt. C. R. 1.] Alpheus and Patty, Dec. 26, 1830. [Dec. 28, a. 3 y. C. R. 1.]
Lidia, w. Edward, May 27, 1736.
Lidia, w. Dea. Ephraim [dropsy. C. R. 1.], Aug. 29, 1796. [a. 80 y. C. R. 1; a. 84 y. G. R. 1.]
Lucia, w. Henry, June 11, 1742, a. 33 y. 10 m. 2 d. G. R. 1.
Lucy, w. Peter, June 30, 1786.
Luse, d. Timothy and Rebeckah, Sept. 20, 1717.
Lydia, w. [wid. C. R. 1; "old." P. R. 4.], John, Apr. 16, 1760. [a. 66 y. C. R. 1.]
Lydia, d. Ephraim and Lydia, Sept. 9, 1808, a. 4 d. [Sept. 10. C. R. 1.]
Margret, May 25, 1748.
Mary, d. Edward and Mary, Aug. 18, 1695.
Mary, d. Henery and Mary, Aug. 5, 1733. [in her 10th y. G. R. 1.]
Mary, w. Henry [jr. C. R. 1.], Oct. 2, 1747. [in her 47th y. G. R. 1.]
Mary, d. Henry [jr. C. R. 1.] and Mary [throat distemper, P. R. 4.], Aug. 18, 1749.
Mary, w. Henry, Apr. 29, 1807, a. 91 y. G. R. 1. [a. 92 y. C. R. 1.]
Nabby, w. Jesse, Aug. 4, 1791, in her 23d y. G. R. 1.
Olive, d. Jonathan and Sary, Oct. —, 1756. [bur. Oct. 26. C. R. 1.]
Olive, d. Lt. John and Phebe, Apr. 2, 1759.
Olive, d. Zebulon, jr. and Lidia, Aug. 30, 1778. [Aug. 31, a. 2 y. 7 m. 25 d. G. R. 1.]
Olive, old age, at the almshouse, Mar. 28, 1844, a. 85 y. C. R. 1.
Oliver, s. Lt. Jonathan and Sarah, Mar. 29, 1760.
Patty, jr. [w. Benja[min]. G. R. 2.], Sept. 14, 1829. C. R. 2. [a. 29 y. G. R. 2.]
Peter, Mar. 16, 1801. [a. 67 y. C. R. 1.]
Phebe, w. Lt. John, Nov. 11, 1752. [Nov. 12. P. R. 4; a. 45 y. 10 m. 20 d. G. R. 1.]
Phebe, w. [wid. C. R. 1.] David [L. C. R. 1.], Dec. 20, 1795. [a. 76 y. C. R. 1; a. 77 y. G. R. 1.]
Philip, s. David and Phebe, Oct. 2, 1749.
Rebecah, d. Timothy, Feb. 8, 1727-8.
Rebeckah, w. Timothy, Dec. 9, 1726.
Robert, s. David and Phebe, Sept. 28, 1749.
Robert, s. David and Phebe [killed by a tree. G. R. 1.], Jan. 26, 1771. [in his 21st y. G. R. 1.]

SPAULDING, Robert, Lt., returning from ye army at New York, at Milford, Conn., ———, 1776. C. R. 1.
Ruben, July 11, 1717.
Ruth, d. Lt. [John and Pheby. G. R. 1.], bur. Apr. 8, 1754. C. R. 1. [d. Apr. 6, P. R. 4; a. 21 y. 7 m. G. R. 1.]
Sarah, w. Simeon, Nov. 14, 1746. [a. 29 y. 1 m. 7 d. G. R. 1.]
Sarah, d. Henry [jr. C. R. 1.] and Mary [throat distemper. P. R. 4.], Sept. 4, 1749.
Sarah, w. Jonathan, Nov. 14, 1752.
Sarah, d. David and Phebe, Mar. 29, 1760.
Sarah, b. Billerica, d. Jacob and Mary A., of Billerica, Nov. 5, 1838, a. 3 y. 3 m. P. R. 3.
Sewel, s. Jesse and Elisabeth [fits. C. R. 1.], June 29, 1804. [a. 3 m. C. R. 1; a. 4 m. G. R. 1.]
Sibb[i]l, d. Jonathan and Mary, Sept. 26, 1783.
Sibel, d. Thomas and Mary, May 6, 1754.
Silas [s. Jonathan. P. R. 4.], bur. Apr. 16, 1780. C. R. 1. [d. Apr. 15. P. R. 4.]
Simeon [Col. G. R. 1.], bur. Apr. 11, 1785, a. 71 y. C. R. 1. [Apr. 7. G. R. 1.]
Stephen, bur. May 6, 1785. C. R. 1. [d. May 4. P. R. 4.]
Susanna, w. [wid. C. R. 1.] Jacob, Aug. 16, 1787. [a. 82 y. C. R. 1.]
Sybill, d. Jacob and Susanna, Oct. 19, 1744.
Sybill, d. [Dea. C. R. 1.] Ephraim and Lydia, Sept. 9, 1747. [in her 8th y. G. R. 1.]
Thankful [d. Henry and Mary. G. R. 1.], bur. Sept. 4, 1778. C. R. 1. [a. 16 y. 9 d. G. R. 1.]
Tryphena, d. Isaiah and Martha (Byam), Feb. 16, 1821. P. R. 19.
Will[ia]m, bur. Feb. 19, 1743. C. R. 1.
———, ch. Henry, bur. Dec. 6, 1750. C. R. 1.
———, ch. Henry, bur. July 6, 1752. C. R. 1.
———, inf. ch. Lt. John [and Phebe. G. R. 1.], bur. Nov. 13, 1752. C. R. 1. [d. Nov. 12. P. R. 4.]
———, d. Jonathan and Mary, ———, 1755. [bur. Mar. 21. C. R. 1.]
———, inf. ch. Henry, bur. July 19, 1757. C. R. 1.
———, inf. ch. Henry, bur. Sept. 12, 1758. C. R. 1.
———, s. Lt. Jona[than], in the Army, at Crown Point [bef. Aug. 28], 1760. P. R. 4.
———, inf. ch. Job, jr., bur. Feb. 23, 1764. C. R. 1.
———, inf. ch. twin, John, jr., bur. Apr. 8, 1771. C. R. 1.
———, inf. ch. twin, John, jr., bur. Apr. 29, 1771. C. R. 1.
———, ch. Philip, bur. at Westford, Oct. —, 1773. C. R. 1.
———, ch. Joel, bur. Aug. 26, 1775. C. R. 1.

CHELMSFORD DEATHS 447

SPAULDING, ——, ch. Joel, bur. Sept. 21, 1778. C. R. 1.
——, w. Joel [s. Col. P. R. 4.], bur. Feb. 3, 1780. C. R. 1.
——, w. Jonathan "bro't from Tophet," bur. Dec. 11, 1780. C. R. 1.
——, d. Rob[er]t, deceased, bur. Jan. 19, 1784. C. R. 1.
——, w. Jona[than], formerly Mrs. Emery, bur. Sept. 2, 1785. C. R. 1. [d. Aug. 31. P. R. 4.]
——, ch. Micah, bur. Sept. 15, 1790. C. R. 1.
——, ch. stillborn, Job, bur. Sept. 20, 1794. C. R. 1.

SPAULDYNG (see also Spaulding), Josiah, s. Edward and Lidya, Feb. 2, 1701-2.

SPOLDING (see also Spaulding), Mary, d. Andrew and Hannah, July 18, 1698.

STACEY, ——, ch. William, bur. Jan. 18, 1766. C. R. 1.

START, ——, Mrs., Aug. —, 1821, a. 42 y. C. R. 1.

STEARNS, Josiah [after Nov. 6], 1822, a. 67 y. C. R. 1.

STEAVENS (see also Stevens), Solomon, s. Samuel [jr. C. R. 1.] and Tabatha, Jan. 7, 1765.

STEDMAN, Jonathan [of Cambridge, suddenly. P. R. 4.], bur. Apr. 21, 1761. C. R. 1. [d. Apr. 17. P. R. 4.]

STEPHENS (see also Stevens), Hannah, w. Benjamin, Dec. 24, 1837, a. 61 y. G. R. 1.
——, ch. Sampson, scald, Feb. 3, 1805. C. R. 1.

STETSON, Isaac O[ldham. G. R. 3.], s. Zenas [and Martha. G. R. 3.], Feb. 2, 1849, a. 1 y. 2 m. [Jan. 29. G. R. 3.]
Zenas, Dec. 24, 1847, a. 39 y.

STEVENS (see also Steavens, Stephens), Asa, Oct. 16, 1843, a. 36 y. 2 m. G. R. 2.
Deborah, wid., bur. May 6, 1779, a. 75 y. C. R. 1.
Easter, dropsy, Feb. 12, 1808, a. 65 y. C. R. 1.
Edward, of Boston, consumption, Mar. 12, 1816, a. 52 y. C. R. 1. [Mar. 13, a. 42 y. G. R. 1.]
Eleazer, s. Henry and Deborah, Feb. 25, 1756. [Feb. 26. P. R. 4.]

STEVENS, Elisabeth, d. John and Elisabeth, Oct. 18, 1674.
Elisabeth, d. John, 9 : 2 m: 1678.
Elisabeth, d. Simeon, consumption, Dec. 5, 1841. [a. 22 y. in pencil.] C. R. 1.
Elizabeth, wid., Jan. 19, 1717-18.
Elizabeth, wid. Simeon, May 24, 1823, a. 81 y. C. R. 1.
Ephraim, s. Henry and Deborah, Sept. 27, 1755.
Ephraim, Oct. 13, 1714.
Hannah, wid., Nov. 11, 1755.
Henry, Serg., Oct. 22, 1764. [Oct. 23. P. R. 4; a. 64 y. C. R. 1.]
Joanna, w. Simeon [childbed. P. R. 4.], Nov. 9, 1762. [a. 23 y. 10 m. 12 d. G. R. 1.]
John, Ens., Apr. 6, 1691. CT. R.
John, Aug. 24, 1737.
John [suddenly, "distracted." P. R. 4.], bur. Mar. 2, 1764, a. 58 y. C. R. 1. [d. Feb. 29, P. R. 4.]
Lucy, d. Jonathan and Thankful, Dec. 18, 1802, a. 21 y. G. R. 1.
Phebe, wid. Sampson, old age, Apr. 18, 1849, a. 79 y.
Rebecca, d. Simeon, bur. Sept. 30, 1778. C. R. 1. [d. Sept. 29, a. 16 y. P. R. 4.]
Rebecca, tailoress, d. Simeon, inflammation of the lungs, Nov. 22, 1848, a. 68 y. [1846. G. R. 1.]
Richard, Mar. 3, 1753. [Mar. 4. P. R. 4; a. 79 y. C. R. 1.]
Ruth, w. Ens. Samuel, Oct. 15, 1787. [a. 73 y. C. R. 1; a. 72 y. 3 m. 26 d. G. R. 1.]
Samson, suddenly, Apr. 19, 1817, a. 45 y. C. R. 1. [Apr. 11, a. 48 y. G. R. 2.]
Samuel, Ens., Dec. 21, 1792. [a. 84 y. 8 m. 10 d. G. R. 1.]
Samuel, Capt., of Dunstable, formerly of Chelmsford, Dec. 10, 1805, a. 72 y.
Sarah, wid., bur. Dec. 16, 1757, a. 88 y. C. R. 1. [d. Dec. 14. P. R. 4.]
Sarah [pauper. C. R. 1.], Nov. 29, 1797. [a. 64 y. C. R. 1.]
Simeon, s. Simeon and Elisabeth, Oct. 11, 1777, a. 12 y. 3 m. 26 d.
Simeon, old age, July 22, 1815, a. 80 y. C. R. 1.
Sophia, d. Capt. Samuel and Betty [dropsy in the head. C. R. 1.], May 24, 1808. [a. 12 y. C. R. 1.]
Tabitha, of Dunstable, wid. Capt. Samuel, Mar. 16, 1807, a. 67 y.
Thankful, d. Jonathan and Thankful, intercellular dropsy, Feb. 8, 1841, a. 62 y. C. R. 1.
——, eldest, s. Henry, at Albany [bef. Aug. 28], 1758. P. R. 4.
——, s. Samson, fever [bet. July 12 and Sept. 3], 1816, a. 14 y. C. R. 1.

CHELMSFORD DEATHS 449

STICKELMIRE, Joseph [John J., native of Germany, foreman of Chelmsford Glass Manufactory. G. R. 1.], dropsy by intemperance, Mar. 31, 1814, a. 48 y. C. R. 1.

STODDARD, Elizabeth, w. Sampson, July 26, 1743. [a. 27 y. G. R. 1.]
Elizabeth, d. Col. Sampson and Elizabeth, Oct. 10, 1749. [a. 7 y. 8 m. G. R. 1.]
John, s. Sampson and Elizabeth, Sept. 20, 1739.
John Vriling, s. Maj. Sampson and Margreet, Nov. 10, 1745. [a. 2 m. 13 d. G. R. 1.]
Margaret, Mad[a]m [at Lancaster. P. R. 4.], bur. Mar. 27, 1789, a. 79 y. C. R. 1. [d. Mar. 25. P. R. 4.]
Margret, wid. Rev. Sampson, Sept. 23, 1748.
Mary, sister of Mrs. Bridge, at Westford, Mar. 29, 1759, a. 36 y. P. R. 4.
Sampson, Rev. [3d pastor, ordained 1706. C. R. 1.], Aug. 23, 1740.
Sampson, bur. Apr. 28, 1777, a. 68 y. C. R. 1.
Sampson, bur. Mar. 26, 1779, a. 38 y. C. R. 1.
Vryling, bur. May 8, 1779, a. 32 y. C. R. 1.
William, Jan. 22, 1741-2.
Will[ia]m, s. [Col. G. R. 1.] Sampson [and Margaret. G. R. 1.], Apr. 4, 1750. C. R. 1. [d. Apr. 1. P. R. 4; a. 11 m. 21 d. G. R. 1.]
———, ch. Sampson, bur. July 20, 1743. C. R. 1.
———, ch. stillborn, Sampson, bur. Dec. 20, 1750. C. R. 1.

STOKES, Mary, wid., bur. Sept. 5, 1802. C. R. 1.

STONE, Benjamin, Capt., lost at sea on board the Schooner Roseway, bound to St. Martins from Newburyport, Dec. —, 1825, a. 28 y. G. R. 6.
Eliab, Rev., of Reading, Aug. 31, 1822, in his 85th y. and 61st of his ministry. C. R. 1.
———, only s. Benjamin and Tamezon, Aug. 17, 1828, a. 3 y. 7 d. G. R. 6.

STRATTON, Naomi, w. Richard, Dec. 8, 1687. CT. R.
Richard, Apr. 8, 1724, a. abt. 60 y. G. R. 1.

SULIVAN, Thomas, Irishman, killed by explosion at powder factory, Dec. 11, 1821. C. R. 1.

SUMNER, Joseph, D. D., of Shrewsbury, Dec. 8, 1824, a. 87 y. and 65th y. of his ministry. C. R. 1.

SWALLOW (see also Swalow), Abigail, wid. [at house of wid. Burge. P. R. 4.], Mar. 24, 1771. [a. 79 y. C. R. 1.]
Ambrose, Apr. 29, 1720.
Anna, w. John, May 10, 1735.
Ephraim, s. Jonathan and Hannah, Sept. 30, 1749.
Hannah, w. Jonathan, Mar. 16, 1770. [Mar. 17. P. R. 4; a. 64 y. C. R. 1.]
John [apoplectic fit. P. R. 4.], May 27, 1756. [a. 85 y. C. R. 1.]
Jonathan, s. Jonathan and Hannah, Feb. 4, 1736-7.
Jonathan, s. Jonathan and Hannah, Sept. 27, 1741.
Jonathan, bur. Apr. 23, 1777, a. 71 y. C. R. 1.
Mary, d. Ambros and Sarrah, May 25, 1716.
Sarah, w. [wid. dup.] Ambrouss, Nov. 22, 1756. [Nov. 21. dup.]

SWALOW (see also Swallow), Ambras, Oct. 25, 1684. [Oct. 20. P. R. 31.]

SWEETSER, John A., s. Elias and Mary, Apr. 28, 1826, a. 1 y. 8 m. G. R. 2.
Juliet C., d. Nathaniel and Hannah, Jan. 3, 1847, a. 9 y. 6 m. G. R. 1.
Samuel A. [Alvin. G. R. 1.], s. Charles and Mary, choked with a brass ferule, Nov. 6, 1848, a. 8 m.

SWETT, Elizabeth L., w. Edmund [of Middlesex Village. C. R. 3.], Oct. 25, 1840, a. 45 y. G. R. 3. [a. 55 y. C. R. 3.]
Harriet Newell Howard, d. Charles and Anna (Babcock), Aug. 25, 1842. P. R. 30.
Jane, Miss, Jan. —, 1836, a. 25 y. C. R. 3.
W[illia]m H[enry. G. R. 3.], s. William and Belinda, lung fever, Mar. 7, 1847, a. 4 y.

SWIFT, John, Rev., of Acton, Nov. 7, 1775. C. R. 1.

SYFFERMANN, Catharine M., w. Charles F., July 22, 1846, a. 31 y. 5 m. G. R. 3.

SYMMES, ——, d. William Blaisdel, bur. Jan. 30, 1792. P. R. 4.

TALBUT, Mary, w. Peter, Aug. 18, 1687. CT. R.

TARBEL, Sally, Mrs., suicide, Oct. 12, 1828, a. 56 y. C. R. 1.

TAYLOR, George, spotted fever, Feb. 17, 1812, a. 2 y. R. 1.

TEMPLETON, Martha, unm., fever, Aug. 1, 1829, a. 54 y. c. R. 1.

THOMPSON (see also Thomson), Mary E. [d. Maj. Luke and Betsey. G. R. 1.], croup, Oct. 4, 1821, a. 2 y. c. R. 1.
Simon, at Woburn, abt. 3-4 y. after 13: 9 m: 1655. P. R. 1.

THOMSON (see also Thompson), ——, Mr., bur. Oct. 15, 1841. c. R. 3.

THORNDIKE, Abigail Chamberlin, wid. Hezekiah, Aug. 30, 1843, a. 82 y. G. R. 1.
Hezekiah, May 3, 1842, a. 87 y. G. R. 1.
Nancy [d. Hezekiah and Abigail. G. R. 1.], dropsy in the head, May 28, 1828, a. 40 y. c. R. 1.

TOOTHAKER, Eunice, Dec. "about the middle," 1838. c. R. 2.

TORREY, John T., Apr. —, 1834, a. 28 y. c. R. 3.

TRAHANT, ——, ch. Charles, a French neutral, bur. June 26, 1759. c. R. 1.

TROWBRIDGE, Caleb, Rev., of Groton, Sept. 9, 1760, a. 68 y. and in the 46th y. of his ministry. c. R. 1.

TRULL, David, suddenly, bur. June 24, 1796. c. R. 1.
Margaret, d. Levi and Nancy, Nov. 2, 1847, a. 1 y. 6 m.

TUCK, Daniel, s. Dan[ie]l, Sept. 7, 1825, a. 5 m. c. R. 1.
Daniel, consumption, July 18, 1828, a. 46 y. c. R. 1.

TUCKER, John, s. [Dr. P. R. 4.] John [fever. P. R. 4.], bur. Sept. 7, 1757. c. R. 1. [d. Sept. 5. P. R. 4.]
John, "Commonly Called Doctr", bur. Feb. 3, 1761. c. R. 1. [d. Feb. 1. P. R. 4.]
Martha, d. [Dr. P. R. 4.] John [fever. P. R. 4.], bur. Sept. 9, 1757. c. R. 1. [d. Sept. 7. P. R. 4.]
——, w. John, bur. Feb. 13, 1746. c. R. 1.
——, s. John, bur. Apr. 5, 1754. c. R. 1.
——, w. John, bur. Apr. 11, 1759. c. R. 1.

TUTTLE, Nathaniel, broken leg, mortified, bur. Dec. 29, 1795, a. 66 y. c. R. 1.
Ruth, unm., a pauper, old age, Jan. 10, 1849, a. 87 y.

TUTTLE, ——, wid. [lately to town. P. R. 4.], bur. Nov. 29, 1779, a. 83 y. C. R. 1.

TWISS (see also Twist), Hannah, w. John, bur. Dec. 5, 1795, a. 63 y. C. R. 1.
John [very suddenly. C. R. 1.], May 11, 1796. [a. 74 y. C. R. 1.]
Joseph, s. John and Sarah, Aug. 20, 1775.
Mehitabel, d. John and Sarah, Oct. 12, 1777.
Phebe, w. Benja[min], Sept. 6, 1793.
Sarah, w. John, Dec. 3, 1794.

TWIST (see also Twiss), James, intemperance, Oct. 3, 1826, a. 53 y. C. R. 1.

TYLER, Jacob, dropsy, bur. Oct. 18, 1795. C. R. 1.
Jeremiah, after a short illness, bur. Aug. 23, 1796. C. R. 1.
Jonathan, s. Joseph, killed by the saw mill wheel, Mar. 18, 1772. P. R. 4.
Joseph, bur. Jan. 7, 1775. C. R. 1.
Mary, May —, 1846. C. R. 3.
Nathan, Nov. 1, 1829, a. 72 y. C. R. 1.
Sarah, Jan. 12, 1822, a. 60 y. C. R. 1.
——, d. Joseph, bur. Aug. 30, 1764. C. R. 1.
——, ch. Joseph, bur. Nov. 6, 1764. C. R. 1.
——, wid., bur. Nov. 26, 1783. C. R. 1. [a. 56 y. P. R. 4.]
——, w. Col., at Billerica, Dec. 19, 1785. P. R. 4.

TYNG, Eleazer, Col., May 21, 1782, a. 93 y. P. R. 4.
John Alford, s. Col., at Dunstable, June 24, 1771, a. 42 y. P. R. 4.
Lucy, w. Capt. William, Apr. 25, 1708. [a. 28 y. 4 m. G. R. 1.]
William, Maj., Aug 16, 1710.

UNDERWOOD (see also Undorwood), Aquilla, s. Will[ia]m [drowned. P. R. 1.], June 17, 1657. CT. R. [17: 5 m. P. R. 1.]
Aquilla, Feb. 4, 1723-4.
Asa, Oct. 20, 1826, a. 30 y. C. R. 1.
Asa W., Mar. 12, 1829, a. 2 1-2 y. C. R. 3.
Eliza Ann, Mrs., —, 1837. C. R. 3.
Sarah, w. William, Nov. 5, 1684.
——, ch. Phineas, bur. Dec. 17, 1777. C. R. 1.

UNDORWOOD (see also Underwood), William, Aug. 12, 1697.

VARNUM, Abiah, lockjaw spasms, May 20, 1810, a. 30 y. c. r. 1.
Mary, wid. Col. Joseph [at house of Oliv[e]r Pierce her son-in-law. p. r. 4.], May 18, 1751.
Susannah, bur. Oct. 28, 1800. c. r. 1.
——, Dr., consumption, Mar. 16, 1805, a. 38 y. c. r. 1.
——, d. Bradley [after Nov. 6], 1822, a. 16 y. c. r. 1.
——, Miss, bur. Oct. 20, 1841. c. r. 3.

VINCENT, Nancy, w. John, Apr. 30, 1829, a. 32 y. c. r. 1.

VOSE, Elizabeth, w. Jeremiah, Mar. 23, 1820, a. 30 y. g. r. 2.
Josiah, Feb. 1, 1846, a. 67 y. g. r. 2.
Reuben, b. Milton, June 22, 1765, d. at Westford, July 21, 1822. g. r. 2.
Rufus, s. Jeremiah and Elizabeth, Dec. 11, 1817, a. 20 m. g. r. 2.
——, w. Josiah [bet. Apr. 8 and 17], 1820. c. r. 1.

WAITE, Elizabeth, alias Betty Virgin, bur. May 14, 1776, a. almost 90 y. c. r. 1.
Susan L., b. Weston, Vt., d. Nov. 3, 1846, a. 24 y. 6 m. 10 d. g. r. 1.

WALDO (see also Waldow), Mare, d. Cornelias and Hana, Nov. 29, 1665.

WALDOW (see also Waldo), Cornelys, Dea., Jan. 3, 1701. [1700, a. 75 y. g. r. 1.]

WALKER, Benjamin, Capt., wounded at Charlestown, carried captive to Boston, died in prison of sickness, in ye latter end of August, 1775. c. r. 1.
Ezekiel, suddenly, June 15, 1811, a. 52 y. c. r. 1.
R., ch. David, Apr. 15, 1813, a. 11 m. c. r. 1.
Sarah [d. Robert and Elizabeth. g. r. 1.], bur. Sept. 25, 1775. c. r. 1. [in her 20th y. g. r. 1.]
Zach[ariah], bur. June 22, 1746. c. r. 1.
——, wid., bur. Apr. 6, 1743. c. r. 1.
——, ch. Samuel, bur. Mar. 2, 1778. c. r. 1.
——, ch. David, Feb. 6, 1817, a. 1 y. c. r. 1.

WARREN (see also Warrin), Abigail, d. wid. Abigail, "hemerage upon the lungs," June 7, 1818, a. 22 y. c. r. 1.
Anna, d. Isaac and Lydia, Feb. 16, 1786, a. 3 y. 9 m. g. r. 1.
Benjamin, s. Benjamin and Izebel, Sept. 5, 1761.

WARREN, Benja[min], Lt., at Hollis, Aug. 20, 1800.
Elizabeth, d. John and Elizabeth, Dec. 11, 1749.
Ephraim, Oct. 13, 1837, a. 44 y. C. R. 1. [Oct. 18. G. R. 1.]
Esther, w. Thomas, Jan. 12, 1732-3.
Esther, "old age & a broken bone," Feb. 13, 1812, a. 78 y. C. R. 1.
George, blacksmith, s. Isaac and Nancy, consumption, Sept. 11, 1845, a. 24 y.
Isaac, s. Isaac and Lydia, Sept. 25, 1775, a. 1 y. 5 m. 6 d. G. R. 1.
Isaac, mortification in his foot, Oct. 20, 1812, a. 75 y. C. R. 1.
Isaac, lung fever, Oct. 31, 1840, a. 63 y. 9 m. C. R. 1.
Jeremiah, hung himself by a rope in the barn, Sept. 20, 1810, a. 48 y. C. R. 1. [Sept. 10, a. 46 y. G. R. 1.]
Joannah, w. Joseph [jr. C. R. 1.], Mar. 3, 1763.
Joseph, bur. Sept. 30, 1769, a. 72 y. C. R. 1. [in his 71st y. G. R. 1.]
Joseph, Capt., bur. Mar. 20, 1792, a. 67 y. C. R. 1. [d. Mar. 17. P. R. 4; in his 67th y. G. R. 1.]
Joseph [Lt. G. R. 1.], consumption, July 1, 1807, a. 46 y. C. R. 1.
Lydia, wid., July 13, 1825, a. 83 y. C. R. 1.
Mary, wid., Dec. 17, 1730.
Mary, w. Ephraim, apoplexy, Feb. 14, 1806, a. 70 y. C. R. 1.
Mary [Spaulding. G. R. 1.], Mrs. [w. Joseph. G. R. 1.], inflammation of pericardium, Oct. 25, 1841, a. 69 y. C. R. 1.
Rachel, Miss [d. Jeremiah and Rachel S. P. R. 7.], typhus fever, in a relapse, Nov. 14, 1839, a. 44 y. C. R. 1.
Rachel [S. P. R. 7.], w. Jeremiah, Dec. 7, 1836, in her 72d y. G. R. 1.
Rebecca [Spaulding. G. R. 1.], wid. [w. Joseph. G. R. 1.], dysentery, Aug. 30, 1848, a. 84 y.
Ruth, ——, 1804, a. 75 y. C. R. 1.
Sarah [w. Capt. Joseph. G. R. 1.], old age, Oct. 7, 1815, a. 85 y. 6 m. C. R. 1. [a. 89 y. G. R. 1.]
Silas, s. Ephraim and Easter, Jan. 20, 1756.
Sybil, d. wid. of Jeremiah [Jeremiah and Rachel. G. R. 1.], consumption, Jan. 30, 1816, a. 18 y. C. R. 1. [Jan. 31, a. 19 y. G. R. 1.]
Tabathy, w. Joseph, Feb. 28, 1749-50. P. R. 4.
——, wid., bur. Nov. 14, 1741. C. R. 1.
——, s. Eph[rai]m, bur. Aug. 28, 1751. C. R. 1.
——, d. Eph[rai]m, bur. Sept. 12, 1751. C. R. 1.
——, ch. Ep[hrai]m, jr. [suddenly. P. R. 4.], bur. Mar. 7, 1758. C. R. 1. [d. Mar. 5. P. R. 4.]
——, ch. stillborn, Joseph, jr., bur. May 25, 1760. C. R. 1.
——, ch. Ep[hrai]m, jr., bur. Feb. 11, 1765. C. R. 1.

WARREN, ——, ch. Benja[min], bur. Sept. 5, 1775. C. R. 1.

WARRIN (see also Warren), Arther, s. Arther and Abigaill, Nov. 19, 1668.

WASHER, Betsey, Miss, consumption and palsy, Oct. 15, 1841, a. 67 y. C. R. 1.

WATERHOUSE, Elizabeth, wid., oldest d. Rev. Samson Stoddard, deceased, bur. Aug. 25, 1775. C. R. 1.
——, Capt., "our brother-in-law" [bef. May 22], 1751 P. R. 4.

WATSON, Charles H., s. James M. and Mary L., Aug. 25, 1848, a. 2 y. 5 m.
Harriott L., w. Enoch [of Manchester, N. H. P. R. 3.], consumption, Aug. 22, 1846, a. 28 y.
William P. [b. Manchester, N. H. P. R. 3.], s. Enoch and Harriett L. [of Manchester, N. H. P. R. 3.], cholera infantum, Aug. 1, 1846, a. 8 m. [a. 9 m. G. R. 1.]

WEBBER, Ann, Mar. 13, 1842. C. R. 2.
Benj[amin], s. Josiah, July 19, 1826, a. 4 m. C. R. 1.

WEEBE, John, alias Everett, Oct. 16, 1668.

WELCH, Polly, Mrs., glass house, May 1, 1825, a. 40 y. C. R. 1.

WELD, Patty, wid. J., d. Justice Fletcher, July 4, 1827, a. 60 y. C. R. 1.

WENDEL, Mary [Mrs., mother of Jacob. P. R. 4.], a Dutch woman, bur. Dec. 11, 1765. C. R. 1.

WENTWORTH, Abram W., Dec. —, 1849. C. R. 3.
Frederic M., s. James M. and Lydia [Elisabeth. G. R. 1.], canker, Sept. 26, 1847, a. 9 m.
Lydia E., d. James M. and Lydia [Elisabeth. G. R. 1.], dysentery, Aug. 23, 1847, a. 2 y. 6 m. [a. 3 y. 6 m. G. R. 1.]

WETHERBEE, Geo[rge] Washington, s. Judah, scarlatina and throat distemper, Oct. 26, 1839, a. 2 y. C. R. 1.
Mary Miranda, d. Judah, scarlatina and throat distemper, Oct. 9, 1839, a. 5 y. C. R. 1.

WEYMOUTH, Abby D., d. Converse L. and Betsey A., canker, Oct. 22, 1845, a. 1 m. 21 d.

WHEAT, Sophrona, quinsy, Feb. 12, 1804, a. 9 m. C. R. 1.
——, ch. Joseph, bur. Aug. 14, 1802. C. R. 1.

WHEELER, Abner, mortification in leg, Jan. 25, 1826, a. 65 y. C. R. 1.
Jonathan B., m., manufacturer, b. Amherst, N. H., s. Jonathan and Martha, consumption, Sept. 16, 1849, a. 33 y. [a. 34 y. G. R. 1.]

WHEELWRIGHT, ——, ch. ——, bur. Oct. 24, 1797. C. R. 1.

WHITING, Hannah, w. Capt. Phineas, May 29, 1814, a. 45 y. C. R. 1.
Oliver, at Dracut, bur. Apr. 15, 1803. C. R. 1.
——, ch. Capt. Phineas, Jan. —, 1818, a. 1 m. C. R. 1.

WHITNEY, Anna, w. Amos, consumption, Dec. 30, 1818, a. 52 y. C. R. 1. [Dec. 31. G. R. 6.]
James F., June 23, 1843, a. 31 y. G. R. 1.
Jonas, s. Joseph and Rebecca, Nov. 4, 1745.
Jonathan, s. Daniel and Hannah, May 10, 1763.
Sewell, s. Amos, bur. July 27, 1799, a. 2 y. C. R. 1.
——, ch. Daniel, bur. Jan. 23, 1754. C. R. 1. [d. Jan. 22. P. R. 4.]
——, ch. stillborn, Dan[ie]ll, bur. Nov. 13, 1755. C. R. 1.
——, ch. stillborn, Daniel, bur. Apr. 15, 1761. C. R. 1.
——, ch. stillborn, Dan[ie]ll, bur. Nov. 28, 1764. C. R. 1.
——, ch. stillborn, Dan[ie]ll, bur. Nov. 11, 1765. C. R. 1.
——, ch. stillborn, Dan[ie]ll, bur. Mar. 4, 1767. C. R. 1.

WHITTEMORE, Gidion, July —, 1834. C. R. 3. [June 27, a. 58 y. G. R. 1.]
Mary, d. ——, burn, Mar. 20, 1818, a. 2 y. C. R. 1.
Theodosia, d. James and Susan H., b. 1845, d. Feb. 11, 1846. G. R. 3.

WIER, ——, inf. ch. Jeremiah, bur. Aug. 21, 1786. C. R. 1.

WIGGIN, Mary Louisa, d. True and Martha, Feb. 12, 1845, a. 7 d.

WILDER, Rebecca [wid. Col. Oliver, late of Lancaster. G. R. 1.], suddenly, bur. Oct. 20, 1796, a. 92 y. C. R. 1.

WILLARD, Sally, w. Joseph, of Lowell, grandd. B. Butterfield, Oct. 12, 1827. C. R. 1.

WILLARD, ——, inf. ch. Joseph and Sally, of Lowell, Oct. 12, 1827. C. R. 1.

WILLIAMS, Anselmo, suddenly, May 15, 1810, a. 23 y. C. R. 1.
Betsy, worms, very suddenly, Oct. 15, 1807, a. 32 y. C. R. 1.
David, Jan. —, 1757.
Dorithy, w. [wid. C. R. 1.] Job, Jan. 30, 1790, a. 100 y. wanting 10 d.
Jonathan, bur. Feb. 2, 1757, a. 77 y. C. R. 1.
Jonathan, mortification of the intestines, Sept. 11, 1805, a. 26 y. C. R. 1.
Ruel, s. Seth and Phebe H., Dec. 1, 1839.
——, ch. stillborn, Jona[than], bur. Mar. 3, 1785. C. R. 1.

WILSON, Sally, w. Jona[tha]n, childbirth, very suddenly, May 24, 1809, a. 40 y. C. R. 1.
Samuel, s. Samuel and Hannah, Nov. 20, 1776.

WINSLOW, Sarah, wid. John, late of Boston, at Tyngsborough, Oct. 9, 1791, a. 72 y. P. R. 4.

WOOD, Leaffe, d. Benjamin and Elisabeth, Aug. 28, 1768.

WOODHEAD, William, Apr. 21, 1676. P. R. 31.

WOODS, Jacob, s. Isaac and Mary W., Aug. 17, 1842, a. 4 y. 3 m. G. R. 3.
Mary, w. Samuel, Jan. 21, 1732-3.
——, ch. Will[ia]m, bur. Oct. 16, 1759. C. R. 1.

WOODWARD, see Woodhead.

WORCESTER, George, s. Osgood, Apr. 12, 1807, a. 12 d. C. R. 1.

WORTHIN, Ezra, chief engineer at cotton factory, organic heart trouble, June 18, 1824, a. 44 y. C. R. 1.

WRIGHT (see also Right, Wrighte), Abigail, worms, Dec. 25, 1808, a. 3 y. C. R. 1.
Abigail, w. [Capt. G. R. 1.] Zacheus, Feb. 11, 1827, a. 52 y. C. R. 1.
Eliza, worms, suddenly, Dec. 18, 1808, a. 5 y. C. R. 1.
Jacob, s. John and Abigall, July 4, **1667**.
Jacob, s. Jacob and Abigall, Dec. 19, 1726.

WRIGHT, James Maddison, s. Capt. Zacheus, dysentery, Nov. 2, 1817. C. R. 1.
John, s. John and Mary, Dec. 2, 1701.
John, of Dracut, burnt, at Pelham [bef. Oct. 28], 1750. P. R. 4.
Martha, 2d w. Capt. Zach., typhus fever and dropsy in the head, Aug. 28, 1832, a. 43 y. C. R. 1.
Mary, w. John, Oct. 29, 1701.
Mary, d. John and Mary, Oct. 29, 1701.
Moses, s. Capt. Zach[eus], dysentery, Oct. 14, 1817, a. 5 y. C. R. 1.
Rufus, s. Capt. Zacheus, dysentery, Nov. 4, 1817. C. R. 1.
Samuell, s. John and Abigaill, 13: 9 m: 1683.
Zacheus, fever sores, Jan. 26, 1813, a. 11 y. C. R. 1.
Zacheus, s. Capt. Zach[eus], dysentery, Oct. 17, 1817, a. 5 m. C. R. 1.
Zacheus, widr., farmer, consumption, Dec. 8, 1846, a. 76 y.
——, ch. Caleb, bur. at Westford, Dec. 19, 1768. C. R. 1.
——, "Sister", Oct. 27, 1824. C. R. 2.
——, ch. Washington, Sept. [bet. 2 and 22], 1826, a. 9 m. C. R. 1.

WRIGHTE (see also Wright), John, s. John and Marah, Mar. 7, 1693.

WYET, John, a vagabond, bur. Mar. 22, 1795. C. R. 1.

WYMAN, Edward, s. Dr. Rufus and Ann [liver complaint. C. R. 1.], Nov. 7, 1817. [a. 15 m. C. R. 1.]

YOUNG, Sally Ann, w. John H., blower, Mar. 18, 1821, a. 34 y. C. R. 1.
Sam[ue]l Eli Carpenter, s. John [H. and Sally Ann. G. R. 1.], Feb. 27, 1819, a. 8 m. C. R. 1. [a. 1 y. 10 m. G. R. 1.]

SURNAMES MISSING

——, Mary, w. Thomas [torn] 20, [torn 1670 or 1671?].
[torn], Dec. 25, 1679.
——, ——, ch. "at Nurse at John Davis, said to be ye Child of one Nanny Eliot," bur. Aug. 11, 1747. C. R. 1.
——, ——, Irishman, in General Leach's employ, at iron factory, lockjaw, June 24, 1824. C. R. 1.
——, ——, ch. "Man at the Factory," Feb. 10, 1825. C. R. 1.
——, ——, laborer at Mr. Blood's mills, Sept. 25, 1828. C. R. 1.

CHELMSFORD DEATHS 459

——, ——, young man killed by blasting rocks, Nov. 24, 1829, a. 18 y. C. R. 1.
——, ——, two chn., at Middlesex Village, Sept. —, 1830. C. R. 1.
——, ——, man at Leach's factory, Dec. —, 1831. C. R. 1.
——, ——, inf. ch. ——, of Lynn, at the house of Mr. Lincoln, Dec. 9, 1840. C. R. 3.

NEGROES

Abbot, Cato, formerly belonging to Dr. Abbot, Nov. 16, 1818, a. abt. 80 y. C. R. 1.
Affa, very industrious woman, bur. Sept. 28, 1801. C. R. 1.
Chester, d. at Timo[thy] Clark's, bur. at Dracut, Jan. 10, 1786. C. R. 1. [d. Jan. 8. P. R. 4.]
Coburn, Nancy, d. Peggy, Jan. 18, 1820, a. 14 m. C. R. 1.
Coburn, Smith, Jan. 12, 1820, a. 80 y. C. R. 1.
Colburn, Margaret, consumption, Oct. 28, 1825, a. 42 y. C. R. 1.
Dinah, servant of Andrew Fletcher, bur. Apr. 17, 1787. C. R. 1.
Foster, Catharine Grey, d. Cornwell, at Boston, Sept. 20, 1822, a. 41 y. C. R. 1.
Foster, Cornwell, consumption, Aug. 26, 1806, a. 28 y. C. R. 1.
Foster, Cornwell, Oct. 3, 1813, a. 75 y. C. R. 1.
Foster, ——, s. Cornwall, bur. May 28, 1790. C. R. 1.
Foster, ——, ch. Cornwall, bur. Feb. 9, 1791. C. R. 1.
Foster, ——, ch. Cornwall, bur. Feb. 11, 1791. C. R. 1.
Foster, ——, ch. Cornwall, bur. Mar. 27, 1791. C. R. 1.
George, man belonging to Josi[a]h Fletcher, bur. Oct. 14, 1775. C. R. 1.
Lois, formerly belonging to Capt. Jona[than] Richardson, bur. June 13, 1768. C. R. 1.
Nichols, Miriam, mulatto, putrid fever, July 20, 1806, a. 50 y. C. R. 1.
Nick, man belonging to Eleazer Richardson, bur. Feb. 17, 1776. C. R. 1.
Plantin, Grant, consumption, Feb. 7, 1824, a. 23 y. C. R. 1.
Reed, Phillis, Oct. 9, 1830, a. abt. 80 y. C. R. 1.
Rose, servant of Madœa]m Stoddard, bur. Mar. 19, 1787. C. R. 1. [d. Mar. 18. P. R. 4.]
Sharp, man belonging to Capt. John Butterfield, bur. Sept. 6, 1764. C. R. 1. [d. Sept. 5. P. R. 4.]
Titus, belonging to Wid. Reb[ecc]a Parker, very aged, bur. Aug. 7, 1761. C. R. 1.
Venus, belonging to Eb[ene]z[er] Bridge [throat distemper. P. R. 4.], bur. Mar. 18, 1756. C. R. 1. [d. Mar. 17. P. R. 4.]

——, ch. belonging to Dea. Ep[hrai]m Spaulding, bur. Apr. 29, 1747. C. R. 1.
——, ch. belonging to Gers[ho]m Prockter, bur. Jan. 27, 1748. C. R. 1.
——, ch. belonging to Sam[ue]ll Adams, bur. May 15, 1758. C. R. 1.
——, ch. belonging to Sam[ue]ll Adams, bur. Jan. 24, 1759. C. R. 1.
——, ch. belonging to Joseph Pierce, bur. Dec. 21, 1761. C. R. 1.
——, ch. belonging to Benj[amin] Byham, bur. Feb. 6, 1766. C. R. 1.
——, ch. belonging to Benja[min] Walker, bur. Feb. 23, 1770. C. R. 1. [bur. Feb. 24. P. R. 4.]
——, ch. belonging to wid. Eliza[beth] Fletcher, bur. May 17, 1770. C. R. 1.
——, ch. belonging to W[illia]m Cambell, bur. Aug. 19, 1770. C. R. 1.
——, ch. belonging to Col. Stoddard, bur. Nov. 23, 1773. C. R. 1.
——, woman belonging to Timo[thy] Clark, bur. May 28, 1775. C. R. 1.
——, inf. ch. Rose, servant of wid. Margaret Stoddard, bur. Nov. 19, 1781. C. R. 1.

www.ingramcontent.com/pod-product-compliance
Lightning Source LLC
Chambersburg PA
CBHW071222230426
43668CB00011B/1267